CITIES OF
TOMORROW

Praise for previous editions of *Cities of Tomorrow*

"This is nothing less than a history of the ideology and practice of urban planning through the century. ... It's all in this most readable tour de force, which makes a whole series of fascinating connections." *The Architectural Review*

"This is the one book you have to read." *American Planning Association Journal*

"Peter Hall is renowned for his critical texts on planning and urban studies, and this updated edition of *Cities of Tomorrow* is no exception. Writing with such enthusiasm and flair, Hall takes the reader on an enthralling journey through the history of city planning." *The Geographical Journal*

"This classic history of modern urban planning has now been updated for the new century with a third edition. *Cities of Tomorrow* is an excellent guide to the urban development of the 20th century, and a good platform from which to view the evolution of the 21st." *Urban Land*

PETER HALL

CITIES OF TOMORROW

An Intellectual History of Urban Planning and Design Since 1880

Fourth Edition

WILEY Blackwell

This fourth edition first published 2014
© 2014 Peter Hall

Edition history: Basil Blackwell Ltd (1e, 1988), Blackwell Publishers Ltd (2e, 1996); Blackwell Publishing Ltd (3e, 2002)

Registered Office
John Wiley & Sons Ltd., The Atrium, Southern Gate, Chichester, West Sussex, PO19 8SQ, UK

Editorial Offices
350 Main Street, Malden, MA 02148–5020, USA
9600 Garsington Road, Oxford, OX4 2DQ, UK
The Atrium, Southern Gate, Chichester, West Sussex, PO19 8SQ, UK

For details of our global editorial offices, for customer services, and for information about how to apply for permission to reuse the copyright material in this book please see our website at www.wiley.com/wiley-blackwell.

Library of Congress Cataloging-in-Publication Data

Hall, Peter, 1932–
Cities of tomorrow: an intellectual history of urban planning and design since 1880 / Peter Hall. – Fourth edition.
    pages   cm
Includes bibliographical references and index.
ISBN 978-1-118-45647-7 (paperback)
1. City planning – History – 20th century.   I. Title.
    HT166.H349 2014
    307.1′2160904–dc23

                                               2013047879

A catalogue record for this book is available from the British Library.

Cover image: Rundhaus at Römerstadt, Frankfurt, Germany by Ernst May, 1926–8.
Photo © Photography Eduardo Perez
Cover design by Simon Levy

Set in 10.5/13pt Minion by SPi Publisher Services, Pondicherry, India
Printed in Singapore by C.O.S. Printers Pte Ltd

For Berkeley

Preface to the Third Edition

That original preface might have been written in another age: WordStar (and the operating system on which it ran, CP/M) are historical memories; personal computers, each exponentially more powerful than the last, have come and gone on my desk; much of this revision was produced in direct connection with the World Wide Web. But the history itself has dated less, I think: 13 years out of a century is not a very long time; the main themes remain those that already concerned us in the 1980s, albeit now seen through different intellectual and political filters; there has been an explosion of scholarship in planning history, but no fundamental reinterpretation of it.

I am grateful to many readers for making the book profitable enough to justify this revision, and to those who have told me they enjoyed it. My special thanks go to some 15 generations of students at Berkeley and UCL, who have come to my classes in planning history and helped illuminate my thinking; and to Rob Freestone, for his stupendous labors in organizing the major conference on twentieth-century planning history in Sydney in 1999, which brought together researchers from all over the world and produced such a splendid record.[1] And familial thanks to John Hall, who supplied a fascinating monograph on the pioneer *cité-jardin* in his home town of Suresnes.

This is a more fundamental revision than I attempted in 1996, which simply consisted of a supplementary chapter. That has now been brought forward, so as to retain the basic structural symmetry of the first edition, which was one of its strong organizing principles and remains still relevant today. I have tried to incorporate all relevant new literature in appropriate places, and hope that any omissions will be brought to my notice, so that I can remedy them next time around.

I have also incorporated some short sections derived from my *Cities in Civilization*.[2] As explained in the preface there, this book and that one can in some

---

[1] Freestone, 2000a.

[2] Hall, 1998.

ways be seen as shoots of a single tree. In writing the later book I strove to avoid overlap, but to have ignored the new work would have left this revision incomplete.

My thanks, as ever, to Magda, without whom neither this revision, nor the original, would ever have been possible.

Peter Hall
London, April 2001

away the layers of historical topsoil that have buried and obscured the original ideas; second to understand the nature of their transplantation.

The Anarchist Roots of the Planning Movement

Specifically, the book will argue that in this process of belatedly translating ideal into reality, there occurred a rather monstrous perversion of history. The really striking point is that many, though by no means all, of the early visions of the planning movement stemmed from the anarchist movement, which flourished in the last decades of the nineteenth century and the first years of the twentieth. That is true of Howard, of Geddes and of the Regional Planning Association of America, as well as many derivatives on the mainland of Europe. (To be sure, it was very definitely untrue of Corbusier, who was an authoritarian centralist, and of most members of the City Beautiful movement, who were faithful servants of finance capitalism or totalitarian dictators.) The vision of these anarchist pioneers was not merely of an alternative built form, but of an alternative society, neither capitalistic nor bureaucratic-socialistic: a society based on voluntary cooperation among men and women, working and living in small self-governing commonwealths. Not merely in physical form, but also in spirit, they were thus secular versions of Winthrop's Puritan colony of Massachusetts: the city upon a hill. When, however, the time at last came for their ideals to be translated into bricks and mortar, the irony was that – more often than not – this happened through the agency of state bureaucracies, which they would have hated. How this came about, how far it was responsible for the subsequent disillusionment with the idea of planning, will be a central question that the book must address.

Neither the idea, nor its treatment here, is new or novel. The anarchist roots of planning have been well dissected by a number of writers, notably Colin Ward in Britain and Clyde Weaver in the United States.[2] I owe a great personal debt to them, both through their writings and through conversations with them. And this account will rely, for much of the essential background, on secondary sources; the history of planning now has an extremely rich literature, which I have plundered freely. So this book is to be judged as a work of synthesis, rather than of original research. There is however an important exception: I have tried to allow the key figures, the sources of the main ideas, to tell them in their own words.

A Warning: Some Boulders in the Trail

The job will not always be easy. Visionaries are apt to speak in strange tongues, difficult to interpret; a striking common feature of many – though mercifully not all – of planning's great founding figures is their incoherence. Their primitive disciples, all

[2]   Ward, C., 1976; Friedmann and Weaver, 1979; Weaver, 1984a; Hall and Ward, 1998.

too anxious to undertake the task, may create a gospel at variance with the original texts. The ideas may derive from those of others and in turn feed back into their sources, creating a tangled skein that is difficult to disentangle. The cultural and social world they inhabited, which provided the essential material for their perceptions, has long since vanished and is difficult to reconstruct: the past *is* a foreign country, with a different language, different social mores, and a different view of the human condition.

I have tried, as far as possible, to let the founders tell their own tales. Since some of them tell theirs discursively or obscurely or both, I have wielded a heavy but, I hope, judicious axe: I have eliminated verbiage, removed parentheses, elided thoughts that seemed to require it, thus to try to do for them what they might have wished for themselves.

If all that is hard enough, even harder is the job of understanding how, eventually, the ideas came to be rediscovered and rehabilitated and sometimes perverted. For here, large questions of historical interpretation enter in. A once-powerful, even dominant, school argued that planning, in all its manifestations, is a response of the capitalist system – and in particular of the capitalist state – to the problem of organizing production and especially to the dilemma of continuing crises. According to this interpretation, the idea of planning will be embraced – and the visions of the pioneers will be adopted – precisely when the system needs them, neither sooner nor later. Of course, the primitive simplicity of this reciprocating mechanism is concealed by a complex mass of historical pulleys and belts: Marxist historians, too, allow that time and chance happeneth – within limits – to us all. But the limits are real: finally, it is the technological–economic motor that drives the socio-economic system and, through it, the responses of the political safety-valve.

Anyone purporting to write history at all – and especially in a field such as this, where so many sophisticated Marxian intelligences have labored – must take a stand on such para-theological questions of interpretation. I might as well take mine now: historical actors do perform in response to the world in which they find themselves, and in particular to the problems that they confront in that world. That, surely, is a statement of the blindingly obvious; ideas do not suddenly emerge, by some kind of immaculate conception, without benefit of worldly agency. But equally, human beings – especially the most intelligent and most original among them – are almost infinitely quirksy and creative and surprising; therefore, the real interest in history, beyond the staggeringly self-evident, lies in the complexity and the variability of the human reaction. Thus, in this book, the Marxian basis of historical events is taken almost as a given; what can make history worth writing, and what can make some history worth reading, is the understanding of all the multifarious ways in which the general stimulus is related to the particular response.

Another personal statement had better be made now. Because of the vastness of the subject, I have had to be highly selective. The choice of major themes, each of which forms the subject matter of one chapter, is necessarily personal and judgmental. And I have deliberately made no attempt to conceal my prejudices: for me, however unrealistic or incoherent, the anarchist fathers had a magnificent vision of the possibilities of urban civilization, which deserves to be remembered and celebrated; Corbusier, the Rasputin of this tale, in contrast represents the counter-tradition of authoritarian planning, the evil consequences of which are ever with us. The reader may well disagree with these judgments, at least with the intemperance with which they are sometimes put; I would plead that I did not write the book with cozy consensus in mind.

There is another problem, of a more pedestrian technical kind. It is that many historical events stubbornly refuse to follow a neat chronological sequence. Particularly is this true of the history of ideas: the products of human intelligence derive from others, branch out, fuse, lie dormant, or are awakened in exceedingly complex ways, which seldom permit of any neat linear description. Worse, they do not readily submit to any schematic ordering either. So the analyst who seeks to write an account around a series of main themes will find that they crisscross in a thoroughly disorderly and confusing way. He will constantly be reminded of the advice from the stage-Irishman in that old and over-worked tale: to get to there, he shouldn't start from here at all. The solution perforce adopted here is to tell each story separately and in parallel: each theme, each idea, is traced through, sometimes down six or seven decades. That will mean constantly going back in history, so that quite often things will come out backwards-forwards. It will also mean that quite often, the order in which you read the chapters does not much matter. That is not quite true; I have given much thought to putting them in the least confusing sequence, that is, the most logical in terms of the evolution and interaction of ideas. But a warning is due: often, it will not quite work out.

And this problem is compounded by another. In practice, the planning of cities merges almost imperceptibly into the problems of cities, and those into the economics and sociology and politics of cities, and those in turn into the entire socio-economic-political-cultural life of the time; there is no end, no boundary, to the relationships, yet one – however arbitrary – must be set. The answer here is to tell just so much about the world as is necessary to explain the phenomenon of planning; to seat it firmly, Marxian-fashion, on its socio-economic base, thus to begin the really interesting part of the historian's task. I have subsequently published a more general account of creativity in cities, including that special kind of creativity that is directed to solving the city's problems;[3] much in the relevant section of the later book helps provide a background to this one, and can even be regarded as a complement to it, even though they were written in the wrong order.

But even that decision leaves remaining boundary disputes. The first concerns the meaning of that highly elastic phrase, city (or town) planning. Almost everyone since Patrick Geddes would agree that it has to include the planning of the region around the city; many, again following the lead of Geddes and of the Regional Planning Association of America, would extend that out to embrace the natural

[3] Hall, 1998.

region, such as a river basin or a unit with a particular regional culture. And virtually all planners would say that their subject includes not merely the planning of one such region, but the relationships between them: for instance, the centrally important topic of the relationship between the spreading Megalopolis and the depopulating countryside. But where, then, does the subject stop? It immediately embraces regional economic planning, which is logically inseparable from national economic planning, and thus from the general question of economic development; again, the spreading circles threaten to embrace the whole world of discourse. There has to be a more or less arbitrary boundary line; I shall draw it to include general discussions of national urban and regional policy, but to exclude questions of pure economic planning.

The second boundary problem is when to start. This is, or was, supposed to be a history of planning in the twentieth century. More particularly, since the subject matter originated in reaction to the nineteenth-century city, it is clearly necessary to start there: specifically, in the England of the 1880s. But the ideas that circulated then can be traced back, at least to the 1880s and 1840s, perhaps to the 1500s. As usual, history is a seamless web, a Gordian knot, requiring some more or less arbitrary unpickings in order to get started.

There is yet a third boundary problem: a geographical one. This is supposed to be a global history, yet – given the all-too-evident confines of space and of the author's competence – it must fail in the endeavor. The resulting account is glaringly Anglo-Americocentric. That can be justified, or at least excused: as will soon be seen, so many of the key ideas of twentieth-century western planning were conceived and nurtured in a remarkably small and cozy club based in London and New York. But this emphasis means that the book deals all too shortly with other important planning traditions, in France, in Spain and Latin America, in the Russian Empire and the Soviet Union, in China. I lack the linguistic and other skills to do proper justice to these other worlds. They must provide matter for other books by other hands.

Finally, this is a book about ideas and their impacts. So the ideas are central and front-of-stage; the impacts on the ground are clearly crucial too, but they will be treated as expressions – sometimes, to be sure, almost unrecognizably distorted – of the ideas. This helps explain two of the book's major idiosyncrasies. First, since the ideas tended to come early, it is heavily biased toward the first 40 years of the century. Secondly and associatedly, many key showpieces of actual planning-on-the-ground are treated cursorily, or even not at all. Books, like other noxious substances, should carry warnings, and the message here should read: Do not attempt to read this as a textbook of planning history; it may be dangerous to your health, especially in preparing for student examinations.

All of this, inevitably, is by way of apologia. The critics may have their field day with the book's obvious omissions and confusions; meanwhile – to ward off some of their strictures, and to guard potential buyers against rash expenditure and consequent disgruntlement – I need now to set down the main lines of argument in slightly more detail, so as to provide some guide through the coming thickets.

A Guide through the Maze

The book says, first and by way of preliminary, that twentieth-century city planning, as an intellectual and professional movement, essentially represents a reaction to the evils of the nineteenth-century city. That is one of those statements that are numbingly unoriginal but also desperately important: many of the key ideas, and key precepts, cannot be properly understood save in that context. Secondly, and centrally, it says that there are just a few key ideas in twentieth-century planning, which re-echo and recycle and reconnect. Each in turn stems from one key individual, or at most a small handful of such: the true founding fathers of modern city planning. (There were, alas, almost no founding mothers;[4] of the consequences, the reader must judge.) These sometimes reinforce each other, often come into conflict: one's vision is another's greatest enemy.

Chapter 2 argues the point about the nineteenth-century origins of twentieth-century planning. It tries to show that the concerns of the pioneers arose, objectively enough, from the plight of the millions of poor trapped in the Victorian slums; that, less worthily but quite understandably, those who heeded their message may also have been obsessed with the barely suppressed reality of violence and the threat of insurrection. Though the problem and some of the resulting concern were replicated in every great western city, they were most evident and certainly most felt in the London of the mid-1880s, an urban society racked by huge social tensions and political ferment; hence the chapter's main focus.

Chapter 3 goes on to suggest a central irony: even as the first tentative experiments were made in creating a new planned social order, so the market began to dissolve the worst evils of the slum city through the process of mass suburbanization, though only at the expense – arguably and certainly not as self-evidently – of creating others. Again, for several decades London led the world in this process, though to do so it imported American transportation technologies and entrepreneurship. So, here too, the Anglo-American focus must remain; but with a prolonged sideways glance, to ask why Paris, Berlin, and St Petersburg were so slow to follow suit.

The first and overwhelmingly the most important response to the Victorian city was the garden-city concept of Ebenezer Howard, a gentleman amateur (there being, by definition, no professionals then) of great vision and equal persistence, who conceived it between 1880 and 1898. It proposed to solve, or at least ameliorate, the problem of the Victorian city by exporting a goodly proportion of its people and its jobs to new, self-contained, constellations of new towns built in open countryside, far from the slums and the smoke – and, most importantly, from the overblown land values – of the giant city. As Chapter 4 will show, it reverberated around much of the world, in the process acquiring some strange guises that made it sometimes well-nigh unrecognizable. These manifestations ranged all the way from pure dormitory

---

[4] Exceptions are Jane Addams, treated in Chapter 2, and Catherine Bauer, treated in Chapter 5.

suburbs, which ironically represented the complete antithesis of all Howard stood for, to utopian schemes for the depopulation of great cities and the recolonization of the countryside. Some of these variants, as well as the purer Howardian vision, were executed by his lieutenants, who thereby acquired their own special niche in the pantheon of planning, second only to his: Raymond Unwin, Barry Parker, and Frederic Osborn in Britain, Henri Sellier in France, Ernst May and Martin Wagner in Germany, Clarence Stein and Henry Wright in the United States. Others were conceived independently, like the Spanish Arturo Soria's vision of the Linear City, or Frank Lloyd Wright's decentralized Broadacre City. Each, and the interrelations of all, will demand a special place in the story.

The second response followed logically, if not quite chronologically, on from this: it is the vision of the regional city. It takes Howard's central theme much further, conceptually and geographically; it says that the answer to the sordid congestion of the giant city is a vast program of regional planning, within which each sub-regional part would be harmoniously developed on the basis of its own natural resources, with total respect for the principles of ecological balance and resource renewal. Cities, in this scheme, become subordinate to the region; old cities and new towns alike will grow just as necessary parts of the regional scheme, no more, no less. This vision was developed just after 1900 by the Scots biologist Patrick Geddes and interpreted during the 1920s by the founder members of the Regional Planning Association of America: Lewis Mumford, Clarence Stein, and Henry Wright aforesaid, Stuart Chase, Benton MacKaye. To this group were related others, principally American: the Southern Regionalists led by Howard Odum, New Deal planners like Rexford Tugwell, even – indirectly – Frank Lloyd Wright. This rich and visionary tradition, the tragedy of which was that it promised so much and in practice delivered so little, is the subject matter of Chapter 5.

The third strand is in stark contrast, even conflict, with these first two: it is the monumental tradition of city planning, which goes back to Vitruvius if not beyond, and which had been powerfully revived in the mid-nineteenth century in the hands of such master-planners as Georges-Eugène Haussmann in Paris or Ildefons Cerdà in Barcelona. In the twentieth century, as shown in Chapter 6, it reappeared fitfully in some odd and ill-assorted places: as the handmaiden of civic pride allied to commercial boosterism in America, as the expression of imperial majesty in British India and Africa and of new-won independence in Australia, as the agent of totalitarian megalomania in Hitler's Germany and Stalin's Russia (and, less ambitiously but more effectively, in Mussolini's Italy and Franco's Spain). When and where it was allowed to finish the job – sometimes belatedly, sometimes never – it did the job expected of it: symbolic, expressive of pomp, power, and prestige, finally innocent of – even hostile to – all wider social purpose.

There was yet another tradition that half-relates, confusingly, to both the garden-city and the monumental-city strains. It is the vision of the Swiss-born French architect-planner Le Corbusier, who argued that the evil of the modern city was its density of development and that the remedy, perversely, was to increase that density. Corbusier's solution, whereby an all-powerful master-planner would demolish the entire existing city and replace it by a city of high-rise towers in a park, is discussed in Chapter 7. In its pure full-blooded form it never found favor – perhaps understandably – with any real-life city administration, either in his lifetime or after it. But parts of it did, and the effects were at least as immense as those of Howard's rival vision: one entire new city on the plains of northern India, rivaling in formal scale and sweep Lutyens's definitive neo-classical monument of the Raj at New Delhi; more significant still, in human impact, hundreds of partial bulldozings and rebuildings in older cities from Detroit to Warsaw, Stockholm to Milan.

There is another major line of planning thought, or planning ideology – the two merge imperceptibly and confusingly – that demands separate attention. But again, like the last, it proves to weave in and out of several other major strains, informing and coloring them. It argues that the built forms of cities should, as generally they now do not, come from the hands of their own citizens; that we should reject the tradition whereby large organizations, private or public, build for people, and instead embrace the notion that people should build for themselves. We can find this notion powerfully present in the anarchist thinking that contributed so much to Howard's vision of the garden city in the 1890s, and in particular to Geddesian notions of piecemeal urban rehabilitation between 1885 and 1920. It forms a powerful central ingredient of Frank Lloyd Wright's thinking in the 1930s, and in particular of his Broadacre City. It resurfaces to provide a major, even a dominant, ideology of planning in third-world cities through the work of John Turner – himself drawing directly from anarchist thinking – in Latin America during the 1960s. And it provides a crucial element in the intellectual evolution of the British-American architectural theorist, Christopher Alexander, in that and the following decade. Finally, it culminates in the community design movement, which in the 1970s and 1980s swept the United States and, above all, Britain, there achieving the ultimate accolade of royal patronage. This long and sometimes strange tale is the burden of Chapter 8.

There was yet another tradition, though it is harder to fix in philosophical terms and it is less firmly associated with one dominant prophet. It is the vision of a city of infinite mobility through advances in transportation technology, above all, the private automobile, that is treated in Chapter 9. This is a tradition that runs from H. G. Wells's remarkable turn-of-the-century prediction of the mass suburbanization of southern England, through the visions embodied in transportation plans like that for Los Angeles in 1939 and almost every other place between 1955 and 1965, to Melvin Webber's depiction of the nonplace urban realm in 1963–4. Frank Lloyd Wright's vision of Broadacre City is closely akin to it, as it is to so many other of the major traditions; so is the vision of the Soviet deurbanists of the 1920s; so, in its way, very early on, was Soria's concept of the linear city and all its countless subsequent derivatives. Of all the great traditions, this surely is the one that most melds and interrelates with almost all the others; for Howard, Corbusier, the regionalists all had their own private versions of this particular gospel.

Most of these ideas, though bereft of all possibility of realization when first conceived, were essentially the product of activists, of the doers of this world. Sooner or later, more often sooner, their creators abandoned talk or writing for action; if you seek their monuments, you must look around you. But it is important for any history of the planning movement also to grasp and to emphasize that since the 1950s, as planning has become more and more a craft learned through formal education, so it has progressively acquired a more abstract and a more formal body of pure theory. Some of this theory, so its own jargon goes, is theory *in* planning: an understanding of the practical techniques and methodologies that planners always needed even if they once picked them up on the job. But the other, the theory *of* planning, is a horse of a different color: under this rubric, planners try to understand the very nature of the activity they practice, including the reasons for its existence. And it is here that – as they have a habit of doing – theory has followed theory, paradigm has replaced paradigm, in increasingly fast, often bewildering, sometimes acerbic fashion. Even to seek to make partial sense of this story runs the immediate and obvious risk of joining the whole process, of becoming locked into the very syndrome one seeks to understand. How well Chapter 10 avoids that pitfall, the reader must decide.

While academia was going its way, the world was going another. Stemming indirectly from the community design movement described in Chapter 8, there came a belief that much of what has been done in the name of planning had been irrelevant at the higher and more abstract strategic level, pernicious at the ground level where the results emerge for all to see. This was because, in half a century or more of bureaucratic practice, planning had degenerated into a negative regulatory machine, designed to stifle all initiative, all creativity. Here was yet another historic irony: left-wing thought returned to the anarchistic, voluntaristic, small-scale, bottom-up roots of planning; right-wing think tanks began to call for an entrepreneurial style of development; and the two almost seemed in danger of embracing back-of-stage. Hence the moves, in several countries, for simplified planning regimes and for streamlined agencies that could cut through red tape and generate a vigorous, independent, entrepreneurial culture, without too many hangups or hiccups. During the 1980s this belief, never far below the surface in North America, quite suddenly emerged in countries long thought immune, like the United Kingdom. Tracing these connections, often subtle and very indirect, is a central concern of Chapter 11.

After this great burst of activity, mainly directed at the regeneration of the inner cities, the 1990s represented a period of consolidation. The overwhelming theme of that decade was the search for sustainability, and sustainable urban development became almost a mantra. But, at the same time, city administrators and city planners found themselves increasingly in competition with other cities as they sought to reconstruct their economies, replacing dying or dead industries with new ones, and to rebuild the shattered industrial landscapes that resulted from this cataclysmic economic change. These two themes, the competitive city and the sustainable city, came together in a renewed focus on urban regeneration: forging an urban renaissance, the theme of a key British policy document at the end of the 1990s, would restore the cities' health and produce new, compact, efficient urban forms. This is the story told in Chapter 12.

Meanwhile, amidst all the resulting plethora of agencies and initiatives, cities were continuing to go their ways. And what began disturbingly to suggest itself, even from the mid-1960s onwards, was that instead of improving, some parts of some cities – and definitely some people in those parts of those cities – were worsening, at least in a relative sense, possibly also in an absolute one. As one urban regeneration effort succeeded another, it too often seemed that everyone benefitted save these people, for whom the efforts were very often specifically designed. Further, it might be that they were simply transmitting their plight from one generation to another, becoming steadily less capable of catching up as the mainstream economy and society pulled away from them. These suggestions were indignantly, even vehemently, attacked; but they would not go away, because the phenomenon glaringly remained. This debate, and the phenomena that triggered it, are analyzed in Chapter 13.

So there is an odd and disturbing symmetry about this book: after 100 years of debate on how to plan the city, after repeated attempts – however mistaken or distorted – to put ideas into practice, we find we are almost back where we started. The theorists have swung sharply back to planning's anarchist origins; the city itself is again seen as a place of decay, poverty, social malaise, civil unrest, and possibly even insurrection. That does not mean, of course, that we have made no progress at all: the city of the millennium is a vastly different, and by any reasonable measure a very much superior, place compared with the city of 1900. But it does mean that certain trends seem to reassert themselves; perhaps because, in truth, they never went away.

The City of Dreadful Night

… the great cities of the earth … have become … loathsome centres of forni-
cation and covetousness – the smoke of their sin going up into the face of
heaven like the furnace of Sodom; and the pollution of it rotting and raging the
bones and the souls of the peasant people round them, as if they were each a
volcano whose ashes broke out in blains upon man and upon beast.

John Ruskin, *Letters to the Clergy on the Lord's Prayer
and the Church* (1880)

"What people do you mean?" Hyacinth allowed himself to inquire.

"Oh, the upper class, the people who've got all the things".

"We don't call them the *people*," observed Hyacinth, reflecting the next
instant that his remark was a little primitive.

"I suppose you call them the wretches, the scoundrels!" Rose Muniment
suggested, laughing merrily.

"All the things, but not all the brains," her brother said.

"No indeed, aren't they stupid?" exclaimed her ladyship. "All the same,
I don't think they'd all go abroad".

"Go abroad?"

"I mean like the French nobles who emigrated so much. They'd stay at
home and fight; they'd make more of a fight. I think they'd fight very hard."

Henry James, *The Princess Casamassima* (1886)

Cities of Tomorrow: An Intellectual History of Urban Planning and Design Since 1880,
Fourth Edition. Peter Hall.
© 2014 Peter Hall. Published 2014 by John Wiley & Sons, Ltd.

2

The City of Dreadful Night

Reactions to the Nineteenth-Century Slum City: London, Paris, Berlin, New York, 1880–1900

In 1880 James Thomson, a poet whose Victorian industriousness never quite compensated for monumental lack of talent, published a collection of doggerel named for its initial offering: an overlong, sub-Dante-esque excursion into the underworld. The verse was soon forgotten but the title, *The City of Dreadful Night*, was not. That, perhaps, was because the dreadfulness of the Victorian city, whether by night or by day, soon became one of the major themes of the decade. Thomson's opening lines,

> The City is of Night, perchance of Death,
> But certainly of Night; for never there
> Can come the lucid morning's fragrant breath
> After the dewy morning's cold grey air[1]

might well have described contemporary London, Liverpool, or Manchester. Perhaps W. T. Stead, the sensationalist muck-raking editor of the London evening *Pall Mall Gazette*, consciously or unconsciously recalled the verse when, in an editorial in October 1883, he commented that "The grim Florentine might have added to the horrors of his vision of hell by a sojourn in a London slum."

Stead's leader was headed "IS IT NOT TIME?" In the stentorian tones for which he was already celebrated, he harangued his radical middle-class audience: "the horrors of the slums," he wrote, represented "the one great domestic problem which the religion, the humanity, and the statesmanship of England are imperatively summoned to solve." With a journalist's acute sense of timing, and a special talent for recognizing the cause of the hour, he had seized upon a pamphlet just published by a Congregationalist clergyman, Andrew Mearns. As shrewdly promoted by Stead, *The Bitter Cry of Outcast London* provided a sensation. It had "immediate and

---

[1] Thomson, 1880, 3.

Figure 2.1 Little Collingwood Street, Bethnal Green, *ca.* 1900. The Victorian "respectable poor," probably Booth's Class C, in their cruel habitations. *Source*: © Ian Galt/Museum of London.

cataclysmic" effect:[2] it provoked immediate demands for an official inquiry not only from the *Pall Mall Gazette* but from much more conservative papers like *The Times* and *Punch*, and eventually from Queen Victoria herself, leading directly to the appointment of the Royal Commission on the Housing of the Working Classes in 1884.[3] It proved one of the most influential writings in the whole history of British social reform; Stead later claimed that through its triggering effect on the appointment of the Royal Commission, it was responsible for the birth of modern social legislation.[4]

The Bitter Cry

It was not the first such attempt to shake the smug self-confidence of late Victorian society; but it proved the pin that pricked the bubble. That was because of Mearns's uncanny ability to take his readers inside the slum. Even after a century, the descriptions make the flesh creep and the stomach turn; they have an almost televisual quality. Only extended quotations will convey their impact:

> Few who read these pages have any conception of what these pestilential human rookeries are, where tens of thousands are crowded together amidst horrors which call to mind what we have heard of the middle passage of the slave ship. To get to them you have to penetrate courts reeking with poisonous and malodorous gases arising from accumulations of sewage and refuse scattered in all directions and often flowing beneath your feet; courts, many of them which the sun never penetrates, which are never visited by a breath of fresh air, and which rarely know the virtues of a drop of cleansing water. You have to ascend rotten staircases, which threaten to give way beneath every step, and which, in some cases, have already broken down, leaving gaps that imperil the limbs and lives of the unwary. You have to grope your way along dark and filthy passages swarming with vermin. Then, if you are not driven back by the intolerable stench, you may gain admittance to the dens in which these thousands of beings who belong, as much as you, to the race for whom Christ died, herd together.[5]

Now, Mearns brings his bourgeois visitor into the horrific interior of the slum:

> Walls and ceiling are black with the accretions of filth which have gathered upon them through long years of neglect. It is exuding through cracks in the boards overhead; it is running down the walls; it is everywhere. What goes by the name of a window is half of it stuffed with rags or covered by boards to keep out wind and rain; the rest is so begrimed and obscured that scarcely can light enter or anything be seen outside.[6]

---

[2] Wohl, 1977, 206.
[3] Wohl, 1970, 31–3; Wohl, 1977, 200, 206.
[4] Wohl, 1970, 33.
[5] Mearns, 1883, 4.
[6] Mearns, 1883, 4.

Furniture might include "a broken chair, the tottering remains of an old bedstead, or the mere fragment of a table; but more commonly you will find rude substitutes for these things in the shape of rough boards resting upon bricks, an old hamper or box turned upside down, or more frequently still, nothing but rubbish and rags."[7]

That set the scene for the human horrors within.

> Every room in these rotten and reeking tenements houses a family, often two. In one cellar a sanitary inspector reports finding a father, mother, three children, and four pigs! In another a missionary found a man ill with small-pox, his wife just recovering from her eighth confinement, and the children running about half naked and covered with filth. Here are seven people living in one underground kitchen, and a little child lying dead in the same room. Elsewhere is a poor widow, her three children, and a child who has been dead thirteen days. Her husband, who was a cab driver, had shortly before committed suicide.

In another room lived a widow and her six children, including one daughter of 29, another of 21, and a son of 27. Another contained father, mother, and six children, two of them ill with scarlet fever. In another, nine brothers and sisters, from 29 years of age downwards, lived, ate, and slept together. In yet another was "a mother who turns her children into the street in the early evening because she lets the room for immoral purposes until long after midnight, when the poor little wretches creep back again if they have not found some miserable shelter elsewhere."[8]

The inevitable result was what shocked Mearns's audience as much as the physical horrors:

> Ask if the men and women living together in these rookeries are married, and your simplicity will cause a smile. Nobody knows. Nobody cares. Nobody expects that they are. In exceptional cases only could your question be answered in the affirmative. Incest is common; and no form of vice and sensuality causes surprise or attracts attention … The only check upon communism in this regard is jealousy and not virtue. The vilest practices are looked upon with the most matter-of-fact indifference … In one street are 35 houses, 32 of which are known to be brothels. In another district are 43 of these houses, and 428 fallen women and girls, many of them not more than 12 years of age.[9]

For the Victorian middle class, this was perhaps the most shocking feature of all.

What was certain, Mearns argued, was that for people so literally destitute, crime did pay. Lingering around Leicester Square were "several well-known members of the notorious band of 'Forty Thieves', who, often in conspiracy with abandoned women, go out after dark to rob people in Oxford Street, Regent Street, and other thoroughfares." The arithmetic of crime was inexorable: "A child seven years old is

---

7   Mearns, 1883, 4.
8   Mearns, 1883, 5.
9   Mearns, 1883, 7.

easily known to make 10s.6d. a week by thieving, but what can he earn by such work as match-box making, for which 2 1/4d. a gross is paid …? Before he can gain as much as the young thief he must make 56 gross of match-boxes a week, or 1,296 a day. It is needless to say that this is impossible …"[10]

At the root of the problem was the fact that the people of the slum were overwhelmingly, grindingly poor. Women trouser-finishers worked 17 hours, from five in the morning to 10 at night, for one shilling; for shirt-finishing, the rate was half that. Illness and drink compounded their plight:

> Who can imagine the suffering that lies behind a case like the following? A poor woman in an advanced stage of consumption, reduced almost to a skeleton, lives in a single room with a drunken husband and five children. When visited she was eating a few green peas. The children were gone to gather some sticks wherewith a fire might be made to boil four potatoes which were lying on the table, and which would constitute the family dinner for the day … In a room in Wych Street, on the third floor, over a marine store dealer's, there was, a short time ago, an inquest as to the death of a little baby. A man, his wife and three children were living in that room. The infant was the second child who had died, poisoned by the foul atmosphere; and this dead baby was cut open in the one room where its parents and brothers lived, ate and slept, *because the parish had no mortuary and no room in which post mortems could be performed!* No wonder that the jurymen who went to view the body sickened at the frightful exhalations.[11]

For Mearns, "The child-misery that one beholds is the most heart-rending and appalling element in these discoveries; and of these not the least is the misery inherited from the vice of drunken and dissolute parents, and manifest in the stunted, misshapen, and often loathsome objects that we constantly meet in these localities":

> Here is one of three years old picking up some dirty pieces of bread and eating them. We go in at a doorway and find a little girl twelve years old. "Where is your mother?" "In the madhouse." "How long has she been there?" "Fifteen months." "Who looks after you?" The child, who is sitting at an old table making match-boxes, replies, "I look after my little brothers and sisters as well as I can."[12]

When Mearns came to "What it is proposed to do," he was in no doubt: "We shall be pointed to the fact that without State interference nothing effectual can be performed upon any large scale. And *it is* a fact."[13] The root of the problem was simple economics. The people were overcrowded because they were poor, and because they

10   Mearns, 1883, 9.
11   Mearns, 1883, 11–12.
12   Mearns, 1883, 13.
13   Mearns, 1883, 14.

were poor they could not afford the obvious remedy: to move out where house room was cheaper:

> These wretched people must live somewhere. They cannot afford to go out by train or tram into the suburbs; and how, with their poor emaciated, starved bodies, can they be expected – in addition to working twelve hours or more, for a shilling, or less – to walk three or four miles each way to take and fetch?[14]

This was deliberately intended to make the middle-class flesh creep. For, as James Yelling has shown, the London rookeries were regarded as "plague spots" where disease, crime, vice, and pauperism flourished, spreading their contaminating influence across the city.[15] Worse, they were seen as "dens of vice," the haunt of the violent and the criminal classes; since they were also the most unsanitary areas, they had to go first.[16] Perhaps they were these, but the great majority of the slum dwellers were decent and desperate people who had to live where they did because they depended on casual labor and were too poor to live far away from the chance of work.[17] As late as 1913, 40% of the working class in Westminster said they had to live close to their work. One casual workman put it succinctly: "I might as well go to America as go to the suburbs."[18] As John Burns put it, slums were "created primarily by poverty of pocket. Wherever casual labour was endemic poverty was epidemic, and squalor must prevail."[19]

The worst, and so the first to go, were in a great horseshoe around the City of London, from St Martin in the Fields, St Giles, and Drury Lane through Holborn to Saffron Hill, Clerkenwell, and St Luke's, and thence east to Whitechapel and across the river to Southwark.[20] Here, philanthropic companies like Peabody and Waterlow labored to tear down rookeries and replace them by model tenement blocks.[21] But it became evident by the 1880s that slum clearance could not be done by this means.[22] The legislation (the Cross Act) did allow local authorities to buy and demolish "unfit" property, but there was little provision for rehousing and the machinery was extremely cumbersome, bureaucratic, and slow-grinding.[23] And the new model dwellings were hated for their overbuilding, their lack of greenery, their grim facades, and their petty regulations; no wonder their inhabitants later took to the garden-city idea with such enthusiasm.[24] Besides, because they earned a meagre return of 2–3%,

---

14   Mearns, 1883, 15.
15   Yelling, 1986, 20.
16   Gauldie, 1974, 267.
17   Stedman Jones, 1971, 67, 97, 171, 173.
18   Wohl, 1983, 319.
19   Wohl, 1983, 324.
20   Yelling, 1986, 25, 55.
21   Tarn, 1973, 43.
22   Yelling, 1986, 28.
23   Gauldie, 1974, 277.
24   Gauldie, 1974, 225; Tarn, 1973, 89.

their rents put them out of reach of the casual poor.[25] Small wonder that in the mid-1870s it was estimated that three-quarters of all London houses were subdivided into apartments.[26]

And all the while, road and railway building and the growth of the central business district of London were taking working-class housing away faster than it could ever be replaced.[27] Street clearances displaced about 100,000 people between 1830 and 1880; the railways at least 76,000 people between 1853 and 1901.[28] Far from compensating for these losses, the clearances actually exacerbated them.[29] By 1895, the year in which the first council housing was occupied in London, the three principal philanthropic trusts had between them built only 16,950 dwellings.[30] Indeed, this failure added to the pressures to abolish the old Metropolitan Board of Works and create a directly elected government for the whole of London.[31]

The British Royal Commission of 1885

This evoked a sympathetic chord. Though some commentators, like the Marquess of Salisbury, thought in terms of charitable trusts and others, like Joseph Chamberlain, thought in terms of local authority action, there was a general willingness to see concerted action.[32] Even *The Times*, with evident disapproval, observed that "it can hardly be doubted by any one who watches the tendencies of the time that *laissez-faire* is practically abandoned and that every piece of state interference will pave the way for another."[33] And even Salisbury, in a crucially important speech of November 1884, raised the question of state intervention.[34] The appointment of a prestigious Royal Commission, chaired by Sir Charles Wentworth Dilke and including among its members the Prince of Wales, Lord Salisbury, and Cardinal Manning, followed. But, while the Commission's report of 1885 abundantly confirmed the nature of the problem, it could reach no unanimous conclusion as to remedy. It concluded definitively that

> first, though there was great improvement ... in the condition of the houses of the poor compared with that of 30 years ago, yet the evils of overcrowding, especially in London, were still a public scandal, and were becoming in certain localities more serious than they ever were; second, that there was much legislation designed to meet these evils,

---

[25] Stedman Jones, 1971, 185; Dennis, 2008, 227.
[26] Dennis, 2008, 221.
[27] Gauldie, 1974, 288.
[28] Stedman Jones, 1971, 162, 169; Wohl, 1977, 26.
[29] Stedman Jones, 1971, 200–2.
[30] Tarn, 1973, 58.
[31] Yelling, 1986, 30.
[32] Tarn, 1973, 111–12.
[33] Quoted in Wohl, 1977, 234.
[34] Wohl, 1977, 238.

Figure 2.2 The Royal Commission on the Housing of the Working Classes in Session, 1884. Shaftesbury, center right, gives evidence on the lifestyles of the poor; the Prince of Wales, leaning forward center left, appears aghast.

yet the existing laws were not put into force, some of them having remained a dead letter from the date when they first found place in the statute book.[35]

Abundant evidence confirmed that in London, one family to a room was typical, and that family might number up to eight souls. This was exacerbated by the custom, in the capital, of dividing up houses into one-room tenements, which must then share one water supply and one closet. And, because the front door was seldom shut, at night the staircases and passages might fill up with the ironically titled "appy dossers": the completely homeless.[36] Within the rooms, the widespread practice of home work – often noxious, such as rag-picking, sack-making, matchbox-making, and rabbit-pulling – made bad conditions worse.[37] In the provincial cities, though there were big variations, overall the same problem of overcrowding did not exist as in London.[38]

For some, like the veteran social reformer Lord Shaftesbury, "the one room system is physically and morally beyond all description":

> I was saying that we dare not tell all we know, and I should be very sorry to go into details of things that I do know; but I will give an instance of the evil consequences of the one-room system, and this not an instance of the worst kind. This case only happened last year, but it is of frequent occurrence. A friend of mine, who is at the head of a large school, going down one of the back courts saw two children of tender years, 10 or 11 years old, endeavouring to have sexual connection on the pathway. He ran and seized the lad and pulled him off, and the only remark of the lad was, "Why do you take hold of me? There are a dozen of them at it down there." You must perceive that this could not arise from sexual tendencies, and that it must have been bred by imitation of what they saw.[39]

But others disagreed; and the Royal Commission concluded that the "standard of morality ... is higher than might have been expected."[40]

That perhaps was some small comfort: the remarkable fact that the average tenement dweller had far less space than that mandated by the Victorian state for those incarcerated in prisons or workhouses. Predictably, mortality levels – especially for children – remained alarmingly high. Those who survived, the Commission calculated, lost an average of 20 days' work a year because they "get depressed and weary." And all this was compounded by the fact that "The warmest apologist for the poorest classes would not assert the general prevalence of cleanly habits among them."[41]

---

[35]   GB Royal Commission Housing, 1885, I, 4.
[36]   GB Royal Commission Housing, 1885, I, 7–9.
[37]   GB Royal Commission Housing, 1885, I, 11.
[38]   GB Royal Commission Housing, 1885, I, 8.
[39]   GB Royal Commission Housing, 1885, II, 2.
[40]   GB Royal Commission Housing, 1885, I, 13.
[41]   GB Royal Commission Housing, 1885, I, 14–15.

The root causes, just as Mearns had shown, were stark poverty and consequent inability to move out. Unskilled London workers like costermongers and hawkers earned a mere 10–12s. a week; dockers averaged only 8–9s.; the average Clerkenwell laborer might bring home 16s. Nearly one-half London families, 46%, had to pay over one-quarter of these meagre earnings for rent; and, while rents were rising, wages were not.[42] And poverty was compounded by the casual nature of so much low-paid work, including that of their home-working wives; so that "an enormous proportion of the dwellers in the overcrowded quarters are necessarily compelled to live close to their work, no matter what the price charged or what the condition of the dwelling they inhabit."[43] Middlemen rack-renters, who managed houses on short end-leases, blatantly exploited the housing shortage for all they were worth. And demolitions – for new streets like Charing Cross Road and Shaftesbury Avenue, since London in the 1880s was undergoing a mini-Haussmannization, or for the new board schools that followed the 1870 Education Act – had worsened the problem.[44]

Underlying all this was an incompetent and often corrupt local government system, unable or unwilling to use the powers it had. Outside London, the historic Public Health Act of 1875 had provided the basis for a more effective local government system;[45] but in the capital, an archaic and chaotic pattern still ruled. Only two vestries or district boards, out of 38 in all London, had taken any vigorous action. There were hardly any inspectors: Mile End, a poor area, had one to 105,000 people. And those were hardly competent: in one London parish, the assistant inspector was "formerly something in the jewellery trade," said the vestry clerk, who added, "I don't know that any special training is required. If a man was endowed with good common sense I think that would be about as good a training as he could have."[46]

So the Royal Commission's main recommendations, rather than adding new powers, focused on how to ensure that local authorities used existing ones. These embraced the so-called Torrens Act (The Artisans' and Labourers' Dwellings Act, 1868), which allowed local authorities to build new dwellings for the laboring classes, and the Cross Act (The Artisans' and Labourers' Dwellings Improvement Act, 1875), which allowed them to clear large areas of unfit housing and to rehouse the inhabitants, both of which were very largely dead letters. They did, however, say that these local authorities should be able to borrow money from the Treasury at the lowest possible rate of interest that would not bring actual loss to the national exchequer. And, in London, they proposed that the vestries and joint boards should surrender their powers under the housing acts to the Metropolitan Board of Trade.[47]

42   GB Royal Commission Housing, 1885, I, 17.
43   GB Royal Commission Housing, 1885, I, 18.
44   GB Royal Commission Housing, 1885, I, 19–21.
45   Ashworth, 1954, 73.
46   GB Royal Commission Housing, 1885, I, 22, 33.
47   GB Royal Commission Housing 1885, I, 40–1.

The Housing of the Working Classes Act, 1885, which immediately followed, implemented these recommendations. It also extended Lord Shaftesbury's ancient 1851 Lodging Houses Act, redefining these to include separate dwellings and cottages for the working classes: a powerful suggestion that the Victorian parliament would at last countenance municipal socialism in housing.[48] The problem remained that local authorities would not move; to which the Royal Commission could only suggest that it was time that the depressed working classes of the cities should begin to show an interest in their plight.[49]

Depression, Violence, and the Threat of Insurrection

Perhaps, indeed, they would. For the 1884 Reform Act had extended the franchise to a large part of the urban male working class. And this class was just then suffering the effects of a major depression in trade and industry, comparable in its impact with those that followed in the 1930s and the 1980s. There was indeed an ominous foretaste of what was to come: the problem, a Royal Commission concluded in 1886, was in part a matter not of the trade cycle, but of a structural weakness in British industry compared with its major international competitors, above all Germany. The Germans were about as good at production as the British; and in the arts of winning and keeping markets they were gaining ground.[50] The Commissioners warned that Britain was taking less trouble "to discover new markets for our produce, and to maintain a hold upon those which we already possess ... There is also evidence that in respect of certain classes of products the reputation of our workmanship does not stand so high as it formerly stood."[51] They rejected suggestions that ascribed the cause to "legislative restrictions on the employment of labour and to the action of the working classes themselves by strikes and similar movements" or "to the action of trades unions or similar combinations."[52]

Whatever the causes, there was no doubt about the effects. During the mid-1880s, throughout the cities and, above all, throughout London, there was a spirit of cataclysmic, even violent, change in the air. The questions of the hour, Beatrice Webb later wrote, were "on the one hand, the meaning of the poverty of masses of men; and, on the other, the practicability and desirability of political and industrial democracy as a set-off to, perhaps as a means of redressing, the grievances of a majority of the people."[53] But these discussions were for the intelligentsia: "it was, in

---

48 Wohl, 1977, 248.
49 Gauldie, 1974, 289.
50 GB Royal Commission Depression of Trade and Industry, 1886, xx.
51 GB Royal Commission Depression of Trade and Industry, 1886, xx.
52 GB Royal Commission Depression of Trade and Industry, 1886, xx, xxi.
53 Webb, 1926, 149.

truth, no section of the manual workers that was secreting ... 'the poison of socialism'
... Born and bred in chronic destitution and enfeebling disease, the denizens of the
slums had sunk into a brutalized apathy." The ferment, in her recollection 40 years
later, was within one section of the Victorian governing class; it consisted in "a new
consciousness of sin" which "was a collective or class consciousness; a growing
uneasiness, amounting to conviction, that the industrial organism, which had
yielded rent, interest and profit on a stupendous scale, had failed to provide a decent
livelihood and tolerable conditions for a majority of the inhabitants of Great
Britain."[54] Later historians might doubt that; the predominant emotion, one asserted,
was not guilt but fear. The poor "were generally pictured as coarse, brutish, drunken,
and immoral; through years of neglect and complacency they had become an ominous threat to civilization."[55]

Their reactions often took a heady form. Those apostles of gradualism, the
Fabians, whom Beatrice Webb soon joined, produced an early manifesto bearing the
clear imprint of George Bernard Shaw, and ending with the stark propositions:

> That the established Government has no more right to call itself the State than the
> smoke of London has to call itself the weather.
>   That we had rather face a Civil War than such another century of suffering as the
> present one has been.[56]

H. M. Hyndman, leader of the Social Democratic Foundation, wrote in the same
year that "Even among the useless men and women who dub themselves 'society,' an
undercurrent of uneasiness may be detected. The dread word 'Revolution' is sometimes spoken aloud in jest, and more often whispered in all seriousness."[57] Hyndman
doubted that the ferment was restricted to the middle class; for

> books, pamphlets and fly-leaves are finding their way into workshop and attic, which
> deal with the whole problem from top to bottom. Theories drawn from Dr. Karl Marx's
> great work on Capital, or from the programme of the Social democrats of Germany
> and the Collectivists of France, are put forward in cheap and readable form.[58]

But Hyndman also drew attention to a phenomenon that few could fail to notice:
"Among the ugliest growths of modern society are the numerous gangs of organized
roughs ... who parade our great cities, and too often, not content with mauling one
another, maltreat the peaceful wayfarer."[59] In London alone, he claimed, according
to the police there were 300,000 members of the "dangerous classes."[60] No one,

[54] Webb, 1926, 154–5.
[55] Stedman Jones, 1971, 285.
[56] Fabian Society, 1884b, 2.
[57] Hyndman, 1884, 3.
[58] Hyndman, 1884, 28.
[59] Hyndman, 1884, 25.
[60] Hyndman, 1884, 32.

Hyndman argued, "had taken the trouble to analyze the manner in which these people were fostered into their present brutality."[61]

Some did not even think it worth the trouble. During 1886 and 1887, the respectable citizens of Liverpool began to complain that they were being terrorized by
gangs; "the district from Athol Street to Luton Street" was "infested by these scoundrels," wrote an indignant correspondent to the local paper in February 1887. The
same month the most notorious among them, the High Rip Gang, went on a wild
rampage through the streets of Liverpool, indiscriminately attacking men, women,
and children with knives and slingshot, and stealing from pawnshops. On 20 May
the gang, described as "four rough-looking young men … labourers, entered as
being imperfectly educated," appeared at Liverpool Assizes on eight charges of
malicious wounding with intent to do grievous bodily harm, and robbery with
violence. The trial judge, Mr Justice John Charles Frederick Sigismund Day,
was a mutton-chop-whiskered sexagenarian with a profound distrust of modern
penological theories, whose fixed conviction about violent criminals was that
they needed a particularly short sharp shock; or, as his son quaintly put it, "that the
only appeal to their reason was through their epidermis."[62]

Pronouncing that "With all his experience he has never heard such outrageous
conduct narrated as he had this day heard," he pronounced the most draconian sen-
tences ever recorded in the courts of Victorian England: as well as terms of hard
labor, each of the four was to receive three separate floggings of 20 lashes each. Thus
fortified by his one-man attack on the city's crime problem, Mr Day returned to the
fray at the November Assizes, where – among seven floggings ordered on one day –
he sentenced two men to 20 lashes each for stealing a halfpenny and a plug of
tobacco. The respectable citizens, his son later claimed, were eternally in Mr Day's
debt, though "members of philanthropical societies, and some others, denounced
the 'flogging judge' as a well-meaning brute, and regarded his method of dealing
with criminals as medieval and mistaken."[63]

In any case, there is no evidence at all that Day's reign of terror had any effect at
all on violent crime in Liverpool. The odd fact was that in general, despite the fears
of the citizens, it seems clear that crime in late Victorian England was following a
long secular downward trend, albeit punctuated by periodic outbursts of violence
such as that of the mid-1880s.[64]

The real terror among the middle classes, despite Beatrice Webb's skepticism, was
that the working class would rise in insurrection. And nowhere was this fear greater
than in the seat of government. In February 1886, their worst fears were realized. For
weeks, unemployed workers and socialist intellectuals had been holding meetings in
Trafalgar Square. On Monday, February 8, a huge meeting, including "a considerable
proportion, larger than usual, of the roughest element,"[65] was met by a force of over

[61]   Hyndman, 1884, 25.
[62]   Day, 1916, 120.
[63]   Day, 1916, 121.
[64]   Jones, 1982, 119–20, 123, 143.
[65]   GB Committee Disturbances, 1886, v.

600 police officers. Fearing an attack on Buckingham Palace, they moved into the Mall; the mob, numbering between 3,000 and 5,000 people, instead went on the rampage past the clubs of Pall Mall, into the streets of St James's and Mayfair, breaking windows and looting shops. An official inquiry condemned the Metropolitan Police for inadequate crowd control, and the Commissioner was forced to resign.[66]

The new Commissioner, Sir Charles Warren, was made of sterner stuff. During the autumn of 1887, tension again rose, with huge crowds gathering daily in Hyde Park and Trafalgar Square to hear speeches. Repeated clashes with the police took place. *The Times*, which habitually referred to the "so-called unemployed," called for firm action: "We trust that if these men, or any other of their class, attempt to carry out their threats as they did last year, they will get their deserts, in the form not of a convenient term of imprisonment for a few months, but of hard penal servitude … The only question worth asking is which of the two parties is the stronger – the would-be smashers of windows and wreckers of tradesmen's shops or the guardians of the public peace."[67]

Thus the stage was set. On Sunday, October 23, a huge crowd gathered in the square, raising the red flag, to hear speeches demanding Sir Charles's dismissal. Just before three in the afternoon, headed by the red flag, the mob suddenly moved down Whitehall and invaded Westminster Abbey during the service. The resulting scenes resembled the final act of Brecht's *Dreigroschenoper*, which perhaps they inspired. According to *The Times*, "A large number of boys, youths, and men, many of them of a very dirty appearance" entered as the organ played a voluntary. They mixed with the congregation, "the more manly" of whom "quietly exercised their influence to restrain the most shameless": "The roughs shouted bitter words about 'capitalists', seeming to suppose that all those who were in the Abbey at worship were 'capitalists.'" Canon Rowsell tried to argue with them. "The mob listened quietly." Just outside, Hyndman spoke: "he looked forward to the time when the Socialistic flag and motto of 'Each for all and all for each' should be placed above that abbey, and they should be inside, preaching the doctrine of revolution."[68]

The demonstrators then returned to the square, where "From every side of Nelson's column meetings were being addressed," with a huge crowd spilling out across the square and into neighboring places. The police panicked and had to call in the army to control the crowds; in the mêlée, more than 100 people were injured; later, two of the crowd died. Massive and mutual recriminations followed. One indignant correspondent wrote to *The Times* that the meetings were "an advertisement to all anarchists, here and elsewhere, to flock to the only great capital in the world where they would be tolerated."[69] Hyndman wrote with a different view: "Men and women will not starve any longer. That I, for one, know. The present agitation is quite spontaneous and unorganized."

[66] GB Committee Disturbances, 1886, passim.
[67] *The Times*, Oct. 15, 1887.
[68] *The Times*, Oct. 24, 1887.
[69] *The Times*, Oct. 27, 1887.

The editorial view was predictable: "This capital itself is menaced by riotous mobs, avowing their determination to profit by the example of the party of disorder in Ireland and to extort the concession of their demands by terrorism."[70] Stead's *Pall Mall Gazette* in contrast accused Warren of trying to establish "police rule": in the Abbey, the interruptions during the service had been the result of overcrowding, and the unemployed had left in perfectly orderly fashion. At Bow Street, sundry persons were charged; some were jailed, others fined or bound over. Later, R. Cunninghame Graeme, MP, and the socialist leader John Burns were convicted at the Old Bailey and imprisoned for six weeks; they became popular heroes.[71]

The Booth Survey: The Problem Quantified

Out of the mayhem of these months came at least some rational response. Charles Booth, the Liverpool shipowner, had been inspired by *The Bitter Cry* to go into the East End of London in order to embark on what became the first modern social survey. Highly critical of sensational accounts like Mearns's *Bitter Cry of Outcast London*, he believed the situation was serious but "not visibly fraught with imminent social danger, or leading straight to revolution."[72] The need was to understand the nature of unemployment, and in particular to discriminate between those "who did not really want to work" and those who were "not unemployed but badly employed," as he told the Royal Statistical Society in 1887.[73]

Aided by an army of able young assistants, including Beatrice Potter, later Webb – who here enjoyed her initiation into academic research – he presented his first results before the Royal Statistical Society in May 1887, and a second paper a year later. According to Booth, the poor of East London numbered some 314,000, or over 35% of the entire population; extending that percentage pro-rata, that meant one million Londoners in poverty. They could be divided, he said, into four sub-groups.

The first, Class A, included a mere 11,000 in the East End, perhaps 50,000 in all London: 1.25% of the population. It "consists of some (so-called) labourers, loafers, semi-criminals, a proportion of the street sellers, street performers and others." It included many young people: "young men who take naturally to loafing; girls who take almost as naturally to the streets"; they led "a savage life, with vicissitudes of extreme hardship and occasional excess. Their food is of the coarsest description, and their only luxury is drink."[74] Booth was sanguine that this group was so small: "The hordes of barbarians of whom we have heard who, coming forth from their slums, will some day overwhelm modern

---

[70] *The Times*, Oct. 24, 1887.
[71] Ensor, 1936, 180–1.
[72] Topalov, 1993, 400.
[73] Topalov, 1993, 400.
[74] Booth, 1887, 334–5.

Figure 2.3 Charles Booth. The shipowner-turned-socialist, presumably intent on the results of his survey; perhaps it was the young Beatrice Potter who was reporting. *Source*: Mansell/ Time & Life Pictures/Getty Images.

civilisation, do not exist. The barbarians are a very small and decreasing percentage."[75] But it still represented an irreducible problem:

> They render no useful service and create no wealth; they oftener destroy it. They degrade whatever they touch, and as individuals are almost incapable of improvement … It is much to be hoped that this class may become less hereditary in its character.[76]

"Less hereditary": an odd formulation, but one that echoed widely in late Victorian England, and after. "By 1914, eugenics was seen as complementary to the traditional aims of better housing and sanitation through the shared objective of greater public well-being and efficiency."[77] Nationally and locally, eugenics supporters merged and overlapped with planners, including eminently respectable individuals like the Earl

[75] Booth, 1888, 305.
[76] Booth, 1887, 334–5.
[77] Garside, 1988, 29.

of Meath, Patrick Geddes, Seebohm Rowntree, the Cadburys, and the Chamberlains. The notion that the lower orders should be discouraged from breeding, even forced to do so, had not yet become politically incorrect; it took the Nazis to secure that.[78]

These, then, were the classic Victorian Undeserving Poor: the raw material of the mob, the perpetual nightmare of the respectable classes, albeit much smaller than Hyndman and others had claimed. The second group, Class B, were, however, much more of a problem. For one thing, they were much bigger a group, numbering 100,000 in the East End, perhaps 300,000 in London as a whole: over 11% of the population. Booth described them as being "in chronic want": "These people, *as a class*," he wrote, "are shiftless, hand-to-mouth, pleasure loving, and always poor; to work when they like and play when they like is their ideal."[79] Their problem was the casual nature of their earnings. They included relatively large numbers of widows, unmarried women, young persons, and children. Booth felt that the solution to the problem of poverty was "The entire removal of this class out of the daily struggle for existence," since "they are a constant burthen to the State ... Their presence in our cities creates a costly and often unavailing struggle to raise the standard of life and health."[80]

Immediately above them came Class C, numbering some 74,000 people in the East End or 250,000 in London as a whole: over 8% of the total. They formed "a pitiable class, consisting largely of struggling, suffering, hopeless people ... the victims of competition, and on them falls with particular severity the weight of recurrent depressions of trade."[81] Their basic problem was the irregular nature of their earnings. And finally Class D, those who suffered from regular but low earnings, included about 129,000 East Enders or some 400,000 in London as a whole: 14.5% of the whole population. They "live hard lives very patiently," and the hope for their improvement could come only through their children, since "For the class as a whole the probability of improvement is remote."[82] Thus, the result that was shocking for so many, 35% of the East End population was in poverty; but for Booth, it was equally significant that 65% were not.[83]

Booth's famous map, with its differentially shaded streets – from yellow for respectable to black for the "seats of vice" – was designed for display; it was widely shown, first in the East End version at Toynbee Hall and Oxford House in 1888, and culminating in the full map at the Paris Exposition of 1900. On return from the latter, Patrick Geddes was seized with enthusiasm for the "concrete encyclopaedia."[84]

He was not the only one. One group who read the early Booth results with particular interest was the Fabian Society, in which the patient fact-grubbing of

[78]   Aalen, 1992, 38; Garside, 1988, 42.
[79]   Booth, 1887, 329.
[80]   Booth, 1888, 299.
[81]   Booth, 1887, 332.
[82]   Booth, 1887, 332.
[83]   Topalov, 1993, 401.
[84]   Topalov, 1993, 419.

Sidney Webb was now married to the acid pen of Bernard Shaw. The definitive Fabian classic, *Facts for Socialists*, first published in 1887, was repeatedly reprinted, selling 70,000 copies within eight years. "In London," the researchers found, "one person in every five will die in the workhouse, hospital, or lunatic asylum"[85]:

> Of the 1,000,000 Londoners estimated by Mr. Booth to be in poverty … practically none are housed as well as a provident man provides for his horse. These 200,000 families, earning not more than a guinea a week … and that often irregularly, pay from 3s. to 7s. per week for filthy slum tenements of which a large proportion are absolutely "unfit for habitation", even according to the lax standards of existing sanitary officers. London needs the rebuilding of at least 400,000 rooms to house its poorest citizens.[86]

The results were predictable: while the average age of death among the nobility, gentry, and professional class of England and Wales was 55, among the artisan classes of Lambeth it was 29; the infantile death rate in Bethnal Green was double that in Belgravia.[87] In 1891, the infant death rate in the Strand was 229, almost double that of middle-class Plumstead. Although the infant death rates declined considerably by the end of the Edwardian era, in poor areas such as Shoreditch they were still double those in healthy areas such as Hampstead. Infant mortality among the poor was so common that working-class parents accepted it stoically and passively.[88]

The heart of the problem, as contemporaries saw it, was housing: "The housing problem was central to the social problem of London in the 1880s," and "From 1883 onwards the quarterly journals and the press were full of warnings of the necessity of immediate reform to ward off the impending revolutionary threat."[89] There was but one remedy, in the Fabian view: "The re-housing of London's poor can only be adequately dealt with by London's collective power."[90] Between the first and second editions of the *Facts* pamphlet, that statement had become much more realistic and practicable; for, following the recommendation of the Royal Commission on Housing, the Local Government Act of 1888 had transferred the responsibilities of the Metropolitan Board of Works to a new democratically elected body, the London County Council (LCC). And, in 1890, yet another Housing of the Working Classes Act did what the 1885 Act had failed to do: in Part III, it provided for the redevelopment of large areas, with compulsory purchase if needs be, for the purpose of building working-class lodging houses, defined to include "separate houses or cottages for the working classes, whether containing one or several tenements."[91]

---

[85] Fabian Society, 1889, 7.
[86] Fabian Society, 1889, 25.
[87] Fabian Society, 1887, 14.
[88] Wohl, 1983, 39, 41.
[89] Stedman Jones, 1971, 217, 290.
[90] Fabian Society, 1889, 28.
[91] Wohl, 1977, 252.

Though the Act was actually contradictory on its attitude to local authority own-ership and management of housing – Part I discouraged it, Part III, if it did not encourage it, allowed it – and though it did nothing to compel laggard authorities to act, it did open the way for progressive local authorities to take control. In particular, it specified that in London authorities could purchase as much land as might prove necessary for long-term planning, without the need for every house to be proved unfit.[92] The new LCC seized the opportunity by immediately establishing a Housing of the Working Classes Committee.[93] In 1894, borrowing powers were extended to the relevant section of the Act; in 1900, local authorities, including the LCC and the new London boroughs which had replaced the vestries by a London Government Act the previous year, were enabled to buy land outside their own boundaries to implement this section of the 1890 Act.[94]

The Slum City in Europe

London, rather than any provincial British city, was the stage on which most of this drama was played out. But that was because – as the Royal Commission recognized in 1885 – the housing problem was so much worse there; and that, in large measure, was a simple measure of London's size. With its 5.6 million people at the start of the 1890s, no other British urban area could compete with it; housing densities, land rents, transportation problems, competition for space were all bound to be so much more acute there.

Even on the international scale, against the Paris region's 4.1 million and Greater Berlin's 1.6 million, London was unchallengeably the greatest city in Europe and even the world.[95] But these other cities, being relatively smaller and denser, had their own competitive horror stories to offer. In Paris the historic city's 2.45 million peo-ple, in 1891, lived at a density twice that of the LCC area. Bertillon concluded at that date that 14% of the Paris poor, 330,000, lived in overcrowded dwellings; the poor were even worse housed than in London. Sellier calculated in 1911 that the total was still 216,000, with another 85,000 in the suburbs, living at two or more per room.[96] There, too, legislation – in 1894, 1906, and 1912 – had allowed the construction of low-cost housing for the working classes, and the last provided for local authorities to establish offices to build and manage such housing, backed by state money. Yet down to 1914, only 10,000 such dwellings had been built in the Paris region, an unimpressive total compared with the LCC achievement.[97] The stark fact was that neither the city nor the state had the money for slum clearance: other huge public

[92]   Gauldie, 1974, 293.
[93]   Tarn, 1973, 122; Gauldie, 1974, 294–5.
[94]   Tarn, 1973, 124, 127.
[95]   Mitchell, 1975, 76–8.
[96]   Sellier and Bruggeman, 1927, 1–2; Bastié, 1964, 190.
[97]   Bastié, 1964, 192; Sutcliffe, 1970, 258; Evenson, 1979, 218.

Figure 2.4 Berlin *Mietskasernen* (tenements). In Berlin a model housing design brings congestion and misery. *Source*: © ullsteinbild/TopFoto.

works – building schools and the Sorbonne in the 1880s and 1890s, building the Métro in the decade 1900–10 – took priority.[98]

Berlin, where the population was growing at almost American speed – a near-doubling in 20 years, from 1.9 million in 1890 to 3.7 million in 1910 – was, like Paris, an extraordinarily compact and therefore congested city: its growth was accommodated in densely packed five-story "rental barracks" around courtyards as narrow as 15 feet wide, the minimum necessary to bring in fire-fighting equipment. This kind of development, apparently first developed by Frederick the Great to house soldiers' families, became universal as a result of the city plan of Police-President James Hobrecht, in 1858; apparently designed to achieve social integration, with rich and poor in the same block, it simply produced miserable congestion, and the pattern even spread to new suburban development after a change in regulations there in the 1890s;[99] speculation, guided by the plan and fueled by an exceptionally favorable mortgage system, did the rest.[100]

The result, according to the calculations of the British planning pioneer T. C. Horsfall in 1903, was that while in London in 1891 the average number of inhabitants to a building was 7.6, in Berlin it was 52.6;[101] as late as 1916, no less than 79% of all dwellings had only one or two heatable rooms.[102] And Berliners paid much more to rent their apartments than did their equivalents in Hamburg or Munich – the poor, ironically, paying the highest proportions of their wages.[103] Further, though Germany was faster to electrify its tram systems than Britain, in Berlin the private tram companies did not serve as a means of outward movement in the same way as the LCC, and underground railway development was held up by legal wrangles.[104] Patrick Abercrombie, the British planner, visiting Berlin just before World War One, was intrigued by the contrast with London:

> Berlin is the most compact city in Europe; as she grows she does not straggle out with small roads and peddling suburban houses, but slowly pushes her wide town streets and colossal tenement blocks over the open country, turning it at one stroke into full-blown city.[105]

There was an interesting reaction to growth and overcrowding in the European capitals: both in London and in Berlin, fears began to develop that the city population was in some way biologically unfit. Around 1900, recruitment for the South African War exposed the fact that out of 11,000 young men in Manchester, 8,000 were

---

[98]   Morizet, 1932, 332; Bastié, 1964, 196; Sutcliffe, 1970, 327–8.
[99]   Voigt, 1901, 126, 129; Hegemann, 1930, 170; Peltz-Dreckmann, 1978, 21; Niethammer, 1981, 146–7.
[100] Hegemann, 1930, 302, 317; Grote, 1974, 14; Hecker, 1974, 274.
[101] Horsfall, 1904, 2–3.
[102] Eberstadt, 1917, 181.
[103] Eberstadt, 1917, 189, 197.
[104] Eberstadt, 1917, 431–3.
[105] Abercrombie, 1914, 219.

rejected and only 1,000 were fit for regular service. Later, in World War One, the Verney Commission reasserted that the physique of the urban part of Britain tended to deteriorate, and was maintained only by recruitment from the countryside.[106] Similarly, in Berlin, only 42% of Berliners were found fit for army service in 1913, against 66% of those from rural areas.[107]

From this soon followed the argument that city people – and eventually the whole population – would fail to reproduce itself, an argument first used by Georg Hansen in his book *Die drei Bevölkerungsstufen* in the 1880s, and developed by Oswald Spengler in his classic *The Decline of the West*, in 1918: "Now the giant city sucks the country dry, insatiably and incessantly demanding and devouring fresh streams of men, till it wearies and dies in the midst of an almost uninhabited waste of country."[108] But in both countries, there were wider fears. Charles Masterman, the Liberal MP, suggested in his book *The Heart of the Empire* (1901) that the Londoner was unstable:

> The England of the past was an England of reserved, silent men, dispersed in small towns, villages and country houses … The problem of the coming years is just the problem of … a characteristic *physical* type of town dweller: stunted, narrow-chested, easily wearied; yet voluble, excitable, with little ballast or endurance – seeking stimulus in drink, in betting, in any unaccustomed conflicts at home and abroad.[109]

Similarly, in Germany in the 1920s *die Angst vor der Stadt* was a fear of social decomposition, suggested by evidence of suicide, alcoholism, and venereal disease, "excessive rationality" and lack of political stability.[110]

German cities seemed bad to the Germans; but to visiting Britons and Americans, they provided a model of what cities should be: whether old-fashioned formal or new-style informal, they were seen as orderly, clean, up to date, and picturesque.[111] Above all, this was true of Frankfurt-am-Main. In the United States Benjamin Marsh wrote extensively about its zoning and taxation of undeveloped land and its Lex Adickes, named after its famous *Bürgermeister*, which consolidated plots for redevelopment; in Britain T. C. Horsfall, a Manchester housing reformer, played a similar role.[112] "German Horsfall," born in the 1840s to a family of rich manufacturers, had a German connection through his uncle; from 1895, he argued that Manchester should have powers to buy peripheral land and plan it, as German cities did.[113] Alfred Marshall was shocked: German cities, he told Horsfall, were overcrowded and insanitary, and Horsfall came to see that this charge was true at

---

[106] Bauer, 1934, 21; Purdom, 1921, 111.
[107] Eberstadt, 1917, 214.
[108] Spengler, 1934 (1918), II, 102.
[109] Masterman *et al.*, 1901, 7–8.
[110] Peltz-Dreckmann, 1978, 62–3: Lees, 1979, 65–6.
[111] Phillips, 1996, 170.
[112] Horsfall, 1904; Phillips, 1996, 171–4.
[113] Ward, 2010, 118.

least for Berlin. Out of this, a consensus emerged: "Germany for town planning, England for cottages."[114] In 1905, John Nettlefold, the Unionist chairman of Birmingham's Housing Committee, led a visit to Germany, returning to persuade the City Council that the answer to Birmingham's housing problems was through German-style planned urban extensions – but with British-style garden suburbs rather than German tenements. And this hybrid concept proved central to the new statutory planning process introduced in the 1909 Housing, Town Planning, etc. Act.[115] When the Royal Institute of British Architects organized the Town Planning Conference in October 1910 in London it was dominated by exhibits from Germany,[116] and in the years before 1914 the key pressure groups in town planning organized several continental tours which initially focused almost exclusively on Germany.[117]

And indeed, after World War One a wider consensus emerged throughout Europe, in the form of a "European Model" of state housing subsidy. Conceived as an expedient, sometimes desperate, to meet the seething dissatisfaction of returning soldiers, the programs – in France, Italy, and Britain – soon collapsed, or at least suffered severe modification, in the succeeding economic crisis of 1921–2, but the principle was established: the state was now a key player on the housing scene.[118] America, though, was different from the very start.

New York: The Tumor in the Tenements

Overall, Andrew Lees concludes in his monumental study of nineteenth-century urban attitudes, fear and dislike of the city were very much an Anglo-German phenomenon: "Few Americans displayed the vitriolic dislike of urban living as such that permeated much of the German literature"; yet "many men and women articulated a keen awareness of the moral blemishes that disfigured the face of the American as well as the European city."[119] Yet such fears were openly, even obsessively, expressed in the New York of the 1890s. There, a traditional Jeffersonian concern, that the city was "pestilential to the morals, the health and the liberties of men," a cancer or tumor on the body social and the body politic, was fueled by industrialization and immigration: New York became the greatest city of immigrants in the world, with "half as many Italians as Naples, as many Germans as Hamburg, twice as many Irish as Dublin and two and a half times as many Jews as Warsaw."[120]

[114] Harrison, 1991, 301–8.
[115] Ward, 2010, 119.
[116] Ward, 2010, 117–8.
[117] Ward, 2010, 119–20.
[118] Lebas *et al.*, 1991, 258.
[119] Lees, 1985, 164.
[120] Schlesinger, 1933, 73.

The intellectuals were unanimous on the result. Henry James wrote that "New York was both squalid and gilded, to be fled rather than enjoyed."[121] Many came to accept the judgment of Josiah Strong, in 1885, that to the city was traceable every danger that threatened American democracy: poverty and crime, socialism and corruption, immigration and Catholicism.[122] Alan Forman, in the *American Magazine* in 1885, wrote of "a seething mass of humanity, so ignorant, so vicious, so depraved that they hardly seem to belong to our species," so that it was "almost a matter for congratulation that the death rate among the inhabitants of these tenements is something over fifty-seven per cent."[123] In 1892, no less authoritative a journal than *The New York Times* complained about the invasion of "the physical, moral and mental wrecks" from Europe, "of a kind which we are better without."[124] Even the *American Journal of Sociology*, in 1897, was forced to concede the power of the "popular belief" that "large cities are great centers of social corruption and … degeneration."[125] F. J. Kingsbury in 1895 was moved to comment that "One would think after reading all this about the evils of cities from the time of Cain to the last New York election that nothing short of the treatment applied to Sodom and Gomorrah will meet the necessities of the case."[126]

The man who above all gave expression to these feelings was Jacob Riis: a rural-born Dane who immigrated to New York in 1870, at the age of 21, and became a journalist seven years later. His *How the Other Half Lives*, published in 1890, created a sensation uncannily similar to the impact of *The Bitter Cry* on London seven years earlier.[127] It too was a brilliant piece of journalism. Its descriptions of tenement slum life skilfully combined two contemporary fears: the city as a kind of parasite on the body of the nation, and the immigrant as corrupter of American racial purity and social harmony. These new immigrants, "beaten men from beaten races; representing the worst failures in the struggle for existence,"[128] became a threat to order and to the very future of the Republic, recalling the earlier New York City riots of 1863:

> The sea of a mighty population, held in galling fetters, heaves uneasily in the tenements. Once already our city, to which have come the duties and responsibilities of metropolitan greatness before it was able to fairly measure its task, has felt the swell of its relentless flood. If it rise once more, no human power may avail to check it.[129]

But now the tenements had spread,

> Crowding out all the lower wards, wherever business leaves a foot of ground unclaimed; strung along both rivers, like ball and chain that is tied to the foot of every street, and filling up Harlem with their restless, pent-up multitudes, they hold within their clutch

[121] White and White, 1962, 17, 75, 218.
[122] Gelfand, 1975, 18.
[123] Ford, 1936, 174.
[124] Lubove, 1962a, 53–4.
[125] Boyer, 1978, 129.
[126] Quoted in Cook *et al.*, 1973, 11.
[127] Lubove, 1962a, 55–7.
[128] Quoted in Lubove, 1962a, 54.
[129] Riis, 1890, 296.

the wealth and business of New York, hold them at their mercy in the day of mob-rule and wrath. The bullet-proof shelters, the stacks of hand-grenades, and the Gatling guns of the sub-Treasury are tacit admissions of the fact and of the quality of the mercy expected. The tenements today are New York, harboring three-fifths of its population.[130]

A Tenement House Commission of 1894 estimated that nearly three in five of the city's population lived in tenement houses, so grossly overbuilt that on average nearly four-fifths of the ground was covered in buildings.[131] In these tenement districts, two factors combined to create an acute human problem. First, the incomers were desperately poor and – because of language and cultural barriers – hopelessly immobile. The American planner and housing expert Charles Abrams, who had the rare authority of having grown up in a tenement, later explained: "The landlord cannot be blamed; the builder cannot be blamed. They built to meet a market. The market was determined by what the tenant could pay. What the tenant could pay was determined by the wages he received."[132] If the poor immigrant had not had such an apartment, he would have had nothing. And poor families crowded into them because they were within walking distance of jobs. Nearly 75% of the Russian Jews were packed into three city wards and especially into one, the 10th, which contained a majority from (or with parents from) Russia and Russian Poland. By 1893, with more than 700 people to the acre, this ward was well over 30% more crowded than the most congested part of any European city; part of the adjacent 11th Ward, with nearly 1,000 to the acre, was even more congested than the worst district of Bombay, and so was almost certainly the most crowded urban neighborhood in the world – though, ironically, in the mid-1980s some parts of Hong Kong well exceeded it.[133]

Secondly, they crowded into tenements that, as in Berlin, perversely resulted from a so-called improved housing design: developed in a competition in 1879, the notorious dumbbell tenement allowed 24 families to be crowded on to a lot 25 feet wide and 100 feet deep, with 10 out of 14 rooms on each floor having access only to an almost lightless (and airless) lightwell.[134] Not infrequently, two families crowded into each of these wretched apartments; in 1908, a census of East Side families suggested that half slept at three or four to a room, nearly a quarter at five or more to a room; they depended on a few communal taps, and fixed baths were non-existent.[135] Thus an ordinary street block could house 4,000 people, and in 1900 some 42,700 Manhattan tenements housed more than 1.5 million people, at an average of nearly 34 to each building.[136]

The reaction of respectable society – meaning older-established, White Anglo-Protestant Society – was, up to a point, identical to that in London. Two successive

---

[130]   Riis, 1890, 19–20.
[131]   Ford, 1936, 187–8.
[132]   Abrams, 1939, 72–3.
[133]   Abrams, 1939, 187; Scott, 1969, 10.
[134]   DeForest and Veiller, 1903, I, 101; Lubove, 1962a, 30–1.
[135]   Howe, 1976, 27.
[136]   Glaab and Brown, 1976, 152.

Tenement House Commissions, in 1894 and 1900, confirmed the evils of tenement-house living; the first achieved little, but the second was followed – after a huge political battle – by legislation in 1901, "the most significant regulatory act in America's history of housing," which outlawed the construction of further dumb-bells and compelled the modification of existing ones.[137] Its secretary, Lawrence Veiller, was a young man in his twenties, who had fought vested interests to have it set up.[138] His own view was that many of the city's problems stemmed from the too-sudden transition from European peasant to American urbanite, which he would propose to remedy via mass rural resettlement. But meanwhile, for those trapped in the city, urgent and drastic action was needed to redress the worst evils of tenement life: more light, more air, new bathrooms, better fire protection.[139]

As Veiller described these evils, they were "almost beyond belief":[140] in one block measuring a mere 200 by 400 feet were crowded 39 tenement houses with 605 separate units, housing 2,781 people, with a mere 264 water-closets, and with not one bath among them; 441 rooms had no ventilation whatsoever, another 635 had theirs solely from narrow air shafts.[141] The 1894 Commission's recommendations, which sought to prevent overbuilding, had been largely circumvented, Veiller wrote:

> Unrestrained greed has gradually drawn together the dimensions of these tenements, until they have become so narrowed that the family life has become dissolved, and the members have been thrust out and scattered. The father is in the saloon; the youth teem in procession up and down the lighted streets past concert halls and licensed dens of infamy; the boys rove in hordes in the alley, the girls in the rear yards … The redemption of the tenement classes lies partly in the restoration of the family, the most conservative unit in civilization, to its proper share of space, natural light and air, and the cultivation of the domestic arts, one of which is personal cleanliness.[142]

The Commissioners concluded,

> The tenement districts of New York are places in which thousands of people are living in the smallest place in which it is possible for human beings to exist – crowded together in dark, ill-ventilated rooms, in many of which the sunlight never enters and in most of which fresh air is unknown. They are centres of disease, poverty, vice, and crime, where it is a marvel, not that some children grow up to be thieves, drunkards and prostitutes, but that so many should ever grow up to be decent and self-respecting.[143]

So there was a huge problem; on that, the Commission was at one with the British Royal Commission of 1885. But, when it came to solutions, Veiller and

137 Ford, 1936, 205.
138 Lubove, 1962a, 82–3, 90–3, 125–7, 132–9.
139 Lubove, 1962a, 131–4.
140 DeForest and Veiller, 1903, I, 112.
141 DeForest and Veiller, 1903, I, 112–13.
142 DeForest and Veiller, 1903, 435.
143 DeForest and Veiller, 1903, 10.

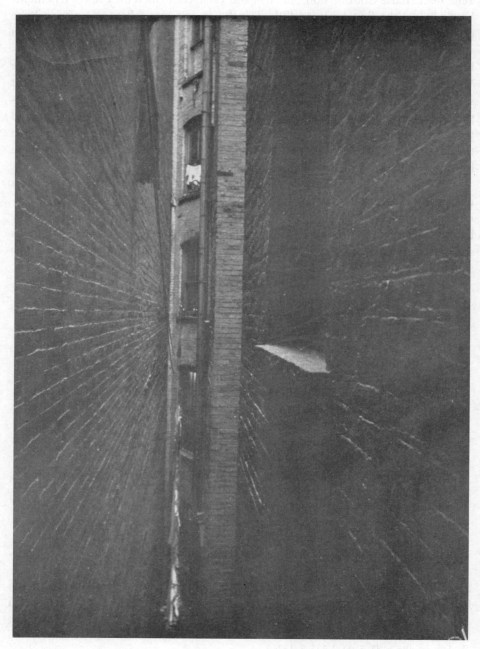

Figure 2.5 and **Figure 2.6**   New York Dumbbells (Old Law Tenements). As in Berlin, so in New York, another "improved" housing design perversely brings no light, no air, but instead monumental overcrowding. *Source*: The Bodleian Library, University of Oxford, 247554 d. 2, vol. 1, facing p. 14 (fig. 2.5).

Source: The Bodleian Library, University of Oxford, 247554 d. 2, vol. 1, facing p. 10 (fig. 2.6).

his commissioners sharply diverged from the British – and indeed the European – road. They looked at the London model of public housing, and decisively rejected it. "No good purpose could be thereby served," they concluded: at most, municipal housing would "better the living conditions of a favored few," and "would furnish no better demonstration than private benevolence has furnished in the past and can be relied upon to furnish in the future"; there would be no way to determine "where should the wage line be drawn between those for whom they should and those for whom they should not provide."[144] Besides, they felt, public housing would mean a ponderous bureaucracy, political patronage, the discouragement of private capital. So it was to be resisted: physical regulation of the private developer was to provide the answer. The 1901 Act, meticulously divided into more than 100 detailed sections, codified space standards, fire protection, plumbing provision.[145] Perhaps, in the conditions of the time and the place, that was a realistic judgment; though soon, other housing reformers – Edith Elmer Wood, Frederick Ackerman – were beginning to take issue with it. Whatever the case, in comparison with Europe, it was to set the cause of public housing back for decades, as Catherine Bauer was to bemoan in the 1930s.[146]

The reasons have intrigued historians – for they entailed a divorce in America between the infant arts of planned housing and planned cities. Early American planning, as will emerge in Chapter 6, was dominated by the City Beautiful movement, and that was planning without social purpose – or even with a regressive one: the zoning movement, which profoundly influenced the subsequent course

---

[144] DeForest and Veiller, 1903, I, 44.
[145] Friedman, 1968, 33–5, 76.
[146] Lubove, 1962a, 178–9, 182–3.

of American suburban development, was, if anything, socially exclusionary in its purpose and its impact. Regional plans, like the celebrated New York Regional Plan of 1931, were largely concerned with better housing for those that could afford to pay. Thus, "Housing, proclaimed as a major concern at the beginning of each of three milestones in the evolution of planning in the United States, in each case becomes joined with other issues; in each case solutions emerge either unrelated to housing or in fact aggravating those very housing conditions that had seemed to beget the effort."[147]

Marcuse's explanation is that of the three reasons why housing emerged as an issue – externalities like fire and disease dangers, concern for social order, and the protection of real estate values – the first two faded after 1910, as public health and fire control improved and as the immigrants were assimilated; thence, planning depended only on "the alliance of real estate interests with middle-income home-owning voters," who had no interest whatsoever in programs for rehousing the poor. And this provided a sharp contrast with Europe, where a strong working-class consciousness allied with an interventionist bureaucracy.[148]

What did emerge, in its place, was something odd and distinctly American: a voluntary movement dedicated to saving the immigrant from his (and, especially, her) own errors and excesses, socializing him into American folkways, and adjusting him to city life. The oddity lies partly in the fact that the idea was borrowed from Europe, and specifically from London's East End. There, a host of social endeavors had developed during the 1870s and 1880s to bring Christian morality and clean habits to the people of the slums. Jane Addams, on her first visit to England at the age of 22, was profoundly affected by the publication of *The Bitter Cry of Outcast London*. On a second trip, in June 1888, she just as providentially heard of Toynbee Hall, Canon Samuel Barnett's Christian settlement in St Jude's in East London, the "worst parish in London."[149] There, a major concern was the welfare of young people. Escaping crowded homes, children played on the streets, where – settlement workers worried – they went unsupervised and unprotected from abusive or corrupting adults.[150] J. J. Mallon, warden of Toynbee Hall, and later a Juvenile Court magistrate, wrote,

> The lot of the East End boy is not a happy one. He is mentally vigorous. He possesses a genius for adventurous play, but is denied opportunities. His district is not furnished with playing grounds; he is too poor to provide apparatus for games. He is cut off from the country and natural things. In these circumstances much of what is healthy and fine in him decays or is deflected into wrong channels. He takes to the streets. He makes evil friends and imitates bad models. He loses any ambition he may have cherished and finally may have only one: the ambition to possess money without working

147   Marcuse, 1980, 38.
148   Marcuse, 1980, 40–9.
149   Bradley, 2009, 286.
150   Bradley, 2009, 288.

Figure 2.7 Jane Addams. The face of compassion and do-goodism, ready to do battle for the bodies and souls of Chicago's slum dwellers. *Source*: Fotosearch/Getty Images.

for it. At this stage the boy is in grave danger, and what may have been an inherently strong and healthy character is marred.

This opened the way for the settlement workers, who – convinced that working-class parents were incapable of or unwilling to supervise their children – overlooked the networks of informal supervision of children on the streets that came from parents, neighbors, and street traders.[151]

The next year, Addams embarked on establishing a similar settlement in Chicago. Located at the middle of four poor immigrant communities – Italian, German, Jewish, Bohemian – Hull House was staffed by idealistic, college-educated young people, almost all female and highly religious: the kind of young woman who earlier would have become a missionary or tried to save a drunken husband, a newspaper reporter wrote, would now go into the settlement house.[152] Some observers, as a result, found the atmosphere insufferable: Thorstein Veblen wrote of "punctilios of upper-class propriety," Sinclair Lewis of "cultural comfort-stations … upholding a standard of tight-smiling prissiness."[153] Their clientele, too, were chiefly

[151] Bradley, 2009, 288.
[152] Davis, 1967, 37.
[153] Davis, 1967, 17.

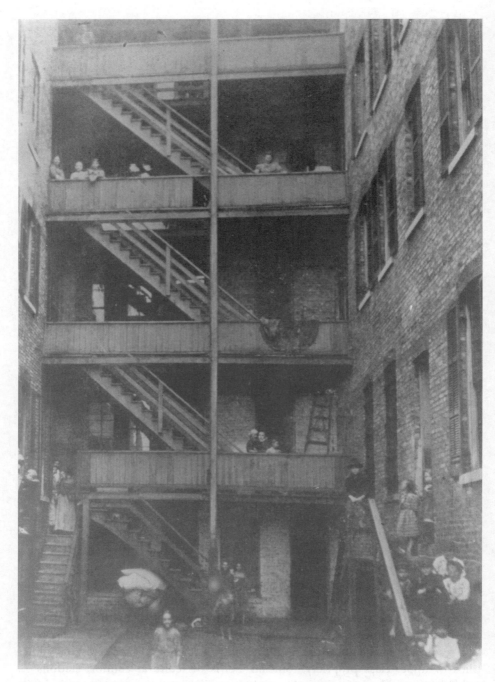

Figure 2.8 and **Figure 2.9**   Chicago tenement life, *ca.* 1900. The immigrant mothers and their children await the reformer from Hull House. *Source*: Photo # JAMC 0000 0198 3117, Jane Addams Memorial Collection, Special Collections & University Archives, University of Illinois at Chicago Library (fig. 2.8) and Photo # JAMC 0000 0190 0275, Jane Addams Memorial Collection, Special Collections & University Archives, University of Illinois at Chicago Library (fig. 2.9).

female: a male immigrant later recalled that "we went there for an occasional shower, that was all."[154] They dispensed continuing education for early school-leavers, summer camps to take children back to nature or playgrounds for those who stayed behind, an old people's club (designed to break down their prejudice against the immigrants), a boarding club for girls, a program to save "fallen women," a day nursery. They also pursued social inquiries consciously modeled on the Booth survey, and worked for reform of the labor laws.[155] Finally, they campaigned against the gin-palace: "These coarse and illicit merrymakings remind one of the unrestrained jollities of Restoration London, and they are indeed their direct descendants, properly commercialized, still confusing joy with lust, and gaiety with debauchery."[156] Years later, after a decade of prohibition had brought mayhem to the streets of Chicago, she still warmly supported it, suggesting that the answer was to disarm the gangsters.[157]

It seems touching. Visitors from Britain – the Warden of Toynbee Hall, John Burns – were puzzled at the evident lack of any municipal intervention: the condition of the houses, where immigrants followed rural folkways in the middle of the city – slaughtering sheep and baking bread in basements – would have made them quite illegal in London, they exclaimed.[158] But the Hull House program was only an especially idealistic, and exceptionally well-publicized, variant of what was happening in every American city before World War One: there were six such centers in the United States in 1891, more than 100 by 1900, more than 400 by 1910.[159] The objective was to integrate the immigrant into the city, first by individual moral example, secondly – if that should fail – through moral coercion and even – so some supporters believed – segregation or repatriation of "the tramp, the drunkard, the pauper, the imbecile."[160] But, thirdly, these were to be accompanied by a systematic upgrading of the urban environment, through parks and playgrounds and eventually through a wider system of city parks which – so argued the father of American landscape architecture, Frederick Law Olmsted – would exert a "harmonizing and refining influence … favorable to courtesy, self-control and temperance."[161] Some supporters went further, arguing for neighborhood revival as a way of restoring the quality of urban life – though Jane Addams herself would have none of such "geographical salvation."[162] And from this grew the notion that the city itself could engender civic loyalty, thus guaranteeing a harmonious moral order; the city's physical appearance would symbolize its moral purity. This became the

[154]   Davis, 1967, 88.
[155]   Addams, 1910, 41–2, 69, 85–9, 98–9, 121, 105–8, 129–31, 136, 146, 169, 198–230: Davis, 1967, 45, 58–9, 61–2, 85.
[156]   Addams, 1965, 87.
[157]   Addams, 1929, 54–5.
[158]   Addams, 1910, 294–5.
[159]   Davis, 1967, 11–12.
[160]   Davis, 1967, 92; Boyer, 1978, 191.
[161]   Quoted in Boyer, 1978, 239.
[162]   Davis, 1967, 76.

central tenet of the City Beautiful movement.[163] Whether it made an adequate substitute for planned public housing, no one apparently thought to ask those most directly affected. In practical terms, Jane Addams followed the Lawrence Veiller prescription: she played a key role in launching Robert Hunter's inquiry into Chicago tenement housing, the exact equivalent of the New York report, which revealed equally horrifying conditions and resulted in a tenement-house ordinance of 1902.[164]

An International Problem

The remedies then were different. But the problem and the perception of it were similar on both sides of the Atlantic. The problem was the giant city itself. The perception of it was the source of multiple social evil, possible biological decline, and potential political insurrection. From 1880 to 1900, perhaps 1914, middle-class society – the decision-makers, the leader-writers, the pamphleteers, the activists – was running scared. Much of this fear was grotesquely exaggerated, some of it deliberately so by practiced self-publicists. But the underlying reality was horrific enough, and it stemmed from poverty. The rich might, through revolution, have given to the poor; it would not have done anyone much good, for there was all too little to go around. That poverty had been endemic since the beginnings of society, but in the countryside it could be more or less hidden; once concentrated in the city, it was revealed. The poor who crowded from Wessex or East Anglia into London, from Italy and Poland into New York, were actually better off than they had been on the land; or at least, they thought they were, and they were in the best position to know.

The difference then lay in the fact of concentration, whereby some thousands of the rich and some millions of the middle classes were brought into close contact with millions of the poor and very poor. In this sense industrialization and urbanization, as the Marxists always say, did create a new set of social relationships and a new set of social perceptions. But that, as argued in Chapter One, just states the obvious. Until 1883–5 in London and Liverpool, until 1900–1 in New York and Chicago, the urban bourgeoisie remained blissfully unaware of the horrific fate of their proletarian counterparts next door. After that, there could be no doubt. Veiller and Hunter described that fate all too graphically. Here is Veiller, interviewing a housewife from the tenements:

THE SECRETARY:	What is the chief trouble with the tenement house in your experience?
MRS. MILLER:	Well, there doesn't seem to be any "chief" about it. It seems to be about all trouble. In the first place, the way the tenements are run. Then the air shaft is the chief and greatest nuisance.

---

[163] Boyer, 1978, 252.
[164] Hunter, 1901, passim; Davis, 1967, 67.

THE SECRETARY:	What is the trouble with the air shaft?
MRS. MILLER:	It is a place of foul odors rather than air. For light, you get light on the top floor, but no place else, and the noises – I do not think it has a very good influence on the people.
THE SECRETARY:	In what way?
MRS. MILLER:	Well, it is not very nice to be waked up in the middle of the night and hear someone yell out "Oh, that is down on the first floor. He has got delirium tremens again." Two houses kept awake by that man yelling. Boys and girls hear it and tease the children about it next day.[165]

And here Hunter, describing life in the frame-house tenements of Chicago:

> To cook and wash for seven, to nurse a crying baby broken out with heat, and to care for a delirious husband, to arrange a possible sleeping-place for seven, to do all these things in two rooms which open upon an alley, tremulous with heated odors and swarming with flies from the garbage and manure boxes, was something to tax the patience and strength of a Titan.[166]

The problem, then, was well-nigh universal. The question for historians must be why, given the similarity of the underlying economic structures and the resulting social relationships in the leading industrial countries around 1900, the subsequent urban outcomes should be so different. That is a question that will recur in the following chapters.

---

[165] DeForest and Veiller, 1903, I, 101.

[166] Hunter, 1901, 63.

The City of By-Pass Variegated

And the newness of everything! The raw, mean look! Do you know the look of these new towns that have suddenly swelled up like balloons in the last few years, Hayes, Slough, Dagenham and so forth? The kind of chilliness, the bright red brick everywhere, the temporary-looking shopfronts full of cut-price chocolates and radio parts.

George Orwell, Coming up for Air (1939)

> Come, friendly bombs, and fall on Slough
> It isn't fit for humans now,
> There isn't grass to graze a cow
> Swarm over, Death!
>
> Come, bombs, and blow to smithereens
> Those air-conditioned, bright canteens,
> Tinned fruit, tinned meat, tinned milk, tinned beans
> Tinned minds, tinned breath.
>
> Mess up the mess they call a town –
> A house for ninety-seven down
> And once a week for half-a-crown
> For twenty years …
>> John Betjeman, "Slough" (*Continual Dew*) (1937)[1]

---

[1]   © John Betjeman. Used by permission of The Estate of John Betjeman and John Murray (Publishers)

Cities of Tomorrow: An Intellectual History of Urban Planning and Design Since 1880,
Fourth Edition. Peter Hall.
© 2014 Peter Hall. Published 2014 by John Wiley & Sons, Ltd.

3

The City of By-Pass Variegated

The Mass Transit Suburb: London, Paris, Berlin, New York, 1900–1940

Almost precisely in 1900, as a reaction to the horrors of the nineteenth-century slum city, the clock of planning history started ticking. But, paradoxically, as it did so, another much older and bigger timepiece started to drown it out. The very problem that the infant planning movement sought to address almost instantly began to change its shape. Most of the philosophical founders of the planning movement continued to be obsessed with the evils of the congested Victorian slum city – which indeed remained real enough, at least down to World War Two, even to the 1960s. But all the time, the giant city was changing, partly through the reaction of legislators and local reformers to these evils, partly through market forces. The city dispersed and deconcentrated. New homes, new factories were built at its suburban periphery. New transportation technologies – the electric tram, the electric commuter train, the underground railway, the motor bus – allowed this suburbanization process to take place. New agencies – building societies, public and nonprofit housing agencies – exploited the opportunities thus offered. Cheap labor and cheap materials reduced the real costs of new housing, especially in the late 1920s and early 1930s. Better, more subtle planning and development regulations curbed the congestion and also some of the tedium of the nineteenth-century cities. The result was an extraordinary and quite sudden improvement in the housing standards of a wide spectrum of the population. But the results were often visually unimpressive and sometimes woeful – not, maybe, to those most immediately affected, but certainly to those who styled themselves expert guardians of the public taste.

And all this took place even while the pioneers were writing, campaigning, exerting influence on the body politic. The resulting dilemma is an unresolvable dilemma for the writer (and the reader) of planning history: it is never clear which came first, the suburbanizing chicken or the philosophical egg. But after all, it does not matter: the story only makes sense if both lines are understood together. So, though it is a logical impossibility, this and the following chapters – above all the next – need to be read simultaneously.

The process of suburbanization, especially the market-led variety, was far more pervasive and more evident in London and New York than in Paris or Berlin or other European capitals. And in certain key aspects – the role of public transport, the importance of cheap long-term mortgages, the relationship between private and large-scale public developments – London remained the most interesting, the most vital, the most evidently problematic of all the great cities in these years. So the story had better focus on it.

The London County Council Starts to Build

Right at the start of the new century, the British Census of 1901 showed just how acute remained London's problems of congestion and overcrowding. Some 45% of families in one inner London borough (Finsbury) still lived in one or two rooms, while in a whole ring of neighboring boroughs[2] the proportion exceeded one-third.[3] That year, Charles Booth published yet another paper, extolling the virtues of "Improved means of locomotion as a first step towards the cure of the housing difficulties of London." What was needed, Booth argued, was "a large and really complete scheme of railways underground and overhead, as well as a net-work of tram lines on the surface; providing adequately for short as well as for long journeys. A system extending well outside the present metropolitan boundaries into the outskirts of London, wherever the population has gone, or may go."[4] True, Booth – never a believer in government action, save in dire necessity – saw this as a means to free the private builder to provide the cure. But the more collectivist mind of the London County Council's (LCC) Progressive Party had already moved in the same direction. Though the Royal Commission of 1885 had recommended rehousing the working classes in the center, during the 1890s that idea was speedily abandoned.[5]

The Progressive – that is, Fabian-influenced – majority dominated the LCC's Housing Committee from the start, in 1890;[6] in 1898 it recommended that the Council itself build on a large scale on vacant land using Part III of the 1890 Act, and the full Council – after much agitation and a big debate – endorsed the policy. Finding that they were precluded from building outside their own constricted inner-London boundaries – even then, almost entirely built up – the LCC pressured Parliament for a 1900 amendment, allowing them to build estates of "working class tenements" on greenfield sites at the edge of the County and even beyond it, which they immediately used to start work on four such estates. And, even though that same year the Moderate (Conservative) party took control, keeping it until 1914, the LCC maintained a big house-building program. Between 1900 and 1914, they

---

[2]   Stepney, Shoreditch, St Pancras, St Marylebone, Holborn.
[3]   Wohl, 1977, 310.
[4]   Booth, 1901, 15–16.
[5]   Stedman Jones, 1971, 329.
[6]   Wohl, 1977, 251.

Figure 3.1   Old Oak Estate, built *ca.* 1913. The LCC Architect's Department out-Unwins Unwin: Germanic vernacular, curves, and gable ends according to Sitte.

provided some 17,000 rooms in rehousing schemes on slum-clearance sites within their own boundaries, and another 11,000 in peripheral and out-county estates.

In 1899, even before they had parliamentary powers, they moved to buy the Totterdown Fields site at Tooting in South London.[7] The means to its development was the electrification of the tramway, which the LCC had acquired from private interests a few years earlier. In May 1903, when the Prince of Wales opened the line from Westminster and Blackfriars Bridges to Totterdown Street, he was also able to visit the first cottages, just occupied. In 10 years, workmen's tickets on the trams rose more than fifteen-fold.[8] A second peripheral estate, at Norbury, outside the LCC area, was slightly more problematic; the LCC trams terminated at the boundary half a mile short. A third, White Hart Lane at Tottenham in North London, 2 miles from the county line, was a bigger challenge still: the LCC had hoped for a tube line as part of the construction mania of the mid-Edwardian years, but it failed to come to pass.[9]

At the fourth site, Old Oak in West London, they were luckier; the estate was planned around an extension of the Central London Railway, which, begun in 1913, was delayed by World War One and opened only in 1920.[10] The whole estate, minuscule though it may be, is thus a classic example of a satellite settlement planned around a transit line from the city; it anticipates by more than a decade what Bruno Taut was

[7]   Tarn, 1973, 137.
[8]   Tarn, 1973, 121.
[9]   Barker and Robbins, 1974, 78–84, 91, 98.
[10]   Barker and Robbins, 1974, 243.

to do at Onkel Toms Hütte in Berlin in the 1920s and, much later, Sven Markelius was to achieve at Vällingby and Farsta in Stockholm in the period 1955–65.

It fell short in one respect, for the LCC: they were not in charge of the underground fares, as on the trams they were. From the outset, they saw the trams as "instruments of social policy":[11] early-morning cheap workmen's fares would ensure that rent and fare combined would be less than central London rentals. "The advantages of air-space and pleasant surroundings can, therefore, be secured at practically no extra cost and even, in the majority of instances, with some reduction of necessary expenses": so they argued in 1913.[12] Thus, though "the Council has not been free to abandon the policy of central housing or rehousing … the policy laid down by Parliament has often led to the retention in central districts of many working-class families who might have been accommodated in the suburbs at less cost to the community and at greater advantages to themselves."[13] By 1914, the trams were carrying 260,000 passengers a day, against 560,000 on the cheap early-morning workmen's trains.[14] About this time, Charles Masterman described the effect in South London, where the LCC routes were especially dense: "Family after family are evacuating the blocks and crowded tenements for little four-roomed cottages, at Hither Green and Tooting. The unaccustomed sign 'To Let' can be seen in almost every street."[15]

So the LCC prescription worked – for some. What Masterman, for all his acuteness of observation, may not have noticed was that the migration was socially selective. It was the better-off skilled artisan who had a bargain from the move: the LCC cottages gave his family more and better-designed space for their money, but they still cost more than the rent of a miserable room near the center, and in them, sub-letting was specifically and stringently barred. So those earning £1 a week or less – the casual laborer, the carman, the market porter, the docker – who had only 7s. left for rent after buying food, were still trapped in the slums; and, during this first full decade of LCC building from 1901 to 1911, overcrowding in London actually worsened.[16]

But for those who could escape, the effect must have been dramatic. Both the early peripheral estates, and the more numerous inner-city slum-clearance schemes, represent some of the earliest examples in Britain of large-scale town planning, and both kinds achieved an extraordinarily high level of architecture and civic design. The credit for that belongs to the new Architect's Department, to which came a group of young and talented architects steeped in the traditions of William Morris, Norman Shaw, and the Arts and Crafts movement. This is the first but not the last point in this story when chronology and organization run awry: this early LCC style

---

[11] Barker and Robbins, 1974, 96.
[12] London County Council, 1913, 113.
[13] London County Council, 1913,115.
[14] Wohl, 1977, 290–3.
[15] Quoted in Barker and Robbins, 1974, 99.
[16] Wohl, 1977, 266, 303.

was in many ways identical, in spirit and in practical outcome, to that practiced in the same years by Raymond Unwin and Barry Parker at New Earswick Garden Village outside York, at Letchworth Garden City, and at Hampstead Garden Suburb, which forms a main focus of Chapter 4.

Where it differed, at least in the earliest examples, was a result not of philosophy but of legal constraint. Working outside existing cities, and sometimes able to pressure traditionalist local authorities, Unwin and Parker were able to set aside the rigid local by-laws which, ironically, had been created 30 or 40 years earlier to guarantee minimum standards of light and air for working-class housing, but which did so at the expense of uniform and dull gridiron layouts. The LCC architects were seldom so lucky. In their earliest scheme of all, completed in 1900 – the Boundary Street estate in Shoreditch, a central-area rehousing scheme on the site of the Jago, a notorious nineteenth-century slum – they had been able to achieve a remarkable effect with five-story walk-up blocks, designed by various hands like large pavilions around a leafy central circus: a kind of palace for the poor, still impressive even more than 120 years later, now restored after years of local authority neglect. But, in their earliest edge-of-town and out-of-town schemes – 1,261 houses at Totterdown Fields (1903–9), 881 houses at White Hart Lane (1904–13), and 472 houses at Norbury (1906–10) – they were stuck with the grid and had to do the best they could with it: by varying the length and setting back some of the terrace rows, by constantly imaginative treatment of the facades, and – at Tottenham – by incorporating a private donation of open space to create a remarkable central quadrangle of houses around a park.[17]

Only after 1910 did they begin to break loose. On a small site for 304 houses at Old Oak in Hammersmith, where they had a free hand, they were able for the first time to build on curving streets to create an Unwinesque townscape of cozy corners, overhanging gable ends, and gateways that provide glimpses into half-hidden interior courts. The whole effect is cunningly conceived around the underground station, and set against the vast green expanse of Wormwood Scrubs, which – like the Heath at Hampstead Garden Suburb – forms a permanent green belt, separating the new satellite from the dense terraces of North Kensington a mile away. Here as in the other estates, the LCC planners labored under extraordinary constraints: costs were as low as £50 a room, densities as high as 30 houses or 130 people to the acre (which, Abercrombie and Forshaw would argue 30 years later, required a high-rise solution), grim prison walls loomed just around the corner. Yet here they created a magic world that, even today, somewhat down-at-heel, has the capacity to astonish. Then, in a second stage (1919–21) at Norbury, they brought off a tour de force in the Unwin–Parker tradition, almost outclassing the masters: they exploited a small hill to create a brilliant courtyard of terrace houses, rising above the by-law streets like a walled German medieval market-town.

---

[17]   London County Council, 1913, 71–6; Tarn, 1973, 138–140; Wohl, 1977, 256, 364.

The First Town-Planning Schemes

Meanwhile, compared with the LCC, the other great urban authorities of England were doing relatively little. And many shared Booth's view that better urban transit, coupled with private house-building, offered the main route to the eventual solution of the problem; the infant art of town planning should concentrate on providing a better framework, within which the developer could work. That logic led to the Liberal government's Housing, Town Planning, etc. Bill, which, bitterly fought through Parliament – the Second Reading deferred no less than 19 times, axed at the end of the 1907–8 session, reintroduced, and with no less than 360 House of Lords amendments – was passed into law in 1909.[18]

Introducing it, John Burns – now, as President of the Local Government Board, retaining some echoes of the oratory that had once swayed Trafalgar Square – intoned,

> The object of this Bill is to provide a domestic condition for the people in which their physical health, their morals, their character, and their whole social condition can be improved … The Bill aims in broad outlines at, and hopes to secure, the home healthy, the house beautiful, the town pleasant, the city dignified, and the suburb salubrious.[19]

The principal means to the "home healthy" would be more extensive slum-clearance and rebuilding powers for the local authorities:

> On its housing side the Bill seeks to abolish, reconstruct, and prevent the slum. It asks – at least, I do for it – the House of Commons to do something to efface the ghettos of meanness and the Alsatias of squalor that can be found in many parts of the United Kingdom.[20]

To that end, the Bill reformed the 1890 legislation, giving local authorities unambiguous powers to retain the houses they built under slum-clearance schemes, thus paving the way for the post-World War One public housing drive; it also allowed the Local Government Board to prod recalcitrant authorities into action.[21] Indeed, it gave fairly draconian powers to the Local Government Board; there was a widespread view, apparently shared by Burns himself, that local councils were not up to the job. And that tradition of central interference – doubtless based on that distrust – has been an abiding feature of British planning throughout the subsequent century.[22]

But the most important section of the Act dealt with the new town planning powers, which, Burns explained,

[18] Gauldie, 1974, 305; Brown, 1977, 144, 150.
[19] Burns, 1908, 949.
[20] Burns, 1908, 949.
[21] Gauldie, 1974, 305–6.
[22] Herbert-Young, 1998, 341, 343–4.

Figure 3.2 Norbury Estate, built *ca.* 1921. Another LCC exercise in Unwinesque vernacular, around a hillside courtyard.

> seek to diminish what have been called bye-law streets, with little law and much monotony. It hopes to get rid of the regulation roads that are so regular that they lack that line of beauty that Hogarth said was a curve.[23]

The by-laws, in contrast, were seen as crudely restrictive; thus culs-de-sac were forbidden because they were seen as bad for public health, and at Hampstead a special Act of Parliament had to be passed to circumvent the Hendon by-laws. And Hampstead was seen as a model in the fight for greater elasticity.[24]

The model was thus the small group of schemes that had already managed to escape from the tyranny of the by-laws:

> They have only to take a motor car or any other vehicle, and go to places like Balham, Millbank, Boundary St., Tooting, Ealing, Hampstead and Northfield to see how modified schemes of town planning, accompanied by schemes of transit, tram, train and tube are progressing.[25]

The objective, accepting that London's population would continue to grow outwards, was to plan for it by gaining agreement between the public and the private

---

23 Gauldie, 1974, 305–6.
24 Booth, 1999, 280–4.
25 Gauldie, 1974, 954.

sector: "to get them to turn together towards one outlook with one scheme, instead of mutually fighting each other to each other's detriment":[26]

Let us take Bournville for the poor and Bournemouth for the rich. Let us take Chelsea for the classes and Tooting for the masses. What do you find? You find in those four instances that your public-spirited corporations and your public-spirited landowners have been at work, and ... you will find very much done without damage to anybody of what we hope to make universal by this Bill.[27]

The press were unimpressed by the oratory. But eventually, on December 3, 1909, the Bill was passed. Its most important provision was to allow and encourage local authorities to make town-planning schemes for large areas liable to be developed for new housing. In them the idea was to recapture the kind of informal yet sensitive control exercised by private developers when they granted building leases, as in the great London estates, through the power to control development – a power added to the 1909 Act, almost accidentally, as an administrative expedient to ensure that necessary building was not impeded by the preparation of town planning schemes.[28] The earliest schemes approved by the Local Government Board were for three linked areas on the west side of Birmingham, Edgbaston, Harborne, and Quinton, a total of 2,320 acres; a scheme for East Birmingham soon followed, with the firm intention eventually to cover the entire periphery of the city. George Cadbury in 1915 commended them for their role in reducing "The great stirrings of social unrest, which are such a striking manifestation in these days," since "Undoubtedly at the present time a large factor in the Labour Unrest is the desire of the masses of the working classes to obtain the means to live a proper life for both themselves and their families."[29] But another prominent Birmingham industrialist and social reformer, J. S. Nettlefold, who had originally conceived of the schemes in imitation of best German planning practice, doubted that they would have any effect of the kind: "Neither of the two Birmingham schemes are in the least degree likely to help those people who so badly need assistance, if only for the sake of their children."[30]

For Nettlefold, the London scheme that was approved at about the same time, at Ruislip–Northwood, was much superior. It was very much larger, covering some 6,000 acres as against 4,000 in the two Birmingham schemes; it set out roads, building lines, open spaces, shopping, factory, and residential areas. With a maximum density of 12 houses to the acre, it included many areas with fewer. At its heart was a design – commended by Burns in the debate – by A. and J. Soutar, the designers of Old Oak, for the Ruislip Manor Company, the winner in a competition assessed by Raymond Unwin and Sir Aston Webb.[31]

---

[26] Gauldie, 1974, 955.
[27] Gauldie, 1974, 956.
[28] Booth, 1999, 277.
[29] Cadbury, 1915, 14, 136.
[30] Nettlefold, 1914, 123.
[31] Nettlefold, 1914, 124–8; Aldridge, 1915, 537.

Figure 3.3   Ealing Tenants' Meeting, *ca.* 1906. Howard's Freedom and Cooperation in full flight in one of the first garden suburbs, but the flavor is decidedly middle-class. *Source*: Reproduced by permission of the London Borough of Ealing.

Today, in a short tour of West London, the earnest student of planning history can take in three early classics: the LCC's Old Oak estate of 1912–14, the Ealing Tenants' nearby cooperative garden suburb of 1906–10, and Ruislip–Northwood. The comparison is not to Ruislip–Northwood's advantage. Speculative builders, even enlightened ones, could hardly compete with the early LCC Architect's Department at its best, or with Unwin and Parker's small gem at Ealing. What additionally disappoints is the quality of the Ruislip layout. The core is the Ruislip Manor scheme, and in turn the core of that is a formal main axis which climbs gradually, through a series of traffic circles, to form the main shopping parade passing under the Metropolitan Railway line that provides the *raison d'être* of the whole development, thence to the summit of a pronounced hill, which looks down the far side to the northern boundary of the scheme, an extensive green belt reserved mainly for recreation.

By the standards of by-law planning, of course, it is a notable advance: there is a coherence of a rather formal kind, the open space is generous and flexibly disposed (a green wedge, for instance, runs alongside the railway, right in to the edge of the shopping center), some pieces of the road pattern are interesting, and the small bit actually designed by the Soutars – one of whom later succeeded Unwin at Hampstead Garden Suburb – is very good.[32] But, surprisingly, there are also long

---

[32]   Miller, 1992, 143.

unbroken lines of almost straight street, of unequalled by-law tedium; Burns, one feels, orated in vain. And, coupled with the uninspired neo-Georgian of the shopping parade – a style to be repeated countless times, all over suburban London, in the 1920s and 1930s – the effect is one of rather crushing formalism: a City Beautiful that isn't very beautiful. It provides an inauspicious start for the golden age of the English suburb.

New York Discovers Zoning

The Americans had already done much better than that. Their classic nineteenth-century and early twentieth-century suburbs, all planned around commuter railroad stations – Llewellyn Park in New Jersey, Lake Forest and Riverside outside Chicago, Forest Hills Gardens in New York – all had a conspicuously high standard of design; Riverside, as we shall see in Chapter 4, was almost certainly one of the models for Ebenezer Howard's Garden City. These suburbs maintained sophisticated systems of social and physical control, in order to maintain homogeneous communities of high quality, with harmonious houses.[33] And, as American cities rapidly extended their basic municipal services outwards, the citizens of these suburbs were the main ben-eficiaries: "They owned the flush toilets and bathtubs that flowed with ample supplies of municipal water; they were the bicyclists who benefited from the fresh asphalt pavements; and they also rode the lengthy streetcar lines to suburban neighbourhoods for a price equal to that paid by inner-city commuters for shorter journeys."[34] The problem was that down to 1900 there were not many of them.

That was especially true in New York and Chicago, which were already too big for effective streetcar access; here, the future would depend on subway or commuter lines. New York opened its first subway segment in 1904,[35] and the system began to spread in the following years.

As its historian has remarked, it was a response to two critical problems, rapid urban growth and awkward geography: with 3,437,000 people in 1900, the world's second city, it sprawled across several islands separated by arduous waterways; Manhattan was 13 miles long but only 2 miles wide at best.[36] So the system had to be good, and it was: it was the first subway in the world with express tracks at up to 40 miles per hour.[37] It opened up huge undeveloped tracts north of 59th Street, especially on the west side, and northwards into the Bronx, for middle- and upper-class occupation.[38] Between 1905 and 1920, the population of Manhattan, above 125th Street, increased by 265% and in the Bronx it increased by 156%;

---

[33]　Sies, 1997, 176.
[34]　Teaford, 1984, 280.
[35]　Cheape, 1980, 90–2.
[36]　Hood, 1992, 192.
[37]　Hood, 1992, 195; Hood, 1995, 105–12.
[38]　Hood, 1995, 198.

from 1910 to 1930 the population living outside Manhattan increased from 51 to 73% of the city total.[39]

But, as the Tenement House Commission had reported in 1900, while "Undoubtedly better transit facilities will enable some of the more ambitious and better paid tenement dwellers to provide themselves with separate houses in the outlying districts ... it is evident that the bulk of the laboring classes will continue to live in tenement houses"; they could not afford to move.[40] Nevertheless, one indirect effect of Veiller's work was the Commission on Congestion of Population, established through the efforts of settlement-house leaders in 1907, which reported in 1911 in favor of decentralization through transit.

But – as the Commission had recognized in its own exhibition on congestion three years earlier, and as civic leaders appreciated – better transit was a double-edged sword: it could also spell even worse congestion in the city's core, by bringing more workers in and raising land values. This was the paradox, and it could be resolved only through a complementary measure: restrictions on the height and massing of buildings.[41]

The Commission's executive secretary was Benjamin C. Marsh, a lawyer and social reformer, who visited Europe at the start of its work in 1907–8 and published an early tome on city planning in 1909, the year of the first National Conference on City Planning in Washington. Both Marsh and a fellow visitor, a New York lawyer called Edward M. Bassett, were most struck by the success of the Germans in zoning land uses and building heights in their cities. Marsh in particular singled out Frankfurt, under its Bürgermeister Franz Adickes, as the model for American cities to follow;[42] Marsh was also impressed by the results of zoning in Düsseldorf and by Werner Hegemann's work in Berlin.[43]

So zoning came to New York from Germany. Perhaps that is an oversimplification: mundanely, American land-use zoning seems to have originated in an attempt to control the spread of Chinese laundries in California, first in the city of Modesto and then in San Francisco, in the 1880s; and from 1909 onwards Los Angeles developed comprehensive land-use zoning.[44] But it was the German model of combined land-use and height zoning that was imported to New York City in its 1916 zoning ordinance, which – so contemporaries believed – was the most significant development in the early history of American city planning.[45] And the Manhattan case was basically different from almost anywhere else in America: here zoning was not residential, it was not concerned with regulating land use, it was commercial and it was concerned with the bulk and massing of buildings. It was supported by

[39]   Hood, 1995, 204.
[40]   Veiller, 1900, 6.
[41]   Ford, 1936, 226–7; Makielski, 1966, 10; Klein and Kantor, 1976, 427–8.
[42]   Williams, 1916, 81; Williams, 1922, 212–14; Mullin, 1977a, 11.
[43]   Bassett, 1939, 116.
[44]   Williams, 1922, 267; Bassett, 1936, 13; Walker, 1950, 55–6; Toll, 1969, 29; Marcuse, 1980, 32–3.
[45]   Williams, 1922, 272.

powerful commercial interests who saw it as a way of protecting the value of existing real estate against undesirable invasions – principally garment shops and garment workers who would invade the prestige stores of Midtown. Indeed, according to investigators from the Fifth Avenue Association, it was directed against "Hebrews" swarming from nearby lofts at lunchtime.[46] It reflected the conditions of 1916: a real estate depression, in which it mattered more to protect existing values than to create new ones. What the 1916 ordinance failed to do, despite the hopes of one influential and enthusiastic group, was to serve as a prelude to a fuller comprehensive plan.[47]

The main agents were Bassett, who regarded it as his great life achievement, and his fellow New York reform politician George McAneny. Their moment of opportunity came in 1911, when Fifth Avenue garment retailers, worried by the spread of the manufacturing workshops that served them, formed a quasi-official commission to pressure the city into action. It brought speedy result: in 1913, the city's Board of Estimate voted to create a Committee on City Planning, empowered to appoint an advisory Commission on Heights of Buildings. The Commission's report, in December the same year, predictably argued for a system of zoning based on the concept of police power: the notion, anciently developed in American out of English law, that the state had the right to regulate the private use of property so as to guarantee "the health, safety, morals, comfort, convenience, and welfare of the community."[48] A charter amendment to permit zoning followed early in 1914, and a Zoning Commission set to work to prepare the actual ordinance. Skilfully marshalling popular support and disarming opposition, it reported in 1916 in favor of four types of land-use zone, two of which – residential and business – would be subject to height restrictions.[49]

As more than one observer pointed out, both then and subsequently, New York embraced zoning so enthusiastically because it was good for business. The Fifth Avenue merchants were concerned that floods of immigrant garment workers on the noontime streets would destroy the exclusive character of their businesses and would thus threaten their property values; they appealed to "every financial interest" and to "every man who owns a home or rents an apartment"; the Commission on Heights of Buildings confirmed that zoning secured "greater safety and security in investment."[50] The very year of the New York ordinance, John Nolen could agree with an English writer that American city planning essentially aimed at civic improvements that did not interfere with vested interests.[51] And, as the zoning movement rapidly spread from New York across the nation, this was its image.

It was indeed an odd kind of planning. For the relationship between zoning and planning was an indirect and tortuous one. True, the movement spread rapidly in

[46] Schwartz, 1993, 20.
[47] Revell, 1992; Weiss, 1992.
[48] Bassett, 1936, 27–8; Makielski, 1966, 21; Toll, 1969, 17.
[49] Makielski, 1966, 33.
[50] Scott, 1969, 154–5; Toll, 1969, 158–9, 186; Glaab and Brown, 1976, 266.
[51] Nolen, 1916b, 22.

the 1920s: in 1921 Herbert Hoover, as Secretary of Commerce, created an Advisory Committee on Zoning that included Bassett and Veiller; it resulted in a Standard State Zoning Enabling Act of 1923, which was widely adopted; in 1927 it was followed by a Standard City Planning Enabling Act, which was adopted by many States to give legal authority to city master-plans;[52] by 1929 more than 650 municipalities had planning commissions and 754 communities had adopted zoning ordinances.[53] And a series of landmark legal judgments, culminating in the historic 1926 case before the United States Supreme Court, *Village of Euclid et al v. Ambler Realty Co.*, established the validity of zoning as a legitimate expression of the general police power.[54] But city planning was commonly done on an advisory, non-mandatory basis; in 1937, out of 1,178 Commissions, no fewer than 904 had no financial appropriation at all.[55] And in practice, despite the assertions of Bassett and others, planning and zoning were largely divorced from each other. Cincinnati, where the pioneer work of Alfred Bettman had achieved some real powers for the Planning Commission and where zoning was an arm of planning, was unusual.[56] As Bassett explained to his readers in 1936, though zoning was logically part of the city plan, commonly, planning and zoning commissions had to be legally separate.[57]

In any case, the real point was why American cities so enthusiastically embraced the concept of zoning. The sordid reason was self-interest. In practice, as in New York, "zoning became primarily a static process of attempting to set and preserve the character of certain neighborhoods, in order to preserve property values in these areas, while imposing only nominal restrictions on those areas holding a promise of speculative profit."[58] In *Euclid v. Ambler*, the great planner-lawyer Alfred Bettman – whose brief, submitted late in the hearing, may well have proved crucial – argued that the "public welfare" served by zoning was the enhancement of the community's property values.[59] The point, significantly, was whether land should be zoned as industrial or residential; the Court gave the respectable residents of Euclid, a middle-class dormitory village next door to Cleveland, a guarantee that their investments would not be threatened. Bassett, the father of the New York scheme, later wrote that one of zoning's major purposes was to prevent the "premature depreciation of settled localities."[60] Or, as a later commentator put it,

> The basic purpose of zoning was to keep Them where They belonged – Out. If They had already gotten in, then its purpose was to confine Them to limited areas. The exact identity of Them varied a bit around the country. Blacks, Latinos, and poor people

52   Hubbard and Hubbard, 1929, 21; Toll, 1969, 201.
53   Hubbard and Hubbard, 1929, 3.
54   Walker, 1950, 67–77.
55   Walker, 1950, 77; Bassett, 1938, 67; Foster, 1981, 137.
56   Bassett, 1938, 75; Toll, 1969, 203.
57   Bassett, 1936, 35.
58   Walker, 1950, 60.
59   Fluck, 1986, 333.
60   Bassett, 1936, 25.

qualified. Catholics, Jews, and Orientals were targets in many places. The elderly also qualified, if they were candidates for public housing.[61]

Zoning, in fact, simply reproduced arrangements that had informally prevailed in exclusive residential suburbs long before it arrived, and that combined four inter-related elements: careful site selection, comprehensive planning, creation of a defensive framework of property restrictions, local ordinances, and boundary-marking strategies, and underlying communal consensus. The walled and gated exclusive suburban communities that have proliferated since 1980 are merely a latter-day manifestation of a long American tradition – impelled, perhaps, by an ageing cohort's fear of crime.[62]

A standard text of the late 1920s, indeed, could openly promote zoning on the basis that it stabilized property values: in every city with well-established zoning, the authors reported, "property values are reported stabilized and in many instances substantially increased," a fact that had been quickly recognized by financial institu-tions everywhere.[63] "*Zoning and plat control,*" they emphasized, "*divide honors in being reported the most profitable results of city planning.*"[64] As they proudly pro-claimed in a chapter heading, "IT PAYS TO PLAN."[65] Far from realizing greater social justice for the poor locked in the tenements of New York and Chicago, the planning-and-zoning system of the 1920s was designed precisely to keep them out of the desirable new suburbs that were being built along the streetcar tracks and the subway lines.

London: The Tube Brings Suburban Sprawl

Something like that was happening around London and other great British cities – but with an important difference. There, too, the age of mass suburbanization began after World War One. The key, in London and Birmingham as in New York or Chicago, was of course transport; these developments, at any rate in London and the big provincial cities, were well outside walk-to-work range. Booth and others had railed against the lack of cheap trains: despite Gladstone's Penny Trains Act of 1844, the railway companies did little, and sometimes even seemed to share the Duke of Wellington's view that railways might "act as a premium to the lower orders to go uselessly wandering around the country."[66] Parliament in 1864 had allowed the GER extension to Liverpool Street on condition that the railway provided cheap trains, and alone in northeast London did large-scale working-class suburbs develop.[67]

[61] Popper, 1981, 54.
[62] Sies, 1997, 165, 186–7.
[63] Hubbard and Hubbard, 1929, 188–9.
[64] Hubbard and Hubbard, 1929, 188–9, 283.
[65] Hubbard and Hubbard, 1929, 281.
[66] Haywood, 1997, 44.
[67] Haywood, 1997, 44.

The key then was municipal trams and then buses in places like Birmingham, Liverpool, and Manchester, underground railways and commuter railways as well in London. Above all, the growth of speculative housing around London – which roughly trebled the capital's area in 20 years – depended on rail transit. Unlike provincial England, this system was provided by private enterprise: specifically, the Underground group, which had absorbed the London General Omnibus Company in 1912, and the main-line railway companies, of which two – the Southern, and the London and North Eastern – developed major commuter networks.

A significant part of this system was created by American capital and enterprise. But that was not surprising. Americans had been quick to see the commercial potential of land development following new rail or streetcar lines, and some of the earliest textbook examples of the planned railway suburb – Llewellyn Park at West Orange, New Jersey (1853), Chestnut Hill in Philadelphia (1854), Lake Forest, Illinois (1856), and Riverside, Illinois (1869) – all anticipate the first classic British essay in the genre, Bedford Park in West London (1876).[68] From here it was a short step to the notion that an entrepreneur would deliberately lay out rail or streetcar lines in order to develop suburbs around them, as illustrated by the careers of F. M. "Borax" Smith in the San Francisco Bay area or Henry E. Huntingdon in Los Angeles.[69] But the most colorful, if perhaps the least savory, example was provided – first in Chicago, then in London – by the career of Charles Tyson Yerkes (1837–1905).

Yerkes was disarmingly open about his operations: "The secret of my success is to buy old junk, fix it up a little, and unload it on other fellows."[70] Contemporaries called him "a buccaneer from a Pennsylvania penitentiary" (he had been jailed for early fraud) and "not a safe man."[71] He developed the street railway system of Chicago and connected it into a network via the downtown Loop, controlling over 400 miles of street railway.[72] When the time came in 1897 to extend his franchises, he paid one million dollars to buy the State legislature and then the City Council; successful in the first, he was unsuccessful in the second and nearly provoked a riot, after which he felt it provident to leave the city.[73]

London was a natural port of call. For there – as Theodore Dreiser recounts in his last novel, a thinly disguised fiction – he immediately realized that the Circle underground line was a ready-made downtown loop which could be exploited thorough new lines, then projected to start.[74] When Chicago heard of all this, Dreiser wrote, there were "snarls of rage" that "such a ruthless trickster, so recently ejected from that city" should now descend on London.[75] But descend he did; by 1901 Yerkes had acquired a large part of the London network, existing and new, and had welded it

[68]   Stern and Massingale, 1981, 23–4; Stern, 1986, Ch. 4.
[69]   Jackson, K. T., 1985, 119–22.
[70]   Quoted in Roberts, 1961, 344.
[71]   Roberts, 1961, 348, 353.
[72]   Barker and Robbins, 1974, 61–2.
[73]   Malone, 1936, 610–11.
[74]   Dreiser, 1947, 35–6, 200.
[75]   Dreiser, 1947, 125.

Figure 3.4 Charles Tyson Yerkes. "Not a safe man" by Chicago standards, but the builder of three of London's tubes; he died before he could reap his speculative rewards, but his legacy lives on. *Source*: © TfL from the London Transport Museum Collection.

into a new company, the Underground Electric Railways of London Limited (UERL), and was engaged in a titanic struggle with another American tycoon, J. Pierrepoint Morgan, for the right to build new tubes in London.[76] The key to the operation is revealed by the fictional Yerkes:

> maybe you can find out something about the land values that are likely to be made by what we do, and whether it might be worth while to buy in advance in any direction, as we have done here in Lakeview and other places.[77]

[76] Barker and Robbins, 1974, Ch. 4.
[77] Dreiser, 1947, 23.

Figure 3.5   Frank Pick. *Source*: © TfL from the London Transport Museum Collection.

The gains would not come directly from the new lines, however: expensive to construct, these barely reached the built-up edge of London. They would come from tramway feeder lines, developed by separate companies, with syndicates to buy and sell land on the American pattern; UERL already controlled one tramway net, in West London.[78] Unfortunately for him, in 1905, while the new tube lines were actually under construction, Yerkes died.

But at least some of his legacy was to live after him – though stripped of the colorful financial aspects. The year after Yerkes's death his successor as chairman of UERL, George Gibb, brought in a young statistical assistant called Frank Pick. The year after that, the company in deep financial trouble, UERL's directors bowed to the wishes of their American controlling interests and appointed to the post of general manager a 32-year-old British émigré to the United States, then manager of the Public Service Corporation of New Jersey, Albert Stanley. Stanley (later Lord Ashfield) and Pick, men of very different but complementary personalities, were to form arguably the greatest management team ever known in the history of urban

---

[78]   Jackson, 1973, 73; Barker and Robbins, 1974, 63.

Figure 3.6 Albert Stanley, Lord Ashfield. Frank Pick and Albert Stanley, the greatest management team in the history of London Transport, and – through their creation of the interwar suburbs – the true creators of modern London. *Source*: © TfL from the London Transport Museum Collection.

public transport; from 1933, on formation of London Transport, Ashfield would become Chairman, Pick Vice-Chairman and Chief Executive Officer.[79] In 1912, when UERL took over the London General Omnibus Company, Pick – now the company's commercial manager – began to develop feeder buses from the tube termini, on the model of Yerkes's original tramways plan; within six months, with a new slogan "Where the Railway Ends the Motor Bus Begins," he more than doubled the number of routes, and extended the service area five times.[80]

But that was just the provisional start. After World War One, Pick began systematically to analyze the gaps in existing rail services and the possibilities of providing new ones. Successive governments, apparently impressed by the notion that public works would relieve unemployment, provided public money at zero or minimal

[79] Menzler, 1951, 104–5, 110–11; Barker and Robbins, 1974, 140, 142.
[80] Barman, 1979, 66, 70.

rates of interest.[81] The results were presented in a number of papers that Pick – that most academic-minded of managers – gave to learned and professional societies from 1927 onwards: a tube line, running at average speed of 25 miles per hour, would give an urban area of 12-mile radius; by wide spacing of outer stations and by closing inner ones (as Pick did on the Piccadilly Line in 1932–4) this could be edged out to perhaps 15 miles, but hardly anyone would pay the equivalent of more than a 6*d*. fare, so by the late 1930s – when the last tube extensions were being built – the whole system had reached a limit.[82]

South of the River Thames, directed by its equally dynamic general manager Herbert Walker, the Southern Railway (SR) did a similar job, rapidly electrifying its network to trigger a building boom. Over a third of the new stations opened in the London area after 1919 were on the SR and "Almost all the new stations opened in the London suburban area after 1920 had some form of subsidy from interested developers, seventeen of them on the Southern Railway alone."[83]

The development, thus triggered, took two forms, both presaged by the pioneering prewar schemes: first, an explosion of speculative building, above all around London, partly within the framework of town-planning schemes, partly running ahead of them; secondly, a great extension of local authority housing estates, especially around the great cities, generally in the form of dependent satellite towns linked to the parent city by tram, bus, or rail. Both came to be condemned for failures in planning; but while in the first place the condemnation was muted and partial, in the second it was well-nigh universal, providing in the process the fuel that powered the movement for a more effective town and country planning system.

The Legacy of Tudor Walters

Down to World War One, local authorities had provided a negligible share of new housing in Britain: a total of 18,000 houses under the 1890 Act, the great majority of them in London; between 1910 and 1914, indeed, demolitions had outrun completions.[84] And, though there was a deepening crisis in the supply of working-class housing, there was no agreement as to the solution; some, like Nettlefold in Birmingham, thought that the framework of the 1909 Act would serve to release the energies of the private builders; others that co-partnership schemes provided the answer.[85] During the war, the problem actually worsened; rent strikes in Glasgow and in the new munitions factory areas led to the hasty imposition of rent control.[86] At its end, the government faced a dilemma; it wanted to lift rent control, but it did

[81] Barman, 1979, 78, 88, 147–8; Jackson, 1973, 220.
[82] Pick, 1927, 165; Pick, 1936, 215–16; Pick, 1938, Q. 3083–4, 3090–5; Haywood, 1997, 58.
[83] Haywood, 1997, 55.
[84] Gauldie, 1974, 306.
[85] Daunton, 1983, 289–92.
[86] Castells, 1983, 27–37.

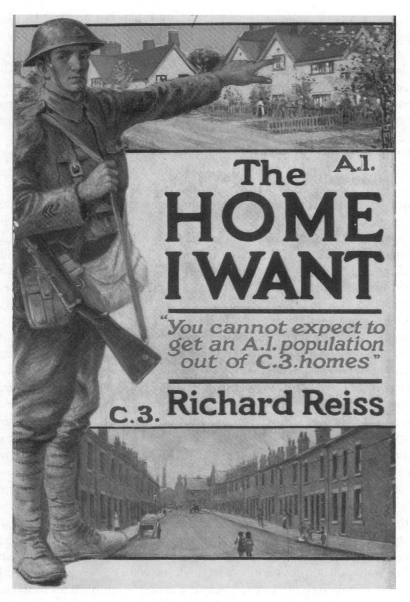

Figure 3.7 Homes Fit for Heroes. The Lloyd George quotation that never was; the actual slogan, though less memorable, decided the Khaki Election of 1918. *Source*: The Bodleian Library, University of Oxford, 24755 e. 77, inside front cover/Hodder & Stoughton.

not dare to unless the supply of new housing increased, and that could come only through local authority intervention.[87] In his highly influential 1918 book *The Home I Want*, the housing reformer Captain Reiss could assert that it was "generally agreed, even by those who believe in private enterprise, that no other policy can be adopted immediately after the war" than local authority building; "It has been a bitter reproach to us that thousands of the men who have gone out to fight for 'Home and Country' have had no home worthy of that name and but little for which to thank their country."[88]

All this was to change. Almost overnight, the housing of the working classes – the term was still openly used, then and for long after – came to be a public responsibility. The result, between the two world wars, was more than a million local authority dwellings, most of them single-family cottage houses, with their own gardens, in the form of satellites at the peripheries of the cities. Sometimes, as with the developments by Manchester at Wythenshawe, Liverpool at Speke, or London at Becontree, these amounted almost to new towns – albeit lacking sufficient industry to make them anything like self-contained. But they were the largest planned developments in England at that time, dwarfing the then garden cities: Becontree reached the 116,000 mark in 1939; Wythenshawe at the end of the 1930s was one-third of the way to the same target.

They represent the supreme achievement, though some would say the supreme failure, of Raymond Unwin. Here, not for the last time, we go out of historical sequence. Unwin's considerable early reputation came from his designs for the first Garden City at Letchworth and for Hampstead Garden Suburb, to be chronicled in Chapter 4. In 1915, at considerable financial sacrifice, he had joined the Local Government Board as Town Planning Inspector in order to influence housing reform. Two years later, his opportunity came: he was appointed a member of the Committee on Housing chaired by Sir John Tudor Walters, which reported a month before the war's end, in October 1918.

That report proved one of the most potent influences on the development of the twentieth-century British city. It essentially argued four propositions. First, that though public utility societies, formed by groups of large employers, "should be made an important auxiliary to the work of the local authorities," the latter alone – subsidized, of course, by government – could complete the task of building some 500,000 houses in a short time, 100,000 a year; speculative builders, the report dismissively declared, "present a rather more difficult problem, but they most certainly have their place." Secondly, that the local authorities must chiefly build on cheap undeveloped land on the outskirts of cities, carefully phasing their plans in with tramway development so that they did not have to pay enhanced value:

---

[87] Bowley, 1945, 9.
[88] Reiss, 1918, 7.

Figure 3.8 Raymond Unwin. Heavily influenced by William Morris and John Ruskin; the creator, with Barry Parker, of the garden-city–garden-suburb architectural vernacular. *Source*: © National Portrait Gallery, London.

> With respect to the large towns, it is most desirable that, in order to avoid further over-crowding in the built-up areas, the new schemes should be provided in the outskirts, and the first step in this direction is to speed up the town-planning schemes coupled with foresight in tramway extension and other means of transit.[89]

Thirdly, it argued that on such sites it was both possible and desirable to build at maximum densities of 12 single-family houses to the acre, each with its own garden, securing economies in land use by skilful design – of which they gave numerous examples. Fourthly, that to ensure good quality of design the plans should be produced by architects and must be approved by local commissioners of the Local Government Board and its Scottish equivalent.[90]

The report represented Unwin's personal triumph. All his basic ideas, carried through from his 1912 pamphlet *Nothing Gained by Overcrowding!*, were here: the minimum

[89] GB Local Government Boards, 1918, 5.
[90] GB Local Government Boards, 1918, 4–7, 13–17, 77.

Figure 3.9   Nothing Gained by Overcrowding! Unwin's enormously influential 1912 pamphlet dealt the death-blow to the by-law street and ushered in the age of the council estate and cottage home. *Source*: The Bodleian Library, University of Oxford, 2479116 d. 4, p. 9.

distance of 70 feet between houses to guarantee winter sunshine, the use of short terraces, the garden for every family, the use of spare backland as recreational space, the emphasis on culs-de-sac for safe children's play. Partly these recommendations stemmed from the remarkable experiment of employing a separate Women's Housing Sub-Committee, of whose recommendations Unwin seems to have taken just so much as he wished – rejecting, for instance, their recommendation that every house must have a separate parlor.[91]

The report was radical enough; what was remarkable was its immediate endorsement. But the fact was that the government was running scared. The day after the Armistice, Lloyd George announced what came to be known as the Khaki Election, promising, in one of those celebrated statements that are always misquoted, "habitations fit for the heroes who have won the war."[92] The next February, back in office at a conference with ministers, the Prime Minister recounted an anecdote:

> A well-to-do man went to remonstrate with the miners. One of them, a fairly educated man and a Scotsman, said "Do you know the place I live in?" He lives in one of those houses that are back-to-back, with all the sewage brought right through the living-room, and he has all his children living in that place. He said "Supposing your children lived in those conditions, what would happen to you?" The well-to-do man said frankly "I should be a Bolshevik."[93]

Neville Chamberlain responded "I agree that our housing problem has got into such a condition that it is a threat to the stability of the State."[94] The next month, in Cabinet, Lloyd George returned to what was evidently an obsession:

> In a short time we might have three-quarters of Europe converted to Bolshevism … Great Britain would hold out, but only if people were given a sense of confidence … We had promised them reform time and time again, but little had been done … Even if it cost a hundred million pounds, what was that compared with the stability of the State?[95]

A month after, the Parliamentary Secretary to the Local Government Board repeated that "the money we are going to spend on housing is an insurance against Bolshevism and Revolution."[96] And this was to be embodied not merely in the fact that a house was built, but also in its design: "The new houses built by the state – each with its own garden, surrounded by trees and hedges, and equipped internally with the amenities of a middle-class home – was to provide visible proof of the irrelevance of revolution."[97]

The insurance policy was duly taken out, in the form of the Addison Act, named for Christopher Addison, Minister of Reconstruction and then of Health: officially, the Housing and Town Planning Act, 1919. It imposed a duty on each local authority to survey housing needs – not just for slum clearance, but generally – and to make and carry out plans. It also guaranteed a state subsidy, independent of costs, to take

---

[91]   GB Ministry of Reconstruction, 1918; Swenarton, 1981, 98.
[92]   Swenarton, 1981, 79.
[93]   Quoted in Johnson, 1968, 370.
[94]   Quoted in Johnson, 1968, 371.
[95]   Swenarton, 1981, 78.
[96]   Swenarton, 1981, 79.
[97]   Swenarton, 1981, 87.

Figure 3.10 Cottage Homes for the People. Basic Unwin plans from the Ministry of Health Manual of 1920, following the Tudor Walters report; they would be repeated in their thousands across the face of England, but the garden-city purists felt betrayed. *Source*: The Bodleian Library, University of Oxford, O.GB/H1c/1920(10), Plate 9.

account of the tenant's ability to pay; the costs were not to be passed on.[98] It also made plan preparation mandatory for all urban areas with 20,000 and more people.

The same year, the Ministry of Health – a brand-new ministry, formed out of the old Local Government Board, and responsible for the new housing program – issued an immensely influential Housing Manual which bore Unwin's stamp all over it; its central argument, that urban densities of 12 houses per acre could be justified on cost grounds, derived directly from *Nothing Gained by Overcrowding!* It also carried over from the Tudor Walters report other key arguments, such as the minimum distance of 70 feet between houses; it "became an unwritten, unexplained, but universally accepted code of practice."[99] But it also repeated another argument, which Unwin had used in a lecture at the University of Manchester in 1912 and which had recurred in the Tudor Walters report: that the resulting developments should take the form of semi-autonomous "satellites" rather than full-fledged garden cities. Unwin, in other words, here made his definitive and immensely influential break with the pure garden-city gospel.

Here, it came to be challenged by another Ministry initiative of 1919: a committee, comprising Chamberlain as chair, George Pepler (Unwin's chief of planning at the Ministry), and Captain Reiss, to report on the problem of unhealthy areas. Its interim report on London, published in March 1920, argued that the capital still suffered from an intolerable housing problem: 184,000 people in the LCC area lived in unhealthy areas, 549,000 in all under unsatisfactory conditions. There were two main remedies: to build up, or to move out. The first was "quite unsuitable for a working-class population who are dependent on their own services for domestic services and the care of their children," as well as putting occupants "at the mercy of any undesirable tenant"; the testimony of Medical Officers of Heath and of social workers made it clear that "the self-contained house is what appeals to working people."[100] So the long-term solution must be garden cities, some based on existing country towns, of 30,000–50,000 people, surrounded by green belts. But, to achieve them, the problem was how to coordinate housing and industrial movement: "the only way to escape from the vicious circle is by the investment of the State ... of a considerable amount of capital ... the return upon which must be delayed for a considerable period."[101] And for this, a first essential was an integrated plan for the development of the whole built-up area of London.[102] Two years later, in its final report, the Committee repeated and underlined this last recommendation; it also asked for government loans to get the garden cities started.[103]

The fact was that the Committee found itself on the horns of a dilemma. Without dispersal, it was difficult to house more than 70% of slum dwellers in five-story

---

[98]   Bowley, 1945, 16–18.
[99]   Edwards, 1981, 106.
[100] GB Ministry of Health, 1920b, 3.
[101] GB Ministry of Health, 1920b, 3.
[102] GB Ministry of Health, 1920b, 4.
[103] GB Ministry of Health, 1921, 4–5.

tenements, and impossible to approach such a figure if development was to be restricted to the three-story blocks favored by the Ministry of Health, let alone the cottages demanded by local authorities like Bethnal Green Borough Council. The dilemma continued throughout the interwar years – to be resolved only by the dramatic reduction in population throughout London – but particularly in the East End – during World War Two bombing.[104]

It was crying for the moon. By 1921, following a sustained campaign by the Beaverbrook and Northcliffe presses against government waste, Christopher Addison – architect of the whole program, first as Minister of Reconstruction, then of Health – had been sacrificed by Lloyd George in order to salvage his precarious coalition government.[105] His successor at Health, Sir Alfred Mond, slashed the program. The era of reconstruction, of Homes Fit for Heroes, was over. To be fair, housing subsidies came back, and with them large-scale local authority house-building: through the 1923 Act, significantly passed when Chamberlain had replaced Mond at Health, and the Labour government's 1924 Wheatley Act, which represented a partial return to the 1919 program. Between 1919 and 1933–4, local authorities in Britain built 763,000 houses, some 31% of the total completions.[106]

They built them, however, according to the latter-day Unwin prescription, in the form of peripheral satellites rather than full-fledged garden cities. The LCC housed 19,000 at Watling in northwest London, 30,000 at Downham in southeast London, 40,000 at St Helier around the new Morden tube station, and no less than 116,000 in the huge satellite at Becontree, the largest planned residential suburb in the world, and bigger than many English provincial towns.[107] They provided an immense improvement in housing standards, though ironically for the artisan, the small tradesman, and the clerk rather than for the really poor, who could not afford the combined burden of rent and fares.[108] Architecturally, they were debased sub-Unwin, following the Housing Manual with little imagination and no inspiration. They are plain dull: a sudden and sad decline from the standards set a few years earlier at Old Oak.

In terms of detailed planning, they aped the worst faults of the speculative builder. The White Hart Lane extension, the Wormholt estate in Hammersmith, and St Helier are all cut in half by huge arterial roads, which were actually built at the same time as an integral part of the plan (though, to tell truth, Unwin and Parker got in the same tangle at the northern edge of Hampstead Garden Suburb); no one, apparently, then anticipated what traffic would do to the local environment. Local jobs were few, and public transport links to jobs poor; by the late 1930s overcrowding on the Morden tube (which served both Watling and St Helier) was the subject of parliamentary questions, and the comedian Max Miller was making questionable

---

[104] Pepper and Richmond, 2009, 168.
[105] Minney, 1958, 176, 185; Gauldie, 1974, 309.
[106] Bowley, 1945, 59.
[107] Young, 1934, 98; Jackson, 1973, 291, 302, 309; Burnett, 1978, 231.
[108] Young, 1934, 118–20; Burnett, 1978, 233.

jokes about it;[109] until the District Line was extended there in 1932, commuters from Becontree faced a 75-minute journey to Charing Cross.[110] None of the estates, even the biggest, had any kind of planned green belt around it, though Becontree had a partial and very narrow park girdle. Becontree was well planted with trees, though, as the sociologist Terence Young reported in his pioneer survey of 1934, "the children have made their existence insecure"; the world was not innocent of vandalism, even then.[111]

Thus the new estates were not always popular with their occupants; at Becontree, the most distant, more than 30,000 left over a 10-year period; more than 10,000 in one year, 1928–9, alone;[112] at Watling in northwest London, surveyed by the young Ruth Glass at the end of the 1930s, some had returned to the slums because they could not afford rent and fares.[113] And some, doubtless, yearned for the bustle of the city:

> One afternoon in the autumn of 1937, early in the history of the Watling Estate, a woman banged loudly at the door of her neighbour. When it was opened she cried out: "What has happened?" "Why," said her neighbour, "what should have happened; what is the matter?" "Everything is so terribly quiet," said the first woman, still frightened to death.[114]

But later research has undermined this view that a move to Watling or Roehampton meant a life of loneliness and desolation. In Roehampton, people became good friends and helped each other. But they kept themselves to themselves and their neighbors at a distance. In Watling the residents went further, building a strong community characterized by friendships, gregariousness, acts of public sociability, and mutual aid. Here, outside hostility played a role.[115] For the prospect of an LCC estate was not popular with locals: at Becontree there were the usual press stories about people who pulled off their front doors for firewood;[116] at an inquiry in the 1930s, an impassioned exchange took place:

> MRS BASTARD: You haved [*sic*] ruined my home! (*turning to LCC officers*) Do any
>   of you gentlemen live near an LCC estate?
>   *receiving no answer*
>   No, I don't suppose you do.
>   (*addressing the Minister's Inspector*):
>   Do you live near an estate?

[109]   Jackson, 1973, 271.
[110]   Young, 1934, 140.
[111]   Young, 1934, 98.
[112]   Young, 1934, 210.
[113]   Durant, 1939, 17–18.
[114]   Durant, 1939, 1.
[115]   Bayliss, 2001, 192.
[116]   Young, 1934, 23.

THE INSPECTOR: They have just bought some land near my house.
MRS BASTARD: Do you like it?
THE INSPECTOR: No.[117]

In fact, the new estates were almost universally regarded as repositories for the working class, which "in many contexts seen as urban, unionized, 'communist,' uncultured, and destructive – was suspect." Sharp predicted barricades and "the bitterest kind of political upheaval." Even Unwin thought the people in one-class estates had become "little more than disorganised crowds." And this explains the concern, at the end of World War II, that the new towns should be of "diverse and balanced social composition."[118]

The Building of Suburbia

This reaction came, of course, from someone on the other side of the great housing divide which by then had sprung up across England, though nowhere more starkly than in the Home Counties around London. On that other side, a new industry had effectively been created, catering for a new market. Before World War One, the overwhelming majority of the entire population had rented their homes. After it, a number of factors conspired to persuade millions of the new middle class to buy. Huge changes in the structure of the economy were creating a new white-collar class, whose numbers rose from 20 to 30% of the workforce between 1911 and 1951.[119] Real incomes for a large section of the population – especially this new white-collar group and the skilled blue-collar workers, whose jobs were disproportionately in and around London – were rising sharply. The Building Societies attracted huge funds, especially in the depression of the 1930s when industrial shares became unattractive. By various devices – insurance guarantees, the development of a "builder's pool" whereby the developer took the risk – the proportion loaned could be raised as high as 95%; at Bexley in the 1930s, keys to the cheapest houses could be had for a £5 deposit, and if this were lacking the estate agent or builder would lend it. Interest payments reached a low point of 4.5% in the mid-1930s.[120]

In Britain, new lending by building societies totaled £7 million in 1918, £32 million in 1923, £75 million in 1929, and £103 million in 1933. Alan Jackson stated that 75% of all new homes in interwar suburban London were bought on a mortgage.[121]

On the supply side, larger established builders like Costain, Crouch, Laing, Taylor Woodrow, Wates, and Wimpey competed with a host of small firms existing on precarious profit margins and cash flows, which often went under but kept prices

---

[117]   Jackson, 1973, 161.
[118]   Bayliss, 2001, 193.
[119]   Burnett, 1978, 247.
[120]   Jackson, 1973, 193, 196; Boddy, 1980, 13–15; Carr, 1982, 244.
[121]   Dennis, 2008, 203.

keen.[122] And, in the depths of an agricultural depression, land was cheap; a plot could be had for as little as £20.[123] So families with modest incomes – skilled manual workers earning as little as £3.50 a week – could now afford to buy.[124] In the 1930s, £1 a week would buy the standard three-bedroomed semi-detached, while those earning £300–500 a year – teachers, bank officials, executive class civil servants – could afford bigger houses, perhaps detached.[125]

But these different agents were merely acting in the service of a deep collective national dream. The worship of the suburban ideal went back a long way, as Dennis Hardy has suggested. Less dramatic than grand metropolitan visions, less innovative than garden cities, it was the vision of suburban life that took pride of place as a populist utopia. People migrated to the new suburbs not only because new houses were available, but also because a house with a garden in a tree-lined avenue was another manifestation of a basic anti-urban feeling. "Owning a small patch of England and turning one's own soil was another demonstration of what Jan Marsh has called 'our collective pastoralism.'"[126]

Paradoxically, the garden-city movement – to be considered in Chapter 4 – fanned the flames of suburban idealism. For, although garden-city purists could not accept anything less than self-standing settlements, others could settle for such terms as "garden suburb" and "garden village" and even, in cases, "garden city," for their own ends. As Gillian Darley has noted, "soon the misused term Garden Suburb, Village or City began to be synonymous with suburbia."[127]

The result was a suburban explosion, on a scale unmatched before or ever after. In the 20 years between 1900 and 1920 the urban acreage of England and Wales increased by 10% (from 2.0 to 2.2 million acres), but in the 20 years from 1920 to 1939 it increased by nearly half (from 2.2 to 3.2 million acres). On these acres went nearly 4.2 million new homes: just under one-third of them (1.2 million) built by local authorities; over two-thirds (3.0 million) by private enterprise, mostly for owner-occupiers. At the peak of the building frenzy, 1934–5, private enterprise built just under 288,000 dwellings, more than double the previous record (1905–6) and never equaled since. Most of them, by far, were built around London. In 1921, the four counties surrounding the County of London – Essex, Kent, Middlesex, and Surrey – accounted for 12.2% of the housing stock; but they accounted for almost double that, 23.6%, of the houses built between 1918 and 1940. Astonishingly, more houses – 983,048 of them – were built here between the wars than had existed at the start.[128]

These circumstances powerfully conditioned the resulting product. "To be saleable, a speculative house had to be emphatically middle-class, but if it had to be middle-class it also had to be cheap": that meant romantic-looking, conservative in

---

[122] Jackson, 1973, 110; Burnett, 1978, 257.
[123] Carr, 1982, 247.
[124] Jackson, 1973, 190–1.
[125] Burnett, 1978, 248.
[126] Hardy, 2005, 40.
[127] Hardy, 2005, 41.
[128] Swenarton, 2002, 267.

style, cheap to build, yet a status symbol.[129] Novean Homes advertised for "Families of good breeding who wish to acquire a house to be proud of at a cost of less than £1 a week";[130] "Every house different" and "No pair of houses alike" were favorite slogans.[131] Because the Royal Institute of British Architects banned speculative architectural practice in 1920, the vast majority of these houses – nearly three million of them, between the two world wars – were designed by unqualified assistants or from pattern books or magazines. Only in the 1930s did the bigger firms begin to use architects.[132]

In the 1920s, at any rate, they were also designed without benefit of much planning. Though local authorities everywhere scrambled to follow the lead of Birmingham and Ruislip–Northwood by schemes under the 1909 and then the 1919 and 1932 Acts, the builders were often as not ahead of them; and in any case, there was a lack of positive direction from the Ministry of Health and a lack of qualified local planners.[133] Councils, frightened of claims for compensation if they refused permission under the then legislation, would gratefully accept gifts of open space from developers in return for an agreement to build denser and cheaper.[134] Many areas must have resembled Edgware, where, in 1927, the Chairman of the Ratepayers' Association said that the Town Planning scheme appeared to be framed by land-development exploiters: "Aesthetic purposes can nowhere be seen in the plans."[135] Thus, the amount of planning depended on what you could pay.

> A carefully-designed development would be marked by a variety of house-styles, winding roads, closes and crescents, generous gardens, tree-plantings and grassed verges. But often the speculative suburb lacked any overall plan, being developed road by road by numerous builders until the land ran out ... The result of such activity was sometimes a long sprawl of monotonously similar semi-detached houses along a busy arterial road, backed by a waste of derelict agricultural land, remote from amenities such as shops, schools and stations.[136]

Since the frontage was the dearest aspect and also the basis of cost, long narrow plots between 25 and 35 feet wide were the rule, producing parallel rows on identical plots. At the bottom end of the market, speed of building was of the essence; a rural landscape could be transformed into a new estate within a month. So trees were uprooted and natural features ignored; roads were laid out in aimless serpentine fashion or simply followed old field paths, giving an impression that managed to be simultaneously restless and monotonous.[137] The result was a segregated landscape of suburbia, in which the kind and density of the housing immediately suggested the

[129] Edwards, 1981, 127–8.
[130] Burnett, 1978, 249–50.
[131] Burnett, 1978, 264.
[132] Burnett, 1978, 253; Edwards, 1981, 133.
[133] Jackson, 1973, 321.
[134] Carr, 1982, 254.
[135] Jackson, 1973, 255.
[136] Burnett, 1978, 249.
[137] Jackson, 1973, 126–7; Burnett, 1978, 256; Carr, 1982, 247.

Figure 3.11 By-Pass Variegated. Osbert Lancaster's merciless rendering of the genre; complete with leaded windows, lace curtains, crazy paving, and the Wall's Ice Cream Tricycle. *Source*: By permission of Clare Hastings.

social status of those within it. And the 1932 Act actually encouraged this, by giving councils the opportunity to lay down variations in density, all the way down to one house per 5, 10, or 25 acres, invariably without liability to pay compensation.[138]

Usually, the starting point was either a concentration of shops and flats in Mock Tudor or Debased Classical, around the railway or tube station; a giant cinema might be another prominent feature. Thence, building proceeded in ribbons, following feeder bus services along the new arterial by-pass roads – designed, ironically, to reduce traffic congestion, and financed under unemployment relief programs in two bursts, in the early 1920s and the mid-1930s – without benefit, until an Act of 1935, of any limitation on frontage development. The resulting pattern was immortalized by the cartoonist Osbert Lancaster, as By-Pass Variegated:

> here are some quaint gables culled from *Art Nouveau* surmounting a facade that is plainly modernistic in inspiration; there the twisted beams and leaded panes of Stockbrokers' Tudor are happily contrasted with bright green tiles of obviously

[138] Burnett, 1978, 249; Sheail, 1981, 77; Carr, 1982, 255.

Pseudish origin; next door some terra-cotta plaques, Pont Street Dutch in character, enliven a white wood Wimbledon Transitional porch, making it a splendid foil to a red-brick garage that is vaguely Romanesque in feeling.[139]

Rustic names like Meadowside, Woodsview, and Fieldsend all too soon became misnomers; the Southern Railway, with three successive stations called Park – Raynes, Motspur, and Worcester – narrowly avoided the appellation being awarded to yet a fourth, Stoneleigh.[140]

The result was universally derided and condemned. The fact was that the prosecutors were all upper-middle-class and the offenders were mostly lower-middle-class: in a typical such suburb, Bexley, which gained 18,000 houses and 52,000 people in the 1930s, the 1951 Census showed that the overwhelming majority came from Social Class III, the skilled manual and junior non-manual grades.[141] Moving as they did from by-law terraces without bathrooms or inside lavatories, they were enjoying a quantum leap in their quality of life, and "whatever their place in the hierarchy of snobbery, all suburbs showed the same characteristic of one-family houses in gardens and in an environment more or less removed from the dirt, noise and congestion of the city."[142]

But suburbia did more for them. Uniform and monotonous as they might seem from the outside, for their new occupants each house embodied tiny variations, built-in or bought-in, which gave it individuality: a stained-glass window, a porch, a kitchen fitting, even a garden gnome. The house itself was designed to express individuality, hence the bay window and the corner door, the great variation in very minor detail, the general lack of collective space around the house, all consciously designed to be as unlike "council housing" as possible.[143]

But architects did not like it. Repeatedly, in their journals, at their congresses, during the 1930s they railed about the suburbs. The suburbs' chief fault seems to have been that they conspicuously diverged from either of the then main standards of good taste: the Neo-Georgian as still taught in leading schools like Liverpool, or the uncompromisingly modern embraced by the young members of the Congrès Internationaux d'Architecture Moderne.[144] Instead, their cozy imitation-vernacular derived from a much older architectural tradition pioneered by John Nash at Blaise Hamlet and Park Village West, and subsequently developed to a high art by such late Victorians as Philip Webb, Norman Shaw, and Raymond Unwin. Perhaps significantly, the first two had opposed the whole idea of a closed architectural profession, and Parker was trained as an interior decorator.[145] But of course, the result was a

---

139 Lancaster, 1959, 152.
140 Jackson, 1973, 128, 170.
141 Carr, 1982, 238, 241.
142 Burnett, 1978, 249; Jackson, 1973, 146.
143 Oliver *et al.*, 1981, 115–17.
144 Oliver *et al.*, 1981, 41, 50, 67–9.
145 Creese, 1966, 255; Oliver *et al.*, 1981, 64.

pastiche; and often an unsuccessful one. Osbert Lancaster put it all better, that is to say more savagely, than any of the professionals:

> If an architect of enormous energy, painstaking ingenuity and great structural knowledge, had devoted years of his life to the study of how best to achieve the maximum of inconvenience, in the shape and arrangement under one roof of a stated number of rooms, and had the assistance of a corps of research workers ransacking architectural history for the least attractive materials and building devices known in the past, it is just possible, though highly unlikely, that he might have evolved a style as crazy as that with which the speculative builder, with no expenditure of mental energy at all, has enriched the landscape on either side of our great arterial roads ... Notice the skill with which the houses are disposed, that insures that the largest possible area of countryside is ruined with the minimum of expense; see how carefully each householder is provided with a clear view into the most private offices of his next-door neighbour and with what studied disregard of the sun's aspect the principal rooms are planned.[146]

The Architects' Revenge

Whether it was sour grapes or not, the architects were angry; they wanted revenge. They were not the only ones, though they led the attack. Their metaphors were sometimes military, sometimes clinical. Clough Williams-Ellis, in *England and the Octopus* (1928), wrote of ribbon development as "The disfiguring little buildings [that] grow up and multiply like nettles along a drain, like lice upon a tapeworm"; bungalows "constitute England's most disfiguring disease, having, from sporadic beginnings, now become our premier disease."[147] By 1933 he was declaring that

> I would certainly sooner go back for another year in wartime Ypres than spend a twelvemonth in post-war Slough. Should that sound like an over-statement I should explain that it is merely the prudent desire of one who desires to remain happily alive, and who would therefore assuredly choose an eighty per cent risk of being shot, gassed or blown up in heroic company to the certainty of cutting his own throat in surroundings of humiliating squalor.[148]

Slough, as also for Betjeman, became the symbol of all that was wrong. Yet Betjeman loved some suburbia, as witness his television labor of love on Metro-land: "A verge in front of your house and grass and a tree for the dog. Variety created in each facade of the houses – in the colouring of the trees. In fact, the country had come to the suburbs. Roses are blooming in Metro-land just as they do in the brochures."[149]

---

[146] Lancaster, 1959, 152.
[147] Williams-Ellis, 1928, 141.
[148] Williams-Ellis, 1933, 105.
[149] Betjeman, 1978, 225.

Figure 3.12   The Great West Road. 1930s By-Pass Variegated *en masse* from the air, clustered around Osterley tube station (foreground), one of Charles Holden's brilliant designs for Frank Pick. *Source*: © English Heritage (Aerofilms Collection).

These, like Surrey, were the *good* suburbs, inhabited by loveable Betjemanesque characters like Pam the great big mountainous sports girl, or Miss J. Hunter Dunn sitting the evening long in the car park in the full Surrey twilight; but Slough, like Ruislip Gardens, from which Metro station,

> With a thousand Ta's and Pardon's,
> Daintily alights Elaine[150]

were quite other places, occupied exclusively by lower-middle-class despoilers of the countryside.

---

[150]   "Middlesex," Betjeman, 1978, 191.

Abercrombie, who had taken the lead in founding the Council for the Preservation (later Protection) of Rural England in 1926, took a more sanguine view of the bungalow disease: "Seriously, is not the damage largely skin deep? ... will many of what you rightly call Blasphemous Bungalows, blaspheme for long? And is not much of England virgin country, *intacta*?"[151] He was more concerned about ribbon growth: "These strips of the countryside are ... being colonised with no more rationale of social grouping, or economies of estate development or aesthetics of rural design than existed during the industrial revolution of last century."[152] But he too was convinced that "This rural England of ours is at this moment menaced with a more sudden and more thorough change than ever before," too rapid to permit automatic adjustment.[153] He wrote wistfully of the Chinese practitioner of *Feng Shui*,

> whose job it is to study and expound the shapes which the spiritual forces of nature have produced and to prescribe the ways in which all buildings, roads, bridges, canals and railways must conform to them, is placed in a position of extreme power; and we ourselves can hardly hope to be able similarly to explode some flaring upstart bungalow or "Satanic Mill" or conflagrate the perpetuation of certain countryside-blasting advertisements in their own spirit.[154]

But, he thought, they certainly showed the right way.

In 1938, Williams-Ellis was back on the attack with *Britain and the Beast*, an edited volume of essays by such leading figures of the day as J. M. Keynes, E. M. Foster, C. E. M. Joad, G. M. Trevelyan, and many others. In it, Joad presented "The People's Claim" to the countryside. "To thousands, nature, newly-discovered, has been a will-o'-the-wisp" as those lured into the countryside find that it has disappeared: "In fifty years' time there will, in southern England, be neither town nor country, but only a single dispersed suburb, sprawling unendingly from Watford to the coast." To guard against this, "the extension of the towns must be stopped, building must be restricted to sharply defined areas, and such re-housing of the population as may be necessary must be carried on within these areas."[155]

Thomas Sharp, perhaps the most prolific writer on planning problems in the early 1930s, took – here as elsewhere – a harder line. For him, the evil started with Ebenezer Howard's vision of Town-Country, which in practice had produced a degenerate mixture:

> From dreary towns the broad, mechanical, noisy main roads run out between ribbons of tawdry houses, disorderly refreshment shacks and vile, untidy garages. The old trees and hedgerows that bordered them a few years ago have given place to concrete posts

---

[151]   Williams-Ellis, 1928, 181.
[152]   Abercrombie, 1926, 20.
[153]   Abercrombie, 1926, 56.
[154]   Abercrombie, 1926, 52.
[155]   Joad, 1937, 81–2.

and avenues of telegraph poles, to hoardings and enamel advertisement signs. Over great areas there is no longer any country bordering the main roads; there is only a negative semi-suburbia.[156]

And, if the present ideals continued to hold sway, under the influence of new technologies – radio, television, the car – things could only get worse.

Tradition has broken down. Taste is utterly debased. There is no enlightened guidance or correction from authority … Rural influences neutralize the town. Urban influences neutralize the country. In a few years all will be neutrality. The strong, masculine virility of the town; the softer beauty, the richness, the fruitfulness of that mother of men, the countryside, will be debased into one sterile, hermaphrodite beastliness.[157]

The root of this sterilization process, it emerged, was fantasy about the countryside:

For a hundred years we have behaved like film-struck servant girls blinded to the filth around us by romantic dreams of worlds as yet and ever likely to be unrealised. More than anything it is this pitiful attitude of escape which has brought the English town from its beauty and hopefulness of a hundred and fifty years ago to its shapeless and shameful meanness of today.[158]

The remedy will be through "great new blocks of flats which will house a considerable part of the population of the future town" – and indeed of the countryside, where old country houses could be demolished to make way for them.[159] Thus Sharp joined the Corbusian camp, distancing himself decisively from the garden-city tradition.

What he shared with them, and with commentators generally at this time, was a terror of what Anthony King has called the democratization of the countryside: the lower-middle-class and working-class invasion of an area that had hitherto been the preserve of an aristocratic and upper-middle-class elite.[160] Joad, in his 1938 essay, expresses it revealingly:

And then there are the hordes of hikers cackling insanely in the woods, or singing raucous songs as they walk arm in arm at midnight down the quiet village street. There are people, wherever there is water, upon sea shores or upon river banks, lying in every attitude of undressed and inelegant squalor, grilling themselves, for all the world as if they were steaks, in the sun. There are tents in meadows and girls in pyjamas dancing beside them to the strains of the gramophone, while stinking disorderly dumps of tins, bags, and cartons bear witness to the tide of invasion for weeks after it has ebbed; there are fat girls in shorts, youths in gaudy ties and plus-fours, and a roadhouse round every corner and a café on top of every hill for their accommodation.[161]

---

[156] Sharp, 1932, 4.
[157] Sharp, 1932, 11.
[158] Sharp, 1936, 98.
[159] Sharp, 1936; 107; 1940, 119.
[160] King, 1980c, 462.
[161] Joad, 1937, 72–3.

This clash of attitudes was neatly expressed when Brighton proposed that, in order to preserve the South Downs from building, it would lease land as a motor racing track. There was immediate expression of outrage from the Society of Sussex Downsmen, *The Times*, the West and East Sussex Councils, and a House of Lords Committee. Lord Buxton, in the Second Reading debate, said, "I say frankly it is not so much the actual track to which I object. It is more the fact of there being that track, which will bring immense numbers of people to the Downs, to the destruction of the amenities." To which the Committee chairman, Lord Redesdale, was forced to point out, "by all means exclude the public from the Downs, but then you must not say you are preserving the Downs for the public. At least be honest and say you are preserving the Downs for the Society of Sussex Downsmen and the actual inhabitants of the Downs.[162]

In all the furore over the English countryside at this time, therefore, there were a few dissenting voices. One significant one was that of the young Evelyn Sharp, secretary of the Town and Country Planning Advisory Committee of the Ministry of Health, who was writing of the need to

> remember that the countryside is not the preserve of the wealthy and leisured classes. The country rightly prides itself on the fact that since the War there has been unparalleled building development, a development which every Government has done its utmost to stimulate, and whose effect has been to create new and better social conditions for a very large number of persons ... persons of very limited means."[163]

Any serious attempt to reverse the policy, she argued, would "undoubtedly run counter to the wishes of a large section of the community."[164] There, indeed, spoke the future Permanent Secretary.

By that time, indeed, Interim Development Orders covered some 19.5 million acres or 50% of the entire country – the half, moreover, where large-scale development was occurring. In Surrey, one of the counties most affected by London's growth, almost all landowners were voluntarily accepting restrictions on development, thus avoiding death and estate duties.[165] The then Permanent Secretary of the Ministry of Health commented that

> nobody who goes about the country today can fail to observe that the tide of sporadic, unregulated development that threatened to engulf the south after the war, is being stemmed, and that planning is beginning to leave a visible mark on the English countryside.[166]

---

[162] Sheail, 1981, 107.
[163] Sheail, 1981, 89.
[164] Sheail, 1981, 89.
[165] Sheail, 1981, 16, 76.
[166] Sheail, 1981, 128.

The 1932 Act was an advance: it allowed local authorities to make schemes for almost any land, including rural areas. By 1942, 73% of all land in England was subject to "interim development control," which, in conjunction with a draft scheme, had become the favored mechanism of control.[167] But not everyone would agree that it was effective – certainly not Professor Joad.

By 1938, the Williams-Ellises and the Joads had a new and a powerful supporter. On every one of his public appearances in the 1920s and 1930s, Frank Pick bemoaned the opportunity that was being lost by the failure to plan. In 1927, "there was much planning, but no plan … The needs of the moment are met sometimes exceedingly well but without reference to the whole … Unfortunately for London it has so far never had a directing head … It is at that low stage of animal development in which the brain is rudimentary and ganglia scattered throughout the organism stimulate such activity as serves to keep the creature alive." In 1936, "Such developments … are almost analogous to a cancerous growth"; in 1938, the risk was of "an amorphous mass of building" in which "London's country would suffer from a confluent pox."[168]

His voice, joined to the chorus, proved irresistible. Neville Chamberlain, on becoming Prime Minister at the end of 1937, almost immediately set up a Royal Commission on the Geographical Distribution of the Industrial Population, chaired by Sir Anderson Montague-Barlow. The following year, in his evidence to the Barlow Commission, Pick had arrived at the argument that if London grew beyond the magic 12–15-mile limit set by the economics of the tube, it "must cease to be intrinsically London … a unitary conception."[169] So, he argued, London's growth should be contained: "It would be possible to go on layering first industry and then residences, and then industry and then residences, and building indefinitely, but that would not be London. It would be putting rings of industrial towns around London, and that would not be London."[170] For this reason, he favored both a green belt at least a mile wide around London, and controls on new industry at the edge of London.[171]

Perhaps Pick's enthusiasm for planning was not entirely disinterested; he wanted controls on London's physical growth but not on further expansion of jobs, which suited London Transport's book; his prophetic fear, that the growth of car ownership would lead to low-density sprawl, was also the view of a public transport advocate.[172] But, in all he wrote, there emerges a consistent, almost cartoon-like, vision of a giant organically planned conurbation, in which a single integrated public transport system would provide the nerve structure for the body, and land-use planning would guide the healthy growth of the organism. Pick was in no

[167]   Crow, 1996, 404–5.
[168]   Pick 1927, 162; 1936, 213; 1938, para. 8.
[169]   Pick, 1938, Q. 3099, 3101.
[170]   Pick, 1938, Q. 3107.
[171]   Pick, 1938, Q. 2999–3001, 3120–1.
[172]   Pick, 1936, 213; 1938, Q. 2989.

doubt, in the 1930s, that the latter was lacking: "What goes by the name is idle and useless so far."[173]

To that extent, Pick was joining his weighty voice to the chorus demanding controls on London's further growth. But there was a subtle difference between them: Frederic Osborn, asked whether he would agree with Pick that a city that was not growing was a city in decay, replied, "I would even go to the other extreme and say that the ideal town, from the rating point of view, is the static town." When the Commission reported in 1940, it recorded Pick's view that London could grow further to a population of 10–12 million, but found against it: it argued on the contrary for the planned dispersal of population to self-contained new towns and an overall reduction in London's population.[174]

So the Barlow Commissioners accepted a limit on London's growth, Osborn-style rather than Pick-style, thus setting in train a course of events that culminated in the 1947 Town and Country Planning Act. Britain at last would have a land-use planning system that could effectively shape the growth of London – and indeed of every city, town, and village in the land.

[173] Pick, 1936, 210.
[174] Haywood, 1997, 58–60.

The City in the Garden

Forget six counties overhung with smoke,
Forget the snorting steam and piston stroke,
Forget the spreading of the hideous town;
Think rather of the pack-horse on the down,
And dream of London, small and white and clean,
The clear Thames bordered by its gardens green.
                    William Morris, *The Earthly Paradise* (1868)

Let every dawn of morning be to you as the beginning of life, and every setting sun be to you as its close:– then let every one of these short lives leave its sure record of some kindly thing done for others – some goodly strength or knowledge gained for yourselves; so, from day to day, and strength to strength, you shall build up indeed, by Art, by Thought, and by Just Will, an Ecclesia of England, of which it shall not be said, "See what manner of stones are here", but, "See what manner of men."

John Ruskin, *Lectures on Art* (1870)
(found in Raymond Unwin's favorite quotations)

Cities of Tomorrow: An Intellectual History of Urban Planning and Design Since 1880,
Fourth Edition. Peter Hall.
© 2014 Peter Hall. Published 2014 by John Wiley & Sons, Ltd.

4

The City in the Garden

The Garden-City Solution: London, Paris, Berlin, New York, 1900–1940

It is invidious, but it needs saying: despite doughty competition, Ebenezer Howard (1850–1928) is the most important single character in this entire tale. So it is important to get him right; even though almost everyone has got him wrong. His many self-appointed critics have, at one time or another, been wrong about almost everything he stood for. They called him a "planner," a term of derogation, whereas he earned his living as a shorthand writer. They said that he advocated low-density prairie planning; in fact, his garden city would have had densities like inner London's, which – so later planners once came to believe – needed high-rise towers to make them work. They confused this garden city with the garden suburb found at Hampstead and in numerous imitations – though, it must be confessed, one of his principal lieutenants, Raymond Unwin, was originally to blame for that. They still think that he wanted to consign people to small towns isolated in the deep countryside, while he actually proposed the planning of con-urbations with hundreds of thousands, perhaps millions, of people. They accuse him of wanting to move people round like pawns on a chessboard, whereas, in fact, he dreamed of voluntary self-governing communities. Most mistakenly of all, they see him as a physical planner, ignoring the fact that his garden cities were merely the vehicles for a progressive reconstruction of capitalist society into an infinity of cooperative commonwealths.

They cannot claim that he made it difficult for them. In his 78 years he wrote only one book, and a slim one at that. First published in 1898 under the title *To-morrow: A Peaceful Path to Real Reform*, it was reissued in 1902 with the title *Garden Cities of Tomorrow*. This was perhaps catchier, but it diverted people from the truly radical character of the message, demoting him from social visionary into physical planner.

Figure 4.1 Ebenezer Howard. The great man reduced to modest humility (or stupefaction) by an unknown orator. The audience seems to share his reaction. Probably photographed at Welwyn Garden City. *Source*: Town and Country Planning Association.

The Sources of Howard's Ideas

Better to appreciate Howard's contribution, he must be set against the background of his time. He developed his ideas in the London of the 1880s and 1890s, the age of radical ferment described in Chapter 1. An eclectic thinker, he borrowed freely from the ideas that were circulating at the time.[1] But there were other, earlier influences. Born in the City of London in 1850 – a fact commemorated by a plaque at the edge of the huge Barbican redevelopment, which almost certainly he would not have liked at all – he grew up in small country towns in southern and eastern England: Sudbury, Ipswich, Cheshunt. At 21, he emigrated to America and became a pioneer in Nebraska, where he met Buffalo Bill[2] but proved a disaster as a farmer. From 1872 to 1876 he was in Chicago, beginning the career as a shorthand writer that he was to follow all his life. We know little about these years, but they must have been important to him. As a farmer on the frontier he had personal experience of the Homestead Act of 1862, which opened up the prairies and the plains to pioneers free of charge, thus establishing an economy and society of prosperous farms and small towns, and an educational system devoted to technical improvement in

---

[1] Osborn, 1950, 228–9.
[2] Ward, 2002a, 16.

agriculture and the mechanical arts. Then, as a resident of Chicago, he saw the city's great rebuilding after the fire of 1871. Still, in these pre-skyscraper days, it was universally known as the Garden City: the almost-certain source of Howard's better-known title. He must have seen the new garden suburb of Riverside, designed by the great landscape architect Frederick Law Olmsted, arising on the Des Plaines River 9 miles outside the city.[3] Howard always denied that he found his inspiration in Chicago, but the broad outlines of the idea must have originated here. Here too he first found the idea of the planned city in a pamphlet of 1876, Benjamin Ward Richardson's *Hygeia, or the City of Health*; its main ideas – low population density, good housing, wide roads, an underground railway, and plenty of open space – all found their way into the garden-city concept.[4]

Back in Britain, he settled himself and his family in a cramped home in a boring street in Stoke Newington,[5] and began in earnest to think and to read. A huge agricultural depression was forcing thousands off the land and into the cities, above all the London slums.[6] He joined a freethinking debating society, the Zetetical Society; it already included George Bernard Shaw and Sidney Webb, with whom he was soon on good terms.[7] Later, in the book, he was adamant that he had thought out the central ideas himself but that he had then found other writers who supplied the details. But there were certainly plenty of precursors. From Herbert Spencer he borrowed the idea of land nationalization, and then from a forgotten predecessor, Thomas Spence, he discovered a superior variant: purchase of farmland by a community, at agricultural values, so that the increased values, which would follow from the construction of a town, would automatically pass back to the community coffers. But Spence nowhere explained how the people are to appropriate the land – which brought him to planned colonization, advocated in J. S. Mill's *Principles of Political Economy*, by the Social Democratic Foundation in its pre-Marxist days, by Keir Hardie, and most notably by Thomas Davidson, a Scottish-American philosopher who founded the Fellowship of the New Life from which the Fabian Society split off (as Shaw inimitably said, "one to sit among the dandelions, the other to organise the docks").[8] Edward Gibbon Wakefield, 50 years earlier, had developed the idea of planned colonization for the poor. The scheme he had promoted, Colonel Light's celebrated scheme for Adelaide in South Australia, provided the idea that once a city had reached a certain size, a second city, separated from it by a green belt, should be started: the origin of the notion of Social City, as Howard acknowledged, though Raymond Bunker has demonstrated that in Colonel William Light's plan North Adelaide was an integral part of the plan from the start, not a subsequent satellite as Howard imagined.[9] Controversy has raged ever since

3   Osborn, 1950, 226–7; Stern 1986, 133–4.
4   Beevers, 1987, 7.
5   Buder, 1990, 31.
6   Beevers, 1987, 9–10.
7   Beevers 1987, 13–14.
8   Meller, 1990, 67.
9   Bunker, 1988, 66.

1986, when Donald Leslie Johnson and his ex-PhD student Donald Langmead argued that Light's deputy, Charles Strickland Kingston, not Light, not only chose the location but was principal designer of the Adelaide plan, adapting a renaissance city template by Pietro Cataneo (1567) to the site. In 2008 they repeated the charge.[10] Robert Freestone caustically records that "While it has not quite resulted in fisticuffs, I have witnessed some terse and heated exchanges in symposia when the issue has been raised (but only in Adelaide)."[11] James Silk Buckingham's plan for a model town gave him most of the main features for his diagram of Garden City: the central place, the radial avenues, and the peripheral industries. Pioneer industrial villages in the countryside, like Lever's Port Sunlight near Liverpool and Cadbury's Bournville outside Birmingham, provided both a physical model and a practical illustration of successful industrial decentralization from the congested city.

The economist Alfred Marshall, in an article of 1884, had suggested the idea that there were "large classes of the population of London whose removal into the country would in the long run be economically advantageous – that it would benefit alike those who moved and those who remained behind."[12] His reasoning had been that new technologies would permit this dispersal – an idea taken up by the anarchist Peter Kropotkin in his *Fields, Factories and Workshops* of 1898, which certainly influenced Howard. And Marshall even suggested the mechanism:

> the general plan would be for a committee, whether specially formed for the purpose or not, to interest themselves in the formation of a colony in some place well beyond the range of London smoke. After seeing their way to buying or building suitable cottages there, they would enter into communication with some of the employees of low-waged labour.[13]

That idea, adopted with enthusiasm by Howard, was based on a critical assumption, as Robert Fishman has pointed out: that workers could find steady employment in a small self-contained city, distant from the metropolis. That proved a prophetic assumption for much of the following century; but entering the twenty-first century, we have returned to the chaotic, flexible job patterns of the 1890s.[14]

Charles Booth, wrestling with the problem of his Class B poor, "the crux of the social problem," had a paternalistic version of the same answer: to withdraw them from the labor force by the formation of labor colonies, "an extension of the Poor Law," outside London:

> my idea is that these people should be allowed to live as families in industrial groups, planted wherever land and building materials were cheap; being well housed, well fed, and

[10] Johnson, 2008, 235.
[11] Freestone, 2008, 222.
[12] Marshall, 1884, 224.
[13] Marshall, 1884, 229.
[14] Fishman, 2002, 62–66.

well warmed; and taught, trained, and employed from morning to night on work, indoors or out, for themselves or on Government account; in the building of their own dwellings, in the cultivation of the land, in the making of clothes, or in the making of furniture. That in exchange for the work done the Government should supply materials and whatever else was needed.[15]

Booth admitted that this solution was draconian: "The life offered would not be attractive" and "The difficulty lies solely in inducing or driving these people to accept a regulated life." His (non-related) namesake, General William Booth of the Salvation Army, was similarly advocating the colonization of the destitute into agricultural smallholding colonies with small-scale industries, within reasonable distance of London but far enough from any town or village to escape the influence of the public house, "that upas tree of civilization,"[16] a feature Howard endorsed in his book and then imposed on bone-dry Letchworth, where the Skittles Inn offered rustic pastimes and wholesome conversation over lemonade and ginger beer.

Canon Barnett's Toynbee Commission of 1892 had followed the same tradition in calling for "industrial regiments" for the "demoralised residuum," providing "compulsory work under humane discipline"; a solution later embraced by the Fabian Society.[17] But Howard, following Marshall, did not see his Garden Cities as colonies for the undeserving poor. On the contrary: they were to be founded, and managed, by the stratum immediately above – Charles Booth's Class C – who were thereby to be freed from the thraldom of the urban slum. So Howard's proposal derives more from the Society for Promoting Industrial Villages, founded by the Reverend Henry Solly, which flourished from 1883 to 1889.[18] His solution was not paternalistic – at least, apart from some residual undertones; rather, it belonged firmly in the anarchistic tradition.

By the end of the 1880s Howard had all the ideas he needed, but he still could not bring them together. The real key was Edward Bellamy's bestselling science-fiction novel *Looking Backward*, which he read early in 1888, shortly after its American publication. He personally testified to the influence it had on him.[19] He began to talk about his ideas to the more progressive London sects, at least from 1892.[20]

Every single one of Howard's ideas can thus, in fact, be found earlier, often several times over: Ledoux, Owen, Pemberton, Buckingham, and Kropotkin all had towns of limited populations with surrounding agricultural green belts; More, Saint-Simon, Fourier all had cities as elements in a regional complex.[21] Marshall and Kropotkin saw the impact of technological development on industrial location, and Kropotkin and Edward Bellamy also appreciated that it would come to favor

[15]   Booth, 1892, 167.
[16]   Booth, 1890, 128.
[17]   Stedman Jones, 1971, 305–6, 334.
[18]   Buder, 1990, 23.
[19]   Beevers, 1987, 18, 27.
[20]   Beevers, 1987, 30.
[21]   Batchelor, 1969, 198.

small-scale workshops. But Howard, attracted as he was to Bellamy's *Looking Backward*, rejected his centralized socialist management and his insistence on the subordination of the individual to the group, which he saw as authoritarian.[22] His biographer, Robert Beevers, points out that all these major influences came from the English dissenting tradition; none, save Kropotkin, were continental European.[23]

More widely, Howard could not fail to be influenced by the Back to the Land movement, which – fueled by urban growth and urban squalor, agricultural depression, nostalgia, quasi-religious motives, anti-Victorian conventions – flourished among the intelligentsia between 1880 and 1914: a genuine alternative movement, similar in many respects to such movements in the 1960s and 1970s.[24] At least 28 such nineteenth-century communities can be traced, all but five or six of which were rural; their inhabitants included utopian socialists, agrarian socialists, sectarians, and anarchists. Few survived for long, though sometimes their settlements do, transmogrified: Heronsgate, established by the Chartists in Hertfordshire after the failure of their political demands in 1848, is today a smart stockbroker community next to the M25 motorway.[25] Behind these manifestations lay a much wider movement, well represented by such writers as Morris and Ruskin, which aimed to reject the grosser trappings of industrialization and to return to a simpler life based on craft and community. So, as Howard wrote, the idea of community-building was everywhere in the air.

The Garden City and the Social City

The ingredients, then, were far from original. What Howard could claim – and did, in a chapter heading, claim – was that his was a unique combination of proposals. He started with the famous diagram of the Three Magnets. Today it has archaic charm, particularly in the colored version of the first edition. But it packs on to one page a set of complex arguments that would take far more space to say in modern jargon. The Victorian slum city, to be sure, was in many ways a horrific place; but it offered economic and social opportunities, lights, and crowds. The late Victorian countryside, now too often seen in a sentimental glow, was, in fact, equally unprepossessing: though it promised fresh air and nature, it was racked by agricultural depression and it offered neither sufficient work and wages, nor adequate social life. But it was possible to square the circle, by combining the best of town and country in a new kind of settlement, Town-Country.

To achieve this, a group of people – necessarily, including several with commercial competence and creditability – should establish a limited-dividend company, borrowing money to establish a garden city in the countryside, far enough from the city to ensure that the land was bought at rock-bottom, depressed agricultural land

---

[22]   Meyerson, 1961, 186; Fishman, 1977, 36.
[23]   Beevers, 1987, 24.
[24]   Marsh, 1982, 1–7.
[25]   Darley, 1975, Ch. 10; Hardy, 1979, 215, 238.

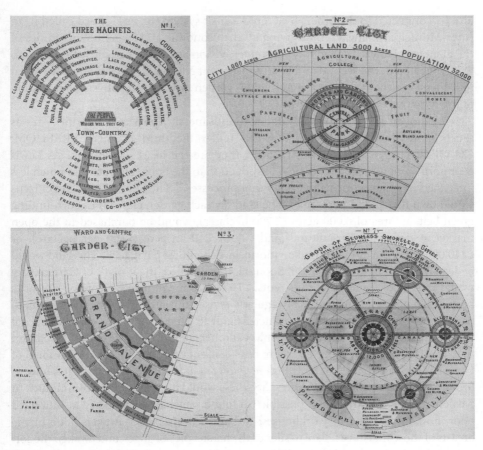

Figure 4.2 Garden Cities of To-morrow. Key diagrams from the first 1898 edition, entitled *To-morrow*, of Howard's classic. The fourth, showing his vision of the polycentric Social City, was never afterwards reproduced in its complete form. *Source*: © British Library Board/Robana.

values. They should obtain agreement from leading industrialists to move their factories there; their workers would move too, and would build their own houses. The garden city would have a fixed limit – Howard suggested 32,000 people, living on 1,000 acres of land, about one and a half times the historic medieval city of London. It would be surrounded by a much larger area of permanent green belt, also owned by the company – Howard proposed 5,000 acres – containing not merely farms, but also all kinds of urban institutions, like reformatories and convalescent homes, that could benefit from a rural location.

As more and more people moved out, the garden city would reach its planned limit; then, another would be started a short distance away. Thus, over time, there would develop a vast planned agglomeration, extending almost without limit; within it, each garden city would offer a wide range of jobs and services, but each would also be connected to the others by a rapid transit system (or, as Howard called it, an Inter-Municipal Railway), thus giving all the economic and social opportunities of the giant city. Howard called this polycentric vision Social City. Because the diagram was truncated in the second and in all subsequent editions, most readers have failed to understand that this, not the individual garden city, was the physical realization of town-country: the third magnet.

But – though almost universally understood as merely a physical blueprint[26] – it was much more than that. The final words under the third magnet, "FREEDOM, CO-OPERATION," are not just rhetoric; they are the heart of the plan. As Lewis Mumford so rightly says in his 1946 introduction to the book, Howard was much less interested in physical forms than in social processes.[27] The key was that the citizens would own the land in perpetuity. The land for each garden city and its surrounding green belt, an area of 6,000 acres (2,700 hectares), would be purchased in the open market at depressed agricultural land values: £40 an acre (£100 per hectare), or £240,000 in all, the money raised on mortgage debentures paying 4%. This land would be legally vested in four trustees.[28] Soon, Howard argued, the growth of Garden City would raise land values, and thus rents.[29] Here was the innovative core of Howard's proposal: rents could and would be regularly revised upwards, allowing the trustees to pay off the mortgage debt, and then increasingly to generate a fund to provide a local welfare state.[30] All this was embodied in yet another colored diagram in the first edition that was subsequently omitted, with dire consequences to the understanding of Howard's message: entitled *The Vanishing Point of Landlord's Rent*, it illustrates how, as urban land values built up in Garden City, these would flow back to the community. In particular, they would make it possible "to found pensions with liberty for our aged poor, now imprisoned in workhouses; to banish despair and awaken hope in the breasts of those that have fallen; to silence the harsh voice of anger, and awaken the soft notes of brotherliness and goodwill."[31]

Howard could thus argue that his was a third socio-economic system, superior both to Victorian capitalism and to bureaucratic centralized socialism. Its keynote would be local management and self-government. Services would be provided by the municipality, or by private contractors, as proved more efficient. Others would come from the people themselves, in a series of what Howard called pro-municipal experiments. In particular, people would build their own homes with capital provided through building societies, friendly societies, cooperative societies, or trade unions. And this activity would in turn drive the economy; 40 years before John Maynard Keynes or Franklin Delano Roosevelt, Howard had arrived at the solution that society could spend its way out of a recession.

[26] Ward, 2002b, 224.
[27] Mumford, 1946, 37.
[28] Howard, 1898, 13.
[29] Howard, 1898, 21.
[30] Howard, 1898, 20–1.
[31] Howard, 1898, 141.

It would do so, however, without large-scale central state intervention. Howard's plan was to be realized through thousands of small-scale enterprises: every man and woman a craftsman, an entrepreneur. It would call, he said "for the very highest talents of engineers of all kinds, of architects, artists, medical men, experts in sanitation, landscape gardeners, agricultural experts, surveyors, builders, manufacturers, merchants and financiers, organizers of trades unions, friendly and co-operative societies, as well as the very simplest forms of unskilled labour, together with all those forms of lesser skill and talent which lie between."[32] It is a peculiarly American vision: the homesteading spirit, brought back home to industrial England. But it is homesteading harnessed to new technology, to create a new socio-economic order: a remarkable vision, not least for its startling modernity, even a century later.

For Howard, communal ownership of land was the essential foundation of his garden city. "But the collective ownership of land was, in Howard's view, as far as things needed to go. Other forms of capital could be privately, cooperatively, or municipally owned. That was entirely up to the people who lived in his new garden city."[33] But collective provision also of housing, through the co-partnership tenants' movement, became a central mechanism in Letchworth and many pre-1914 garden suburbs, as well as some industry at Letchworth.

Letchworth and Hampstead: Unwin and Parker

Howard was thus a dreamer of great dreams, but he was much more: he was quintessentially a doer. The modern reader, going back to his book, is surprised that so much of it consists of pages of calculations about finance; Howard was writing not for utopian simple-lifers but for hard-nosed Victorian businessmen who wanted to be sure they would get their money back. These calculations appeared realistic: in low-inflation late Victorian England, consols might pay as little as 2% a year; "philanthropy plus five per cent" was a well-known concept.[34]

One of the many brilliant features of the plan was that it could be achieved incrementally, by a series of separate local initiatives which would progressively reinforce each other. As Dennis Hardy has written, the garden city was a "quasi utopia," a perfect city that was achievable in an imperfect world.[35] So, eight months after the book was published, at a meeting at the Memorial Hall in Farringdon Street in London on June 21, 1899, Howard took the lead in setting up a Garden City Association (GCA) to discuss his ideas, and "ultimately to formulate a practical scheme on the lines of the project with such modifications as may seem desirable"; he took care to make it politically bipartisan and to include manufacturers, merchants, and financiers as well as cooperators, artists,

---

[32] Howard, 1898, 140.
[33] Ward, 2002a, 23.
[34] Hall and Ward, 1998, 26.
[35] Hardy, 2000, 73–4.

Figure 4.3 New Earswick. A classic Unwin–Parker design around an enclosed green space, intended to recapture the communal quality of the medieval quadrangle. *Source*: The Joseph Rowntree Archive.

and ministers.[36] By 1902, when the second edition of the book appeared minus those key diagrams, membership had risen to over 1,300; there were two peers, three bishops and 23 members of parliament, a few academics including Marshall, and half a dozen industrialists, including Cadbury, Lever, and Rowntree. Ralph Neville, a distinguished lawyer who soon afterwards became a judge, became Chair of Council in 1901, injecting hard practical sense; and a young and able Scots journalist, Thomas Adams, provided some more on his appointment as secretary.[37] But before that, in 1900, the young GCA had already resolved to form the First Garden City, Limited, with capital of £50,000 and a 5% dividend; two years after that, the Garden City Pioneer Company was registered with a capital of £20,000, in order to survey potential sites.[38]

The directors of the Pioneer Company laid down criteria closely following Howard's: a site of between 4,000 and 6,000 acres, with good rail connections, a satisfactory water supply, and good drainage. The favorite site, Childley Castle east of Stafford, was rejected as too far from London. Letchworth, 34 miles from London in an area of severely depressed agriculture and low land prices, met the criteria and – after delicate secret negotiations with 15 owners – the 3,818-acre site was bought for £155,587. The First Garden City Company was registered on September 1, 1903, with a £300,000 capital, of which £80,000 was to be raised immediately, and a 5% dividend.[39] After a limited competition, Raymond Unwin and Barry Parker were chosen as architect-planners in 1904.[40]

Now, crucially, more business expertise needed to be injected: the First Garden City Company had Neville in the chair, and seven industrialists including Cadbury, Lever the soap king, Idris the soft-drink manufacturer who traded under the slogan "Idris because I'se dry," plus a cotton-spinner, a newspaper proprietor, and an ironmaster. Thomas Adams was borrowed part-time from the Garden Cities Association, on a disarmingly casual basis, to run the new company; with abundant energy, imagination, shrewdness, charm, tact, and unfailing good humor, he lacked management experience.[41]

There was very successful publicity, and in the summer of 1905, 60,000 people came to see progress with the new city.[42] But, as Denis Hardy concludes,

> The kind of money that was needed to build a new city drew Howard away from any immediate hope of financing the venture primarily from within the ranks of fellow radicals, excited by the prospect of a "co-operative commonwealth", and, increasingly, into the world of Edwardian company boardrooms and the panelled lounges of gentlemen's clubs.[43]

---

[36] Macfadyen, 1933, 37; Beevers, 1987, 72.
[37] Macfadyen, 1933, 37; Simpson, 1985, 2; Beevers, 1987, 72–3, 79–80.
[38] Macfadyen, 1933, 37–9; Simpson, 1985, 14.
[39] Culpin, 1913, 16; Simpson, 1985, 14–17.
[40] Miller, 1992, 52–4.
[41] Simpson 1985, 17.
[42] Beevers, 1987, 86, 98–100; Hardy, 1991a, 47, 52.
[43] Hardy, 1991a, 47.

George Bernard Shaw, who was one of Howard's lifelong staunchest supporters yet one of his most trenchant critics, brilliantly caught his limitations:

> We went down to Hindhead from Saturday to yesterday. On Monday Ebenezer the Garden City Geyser lectured in Hindhead Hall, with a magic lantern giving views of that flourishing settlement in the manner of Mr. Scadder in Martin Chuzzlewit. I had to make a speech which had so fell an effect, in spite of my earnest endeavors to help him over the stile, that the audience declined to put up a single hand for the resolution. Finally the chairman put it again, coupling it with a vote of thanks, when, the situation becoming too poignant, I ostentatiously held up my paw, on which the others followed suit and Eb was saved. I pointed out that manufacturers were ready enough to go into the country; but what they went there for was cheap labor. I suggested that half a dozen big manufacturers building a city could give good wages, and yet get so much of them back in rent and shop rent, or in direct butcher, baker and dairy profits, that the enterprise might pay them all the same. At this the Hindhead proletariat grinned from ear to ear, and concluded that I was the man who really understood the manufacturing nature, the Geyser being a mere spring of benevolent mud.[44]

Shaw, with his usual brilliance, had grasped the key point. As early as 1901, he wrote a letter to Neville, in which he questioned whether capitalists would ever agree to a trust deed limiting their freedom; they might tolerate a maximum 5% dividend but they would not distribute their profits; to realize the ideal, the only way might be to nationalize the garden city like the telegraphs and public roads.[45] He was soon proved right. Letchworth was chronically undercapitalized: at the formal opening in 1903, only £40,000 out of a projected £300,000 had been subscribed, all by the directors; a year later, it was clear that firms were not being attracted; it was a major breakthrough when the printing and binding works of J. M. Dent, a major publisher, was attracted;[46] in the first two years, only one thousand residents arrived, and most were idealist, artistic folk who gave Letchworth a permanent reputation for crankiness that it later ill-deserved: "here was a whole colony of eccentrics making an exhibition of themselves rather too near our sacred borders. We wished they would remove their mad city a little nearer Arlesley."[47] Arlesley was the local mental institution. That was doubtless overdone, but there were grounds for suspicion.[48] At The Cloisters, a residential college where residents slept on hammocks separated by canvas screens arranged in a horseshoe around a marble fountain, they grew wheat according to what were thought to be Kropotkinesque principles, each grain receiving individual attention; the result was mainly weeds and thistles.[49]

[44] Quoted in Beevers, 1987, 70.
[45] Beevers, 1987, 73–6.
[46] Jackson, F., 1985, 71; Simpson, 1985, 20, 35.
[47] Macfadyen, 1933, 47.
[48] Marsh 1982, 238–9.
[49] Marsh, 1982, 238–9.

For a long time it was not possible to build houses, shops, factories, or public buildings; no dividend was paid until 1913, and then only at 1%.[50] Soon, the directors excluded Howard from any managerial function; maybe he already realized that he was not cut out for the work.[51] "The directors, a constantly changing group, were nervous men, anxious for instant profitability and fearful of imminent collapse."[52] In August 1905, after little more than a year; they replaced Adams by W. E. H. Gaunt, manager of Trafford Park and the kind of man who should have been appointed in the first place.[53]

Already, there was no mention in the Memorandum and Articles of Association of any legal obligation to transfer power progressively to the community.[54] Then, the directors faltered on the key issue of the gain in value to the community, and there was a compromise: tenants would be offered a choice between a "Howard lease" with ten- (not five-) year revisions and a normal 99-year fixed lease; most predictably settled on the second.[55] Effectively, Howard and his central ideas were being eased out of the frame; Adams resigned from the Board, probably because he opposed the "New Policy."[56] As Robert Fishman has commented, instead of a peaceful alternative to capitalism the garden city became a device for preserving it.[57]

The directors proved equally conservative on other matters: when, in 1905, they gave away part of the proposed town center – a Buxton-style Crescent – for a cottage housing exhibition that was to become permanent, Raymond Unwin turned his energies to Hampstead Garden Suburb. In fact, even this attempt was insufficient; it showed that houses could be built for as little as £150 and let at rents from 22p to 82p per week, but even this was too much for unskilled workers who had to find poorer housing outside the garden city; ironically, the press saw them as more suited for weekenders than for the deserving poor, and the *Manchester Evening Chronicle* described middle-class ladies gushing over them: "what a darling wee, little place"; "oh, how too, too charming!"[58] Many of the first houses were built by speculative contractors with eccentric designs that Parker and Unwin had wanted to banish.[59] Unwin did, however, remain consultant architect until dissolution of his partnership with Parker in May 1914; C. B. Purdom's statement that "Unwin, fighting a losing battle, fled during 1906 to Hampstead Garden Suburb ... and Letchworth hardly saw him again" was, it seems, a melodramatic overstatement.[60]

Soon, though, the original middle-class eccentrics had been overwhelmed by the blue-collar workers who were to provide the *raison d'être* for the garden city's existence.

50 Creese, 1966, 215–16; Fishman, 1977, 71.
51 Beevers, 1987, 82, 86–9.
52 Simpson, 1985, 35.
53 Simpson 1985, 35.
54 Beevers, 1987, 90.
55 Beevers, 1987, 93–6.
56 Simpson, 1985, 38.
57 Hardy, 1991a, 47.
58 McGahey, 1990, 17–18.
59 Fishman, 1977, 71–2; Beevers, 1987, 113–14, 131; Sutcliffe, 1990, 262.
60 Miller, 1992, 75.

But ironically, far from participating in the cooperative spirit of the enterprise, they embraced trades unionism and socialism.[61] Many, in a development that had its own special irony, joined in-commuters from neighboring Hitchin in the giant Spirella factory, "to make corsets which Letchworth women obviously never wear, but which their husbands sell at great profit to the less enlightened women in other towns."[62]

What survived from all this was, however, a watered-down essence of the Howard vision. The town began to pay dividends after a decade; it continued to grow, more slowly than the promoters hoped, to reach 15,000 – less than half its planned target – in 1938; after World War Two, aided by government-subsidized decentralization schemes, it was at last completed, on a slightly smaller scale than originally planned. Ironically, at that point it became the victim of land speculation, from which it was rescued by a 1962 Act of Parliament that put its management in the hands of a special corporation.[63] Above all, it found its perfect physical realization in the hands of Raymond Unwin and Barry Parker. Almost too perfect, in fact; Unwin–Parker architecture clothed the Howard skeleton so memorably that, ever after, people could hardly distinguish one from the other.

To understand what Unwin and Parker so memorably achieved, here and at Hampstead and in other places, they need to be set in a context of place, time, and culture. Unwin was born in 1863, Parker in 1867, within a dozen miles of Sheffield in northern England; they were half-cousins, and Unwin married Parker's sister. Neither was formally trained as an architect; Unwin started as an engineer, Parker as an interior decorator. They grew up in an intense ferment of ideas, deriving in large measure from William Morris, which were to influence all their subsequent work. As a young man Unwin considered a career as a priest; asked by Samuel Barnett, Vicar of St Jude's in Whitechapel, whether he was more troubled by man's unhappiness or by his wickedness, Unwin replied unhappiness; Barnett advised him not to enter the church.[64] He and Parker shared the view that creativity came from an imaginative understanding of the past; that the Middle Ages provided an historic standard; that old buildings grew out of the ground they stood on; that the village was an organic embodiment of the small, personally related community; that the architect and planner were guardians of social and aesthetic life, maintaining and enhancing the traditional values of the community for future generations.[65]

Unwin early became a socialist in the William Morris tradition, joining the Sheffield group started by Edward Carpenter, a founder of the Fabian Society; here Kropotkin lectured on the union of craft and intellectual work.[66] Before 1900, he was working on the design of cottages for mining villages in his local area.[67] From this stemmed his book *Cottage Plans and Common Sense* (1902), an impassioned plea for

[61]   Simpson, 1985, 34.
[62]   Macfadyen, 1933, 51; Marsh, 1982, 234.
[63]   Miller, 1983, 172–4.
[64]   Miller, 1992, 12.
[65]   Creese, 1966, 169–70; Jackson, F., 1985, 41, 168.
[66]   Jackson, F., 1985, 17.
[67]   Creese, 1966, 184–5.

Figure 4.4 Letchworth. The medieval village green motif as interpreted by Parker and Unwin in the First Garden City. *Source*: Peter Hall.

better working-class housing: "It does not seem to be realized that hundreds of thousands of women spend the bulk of their lives with nothing better to look on than the ghastly prospect offered by these back yards, the squalid ugliness of which is unrelieved by a scrap of fresh green to speak of spring, or a falling leaf to tell of autumn." Yet, "If, instead of being wasted in stuffy yards and dirty back streets, the space which is available for a number of houses were kept together, it would make quite a respectable square or garden"; cottages, each correctly orientated to give a sunny aspect to the chief room, would be planned around "quadrangles opening one into the other" after the manner of Oxford and Cambridge colleges.[68]

Already, that year, Parker and Unwin were working on their first major commission: the garden village of New Earswick for the Rowntree chocolate family, to be developed not as a charity but as an independent trust, close to their factory on the northern edge of York. It contains in embryo many of the features that were to be worked out on a much larger canvas at Letchworth and then at Hampstead. The village is separated from the factory, and from the city, by a narrow but quite distinct green belt, part natural, part in playing-fields. The cottages are disposed in terraces and grouped either around communal greens, or along pedestrian ways – thus anticipating the Radburn layout by more than a quarter-century – and, later in the design process, culs-de-sac. A village green and a folk hall are prominent central features. Everywhere, natural features – trees, a small brook – are integrated into the design. It has in

[68] Unwin, 1902, 4.

Figure 4.5 Barry Parker. Unwin's partner and co-designer at New Earswick, Letchworth, and Hampstead; later the sole author of the plan for Manchester's Wythenshawe, truly England's Third Garden City. *Source*: © Garden City Collection, Letchworth Garden City Heritage Foundation.

supreme measure what Parker and Unwin themselves called "the first essential in the form and design of any decorative object … reposefulness": the visitor, arriving in whatever psychological state, immediately receives a quite extraordinary impression of calm, of an informal but natural order of things, which is all-pervasive. Beautifully preserved, sympathetically restored to Unwin and Parker's original intentions, New Earswick is a small gem, dazzling to the eye at the age of more than 100. In one respect only it failed: the standards of design were so high that the lowest-paid could not afford it. That, indeed, was to prove a recurrent defect.

At Letchworth they had a larger and more complex problem. For one thing, industry had to be integrated in with the housing. The fact that a railway line bisected the site determined that here the industry must be. As against New Earswick's modest village hall and row of shops, a whole town center had to be planned. Writing later in his great textbook of planning, Unwin exhaustively analyzed the town plans of the past, concluding that both formal and informal approaches had their merits; though it was never in doubt that his tastes lay toward the informal, Letchworth also has more formal elements in the form of radial avenues, ronds-points, and, above all, the big central Town Square dominated by the major municipal buildings. It does not work out right. The best of the informal housing layouts are as good as New Earswick, some – planned around huge village-green-like spaces – maybe even better. And the Spirella factory is a joy, designed – perhaps to try to avoid the associations – in a very free Viennese *Jugendstil*. But the town center is a terrible mess, with streets that seem to lead nowhere in particular, lined (well after Unwin and Parker departed) by an amorphous mixture of the worst interwar commercial Neo-Georgian and even worse sixties tatty, all gone slightly to seed.

Significantly, Unwin confesses that when designing it all he had not yet read Camillo Sitte's book *Die Städtebau nach seinen künstlerischen Grundsätzen*, published over a decade previously, with its stress on the informal qualities of medieval cities. It was a lesson Unwin was not to forget; *Town Planning in Practice*, published in 1909 – a mere half-decade after Letchworth – is memorable above all for the brilliant line drawings of old English and French and German towns and villages, from which he developed his understanding of the relationships of buildings and spaces. Or, rather, *their* understanding: together, Unwin and Parker raised the art of civic design to a level of pure genius, after which almost everything else was pedestrian anticlimax. They were specific that their job was above all to promote beauty or amenity, terms which for them were interchangeable: "above all, we shall need to infuse the spirit of the artist into our work."[69] But, as well, their thoughts were always imaginatively with the people who would live in the buildings, walk, or play in the spaces they created. And this went down to minute particulars: good architecture and planning, for them, was the multiplication of right details:

> The children, too, must not be forgotten in the open spaces. The *kinderbank*, or low seat to suit their short legs, should always be provided, and where possible spaces of turf be supplied with swings or seesaws, with ponds for sailing boats, and with sand pits where these can be kept sufficiently clean.[70]

They wanted, too, to pursue social ends. "Both in town and site planning it is important to prevent the complete separation of different classes of people which is such a feature of the modern English town."[71] But, in Edwardian England, there were limits. Both at Letchworth and at Hampstead, areas are shown for "cottages," away from the grander middle-class houses: close enough, but not too close.

Hampstead was a turning-point, both for the English garden-city movement in general and for Unwin in particular. For it was self-confessedly not a garden city but a garden suburb; it had no industry, and was openly dependent on commuting from an adjacent tube station, which opened just as it was being planned. In

[69]   Unwin, 1920, 225, 9.
[70]   Unwin, 1920, 287.
[71]   Unwin, 1920, 294.

fairness, and for the historical record, it must be said that it was not the only or even the first in this genre. Ealing Tenants Limited, the first London housing cooperative, had been founded in 1901 and had bought their 32-acre Brentham Estate site off The Mount Avenue in 1902, even before Letchworth; they had hired Unwin and Parker to design a model garden village by 1906, a year before the Hampstead commission.[72] It was a garden village suburb, little different in scale from New Earswick, distinguished by the high quality of its design, its inimitable feeling of easeful domesticity, its central social club (a notion borrowed from New Earswick, and indeed from the first garden suburb at nearby Bedford Park 30 years previously), its central communal superblocks for small-scale cultivation (an innovation copied 20 years later by Stein and Wright at Sunnyside Gardens, by Geddes in Tel-Aviv, and then in a great variety of places), and its proto-green-belt, formed by the meadows of the adjacent River Brent.[73]

Ealing is interesting for more than design, though. It represents the way that garden cities and garden suburbs were supposed to be built: Howard's Freedom and Cooperation in action. Unwin had commended cooperative housing in a pamphlet of 1901, arguing that this way groups of prospective owners could obtain housing at low cost on land bought at farm value: Howard's argument again. But additionally, "The houses could be grouped together and so arranged that each would obtain a sunny aspect and an open outlook; and portions of the land could be reserved for ever from being built on to secure these views"; and common rooms could be provided for music and general recreation, and also for meals. Groups of houses, he suggested, could be developed around quadrangles, each with a common room; the quintessence of that medieval spirit of community that Unwin so earnestly wanted to recapture.[74] Unwin sat on the executive committee of the Co-Partnership Tenants Housing Company; he and Parker developed not only Ealing, but also suburbs outside Leicester, Cardiff, and Stoke-on-Trent.[75] The 1909 Housing and Town Planning Act allowed such "Public Utility Societies" (PUS) to borrow public money at low rates of interest, and by 1918 there were more than 100 of them.[76] They had two distinct advantages: loans from the Local Government Board carried lower rates of interest than available in the market, and they were also able to borrow a higher proportion of the value of their development costs than other limited profit organizations. Probably a majority of the 128 PUS registered and active before 1914 were co-partnership societies, drawing part of their capital from shareholders who were (or intended to become) tenants of the society. The close identification of the PUSs with prewar garden suburb developments, as well as Letchworth, might be seen as strengthening their claim to be involved after the war because of the government's commitment to a new standard of housing for the working class, based on

[72] Jackson, F., 1985, 73; Co-Partnership Tenants, 1906, 70–1; Abercrombie, 1910a, 119.
[73] Reid, 2000, passim.
[74] Parker and Unwin, 1901, 96–7, 106; Hayden, 1984, 126, 129.
[75] Jackson, F., 1985, 73, 109–10.
[76] Reiss, 1918, 85–6.

Figure 4.6 Ealing Garden Suburb. Construction in progress, Denison Road, *ca.* 1907. *Source*: Reproduced by permission of the London Borough of Ealing.

garden-city principles.[77] But the Treasury resisted a clause which would have allowed them to borrow money on the same terms as local authorities, and this constrained them as local housing development agencies.[78] In 1913, when Henry Vivian – who had founded Co-Partnership Tenants in a pub in Ealing in 1901 – became a member of the Garden Cities and Town Planning Association (GCTPA) Council, effectively the two movements began to merge.

But Hampstead was an altogether bigger affair. Its begetter was Dame Henrietta Barnett, redoubtable wife of the Warden of Toynbee Hall. They had a weekend house at Hampstead, and heard in 1896 of a plan to build a new tube station next door. (The line soon became part of the empire of Charles Tyson Yerkes.) In true English middle-class fashion, she resolved to campaign to buy up land to extend Hampstead Heath and frustrate the real-estate ambitions of the promoters. After a five-year campaign involving the dispatch of 13,000 letters, the 80-acre Heath extension was bought by the London County Council (LCC) for £43,241; the tube station, stopped in mid-construction, became one of the London underground's several ghost stations. In the middle of it all, someone suggested the idea of a garden suburb; it took another 243-acre purchase from the Eton College Estate, using £112,000

77 Malpass, 2000, 379.
78 Skilleter, 1993, 139.

Figure 4.7 Henrietta Barnett. The Dame takes charge: plan of Hampstead Garden Suburb in her hand, moral fervor and reforming zeal in her eyes. *Source*: Hampstead Garden Suburb Archive Trust.

invested from the appeal, in 1907. A trust was already set up to provide 8,000 houses; Unwin and Parker were appointed architects – a dilemma, since Unwin had attacked suburbs in *The Art of Building a Home*, in 1901, quoting his hero Morris.[79]

From the first, the suburb had high social purposes: as a contemporary put it, it would be a place "where the poor shall teach the rich, and the rich, let us hope, shall help the poor to help themselves"; the first plan included barns for the storage of coster barrows.[80] But soon, land values and rents began to rise, and – like Letchworth, or Bedford Park before that – the suburb began to acquire a reputation, which Dame Henrietta was at pains to refute: it was untrue that the inhabitants were "all eccentric, sandalled, corsetless 'cranks' – we are just ordinary men and women":

> Some of us keep servants, some don't; some of us have motors, others use "Shanks' pony"; some read, some paint, some make music, but we all work, we all wash ("no house, however small, without a bathroom" – vide advertisement) – and we all garden … relieved

---

[79] Miller and Gray, 1992, 46.
[80] Jackson, 1973, 78.

from the oppression of wealth, and able to meet each other on the simpler and deeper grounds of common interests and shared aspirations.[81]

Of the three separate house-building organizations that provided the great bulk of the houses, two were co-partnerships.[82] But the objective, "day-to-day coexistence which would sooner heal the estrangement of the classes,"[83] was frustrated by the suburb's own success; today, even the tiny artisans' cottages are well and truly gentrified.

What does survive is the physical quality. In some ways it is curiously transitional. Unwin was by now heavily influenced by Sitte and by his own German wanderings; restrictive local by-laws were overcome by using special parliamentary powers.[84] So Unwin was free to demonstrate on the ground what a few years later, in his enormously influential pamphlet *Nothing Gained by Overcrowding!*, he demonstrated on paper: that a proper planning scheme could give everyone much more space, without using more land. The key to this trick was to cut the land needed for roads from 40% (as in the typical by-law scheme) to 17%, thus raising the land available for gardens and open space from 17% to no less than 55% of the total area.[85] This new freedom is used at Hampstead to produce a typically informal layout, with irregular curving streets, culs-de-sac, and great variety of housing types; Unwin aimed, even at this early date, to design traffic out, and today it notably still proceeds with respectful sedateness.[86] And the design consciously, even winsomely, recalls German medieval models: there is a town wall against the Heath extension, with gatehouses; next to the shopping parade on the Finchley Road, Unwin places a huge gateway that was modeled on the Markusthurm at Rothenburg, which on first sight in 1900 – so his wife Etty later recalled – he greeted with "tears of joy."[87]

But in the central Town Square, placed by desire of the Dame on the suburb's highest point,[88] and in the adjacent streets, Unwin defers completely to Lutyens, the designer of the two big churches and the adjacent Institute. The result is an anomalous, heavily formal exercise in the City Beautiful tradition: approaching through the main gateway from the Heath, the expectant visitor expects to find a pastiche of Rothenburg ob der Tauber, with narrow streets leading to the kind of market place Unwin delighted to draw, but instead finds a processional way that looks suspiciously like a dummy run for the approach to the Viceroy's Palace at New Delhi (Chapter 6). And the whole concept, vast in scale, is curiously dead; hardly anyone ever goes there, and the square looks as if it is waiting for an Imperial Durbar that will never now take place. Perhaps, though, as Creese said, the intention was not to entertain the inhabitants, or offer them recreation or shopping, but to impress them;

81   Barnett, 1918, 205.
82   Abercrombie, 1910a, 32.
83   Creese, 1966, 227.
84   Jackson, 1973, 79.
85   Unwin, 1912, 6.
86   Creese, 1966, 239.
87   Miller, 1992, 99, 112.
88   Creese, 1966, 223.

· PROPOSED SHOPS · HAMPSTEAD GARDEN SUBURB ·   BARRY PARKER AND
                                                    RAYMOND UNWIN ARCHITECTS

Figure 4.8 Hampstead Garden Suburb. Old Nuremberg (or is it Rothenburg?) comes to the Finchley Road; the product, most likely, of Unwin's last summer sketching holiday. *Source*: The Bodleian Library, University of Oxford, 2479116 d. 5, p. 172.

and it presumably did that.[89] But Unwin had blessed it; and at Letchworth, he too had formal moments.

But Hampstead thoroughly confused the faithful. From the start, as Abercrombie pointed out in 1910, the Garden City Association had as objectives, as well as the "building of new towns in country districts on well thought out principles," also "the creation of Garden Suburbs, on similar principles, for the immediate relief of existing towns" as well as "the building of Garden Villages … for properly housing the working classes near their work."[90] In 1906, the Association added garden suburbs to its objectives; at the November AGM, after a lecture by Henrietta Barnett, Rider Haggard proposed a motion and secured a unanimous vote in favor of garden suburbs; the garden suburb and garden village appeared more realistic objectives than the garden city.[91] In 1909, a Special General Meeting agreed to make the promotion of town planning the Association's primary objective, and to change the name to Garden Cities and Town Planning Association; henceforth, garden cities were relegated to a subsidiary role.[92] At a dinner in honor of Howard in 1912, well-planned garden suburbs were not only acknowledged in their own right, but were commended as worthy of support.[93] But the question would increasingly be whether the good was not the enemy of the best. Hampstead in Unwin and Parker's hands was

[89]   Creese, 1966, 234.
[90]   Abercrombie, 1910a, 20.
[91]   Sutcliffe, 1990, 265; Ward, 1992, 8.
[92]   Sutcliffe, 1990, 266–7.
[93]   Hardy, 1991a, 61.

Figure 4.9 Sunday lunch in Welwyn Garden City. Howard's ideal personified; the working man and his wife come into their patrimony. *Source*: Town and Country Planning Association.

allowable, even commendable; so, presumably, were most of the dozen or so schemes coordinated by Co-Partnership Tenants between 1901 and World War One;[94] but the "purist" wing of the Association reacted with fury to the fact that "many of the schemes that are called garden city schemes have nothing in common with the garden-city movement but the name, which they have dishonestly appropriated. Schemes of the wildest speculation, land-sweating and jerry-building have all been

[94]   Culpin, 1913, passim.

Figure 4.10   The Mall, Welwyn Garden City. Louis de Soissons brings classical formality and Georgian good taste to the Second Garden City. *Source*: Town and Country Planning Association.

promoted in the hope that the good name would carry them through," Ewart G. Culpin complained in 1913.[95]

After the war, C. B. Purdom, the new editor of the Association's magazine, complained: "There is hardly a district in which the local council does not claim to be building one, and unscrupulous builders everywhere display the name on their advertisements … The thing itself is nowhere to be seen at the present date, but in Hertfordshire, at Letchworth and Welwyn Garden City."[96] In 1918, a breakaway movement emerged: the National Garden Cities Committee, led by Purdom, together with Howard, F. J. Osborn, Abercrombie and G. D. H. Cole; it produced a pamphlet, *New Towns after the War*, by "New Townsmen," in fact by Osborn. It caused a frisson in the Association, though eventually a merger was arranged.[97] But even Welwyn was dubious, for, as Michael Hebbert points out, it "was developed and marketed in the first decade as a middle-class dormitory for city commuters, and its values protected in a manner not envisaged by Ebenezer Howard involving the segregation of factories and weekly rented housing to the further side of the railway tracks."[98] When, at the end of the 1920s, Abercrombie was appointed to assess the feasibility of Wythenshawe and Parker was appointed architect, the Association referred to it condescendingly as a "semi-garden city," which, in fact, it was.[99]

In 1919, the Association adopted a carefully restrictive definition of the "thing itself"; the following year, embarrassed by the 69-year-old Howard's unilateral purchase of a huge tract of land at Welwyn without the money to pay for it, they bailed him out and started the Second Garden City there.[100] Designed by Louis de Soissons in the neo-Georgian style that by then had swept the Unwin–Parker neo-vernacular off the stage – Unwin himself had turned coat – it is much more formal than either Letchworth or Hampstead, especially in its huge Lutyens-like central mall, almost a mile long: a kind of Garden City Beautiful. But the architecture shows how very good Neo-Georgian can be in the right hands. And it has been beautifully cared for; a cheat, perhaps, because unlike Letchworth it soon became popular with middle-class commuters. The fact, heretical though it may be to say out loud, is that it is actually much more appealing than Letchworth.

The Garden-City Movement between the Wars

Meanwhile, in 1918 and 1919 the movement had faced a double crisis. In 1912 Unwin had already committed what for some was the great apostasy: in a lecture at Manchester University, he had commended the building of "satellite towns" next to cities, garden suburbs depending on the city for employment. In 1918, placed in a position of unequalled power as key member of the Tudor Walters Committee, he wrote that into the official prescription for the postwar public housing program, which received legislative blessing in the Addison Act the next year; the conse-quences have been detailed in Chapter 3. The result was that of the million or so publicly subsidized dwellings built by local authorities between the wars, none – with the exception of a handful at Letchworth and Welwyn – was built in the form of true garden cities. This was a severe blow to the Association, which was cam-paigning simultaneously for a vastly expanded public housing program and for gar-den cities. Howard himself had no faith at all in the capacity of the state to do the job, and perhaps no ideological relish for the idea either: as he told his faithful lieutenant Frederic Osborn in 1919, "My dear boy, if you wait for the Government to do it you will be as old as Methuselah before you start."[101]

There was another blow: the co-partnership societies simply faded away. When the emergency housing program was abandoned in 1921, they had made a negli-gible contribution: less than 2%. A civil servant wrote an acid note to the Minister of Health in February 1922: "These societies have performed pitiably in the way of

---

[98]   Hebbert, 1992, 168.
[99]   Hardy, 1991a, 178.
[100] Purdom, 1921, 34; Osborn, 1970, 9–10.
[101] Osborn, 1970, 8.

helping on housing." Sir Arthur Robinson, Permanent Secretary at the Ministry of Health from 1920 to 1935, could observe the performance of the PUSs from close quarters, and he was not impressed. Ten years of experience, he commented, showed that *they were bodies neither efficient nor easy to deal with*, as their members were not normally men of affairs. He considered, therefore, that they had only a very small contribution to offer at the price of much inconvenience. That seems to sum up the achievement of the PUSs since the end of the war: they had built very few houses, and had alienated the top civil servants in the Ministry of Health.[102]

So Howard obtained Welwyn by his own unconventional methods, the country was given satellite towns, the co-partnership ideal collapsed, and the cause of large-scale new-town building in Britain was set back 30 years. Perhaps it was inevitable: the political objections to the large-scale removal of urban slum dwellers into the countryside, coupled with the threat of massive boundary extensions, would have been huge, as the LCC's troubles in planning its satellite estates, and Manchester's at Wythenshawe, amply demonstrated.

Partly the problem was one of failure of imagination. Some of the so-called satellites – above all the LCC's Becontree, in Essex – were huge, many times Howard's planned 30,000 target, and equal to a medium-sized English town. And they were distant from their parent urban authority. But they lacked the necessary industry to make them self-contained – though, after 1928, Becontree had the windfall of the Ford Dagenham plant – and they even lacked decent public transport links. And, too often, they were design failures too. The housing was worthy enough, and it conformed to Unwin's pattern books; it, and the layouts within which it was embodied, were just plain dull.

The provincial satellites were partial exceptions. And Wythenshawe, designed by Barry Parker for Manchester in 1930, really is a rather outstanding one. Its early history was tortuous. Abercrombie, appointed as consultant, had recommended that the city buy the 4,500-acre estate; it purchased half of it in 1926. At the public inquiry, Unwin was inspector; he recommended his old partner Parker as consultant.[103] In 1927 the city had commissioned Parker to produce a plan. On a huge site of 5,500 acres, he was given a free hand to design a virtual new town. There had followed a huge battle by Manchester to incorporate the area, won in Parliament in 1931; it was unsuccessful in obtaining an order to buy the rest of the land. By 1938, with over 7,000 corporation and some 700 private houses, it was already bigger than either Letchworth or Welwyn and was still only one-third of the way to its planned target of 107,000.[104] Parker himself described it, in 1945, as "now the most perfect example of a garden city."[105] It is, to be sure, an imperfect one. The population target was three times that recommended by Howard, though close to that of the larger post-World War Two new towns. Though the land was purchased at near-agricultural values, it

[102]   Malpass, 2000, 388.
[103]   Miller and Gray, 1992, 107.
[104]   Macfadyen, 1933, 115–21; GB Royal Commission Distribution, 1937–9, passim.
[105]   Creese, 1966, 255.

Figure 4.11   Frederic Osborn. First Howard's lieutenant, then his successor as indefatigable campaigner-in-chief for garden cities; in his Welwyn garden, aged 80, the next polemic ready for the printer. *Source*: Town and Country Planning Association.

was separated from the city only by a half-mile-wide, thousand-acre green belt along the River Mersey. Though a large industrial area was planned – like Letchworth, alongside the railway that bisects the site – it could not provide jobs for all the working inhabitants; a subsidized express bus service to the city was necessary.

Its achievement lay in introducing three American planning principles, borrowed directly by Parker from the New York region, which he had visited in 1925.[106] The first of these was the neighborhood-unit principle, the origins of which will need to be discussed later in this chapter. The second was the principle of the Radburn layout, which Clarence Stein and Henry Wright had developed in their 1928 plan for the garden city of the same name, also to be described later in this chapter, which they had discussed with him as early as 1924.[107] The third was the principle of the parkway, which Parker – visiting New York with Unwin and Howard in 1925 for the International Federation for Garden Cities and Town Planning Conference, staying on as guests of the Regional Planning Association of America[108] – had observed in Westchester County, but which he now used in a completely original way.

[106]   Creese, 1966, 261.
[107]   Creese, 1966, 266.
[108]   Miller, 2002, 125.

The original New York parkways – the Bronx River Parkway of 1914, and the examples developed by Robert Moses as part of his recreational parks plans of the 1920s – were limited-access highways designed for private car traffic only, and deliberately landscaped to provide a recreational experience.[109] Parker's genius at Wythenshawe was to combine these with another, older American parkway tradition, conceived by Frederick Law Olmsted and widely used by planners in the City Beautiful tradition at the start of the century: the idea of parkways as access roads to residential areas, linked to civic parks[110] – an idea that had been tentatively employed in Britain, by Soissons at Welwyn and by the landscape architect T. H. Mawson around Stanley Park, Blackpool, in the 1920s – to provide the main element of the circulation plan for an entire garden city.[111] Thereby he planned to avoid one of the principal planning defects of the 1930s, so evident around London, of ribbon development along new arterial roads. At Wythenshawe, he explained,

> such roads … will lie in strips of parkland and they will not be development roads. They have been planned to skirt existing parks, future recreation grounds, school playing fields, existing woodlands, coppices and spinnies, the proposed golf course, the banks of streams and everything which will enhance their charm and will widen them out into great expanses of unbuilt upon country.[112]

These roads, he argued, should in American terminology properly be called "freeways," not "parkways," because they were not restricted to recreation and would be used by all kinds of traffic. (Indeed, they were akin to the notion of segregated arterial roads as the highest level in a hierarchical system of traffic planning, as enunciated by Alker Tripp in 1938 and then borrowed by Abercrombie and Forshaw as a major element in their County of London Plan in 1943.) But eventually, once finished, Parker's main north–south artery was called the Princess Parkway. Its fate was ironic: originally planned with junctions to the local street system at grade, 30 years later it was upgraded into a motorway by the transport planners. Approached from the city through a mass of concrete spaghetti, it is now a freeway, in the Angeleno sense of that word, with a vengeance. The other planned parkway, unaccountably, was abandoned halfway, the park strip wandering on shorn of its original point.

Manchester, in fact, has not dealt kindly with its masterpiece. The shopping center, completed very belatedly, is 1960s-tawdry; some of the postwar flats are monstrosities. A second and third generation of incomers have not treated the place as kindly as the original arrivals; there is all too much evidence, for those who would like to believe that civilized surroundings will engender civilized behavior, of graffiti, vandalism, and petty crime. The place looks down-at-heel in that distinctively English way, as if the city has given up on it; it now appears a distinctly poor relation to the booming city center. But despite its best efforts, it could not obliterate Parker

---

[109]   Caro, 1974, 10–11; Jackson, K., 1985, 166–7.
[110]   Gregg, 1986, 38, 41–2.
[111]   Mawson, 1984, 195.
[112]   Parker, 1932, 40.

entirely. The huge green space of Wythenshawe Park, right in the center, almost turns the green-belt concept inside-out; this is a green-heart city. The housing, which deftly embodies Georgian motifs into the vernacular of Letchworth, is cunningly grouped round a multitude of small green spaces. For all its latter-day shabbiness, it fully deserves the appellation of Third Garden City.

Meanwhile, the faithful soldiered on. Chamberlain, always the friend of garden cities while in office, had government subsidy written in to legislation in 1921, 1925 and – in the face of treasury opposition – in 1932.[113] But it did not do much good. By the 1930s the Permanent Secretary of the Ministry of Health, Sir Arthur Robinson, was openly confessing that "beginning as a supporter of garden cities, properly so called, I have in the course of time changed my views on them – they are fine in theory but in practice they do not seem to work. What is properly called a satellite town is a much better method of approach … But the satellite town is just what several of the large housing schemes of local authorities are producing, and the line of progress is to encourage it."[114] And, once Chamberlain had managed to create the Barlow Commission, Unwin, giving evidence to it in 1938, could argue that Howard's great contribution had been the garden suburb, not the garden city; satellite development would be sufficient to guard against the continued sprawl of London.[115]

In vain, Osborn railed at the consequences: "To build cottage estates on the outskirts gives people good immediate surroundings, but imposes on them an intolerable burden of journeys, costing money, energy and leisure. It also cuts off London as a whole from playing fields and open country."[116] The only way out of this, he was arguing in 1938, was to establish a London Regional Planning Commission with powers to establish executive boards to build new towns or expand existing ones," and to decentralize industry and business within an enlarged London region.[117] Against that view, of course, it could be argued that London was special; for the much smaller provincial cities, satellites – like Manchester's Wythenshawe or Liverpool's Speke – were perfectly acceptable. But Osborn would have none of that: "the fate of London may give cause to those responsible for the great towns and town-conglomerations of the North and Midlands … what Londoners can be got to stand today, England will be asked to stand tomorrow."[118] The establishment of the Barlow Commission – one of the first acts of Neville Chamberlain on becoming Prime Minister – at last gave him his chance; he did not miss it. As he confessed shamelessly to Lewis Mumford, he redrafted for Abercrombie some of the key paragraphs of the 1940 majority report and of Abercrombie's own minority report, which recommended sweeping controls on industrial location and which finally – in 1945 – was embodied into legislation.[119] After years in the political wilderness, the friends of the garden city were at last about to come into their own.

[113] Macfadyen, 1933, 104; Sheail, 1981, 125–6.
[114] Sheail, 1981, 126.
[115] GB Royal Commission Distribution, 1938, Q. 7221.
[116] Osborn, 1937, 51.
[117] Osborn, 1938, 100–2.
[118] Osborn, 1934, 5–6.
[119] Hughes, 1971, 271.

The Garden City in Europe

Over the water on the European mainland, the garden-city notion soon became just as thoroughly diluted or, as the faithful would say, traduced. As Stephen Ward has shown, in these years planning ideas were being furiously exchanged from country to country: Britain went to Germany for town extensions, zoning, and organic urban designs; the Germans admired British housing and above all the garden city; the French borrowed German zoning and the British garden city; but in the process, the idea became subtly transmogrified.[120] One problem was that several countries each had a home-grown garden-city advocate, who could – and sometimes did – claim that he thought of the idea independently. Insofar as these claims can ever be settled, all did; but in any case, their notions are subtly but importantly different from Howard's.

The first in time was undoubtedly the Spanish engineer Arturo Soria y Mata (1844–1920), who conceived of his ideal of *La Ciudad Lineal* in a magazine article of 1882 and developed it into a detailed proposal in 1892. Its essence was that a tramway, or light rail, system running out from a big city could give extraordinary linear accessibility, which would permit the development of a planned linear garden city: "A Cada Familia, Una Casa, En Cada Casa, Una Huerta y un Jardín," as an advertisement put it.[121] But the linear city was never more than a commuter suburb, developed as a commercial speculation. Started in 1894 and completed in 1904, the first section of the planned 48-kilometer (30-mile) city ran for 5 kilometers (3 miles) circumferentially between two major radial highways east of Madrid; on either side of a main axis 40 meters wide, carrying the tramway (originally worked by horses, and not electrified until 1909), villas were laid out on superblocks measuring approximately 200 meters in depth and with 80- or 100-meter frontages.[122] That was all that was built, and in 1934 the *Compañía Madrileña de Urbanización* gave up the ghost.[123] After World War Two the stupendous growth of the city almost buried the linear city; travelers from the airport pass under it without noticing. Those curious enough to divert will find it still quite recognizably there, with the tram replaced by a metro; they thoughtfully named a station for Arturo Soria. Some of the original villas, too, are still standing; but one by one, they are being replaced by apartment blocks, and soon the linear city will be a memory. Soria had grander dreams of linear cities across Europe, which in 1928, after his death, inspired an *Association Internationale des Cités Linéaires* masterminded by the influential French planner Georges Benoît-Lévy; echoes of his scheme can be found in the Russian deurbanists of the 1920s and in Corbusier's thinking of the 1930s, where we shall encounter them later.

The French Howard was Toni Garnier, an architect from Lyon, whose *Cité Industrielle* was first presented as a student study, rejected by the examiners, at the École des Beaux-Arts in Paris in 1899–1900 and first exhibited in 1904, to be revised

---

[120]   Ward, 2000b, 45.
[121]   Soria y Puig, 1968, 35, 43, Fig. 7.
[122]   Soria y Puig, 1968, Figs. 2–10.
[123]   Soria y Puig, 1968, 44–9, 52.

in the version we know now in 1917.[124] Garnier was a strangely isolated figure, even in his native France: serving on a policy committee, the only foreign book he could mention was one written by a Belgian; he recommended to the mayor, Edouard Herriot, to read Camillo Sitte in 1918, 16 years after its French translation was published.[125] If there is an intellectual provenance, it is the French regional thinking of Le Play and of the French school of geography, with its anti-metropolitan stress on the development of vigorous provincial craft culture; it is anarchist in its emphasis on common property and its rejection of such symbols of bourgeois repression as police stations, law courts, jails, or churches, and its large central building where 3,000 citizens could meet together.[126] All the odder, then, that Garnier makes his city depend economically on a single huge metallurgical plant (though questions of economics are given short shrift), and that the physical plan is dominated by strong axial boulevards and housing on rectangular grids; rather, as Reyner Banham put it, like Camillo Sitte with the serpentinings taken out.[127] His was an architect's vision, more utopian than Howard's, and was never built.[128]

If Garnier is not quite of one piece, his German equivalent is even weirder. Theodor Fritsch published his *Die Stadt der Zukunft* two years before Howard, in 1896; he had an obsession that Howard had stolen his ideas, though it seems clear that Howard had developed his independently before that.[129] True, in purely physical terms there are similarities between Garden City and City of the Future: the circular form, the division between land uses, the open land at the center and the surrounding green belt, the low-rise housing, the peripheral industry, the communal landownership. But these recur in other ideal plans, including Buckingham's, which Howard specifically acknowledged. And Fritsch's city, "eine Mischung von Grossstadt und Gartenstadt," lacks the specific function of urban decentralization which is central to Howard's thinking; it apparently would have been much bigger, with up to one million people.[130] Most important, the underlying ideology is totally different: Fritsch, a rabid propagandist of racism, plans a city where each individual immediately knows his place in a rigid, segregated social order.[131] Overall, any resemblance between Fritsch and Howard is one of surface appearance; and, as already seen, Howard was not in the least concerned about that. Fritsch remained a "lonesome preacher in the desert"; Fritsch's version of the garden city was largely ignored by the Deutsche Gartenstadtgesellschaft (DGG; German Garden City Association), founded in 1902. Howard was honored as the sole inventor of the garden city, even in Germany. For the DGG had a social reformist garden-city vision. In return, Fritsch never mentioned the existence of Letchworth, Welwyn, or all the German garden suburb developments, such as Hellerau

[124]   Ward, 2000a, 29.
[125]   Saunier, 1999, 38.
[126]   Wiebenson, 1969, 16–19; Veronesi, 1948, 56.
[127]   Banham, 1960, 36–8.
[128]   Ward, 2000a, 29.
[129]   Bergmann, 1970, 145–7; Hartmann, 1976, 33.
[130]   Reiner, 1963, 36–8; Peltz-Dreckmann, 1978, 45.
[131]   Peltz-Dreckmann, 1978, 45–7.

or Margarethenhöhe: "Fritsch ignored the DGG, accused Howard of plagiarism and wrote later that he was probably a Jew."[132]

For, before long, it was Howard's ideas which – to the chagrin of Fritsch – were carried across the water to influence thinking on the European mainland; but there, almost immediately, they were misunderstood. One of the earliest foreign interpretations of Howard's ideas, Le Cité Jardin by Georges Benoît-Lévy, managed to make an elementary confusion between garden city and garden suburb, from which French planners never afterwards extricated themselves.[133] Or, perhaps, they thought that the pure Howard gospel would not work for the incurably urban French.

Henri Sellier was the person who made it happen. Originally a trade unionist, then an active local socialist and national politician,[134] he was committed to the notion that the ordinary manual worker should become accustomed to bourgeois standards of respectability and comfort, so fostering the emergence of a new middle class.[135] As director of the Office Public des Habitations à Bon Marché du Département de la Seine, planning 16 cité-jardins around Paris between 1916 and 1939, he certainly understood that his interpretation was not pure Howard, but Unwin's Hampstead variant; he took his architects to visit Unwin in England, in 1919, and used the Unwin text as a basis for design.[136]

What they shared was some key aspects of the Unwin prescription, albeit translated into French terms: small size, between 1,000 and 5,500 units; land bought outside the city at low agricultural prices; densities that were low for Paris, 95–150 persons to the hectare (40–60 to the acre), and plenty of open space. Then, rising land and housing costs, plus population pressure, brought modifications: more and more blocks of five-story flats were included; densities rose to 200–260 to the hectare (80–105 per acre), though still with generous open space and social services.[137] Visited today, a typical example like Suresnes – 6 miles from the center of Paris, a mere mile from the Bois de Boulogne, and the city for which Sellier was mayor during virtually all the interwar period – looks like nothing so much as an LCC inner-London apartment-block scheme of the same period: until one wanders into some of the peripheral streets, Unwin's, certainly, is not the first name that springs to mind.[138] And in the 1930s, as the proportion of apartment blocks rose even higher and the architects joined the modern movement, as at Le Plessis-Robinson in the southern suburbs, the divergence was complete.

In Germany, they did better. In 1902 a salesman visiting England, Heinrich Krebs, brought back Howard's book, had it translated, ran a conference, and started a German equivalent of the Garden City Association. There was an enthusiastic response: German industrialists, almost unbelievably, thought that the garden-city

[132]   Schubert, 2004, 14–15.
[133]   Batchelor, 1969, 199.
[134]   Gaudin, 1992, 55.
[135]   Gaudin, 1992, 63.
[136]   Read, 1978, 349–50; Swenarton, 1985, 54.
[137]   Read, 1978, 350–1; Evenson, 1979, 223–6.
[138]   Ville de Suresnes, 1998, passim.

movement helped explain good British industrial labor relations.[139] That, to be sure, was some kind of obsession with German industrialists.

Before World War One, its outstanding expression was the garden village of Margarethenhöhe at the edge of Essen in the Ruhrgebiet, developed by the Krupp family in 1912 as the latest in a long line of such industrial housing estates that went back as early as 1863. It served Krupp workers, including 4,000 white-collar workers at the time of foundation, but not exclusively so: in 1913 less than half the tenants were "Kruppianer."[140] Small, with only 5,300 people at the end of the 1930s, it is physically a transplanted New Earswick. Its architect, Georg Metzendorf, faithfully followed the Unwin–Parker tradition to create a magic little town, separated from the city by a wooded mini green belt, its entrance gateway, its central market square, its medieval-looking inn, its narrow curving streets from which all through traffic is excluded. Thus, ironically, it out-Unwins Unwin; it really does look like a twentieth-century Rothenburg. Perhaps it took a German architect, working in a German environment with a top German planner – Metzendorf worked hand in hand with Essen's municipal architect Robert Schmidt – to achieve what Unwin so zealously strived for. Whether it served Krupp's purposes is another question altogether; apparently, by herding his workers together in their own town, it made them even more class-conscious.[141]

The *Gartenstadtbewegung*, however, aimed higher: they wanted a German Letchworth, as their leader Hans Kampffmeyer said in 1908.[142] They never quite achieved it, though they came near. The garden city at Hellerau, 8 kilometers (5 miles) outside Dresden, was – like Margarethenhöhe – essentially a garden suburb at the end of a tram line. But, like Letchworth in its heady early years, it – and the movement in general – was heavily imbued with principles of the Life Reform Movement: not merely housing, but eating, clothing, and lifestyle generally were to be simplified and stripped of nineteenth-century dross. Hellerau contained the Deutsche Werkstätte für Handbaukunst, and even a Society for Applied Rhythmics.

The latter-day pilgrim, visiting it, goes into a time warp. It is isolated from the city, in open heathland that provides a natural green belt against the city, but that once served as a Red Army training ground, punctuating the arcadian peace with eerie explosions. Now it is peaceful once again, as it should be. The GDR government lacked resources to do much with it, leaving it rather charmingly down-at-heel; since reunification money has been lavished to restore it as a national monument, which it certainly is. Heinrich Tressenow's terrace and semi-detached houses, utterly faithful to the Unwin–Parker tradition, wear their years lightly. There is even a Radburn-style pedestrian layout, anticipating Radburn itself by two decades. It leads to the Werkstätte, long a People's-Owned Enterprise, now restored to its original management. The market square, reminiscent of Margarethenhöhe – which, surely,

---

[139]   Kampffmeyer, 1908, 599.
[140]   Petz, 1990a, 6.
[141]   Peltz-Dreckmann, 1978, 50; Petz, 1990a, 7, 9.
[142]   Kampffmeyer, 1908, 595.

Figure 4.12 Margarethenhöhe. Georg Metzendorf's brilliant exercise in the Sitte tradition, for the Krupp family, outside Essen: the essence of German industrial paternalism. *Source*: Historisches Archiv Krupp, Essen.

Tressenow must have visited – manages to achieve what Unwin and Parker should have done at Letchworth and Hampstead, but unaccountably never did. It is an anomalous small gem.

It represents what could be called the left-wing side of the German garden-city movement; but there was always another side too, and over time it became more and more insistent. It stemmed from the fear of the giant city; it spoke of biological decline of the race in the great cities, and of the need to recolonize the declining countryside, especially on the borders of German settlement against Slav Europe. Already, ominously, in the middle of World War One, the word *Lebensraum* was in use; it entailed the removal of population that was harmful to the "national character"[143]. In the 1920s, these themes were to become a potent element of Nazi thinking.

But that, still, was in the realm of intellectual speculation. In the real world, immediately after World War One, the reality was similar to that in Britain: a fear of revolution. And perhaps in Germany it had sounder foundation. In Frankfurt, as elsewhere, a Workers' and Soldiers' Council dominated politics for a year after the

---

[143] Bergmann, 1970, 169–71.

1918 armistice. When the Social Democrats finally achieved power in the city, their strategy under Mayor Ludwig Landmann (1924–33) was to restore social peace through an implicit compact between capital and labor: a theme that was to recur in the creation of the *Wohlfahrtsgesellschaft* after World War Two. Frankfurt's central business district was to be preserved and enhanced as Germany's leading financial center; the banks of the Main were to be developed for high-technology industry. But, to satisfy the demands of labor, the city would also embark on an active housing policy.

Landmann attracted the architect-planner Ernst May, who had acquired a considerable reputation with his plans for the city of Breslau (Wrocław). Thanks to the far-sighted policies of Frankfurt's famous prewar mayor, Franz Adickes, the city had acquired enormous landholdings, at rock-bottom agricultural prices, in the open countryside around.[144] Thus, on arrival in 1925, May had all he needed to evolve a startlingly innovative development plan.

May, like Sellier in Paris, was heavily influenced by the garden-city movement; he had worked with Unwin, in 1910, on both Letchworth and Hampstead; he maintained close contact with him. His original notion was a pure garden-city one, with new towns 20–30 kilometers (15–20 miles) distant, separated from the city by a wide green belt. It proved impossible to realize politically; May fell back on a compromise, the development of satellite cities (*Trabantenstädte*), separated from the city by only a narrow green belt, or "people's park," dependent on it for jobs and for all but immediate local shopping needs, and therefore linked to it by public transportation.[145] But these were to be developed by the city, as public housing; the comparison is with the British housing program after the 1919 Act (Chapter 3), not with the early British garden cities and garden suburbs.

In another important respect May broke away completely from Unwin, and indeed from the British tradition of the 1920s: his satellites were to be designed uncompromisingly as modern architecture, in the form of long terraces of flat-roofed houses with roof gardens, on which people could breakfast, sunbathe, raise plants. But that difference is skin-deep: in his insistence on single-family homes with gardens, carefully aligned in relation to the light of the sun, May proved an apt pupil of his master. Indeed, he took issue with Walter Gropius, his fellow-German member of the Congrès Internationaux d'Architecture Moderne (CIAM), at a 1929 meeting in Frankfurt: Gropius favored high-rise 10-story steel-frame construction, May low-rise three- and four-story prefabricated concrete and brick.[146]

The entire program was not large: 15,000 houses, though it did constitute the great bulk of all housing built in the city in that period, 1925–33. May's tenure would last only five years, but during that time his program, dubbed the "New Frankfurt," rehoused over 10% of Frankfurt's population, some 60,000 people in 15,000 units of housing and 14 new settlements. In all of Europe, only Berlin built more. And it was

[144]   Yago, 1984, 87–8, 94, 98–9.
[145]   Fehl, 1983, 188–90.
[146]   Fehl, 1987, 204, 206.

never completed as planned; the money ran out, and the community halls – an echo, perhaps, of Unwin – were never completed. The individual schemes, for all their fame then and subsequently, were minuscule, and many of them were disposed unmemorably on small plots around the city; only a few, strung out along the valley of the river Nidda northwest of the city, represent the classic satellites, and even these are surprisingly small: 1,441 dwellings at Praunheim, 1,220 at Römerstadt.[147] What made them memorable was the disposition of the houses in long rows alongside the river, the placing of schools and *Kindergarten* on the lower land, and the use of the valley as a natural green belt between the city and the ring of new settlements, in which are concentrated all kinds of uses: allotments, sports grounds, commercial garden plots, gardening schools for young people, even perhaps a fairground.[148] Here May worked with Max Bromme, who had sought to preserve the valley as parkland. The great central basin became the seat of recreation, sport, and outdoor education:

> With its vast meadows, bounded by forests and terraced housing, sports facilities and vegetable gardens, the Nidda River Valley became the great leisure realm of the northwest settlement zone. Botanical and school gardens replaced formal gardens and new types of leisure facilities abounded: wading pools and sandboxes for the children, and swimming pools, gymnasia, sunning terraces, dressing rooms and copses scattered with hammocks for adults. Working-class families who could not afford the trip to the seaside now only had to look in their own backyard.[149]

Römerstadt, largely completed in a single year (1928), was the quintessence in which May sought to recapture the idyll of Hampstead Garden Suburb, experienced in a two-year sojourn in Raymond Unwin's Hampstead office (1910–11).[150] It had a low density, a predominance of single-family row houses (comprising over half the total 1,220 units), garden allotments for all, and a generous allowance for streets and pedestrian pathways. The original 1927 plan also had extensive community facilities: two schools, a day care center, shops, a cooperative store, a community center, a church, a guesthouse, a communal laundry, a theater, cable radio, and a youth clubhouse, most of which disappeared in cutbacks in 1928, but still left it the most complete and generously equipped among the Frankfurt settlements.[151]

Count Henry Kessler took the French sculptor Aristide Maillol on a tour of the Frankfurt Forest Stadium in June 1930; looking at the nude bodies he said, "A people really want to *live* in the sense of enjoying light, happiness, and the health of their bodies. It is not restricted to a small and exclusive circle, but is a mass movement which has stirred all of German youth."[152] And here lay the essence. One publicity picture (and there were many) shows a young couple enjoying open-air freedom on

---

[147]   Gallion and Eisner, 1963, 104.
[148]   Fehl, 1983, 191.
[149]   Henderson, 1994, 208.
[150]   Henderson, 2010, 324.
[151]   Henderson, 2010, 327.
[152]   Henderson, 1994, 211.

a roof garden of one of the new houses; she is the archetype of the "New Woman" with bobbed hair, loose clothing, and short skirt.[153] The Nidda Valley settlements, one might say, were designed for her and her sisters.

After the war, Frankfurt dealt brutally with its miniature masterpiece: two urban motorways now slice across the valley, one cuts Römerstadt in half, and the satellites are totally swallowed up in a much larger and completely amorphous satellite town called – with appropriate impersonality – Nordweststadt. But still, with the eye of imagination and the eye of faith, one can get a feeling for what it might have been, what it was, and what it still remarkably is. It is almost totally gentrified, with only 11% of the blue-collar workers for which it was designed; but it is beautifully maintained. After more than half a century the vegetation is mature, making of it the garden city that May imagined. In the summer sunlight the hard clean lines of the long cream-colored terraces are masked, almost submerged, by the trees and flowers; across the valley, the blue industrial haze achieves the serendipitous effect of making the city's new high-rise townscape appear almost like a magical world.

What has vanished is the spirit. And that, now, is hard even to imagine. May differed on many things with the other great planner of the Weimar time, Berlin's Martin Wagner; but both shared a belief in a new social partnership between capital and labor, and in a reintegration of working and living. This they also had in common with Howard and Unwin; but there was an absolutely crucial difference. The May–Wagner variant was a collective one, diverging sharply from the anarchist-cooperative sources of the Howard–Unwin tradition: in May's own words, it aimed at "the collective ordering of the elements of living."[154] For May, a well-planned residential environment could complement the pursuit of efficiency in the workplace, and – to quote May again – "The uniform box-shapes of the roof gardens symbolize the idea of collective living in a uniform style, like the similarly shaped honeycombs of the beehive, symbolizing the uniform living conditions of their inhabitants."[155]

It all sounds too perfectly like raw material for a Marxist PhD thesis: the capitalist state coopting the local state in a plot to secure the reproduction of the labor force. In any event, both Howard and Unwin would have hated it; no wonder, perhaps, that Unwin made himself thoroughly unpopular by holding out against modern architecture to the end. And no wonder either, perhaps, that after Frankfurt May went on to design model cities in the Soviet Union – none of which, ironically, were ever built as planned, for by then the spirit of Stalin had descended on the Soviet City.

But Wagner went significantly further – much further. Appointed Berlin City Planner in 1925, aged 30[156] and a leading Social Democratic intellectual figure, in April 1931 he resigned from the party, disillusioned by corruption over support for land speculation and privatization of public bodies. He wrote incessantly, editing 12 issues of *Das Neue Berlin* in 1929, and then contributing a two-volume unpublished book of

[153] Henderson, 1994, 199–200.
[154] Fehl, 1983, 186.
[155] Fehl, 1983, 190.
[156] Frisby, 2001, 271–2.

the same title, in 1932.[157] In often very abstract German, he argued for a new collective style of architecture.[158] In 1929, he was demanding

> the leadership with clear aims that can provide a comprehensive direction of all forces into a cosmopolitan tapestry. The director (*Regisseur*) of the world city of Berlin is lacking. The ordering, demanding dynastic will has died out. Today, the world city of Berlin is not governed by a single democracy but by a whole system of democracies that lack decisive and unified leadership."[159]

David Frisby, the chronicler of modernism, comments, "The post of director to which Wagner refers is, at the very least, ominously reminiscent of the charismatic leader."[160]

Later, in 1932, he had made a radical shift, calling for new urban areas for 50,000 people in Brandenburg, his "fifties." He emphatically declared that these were not garden cities, at least architecturally:[161] they were to be "ribbon cites (*Bandstädte*), new cities [built] in accord with the idea of the perfect machine."[162] He demanded a technocratic leader, free of politics, to make it happen:

> Leader to the back! Leader to the front! Politicians and lawyers to the resting place, engineers to the front! This *must* happen and it *will* happen. ... *City planning* is *economic planning*, and economic planning is only possible if we work *with* the machine but not *against* the machine.[163]

These are to be organic communities set in the countryside. But, Frisby rather politely remarks, "The moral rhetoric directed at 'the sin against the holy spirit of the machine'... and assertions (with reference to the new form of life in the new cities) that 'the new form grows out of the organic' are difficult to reconcile."[164]

He was dismissed by the Nazis in 1933 and emigrated, first to Istanbul and then, in 1937, to Harvard where he remained until his death in 1957.[165] There, he joined his fellow émigré Walter Gropius in promoting a modernist CIAM-based urbanism, playing a key part in shaping the postwar American landscape. In the process, from 1944 onward, "the city and its future became the subject of a simmering feud between Hudnut and Gropius, which finally escalated into a raging battle" from which Gropius and Wagner emerged victors, playing a key part in shaping the postwar American landscape.[166] Hudnut, however, had a strange posthumous revenge: in 1945 he coined the phrase "postmodern" to oppose the modernists' obsession with

---

157   Frisby 2001, 282–3.
158   Frisby 2001, 275.
159   Quoted in Frisby, 2001, 284.
160   Frisby, 2001, 284.
161   Frisby, 2001, 293.
162   Frisby, 2001, 296.
163   Quoted in Frisby 2001, 295.
164   Frisby 2001, 298.
165   Frisby, 2001, 273.
166   Pearlman, 2000, 204.

technology, efficiency, economy, and social expediency and their neglect of individual needs, local customs, and the spiritual qualities of form.[167]

Wagner, like May, was coordinating a major housing and planning program, albeit on a much larger scale. His big difference with May concerned the role, and thus the character and the location, of the new estates. Wagner did not believe at all in satellites; his ideal was the *Siedlung* – the concept and the term were first developed by the coal and iron barons of the Ruhrgebiet – wherein houses were grouped around a factory, but with no independent – or even semi-independent – existence from the rest of the city.[168] The ideal is Siemensstadt, developed by the giant electrical company around their complex of works in the northwest sector of the city between 1929 and 1931. It is a *Grosssiedlung*, a complex of housing areas, planned and executed on a lavish scale; every name in German architecture of the 1920s has his piece of it; it is a place of reverent pilgrimage, and pieces are being restored by the Federal government as historic monuments. The pilgrims arrive at the U-Bahn station, Siemensdamm, a busy urban boulevard just over 20 minutes from the center of West Berlin; this announces itself from the start as an urban development. Yet, a couple of minutes away, they are in another world: the masters – Scharoun, Bartning, Häring, Gropius, and others – have placed their four- and five-story apartment blocks in a huge garden, that – as with the two-story rows of Römerstadt – has grown over the decades so as to seem almost to envelop them.[169]

The overwhelming impression, just as much in any English garden city, is that of peacefulness. Any sceptic from Britain or the United States, who believes that collective apartment schemes mean slum living, any indeed who believes that an apartment garden city is a contradiction in terms, should see Siemensstadt and think again. The reflections have to be these: first, uncompromisingly modern apartment blocks, so long as kept moderately low and strongly horizontal, can be as reposeful – that special Unwin–Parker quality – as uncompromisingly modern houses, or as traditional ones. Secondly, the quality of the surrounding garden space is crucial. And thirdly, maintenance is all: Siemensstadt works, as does Römerstadt, because it is in good heart.

The same goes, outstandingly, for the two other great developments of the Wagner years in Berlin: the *Grosssiedlungen* Onkel-Toms-Hütte (1926–7), at Zehlendorf in the southwest sector of the city, and Britz (1925–7), in the south. Both were developed by Gehag, the great housing agency formed in 1924 through the merger of several building societies with trade union funds and the Berlin Social Housing Society, which was responsible for so much publicly subsidized housing in Berlin at that time and in the Federal Republic after World War Two: a living illustration of the kind of agency Howard wanted to build his garden city, but never had on the scale needed.[170] (Ironically, its postwar successor was racked by scandal in the 1980s.) Both were and are pure garden suburbs, at the then-periphery of the city, developed on extensions of the U-Bahn system.

[167] Pearlman, 2000, 205.
[168] Uhlig, 1977, 56.
[169] Rave and Knöfel, 1968, 193.
[170] Lane, 1968, 104.

Figure 4.13 Römerstadt.

Figure 4.14 Siemensstadt.

Figure 4.15   Onkel-Toms-Hütte. The garden suburb reinterpreted by the masters of the modern movement, May in Frankfurt, Gropius and Taut in Berlin: functionalism, even in four-story apartments, can prove liveable too.

Onkel-Toms-Hütte, built between 1926 and 1931, calls itself a forest-settlement (*Waldsiedlung*) and indeed the first impression is of the huge canopy of tall trees that extends, with almost military uniformity, across the whole site. Under its cover are two- and three-story houses, the bulk of them by Bruno Taut and Hugo Häring, uncompromisingly in 1920s modern idiom, washed in pastel shades, developed in rows along long gently curving or shorter straight streets.[171] Again – especially to those hardened by experience of British council estates – the astonishing feature is the level of upkeep: the houses, still owned by the housing association, convey the unreal impression that they are almost brand-new. Britz (1925–31), designed by Bruno Taut and Martin Wagner, is more formal: its two- and three-story terraces of houses are grouped around the celebrated *Hufeneisensiedlung*, where the four-story block wraps itself in a huge horseshoe round a lake.[172] In the streets around, the houses – again impeccably maintained – show an unexpected counterpoint: Bruno Taut's are respectably conservative, Martin Wagner's Disneyland-fantastic. An underground station stands at each end of the settlement, which on its east side faces out on to the huge open space of the Köningsheide.

Both these developments are splendid; both, ironically, represent the very antithesis of the garden-city idea. It might be argued that May in Frankfurt, like Parker in

[171]   Rave and Knöfel, 1968, 146.
[172]   Rave and Knöfel, 1968, 79.

Manchester, was dealing with a spatial scale different in kind from that of London, which provided Howard's model urban problem; both were quintessentially medium-sized provincial cities, with between half and three-quarters of a million people, and so a satellite solution might seem more workable and more appropriate. But the same could hardly be said of the Greater Berlin of the mid-1920s, already – with some four million people – the second greatest single urban mass in Europe. The fact was that by this time, racked by lack of funds and by political realities, the planners of the Weimar Republic no longer thought that the self-containment of the garden city was worth fighting for.[173]

Garden Cities in Far Places

What was astonishing about the garden-city movement was how easily it was exported from its homeland, but also how strangely it became transformed in the process.

The Japanese took it up as enthusiastically as any; railway companies built them around Tokyo and around Osaka in the 1910s and 1920s. The Japanese name, *den-en toshi*, suggests green paddy fields, quiet rural villages, and a beautiful breeze; these were to be oases of rural calm, appealing to people who had migrated from the countryside into a polluted industrial city. But of course they were pure commuter suburbs, without any social purpose: the profits went not to the community, but straight into the account books of the train companies.[174]

Down in Australia, as in Britain, the movement was strongly associated with the idea of building "homes for heroes" after the 1914–18 war.[175] Colonel Light Gardens, in the southern Adelaide suburb of Mitcham – initially known (in 1917) as the Mitcham Garden Suburb but, in 1921, in deference to Charles Compton Reade's wish to commemorate "the Pioneer Town Planner of South Australia," renamed in honor of the first Surveyor-General of Adelaide, Colonel William Light[176] – would not have appealed to Howard as illustrating the correct principles of city growth; it was a pure tram-based garden suburb. It was administered by a Garden Suburb Commission comprising a sole Commissioner responsible to the Parliament, and having the powers both of a development corporation and of a municipality, a distinction that sets it apart from Letchworth and Hampstead, and anticipating the post-1945 UK new towns.[177] It was and is a remarkable piece of urban design, distinguished by very generous park space, from formal parks to neighborhood parks used for tennis clubs, by a hierarchy of streets designed to exclude through traffic, and by provision of community facilities.[178] It was the work of Charles Compton Reade (1880–1933), a New Zealander who as an Auckland journalist had unsuccessfully campaigned for

[173]   Hartmann, 1976, 44.
[174]   Watanabe, 1992, 69–84.
[175]   Hutchings, 1990, 15.
[176]   Garnaut and Hutchings, 2003, 277–8.
[177]   Garnault and Hutchings, 2003, 278.
[178]   Hutchings 1990, 18–19.

garden cities in his homeland[179] and had then spent time in London as Assistant Secretary to the GCTPA before becoming Government Town Planner for South Australia, and who designed the new suburb as part of a comprehensive metropolitan plan.[180] But he was by all accounts a difficult and even tragic person: though "a man of delightful personality with a strong sense of humour and a rich fund of anec-dotes,"[181] a member of the South Australian Legislature said of him "When a visitor to your house calls your paintings oleographs, your silver spoons brass, and your dog a mongrel, he is hardly the man you would want to meet again."[182] In 1921, apparently frustrated by political battles to secure adequate planning legislation, he left Australia to become Government Town Planner in the Federated Malay States, but, after bureaucratic battles there and in Africa, he shot himself in a Johannesburg hotel.[183]

Garden Cities for America

Across the Atlantic Ocean, too, the garden-city tradition never quite developed as Howard had hoped. It was not, however, for want of trying. During the 1920s, the Regional Planning Association of America (RPAA) not only acted as guardians of the sacred treasures; rather in the manner of a reforming church, they actually extended and purified the gospel, writing the holy texts that Howard might have delivered if appropriate disciples had been at his sleeve. But their god was a twin god, Howard–Geddes, and their creed embraced the planning of entire regions; so they deserve a goodly part of a chapter to themselves, which they will have in Chapter 5. Here, we need to talk of their contributions to the garden city without benefit of that context; difficult, illogical even, but necessary in the interests of coherence.

The architects in this small and distinguished group were Clarence Stein and Henry Wright. Their unique contribution to the garden city lay in the handling of traffic and pedestrian circulation through the so-called Radburn layout, which they developed for the garden city of the same name in 1928. But to appreciate it fully, they need to be related to another figure, oddly not associated with the RPAA group at all: Clarence Perry.

Perry was a very early example of a breed that was to become commoner, the sociologist-planner. He worked as a community planner for the New York-based Russell Sage Foundation from 1913 until his retirement in 1937. Even before this, he had become interested in a movement – clearly derivative from the approach of Jane Addams in Chicago – to develop local schools into community centers through the involvement of parents. He was also profoundly influenced by the writings of the American sociologist Charles Horton Cooley, who had stressed the importance

---

[179]   Schrader, 1999, 398, 408; Miller, 2002, 51.
[180]   Garnaut, 2000, 56–8, 63.
[181]   Quoted in Home, 2013, 169.
[182]   Quoted in Home, 2013, 169.
[183]   Home, 1990, 28–9.

of the "primary group," "characterized by intimate face-to-face association and cooperation," which he held to be "fundamental in forming the social nature and ideals of the individual" and which was especially important in the dense, highly fragmented life of the modern city.[184]

That was a theme taken up by leaders of the settlement house movement, who had argued that the time had come for "a great renewal of confidence in the vitality of the neighborhood as a political and moral unit," especially in those "Disorganized neighborhoods … which have lost their responsible leadership," whereby "under-average mothers in relatively resourceless neighborhoods … can be trained and held to their task" and "the loss of productive power" could be corrected by "the vocational extension of our public school system."[185] Socialization of the immigrant, and of the immigrant's children, was clearly the object here.[186] But it was more than that; as a resident in the model garden suburb of Forest Hills Gardens, developed by the Russell Sage Foundation from 1911 – itself a railroad suburb, some 9 miles from Manhattan, where Grosvenor Atterbury's plan is clearly derivative from Chicago's Riverside and London's Bedford Park – Perry learned just how much good design could contribute to the development of a neighborhood spirit.[187] It derives in spirit from Unwin and Parker's quasi-Teutonic at Hampstead, and from the real thing at Margarethenhöhe and Hellerau; but it goes beyond any of them, to create a kitsch-like quality that anticipates Hollywood. Supreme irony: in true American fashion, Atterbury used prefabricated panels with embedded electrical wiring, which he then incorporated into experimental Tudor-style houses.[188] Yet, like all the best suburban dream environments before it, from Nash's Blaise Hamlet onwards, the point is that it works: in the presence of this superb theatrical set, disbelief is immediately suspended.

But theater is put to serious purpose. Life in Forest Hills Gardens gave to Perry the concept of the neighborhood unit, which he first developed at a meeting of the American Sociological Association and the National Community Center Association in Washington, DC, on December 16, 1923, and subsequently developed in greater detail in his monograph of 1929 for the Regional Plan of New York, which was financed by Russell Sage and in which Perry played a principal role as a social planner.[189] Its size would be set by the catchment area of the local elementary school, and so would depend on population density; its central features would be this local school and an associated playground, reachable on foot within half a mile; local shops, which, by being placed at the corners of several neighborhoods, could be within a quarter-mile; and a central point or common place for the encouragement of community institutions:

> The square itself will be an appropriate location for a flagpole, a memorial monument, a bandstand, or an ornamental fountain. In the common life of the neighborhood it

[184] Cooley, 1909, 23, 408–9.
[185] Woods, 1914, 17–18, 20–1.
[186] Lubove, 1962a, 205.
[187] Perry, 1929, 90–3; 1939, 205–9, 217; Mumford, 1954, 260; Lubove, 1962a, 207.
[188] Radford, 1996, 33.
[189] Perry, 1939, 214; Lubove, 1962a, 207.

Figure 4.16 Clarence Stein. Campaigner for new towns in America, and builder of three brilliant designs; he gave the Radburn layout to the planner's vocabulary. *Source*: Clarence Stein Papers # 3600. Division of Rare and Manuscript Collections, Cornell University Library.

> will function as the place of local celebrations. Here, on Independence Day, the Flag will be raised, the Declaration of Independence will be recited, and the citizenry urged to patriotic deeds by eloquent orators.[190]

The inspiration is unmistakable: it is a latter-day reinterpretation of Jane Addams' desire to integrate the new immigrant, now become the immigrant's American-born children, as they move out from the city slums to their new suburban homes.

The *raison d'être* then was socio-cultural; but, Perry already argued at the end of the 1920s, "the automobile menace" had made the definition of such neighborhood units imperative, proving thus "a blessing in disguise."[191] The arterial streets, wide enough to carry all through traffic, would thus provide logical boundaries; the internal street network would be designed to facilitate internal circulation but to discourage through traffic.[192]

[190]   Perry, 1939, 65.
[191]   Perry, 1929, 31.
[192]   Perry, 1929, 34–5.

Figure 4.17 and **Figure 4.18**   Forest Hills Gardens. The New York commuter garden suburb where Clarence Perry discovered the principle of the neighborhood unit. *Source*: Peter Hall.

In the celebrated diagram in the 1929 report, one element only is missing: a clear indication of how, precisely, the unwanted traffic was to be kept out. Perry himself knew this to be the only real defect of the Forest Hills Gardens plan.[193] But already, a few miles nearer Manhattan along the same commuter rail line,

193   Perry, 1939, 211.

Stein and Wright were tentatively showing the way. In 1924, Alexander Bing, a successful developer, had been inspired by Stein to launch the City Housing Corporation (CHC) in order to build an American garden city. As a first trial, from 1924 to 1928, they took Sunnyside Gardens, a still-undeveloped 77-acre inner-city site only 5 miles from Manhattan, planning it on the basis of big traffic-free superblocks to create vast interior garden spaces – albeit frustrated by the same kind of rigid restrictions against which Unwin had fought in England (and had overcome at Brentham).[194] Lewis Mumford, who was one of the first residents, long after testified to the quality of life, both physical and social, there;[195] but it was no garden city.

There was a strange contemporary echo far away in Tel-Aviv. There, in 1925, Patrick Geddes – to receive attention in Chapter 5 – who had been working for the Zionist Congress, accepted an invitation to produce a new plan for the city. There was a contradiction: Geddes was a devout believer in new towns, but the Zionist agenda stressed agricultural settlement and urban consolidation. But Geddes squared this circle by making the city into a garden: the major Jewish urban center in Palestine would be partially rural.[196] Geddes's concept of the "home block" consists of groups of small residential blocks connected by short inner streets, organized around an inner open space reached by pedestrian alleys, 1.5 meters wide, and envisaged by Geddes as lanes covered with roses and vines. These passages, at the back of the private plots, allow the residents easy access to communal facilities located in the central open space.[197] Alas, as Tel-Aviv mushroomed from 40,000 people in 1925 to 180,000 at independence in 1947, his vision did not survive the vast urban development, the extensive demands for building land, and the speculative character of development.[198]

Meanwhile, apprenticed in Sunnyside Gardens, Stein and Wright moved on to the real thing. In the borough of Fairlawn in New Jersey, 15 miles from Manhattan – a place with no zoning ordinance and no roads plan – the CHC bought 2 square miles, on which Stein and Wright planned three neighborhoods.[199] The trick was to take the Sunnyside superblock, release it from the rigid New York City grid, and combine it with cluster housing so that not merely through traffic, but all traffic, was excluded. As one of the consultants on the design put it, "we abolished the backyard and made it the front yard … we are building houses that have no backs, but have two fronts"[200] – a feature Wright had noticed in Irish peasant houses.[201] But the main influence, interestingly, was Unwin: Bing had sent Stein and Wright to England in 1924 to study new towns and housing designs; they met Howard in Welwyn and Unwin at his home on

---

[194]   Stein, 1958, 21.
[195]   Mumford, 1982, 411–21.
[196]   Kallus, 1997, 289.
[197]   Kallus, 1997, 294.
[198]   Kallus, 1997, 313.
[199]   Stein, 1958, 39–41; Schaffer, 1982, 147.
[200]   Quoted in Schaffer, 1982, 156.
[201]   Stein, 1958, 48.

Hampstead Heath, afterwards reflecting that the Letchworth plan "did not altogether work,"[202] but impressed by the urban design in Hampstead, which – in culs-de-sac like Reynolds Close off Hampstead Way – has minor elements of the Radburn layout; and in 1928, on a visit to Radburn, Unwin became deeply involved in its design.[203]

Years later, after World War Two, Arthur Ling in Coventry would return the compliment by designing the first British Radburn layout at Willenhall Wood.[204] And here lay a tale: Gordon Stephenson, then editor of the *Town Planning Review*, who had studied city planning at the Massachusetts Institute of Technology in the 1930s when Stein was sometimes a visiting lecturer, published the projects of Stein, Wright, and associates in 1949–50 and then Stein's book *Toward New Towns for America* in 1951. This had a direct influence on UK design, first in Stephenson's own project in Wrexham and then in the New Towns. Stephenson appointed Stein as consultant for the Stevenage central business district in mid-1950, and this became the first pedestrianized New Town shopping center in Britain. Ling's Willenhall Wood was designed from 1955, evoking public resistance because people wanted the "front door" to face the road where people arrived by car.[205] Though there is no evidence of direct contact between Stein and Arthur Ling, Hugh Wilson, or Paul Ritter before the 1960s, British planners were much influenced by Ling's Coventry schemes and by Wilson's designs for Cumbernauld with its extensive pedestrian system, extending outside the town, which – as Kermit Parsons concludes – are "among the most successful and complete such facilities in existence anywhere, exceeded for the comprehensive, continuous pedestrian path system only by several of the Stockholm suburban communities planned from 1948 to 1973 ..."[206]

There seems to be some kind of general law in planning history that the first time is the best. Certainly that was true of New Earswick and Letchworth; certainly it is so here. Radburn is the best Radburn layout. The hierarchical arrangement of roads – here used for the first time, though almost immediately copied by Parker at Wythenshawe – is very natural and easy. The houses, modest enough in themselves, cluster cozily alongside the short culs-de-sac from the distributor roads – a motif borrowed directly from Unwin and Parker at Hampstead and the later part of New Earswick, as Stein freely acknowledged;[207] obscured by the rich New Jersey summer vegetation, they look almost as if they grow out of the ground. The central open space, with its serpentine pedestrian and bicycle paths diving under rusticated overbridges, has an informal naturalness. It looks and feels right.

The feeling was bought at a cost. Though a Radburn Association controlled and managed the space, the houses were sold, and – despite the hopes of social mix – by 1934 three in five family heads were at least middle executives; there were no blue-collar

[202] Parsons, 2002, 131.
[203] Parsons, 1992b, 184; Miller, 2000, 21.
[204] Parsons, 1992b, 191.
[205] Parsons, 2002, 135–7, 145.
[206] Parsons, 2002, 150.
[207] Stein, 1958, 44.

Figure 4.19   Radburn.

workers at all. Even worse, the realtors kept out Jews and blacks.[208] From the start, the site was too small to allow for a proper green belt. The depression stopped further development, keeping the population pegged at 1,500: far too low to support the elaborate range of community programs and services originally envisaged. Even to maintain the communal part of the development, the Association depended on CHC and Carnegie grants. It proved difficult to attract industry; so, to keep up cash flow, the CHC was forced to abandon all hope of creating a true garden city, advertising it as a pure commuter suburb. Many owners were forced to sell; finally the CHC too, over-whelmed by land-carrying costs, went down in a sea of acrimony and legal actions.[209] Finally, Stein reflected more than 20 years after, the Radburn experience showed that a private corporation had at best a gambler's chance to build a new community.[210]

And, of course, it was not and would never become a true garden city. Stein later wrote that "Radburn had to accept the role of a suburb."[211] But what Mumford called the "Radburn idea" provided the basis for virtually every American new town from then to 1980, including the green-belt towns, Reston and Columbia, the federal new communities of the 1960s and 1970s, and Californian "master-planned communities" like Irvine, Valencia, and Westlake Village.[212]

---

[208]   Schaffer, 1982, 173–4, 177.
[209]   Stein, 1958, 39, 41 68–9; Schaffer, 1982, 149–50, 160, 186–7.
[210]   Stein, 1958, 69.
[211]   Fulton, 2002, 162.
[212]   Fulton, 2002, 163.

There were, immediately, two other Radburns, on both of which Stein served as consultant: Chatham Village (1932) in Pittsburgh, a pioneer venture in low-rent housing only 2 miles from the Golden Triangle; and Baldwin Hills Village (1941) in Los Angeles. Both were financial successes. At Baldwin Hills, the planners significantly modified the layout, substituting collective vehicle courts for the culs-de-sac, and throwing some of the three linked central open spaces – vast enough, to be sure – into private enclosed space, thus saving maintenance costs.[213] But the shopping center and three childcare centers disappeared in budget cuts, and a second phase was never started; worst irony of all, though the project was at first racially integrated, after a decade many white families left complaining of problem families; in the 1970s a rescue group converted the development from rental housing to condominiums, banned children under 18, and – final ignominy – renamed it The Village Green.[214] Today, though Baldwin Hills still has an extraordinary physical quality, its nearness to a low-income public housing project gives unease to its predominantly older residents; after nightfall motor-bike patrols guard the estate, making mockery of the very qualities it was designed to protect.

The Stein-Wright Radburn cities are unquestionably the most important American contributions to the garden-city tradition. True, on strict criteria, like their European counterparts they fail to qualify; all three are now long since submerged in the general sprawl of suburbia, and to seek them out on the ground demands a good map and some degree of determination. But as garden suburbs, they mark perhaps the most significant advance in design beyond the standards set by Unwin and Parker. They are not, however, the only examples of new towns in America. Most of the others are one-off examples associated with particular initiatives, like the new town of Norris in Tennessee, developed as part of the Tennessee Valley Authority exercise in regional development, which will be briefly discussed in the appropriate place (Chapter 5). But the green-belt cities, developed by Rexford Guy Tugwell's Resettlement Administration in the early years of Franklin Delano Roosevelt's New Deal (1935–8), deserve separate and special attention.

There are curious historical parallels between their origin and that of Howard's idea: both were conceived in the depths of a major depression; in both, destitute ex-farm workers were crowded in poverty-stricken cities, which could offer them no work. By 1933, there was an embarrassing shanty town of the unemployed right in the heart of Washington. FDR's original notion was a back-to-the-land movement; Tugwell, a Columbia University economist who had become one of the most innovative members of his brains trust, persuaded him that this path led nowhere.[215] His idea was "to go just outside centers of population, pick up cheap land, build a whole community, and entice people into them. Then go back into the cities and tear down whole slums and make parks of them."[216] He used a threat of resignation to force Roosevelt, in April 1935, to create the Resettlement Administration, which neatly bracketed the land and

213   Stein, 1958, 189–90, 193, 198.
214   Hayden, 1984, 10–11; Moore *et al.*, 1984, 282.
215   Myhra, 1974, 178–81; 1983, 231.
216   Jackson, 1985, 195.

Figure 4.20 Greenbelt. The first Radburn layouts applied to entire neighborhoods; in Greenbelt, as earlier in Weimar Germany, functional architecture is successfully married to garden-city–garden-suburb tradition.

the poverty problem; under the Emergency Relief Appropriation Act of 1935, this was given the power of eminent domain (compulsory purchase of land).[217]

"Just outside the cities" was the critical phrase: intended essentially to be self-contained, the green-belt cities would also have to offer the possibility of commuting to the city, so a suburban fringe location was essential; this also represented the existing trend of population.[218] Tugwell hoped for 3,000 of them; but of the first list of 25, the program was allocated funds only to start eight; Congress whittled this to five, of which two (in New Jersey, and outside St Louis) were blocked by legal action. So the eventual program consisted of just three towns: Greenbelt, Maryland, outside Washington; Greenhills, Ohio, outside Cincinnati; and Greendale, Wisconsin, outside Milwaukee.[219] Persuaded out of a prejudice against architects, Tugwell – working at speed against a deadline – hired separate teams for each town: so Greenbelt and Greenhills have Radburn-style superblocks; Greendale also has a Radburn layout but without superblocks or major park areas – it has conventional streets and traditional architecture. But all have very low densities of between four

[217] MacFarland, 1966, 221; Arnold, 1971, 24–6; Myhra, 1974, 181; Weaver, 1984b, 228.
[218] Conkin, 1959, 307; Arnold, 1971, 26, 201.
[219] Conkin, 1959, 308; Glaab and Brown, 1976, 277.

and eight units per acre.[220] And the largest of the three – Greenbelt, designed with advice from Stein and from fellow-RPAA architect Tracy Augur – is a classic adaptation of the Radburn layout: the houses, built in five superblocks forming a huge horseshoe around a central open space, all have direct pedestrian access to parks, shops, and community facilities.[221] The architecture is more uncompromisingly modern-movement than at Radburn, and the overall effect is curiously reminiscent of the best German schemes of the 1920s: an exclave of Frankfurt, or Berlin, in the middle of the Maryland countryside.

All too soon, the program was at an end. As a leading New Deal planner, Tugwell was an obvious target for conservative congressmen, the media, the building and real estate industries, and the banks, to whom the "Tugwelltowns" represented the start of a socialist takeover; they complained about "shifting people around from where they are to where Dr Tugwell thinks they ought to be."[222] The United States Court of Appeals, in May 1936, held that the provisions of the 1935 Emergency Relief Appropriations Act were invalid; and, though the ruling applied only to the proposed town at Greenbrook, New Jersey, few doubted that this was the end of the road.[223] Construction was virtually complete by mid-1938, when the three towns were transferred to the Federal Public Housing Agency; in the 1950s, they were sold off.[224] At Greenbelt, by far the largest of the three, the original core of the development went to a cooperative housing association which has managed to maintain it intact; extensively (and expensively) rehabilitated with federal loan money between 1979 and 1983, it is now on the National Register of Historic Places. But the rest of the huge site has been cut through by major highways and developed piecemeal by different developers, with no continuity of style at all.[225] And post-1945 urban dispersal has overwhelmed the entire notion of planned dispersal: Greenbelt, like its illustrious post-1945 successors – among them Reston, and Columbia, built nearby in Maryland a few years later, both built by private agencies but financed with federally guaranteed loans – are "deeply enmeshed in the 'vast, formless sprawl' of the regional new city."[226]

In purely quantitative terms, therefore, the green-belt towns were almost a non-event: "providing an attractive environment for only 2,267 families can hardly be called that significant."[227] And, as experiments in planning, they were – like so much that FDR did – curiously circumspect: blacks were excluded; the rents, though moderate, excluded the poorest; unit costs were high; local jobs were lacking; public transportation links with the parent cities were often poor; the houses, parking areas, and shops are now all too small-scale to meet the needs of affluent Americans.[228]

[220]   Myhra, 1974, 183–5; 1983, 241; Perkins, 2007, 34–5.
[221]   Arnold, 1983, 199.
[222]   Arnold, 1971, 31, 97, 209.
[223]   Myhra, 1974, 185.
[224]   Conkin, 1959, 322–5.
[225]   Arnold, 1983, 201–2, 204.
[226]   Fishman, 1992, 153, 158.
[227]   Glaab and Brown, 1976, 278.
[228]   Stein, 1958, 130; Arnold, 1971, 143–4, 153; Wilson, 1974, 159–60; Arnold, 1983, 202.

Figure 4.21 Rexford Guy Tugwell. Creator of the experimental green-belt communities of the mid-1930s: bitterly attacked in Congress as socialistic, and indeed a model for Britain's postwar government-funded new towns. *Source*: Courtesy of University Archives, Columbia University in the City of New York.

They are less important, in fact, for what they did than for what they symbolized: complete federal control over development, bypassing local government altogether; thus complete discretion to Tugwell in choice of sites; compulsory purchase of the land; control over construction by the same agency; even, because the land was federal, no right to local authorities to levy property taxes. Doing what successive interwar British governments never dared do, they, in fact, provided a model for the postwar new towns.[229] No wonder that almost everyone was against them.

History would repeat itself, when, in 1968 and 1970, Congress passed new towns legislation. The brainchild of Robert Weaver, chief administrator of the Housing and Home Finance Agency and then Secretary of Housing and Urban Development, and an economist with a long-time interest in comprehensive urban planning, who hailed the legislation as a victory for planning that would "eliminate the costly clutter of blindfold growth and blunderbuss expansion," the Johnson administration gave financial assistance to private developers who built 13 new towns in various locations

[229] MacFarland, 1966, 219–23.

around the country. But, it soon emerged, everyone was against it: not only the business organizations that traditionally opposed all varieties of housing reform as a threat to free-market capitalism, but also big city mayors who resisted support for any form of suburbanization. By the time these interests had been sufficiently mollified, the Johnson Administration was entering its last days. Like so many other Great Society programs that foundered in the Nixon era, the new towns suffered when a Republican White House suffocated the program in bureaucracy and refused to provide the financial support authorized by Congress. "Simply put, the new towns perished in floods of red tape and red ink."[230] By the early 1980s, officials of the US Department of Housing and Urban Development concluded that the experiment had failed in all but one of them, and arranged for bankruptcy and foreclosure proceedings.[231]

The green-belt towns provide, therefore, something of an exception in the first 40 years of the garden-city movement. Though private initiative built two true garden cities (Letchworth, Welwyn), and though sometimes municipalities built satellite towns (Wythenshawe, Römerstadt), nowhere else did government move in to produce the real thing. There is a slight irony in that it all happened in the United States, which is almost the last country anyone would expect it to happen. And there, it is hardly surprising that it failed.

New Towns for Britain: The State Takes Over

It is hardly surprising either that after World War Two Britain again seized the lead; or that, this time around, the state took control. But even then, it was touch and go. There was a Labour government, but one dominated by Fabian socialists, who believed in gradual change through municipal government (above all, the London County Council) and a working-class majority in Parliament and, thus, poured scorn on the "unpalatable dough" of Howard's blueprint. They had long argued that "we have got to make the best of our existing cities, and proposals for building new ones are about as useful as would be arrangements for protection against visits from Mr Wells's Martians." In a similar vein, George Bernard Shaw had some years earlier dismissed attempts to form new communities in the countryside, compared with addressing urban problems directly, with the words "one to sit among the dandelions, the other to organise the docks."[232]

On the other hand, the wartime coalition government nailed its flag to the private enterprise mast. Peter Malpass has shown that planning for postwar housing had begun as early as 1941, and that a detailed and ambitious policy was in place well before the end of the war. It provided that local authorities would play a major role in the transitional period, but that, in the longer run, the majority of new building would be left to the private sector, with the local authorities reverting to their prewar

---

[230]   Biles, 1998, 127–8.
[231]   Biles, 1998, 113.
[232]   Hardy, 2005, 41.

role concentrating on slum clearance and provision for the least well off.[233] Labour fought this: already, in May 1942, Ernest Bevin proposed a National Housing Corporation, to provide mortgages at cheaper rates and to ensure that purchasers were given value for money, but he got nowhere. Both he and Clement Attlee had expressed "grave misgivings" about subsidy for private enterprise, which appeared in a White Paper. Abandoning this position, Malpass points out, was one of the most significant changes made to housing policy by the Labour government elected in July 1945.[234] But the established Labour position was that the local authorities – Labour-controlled, of course – should do the job.

In Britain, Lewis Silkin, the incoming Labour minister, conscious of possible reluctance among colleagues to launch a new towns program, appointed a committee in October 1945 to tell him how they should be built. At its head he put Lord Reith, the ex-director of the BBC, an intense, driven man who had managed to offend almost everyone in British public life and who had, in consequence, become virtually unemployable. Osborn was a member; the others were L. J. Cadbury of Birmingham and Monica Felton of the LCC, both known new-town advocates.

Unsurprisingly, given this composition, within a mere three months the committee emerged with interim recommendations. It faced three possible mechanisms: local authorities, intermediate nonprofit organizations, for which Letchworth and Welwyn offered "ambivalent precedents," and ordinary profit-seeking private developers. But there was a possible built-in bias, for the committee included only two private-sector members. Volume builders – like Taylor Woodrow, John Laing, and Wates – said they could take contracts to build new towns, and the financial institutions agreed. But, given the composition, the conclusions were predictable: new towns should be in the size range 20,000–60,000, just as the Town and Country Planning Association (which had now dropped garden cities from their name) had always said; they should generally be built by public corporations, one for each town, financed directly by the Exchequer. In certain cases, one or more local authorities might do the job; and, though housing associations probably lacked both legal authority and competence, specially constituted "authorised associations," promoted for this specific purpose, would be appropriate. So the committee paid its lip service to Ebenezer Howard; but the public corporation was "our primary choice of agency."[235] Thus, ironically, at one stroke they resolved the perennial problem of how to fund the new towns but also destroyed the essence of Howard's plan, which was to fund the creation of self-governing local welfare states. Top-down planning triumphed over bottom-up; Britain would have the shell of Howard's garden-city vision without the substance.

Against all odds, the Reithian position won out. Osborn was not to be as old as Methuselah before the government started on new towns; he was 61 when, on August 1, 1946 (even before the Reith Committee's final report was out), the New Towns Act

[233]   Malpass, 2003, 177.
[234]   Malpass, 2003, 192.
[235]   GB Ministry of Town and Country Planning, 1946, 11; Hebbert, 1992, 172.

received the royal assent; on November 11 the first, Stevenage, was already designated.[236] Between then and 1950, the Labour government designated 13 new towns in Britain: eight for the London area, two for Scotland, two in northeast England, one in Wales and one in the English Midlands. That emphasis, again, underlines that in the 1940s as in the 1890s the core of the British urban problem was still seen to lie in London; though new towns were actively considered for Manchester, Liverpool, and a number of other cities, and though sites for Manchester at Mobberley and Congleton in Cheshire were seriously considered, both ran into objections.[237]

Four of the eight London new towns were in one county, Hertfordshire; and three of them form a group, running along the Great North Road and the parallel main railway line north of London. Stevenage, the first to be designated, was soon joined by Welwyn Garden City, which was given the dignity of a development corporation shared with next-door Hatfield, where there was an urgent need to tidy up some messy development around a big aircraft factory. And, though Letchworth remained fiercely independent, it forms effectively part of the group; so that here, uniquely, the student can see Howard's vision of the Social City on the ground. Each garden city is surrounded by its own green belt, so that each appears as a separate urban community against a background of agricultural land. But all four are tied together by the modern equivalent of Howard's inter-municipal railway: the electrified commuter line that also joins them to central London, and the motorway completed in the mid-1980s. Passing from one to another in a few minutes, you go from the roar of the motorway into a serene, green world; none of the new towns is any longer new, and the vegetation long ago lushly enveloped them, softening some of the over-simple lines of the budget-conscious housing. There are detailed quibbles in plenty, to be sure; but it looks and feels very much like that final chapter of *To-Morrow*.

It had, however, come about by a route of which Howard would probably have disapproved. In the land of its birth, the garden city was now nationalized and bureaucratized, as the coal mines and the railways were shortly to be. That is unsurprising, in a way; the Attlee government was committed to that particular variety of socialism; Reith, who was convinced that his BBC was God's own design for broadcasting, could be relied on to repeat a similar prescription for new towns or indeed any other new institution. And there was wisdom in it too: if London's persistent housing problem was as bad after half a century as Abercrombie's Greater London Plan was just then saying, and if the evident mistakes of the interwar years were not to be repeated, then some very tough and resilient machinery must be provided, capable of rolling roughshod over local special interests if needs be. Almost immediately, the unholy row that broke out over the Stevenage designation was to underline that point; and later, after 1951, when the incoming Conservative government resisted further designations, the resulting strains and stresses caused them within a decade to reverse that decision.[238]

The Marxist commentators can of course again have their field day: once again, the capitalist state was managing the system to make it acceptable; new towns had become

---

[236]   Cullingworth, 1979, 29–30.
[237]   Cullingworth, 1979, 95–101, 112.
[238]   Cullingworth, 1979, 27–31, 127, 165.

an essential part of that welfare-state management, designed to guarantee the reproduction of the skilled labor force for the high-technology industries that so enthusiastically moved there. Yet as usual, all this misses the rich complexity of the decision process. There was a new, fresh, radical Labour government, swept into power not by the machinations of the capitalist machine but by the votes of the armed forces. It was determined to make a fresh start. New towns were an important part of its ideology; Attlee himself had written in favor of the national planning of towns and countryside.[239] The garden-city propaganda machine had swung into action, led by Osborn; and Osborn, unlike his erstwhile mentor, had campaigned for a quarter-century in favor of state new towns. Of course, they might all be mere puppets, agents of the system; but difficult, for anyone who knew him, thus to view Osborn.

What is certain is that in the process a great deal was gained and something was lost. The new towns were built, and, in the imperfect world of politics, that was something of a miracle: eight of them around London, almost as Abercrombie had prescribed, and roughly according to a timetable laid down. True, they were criticized at first, often by people who had no sympathy from the start: their architecture was boring; they had no urban feel; the people moving into them, deprived of the crowds of London and often suffering from belated building of shops and other services, suffered from "new town blues." (This last was a distinct sociological curiosity; the phenomenon was discovered not in a new town at all, but in one of the LCC's inadequately planned and hastily built satellite estates; yet the media either did not know or did not want to know the difference.) True, too, the new towns absorbed a mere 400,000, a fraction of the population growth in the belt around London in the 1950s and 1960s; Abercrombie's sums had failed to allow for the baby boom.

All that said, the new towns were built as planned, according to the latter-day Reithian version of the Howard gospel; and, so far as anyone can judge, they did what their supporters always expected of them. Mark Clapson has shown that, contrary to some sociological interpretations, working-class households moved to them in search of better housing, and if they were given the housing they expected, they settled in quite happily; they did not, however, retreat behind lace curtains, but actively joined organizations. Thus, he concludes, "the grim diagnoses of suburban neurosis and new town blues ... were misleading. The undoubted problems of moving on and settling in were, for the majority, overcome as newcomers sought to make a fresh life for themselves. They attempted to achieve a meaningful balance between home, wider family and the social and material opportunities offered by the suburban and new towns context."[240] When, in 1979, the Milton Keynes community television station announced as an April Fool joke that the entire new town would be ploughed into the ground, a viewer declared he would not go back to London: "Milton Keynes had given him a garden, something he'd never had before, and he was damned if he was going to give it up now."[241] The new towns are still rather good places to work and to live, and the best thing that can be said about them is that half a century after the first

[239] Wilde, 1937, 24.
[240] Clapson, 1998, 197.
[241] Clapson, 1998, 104.

of them were started, they are almost completely non-newsworthy: the media notice them only on the rare occasions when (like *The Guardian* in August 1986) they want to write about a place without problems.

The irony is that Milton Keynes and its American equivalent, Reston outside Washington, both planned during the 1960s, have proved so popular with their residents because of their low densities and suburban ethos. Yet their planners had very different intentions. They aimed for compact living clusters set in a tamed countryside of parks and open spaces, characterized by late-modern urban housing styles. In both places, popular tastes later led their managers to embrace traditional–vernacular models, complementing their countrified setting.[242]

There was yet a further irony. During a lecture tour of North America in the 1940s, Frederic Osborn confessed to his audience that he had "not realised the extent and high quality of your better-class residential developments": "The pattern of living in these places, with the detached family home in well-planted surroundings, represents I am sure the ideal of a way of life held at heart by most Americans, as by nearly all English people."[243] That "ideal" had been at the heart of the appeal of both Reston and Milton Keynes.

Nor did the vision prove enduring in other places. Howard's notion, "that the community should primarily grow from a collective sense of ownership of the garden city by its people. Physical planning and design would reflect this common ownership rather than be a substitute for it,"[244] did not find traction. With a few notable examples, like Curitiba and Singapore, "The most telling feature of the Howard legacy is that a majority of the world's city dwellers remain completely disinherited from it."[245] Eugenie Birch finds echoes of garden-city thinking in such diverse designs as Celebration, Florida, with its 4,700-acre green belt and 18-acre mixed-use downtown, replete with retail, civic, open-space, public-facility, and residential uses; or Tampines, Singapore, an 824-acre town with a population of about 180,000 that "shows the Howard influence," despite its extremely high density, because it combines living, working, and other uses.[246] But one senses that, aroused by a spiritual medium from the shades, Howard would fail to see much resemblance to his vision in either place.

And in the wider view, that vision is nowhere to be found: the shell is there, but not the substance. These are not anarchist self-governing commonwealths of free artisans; in them, the link is missing between industry and the land; the rich cooperative life, recapturing the traditions of the middle ages, is nowhere to be seen. Perhaps it was a chimera from the start; perhaps, if all this ever was a faint hope, the realities of the late capitalist economy and the post-industrial society have finally dashed it. But in order to judge that better, it will be necessary to understand that there was yet a further and even more radical strand to this thinking, which requires another chapter to itself.

---

[242] Clapson, 2002, 145.
[243] Clapson, 2002, 159.
[244] Clapson, 2002, 159.
[245] Ward, 2002b, 244.
[246] Birch, 2002, 187, 198.

The City in the Region

Thus they went along towards the Gate, now you must note that the City stood upon a mighty hill, but the Pilgrims went up that hill with ease, because they had these two men to lead them up by the arms; also they had left their *Mortal* Garments behind them in the River: for though they went in with them, they came out without them. They therefore went up here with much agility and speed though the foundation upon which the City was framed was higher than the Clouds. They therefore went up through the Regions of the Air, sweetly talking as they went, being comforted, because they had safely got over the River, and had such glorious Companions, to attend them.

John Bunyan, The Pilgrim's Progress (1678)

And as the moon rose higher the inessential houses began to melt away until gradually I became aware of the old island here that flowered once for Dutch sailors' eyes – a fresh, green breast of the new world. Its vanished trees, the trees that made way for Gatsby's house, had once pandered in whispers to the last and greatest of all human dreams; for a transitory enchanted moment man must have held his breath in the presence of this continent, compelled into the aesthetic contemplation he neither understood nor desired, face to face for the last time in human history with something commensurate to his capacity for wonder.

Cities of Tomorrow: An Intellectual History of Urban Planning and Design Since 1880,
Fourth Edition. Peter Hall.
© 2014 Peter Hall. Published 2014 by John Wiley & Sons, Ltd.

And as I sat there brooding on the old, unknown world, I thought of Gatsby's wonder when he first picked out the green light at the end of Daisy's dock. He had come a long way to this blue lawn, and his dream must have seemed so close that he could hardly fail to grasp it. He did not know that it was already behind him, somewhere back in that vast obscurity beyond the city, where the dark fields of the republic rolled on under the night.

F. Scott Fitzgerald, The Great Gatsby (1926)

5

The City in the Region

The Birth of Regional Planning: Edinburgh, New York, London, 1900–1940

If the garden city was English out of America, then the regional city was undoubtedly American out of France via Scotland. Regional planning began with Patrick Geddes (1854–1932), an unclassifiable polymath who – after four unsuccessful attempts to secure a University chair – officially taught biology (more probably, anything but biology) at the University of Dundee,[1] gave India's rulers idiosyncratic advice on how to run their cities, and tried to encapsulate the meaning of life on folded scraps of paper. From his contracts with French geographers at the turn of the century, Geddes had absorbed their creed of anarchistic communism based on free confederations of autonomous regions. Through his meeting in the 1920s with Lewis Mumford (1895–1990), a sociologist-journalist who could make his thoughts coherent in a way Geddes never could, this philosophy passed to a small but brilliant and dedicated group of planners in New York City, whence – through Mumford's immensely powerful writings – it fused with Howard's closely related ideas, and spread out across America and the world; exercising enormous influence, in particular, on Franklin Delano Roosevelt's New Deal, in the 1930s, and on the planning of the capitals of Europe, in the 1940s and 1950s. But, ironically, in this process – just as with Howard – the truly radical quality of the message was muffled and more than half-lost; nowhere on the ground today do we see the true and remarkable vision of the Regional Planning Association of America (RPAA), distilled via Geddes from Proudhon, Bakunin, Reclus, and Kropotkin.

Geddes and the Anarchist Tradition

The tale must start with Geddes: a hard thing to do, since he always went round in increasing circles. A secretary, who (like all secretaries) was in the best position to judge, once said, "Geddes must be accepted … as a good Catholic accepts grief, with

---

[1] Meller, 1990, 6.

an open heart and no reserves, if he is to benefit those whom his presence scourges."[2] He was the archetypal comic professor: "he had never mastered the art of making himself audible, either on the platform or in closer quarters"; he was "always forgetting engagements, or making two or three for the same time"; "The unformed theses, the unwritten books, mostly remained unformed and unwritten";[3] "in every short article he began again at the beginning, outlining and repeating his basic ideas endlessly";[4] he was, Abercrombie related, "a most unsettling person, talking, talking, talking ... about anything and everything."[5] He obsessively developed his ideas on sheets of paper divided into nine blocks, his "machines," which he filled with his endless intuitive ruminations, but which proved barriers to communication: when he gave a major lecture, the reporters refused to report it.[6] One biographer said of him that

> Geddes' contributions to the academic social sciences were ... at best marginally illuminating, and at worst, counter-productive ... by his many idiosyncrasies, he cast himself and his ideas into the wilderness, where he remains in terms of modern scholarship.[7]

Early on, he had "begun on the idiosyncratic path which was to take him out of the mainstream of academic life, and eventually from the natural to the social sciences."[8] Through T. H. Huxley, under whom he studied briefly, he was enabled to work at the marine station at Roscoff in Brittany, from where, in 1878, he first visited Paris and became a fluent French speaker.[9] Here he found his key ideas: "the central and vital tradition of Scottish culture," he argued, "has always been wedded with that of France."[10] He took his central concepts from the founding fathers of French geography, Élisée Reclus (1830–1905) and Paul Vidal de la Blache (1845–1918), and from the early French sociologist Frédéric Le Play (1806–1882), whose new academic disciplines acquired respectability in France some years before they did in Britain or the United States.[11] Le Play – engineer, practical social scientist, and trusted counsellor of Napoleon III – played a key role as organizer of the 1867 Paris Exhibition, organizing it around work and social life; at the subsequent 1878 exhibition, Geddes first encountered Le Play's ideas, with their trinity of *Lieu, Travail, Famille*: they stressed the family as the basic social unit, in the context of its environment.[12] After

2   Mumford, 1982, 319.
3   Mumford, 1982, 321, 326, 331.
4   Meller, 1990, 3.
5   Defries, 1927, 323.
6   Meller, 1990, 45, 49, 55 note 64.
7   Meller, 1990, 122.
8   Meller 1990, 19.
9   Meller, 1990, 31–2.
10 Defries, 1927, 251.
11 Weaver, 1984a, 42, 47–8; Andrews, 1986, 179.
12 Meller, 1990, 35.

Figure 5.1 Patrick Geddes. The indefatigable folder of paper and drawer of diagrams here conducts an incomprehensible experiment on himself. *Source*: Reproduced by permission of the National Library of Scotland, MS 10606.

Figure 5.2   Lewis Mumford. His only meeting with Geddes was a disaster, but at last the professor had found his scribe; the Regional Planning Association of America would bring the master's message to the world. *Source*: Time & Life Pictures/Getty Images.

his death, Le Play's disciples devoted a pavilion to his work; and here Jane Addams met Henrietta Barnett.[13]

From them he gained his idea of the natural region, as exemplified by his famous valley section, which he based on the ideas of Reclus.[14] And it is significant that, like them, he preferred to study the region in its purest form, far from the shadow of the giant metropolis:

> Coming to concrete Civic Survey, where shall we begin? ... London may naturally claim pre-eminence. Yet even at best, does not this vastest of world cities present a less or more foggy labyrinth, from which surrounding regions with their smaller cities can be but dimly described ... For our more general and comparative survey, then, simpler beginnings are preferable ... the clear outlook, the more panoramic view of a definite geographic region such, for instance, as lies beneath us upon a mountain holiday ... Such a river system is, as one geographer has pointed out, the essential unit for the

13   Meller, 1995, 296–8.
14   Meller, 1990, 40.

student of cities and civilisations. Hence this simple geographical method must here be pled [*sic*] for as fundamental to any really orderly and comparative treatment of our subject.[15]

Planning must start, for Geddes, with a survey of the resources of such a natural region, of the human responses to it, and of the resulting complexities of the cultural landscape: in all his teaching, his most persistent emphasis was on the survey method.[16] This also he derived from Vidal and his followers, whose "regional monographs" were attempts to do just that.[17] In the famous Outlook Tower, that craggy monument that still stands at the end of the Royal Mile in Edinburgh, he created a model for what he wanted to see everywhere: a local survey center, in which people of all kinds could come to understand the relationship of Le Play's trilogy of Place–Work–Folk.[18] The student of cities, he asserted, must go first to the study of such natural regions: "Such a survey of a series of our own river basins … will be found the soundest of introductions to the study of cities … it is useful for the student constantly to recover the elemental and naturalist-like point of view even in the greatest cities."[19]

It sounds deceptively simple; but, as the great British planner Patrick Abercrombie once said, Civic Survey in actuality "is a sinister and complicated business," the more so since it must widen to embrace the region and finally the world. Yet Abercrombie, who, if anyone, should have known, believed that in Britain in the early 1920s "the errors of our national reconstruction can be attributed to the neglect of this teaching of Geddes."[20]

For this great work, Geddes constantly argued, the planner's ordinary maps were useless: you must ideally start with the great globe which Reclus proposed, but which was never built; failing that, you must draw cross-sections "of that general slope from mountains to sea which we find everywhere in the world" which "we can readily adapt to any scale, and to any proportions, of our particular and characteristic range, of hills and slopes and plain." Only such a "Valley Section, as we commonly call it, makes vivid to us the range of climate, with its corresponding vegetation and animal life … the essential sectional outline of a geographer's 'region,' ready to be studied"; examined closely, it "finds place for all the nature-occupations": "Hunter and shepherd, poor peasant and rich: these are our most familiar occupational types, and manifestly successive as we descend in altitude, and also come down the course of social history."[21] In turn,

These variously occupied folk each come to develop their own little hamlet or village, with its characteristic type of family, and folk-ways, even institutions; not simply of

[15] Geddes, 1905, 105.
[16] Mairet, 1957, 216.
[17] Weaver, 1984a, 47.
[18] Mairet, 1957, 216.
[19] Geddes, 1905, 106.
[20] Defries, 1927, 323–4.
[21] Geddes, 1925c, 289–90, 325.

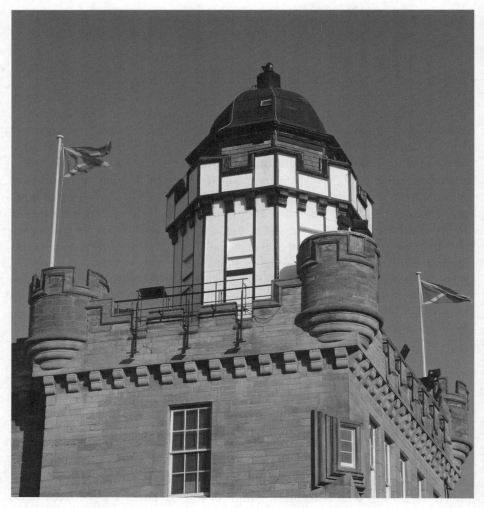

Figure 5.3   The Outlook Tower. From its castellated top, complete with camera obscura, Geddes ranged the rooftops of Edinburgh and taught the lesson of Survey before Plan. *Source*: © David Davies/Alamy.

> home-building, though each with its germ of appropriate architectural style. In this way their villages are ranged, from fishing port to forest and mountain pass, from gardens and fields below to mine and quarry usually above.[22]

And at the center of this region lay "The Valley in the Town," where "we must excavate the layers of our city downwards, into its earliest past – the dim yet heroic cities over and upon which it has been built; and thence we must read them upwards, visualizing them as we go."[23]

[22] Geddes, 1925c, 415.
[23] Geddes, 1925c, 396.

MINER   WOODMAN   HUNTER   SHEPHERD   PEASANT   GARDENER   FISHER

Figure 5.4   The Valley Section. The essence of Geddes's regional scheme, from a paper of 1905: Folk–Work–Place in perfect harmony, the city in the center of things. *Source*: Reproduced by permission of the National Library of Scotland, OF.1314.6.20.

Much of that, in outline, has become familiar, even trite; every freshman planner knows that the aphorism, Survey before Plan, comes from Geddes. And it derives from a kind of traditional regional geography, which – vulgarized in a thousand staple school texts – has long since been derided and swept away. But that misses its truly radical point. For Vidal and his followers, as for Geddes, regional study gave understanding of an "active, experienced environment" which "was the motor force of human development; the almost sensual reciprocity between men and women and their surroundings was the seat of comprehensible liberty and the mainspring of cultural evolution," which were being attacked and eroded by the centralized nation-state and by large-scale machine industry.[24] (He believed that a woman's function was to shape civilization through the upbringing of children.[25]) So the deliberately archaic quality of the regional survey, the emphasis on traditional occupations and on historic links, was no mere quirk: like Geddes's attempts to recapture past civic life through masques and pageants,[26] it was a quite conscious celebration of what, for him, was the highest achievement of European culture.

But this, quasi-mystical though it might be, has a very radical purpose. For Geddes, as for Vidal, the region was more than an object of survey; it was to provide the basis for the total reconstruction of social and political life. Here, again, Geddes was indebted to geography and to the French tradition. Élisée Reclus and Peter

[24]   Weaver, 1984a, 47.
[25]   Meller, 1990, 81.
[26]   Boardman, 1978, 234–40.

Kropotkin (1842–1921) were both geographers; but both were also anarchists. Kropotkin, who was exiled from his native Russia, was expelled from both France and Switzerland and lived for 30 years as a refugee in Brighton;[27] Reclus had indeed been expelled from France for fighting on the Communard side in 1871, and lived in exile, though curiously he was commissioned to design the great globe for the 1900 Exposition, which was supposed to convey a notion of universal citizenship.[28] Both based their ideas on Pierre-Joseph Proudhon (1809–65), the French anarchist best known for his declaration "Property is Theft." Ironically, Proudhon's writings had been dedicated to proving the exact opposite; his argument was that individual property ownership was the essential guarantee of a free society, so long as no one owned too much. Such a society, he believed, could alone provide the basis for a decentralized, non-hierarchical system of federal government:[29] an idea shared by the Russian anarchist Michael Bakunin (1814–76), whose defeat and expulsion by Karl Marx in the First International conference at The Hague in 1872 was one of the decisive events in the history of socialism.[30]

Reclus and Kropotkin were the inheritors of this tradition; and both met Geddes more than once during the 1880s and 1890s. Reclus's most important work, a huge multi-volume study called *L'Homme et la Terre*,[31] argued that the naturally collec-tivist small-scale societies of primitive peoples, living in harmony with their envi-ronments, had been destroyed or distorted by colonialism. But Kropotkin was even more significant; for he developed the anarchist philosophy and translated it into the conditions of the early twentieth century, and through him it had incalculable influence on both Howard and Geddes. His creed was "Anarchist Communism, Communism without government – the Communism of the Free":[32] society must rebuild itself on the basis of cooperation among free individuals, such as can be found naturally even in animal societies; this, he thought, represented the logical tendency toward which human societies were moving.[33]

More than this, Kropotkin developed a remarkable historical thesis: that in the twelfth century, a "communalist" revolution had taken place in Europe which had saved its culture from suppression by theocratic and despotic monarchies. This revolution expressed itself both in the local village community, and in thousands of urban fraternities and guilds. In the late medieval city, each section or parish was the province of an individual self-governing guild; the city itself was the union of these districts, streets, parishes, and guilds, and was itself a free state.[34] And, he argued,

[27]   Woodcock, 1962, 181–96.
[28]   Mairet, 1957, 89; Meller, 1995, 300.
[29]   Edwards, 1969, 33, 107.
[30]   Lehning, 1973, 71, 169, 236.
[31]   Reclus, 1905–8.
[32]   Kropotkin, 1906, 28.
[33]   Kropotkin, 1906, 90; 1971a, 96.
[34]   Kropotkin, 1920, 14–17.

In those cities, under the shelter of their liberties acquired under the impulse of free agreement and free initiative, a whole new civilization grew up and attained such expansion, that the like has not been seen up till now … Never, with the exception of that other glorious period of ancient Greece – free cities again – had society made such a stride forwards. Never in two or three centuries, had man undergone so profound a change nor so extended his power over the forces of nature.[35]

These achievements had been swept away by the centralized state in the sixteenth century, which represented the triumph of what Kropotkin called the Roman-imperial-authoritarian tradition. But now, he believed, this was in turn again challenged by its opposite, the popular-federalist-libertarian movement.

The reason, he thought, was the technological imperative: new sources of power, hydraulic and especially electric, meant that a big central unit of power was no longer needed; industries that depended chiefly on skilled labor had no economies of scale; observably, the newer industries tended to be small in scale. Thus, big industrial concentrations represented pure historical inertia: "There is absolutely no reason why these and like anomalies should persist. The industries must be scattered all over the world; and the scattering of industries amidst the civilized nations will be necessarily followed by a further scattering of factories over the territories of each nation."[36] And

This scattering of industries over the country – so as to bring the factory amidst the fields, to make agriculture derive all those profits which it always finds in being combined with industry … and to produce a combination of industrial with agricultural work – is surely the next step … This step is imposed by the very necessity of *producing for the producers themselves*; it is imposed by the necessity for each healthy man and woman to spend a part of their lives in manual work in the free air.[37]

This was one of the most crucial insights that Geddes borrowed from Kropotkin; already in 1899, presumably just after reading the first edition of *Fields, Factories and Workshops*, he had christened the new age of industrial decentralization the *neotechnic* era;[38] the following year, in a display at the great Paris Exposition, he was using the terms "palaeotechnic" and "neotechnic."[39] As he later wrote, "we may distinguish the earlier and ruder elements of the Industrial Age as Palaeotechnic, the newer and still often incipient elements disengaging themselves from these as Neotechnic."[40] Only in this new era – here he directly followed Kropotkin – would we "apply our constructive skill, our vital energies, towards the public conservation instead of the private dissipation of resources, and towards the evolution instead of the destruction of the lives of others."[41]

[35] Kropotkin, 1920, 18–19.
[36] Kropotkin, 1913, 357.
[37] Kropotkin, 1913, 361.
[38] Mairet, 1957, 94.
[39] Kitchen, 1975, 188–9.
[40] Geddes, 1912, 177.
[41] Geddes, 1912, 183.

From Reclus and Kropotkin, and beyond them from Proudhon, Geddes also took his position that society had to be reconstructed not by sweeping governmental measures like the abolition of private property, but through the efforts of millions of individuals: the "neotechnic order" meant "the creation, city by city, region by region, of a Eutopia." He was hostile to the Fabian centralized approach, and thus took himself out of the mainstream political debate of his time; he sought solutions capable of immediate implementation.[42] After World War One he believed that the League of Nations should be a league of cities – and not of the capitals, which were the centers of the war-machines, but of the great provincial cities, which, regaining their former independence, would then voluntarily federate on a Swiss model.[43] This idea prompted a characteristic outpouring, which demands extended quotation – though, in Geddesian terms, it is a mere fragment:

> The natural eugenic centre is in every home; its young go out to make new homes; these make the village, the town, the city small or great; so the would-be Eugenist has to work at all these towards their betterment. Federate homes into co-operative and helpful neighbourhoods. Unite these grouped homes into renewed and socialized quarters – parishes, as they should be – and in time you have a better nation, a better world ... Each region and city can learn to manage its own affairs – build its own houses, provide its own scientists, artists and teachers. These developing regions are already in business together; can't they make friends and organize a federation as far as need be ... May not this be the time prophesied by Isaiah? ... "When it shall come, then I will gather all nations and all tongues and they shall come" and "there shall be a new heaven and a new earth ... and the former shall not be remembered ... they shall build houses and inhabit them ... and I will direct their work in truth."[44]

When his bemused questioner tried to have him explain himself, he replied that a flower expressed itself by flowering, not by being labeled.[45]

Indeed there was more to come; much more. There were the themes first developed by Geddes's equally discursive collaborator, Victor Branford: the role of the church and the university in practical relationship to the civic community;[46,47] the union of eugenics and civics with town planning and social welfare in a system of civic education;[48] "the increase, within the civic domain, of woman's influence and that of her friends and allies, the artist, the poet and the educationalist," so to meet "the need to provide the women [*sic*] of the people with this cultural environment, necessary ... for her full dignity as a spiritual power."[49] Repetitively, circuitously, too

[42]   Meller, 1990, 67–8.
[43]   Defries, 1927, 268; Boardman, 1944, 382–3.
[44]   Defries, 1927, 218–19, 230–1.
[45]   Defries, 1927, 231.
[46]   Branford, 1914, 294–6, 323.
[47]   Clavel, 2002, 50.
[48]   Branford, 1914, 283.
[49]   Branford and Geddes, 1919, 250–1.

often obscurely, the ideas pour out: the raw material for a score of still-unwritten dissertations. But there is one further concept, central to Geddes's thesis of regional planning as part of social reconstruction.

In 1915, Geddes published his book *Cities in Evolution*. It is the most coherent exposition of his views, save for the articles collected in the American magazine *The Survey* a decade later (which, based on his 1923 lectures, it took two years to render into sense.)[50] In it, he drew attention to the fact that the new neotechnic technologies – electric power, the internal combustion engine – were already causing the great cities to disperse and thus to conglomerate: "Some name, then, for these city-regions, these town aggregates, is wanted. Constellations we cannot call them; conglomerations is, alas! nearer the mark, at present, but it may sound unappreciative; what of 'Conurbations'?"[51] In Britain he identified Clyde–Forth, Tyne–Wear–Tees, "Lancaston," the West Riding and "South Riding," "Midlandton," "Waleston," and Greater London; among the great European "World-Cities," Paris, the French Riviera, Berlin, and the Ruhr; in the United States, Pittsburgh, Chicago, and New York–Boston.[52] Presaging Gottmann's celebrated study of *Megalopolis* half a century later, he wrote, "the expectation is not absurd that the not so distant future will see practically one vast City-line along the Atlantic Coast for five hundred miles; and stretching back at many points; with a total of, it may well be, well-nigh as many millions of people."[53]

The problem was that these spreading cities were still the outcome of the bad old palaeotechnic order, which he saw "as dissipating resources and energies, as depressing life, under the rule of machine and mammon, and as working out accordingly its specific results, in unemployment and misemployment, in disease and folly, in vice and apathy, in indolence and crime."[54] The first step, since "the children, the women, the workers of the town can come but rarely to the country," was that "we must therefore bring the country to them," "make the field gain on the street, not merely the street gain on the field";[55] "Towns must now cease to spread like expanding ink-stains and grease-spots," but must grow botanically, "with green leaves set in alternation with its golden rays":[56] the people of the city would thus grow up amidst the sights and smells of the country.

His ideas found an echo in Germany. Robert Schmidt (1869–1934), a councilor in the city of Essen between 1907 and 1920, then moved to head a new regional organization, the *Siedlungsverband Ruhrkohlenbezirk* (SVR; Ruhr Planning Association, today *Kommunalverband Ruhr* or Intermunicipal Association of the Ruhr District). Already, in 1913, he had formulated a comprehensive "open space" policy and also a strategy to optimize the traffic infrastructure.[57] In this he was clearly influenced by

[50]   Boardman, 1944, 412.
[51]   Geddes, 1915, 34.
[52]   Geddes, 1915, 41, 47, 48–9.
[53]   Geddes, 1915, 48–9.
[54]   Geddes, 1915, 86.
[55]   Geddes, 1915, 96.
[56]   Geddes, 1915, 97.
[57]   Petz, 1999, 163–4.

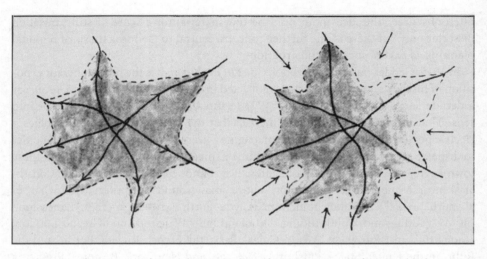

Figure 5.5   The Process of Conurbation, right and wrong. Diagram from Geddes's *Cities in Evolution* (1915) showing urban sprawl and its remedy. *Source*: Reproduced by permission of the National Library of Scotland, J. 231.a.

that of Charles Eliot for the City of Boston, with urban areas "penetrated by contiguous systems of parks and playgrounds, immediately connected with large forest areas and other open spaces outside the city," as Werner Hegemann writes in a book commemorating a 1910 town-planning exhibition in Düsseldorf.[58] In a *Denkschrift* (Think Piece) of 1912, he proposed that the city should be encircled by a green ring and traversed by radial wedges of "green." There would be a differentiated network of traffic routes serving long-distance and short-distance traffic, both for passengers and goods. This was the origin of the regional green open space by the SVR soon after its foundation in 1920.[59]

All of these ideas of Geddes were no more than Howard had said, in one sense; but Geddes was saying it at the level of the entire city region, and that constituted its unique novelty. "Regional Survey and their [*sic*] applications – Rural Development, Town Planning, City Design," he concluded,

> these are destined to become master-thoughts and practical ambitions for the opening generation, not less fully than have been Business, Politics, and War to the past, and to our passing one … Already, for thinking geographers here and there, for artists and engineers, for town planners also, the neotechnic order is not only becoming conscious, but generalised, as comprehensively geotechnic; and its arts and sciences are coming to be valued less as intellectual pleasures, attainments, distinctions, and more in the measure in which they can be organised into the geographical service, the regional regeneration of Country and Town.[60]

[58]   Petz, 1999, 172.
[59]   Petz, 1999, 177.
[60]   Geddes, 1915, 400.

To say that geography is an essential basis of planning did not sound very radical in the 1980s, or indeed for 30 years before that; but in 1915, when for most people town planning still equaled the City Beautiful, it was revolutionary. The trouble was that, revolutionary as it was, it was also quintessentially incoherent; that quotation gives the all-too-characteristic flavor of the 402 pages, as of the many thousands of others that Geddes wrote. He was a lot better at exhibitions: he organized one for the very important 1910 London Town Planning Conference, stressing Le Play's sociology and his own evolutionary perspective, which evidently influenced key figures like Unwin and Abercrombie.[61] And it was at this time that he began to influence contemporaries, above all Patrick Abercrombie, then just beginning his academic career at the University of Liverpool. Practitioners, especially architects, turned to him because he seemed to have ready answers to vital questions.[62] Abercrombie wrote in 1927,

> It is perhaps safe to say that the modern practice of town-planning in this country would have been a much simpler thing if it had not been for Geddes. There was a time when it seemed only necessary to shake up into a bottle the German town-extension plan, the Parisian Boulevard and Vista, and the English Garden Village, to produce a mechanical mixture which might be applied indiscriminately and beneficently to every town in this country; thus it would be "town-planned" according to the most up-to-date notions. Pleasing dream! First shattered by Geddes, emerging from his Outlook Tower in the frozen North, to produce that nightmare of complexity, the Edinburgh Room at the great Town Planning Exhibition of 1910.[63]

And a quarter-century later, at a meeting to celebrate the centenary of his birth, his academic successor William Holford quoted the Greek epigram on Plato: "Wherever I go in my mind I meet Geddes coming back."[64] But he needed an amanuensis. That is why Mumford and his fellow-members of the Regional Planning Association of America were such critically important torchbearers. "Geddes," Mumford wrote, "gave me the frame for my thinking: my task has been to put flesh on his abstract skeleton."[65] In the preface of his greatest and most influential work, *The Culture of Cities* (1938), he was at pains to acknowledge that debt.

His fateful meeting with Geddes, in New York in 1923, was a disaster: on meeting him, Geddes wept, saying, "You must be another son to me," and then proceeded to treat Mumford "more like an acolyte than an associate, dominating his time, ordering him around like a grammar school pupil, and even subjecting him to a blackboard grilling in the elements of his complicated graphs and diagrams";[66] accommodated for a few days in the New School, he refused to move and stayed there all summer,

[61]   Meller, 1995, 304–5.
[62]   Meller, 1990, 156, 181.
[63]   Meller, 1990, 157.
[64]   Meller 1990, 325
[65]   Boardman, 1978, 345.
[66]   Miller, D. L., 1989, 220.

taking possession of the entire building and filling it with his papers, which he had shipped in advance.[67]

Geddes wanted to turn the 28-year-old rising star into an assistant. Mumford found no embarrassment in addressing Geddes as "Master," which he did ever after; he was under Geddes's spell, but found that the older man was seeking a kind of super-secretary to convert his "midden" of papers, his own term, into a coherent whole. Mumford's own career as writer was just taking off, and he had neither the time nor the inclination for this role. So, for another nine years, their regular correspondence took on an increasingly anguished tone: Geddes with the sense that his life was ebbing away, with too little to show for it; Mumford, making elegant excuse after excuse for postponing his proposed visit to Europe.[68]

Mumford, wrestling with Geddes's writings, found a basic deficiency never evident when they met: "Geddes, by confining so much of his thought to his limited graph-bound vocabulary, was incapable except in spontaneous speech of drawing on the fullness of his own life experience."[69] At the age of 80, in one of his last writings, Mumford composed a moving epitaph for his "Master":

> For me, Geddes' greatest service was to open up the House of Life, from rooftop under the open sky to labyrinthine cellar. But I cannot forget that there are many chambers in that house we shall never, to the end of our days, penetrate; and that no single life, no single culture, no single philosophic or religious outlook, no single period or epoch, nor yet all the assembled products of science and technics, however condensed and computerized, will ever exhaust life's boundless and unpredictable manifestations of creativity. Nothing less than the total effort of all creatures and all minds, aided by stars in their courses, is necessary to convey even faintly the meanings and values of life. And from whom did I first learn this lesson? From Patrick Geddes. But I did not find it in any of his graphs.[70]

Yet Geddes, without knowing it throughout this long and anguished correspondence, had found the author for his gospel.

The Regional Planning Association of America

In his autobiography, Mumford recalls how the RPAA came into being. Already, in 1917, when he was only 22, he had written a piece, apparently unpublished, *Garden Civilizations in Preparing for a new Epoch*, on industrial decentralization and garden cities. In the autumn of 1922 he met Clarence Stein, an architect. The RPAA arose from a chance association of Mumford, Stein, Benton MacKaye (whose proposal for an Appalachian Trail Stein had published in the *Journal of the American Institute of*

[67]   Miller, D. L., 1989, 220–1.
[68]   Novak, 1995, 243–7, 259–63, 275, 283, 288, 313–15, 323, 325, 339.
[69]   Novak, 1995, 368.
[70]   Novak, 1995, 372.

Architects in 1921), and Charles Harris Whitaker. Other founder members of the group, at its inception around March 1923, included the economist Stuart Chase, the architects Federick Lee Ackerman and Henry Wright, and the developer Alexander Bing; Catherine Bauer was appointed Executive Director and Research Assistant to Stein.[71] It was a small and diverse group, never exceeding 20 in number, mainly but not exclusively New York-based, with "no prima donnas"; its core members seem to have been Mumford, Stein, Wright, Ackerman, and MacKaye.[72] In June 1923, during Geddes's visit to New York, it adopted a fivefold program which included the creation of garden cities within a regional plan; development of relationships with British planners, especially Geddes; development of regional projects and plans to further the Appalachian Trail; collaboration with the American Institute of Architects' committee on Community Planning to propagate regionalism; and surveys of key areas, notably the Tennessee Valley basin.[73]

This ideology came from the RPAA. Formed in April 1923, it included several of the most remarkable people the twentieth-century planning movement has ever produced. They came from very diverse backgrounds and had very different personalities: Benton MacKaye was a Scottish New Englander, son of a playwright and student of the great Harvard geographer W. M. Davis, a lover of the country and small-towns, and a wilderness/rural conservationist; Clarence Stein was a cosmopolitan Jewish socialist and urbane community planner; Henry Wright was an established architect who worked with Stein on projects; Mumford was the literate urban critic. Finally, Alexander Bing, a real-estate financier who was elected President of the RPAA in 1923, played a crucial role in turning its ideas from theory into action; his City Housing Corporation provided mortgage guarantees to the Association's two projects at Sunnyside Gardens in Queens and Radburn in New Jersey, which made them affordable for working people. Each of these people was individually talented, even a genius; but they had the capacity to work together in small creative groups. They became great friends, and their ideas fused into the concept of a "regional city": a "utopian urban form" in which a great variety of urban communities would be sited upon a continuous green backcloth of farms, parks, and wilderness areas. The concept derived from Ebenezer Howard's garden-city/greenbelt idea; but it took it much further.[74]

The RPAA believed that new technologies – electric power, the telephone, the car – were liberating agents, allowing homes and workplaces to escape completely from the constriction of the nineteenth-century city: a notion that Mumford had derived from Geddes's notion of the palaeotechnic and neotechnic economies, which he would so effectively employ in his 1938 masterpiece *The Culture of Cities*.[75] Mumford would later come to doubt and then to reject that hypothesis, as he saw what mass

---

[71]   Dal Co, 1979, 231; Mumford, 1982, 337–9; Goist, 1983, 260.
[72]   Lubove, 1967, 17; Mumford, 1982, 339–40.
[73]   Dal Co, 1979, 232.
[74]   Parsons, 1992b, 466–7, 470, 475; Spann, 1996, 20–4.
[75]   Parsons, 1992b, 478.

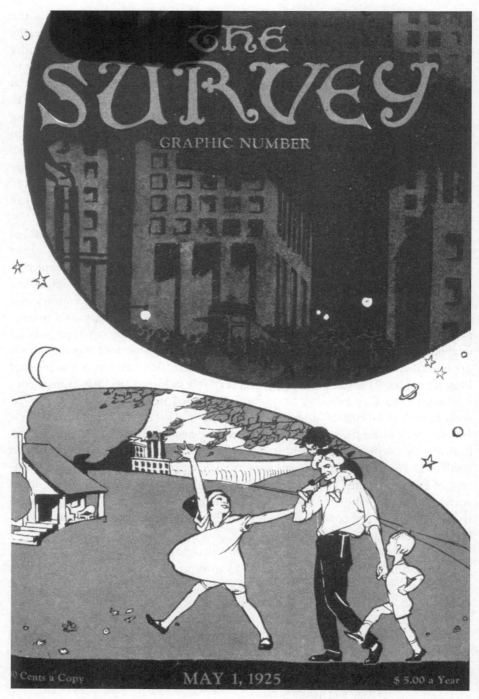

Figure 5.6 The RPAA Manifesto. Edited by Lewis Mumford, this collective issue was the definitive statement of the philosophy of the small New York group, which proved one of the most important documents of planning's history. *Source*: Peter Hall.

automobility did to post-World War Two America; but at the end of the 1920s, it was still possible to see the car as a benign technology.

These ideas came together in the State Plan which Henry Wright drew up for the New York State Commission of Housing and Regional Planning, of which Clarence Stein was the chair. Condemning past trends which had resulted in 80% of the people living on only 15% of the state's land, notably in the 400-mile-long, 25-mile-wide Hudson-Mohawk corridor, Wright pointed to the contrast between congested cities and deserted countryside, and argued for planned long-distance dispersal of people and jobs throughout the state. It became the RPAA's credo: their counter-plan, their radical alternative to Adams's business-as-usual proposals. Unfortunately, Governor Alfred E. Smith, the plan's patron, withdrew his support: he had his eyes on the White House and turned to support Robert Moses, the sworn enemy of planners and above all the RPAA.[76]

Two years later came the RPAA's first major opportunity: *The Survey*, a magazine with an influential circulation among liberal intellectuals and a special link with the social work movement, invited it to produce a special number for the New York meeting of the International Town Planning and Garden Cities Association. Conceived by MacKaye, it was commissioned and edited by Mumford.[77] Out of print for half a century until reprinted by Carl Sussman in his book *Planning the Fourth Migration*, it remains – apart from *The Culture of Cities* – the group's definitive manifesto, and constitutes one of the most important documents of this history.

It opens as only Mumford could.

> This is the Regional Plan number of Survey Graphic. It owes its underlying idea to a long-bearded Scot whose curiosity would not let him rest until from his Outlook Tower in Edinburgh he had seen clear through the pother of civilization to the land which sustained it and, in spite of human fumbling, nurtured it.
>
> This number has been produced by a group of insurgents who, as architects and planners, builders and rebuilders, have tried to remold cities in conventional ways and, finding the task a labor of Sisyphus, have pinned their faith boldly to the new concept of the Region.[78]

He had his audience in his hand: Geddes's message would at last be understood. The opening article, *The Fourth Migration*, also came from Mumford. He wrote of two Americas: "the America of the settlement," the coasts and the plains developed by 1850, and "the America of the migrations; the first migration that cleared the land west of the Alleghenies and opened the continent, the work of the land pioneer; the second migration, that worked over this fabric a new pattern of factories, railroads and dingy industrial towns, the bequest of the industrial pioneer; and finally … the America of the third migration, the flow of men and materials into our financial

[76] Simpson, 1985, 220–2.
[77] Mumford, 1982, 344–5.
[78] Anon, 1925, 129.

centers, the cities where buildings and profits leap upwards in riotous pyramids."[79] But now, "we are again in another period of flow," a fourth migration, based on "the technological revolution that has taken place during the last thirty years – a revolution that has made the existing layout of cities and the existing distribution of population out of square with our new opportunities." The automobile and the trunk road had opened up markets and sources of supply: "The tendency of the automobile ... is within limits to disperse population rather than to concentrate it; and any projects which may be put forward for concentrating people in Greater-City areas blindly run against the opportunities the automobile opens out"; the telephone, the radio, and the parcel post had the same effect; so did electric power.[80] The difference, as against the first three migrations, was that this time we had the capacity to guide the movement: "Fortunately for us, the fourth migration is only beginning: we may either permit it to crystallize in a formation quite as bad as that of our earlier migrations, or we may turn it to better account by leading it into new channels."[81]

Clarence Stein, in the following article, takes up Mumford's theme: unknown to almost everyone living and working in them, the new technologies were making New York, Chicago, Philadelphia, Boston, and the rest into "Dinosaur Cities," which were breaking down under the weight of congestion, inefficiency, and escalating social cost, and finally complete physical collapse. The result was that these cities were fast becoming the least logical places to locate industry. In a remarkable prophecy – this, remember, was 1925 – Stein wrote,

> When the local overhead cannot be shifted, and when smaller centers are, in spite of their poorer financial and business facilities, able to make their industrial advantages felt, the great city's industries will have to migrate or declare bankruptcy. We are still in the day of postponement; but the day of reckoning will come; and it behooves us to anticipate it.[82]

Robert Freestone has traced Stein's regional city concept, "galaxies of modest-sized communities (not satellite towns) linked by modern means of communication," back to Howard's Social City via Geddes's *Cities in Evolution* and the 1922 regional plan by Patrick Abercrombie and Henry Johnson for Doncaster and district.[83] The transatlantic connections were already busy at work.

In turn the group's economist, Stuart Chase, developed the argument further: much of the American economy consisted in carrying "Coals to Newcastle," moving goods across the continent that had no need to be moved at all. He asks,

> Now what, specifically, is the matter? Where does the energy, particularly transport energy, go to waste, and how would planned communities reduce this waste so that the

[79]   Mumford, 1925a, 130.
[80]   Mumford, 1925a, 130, 132–3.
[81]   Mumford, 1925a, 133.
[82]   Stein, 1925, 138.
[83]   Freestone 2002, 86.

wayfaring man instead of falling behind, or making unheard-of efforts to keep where he is, can begin to make ground against the cost of living?

This marks an important shift in the argument: it is necessary not merely to go with the flow of technological change, as Mumford and Stein had argued, but to intervene in order to correct the grosser inefficiencies of the system. A "national plan" would involve "regions delimited on the basis of natural geographic entities"; "a maximum of foodstuffs, textiles and housing materials grown and manufactured in the home region"; "a minimum of interregional exchanges based only on such products as the home region cannot economically produce"; plus regional power plants, short hauls by truck, and "a decentralized distribution of population":[84]

> The regional planning of communities would wipe out uneconomic national marketing, wipe out city congestion and terminal wastes, balance the power load, take the bulk of coal off the railroads, eliminate the duplication of milk and other deliveries, short circuit such uneconomic practices as hauling Pacific apples to New York customers by encouraging local orchards, develop local forest areas and check the haulage of western timber to eastern mills, locate cotton mills near cotton fields, shoe factories near hide producing areas, steel mills within striking distance of ore beds, food manufacturing plants in small giant power units, near farming belts. Gone the necessity for the skyscraper, the subway and the lonely country-side![85]

It was again prophetic: the argument for conservation, half a century before the Club of Rome. But it involved a plan, and a consequent interference with private business, that was frankly socialist; well did Chase say, a few years later, "We were mildly socialist, though not at all communist; liberal but willing to abandon large areas of the free market in favor of a planned economy. So we were not doctrinaire socialists. We were open-minded; kind of Fabian Socialists."[86]

That emerges clearly enough as the group moves into proposals. Mumford now returns specifically to that choice for the coming neotechnic era: society can have already-overgrown cities becoming bigger and bigger, "in Professor Geddes' sardonic phrase, more and more of worse and worse."[87] Or it can have regional planning.

> Regional planning asks not how wide an area can be brought under the aegis of the metropolis, but how the population and civic facilities can be distributed so as to promote and stimulate a vivid, creative life throughout a whole region – a region being any geographic area that possesses a certain unity of climate, soil, vegetation, industry and culture. The regionalist attempts to plan such an area so that all its sites and resources, from forest to city, from highland to water level, may be soundly developed, and so that the population will be distributed so as to utilize, rather than to nullify or destroy, its

[84]   Chase, 1925, 144.
[85]   Chase, 1925, 146.
[86]   Quoted in Sussman, 1976, 23.
[87]   Mumford, 1925b, 151.

natural advantages. It sees people, industry and the land as a single unit. Instead of trying, by one desperate dodge or another, to make life a little more tolerable in the congested centers, it attempts to determine what sort of equipment will be needed in the
new centers.[88]

Here it is, at last, what Geddes was struggling, through all those torrents of words, to
say. But it is Geddesian, too, in its purpose: neotechnic technology can be the means
not merely to greater mechanical efficiency, but also to

> a fuller quality of life, at every point in the region. No form of industry and no type of
> city are tolerable that take the joy out of life. Communities in which courtship is fur-
> tive, in which babies are an unwelcome handicap, in which education, lacking the
> touch of nature and of real occupations, hardens into a blank routine, in which people
> achieve adventure only on wheels and happiness only by having their minds "taken
> off" their everyday lives – communities like these do not sufficiently justify our
> modern advances in science and invention.[89]

This is where Howard comes in. For if regional planning provides the framework,
the garden city provides the "civic objective"[90]: "not as a temporary haven of refuge
but as a permanent seat of life and culture, urban in its advantages, permanently
rural in its situation." But it meant "a change in aim as well as a change of place": "our
garden cities represent fuller development of the more humane arts and sciences –
biology and medicine and psychiatry and education and architecture ... all that is
good in our modern mechanical developments, but also all that was left out in this
one-sided existence, all the things that fifth century Athens or thirteenth century
Florence, for all their physical crudity, possessed."[91]

Kropotkin, again. But it is more than Kropotkin, more even than Geddes: there is
another strain, which is specifically American.

> Regional planning is the New Conservation – the conservation of human values hand
> in hand with natural resources ... Permanent agriculture instead of land-skinning,
> permanent forestry instead of timber mining, permanent human communities, dedi-
> cated to life, liberty and the pursuit of happiness, instead of camps and squatter-
> settlements, and to stable buildings, instead of the scantling and falsework of our
> "go-ahead" communities – all this is embodied in regional planning.[92]

That American theme is taken up by Benton MacKaye in his article *The New
Exploration*. At one level it is pure Geddes: long transects through valley sections at
different scales, from the Berkshires of upstate Massachusetts down to Boston and

88   Mumford, 1925b, 151.
89   Mumford, 1925b, 151.
90   Mumford, 1925b, 151.
91   Mumford, 1925b, 152.
92   Mumford, 1925b, 152.

the ocean, down the little Somerset Valley along the Upper Deerfield River. And the plan for the Somerset Valley is intended to achieve just that ecological balance that Vidal and his followers found in those long-settled regions of France. The difference is that it is planned: it is based on *"forest culture* against *forest mining,"* for this alone "will keep Somerset Valley in a truly settled state."[93] America, this relatively new-settled land, must learn the same time-scales, the same unconscious capacity for natural regeneration through good husbandry, that European peasants had passed on from generation to generation through centuries. This emphasis goes back to several different strands of nineteenth-century American thinking: to the concept of "structure, process and stage" of the early Harvard physical geographers, Nathaniel S. Shaler and William M. Davis; to the views of an even earlier geographer, George Perkins Marsh, on ecology and resource planning; to David Thoreau's emphasis on the return to living amidst nature, and on natural balance.[94] And in addition, there was a newer skein of intellectual movements in the universities of the depressed rural South. There were the conservative Southern Agrarians at Vanderbilt University in Nashville, Tennessee, with their rejection of northern industrialism and their model of the rural medieval or early New England economy.[95] And, in sharp ideo-logical contrast, there were the Southern Regionalists around Howard Odum, with their emphasis on decentralization of wealth and power, and on balanced regenera-tion of the region's rich legacy of badly exploited natural resources, who were just then beginning to develop their thinking at the University of North Carolina, but whose major work would come in the 1930s.[96]

These developing – though sometimes inconsistent – strains come together in MacKaye's complete statement of his own brand of RPAA philosophy, "The New Exploration."[97] Here, he developed the notion of two contrasting Americas: the indigenous, "a compound of the primeval and the colonial," and the metropolitan, "a compound of the urban and the world-wide industrial." The job of the regional planner was painstakingly to reconstruct and conserve the environments of that older indigenous America, the primeval wilderness, the early village communities of New England, and "the real city, the complement of the real village."[98] But this would be difficult, for

> The contest in the country will be between Metropolitan America and Indigenous America. These now stand vis-à-vis, not only psychologically, but also physically and geographically. The metropolitan world ... is a mechanized molten framework of industry which flows ... mightiest in the valleys and weakest on the mountain ridges. The strategy of the indigenous world is just the other way. It is still mighty within the primeval environment, as along the ridgeways of the Appalachian barrier ... strong

[93] MacKaye, 1925, 157.
[94] Lubove, 1963, 91–6.
[95] Ciucci, 1979, 341–2.
[96] Odum, 1936; Odum and Moore, 1938; Kantor, 1973c, 284–5; Friedmann and Weaver, 1979, 35–40.
[97] MacKaye, 1928.
[98] MacKaye, 1928, 64.

also in such regions as up country, where, although the farms and villages are depleted, the resources both physical and psychologic are still there, and are yet open to restoration and renewed development.[99]

The problem, then, "concerns the remolding of the Metropolitan America in its contact with the Indigenous America." For indigenous America was Mumford's America of the settlement; Metropolitan America, his America of the migrations.[100] And Mumford's fourth migration was a "backflow," "a relocation of the populations and industries resulting from the second and third migrations," which had become a flood from a broken reservoir.[101] The question for regional planning then was "What manner of embankments ... can we construct downstream to hold our deluge in check?"[102]

MacKaye's answer was a typical RPAA stratagem: it was to harness the new technology, but thereby to control its impact on the natural environment. The metropolitan environment would be extended by "motor ways"; between these, the hill areas would be kept as a primeval (or "near-primeval") "wilderness area," "serving the double purpose of a public forest and a public playground," through which a system of open ways, "equipped for actual use as a zone of primeval sojourn and outdoor living," would serve as "a series of breaks in the metropolitan deluge": it would divide – or tend to divide – the flood waters of metropolitism into separate "basins" and thereby seek to avert their "complete and total confluence."[103] Additionally, "as an adjunct of the motor way system" would run an *intertown*: "a series of open ways, or zones, straddling the motor road between successive towns and villages" and free of all inappropriate structures and land uses.[104] This was the very opposite of "Roadtown," "the embodiment of the metropolitan flood."[105] It would not be bereft of buildings – "Fear not, we have no notion of sounding a civic curfew" – but these buildings would not be "chucked together," they would be "assembled" through good planning.[106] And, developing the idea two years later, he came up with the notion of the Townless Highway: a limited access road around Boston, with service stations at intervals, but with no other access. No wonder that, nearly 40 years after, Lewis Mumford credited MacKaye with the invention of the modern motorway; not quite true, as Chapter 9 will show, but fair testimony to the remarkable prescience of the RPAA founders.[107]

How in practice this would look can be seen from the maps and charts prepared by Henry Wright for the New York State Commission of Housing and Regional

99   MacKaye, 1928, 73.
100 MacKaye, 1928, 75–6.
101 MacKaye, 1928, 170.
102 MacKaye, 1928, 178.
103 MacKaye, 1928, 179–80.
104 MacKaye, 1928, 182.
105 MacKaye, 1928, 186.
106 MacKaye, 1928, 186–7.
107 MacKaye, 1930; Mumford, 1964; Guttenberg, 1978.

Planning: "Epoch I" (1840–80), of "State-Wide Activity and Intercourse" is followed by "Epoch II" (1880–1920), in which population concentrates along main-line transportation. But in "Epoch III" we see "The possible state of the future in which each part serves its logical function in support of wholesome activity and good living." A magnified close-up, "an ideal section," proves to be Geddes's familiar diagram applied to the land fronting on to Lake Erie: forests and storage reservoirs in the highlands, dairy farms in the bordering upland, two parallel motorway highways flanking the highway and railroad on the fertile plain, cities and towns neatly disposed like beads on a string.[108]

Not much of this, in the America of the 1920s, was practical policy; even the constitutionality of zoning was in doubt until the historic Supreme Court decision of 1926.[109] True, as Governor of New York, Franklin Delano Roosevelt bought at least Stuart Chase's prescription, for – by manipulating dairy health regulations – he protected New York dairy farmers against out-of-state competition.[110] And, through the agency of Alexander Bing, the RPAA did manage to float the two experimental communities at Sunnyside Gardens in New York City and at Radburn in New Jersey (Chapter 4). But mostly, the RPAA was in the business of marketing long-term dreams.

The RPAA versus the Regional Plan of New York

In their one major clash over policy, they found an unlikely adversary. Thomas Adams had been one of the founding fathers of British town planning: first general manager of Letchworth Garden City, first planning inspector, founder-member and first president (though barely qualified)[111] of the Town Planning Institute.[112] And, arrived in North America, fully four years before the foundation of the RPAA he had emphasized "the importance of one of the most modern aspects of town planning, namely, the direction and control of the growth taking place within the rural and semi-rural districts where the new industries are being established," arguing that "no city planning scheme can be satisfactory which is not prepared with due regard to the regional development surrounding the city."[113] So when Charles Dyer Norton – former Chairman of the Commercial Club of Chicago and thus commissioner of the Burnham plan, now treasurer of the Russell Sage Foundation – approached him to direct an ambitious survey and plan for the whole New York region, it was a challenge he could hardly refuse. Confirmed after Norton's death by his successor Frederic Delano, he was appointed Director of Plans and Surveys in July 1923.[114]

---

[108]   Smith, 1925, 159–60.

[109]   Fluck, 1986.

[110]   Roosevelt, 1932, 484.

[111]   Simpson, 1985, 67.

[112]   Simpson, 1985, 191.

[113]   Scott, 1969, 178–9.

[114]   Hays, 1965, 7–11; Simpson, 1985, 136.

This, as Robert Fishman has pointed out, was the culmination of a profound shift in American planning: from the City Beautiful to the City Functional, which emphasized business-like, technocratic, and survey-based approaches. Starting as early as 1907 in New York, St Louis, Grand Rapids, and Dubuque, it blossomed in the 1920s: John Nolen could report in 1928 that 200 cities with a total population of 26.5 million had been "broadly replanned." These replannings – produced for city-planning commissions, predominantly advisory, sitting outside urban government proper and dominated by unpaid, middle-class, "public spirited" citizens and business leaders – were the work of a small and select band of private practitioners: Harland Bartholomew, George Ford, Frederick Law Olmsted, Jr, and John Nolen. There was another significant trend here, presaged as early as 1909 in the Burnham Plan for Chicago: a shift in some places – Allegheny County (the Pittsburgh area), Los Angeles, Hamilton County (Greater Cincinnati) – from a focus on the central city to a wider metropolitan region.[115]

Always a team player, Adams recommended that the New York Plan be drawn up by a group including an engineer, an architect, a lawyer, and a regional planner who would act as coordinator. There was, however, another respect in which he was the perfect candidate, for this was to be a businessmen's plan, the core movers of which were ex-Chicago business leaders, that would cost them a total of more than $1 million over a decade,[116] and Adams, in his fifties, "his philosophical mould long set," was a businessman's planner. He believed that the plan must represent the art of the possible: "the Regional Plan was to be no revolutionary prescription but rather the imposition of mild public controls on a free development pattern so as to improve metropolitan efficiency and curb the market's worst abuses while adding non-controversial public benefits like modern motor roads, parks and beaches."[117] This, needless to say, was a recipe for headlong conflict with the idealists of the infant RPAA.

It was not the geographical scope of the plan that was wrong. For Norton had called for a wide compass: "From the City Hall a circle must be swung which will include the Atlantic Highlands and Princeton; the lovely Jersey hills back of Morristown and Tuxedo; the incomparable Hudson so far as Newburg; the Westchester lakes and ridges, as far as Bridgeport and beyond, and all on Long Island."[118] The resulting area – over 5,000 square miles, with nearly nine million people – was a far bigger canvas than any plan before had covered.[119] Nor was it the survey methodology: Adams assembled an unrivalled team, whose detailed volumes constitute some of the uncontested classics of planning literature, with conclusions that echo those of Mumford, Chase, and Stein. Here is Robert Murray Haig on the urban economy,[120] showing that many activities

[115] Freestone, 2000a, 303–4.
[116] Kantor, 1973a, 36–7; Wilson, 1974, 136.
[117] Simpson, 1985, 135.
[118] Scott, 1969, 177.
[119] Regional Plan of New York, I, 1927, xii; Kantor, 1973a, 39.
[120] Regional Plan of New York, I, 1927, 23–8.

were already moving out because they had less need of a central location, and arguing for zoning controls to take account of negative externalities: "Zoning finds its economic justification in that it is a useful device for ensuring an approximately just distribution of costs, of forcing each individual to bear his own expenses."[121] Here is the volume on population and land values, arguing that the problem was the excessive concentration of transportation facilities which in turn encouraged excessive concentration of economic activities, hence further congestion, hence economic waste.[122] Here is the volume on zoning and land use, arguing that high land values in New York are the direct result of the permitted height and bulk.[123] And here is Perry's volume on neighborhood units, with its recognition that the automobile was naturally creating the cellular city.[124]

It was none of this: it was the philosophy, which Adams shared with his committee. It was the belief that in practice the form of the region was fixed and that only incremental, marginal change was possible. It expressed itself in a hundred ways: in the acceptance of the existing highway plan, with merely "by-passes or belt lines ... to permit free circulation between the major subdivisions of the Region"; in the costly investment in yet more radial commuter rail links into Manhattan;[125] in the advocacy – though his name was nowhere mentioned – of the Corbusian principle of widely spaced skyscrapers in a park;[126] above all, in the suggestion that "what is needed in connection with the problems of concentrated industrial and business growth in a region is not decentralization but a reorientation of centralization on the basis of making all its centers and sub-centers healthy, efficient and free from congestion";[127] and the resulting suggestion that "recentralization" of business and industry into sub-centers within the region could relieve congestion;[128] in the associated rejection of the garden city as a general solution, "except for the very small part of industry and population that could be made to move to new centers";[129] in the rejection of any wider unit of government to plan for the entire region.[130] Above all, it was in the passive assumption that the region would continue to grow, from 14.5 million people to perhaps 21 million by 1965, coupled with the lack of any firm proposals as to where the extra people were to go;[131] the basic aim was "to decentralize and decongest New York enough for it to continue functioning in traditional ways."[132]

[121]   Regional Plan of New York, I, 1927, 44.
[122]   Regional Plan of New York, II, 1929, 25–6.
[123]   Regional Plan of New York, VI, 1931, 102–3.
[124]   Regional Plan of New York, VII, 1931, 30.
[125]   Regional Plan of New York, III, 1927, 126–32.
[126]   Regional Plan of New York, VI, 1931, 103–5.
[127]   Regional Plan of New York, II, 1929, 31.
[128]   Regional Plan of New York, II, 1929, 31; Hays, 1965, 20; Scott, 1969, 262.
[129]   Regional Plan of New York, VI, 1931, 25.
[130]   Regional Plan of New York, II, 1929, 197.
[131]   Regional Plan of New York, II, 1929, 35.
[132]   Wilson, 1974, 137.

Predictably, it provoked a bitter response. In a celebrated review, Mumford condemned the plan in almost every last particular. Its spatial frame, wide as it might seem, was too narrow; it accepted growth as inevitable, ignoring the potential of planning to influence it; it failed to consider alternatives; it continued to allow overbuilding of central areas; it condemned the last remaining piece of open space near to Manhattan, the Hackensack Meadows of New Jersey, to be built over; it dismissed garden cities as utopian; it condoned the filling-in of suburban areas; through its rejection of the principle of public housing, it condemned the poor to live in poor housing; it favored yet more subsidy for the commuter lines into Manhattan, thus helping create more of the very congestion it condemned; its highway and rapid-transit proposals were an alternative to a community-building project, not a means toward it. Its central fault was that it appeared to support everything: concentration and dispersal, planning control versus speculation, subsidization versus the market. But, despite appearances to the contrary, it really meant a drift to yet more centralization.[133] Mumford concluded,

> In sum: the "Plan for New York and its Environs" is a badly conceived pudding into which a great many ingredients, some sound, more dubious, have been poured and mixed: the cooks tried to satisfy every appetite and taste, and the guiding thought in selecting the pudding-dish was that it should "sell" one pudding to the diners, specially to those who paid the cooks. The mixture as a whole is indigestible and tasteless: but here and there is a raisin or a large piece of citron that can be extracted and eaten with relish. In the long run, let us hope, this is how the pudding will be remembered.[134]

Adams, clearly irritated, decided to sting Mumford by calling Geddes in aid:

> This is the main point on which Mr Mumford and I, as well as Mr Mumford and Geddes, differ – that is whether we stand still and talk ideals or move forward and get as much realization of our ideals as possible in a necessarily imperfect society, capable only of imperfect solutions to its problems.[135]

That was the essence of a profound philosophical gap that would never be bridged. Mumford, he suggested, was guilty of being "prepared to let the wish become father to the thought. How happy I would be if I could do the same!"[136]

That was the end of this extraordinary exchange: "Adams and Mumford, committed reformers both, had sailed past each other like ships in the night."[137] The irony was that the car would before long create a sprawling city, equally unacceptable to either party.[138]

---

[133]   Sussman, 1976, 227–47.
[134]   Quoted in Sussman, 1976, 259.
[135]   Quoted in Sussman, 1976, 263.
[136]   Johnson, 1988, 181.
[137]   Johnson, 1996, 193.
[138]   Fishman, 1992, 122; Simpson, 1985, 158.

There were rich paradoxes here. Adams, too, continued to believe that New York was too big and that "from an economic, and perhaps from a health standpoint we should get as many people and industries out of their central areas and into garden cities as is possible."[139] But the very success of garden cities, he argued, was lessening the need for them as a solution: the solution "is not to be found in an indiscriminate process of decentralization, but both in well-planned decentralization in Garden Cities and equally well-planned diffusion in urban regions."[140] And Mumford's alternative prescription was not as straightforward as it might seem. He wrote of

> the conditions that are precedent to finding a solution. These are: (1) lessen the pressure of congestion in Manhattan by recentralizing the business areas of the metropolis; (2) lay down new cities and direct the exodus to these new cities *outside* the New York region: this means a widespread system of state aid for city building and housing, such as that promoted in England, Germany and Russia; (3) rebuild the blighted areas and take care of part of the increase of population, while it continues, by a process of intensive internal colonization.[141]

This is not the Mumford most of his readers recognize: he argues against overspill of population from blighted areas, and for razing and rebuilding them as neighborhood communities, more intensively but with an increase of usable open space. Here, he seems almost Corbusian in his enthusiasm for the bulldozer: he estimates that there may be room for five million more people in these blighted areas, in which he includes recently developed areas like Queens, which must be totally rebuilt.[142] For "the building of houses fit for the nurture of human beings is dependent upon making production and distribution directly subservient to biotechnic standards of consumption, available for the whole community."[143] Machines for living in, indeed. Nor was this an isolated aberration. In 1934, the year the New York City Housing Authority (NYCHA) was formed, the Housing Study Guild – Mumford, Wright, Mayer, and Carol Aronovici – made a study which concluded that high land values made high-rise the most economic form of building for New York. (And reviewing the NYCHA's first project after the 1937 Federal Housing Act, the Red Hook Houses in Brooklyn, with its bleak low-cost 25-story blocks, Mumford criticized its repetitive quality but found it "miles above the product of any commercial apartment builder.")[144]

In any event, Adams and Mumford parted ways; Adams tried to set up a continuing dialogue, but Mumford – though remaining personally amiable – became ever more savage in his criticism.[145] The New York plan went ahead, through the medium of a

---

139   Adams, 1930, 142–3.
140   Adams, 1930, 146.
141   Mumford, 1932, 150–1.
142   Mumford, 1932, 151.
143   Mumford, 1938, 470–1.
144   Mumford, 1995, 22, 25.
145   Simpson, 1985, 155.

Regional Plan Association under business elite leadership, and Planning Commissions for each area; it was particularly successful in its highway, bridge, and tunnel proposals, mainly because the master-builder Robert Moses was in charge.[146] Meanwhile, Mumford's alternative prescription – state-aided new cities and the extensive rebuilding of blighted areas – remained on paper.[147]

New Deal Planning

This might seem a strange outcome; for in 1933 Franklin Delano Roosevelt was inaugurated as President and the New Deal began. And Roosevelt was heavily committed in principle to a program along pure RPAA lines. In 1931, he had floated the idea of a mass return to the land, by providing a house and a few acres and money and tools; he was also borrowing RPAA ideas when he argued that electric power and the truck were aiding decentralization of industry to small communities and rural areas, while electricity, radio, cinema, and parcel post were bringing an urban quality of life to the countryside; he specifically proposed a State Commission on Rural Homes, to establish a plan based on "cooperative planning for the common good."[148] A few months later, he had called for "a definite plan by which industry itself will seek to move certain firms ... out of the congested centers where unemployment is greatest into the smaller communities, closer to the primary food supply."[149] And in 1932, just before election, he asked "if out of this regional planning we are not going to be in a position to take the bull by the horns in the immediate future and adopt some kind of experimental work based on a distribution of population."[150] His uncle Frederic Delano had guided the New York Regional Plan, and had given him, he said in 1931, an abiding interest in the question; the day might not be far distant, he said, when planning would become part of the national policy of the country.[151]

He was as good as his word: following Rexford Tugwell, who in turn was advised by Stuart Chase, he pushed a Public Works Bill through Congress in June 1933, providing $25 million to resettle people on the land, thus giving people the chance "to secure through the good earth the permanent jobs they have lost in the overcrowded, industrial cities and towns";[152] but the people would not go.[153] The response was the green-belt towns program of the Resettlement Administration, in 1935, already described in Chapter 4: a glorious failure, with hardly anything to show on the ground.

[146]   Hays, 1965, 25–31, 36–40; Sawers, 1984, 234.
[147]   Sussman, 1976, 250.
[148]   Roosevelt, 1938, 505, 508–9, 510–11, 514.
[149]   Roosevelt, 1938, 518.
[150]   Roosevelt, 1932, 506.
[151]   Quoted in Lepawsky, 1976, 22.
[152]   Gelfand, 1975, 25.
[153]   Gelfand, 1975, 25–6; Schaffer, 1982, 222.

The RPAA were deeply disillusioned; always a loose and informal group, perhaps too loose ever to be effective, they went into suspension in 1933.[154] They had reasons for disillusionment. Despite the New Deal, despite the hopes they still had of Roosevelt, they may already have felt that the political inertia was just too strong. Or perhaps they were simply exhausted, not least by the vehemence of the great debate on the Adams plan. Mumford, bruised by a relationship with Catherine Bauer that had turned steamily unplatonic and then stormy (partly, at least, when she pipped him for an important magazine prize),[155] retreated in stages with his long-suffering Sophie to Amenia in rural New York, to write his masterpieces *Technics and Civilization* (1934) and *The Culture of Cities* (1938). In the latter book, which brought him great fame, he broadened and deepened his attack on the "Insensate Metropolis," the "Megalopolis" that became almost the quintessence of evil: "Concentrated upon war, the metropolitan regime opposes these domestic and civic functions: it subordinates life to organized destruction, and it must therefore regiment, limit, and constrict every exhibition of real life and culture."[156] He contrasted this with "the organic order" based on "the primacy of life, and of autonomous but perpetually inter-related organisms as vehicles of life" in which "to maintain its life-shape the organism must constantly alter it and renew itself by entering into active relationships with the rest of the environment."[157] But to achieve that would demand that the neotechnic era be succeeded by a new eotechnic order, and that – though he never brings himself to use the word – would require the replacement of American capitalism by a socialist, or at least a social democratic order:

> The increase of collectivism, the rising of municipal and governmental housing, the expression of co-operative consumers' and producers' associations, the destruction of slums and the building of superior types of community for the workers – all these are signs of the new biotechnic orientation.[158]

Indeed, when he spoke in 1932 to students at Barnard College, he seemed to be thinking of a general communist-style upheaval; he had no faith in FDR, regarding him as "a sort of political Mary Baker Eddy," a political faith healer who would never cure a disease because he did not believe in radical operations.[159] But, as his biographer Donald Miller has stressed, his great problem was that he always believed in the primacy of mind over matter; apolitical in early life, he lacked an effective concept of political action. "Mumford's so-called communism was a creature of his own creation";[160] throughout his life, "he maintained an almost Erasmian aloofness from all organized political movements."[161] That, Donald Miller convincingly demonstrates,

154 Parsons, 1992b, 462; Spann, 1996, 41, 82.
155 Oberlander and Newburn, 1999, 73.
156 Mumford, 1938, 278.
157 Mumford, 1938, 301.
158 Mumford, 1938, 464.
159 Spann, 1996, 164.
160 Miller, D. L., 1989, 288.
161 Miller, D. L., 1989, 291.

finally makes *The Culture of Cities* a magnificent failure; as Bauer said of its successor, *The Condition of Man* (1944), he was always seeking a messiah, to begin some spiritual transformation. The comment was so on-target that it stung Mumford to vehement response. Significantly, after laboring for many years to rewrite *The Culture of Cities*, he published it in 1961 as *The City in History*, missing out the prescriptive part. And, in the long correspondence with Frederic Osborn, the contrast is palpable: Osborn chides Mumford for not founding an American Town and Country Planning Association, Mumford pleads that he has to earn his living as a journalist.[162]

Stein, the Association's true mover-shaker, was consultant to Tugwell's Resettlement Administration and its green-belt new towns program, but soon became disillusioned when Roosevelt failed to overcome the rooted opposition of Congress to the program. Stein's letters, magnificently published,[163] reveal both his admiration for Roosevelt's intellect and charisma (and, it emerges, his habit of hardly ever allowing anyone a word in edgeways), but also his deep suspicion of Roosevelt's capacity to agree with everyone he ever spoke to. Stein's perception of his failure had tragic consequences: in the mid-1930s, he fell victim to a manic-depressive illness that incapacitated him increasingly over the decade that followed. It stemmed not merely from the failure of his campaigns and his difficulty in finding professional commissions, but also from the extraordinary strain of his marriage to the stage and movie actress Aline MacMahon, whom he married in 1928 but who spent much of her time on the other side of the continent in Hollywood. He emerged from this mid-life crisis as an international guru of the planning movement, in constant contact not merely with old fellow-warriors like Benton MacKaye and Lewis Mumford, but with the increasing circle of international correspondents like F. J. Osborn and Göran Sidenbladh, and Gordon Stephenson, whom he assisted on the design of the pioneer exercise in pedestrianized town-center design at Stevenage in 1950; he survived to the age of 94.[164]

But Stein's letters also confirm what students of the RPAA have long surmised: that they were effectively closet socialists, who admired the Russian model (Stein visited the Soviet Union in the late 1920s), but who were ambivalent and confused about introducing it to the United States. Of course, at the time of the Great Depression the great majority of liberal thinkers in every western democracy had effectively embraced socialist planning: Stein and Mumford and their colleagues were hardly unique. What was unique was their dilemma. They looked to FDR to make the transition, ignoring the huge inbuilt forces of conservatism that were and are inherent in the American federal system. The tragedy of this small and select band of brilliant individuals was simply that they lived in the wrong country at the wrong time.

This was clear enough in Mumford's exchange with Adams, when he affirmed that no effective plan could be produced under the existing order.

---

[162]   Hughes, 1971, 145, 148–9.
[163]   Parsons, 1998.
[164]   Parsons, 1998, passim.

It may be more *effective*, as well as more clear-sighted and honest, to say that no comprehensive planning for the improvement of living conditions can be done as long as property values and private enterprise are looked upon as sacred, than it is to draw pictures of parks that may never be built, playgrounds that may never be opened to children, and garden cities that will never be financed.[165]

Because the Regional Plan avoided any proposal for effective public control of land or property values, buildings, or human institutions, it could effect no substantial change; and so it must be condemned.[166] It was vital not to accept the existence of the metropolis, as Adams had done, but to fight against it; "for to carry it further is only to broaden its capacities for mischief."[167]

Bauer, the sole woman in the group, was the great exception, the truly effective operator; she used her prize to make a second professional trip to Europe, where she visited top German planners like May and Wagner,[168] and came back to write a book on modern housing, which made a big stir. Her thesis was that the European programs had achieved several breakthroughs: modern housing as for use rather than profit, built as part of comprehensively planned neighborhoods with social facilities, and built in a modernist style. Whether the residents appreciated this last feature was not made clear.[169]

She was now drawn into the New Deal's housing effort. With Mumford's encouragement, she took a position in Philadelphia as principal adviser and executive secretary of the Labor Housing Conference, where she became involved in an affair with Oskar Stonorov, the chief designer; she threw herself into lobbying and into writing her book, and now returned to New York only infrequently.[170] She now began to attack Mumford and the RPAA, for their ineffectuality: "There isn't a society in which the isolated intellectual, an intellectual, as an *individual* writing and talking to the general public, can expect to provide *direct* leadership, straight-line influence on policy and action."[171] In 1934 they quarreled and parted as lovers, just before the appearance of *Technics and Civilization*; she had not the time to read even part of it.[172]

Established in Philadelphia, over three long years of lobbying, after many setbacks, she proved brilliantly effective in securing the 1937 Federal housing legislation.[173] She alone managed both to recognize the political forces, and to work around them; but, as one of America's greatest academic planners said of her shortly before his death, she could make every man in the room fall in love with her and do exactly

165 Mumford, 1932, 124.
166 Mumford, 1932, 154.
167 Mumford, 1932, 150.
168 Oberlander and Newburn, 1999, 61, 74, 86.
169 Radford, 1996, 76–7.
170 Miller, D., 1989, 333.
171 Miller, D., 1989, 334.
172 Miller, D., 1989, 335.
173 Oberlander and Newburn, 1999, 118–56.

Figure 5.7 Catherine Bauer. Educating herself in the Regional Planning Association of America, then disillusioned with them in general and with Mumford in particular, she brilliantly steered Congress to pass the first federal housing legislation. *Source*: William W. Wurster/ WBE Collection, Environmental Design Archives, University of California, Berkeley.

what she wanted.[174] Charles Abrams, another great figure in the American housing movement, coined a limerick:

> There was a young lady named Bauer
> Who resolved to help housing to flower
> She fought and she battled
> And couldn't be rattled
> No power could cow her – this Bauer.[175]

Beyond that, New Deal policy on regional planning mainly meant a prodigious multiplication of paper. The National Resources Planning Board and its variously named predecessor organizations, which survived exactly a decade (1933–43), have been described as "the most nearly comprehensive national planning organization this

[174] Lloyd Rodwin, personal conversation, Cambridge, Massachusetts, October 14, 1999.
[175] Oberlander and Newburn, 1999, 156.

country has ever known";[176] when first created in 1933 as the National Planning Board, they numbered three of the most distinguished names on the roll of American planning, Frederick Delano, Charles E. Merriam, and Wesley C. Mitchell; in all they produced some 370 printed and major mimeographed reports, totaling 43,000 pages.[177] Yet for all that, it is hard work to find anything out there on the ground. The 1935 report of the National Resources Committee (as it was then known), *Regional Factors in National Planning*, recommended regrouping the field districts of the various federal agencies in a limited number – say 10 or 12 – of major regional centers; the resulting regional planning commissions would have no regional executive, so that they would require "a conduit running to an established executive," a National Planning Agency.[178] But there is no record of the outcome. And their 1937 report, *Our Cities: Their Role in the National Economy*, though it drew attention to the problems of blight, speculation, social disruption, crime, and urban public finance that were even then wracking American cities, failed in its recommendations to take explicit note of the regional dimensions; on the critical question of centralization versus decentralization it sat firmly on the fence, stating that "the most effective environment for the urban dweller and for the effective use of human and material resources is more likely to be found between these two extremes"; the aim, it concluded vaguely enough, was "to loosen up the central areas of congestion to create a more decentralized urban pattern," a statement to which both Adams and Mumford would doubtless have acceded.[179] Both FDR and Congress proved massively uninterested, and the report fell into a political limbo.[180]

The TVA

To the mountain of paper, of course, there was one shining counterweight on the ground: the Tennessee Valley Authority (TVA), undeniably the greatest achievement of New Deal planning, and – at least in legend – the realization of the most radical ideas of both the RPAA and the Southern Regionalists. Addressing the last RPAA conference in 1932, Roosevelt described the TVA idea as an example of regional planning; but this, like so much of his language, was "a phrase so loose and imprecise that it could fit almost any program, and yet so elusive that it involved few specific commitments."[181] In fact, it brought together several strands: to improve navigation at Muscle Shoals in Alabama (a pet Corps of Engineers project since the previous century), develop power there, provide an armaments production facility there, and control floods; Roosevelt's achievement was to pull all this together with

176 Clawson, 1981, xvi.
177 Karl, 1963, 76; Clawson, 1981, 7.
178 US National Resources Committee, 1935, IX; Clawson, 1981, 168.
179 US National Resources Planning Board, 1937, VIII–XI, 84; Clawson, 1981, 162–4.
180 Gelfand, 1975, 97.
181 Conkin, 1983, 26.

notions of rural planning and regional development, and to drop arms production.[182] Yet all these concerns proved tangential in the actual negotiations that led to
passage of the Act; and the directors in consequence had little notion of what the
planning sections mandated or allowed.[183] FDR certainly did not offer them any
guidance, perhaps because he did not know either.[184]

Geography ensured also that the TVA was bound to make an odd example of
regional river-basis planning. The river was 650 miles long, its basin the size of
Britain, the region diverse in climate, resources, racial composition, and cultural
patterns.[185] What it had in common was poverty: the eastern Appalachian half was
possibly the poorest part of the poorest region in the United States, with thousands
of families subsisting on cash incomes of less than $100 a year.[186] They were to be
lifted out of their condition by a set of multipurpose dams – themselves a challenge
to the conventional engineering wisdom – around which a series of programs would
develop the region's natural resources. At least, that was the theory implicit in the
passage of the Act and in the early policy of the TVA Board.[187]

Soon, however, it blew apart. To the TVA Board, Roosevelt appointed three members who would make a totally, explosively incompatible mixture. In the chairman's
seat he put A. E. Morgan, President of Antioch College: a utopian, ascetic, almost mystical visionary, who – though neither a socialist nor a Christian – had much in common
with the early utopian communitarians.[188] He saw the job as his life's opportunity to
realize his personal vision of a new physical and cultural environment: a vision he
believed FDR to share.[189] As second member, and as the expert on public power
development, he put David Lilienthal: an immensely ambitious, driving young man
with the reputation of stealing any show he joined.[190] And as third he chose Harcourt
A. Morgan, no relation of the chairman: President of the University of Tennessee, representative of the conservative agrarian interests at Vanderbilt, obsessed with the idea
of rural extension services and in particular with a scheme for a phosphate fertilizer
program, he readily made common cause with Lilienthal. Within five months they
were condemning the "variety" – later to become "vagaries" – in the chairman's grand
design.[191] Within two years, the chairman was openly criticizing his colleagues in the
public prints: a major tactical error, as it proved.[192]

Soon, Lilienthal and Harcourt A. Morgan outvoted the chair and divided responsibilities: Lilienthal was given power development, H. A. Morgan agricultural

[182]   Conkin, 1983, 20.
[183]   Conkin, 1983, 26–7.
[184]   Tugwell and Banfield, 1950, 47.
[185]   Lowitt, 1983, 35; Conkin, 1983, 26.
[186]   Morgan, 1974, 157; Lowitt, 1983, 37.
[187]   Neuse, 1983, 491–3; Ruttan, 1983, 151.
[188]   McCraw, 1970, 11; 1971, 38–9.
[189]   Morgan, 1974, 54–5, 155.
[190]   Morgan, 1974, 22.
[191]   Morgan, 1974, 55.
[192]   McCraw, 1970, 95, 107.

extension work. From now on, these were to be the TVA's work: A. E. Morgan's vision of a regional planning authority – for many, the true TVA mission – was simply buried.[193] The agriculturalists were sworn enemies of the Land Planning Division, whom they pejoratively called "the geographers"; they fought over powers to acquire public lands around reservoirs, which were progressively whittled down to the absolute minimum.[194] Their opponents described the agriculturalists as "fanatical," identifying less with the Authority than with local interests.[195] Finally, after two years of agonizing indecision – during which both A. E. Morgan and Lilienthal suffered nervous breakdowns – in 1938, FDR dismissed A. E. Morgan for "insubordination and contumacy"; "contumacy" was a word he was rumored to have found in a dictionary and used it in the hope no one would look it up; Morgan was later exonerated by a Congressional Committee.[196] Thus, despite Lilienthal's insistence in the much-read popular official account that policies were based on "principles of unity,"[197] they had evidently long since ceased to be based on anything but violent dissension.

That was the effective end of the TVA as a regional planning agency. One victim of these bitter battles was Benton MacKaye. He had written about Appalachian regional development as early as 1921–4, before his work on the New York Plan, apparently coining the term "New Deal"; his vision for Appalachia was based on hydro-electric power as the source of a new industrial revolution, as the basis for a 2,000-mile linear city, of which his famous wilderness trail would be but a small feature. Spelling out his ideas for the Tennessee Valley in an article of 1932, he was hired together with the architect-planner Tracy Augur, another RPAA supporter, to work in Earle Draper's Department of Regional Studies.[198] Hired to produce a comprehensive regional plan, what he called "The American Magna Carta of regional planning,"[199] he worked for the TVA for just two years between spring 1934 and summer 1936. Very soon, he became the "resident philosopher in a world occupied largely by builders and bureaucrats," and never moved beyond general principles;[200] soon sidelined, he was finished when Morgan went.[201] Thus, "Except for initiatives at Norris Reservoir, the TVA's regional planning ideas remained more rhetoric than reality";[202] MacKaye left when it became clear that his ideas could not be turned into a practical blueprint, though he did inspire a younger generation of TVA planners to carry the torch.[203]

[193] Selznick, 1949, 91–2, 149.
[194] Selznick, 1949, 152, 186–205.
[195] Selznick, 1949, 211–12.
[196] Creese, 1990, 9; McCraw, 1970, 108; Lowitt, 1983, 45.
[197] Lilienthal, 1944, 51.
[198] Creese, 1990, 57–60; Spann, 1996, 153–4.
[199] Spann, 1996, 155.
[200] Schaffer, 1990, 8.
[201] Creese, 1990, 57.
[202] Schaffer, 1986, 39.
[203] Schaffer, 1990, 11, 40.

Yet to the outside world at the time, the TVA was a triumphant example of "grass-roots democracy." Lilienthal's argument was that it was "a policy, fixed by law, that the federal regional agency work co-operatively with and through local and state agencies."[204] The reality seems to have been that this was a "protective ideology," allowing the TVA to appear as the champion of local institutions and interests; in order to justify its autonomy, and head off possible opposition from powerful local groups and individuals, it delegated the agricultural program to an organized constituency, the land-grant colleges, thus compromising much of its role as a conservation agency. (Selznick's study of the TVA acidly commented that "The way to get democratic administration is to begin by organizing a central government strong enough to eliminate those conditions which make much of our life grossly undemocratic."[205])

In one way, however, the TVA went against the ideology of the rural fundamentalists at Vanderbilt University. They, recall, had shared with RPAA the notion that movement from the land should be slowed and even reversed; and FDR had appeared to side with them. Yet in practice, under the Lilienthal–H. A. Morgan alliance, the TVA became more and more a power-generating authority, devoted to creation of a big industrial-urban base. As Tugwell put it, "From 1936 on the TVA should have been called the Tennessee Valley Power Production and Flood Control Corporation."[206] By 1944, it was already the second largest producer of power in the United States, generating half as much as the entire national production of 1941.[207] The reason was ironic: it was the huge increase in power demand arising from the establishment of the Atomic Energy Authority's plutonium production plant at Oak Ridge, as basis for production of the Atomic Bomb.[208] The one element that Roosevelt had removed from the TVA prescription, munitions production, was now driving the economic development of the Valley.

The dams and the reservoirs must have looked good to the pilgrim tourist, rather like all those dams on the Volga and the Dnieper, over which left-wing visitors enthused at the end of the 1930s. But of regional planning – especially that radical variant espoused by the RPAA – there was an imperceptible residue: community development, health, and educational services received a minuscule sliver of the total budget;[209] the new town of Norris next to the great Tennessee dam, though planned by an RPAA member (Tracy Augur) and extolled by Benton MacKaye as a first step in regional community development, was most accurately described by the TVA's Planning Director as a "rural village."[210] A. E. Morgan's idealistic hopes for Norris – a town where rich and poor would live together, and where the inhabitants

---

[204]   Lilienthal, 1944, 153.
[205]   Tugwell and Banfield, 1950, 54.
[206]   Tugwell and Banfield, 1950, 50; Ruttan, 1983, 151–2.
[207]   Lilienthal, 1944, 17.
[208]   Hewlett and Anderson, 1962, 77, 105–8, 116–22, 130; Allardice and Trapnell, 1974, 15–17.
[209]   Ruttan, 1983, 157–8.
[210]   Johnson, 1984, 35.

Figure 5.8 Norris, Tennessee. Tracy Augur's small gem for the Tennessee Valley Authority: one of the few manifestations of its original regional planning ideals, which it soon lost. *Source*: Peter Hall.

would combine agriculture and craft industries – were never fulfilled. Built in a hurry, minimally financed, the tiny town – a mere 1,500 people – is almost buried in dense woods; so informal is its layout that its origins might never be guessed.[211] Designed for 1,000 houses on 4,500 acres, it ended up with only 294 houses, at 2.7 families per acre, tucked away in the woods.[212] This was deliberate. The form was to be anti-urban, "loose, bucolic, pastoral, running free."[213] It was "a large model implemented in a small way":[214] an interesting footnote to garden-city history, in terms of the RPAA's grand vision it represents a ridiculous mouse. The fact was that America – even New Deal America – was not politically ready for that vision.[215] Morgan's two partners told Morgan there would be no more Norrises; they sensed that Congress was implacably opposed to public housing.[216] Catherine Bauer's lobbying would change that, not long after, but in a very different geographical context.

There was another more sinister aspect, glossed over in Creese's description of idyllic parks where "people, particularly in the South, tended to bridge over social

[211] Schaffer, 1984, passim; Creese, 1990, 248.
[212] Creese, 1990, 240, 262.
[213] Creese, 1990, 251.
[214] Creese, 1990, 249.
[215] Schaffer, 1982, 224–5, 230.
[216] Creese, 1990, 261.

and economic difficulties with great politeness and courtesy," helping to stave off armed insurrection. In reality, as illuminated by Nancy L. Grant, in 1938 and again in 1940 the park management reiterated that there were no plans to provide Negro facilities at Norris. Among the reasons given was another plan to build Booker T. Washington Park in Chattanooga, over 100 miles away, where surveys had shown over 400,000 black people living within 200 miles of the site. The park at Chattanooga was built, with facilities for swimming, boating, picnicking, and two unusual features: a camping ground and vacation camps. "These last two features," Grant notes, "were provided because no private tourist areas admitted blacks." She finds that there were complaints about the park's proximity to an industrial site and about the swimming pool (for 400,000 people) that remained closed for lack of pumping equipment. (Donald Krueckeberg drily comments that the TVA is primarily a hydro-power authority; moving water is what they do!) And, "in addition, there were no lavatories in the park."[217] Krueckeberg comments that this "certainly helps explain why there were no armed insurrections. There were more pressing matters, little difficulties that evidently did not appear in Creese's glossy pictures."[218]

The Vision Realized: London

Thus, by one of the many ironies in this history, the real impact of Mumford and Stein and Chase and MacKaye was not to be on their own unsympathetic country, but on Europe's capitals. And there London was to provide the exemplar. Throughout the 1920s and 1930s, British and American planners continued a vigorous two-way transatlantic traffic. Thomas Adams crossed the ocean almost every year, sometimes three or four times a year, between 1911 and 1938; Stein and Wright met Howard and Unwin in England in 1923; Geddes met the RPAA in 1923, Unwin and Howard in 1925.[219] So, throughout these doldrum years, a small group of planners was already applying American ideas in a variety of British contexts.

One of the most successful, ironically, was the RPAA's *bête noir*. During his years on the New York Regional Plan, Thomas Adams continued as a partner in the planning practice of Adams, Thompson, and Fry, who between 1924 and 1932 produced eight out of twelve exercises in the emerging field of advisory regional plans for the area around London. To these plans Adams brought many American concepts: parkways in West Middlesex and the Mole Valley, green girdles and green wedges to limit urban sprawl.[220] But the philosophy, as in New York, was planning as the art of the possible: planning should remain an advisory function, it should not try to achieve more than marginal changes, and it must work within the limits of existing powers.

---

[217]   Grant, 1991, 88.
[218]   Krueckeberg, 1997, 274–5.
[219]   Simpson, 1985, 193; Dal Co, 1979, 233.
[220]   Simpson, 1985, 174–5, 181, 193.

The remaining four plans carry an equally significant name: they come from the partnership of Davidge, Abercrombie, and Archibald. Leslie Patrick Abercrombie (1879–1957), ninth child of a Manchester businessman, oddly owed his career to gutter journalism; starting his career as an architect, he converted to town planning through a research fellowship established at the University of Liverpool by the soap magnate William Hesketh Lever, founder of Port Sunlight, with the proceeds of a successful libel action against a newspaper. He proved so apt that in 1914, when the first Professor of Civic Design at Liverpool, Stanley Adshead, moved to a new chair in London, Abercrombie was his logical successor.[221] Through his editorship of the *Town Planning Review*, he early acquired unrivalled knowledge of what was happening in the world of planning. Even before World War One he won a prize for a town plan for Dublin, which, setting the city in its regional context, demonstrated his debt to Geddes (who happened to be on the jury).[222] But it also interestingly demonstrated two contrasted aspects of his personality and approach, which would persist. The city center would be Haussmannized, with boulevards, street widenings, a Dublin "Place de la Concorde" and sites for new public building – even a bourse. But outside the center, to accommodate 60,000 people to be "thinned out" from the city-center slums, Abercrombie and his Liverpool colleagues developed suburban housing layout plans reflecting the new ideas being developed across the Irish Sea in response to the 1909 Housing and Town Planning Act of England and Wales. In parallel, the plan provided for a hierarchy of open spaces, metropolitan bus and underground transport systems, the suburbanization of industry, and even extensive infilling of Dublin Bay to accommodate housing, open space, and industry.[223]

After it, his growing reputation led him to a pioneer exercise in regional planning for the Doncaster area, in 1920–2, and thus in 1925 to a plan for East Kent: a new coalfield, set in the garden of England, in which Abercrombie boldly set out to demonstrate a Geddesian thesis that in the neotechnic age, even palaeotechnic industry could be absorbed into the landscape. He proposed eight small new towns, each in a fold in the rolling chalk landscape, set within a continuous green belt;[224] a prophetic echo, down to the precise number, of his strategy 18 years later for Greater London. That report, widely reviewed though in practical terms a failure, set him on a career in regional planning that would lead him on to the heights of the Greater London Plan.

But Abercrombie owed another important debt, to a report that has almost been forgotten but that he himself acknowledged. The London Society, founded in 1912, was an extraordinary assemblage of the Great and the Good. Its chair was Sir Aston Webb, architect of the Victoria and Albert Museum, Admiralty Arch, and the facade of Buckingham Palace. Its Council and Executive Committee members included Sir Reginald Blomfield, President of the Royal Institute of British Architects, Raymond Unwin, Stanley Adshead, and a host of architects including T. H. Mawson

[221] Dix, 1978, 329–30.
[222] Dix, 1978, 332.
[223] Dix, 1978, 151.
[224] Dix, 1978, 337.

and E. L. Lutyens; its Vice-Presidents included Lord Curzon, former Viceroy of India, John Burns, then President of the Local Government Board, Lord Northcliffe, the owner of *The Times*, and the retail tycoon Gordon Selfridge.[225] Fundamentally, despite a mission to evangelize ordinary Londoners, the Society was a middle-class group of male professionals; *The Builder* in March 1914 commented, "Architects are the backbone of the London Society."

Significantly, it was on October 1, 1914, that a special meeting was called to discuss an opportunity for providing employment for architects and planners during war time: the creation of a Development Plan for London, "special consideration being given to the new arterial roads and the provision of open spaces." Those attending were architects: Sir Aston Webb, Carmichael Thomas, Raymond Unwin, H. V. Lanchester, and Professor Adshead. A Plan Committee was formed (other members included Arthur Crow, W. R. Davidge, H. J. Leaning, and D. B. Niven), and by 1916 they had virtually finished; they called it their "War Work."[226] By 1920 it was published and exhibited "at various Town Planning exhibitions around the country"; in 1929 it was the subject of an exhibition at the London Museum. Although it never became the "official" plan for London, in December 1925, Abercrombie presided over a meeting of the Society in which he wholeheartedly supported the work. When Abercrombie finally produced his own plan for the London County Council (LCC) almost 20 years later, he acknowledged his debt to contributions made by "the great voluntary societies either taking in the whole scope of the physical environment or devoted to some special aspect of it," saying,

> There is finally the London Society, pioneer of Metropolitan Planning; to its Vice-Chairman, Mr. W. R. Davidge, PPTPI, we owe a debt for help and guidance given, out of his inexhaustible knowledge, towards the solution of London's problems, so many of which he himself is actively engaged in resolving.[227]

The failure in implementation, though, was indicative: here as elsewhere, regional plans were advisory; they depended on cooperation among many different small district planning authorities, often not forthcoming. Particularly this applied to limiting suburban sprawl, which just then (Chapter 3) was becoming a very vexed question in southern England. Abercrombie in East Kent thought that even with existing powers, local authorities could buy up the land to build new towns; the North Middlesex Joint Committee also advocated satellite towns.[228] But nothing was done in either place. Otherwise, both Adams's and Abercrombie's plans sought to achieve control by rural – that is, very-low-density – zoning; on the efficacy of that, opinions differed. Even so, according to one calculation the 12 plans together set aside enough land to house 16 million people at the then prevailing densities.[229]

[225] Beaufoy, 1997, 135–6.
[226] Beaufoy, 1997, 149.
[227] Beaufoy, 1997, 150.
[228] Abercrombie, 1926, 39–40; Cherry, 1974, 91.
[229] Beaufoy, 1933, 201, 204, 212; Simpson, 1985, 176, 180–1.

The fact was that these plans, impressive as they might look on paper, were little more than ameliorative exercises. Indeed, they were probably less effective than Adams's New York plan for the simple reason that in England organized business had less clout. The more radical concept of regional planning, represented by the RPAA, could come only if by legislation the British government gave comprehensive powers to plan a whole region, including the ability to stop urban sprawl; and of this, as seen in Chapter 3, there was no trace down to 1939. This is well illustrated by the sad story of Raymond Unwin's Committee.

In 1927, Neville Chamberlain used his position as Minister of Health to give a boost to regional planning by the creation of a Greater London Regional Planning Committee, covering some 1,800 square miles within a 25-mile radius of central London, and with 45 members from local authorities; in 1929, on retirement from the Ministry of Health, Raymond Unwin was made its technical adviser.[230] Its interim report of the same year proposed a complete reversal of the then planning system; instead of planning authorities trying to reserve pieces of land for open space, they should allocate certain areas for building, on the assumption that all the remainder be left open: towns against a background of open space. This was more radical than the simple idea of limiting London's growth by a green belt, which had been invented as early as 1892 by Reginald Brabazon, twelfth Earl of Meath, after a visit to American parkways, and had been taken up by the influential London Society in 1915.[231] It would require an overall Joint Regional Planning Authority with executive powers over larger regional matters, including reservations for building. Local authorities, it thought, should be able to deny development without compensation, but offer ex gratia payments from a common pool owned by all the local landowners – a proposal, originating from Unwin, that the then Minister found impracticable.[232]

Meanwhile, in a major address of 1930, Unwin had spelt out his concept of regional planning: "Regional Planning schemes should be made effective," he said, "…without depriving the local authorities within the region of their freedom to make Town Planning Schemes for their areas." "The main purpose of the plan," he went on, "is to secure the best distribution of the dwellings, the work and the play places of the people. The method shall be to lay out this distribution in a convenient pattern on a protected background of open land."[233] "If development were guided into reasonably self-contained nuclei, forming attractive urban groups of different sizes, spaced out on an adequate background of open land, there would be ample space in the Region for any increase in population which may reasonably be expected, still leaving the greater part of the area as open land."[234] But at present, "All land is potentially building land"; anybody could build anywhere, so that sporadic building and ribbon development would continue.[235]

---

[230] Miller M., 1989b, 24; Miller, M., 1992, 189.
[231] Aalen, 1989, 141–3; Miller, M., 1989b, 18–19; Beaufoy, 1997, 150.
[232] Greater London Regional Planning Committee (hereafter GLRPC), 1929, 4–7; Jackson, F., 1985, 147.
[233] Unwin, 1930, 186.
[234] Unwin, 1930, 189.
[235] Unwin, 1930, 186.

At this point Robert Schmidt made an appearance in London, revealing the interest within the Ministry of Health in his regional planning work in the Ruhr. In 1928 he was invited to London to speak at the Town Planning Institute. Although fog prevented his flight, an impressive audience heard George Pepler read Schmidt's paper. They included the future leader of the LCC and Deputy Prime Minister, Herbert Morrison, who had met Schmidt in the Ruhr while part of a Labour Party delegation the previous year. Schmidt's work was particularly close to Pepler's heart because at the time he was trying to persuade British local authorities to join together voluntarily to undertake regional planning to guide and coordinate their own local statutory plans. He naturally envied the legal force that Schmidt could theoretically wield to compel the Ruhr's local authorities. Yet he increasingly understood that, compulsion or not, Schmidt's powers of persuasion remained essential to carry through the regional plan.[236] In 1929, Harris reported on this and other German developments to the recently formed Greater London Regional Planning Committee, of which he was part-time secretary. Unwin, its chief planner, enthusiastically adopted the proposal for a "green girdle" around London. *The Times* newspaper in 1924 had already reported on Fritz Schumacher and Konrad Adenauer's notable plan, initiated shortly before, to create a double green belt (Grüngürtel) for Cologne. This was reported on more fully for the Committee in 1929, detailing the special land readjustment powers by which it had been created.[237]

The Committee's final report appeared in 1933. It came back to the same theme: there should be a narrow green girdle around the existing built-up area of Greater London, to provide space for playing fields and open spaces; through this could run an orbital parkway; outside that, "every effort should be made by full powers in the Town and Country Planning Act to define the areas ... which may be allowed [for] building development, and thus secure the background of open lands from which public open spaces may be obtained as and when needed."[238] New industrial areas should be planned in self-contained satellites within 12 miles of central London, and in garden cities between 12 and 25 miles distant. And both industrialists and developers, the report argued, could benefit from such a clear plan; the problem, again, was to compensate those whose land would not be developed, and this would require legislation.[239] All this would call for a new ad hoc authority, empowered to acquire and manage land and open space and to coordinate local planning schemes. As an alternative, local authorities could buy unbuilt land in their area, but compensation would present enormous problems.[240]

Already, when this final report emerged, it had effectively been put in cold storage by government spending cuts.[241] As early as 1931, Unwin was deeply depressed about the

236   Unwin, 1930, 122.
237   Ward, 2010, 121.
238   GLRPC, 1933, 83.
239   GLRPC, 1933, 95–9, 101–2; Crow, 1996, 405–9.
240   Miller, M., 1992, 202.
241   GB Royal Commission Geographical Distribution, June 16, 1938, paras 59, 66, 69.

Committee's future: "My chance of a Green Belt is gone ... and I expect our Regional work to be cut down to ⅓ or ¼ this year."[242] On that much he proved wrong: when Labour gained control of the LCC in March 1934, its leader Herbert Morrison was a supporter, and after a long-running Public Inquiry approval was granted in May 1935.[243]

That was a minor victory, but there were major defeats. The Town and Country Planning Bill, before Parliament in 1931, fell victim to the election; it was revived and passed in 1932, but in a weakened form. Unwin, embittered, decided that the possibility of good legislation had been put back for years;[244] in a sense he was right, since it took until 1947 to secure the powers his committee had thought vital. Increasingly he deserted Britain; in 1936 he succeeded Henry Wright as Visiting Professor at Columbia.[245] Arriving in the United States just before the outbreak of war for an international forum which was canceled, he and his wife were stranded there; after a two-month illness, he died of jaundice in his daughter's country home at Old Lyme, Connecticut, on June 28, 1940.[246] A few weeks before, his home, Wyldes, had been hit by an incendiary bomb, destroying many of his papers;[247] a sad and ironic outcome, given his passionate love of German cities.

One thing he had, however, achieved: there was at least a clear vision of a future planned region. Not all of it was new; as with Howard's ideas, curious students can find individual elements of the plan in George Pepler's "green girdle" and associated parkway, of 1911, or Austin Crow's plan for 10 "cities of health" at a distance of 14 miles from London, the same year.[248] And, of course, Howard's diagram of Social City provides the theoretical basis for almost all subsequent schemes.[249] But it is more fully worked out than any of these; and the link between it and the 1944 Abercrombie plan is clear. Unwin had, in a sense, atoned for his great apostasy of 1918–19, when he had steered the course of English urban development away from garden cities and towards suburban satellites. It was a trend that, much later, even Osborn said he could probably have not avoided, given the state of opinion at that time.[250]

But in the 11 years between Unwin's final report and the Abercrombie plan, as seen in Chapter 4, a lot of water had flowed under Thames bridges. Neville Chamberlain, on becoming Prime Minister, had almost as a first step created the Barlow Commission. Patrick Abercrombie, appointed to it, had been carefully steered by Frederic Osborn to his minority report and his dissentient memorandum with their demands for a national planning framework, for stringent general powers over industrial location, and for powers to make regional plans stick;[251] Reith had

[242] Miller, M., 1989b, 35.
[243] Miller, M., 1989b, 37; Miller, M., 1992, 205.
[244] Jackson, F., 1985, 154.
[245] Miller, M., 2000, 23.
[246] Miller, 2000, 25.
[247] Miller and Gray, 1992, 108.
[248] Pepler, 1911, 614–15; Crow, 1911, 411–12.
[249] Hall, 1973, II, 52–5.
[250] Hughes, 1971, 62.
[251] Hughes, 1971, 271–2; Dix, 1978, 345–6.

Figure 5.9 The New Town idea from Howard to Abercrombie. The notion of a host of satellite cities around a metropolis, from Howard (1898), through Purdom (1921) and Unwin (1929–33), to Abercrombie's definitive Greater London Plan of 1944. *Source*: Unwin Hyman.

come and gone as first Minister of Planning. And Abercrombie had collaborated with Forshaw, the LCC's Chief Architect, on the County of London Plan.

For purists like Mumford or Osborn, Abercrombie could never be forgiven for selling the pass, in the County Plan, on the vital question of density and decentralization: "I was too confident about Abercrombie," Osborn wrote to Mumford, "I kick myself that I didn't sit on his doorstep at County Hall as I did on Barlow's doorstep during the sittings of the Commission. But I could not have believed that any planner could state in full detail the case for Decentralization, and then produce a Plan that doesn't do the main thing necessary – permit the majority of people to have decent family homes."[252] A year later, in his Greater London Plan, when Abercrombie was free of the LCC influence, he came closer to the Osborn view in arguing for densities of 100 and 70 persons per acre, the latter allowing everyone to go into houses, the former giving 80% houses, so that no family need go into a flat unless it wanted one. But the LCC, for Osborn, were too concerned at the loss of votes and rateable value, and so settled for what he called "token" decentralization, or just over a million people.[253]

Osborn, of course, was less than fair; Abercrombie, working with LCC officials, must have been acutely sensible that here above all, planning was the art of the possible. And, viewed as half of the single regional plan which the two volumes represent, the County Plan has striking qualities that should have commended it to the most pure-minded RPAA member. There is, first, its insistence on Geddesian survey methods to tease out the elusive community structure of London, that metropolis of villages. Then, there is its brilliant combination of Perry's neighborhood-unit principle with Stein and Wright's roads hierarchy – as interpreted by a Scotland Yard traffic policeman, Alker Tripp, in two influential books[254] – to create a new spatial order for London in which fast-traffic highways not only solve the traffic congestion problem but also give definition and shape to the reconstruction communities they separate, by flowing through green strips which additionally bring much-needed open space to London. Georgian and Victorian London's major problems – congestion, obsolescence, incoherence, lack of greenery – are tackled simultaneously, in a solution that imposes order on the world's least orderly great city; but in a way so natural that no one would notice.[255]

Specifically, the County Plan used the new road system to create a cellular London; the new order was to be implicitly organic.[256] Abercrombie's debt to Geddes is clear here, though there was also an important strain that came from Perry via Wesley Dougill, Abercrombie's inspired assistant and ex-Liverpool colleague, an enthusiastic advocate of the neighborhood-unit principle for London, who died as the plan was nearing completion.[257] The important point is that in going from the County Plan to the Greater London Plan, Abercrombie retains this same organic structure. There is first the basis in concentric rings, of decreasing intensity of popularity and activity: Inner (slightly larger than the County, with central London forming an innermost ring), Outer or suburban, Green Belt, Outer Country. Then, again, there is the way in which each of these is neatly defined by a ring road, part of the

252 Hughes, 1971, 40.
253 Yelling 1994, 140; Hughes, 1971, 40; for further discussion see Chapter 7.
254 Tripp, 1938; 1942.
255 Forshaw and Abercrombie, 1943, 3–10; Hart, 1976, 54–87.
256 Hart, 1976, 58–9, 78–9.
257 Forshaw and Abercrombie, 1943, v; Perry, 1939, 79–80.

hierarchical system that produces the cells: the innermost A ring encloses the central area, the arterial B ring effectively defines the edge of inner London, the C ring runs through the suburbs and the arterial D ring encloses them, the parkway E ring is the central feature of the green belt and helps define the start of the outermost ring.[258]

And again, there is the use of open space as a structuring element. Here, Abercrombie pays his debts to Unwin:

> Sir Raymond Unwin first posed the alternative solutions to London's outward spread: either a continuous zone of free-entry for universal building at varying degrees of density (some of them, in high-class [*sic*] districts, quite low), its continuity broken at intervals by areas of green (as public open space) and, in practice, by patches of farm-land left over from the builder's demand: or a continuous green background of open country in which are embedded at suitable places compact spots of red, representing building. We have unhesitatingly adopted the second alternative, which he advocated, for the two outer rings.[259]

There would be "a gigantic Green Belt around built-up London," with special stress on outdoor recreation; but there should also be "lesser girdles for the separate communities, old and new; this local girdle need not be wide, if beyond it is open agricultural country." Finally, green wedges would run inward from the Green Belt into the heart of built-up London.[260]

Of the total of 1,033,000 people to find new homes as a result of reconstruction and redevelopment in inner London, all but 125,000 would move beyond the Green Belt: 644,000 would go to the Outer Country Ring (383,000 to new towns, 261,000 to extensions of existing ones), nearly 164,000 just beyond this ring but within 50 miles of London, 100,000 farther still. There would be eight new towns, of maximum population 60,000 people, between roughly 20 and 35 miles from the center of London.[261] The point was that out here, the organic structure would be retained; but it would now be turned inside out. Instead of highways and narrow park strips defining the communities, the basic element would now be the green background, against which the individual communities – each, like those in London, consisting of smaller cells or neighborhoods – would appear as islands of urban development.

It was the vision of the RPAA, at last realized. Mumford himself, in a letter to Osborn, called it "the best single document on planning, in every respect, that had come out since Howard's book itself; in fact it may almost be treated as the mature form of the organism whereof *Garden Cities of Tomorrow* was the embryo."[262] "The original job of making the ideal credible has been performed," he continued, "and the main task now is to master the political methods that will most effectively translate it into a reality. We have not yet reached that stage here ... And

---

[258]   Abercrombie, 1945, 7–10.
[259]   Abercrombie, 1945, 11.
[260]   Abercrombie, 1945, 11.
[261]   Abercrombie, 1945, 14.
[262]   Hughes, 1971, 141.

I fear the results of our immaturity here once the post-war building boom ... gets under way."[263]

A latter generation of academic planners has deconstructed Abercrombie. Michael Hebbert has powerfully argued that London's uniquely chaotic structure – the collection of villages celebrated in the traditional (but true) cliché – simply needed leaving well alone.[264] But Abercrombie's vision could have preserved all this, and more: it would have enhanced the structure, because the villages would have been more clearly defined by his planned urban motorways, and the buses would still have trundled along the radial roads past the shopping centers, now free of the chaos of the other traffic. Abercrombie loved London, his adopted city. His plans did no violence to it.

His vision was so compelling because it was expressed in powerful visual imagery.[265] Aerial photographs portrayed endless vistas of haphazard and uncoordinated urban growth stretching to the horizon.[266] Lord Latham, Labour Leader of the LCC, emphasized the point: the plan centered on the visualization of a "series of great projects extending over the next half century ... forming part of a general pattern by which ordered progress could be achieved."[267] And the timing was propitious; the launch, on July 9, 1943, coincided with the allied invasion of Sicily, and a fresh Soviet offensive on the eastern front, together with intensified bombing of German cities. The London *Evening News* placed its announcement of the "50-Year Plan to Rebuild London" next to front-page banner headlines and photographs showing the devastation in Cologne.[268]

But there was another turning point, on the Home Front. In December 1942, William Beveridge announced his comprehensive review of the social security system, *Social Insurance and Allied Services*. Six months later, almost simultaneously with the *County of London Plan*, R. A. Butler, the Education Secretary, produced his far-reaching white paper on postwar state education. Key LCC Labour politicians, such as Herbert Morrison and Lewis Silkin, worked to position the plan as part of this debate over national reconstruction. In his foreword, Latham deliberately echoed Beveridge – as there were giants blocking the path to social security, so similar giants obstructed the march of planning: "conflicting interests, private rights, an outworn ... scale of values, and lack of vision." The *Daily Mirror* presented the plan as part of a radical agenda, a "war without end."[269]

Abercrombie's own view of the world, reflecting his youth in late Victorian and Edwardian liberal England, was "grounded in his belief in the power of professional expertise and in the confidence of a genteel, high-bourgeois outlook," shared by

[263] Hughes, 1971, 141.
[264] Hebbert, 1998, passim.
[265] Mort, 2004, 124.
[266] Mort, 2004, 134.
[267] Mort, 2004, 125.
[268] Mort, 2004, 126.
[269] Mort, 2004, 126–7.

many of his generation, intellectuals like Keynes and Beveridge, politicians like R. A. Butler and Anthony Crosland. It was an eclectic, even contradictory, set of values: Frank Mort writes that "In Abercrombie's case competing accounts of the urban future struggled for ascendancy, often within the same planning statement and within his own social personality: monumental civism versus communityminded programs, a grandiose urban aesthetic as opposed to an intense localism, state-driven schemes versus more commercially nuanced expansion. This complex legacy continued to shape political and professional debate about the future of London during the postwar years."[270]

The "political methods" were learned soon enough. The new Minister for Town Planning, Lewis Silkin, quickly told the planning authorities that the Abercrombie plan would serve as the interim development guide for the region.[271] Even before this, as told in Chapter 4, he had accepted the principle of the new towns and had appointed John Reith to head a committee to tell him how to build them. With equal dispatch the committee gave him the answer: establish bureaucracies, in the form of development corporations, to bypass the complexities and foot-draggings and com-promises of local democracy. In a strictly instrumental sense, it proved right: the New Towns Act received the Royal Assent in the summer of 1946, just as Abercrombie was retiring from his academic chair to an afterlife of consultancy and touring (dur-ing his Australian visit in 1948 a councilor referred to him as "Saint Patrick," which was brilliantly right);[272] all the eight Abercrombie new towns were designated by 1949 (though not always in the places he proposed), and were well on the way to completion by the mid-1960s. The machinery for the other major element of the plan, the expansions of existing towns, took longer to establish and even longer to put into motion: the relevant Town Development Act was passed in 1952, the first notable results did not appear until the 1960s.

But they too finally appeared as major elements of the Abercrombie landscape. Even though during the 1950s and 1960s implementation almost became over-whelmed under unexpected population growth and continued industrial development in and around London – necessitating three further and much bigger new towns, started in the second half of the 1960s – an odd fact is that the basic Abercrombie principles proved remarkably resilient to stresses and strains. Odd, because as the American commentator Donald Foley noticed, the Abercrombie plan's most striking feature was its fixed, unitary quality, which "stresses the primacy of striving toward a positively-stated future spatial form as a physical environmental goal product. The plan is characteristically presented for a hypothetical future point or period of time."[273] Yet, as Foley also noticed, it soon came to be absorbed into a political and economic process within central government that represented the very opposite: an adaptive approach, evolutionary rather than deterministic, that

[270]   Mort, 2004, 150–1.
[271]   Hart, 1976, 55.
[272]   Gawler, 1963, 24, quoted in Amati and Freestone, 2009, 619.
[273]   Foley, 1963, 56.

recognizes the importance of political and economic decisions in the planning process.[274] And, in this very different context, it worked: it proved capable of being bent without breaking. Details soon had to be changed: Abercrombie's new town at Ongar was dropped, while one in the Pitsea–Laindon area appeared; White Waltham, west of London, was dropped and replaced by Bracknell nearby;[275] later, after a change of government, the whole policy came into question, and was nearly truncated prematurely.[276] Somehow, it survived; and the London region is one of the few places in the world where it is possible to see the Howard–Geddes–Mumford vision of the world made actual.

But finally, doubts remain. One is that the policy did survive precisely because, in a complex and also conservative society, it served – imperfectly, to be sure – as a consensus among very different, indeed conflicting, political views. Liberal–socialist idealists could join forces with the conservative squirearchy to support a plan that simultaneously preserved the English countryside (and the traditional English rural way of life), and also provided model communities that would consciously seek to erode traditional English class barriers. It was useful that, as Robert Freestone has commented, "Greenbelts are said to be practically the entire issue on which all parties agree."[277] "They are able to transcend local tensions by a kind of mystical, symbolic status, which deems them capable of delivering all things to all people."[278] So this fragile alliance did survive, at least until the late 1970s when it fell victim to demographic and economic stagnation; but the result was far from the original vision of the founders, which in the process almost became obscured. The inhabitants of Stevenage and Bracknell were certainly part of the neotechnic economy, but they did not, as Kropotkin had supposed, spend part of their days in the fields.

What in fact triumphed was a very different vision: a top-down patrician vision devised and imposed by benign and superbly capable politicians and devoted public servants. And, for two decades, it worked. In 1967, the peak year for housing completions in the United Kingdom, the machine was producing regional plans for the South East and the West Midlands and the North West, starting Milton Keynes and Peterborough and Telford and several other new towns, and beginning the first subregional plans based on the new systems-planning methods imported from American planners like West Churchman. Brian McLoughlin was working on the Leicester–Leicestershire study while writing a textbook of the new planning approach in his spare time. The Redcliffe–Maud Commission was commissioning research on city regions as the basis for reorganizing English local government. The Roskill Commission was using a similar evidence-based approach to find a location for the third London airport. The government had a vast phalanx of professional planners embedded in the Ministry of Housing and Local Government (MHLG),

[274]   Foley, 1963, 173.
[275]   Cullingworth, 1979, 53, 82–6, 89–93.
[276]   Cullingworth, 1979, 147.
[277]   Freestone, 2002, 79.
[278]   Freestone, 2002, 79.

the precursor of today's Department for Communities and Local Government; the legendary Jimmy James was succeeded as Chief Planner by the legendary Wilfred Burns. A high-level Planning Advisory Group (PAG), including leading professionals from local government, the private sector, and officials from MHLG, the Ministry of Transport, and the Scottish Development Department, had published its report on the design of a Mark II development plan system.[279,280] John Delafons, who was the Group's Secretary, commented long after that "perhaps the most significant effect of the PAG report was the fillip that it gave to planning and to planners at a time when the statutory planning system had run slowly into an impasse ... By expressing such positive confidence in the potential of planning, PAG released a lot of pent-up energy in the planning profession and provided the stimulus that was needed."[281]

Bliss it was in that dawn to be alive, but to be young was very heaven.[282] It was, in retrospect, the high-water mark of a belief in such a total, centralized, top-down, expertly based but also benign planning. The inspirations were many: our own garden-city/new-town movement, so successfully pursued by the Town and Country Planning Association; ideas from Stockholm and Copenhagen; the French style of indicative planning, then enjoying a huge vogue. And one can precisely date the point of its reversal: the collapse in 1967 of the National Plan, center of the Wilson government's policy package, in a classic balance-of-payments crisis; the huge weakening of the Department of Economic Affairs, created by Wilson to replace the Treasury as manager of macro-economic policy, and its subsequent rapid disappearance. Then came the Heath government of 1970 and the abandonment of the Redcliffe–Maud recommendations for city-region government across England, which fatally compromised the implementation of the new structure-plan/local-plan system of planning proposed in the PAG Report and embodied into legislation in the dying days of the Wilson government. The vision imploded from within, because the critical implementation mechanisms were lacking.

Planning, it can be seen in retrospect, then went on a long downward slide. And it was much criticized even at the time, for being too prescriptive and too restrictive; even then, a group of us concluded in a study in 1973, it was failing to generate enough development of the right kinds in the right places; even then, local politics were intervening to paralyze the process.[283] And in the 1970s, as deindustrialization gripped the economies of the great cities, the energies of planners and other urban professionals were massively diverted into the task of urban regeneration. That continued into the 1980s; though the means – urban development corporations, enterprise zones – were radically different, the underlying objectives were the same as under the previous Labour administration.

279   Delafons, 1997, 374–5.
280   Delafons, 1997, 373–4.
281   Delafons, 1997, 384.
282   Wordsworth, "The French Revolution as It Appeared to Enthusiasts at Its Commencement," cited in Hall, 2012, 252.
283   Hall, Thomas, Gracey, and Drewett, 1973.

But then and subsequently, the wider task of planning the overall pattern of town and country development remained. And, because demographic growth has continued to be strong, the underlying pressures and the tensions have never gone away. In the early years of the Blair government, there was a fitful return to the grand strategic planning visions of the 1960s, in John Prescott's Sustainable Communities Strategy of 2003. And there was a determined attempt again to develop regional plans with regional and sub-regional development targets, above all for new housing. But again there was a tragic failure, comparable to the abandonment of city regional government in 1974: the rejection by voters in the North East, in a sample referendum intended to unleash a process across England, of a democratically elected regional assembly. This idea, which echoed a similar proposal in the Redcliffe–Maud report 40 years earlier, was vital to give democratic legitimacy to the whole planning process. Without it, it became all too easy for the Coalition to consign the entire regional structure to the waste bin, bringing us back full circle to the 1980s.[284]

The concluding verdict is a very paradoxical one. The Abercrombie plan showed no sign of challenging the autonomy of one of the most centralized and monolithic bureaucracies to be found in any western democracy; on the contrary, the processes of implementation actually strengthened it, and the quality of civilization in Basildon or Crawley does not yet recall the glories of fifth-century Athens or thirteenth-century Florence. Nor, though the planning system did preserve the countryside, did it produce anything like the integrated regional development of which Chase and MacKaye dreamed; the people of the Berkshire and Hertfordshire countryside eat vegetables flown in the holds of 747s from all over the world and brought to them via London wholesale markets, and the grubbed-up hedgerows and industrialized farm buildings bear witness to the fact that for the British farmer it is the account-book that rules.

Of course, much does remain of the vision of the pioneers: the new towns are self-evidently good places to live in and above all to grow up in, they do exist in harmony with their surrounding countryside; the sheer mindless ugliness of the worst of the old sprawl has been eliminated. But it is not quite as rich, worthy, and high-minded as they hoped: a good life, but not a new civilization. Perhaps the place was wrong; the English, those archetypally cozy people of low expectations, were the last people to achieve it. Or, as with Gatsby's dream, it was already out there behind them, never to be realized.

[284] Hall, 2012, 252–3.

The City of Monuments

Make no little plans. They have no magic to stir men's blood and probably
themselves will not be realized. Make big plans; aim high in hope and work,
remembering that a noble, logical diagram once rewarded will never die, but
long after we are gone will be a living thing, asserting itself with ever-growing
insistency. Remember that our sons and grandsons are going to do things that
would stagger us. Let your watchword be order and your beacon beauty.

Daniel Burnham, *The Plan of Chicago* (1909)

Why always the biggest? I do this to restore to each individual German his
self-respect.

Adolf Hitler, speech to construction workers (1939)
(quoted by Albert Speer, *Inside the Third Reich*, 1970)

Cities of Tomorrow: An Intellectual History of Urban Planning and Design Since 1880,
Fourth Edition. Peter Hall.
© 2014 Peter Hall. Published 2014 by John Wiley & Sons, Ltd.

6

The City of Monuments

The City Beautiful Movement: Chicago, New Delhi, Berlin, Moscow, 1900–1945

The City Beautiful movement had its nineteenth-century origins on the boulevards and promenades of the great European capitals: Haussmann's reconstruction of Paris under Napoleon III and the almost simultaneous construction of the Vienna Ringstrasse were its classic models. Yet its twentieth-century manifestations came mainly in other places and cultures: in the great commercial cities of middle and western America, where civic leaders built to overcome collective inferiority complexes and boost business; and in the newly designated capitals of far-flung pieces of Empire, where British civil servants commissioned plans that would express imperial dominance and racial exclusiveness. Then, ironically, the City Beautiful came back full circle to its geographical and spiritual point of origin: in Europe, culminating in the 1930s, totalitarian dictators sought to impose megalomaniac visions of glory on their capitals. Despite the superficially very different contexts, there are strange similarities in the outcomes, with implications that perhaps should be disquieting.

Burnham and the City Beautiful Movement in America

Each of the great planning movements in this account has its prophet, and this one is no exception. He was Daniel Hudson Burnham (1846–1912), partner in the architectural practice of Burnham and Root in Chicago, designer of several of the classic early skyscrapers in that city during the 1880s and 1890s, and chief of construction for the World's Columbian Exposition, one of the definitive World Fairs of all time, held there in 1893. The money that flowed from the lucrative architectural work, allowing him to take planning commissions at little or no fee, was one impulse that turned the young architect into the middle-aged city planner. The other was the experience of designing the magical White City of the shores of Lake Michigan: if a citizen elite could harness professional skills to create an instant city of beauty, to last

Figure 6.1   Daniel Burnham. The maker of no small plans, in a suitably large and magisterial pose. *Source*: Daniel H. Burnham Collection, Ryerson and Burnham Archives, The Art Institute of Chicago. Digital File #194301_110614-007 © The Art Institute of Chicago.

a mere summer long, it should surely be feasible to do the same thing for a real-life work-soiled American commercial city, to longer-lasting effect.[1]

The notion struck a responsive chord; for, as seen in Chapter 2, the 1890s were a period of intense introversion in urban America. For many among the civic-minded bourgeoisie, faced with increasing ethnic and cultural heterogeneity and escalating threat of disorder, the problem appeared to be the very preservation of the urban social fabric. Henry Morgenthau, banker and real-estate figure, put it plainly enough at a conference of 1909: the planner's first aim was to eliminate the breeding places of "disease, moral depravity, discontent, and socialism."[2] And nowhere was this truer than of Chicago, the scene of ugly riots in the 1880s that ended in the execution of the ringleaders in an atmosphere of near-insurrectionary tension.

The Chicago Plan of 1909 was indeed Burnham's greatest achievement. But he came back to his own city via some triumphs and some failures in other places. The first, which was nearly all triumph, was the long-fought battle for the reconstruction

[1]   Wilson, 1989, 66.
[2]   Quoted in Boyer, 1978, 269.

Figure 6.2 The Chicago Plan of 1909. A complete scheme of classical civic order is laid down on the Illinois grid. And amazingly, spurred by civic boosterism, by 1925 much of it is complete. *Source*: © The Art Institute of Chicago.

of the Mall in Washington, DC, which began in 1901. In his plan of 1791, L'Enfant, following George Washington's original ideas, had intended it as a great park, 400 feet broad and more than a mile long, from the Capitol to the Potomac – then lapping as far east as the front of the White House. But the plan was never completed; the strip remained as common pasture ground, invaded by commercial land uses; and in the 1870s, final indignity, a railroad was built across it. For many, both in and out of Congress, the disfigured Mall came to stand as a symbol of all that was wrong with America's cities.[3]

In 1901, prompted by the architect Charles Moore, Senator James McMillan of Michigan, Chairman of the Committee on the District of Columbia, successfully proposed a resolution permitting it to study the park system, including appointment of experts; soon after, Burnham became head of a three-man commission; the other members were Frederic Law Olmsted, Jr, and the New York architect Charles McKim; later, a sculptor, Augustus St Gaudens, joined them. Burnham insisted that they all went to Europe to study the finest urban models, ignoring the obvious irony that many of these had been created by the very tyrannies against which Americans

---

[3] Hines, 1974, 140–1.

had revolted. Later, he insisted that the report contained enough purple passages for it to receive plenty of notice from the press as well as from his architectural peers.[4]

The result was the original L'Enfant concept, writ large, with a Mall doubled to 800 feet in width, nearly doubled in length to take in the reclaimed floodplain of the Potomac, and intersected by two major cross-park strips. It received much praise but also, inevitably, some opposition that for a time almost seemed to kill it. Eventually the whole scheme was completed, just as Burnham had intended it, with the dedication of the Lincoln Memorial in 1922.[5] It was an exercise in pure Beaux Arts design; behind it, appalling slums continued to proliferate.[6]

But Washington, as everyone would insist, was special: a city apart from other American cities, in which the ceremonial and symbolic aspects must loom large. The point was that other cities too – New York, Philadelphia, Baltimore, Cleveland, and Denver – felt that they should hire an architect to draw up a plan.[7] Significantly, the movement took root in the great commercial cities of the Midwest and West: Kansas City, Denver, and Seattle.[8] The enthusiasts were mostly male and middle class, often owners or managers of large businesses – newspaper editors, factory managers, or retail titans; they generated intensive publicity campaigns through boards of trade, chambers of commerce, or various ad hoc groups.[9] Burnham now moved on to bolder enterprises still: attempts to bring a missing civic order to the great industrial and port cities of the United States. He started in an unpropitious enough environment: Cleveland, the Ohio lakefront city, a place of rampant uncontrolled industrialism, racked by pollution, labor unrest, and violence. Burnham was appointed head of a commission in 1902; it reported the next year. It predictably recommended a new civic center in which half a dozen major civic buildings would be grouped in a set of linked public parks, alongside the lakefront and on a broad mall at right angles to it, which together would form an impressive open space in front of the city's relocated main railway station: a clear echo of the Washington plan, which had also included a resited Union Station. It demanded the clearance of over 100 acres of dense, miserable slums including the city's red light district. The city leadership applauded the plan and set vigorously to work on it; only the station, which depended on agreement among competing railroads, failed to see the light of day. No one apparently gave any thought at all to the fate of the slum dwellers; the market, presumably, would take care of them.[10]

But Cleveland was essentially Washington by Lake Erie; ambitious as it was, it was still a pure city-center plan. For San Francisco, in 1906, Burnham proposed

4   Hines, 1974, 150–1.
5   Moore, 1921, passim; Hines, 1974, 140–155, 354–5; Gutheim, 1977, 133–4.
6   Green, 1963, 132–46; Scully, 1969, 74–5, 140.
7   Wilson, 1989, 69.
8   Wilson, 1989, 292.
9   Wilson, 1989, 75.
10 Hines, 1974, 159–68.

something far grander. Here, a new civic center complex – strategically located at the junction of Market Street, the city's main commercial street, and Van Ness Avenue – was to be the focus of a set of radiating boulevards, from which in turn subsidiary radials would take off at intervals; thus the city's regular grid would be brought into "miraculous formal equilibrium" by another logic of angular abutments and natural irregularities used as sites for boulevards and formal buildings.[11] One of these would form a continuous park strip leading to the Golden Gate Park on the west side of the city. There would be a formal architectural treatment on the Twin Peaks which dominate the city's southwest side, with an Athenaeum and a monumental statue facing out over the Pacific Ocean.

Ironically, despite the extraordinary accident of the earthquake and fire, which uniquely gave the city a virtually clean slate on which to implement the plan, commercial pressures doomed it; only fragments, including the oddly dispiriting civic center put in a different place than Burnham intended, form a partial memorial. Today, many San Franciscans are profoundly relieved that Burnham's grand boulevards and ronds-points have not drowned out the gridiron streets that climb up and down the hills, and the Victorian gingerbread houses that line them, which help give the city its unique charm.[12]

Chicago, then, is the definitive Burnham plan: the big one that amazingly, despite apparently insuperable odds, was for the most part carried out. Its basic concept was grand enough, even if singularly vague as to instrumentalities: it was "to restore to the city a lost visual and aesthetic harmony, thereby creating the physical prerequisite for the emergence of a harmonious social order";[13] the chaotic city, that had arisen through too-rapid growth and too-rich a mixture of nationalities, would be given order by cutting new thoroughfares, removing slums, and extending parks.[14] Its very confusion of social objectives and purely aesthetic means was, apparently, the quality that endeared it to the upper and middle classes who backed the Progressive movement.[15]

Introducing the plan, Burnham was confident about the standard of comparison: it was the great European cities. "The task which Haussmann accomplished for Paris corresponds with the work which must be done for Chicago."[16] But, since the backers were the businessmen first of the Commercial Club, then of the Merchants Club, there was a gloss to the argument: Napoleon III's City Beautiful had proved a good investment.[17] "The changes brought about by him made that city famous, and as a result most of the idle people of great means in the world habitually linger there, and I am told that the Parisians annually gain in

[11] Manieri-Elia, 1979, 89.
[12] Hubbard and Hubbard, 1929, 264; Burnham and Bennett, 1971, passim; Hines, 1974, 182–95.
[13] Boyer, 1978, 272.
[14] Boyer, 1978, 272.
[15] Peterson, 1976, 429–30.
[16] Burnham and Bennett, 1970, 18.
[17] McCarthy, 1970, 229–31.

profits from visitors more than the Emperor spent in making the changes."[18] So too in Chicago:

> We have been running away to Cairo, Athens, The Riviera, Paris, and Vienna, because life at home is not as pleasant as in these fashionable centers. Thus a constant drain upon the resources of the town has been going on. No one has estimated the number of millions of money made in Chicago and expended elsewhere, but the sum must be a large one. What would be the effect upon our retail business at home if this money were circulated here? ... What would be the effect upon our prosperity if the town were so delightful that most of the men who grow independent financially in the Mississippi Valley, or west of it, were to come to Chicago to live? Should we not without delay do something competent to beautify and make our city attractive for ourselves, and especially for these desirable visitors?[19]

He even went on to argue that Pericles's "investment" in ancient Athens was still paying off in tourist revenue. Burnham, who certainly understood the Chicago ethos only too well, may have had tongue in cheek; he knew how to make a sales pitch when he had to. All this was by way of preliminary to the exposition of the actual plan, which had a huge price tag attached. The Lake Front was to be reclaimed and turned into a park, with a parkway running through it. One of the streets running at right angles from this park, Congress Street, was to become the principal axis of the new Chicago, with a park strip 300 feet wide. A mile inland, where this axis intersects Hubbard Street, wide diagonal avenues would radiate from a huge domed civic center: the focus of the whole plan, and ironically one of the few features that was never built. The banks of the Chicago River, which here run parallel to the lake between it and Hubbard, were to be straightened, reclaimed, and lined with new streets and buildings. Large public buildings were to be placed at prominent positions in the park strip. There was to be "a stately white Museum, resting on the Grand Terrace called the Lake Front, and dominating all the elements of it; the lawns, the fountains, the monuments, all of which should be placed so as to have some reference to that particular building. No structure in the world has ever had a nobler setting than this would be."[20] There was to be a seven-and-a-half-mile Shore drive, reached from the land by seven viaducts, and a lagoon 30,000 feet in length. In describing it, Burnham waxed lyrical:

> Both shores of the Lagoon should be ornamented with trees and shrubs adapted to our climate, and especially with those that blossom – the apple, the pear, the peach, the horse-chestnut, the wild-chestnut, the catalpa, the crab, the lilac, syringas, acacias, dogwood. The days of May and June should be a festival-time upon the water. In the spring and summer, and in the autumn, when floating upon the Lagoon, one

[18]   McCarthy, 1970, 102.
[19]   Burnham and Bennett, 1970, 102–3.
[20]   Burnham and Bennett, 1970, 105.

Figure 6.3 Chicago Civic Center. Jules Guerin's haunting pastel vision of a magnificently Haussmannized Chicago: formal, symmetrically ordered, but devoid of broader social objective or content. Ironically, this central element was the part that was never completed. *Source*: © The Art Institute of Chicago.

should be conscious of the presence of flowers. On the banks should be sweet-briar, heliotrope, mignonette, and wild sweet grasses – the plants that fill the air with fragrance.[21]

And he concludes with his vision of the future Chicago:

Before us spreads a plantation of majestic trees, shadowing lawns and roadways, upon the margin of the Lake. In contrast with it, the shining Lagoon stretches away to the north. Behind this the soft banks of the shore, and trains glancing in and out through waving willows. Behind all, the wall of a stately terrace, covered with clinging vines and crowned with statues, and upholding quiet lawns, surrounding lovely homes.

The Lake has been singing to us many years, until we have become responsive. We see the broad water, ruffled by the gentle breeze; upon its breast the glint of oars, the gleam of rosy sails, the outlines of swift gliding launches. We see racing shells go by, urged onward by bronzed athletes. We hear the rippling of waves, commingled with youthful laughter, the music swelling over the Lagoon dies away under the low branches of the trees. A crescent moon swims in the western sky, shining faintly upon us in the deepening twilight.

[21]   Burnham and Bennett, 1970, 109.

We float by lawns, where villas, swan-like, rest upon their terraces, and where white balustrades and wood-nymphs are just visible in the gloaming. The evening comes, with myriad colored lights twinkling through air perfumed with water-lilies, and Nature enfolds us, like happy children.[22]

It is an extraordinary, poetic picture; one of the very few in the history of planning. And the haunting pastel washes by Jules Guerin, which show the great city from the air, and radiating boulevards marching away into the vast prairies of Illinois at last light, are like no other urban visions that have ever been; the muted flat colors, the luminosity of reflected light on wet pavements, these faintly recall Whistler, but Whistler never achieved such panoramic sweep.

It was also, of course, superb public relations. But, finally, for whom? Burnham's answer brings us brutally back to earth: "Not for rich people solely or principally, for they can take care of themselves," but rather for the mass of the people; yet "Do not these latter depend upon the circulation among them of plenty of ready money, and can this be brought about without the presence of large numbers of well-to-do people?"[23] This is, with a vengeance, trickle-down urban development; implicit in it, never spelt out, is a notion of an urban economy led by what Thorstein Veblen was just then castigating as conspicuous consumption, on the part of a European-style leisure class.

It is also too easy to deride this; and plenty of critics, from traditional left-liberals to Marxists in need of an easy case study, have had a field day. Already in 1922, when the plan was in course of implementation – coordinated through an Executive Committee of the Plan Commission, which was dominated by Commercial Club members, at a cost of over $300 million[24] – Lewis Mumford was castigating the Burnham approach as "municipal cosmetic"; later he was to compare the results with planning exercises of totalitarian regimes.[25] Everyone attacked it for ignoring housing, schools, and sanitation; Burnham might have claimed in defense that he did say at one point that Chicago might have to go the London route of subsidized housing, but, to put it at its mildest, it was clearly not his central concern.[26] Of the three objectives of planning that Abercrombie was to lay down in his slim textbook of 1933,[27] beauty clearly stood supreme for Burnham, commercial convenience was significant, but health, in its widest sense, came almost nowhere. Later commentators have been kinder: elites like the Commercial Club were simply battling the pervasive ugliness of the late nineteenth-century American city; they thought that a beautiful city would make its inhabitants better people; and, though theirs was a movement for social control, they were not authoritarians, for their rhetoric was belied by their actions.[28]

[22] Burnham and Bennett, 1970, 110–11.
[23] Burnham and Bennett, 1970, 111.
[24] McCarthy, 1970, 248; Hines, 1974, 340.
[25] Lubove, 1962a, 219; Boyer, 1978, 289.
[26] Hines, 1974, 333; Schlereth, 1983, 89.
[27] Abercrombie, 1933, 104–9.
[28] Wilson, 1989, 78–81.

More subtly, the plan – like those for San Francisco and Cleveland before it – could be called centrocentrist: it was based on a civic and business core with no conscious provision for business expansion in the rest of the city.[29] As Mel Scott put it, "the Chicago of the Burnham plan is a city of the past that America never knew," an aristocratic city for merchant princes.[30] In that respect, it was like many other urban development strategies to come. But even there, it contained a basic contradiction: as Herbert Croly pointed out at the time in the New York *Architectural Record*, posited as it was on formal qualities, it accorded ill with the realities of downtown real estate development, which demanded overbuilding and congestion.[31]

That proved its downfall in its native land. At the First National Conference on City Planning and Congestion in 1909, some planners and their business supporters came to see that utopia would demand more than some were willing to pay. The City Beautiful rapidly gave way to the City Functional, to be achieved by zoning – a topic to which the Burnham Plan had devoted scant attention.[32]

Burnham died in 1912 at the height of his fame. The job of implementing his plan was given to his trusted lieutenant, Edward H. Bennett. Born in Bristol in 1874, son of a master mariner, emigrating to California at 16, Bennett learned his trade first with the visionary architect Bernard Maybeck and then – through a scholarship funded by the mother of William Randolph Hearst – at the École des Beaux-Arts in Paris. Burnham, for whom he worked from 1903,[33] immediately took to this "poet with his feet on the earth,"[34] using him first at San Francisco and then in Chicago.[35] So he was always Burnham's logical successor, becoming Consulting Architect to the Chicago Plan Commission in 1913 and staying until 1930.[36] He designed the key architectural features of the Plan, in particular the Union Station and the great bridges across the Chicago River and the ornamental Grant Park, though always in collaboration with others as a consultant, never supervising the work; but he failed to implement the keystone of the plan, the Civic Center; in 1930 it was abandoned after opposition by City Engineer Hugh E. Young, and at that point Bennett was effectively fired.[37]

But Bennett's role and reputation extended far beyond Chicago. After 1906 Burnham declined all planning work, referring potential clients to Bennett or Frederick Law Olmsted, Jr, his collaborator on the McMillan Commission plan for Washington. Bennett set up his own firm in 1910, and was soon preparing plans for Detroit, Minneapolis, Portland, Brooklyn, and central Ottawa. In the years that

[29] Schlereth, 1983, 89.
[30] Scott, 1969, 108.
[31] Kantor, 1973b, 171.
[32] Walker, 1950, 273; Klein and Kantor, 1976, 430–1.
[33] Draper, 1982, 7–8.
[34] Draper, 1982, 10.
[35] Draper, 1982, 8, 13.
[36] Draper, 1982, 17.
[37] Draper, 1982, 21, 24.

followed, he prepared plans for Denver, Buffalo, St Paul, the New York Regional Plan, the Federal Triangle in Washington, and the 1915 San Francisco and 1933 Chicago World's Fairs. Bennett was clearly the leading American City Beautiful planner, making a 40-year career as a planning consultant.[38] His status was confirmed by his appointment to the elite team of technical advisors to New York's Regional Plan Association, with Thomas Adams, Harland Bartholomew, George Ford, John Nolen, and F. L. Olmsted, Jr. The 1929–31 Regional Plan of New York was Bennett's last major land-use planning project, as his consulting practice dried up in the Depression of the 1930s.[39]

Meanwhile, even on his death, Burnham's fame had spread far afield: Europe was returning his compliment. He had urged Chicagoans that "as a people we must, if we can, do for ourselves what elsewhere has been done by a single ruler."[40] But in Berlin, the Kaiser – so wrote the Berlin correspondent of the *Chicago Record-Herald* – had already appointed a commission to prepare a similar plan, only regretting that Berlin was too solidly built up and lacked Chicago's lake frontage.[41] The initiative seems to have died a death; but it was to be revived, with a vengeance, a quarter-century later.

The City Beautiful in the British Raj

But before the City Beautiful came back to its European homeland, it first spread out over the world. Its most spectacular manifestations, between 1910 and 1935, came in the last flowering of the British Raj. And this was no accident: seeking to establish what were often new and precarious holds on conquered territory, anxious therefore to build visible symbols of authority and domination, concerned also to house their servants in the style of life to which they were accustomed, the British India Office and Colonial Office found themselves employing consultants to create instant capital cities in far corners of the globe.

Many, constrained by an anxious Treasury in the Depression years, were decidedly modest exercises: no pomp, straitened circumstance. But one, appropriately, was not: it was the jewel in the crown. At his Coronation Durbar in 1911, George V made the momentous announcement that the capital of British India would be transferred from Calcutta to Delhi: a site suitable for its central position, easy access, and healthy climate, it also had political significance as the historic capital, important symbolically in a country already torn by Hindu–Moslem conflict. So the new capital would be the concern of a great monumental exercise by a people lacking the taste for monumentality: "an Anglo-Indian Rome … one size larger than life."[42] Ironically, taking 20 years to finish, it was then to fill that role for a mere 16 years.

[38]   Gordon, 1998, 280.
[39]   Gordon, 2010, 234.
[40]   Burnham and Bennett, 1970, 111.
[41]   Hines, 1974, 344.
[42]   Hussey, 1953, 237, 240.

Figure 6.4 New Delhi. The Lutyens–Baker plan: symbolic of the awesome power of the Raj, and completely unrelated to the organic life of the indigenous city next door. *Source*: © Country Life.

The architect-planners chosen for this historic mission were in many ways an odd pair. Herbert Baker had early established a claim as the architect of imperialism, having progressed from the Pretoria railway station to the government buildings for the new Union of South Africa; his architectural ideas were "nationalist and

Figure 6.5   Planning New Delhi. Captain Stanley, Edward Lutyens, Herbert Baker, and an unidentified elephant wallah practice the Geddesian principle of Survey before Plan. *Source*: © Adam Pallant, care of The Lutyens Trust.

Imperialist, symbolic and ceremonial."[43] The Indian Viceroy, Hardinge, wanted him for New Delhi but – after pressure from London – chose Lutyens, then best known as a country-house architect; Lutyens, realizing that he could not do all the work himself, then asked for Baker as collaborator.[44] At his first encounter with Lutyens,

---

[43]   Stamp, 1982, 34.
[44]   Baker, 1944, 57–63; Irving, 1981, 278–9; Stamp, 1982, 35.

Baker appreciated the "wilful masterfulness which early success had developed in him."[45] But Baker relished the challenge, writing to Lutyens,

> It is really a great event in the history of the world and of architecture – that rulers should have the strength and sense to do the right thing. It would only be possible now under a despotism – some day perhaps democracies will follow … It must not be Indian, nor English, nor Roman, but it must be Imperial. In 2000 years there must be an Imperial Lutyens tradition in Indian architecture … Hurrah for despotism![46]

There was, however, a third senior partner in the design team: the Viceroy himself. The first question on which he proved decisive was that of a site. Delhi in 1911 consisted of two cities: the densely packed "native city," where 233,000 people lived on just over one and a half square miles, and the British "civil lines" a safe sanitary distance away to the northwest; there was also a nearby military "cantonment," vacant since 1861 but reserved for army use, the scene of the historic Durbar.[47] A powerful interest wanted the new capital here for reasons of tradition and sentiment.[48] But the Viceroy saw that it offered no room for the new 10-square-mile city and 15-square-mile cantonment, and took appropriately viceregal action:

> I then mounted and asked Hailey … Commissioner of Delhi, to accompany me to choose a new site, and we galloped over the plain to a hill some distance away. From the top of the hill there was a magnificent view … I said at once to Hailey, "This is the site for Government House", and he readily agreed.[49]

Splendid, but historically somewhat simplified: the architecture-planning committee in fact had recommended this site to the south of the Indian city, known as Raisina, in June 1912; Hardinge, who had originally favored a site on top of the ridge to the west, dominating the city, seems to have given his agreement in November. Meanwhile, Lutyens and Baker, who only received their formal appointments in January 1913, had taken the result for granted and had begun design work, taking the crucial decision to put the Viceroy's House and Secretariat Building at the same level on the flat hilltop; the Viceroy, at first evidently affronted by the disrespect to his majesty, was persuaded.[50]

The critical decisions on the plan of the new city came very quickly in February–March 1913; the choice of the southern site was ratified on March 7, the plan outlines were confirmed on March 20. From the acropolis on the heights of Raisina, the main axis would run east to the ancient capital of Indrapat, symbolizing "the keystone of the rule over the Empire of India," as the committee's report had it; two

---

[45]   Baker, 1944, 64.
[46]   Quoted in Hussey, 1953, 247.
[47]   King, 1976, 228–30.
[48]   Baker, 1944, 65.
[49]   Hardinge of Penshurst, 1948, 72.
[50]   Baker, 1944, 65; Hussey, 1953, 261–2; Irving, 1981, 46, 51, 67–8.

other major radials would also fan out from it, in classic City Beautiful fashion; a cross-radial, joining the new Anglican cathedral on the south and the railway station on the north, would intersect them.[51] The resulting final plan reflects Lutyens's passion for formal geometry: the Secretariat and the War Memorial Arch both have seven radiating routes, the great railway station circle no fewer than 10; virtually all main roads make 30° or 60° angles with the routes connecting these three foci, and all major buildings are at centers or angles or mid-sides of hexagons. As Baker came to realize years after, there are uncanny similarities with L'Enfant's plan for Washington.[52] Here, a major role was played by a less illustrious figure: John Brodie, City Engineer of Liverpool, of whom it was commented,

> Mr Brodie, of course, was a great man on roads, and when he went to Delhi his intention probably was to try to make the longest and widest avenue in the world. Mr. [*sic*] Brodie had got two roads three miles long, so he had done very well.[53]

The buildings sometimes match up to the roads, more often not. The big ones are very grand indeed. In Lutyens's Viceregal House, the staff quarters for the top officials are virtually palaces in themselves; at the close of British rule, there were more than 2,000 servants in all.[54] Beside it is Baker's Secretarial building: nearly a quarter-mile long, designed to impress, "a majestic stage set for the spectacle of the Indian Civil Service, the tiny corps who were governors over a quarter of the human race ... known in common parlance as the 'heaven-born.'"[55] Between them is a hump in the road that represented the parting of the ways between Baker and Lutyens, and in doing so shook the British Empire to its foundations.

Very early, as already seen, the two architects had agreed that the Viceregal House and Secretariat should share the same level. But for Lutyens, it was central and crucial to the whole plan that the main east–west radial should rise at a constant gradient to Raisina, so that the Viceroy's House should be continuously visible between the wings of the Secretariat. Nevertheless, in March 1913 – tired, ill (almost certainly with dysentery), and anxious to return to England – he signed a minute agreeing to a final gradient that would obscure the view. Baker thought he understood the consequences; Lutyens ever after claimed that he was deluded by perspective drawings, exhibited at the Royal Academy in May 1914, which were drawn from an imaginary point 30 feet above the ground.[56] Discovering his error in 1916 when construction was well advanced, Lutyens pressed for a change; the committee refused him on the ground that it would cost £2,000. Lutyens, increasingly obsessed by the idea that he was victim of a trick, appealed to everyone: to the Viceroy, who was unsympathetic, then to King George V on no less than two occasions; one feels that he would have

51   Irving, 1981, 67–8, 71, 73.
52   Irving, 1981, 79, 84.
53   Quoted in Home, 2013, 45.
54   Irving, 1981, 227.
55   Irving, 1981, 280.
56   Hussey, 1953, 286–7, 323; Lutyens, 1980, 126; Irving, 1981, 143–50.

appealed to God (in Hindu, Moslem, and Christian versions) if appropriate channels had been open. In vain, Baker wrote to ask why he wouldn't play cricket; Lutyens later said that he had met his Bakerloo.[57]

They were not the only problems. The Viceroy found Baker's plans "admirable" and within the stated cost limits; not so Lutyens, whose plans, "though beautiful, were made absolutely regardless of cost."[58] The Public Works Department, furious at being displaced by outside architects, wanted an Indian style of architecture; Hardinge too, as he stressed in a letter to Lutyens just before his formal appointment, believed that for political reasons there must be a strong Indian motif. And Lutyens, though insisting on his formal classical plan, came round to their view.[59] But Lutyens was not an easy person: once, asked what he thought an asinine question by a Royal Commission, he allegedly answered "The answer is in the plural and they bounce." Later, Baker reflected that their natures were too different: Lutyens was the abstract geometrician, devoid of human concerns; Baker cared more for "national and human sentiment." "What more might we have achieved with unity of counsel!" he bewailed.[60]

And, perhaps, with more money. Most of the huge axial boulevards contain no such seeds of controversy; they are lined with one-story bungalows.[61] Within the hexagonal grids, houses were allocated according to a bewilderingly complicated formula of race, occupational rank, and socio-economic status: "From the Viceroy, via the Commander-in-Chief, Members of the Executive Council, senior gazetted officers, gazetted officers, down to superintendents, peons, sweepers and *dhobis*, a carefully stratified spatial order was integrated, both in terms of physical distance and spatial provision, to the social structure of the city."[62] This feat, to conceive intellectually of an elaborate social structure then to render it literally in concrete on the ground, was a triumph of highly abstract planning; it had nothing to do with the traditional structure of "civil lines" in India, which had evolved in a very British fashion, that is to say informally.[63]

And, as so often in post-colonial cities, it all goes on to this day: architectural styles and housing standards are still colonial, the by-laws are obsolete, the subsidy structure favors the upper-income groups, there are almost unbelievable disparities between the standards of the rich and the poor;[64] so pervasive are the ways of the past that, when Anthony King visited the Connaught Circus shopping center in 1970, the music shop was still adorned with pictures of Harry Roy, Geraldo, Evelyn Laye, and Albert Sandler.[65] The ways of the Raj indeed die hard.

---

[57] Hussey, 1953, 355–6, 363– 6, 410–12.
[58] Hardinge of Penshurst, 1948, 96.
[59] Hussey, 1953, 260, 265, 268, 300; Stamp, 1982, 37–8.
[60] Baker, 1944, 68–9.
[61] Baker, 1944, 79.
[62] King, 1976, 246.
[63] King, 1976, 264.
[64] Bose, 1973, 184–5.
[65] King, 1976, 259.

Figure 6.6   New Delhi: Lutyens's "Bakerloo." Obscuring the view of the Secretariat and the Viceroy's palace, the kink in the great processional way caused a fatal rift between Lutyens and Baker and nearly shook the Empire. Lutyens–Baker plan of New Delhi.

And not merely in India. In South and East Africa, where the British came late and did not stay long, they produced a number of instant mini-capitals: Salisbury (later Harare), Lusaka, Nairobi, Kampala. In all, consultants produced plans based on the fiction that these cities were completely white with, perhaps, a separate Indian bazaar area at a respectful distance; Africans were either assumed not to exist, since they were officially supposed to be farmers, or were herded into squatter reservations with the aid of mass deportations and pass systems.[66] In Nairobi between 1932 and 1947, the city spent a total of £1,000–2,000 a year, between 1 and 2% of revenue, for 20,000 Africans.[67]

The basis was hygienic: the government medical service, invariably of military origin, had a virtual stranglehold over the planning system. Since the British settlers fell like ninepins to tropical diseases, they had to take themselves to the hills, segregate themselves as best they could, and live bungalow-style at exceedingly low densities, even when that meant – as it invariably did – high infrastructure costs and long journeys.[68] Typically, as in Nairobi, the Europeans would be given the best – that is, highest – areas, the Indians the next best, the Africans anything that was

[66]   Van Zwanenberg, 1975, 261, 267, 270–1.
[67]   Van Zwanenberg, 1975, 268.
[68]   Southall, 1966, 486; King, 1976, 125; King, 1980b, 211–15.

left.[69] Here, the Feetham Committee in 1927 recommended strict control over "ingress of natives" to control "idle, vicious, or criminal" elements.[70] A town plan was produced in 1926 by F. Walter Jameson (popularly known as Jacaranda Jim), of Kimberley, and Herbert Baker; another came from a further South African consultancy in 1948. Both, unsurprisingly, accepted and reinforced the existing racial divisions;[71] the latter observing that it must note the fact that the government had disowned segregation between whites and Asians, then commented that many people wanted it, and proceeded to take refuge in "the principles of planning which take their measure on the human and technical needs," which presumably meant back-door segregation. The Africans were dismissed on the ground that though they were the most numerous they were also the most transitory; the plan did not even show African housing areas.[72] Robert Home comments that "The contrast could not have been greater between this type of accommodation and that which British administrators thought suitable for themselves," typically a bungalow set in a 1- or 2-acre (0.4- or 0.8-hectare) compound.[73] Lugard said in 1893 that the colonial official's "dwelling house should be as superior to those of the native as he is himself superior to them."[74] In South Africa, the mining compounds – where cabins of 700 square feet (65 square meters) housed 25 workers – produced a death rate from tuberculosis and pneumonia so high, 7–10% per year, that a commission recommended a minimum of 200 cubic feet (5.7 cubic meters) per worker.[75]

After the Anglo-Boer South African War (1899–1902), a reconstruction program for the former Boer republics was launched by the imperialist proconsul, Lord Milner. Natal, a British colony, occupying a key strategic location in the British Empire on the sea routes between Africa and Asia, was not part of it, but was already beginning to play a key role in shaping the segregationist policies of the apartheid state.[76] It originated the so-called "Durban system," using revenues from a municipal monopoly of beer sales to fund African worker housing and social facilities, and thus allowing white ratepayers to avoid financial obligations. It became a model for urban control throughout British East, Central, and South Africa and was thus one of "a nexus of institutions including labor compounds, townships and rural reserves within which Africans were in some senses incarcerated."[77] Clarified by adoption of the Natives (Urban Areas) Act No. 21 in 1923,[78] it eventually became a central feature of the National Party's program of "township development."[79] Even before that,

[69] Halliman and Morgan, 1967, 106.
[70] Hake, 1977, 44.
[71] Hake, 1977, 56–7.
[72] Thornton White *et al.*, 1948, 21 and maps.
[73] Home, 2013, 104
[74] Quoted in Home, 2013, 104.
[75] Home, 2013, 107–8.
[76] Home, 2000, 332–3.
[77] Home, 2000, 333–5.
[78] Mabin and Smit, 1997, 199.
[79] Harrison, 2002, 163.

in 1944, a report on "Regional and Town Planning" of the South African Social and Economic Planning Council, set up by Premier Jan Smuts, was quoting approvingly from British reports (Barlow, Scott, Uthwatt) to back up recommendations for coherent communities separated by green belts, together with careful planning of residential and employment sites and the transport between them. But in the South African context, this effortlessly mutated into the idea of planning racially distinct, well-separated zones:

> The Union has a large and growing permanently urbanized non-European population. The Council ... therefore, urges that in the lay-out of new townships, the replanning of existing ones and the erection of state-subsidised housing schemes, full use should be made of the principle of planned neighbourhoods, protected from other neighbourhoods by "green belts" of cultivated and park land and at the same time reasonably close to work places.

The official correspondence leaves no doubt that what bureaucrats had in mind was urban segregation:

> The [Social and Economic] Planning Council has indicated in the Fifth Report that it regards the separation of residential areas of different races ... as a function of town planning in this country ... Residential segregation must be the result of a valid and accepted *National* policy ... no legal basis exists for it at the present time ...[80]

When the Herenigde Nasionale Party (Reunited National Party) came to power in May 1948, it provided for that legal basis.[81]

Within these segregated areas, the invariable settlement form was the barracks, renamed "hostels" in the 1923 Act, which empowered local authorities to build African housing in "locations" outside the urban areas. Usually placed in a compound (a word derived from the Malay *kampong*, or village), the location was the demarcated land parcel to which African housing was restricted.[82] Even as late as 1975, Durban's compounds accommodated over 200,000 people in single-sex hostels. Barracks for indentured laborers still survive on many Natal sugar estates to this day; dozens of barrack/hostel structures remain a grim feature of the South African urban landscape.[83]

In other parts of southern and eastern Africa, still under direct British control after World War Two, the garden-city and new-towns movement was exerting a major influence inside the Colonial Office, as evidenced by this minute of 1943:

> a layout on a garden city basis is most attractive to Africans, who do not like to bring their wives to a township where they will have nothing to do but gossip and get into

---

[80]   Mabin and Smit, 1997, 203–4.

[81]   Mabin and Smit, 1997, 205.

[82]   Home, 2000, 337.

[83]   Home, 2000, 338.

mischief. The African likes his wife to have a garden to tend, and this desire deserves every encouragement for its influence on nutrition.[84]

Thus, Robert Home points out, a design for working-class housing in Britain, espoused by the town-planning and garden-city movement, could also be reproduced in a colonial context to form a model of social control based around the stable family unit and concepts of citizenship.[85] But the history is a tortuous one. As early as 1907 the journal *Garden City* had pronounced "We want not only England but all parts of the Empire to be covered with Garden Cities."[86] Fifteen years after that, at the 1922 conference of the International Garden Cities and Town Planning Association at Olympia, a presentation was titled "How to get Garden Cities Established throughout the World?"[87] In the following decade, European – particularly British – colonial town planners implemented "garden cities" throughout Africa. The 1931 plan of Lusaka, at the time the colonial administrative capital of Northern Rhodesia (present-day, Zambia), by Stanley Adshead, Professor of Town and Country Planning at the University of London, is illustrative.[88] Here as elsewhere, the garden city was strictly for the white colonials. Adshead's Lusaka plan embodied the usual division between the spacious European quarters and the primitive African areas, which mostly lacked the most elementary services.[89] Adshead bluntly stated the view that "it would be a mistake to treat the Africans as if they were Europeans … it would be foolish to offer them those bodily comforts which they had never known and which generations and generations of habit have made necessary to the white man";[90] as in Kampala, the plan – despite emerging contrary evidence – took refuge in the myth that the African was migratory.[91] Within the European area, there were to be three classes of housing (though the Professor noted that it would be objectionable to call them that); even in official correspondence, the top class, next to the offices on top of the ridge, came to be known as Snob's Hill.[92] Over the next 20 years, Adshead's already low densities were thinned out still further; his grandest concept – a 400-foot-wide Independence Avenue, along the ridge – became a relatively minor link between three far-flung garden suburbs.[93]

Common to all these plans was the land-use and settlement structure. There would be a central government office node and a nearby commercial office area; the central shopping area would be adjacent to both. All these would be designed around a formal geometrical road layout, with broad avenues meeting at traffic circles. They

[84]   Home, 2000, 341.
[85]   Home, 2000, 343.
[86]   Njoh, 2009, 310.
[87]   Njoh, 2009, 310.
[88]   Njoh, 2009, 311.
[89]   Davies, 1969, 101–12.
[90]   Quoted in Kay, 1967, 114.
[91]   Collins, 1980, 232.
[92]   Collins, 1980, 119.
[93]   Collins, 1969, 17–19.

would be surrounded by very low-density European residential areas, within which individual bungalow-style houses hid themselves in huge private grounds; a style known in Lusaka, and elsewhere, as "garden city," which usage might make the recently dead Ebenezer Howard return to complain. The African compound, revealing title, was relatively very small and was clearly segregated on one side of the city, separated as far as possible from the European areas by a physical barrier such as a railway track. There might be an older shopping area in or near the African area, the assumption being that shopping too would be racially segregated. In general, the interesting basic assumption was that apart from a necessary quota of house servants, the Africans did not exist.

There were, however, key differences as against New Delhi, and they were not just a matter of money. The consultants' plans for the African capitals, though they imposed a degree of formal organization on the European center and suburbs, never aimed at Lutyens's geometrical complexities. Nor, though the government house was always given a prominent and dignified position, was there anything like the elaboration of the great structures of Raisina; there were, presumably, fewer people who needed impressing, and perhaps it was assumed that they could be impressed more easily. Nor, despite the three-caste system in Lusaka, did their plans reflect an elaborate occupational and social hierarchy – presumably because running Kenya or Northern Rhodesia did not require such elaborate distinctions.

But change was afoot. In Kenya, encouraged by London, as early as 1939 the Kenyan government began to promote a policy of development which implied that Africans would move to the cities.[94] The Colonial Development and Welfare Act of 1940 empowered the British government to provide money for development projects in its colonial territories.[95] Thus, by the mid-1950s, an impressive amount of housing had been built by, and with the encouragement of, the colonial state.[96] Local administrators adapted the idea of neighborhood planning in garden suburbs to local circumstances.[97] When Fenner Brockway, a maverick socialist politician from Britain whose support for nationalist causes earned him the title of "member for Africa," undertook an inspection tour of African locations in Nairobi together with Jomo Kenyatta, he was "delighted" by the only postwar project that he saw – probably Makongeni/Kaloleni, where he saw an "architecturally beautiful ... garden village of red-stone bungalows ... each with a small kitchen" and grudgingly concluded that "the advance in public housing over thirty years ... gave some ground for hope at last." Unfortunately, such family projects were expensive to build, and most of what was actually built was still barracks for single men, where even families were shoehorned in.[98]

Here, as elsewhere, the end of the Raj brought its own ironies: the rulers of the newly independent states, finding themselves faced with the same problems of

[94]   Harris and Hay, 2007, 195.
[95]   Harris and Hay, 2007, 203–4.
[96]   Harris and Hay, 2007, 210.
[97]   Harris and Hay, 2007, 216.
[98]   Harris and Hay, 2007, 216–7.

squatter settlement as the old colonial officials, reacted identically. In Lusaka, where a Cabinet minister referred to "90,000 uninvited guests," the local newspaper in 1970 indignantly argued that "If the people living in these terrible areas used more initiative instead of sponging from a city to which they are contributing nothing, they need not suffer in any way by being moved away from their hovels." So occasional bulldozings took place, and even pass laws were suggested.[99] In Nairobi, the government in 1969 began systematic demolition and the mayor, Isaac Lugonzo, argued that the government should stop people without means of support moving into the city.[100]

In both places, of course, the policies were determined by an African elite who had moved into the houses vacated by the colonials: "You forget the smell of the dust after only a few days," said one, a civil servant in Nairobi: "There is a bigger gap between my father and myself than between myself and the average European."[101] In such ex-European areas, Mabogunje reported in 1978, the officials knew the old building standards by heart, even when they could not find the original colonial documents.[102] To give them due credit, they changed their policies later: to upgrading in Nairobi, to upgrading and self-build in Lusaka.[103] Meanwhile, even New Delhi had spawned numberless informal settlements, some packed into the very spaces that Lutyens had provided so generously along his ceremonial streets.[104]

Canberra: City Beautiful Exceptional

So, transmuted to a colonial or ex-colonial context, the City Beautiful turned out to have a few blemishes. There was, however, one outstanding exception, though perhaps that was because for a long time most of it remained on paper: Canberra. Its early history verged on the tragi-farcical. The new Commonwealth of Australia government, established on New Year's Day 1901, immediately started to fulfill its remit to find a new capital within New South Wales outside a 100-mile radius of Sydney. In 1908 it chose Canberra and the site was set aside as Australian Capital Territory; in 1911 it organized an international competition to plan the city. But it was so mean about the prize (a paltry £1,750) that both the British and the American institutes of architects effectively boycotted it: obvious names like Abercrombie, Burnham, and Olmsted were missing. One hundred and thirty-seven architects, presumably including a quota of starving students, competed; Walter Burley Griffin, an American student who had worked in Frank Lloyd Wright's office, entered with his wife, Marion Mahoney, and won. The government then appointed a board to report on the design; it pronounced it impracticable and promptly designed its own,

99 Van Velsen, 1975, 295–6, 307.
100 Hake, 1977, 99, 123.
101 Quoted in Hake, 1977, 74.
102 Mabogunje *et al.*, 1978, 64.
103 Hake, 1977, 164–70; Martin, 1982, 259–61.
104 Payne, 1977, 138–9.

COMMONWEALTH OF AVSTRALIA
FEDERAL CAPITAL COMPETITION

CITY AND ENVIRONS·

SCALE

Figure 6.7 Canberra. Walter Burley Griffin's prizewinning plan of 1912; ignored, circumvented. Maybe – over a century afterwards – almost complete. *Source*: National Archives of Australia: A710,38.

which it started to implement. This was so terrible that public opinion, hitherto lukewarm, swung behind Griffin; in England, Abercrombie said of it that "It is the work of an amateur who has yet to learn the elementary principles."[105]

There was a change of government; in 1913 Griffin was appointed Federal Capital Director of Design and Construction. For seven years he nearly went mad as his attempts were systematically sabotaged: plans went astray, his own drawings disappeared from his desk to resurface only 30 years later. In 1920 he gave up and his post was abolished. Numerous attempts were made in parliament to scrap the plan, until finally it was fixed; but nothing was done to implement it. The suburbs began to grow in typical Australian fashion, that is to say sprawlingly, without plan. Finally, in 1955 a Senate Committee of Enquiry recommended a new central authority for planning, construction, and development. In 1957 William Holford came from England to recommend plan modifications; the next year John Overall was appointed National Capital Development Region Director.[106] Almost unbelievably, after 45 years Griffin's plan began to take shape; by the millennium, it was effectively complete.

But the buildings are not his; only their disposition. The aboriginal name, Kamberra, means a meeting place: the site, as Griffin's introduction to the plan put it, "may be considered as an irregular amphitheatre," on which he proposed to stage a great drama of government. Today's tourist map, which is oriented upside-down, is perversely correct: that is how, for Griffin, his audience would see it. From the mountains on the northeast, which would form the rear galleries, the land fell gently to form the auditorium; the spectators, facing southwestwards with the sun behind them, would look down to the lowest point of the basin, which would be flooded to become the arena; behind that, the land rose in steps, to form a stage on which would be placed in rising order the symbolically important buildings of the Commonwealth: the Court of Justice, the Parliament House, finally – on the highest internal hill within the basin – the Capitol building.

To accent the drama, stage and arena would form a triangle, with the Capitol Hill as the rear apex and – both these on the audience's side of the water – the military establishments and market center to their front left, the national university and municipal center to front right. (Here, though the plan's command of theatrical metaphor at this point fails it, drinks and ice creams would be available; this would be the commercial center.) These two would be joined to the apex by broad highways crossing the lake. Bisecting the triangle, on the audience's side, would be a huge central processional aisle leading towards them. And, behind the stage, the nearer hills and the far-distant blue mountain ridges would form "the back scene of the theatrical whole."[107]

Latter-day interpretation has it that the whole plan has a much deeper quasi-religious significance, stemming from Madame Helena Blatavsky's theosophical movement, which also was said to influence Lutyens: "The double triangle within the Vesicle can be interpreted as a symbolic restructuring of both Western and

[105] Boyd, 1960, 13; Manieri-Elia, 1979, 112.
[106] Boyd, 1960, 14–15.
[107] Commonwealth of Australia, 1913, 3.

Eastern cosmogonies; a clear parallel with the Chaldean and Hindu geometry as well as that of Stonehenge, Glastonbury and varied visualizations of the conjectural New Jerusalem – 'the world within the universe.'"[108] Maybe; but it comes out well enough as just an exercise in plain old formal geometry.

Remarkably, it has all come out like that, with a few more changes of cast. The play has been rewritten to give a bigger role to the parliament, which in 1988, Australia's bicentennial, was moved up to a new home on Capitol Hill. An elegantly monumental art gallery and national library have joined the Courts of Justice at front of stage. Visually, that right edge of the triangle has become the dominant feature: it leads the eye back from the municipal-commercial center, past a traffic circle, via a broad highway across Lake Burley Griffin and so up to the new Parliament House, low-slung and half-buried into the hill; low-key government, this. On the lake itself, strong decorative vertical features – the carillon clock at extreme left, the huge Captain Cook memorial water-jet close to the central axis, the telecom tower at extreme right – define and frame the stage. The heavily neo-classical Anzac Parade, a post-World War One war memorial and hence a very early feature, forms the central processional aisle to the auditorium. Most notably, because the actual building came so late, the architecture is of the 1970s and 1980s: in style it is international modern respectful. It lacks some of the zest of Niemeyer's Brasília (of which more in Chapter 7); it also lacks its monumental excesses. It is all exceedingly grand, dignified, elegant, yet (that Parker–Unwin word) reposeful; it will soon rank with Washington as one of the world's great monumental capitals, an eloquent testimony to the wisdom of making haste slowly.

Most remarkably, Griffin made some of his most innovative leaps in designing the residential suburbs. He was, remember, not a true-blue City Beautiful planner: he admired the work of the garden-city movement, and of Geddes.[109] A decade before Perry, he anticipated the neighborhood unit. He wrote that

> the segregated sections, formed and separated by the general traffic lines, furnish not only suitable individual home sites, but comprise social units for that larger family – the neighbourhood group, with one handy district school or more for the children, and with local playground, game fields, church, club, and social amenities accessible without crossing traffic tracks, or encountering the disturbing elements of temptations of business streets, since these family activities may best be directed internally toward the geographical centers of their groups for their special congregation.[110]

It sounds almost like a pre-Radburn Radburn. The original diagram shows the units as hexagons, a device Parker used later in his Radburn layouts at Wythenshawe.[111] And, in these later neighborhoods, that is how it all came out: a morning jogger may emerge from the front door, go from path via linear park to a vast central space of playing fields, making a circuit of a mile or more without ever seeing traffic.

---

[108]   Proudfoot, 1996, 251.
[109]   Manieri-Elia, 1979, 113.
[110]   Commonwealth of Australia, 1913, 13.
[111]   Creese, 1966, 266–8.

Figure 6.8 Walter Burley Griffin. The Chicago landscape architect who worked with Frank Lloyd Wright before winning the Canberra competition. *Source*: National Archives of Australia, A1200, L32618.

These neighborhoods, and the new towns that are supplementing them farther out, are strung like beads on the strings of the traffic roads which pass between and around them. So Canberra achieves the difficult feat of being one of the last Cities Beautiful, and also the world's biggest Garden City. It is even, in its way, one of the few extant realizations of Howard's polycentric social city: no small achievement for a city that for a long time never looked like growing up. Thus, unlike a number of other examples of the City Beautiful genre, it manages to be rather likeable.

The City Beautiful and the Great Dictators

The return of the City Beautiful to Europe was altogether less happy. It came in the age of the Great Dictators, and it too was theater: bad melodrama. Mussolini's Rome was the curtain-warmer: "Mussolini *was* the chief architect of fascism as a political system, and he did turn out a prodigious amount of building, including the construction of 13 towns and more than 60 rural settlements *ex novo* in Italy between 1928 and 1940."[112] For him, great public works would not only recall the triumphs of imperial and medieval Italy; they would surpass them.[113] But fascist ideology

---

[112] Ghirardo, 1989, 24.
[113] Ghirardo,1989, 25.

concerning the city was in many ways close to Nazi: only rural family life was truly healthy; the metropolis was the origin of most things bad, including labor unrest, revolution, and socialism.[114] Ironically – an experience soon to be repeated in Franco's Spain – under Mussolini the cities boomed as never before; fascism proved good for business. Mussolini's response was to pass laws – in 1928, in 1939 – to control migration; by one of those many ironies, the latter only became effective after World War Two.[115] It was also to carry through well-publicized rural land-reclamation schemes like those in the Pontine Marshes south of Rome, with five completely new towns. Here, too, there was a tradition that went back at least as far as the Roman Empire. The fascist town plans followed Roman models, with modified orthogonal grids, normally with four quadrants and a rectangular piazza as the civic center.[116] The garden-city model was rejected, but the skylines evoked medieval echoes, particularly by using towers for symbolic purposes: "In effect, the Fascists erected a medieval skyline on a Roman ground plan."[117]

Within the metropolis, however, the role of planning was to be monumental: to rediscover the glories of Rome by removing most of the traces of the subsequent two millennia. Mussolini gave his instructions to the 1929 Congress of the Housing and Town Planning Federation in Rome:

> My ideas are clear. My orders are precise. Within five years, Rome must appear marvellous to all the people of the world – vast, orderly, powerful, as in the time of the empire of Augustus … you shall create vast spaces around the Theater of Marcellus, the Capitoline Hill, and the Pantheon. All that has grown around them in the centuries of decadence must disappear.[118]

In matter of fact, the new plan – promulgated in 1931 – was internally contradictory: the street widenings, the focus on the Piazza Venezia as ceremonial square, would have covered up or destroyed imperial Rome rather than revealing it. But it did not matter; despite sweeping powers, despite generous injections of money, despite the *imprimatur* of *Il Duce* himself, life in Rome continued in the old sweet way. When the sweeping lines of the Master Plan were finally translated into detailed plans, broad boulevards and panoramic squares had mysteriously turned into building lots; old-fashioned chaos, compromise, and corruption saved Rome from the depredations of the master-builder.[119]

There was the same inbuilt contradiction in Nazi as in fascist thinking about the city. The party's theoretical wing at the end of the 1920s was strongly anti-urban, arguing that the Nordic people were quintessential farmers, never successful in founding cities and nearly destroyed by them; its newspaper, the *Völkischer*

---

[114]   Ghirardo, 1989, 39.
[115]   Treves, 1980, 470–86.
[116]   Calabi, 1984, 49–50; Ghirardo, 1989, 27, 65.
[117]   Ghirardo, 1989, 66.
[118]   Quoted in Fried, 1973, 31.
[119]   Fried, 1973, 35–9.

Beobachter, described the metropolis as "the melting-pot of all evil ... of prostitution, bars, illness, movies, Marxism, Jews, strippers, Negro dances, and all the disgusting offspring of so-called 'modern art.'"[120] Shortly after the Nazis seized power, their policies – borrowing from Weimar ideas – emphasized *Kleinsiedlungen* at the edge of the big cities, such as Marienfelde, Falkensee, and Falkenberg outside Berlin; then the emphasis shifted to rural areas, but by that time the rival claims of rearmament were shrinking the whole program.[121]

The definitive Nazi statement on urban policy, Gottfried Feder's *Die neue Stadt* of 1939, has odd echoes of the *Gartenstadtbewegung* in its emphasis on developing small self-sufficient rural towns of some 20,000 people which would combine the best features of urban and rural life, both economically and socially, while minimizing the attendant disadvantages.[122] But perhaps not quite so odd; for, as seen in Chapter 4, that movement in Germany did have its strongly conservative wing. And, following ideas that developed in the 1920s, these garden cities were to be built not near the major metropolitan centers, but in thinly populated agricultural districts like Mecklenburg and East Prussia: a return to the countryside, with a vengeance. Within them, Nazi planners borrowed and adapted perfectly conventional planning concepts: the neighborhood unit was imported from America, becoming *Die Ortsgruppe als Siedlungszelle*, a cellular unit that combined nationality, community, kinship, neighborhood, and quasi-military camaraderie.[123]

All of which seems hundreds of miles away, both literally and figuratively, from the plans that Hitler and his *Generalbauinspektor*, Albert Speer, were hatching for the reconstruction of Berlin. But running through it all was a perverse logic: Germany's cities, and above all Berlin, were to perform a psychological, a quasi-religious, even a magical function as gathering-points for vast public ceremonies, while the productive population was removed to *Lebensraum* in the countryside.[124] Appropriately, the plans would have involved unparalleled destruction of the old medieval town centers to make way for ceremonial axes, assembly areas and halls, vast towers, and sprawling administrative complexes, at a bill exceeding 100 billion marks.[125] The resulting irony was that the Nazis, having embraced the cult of rural virtue and the small medieval city and excoriated the giant city, ended by trying to produce a totally mechanized, totally anti-human city of parade and spectacle.[126]

Berlin was, however, a very different canvas from Rome – here was no old master awaiting restoration, but a piece of nineteenth-century commercial art. And the retouching artist had very decided views: Hitler had failed to enter the Vienna academy to study art, and was prone to repeat to Speer, again and again, "How I wish

[120] Quoted in Lane, 1968, 155.
[121] Peltz-Dreckmann, 1978, 102, 122, 144.
[122] Peltz-Dreckmann, 1978, 194.
[123] Schubert, 2000, 128.
[124] Thies, 1978, 422–4. But much planning under the Nazis simply continued policies of slum clearance and urban renewal: Petz, 1990b, 185.
[125] Thies, 1978, 417–8.
[126] Schorske, 1963, 114.

I had been an architect."[127] He had an amazingly detailed knowledge of earlier City Beautiful plans for Vienna and Paris; he knew the exact measurements of the Champs Elysées, and was obsessionally determined that Berlin should have an east–west axis two and a half times as long; the disposition of the buildings – huge and monumental, with wide spaces between them – recalls the Vienna Ring remembered from his youth.[128] He showed Speer two sketches from the 1920s, which already showed his dreams for a 650-foot domed building and a 330-foot arch: "he had been planning triumphant monumental buildings when there was not a shred of hope that they could ever be built."[129] "Why always the biggest?" he rhetorically asked an audience of construction workers in 1939; "I do this to restore to each individual German his self-respect."[130]

His obsession with the monumental was such that he ignored wider aspects: "He would look at the plans, but really only glance at them, and after a few minutes would ask with palpable boredom, "Where do you have the plans for the grand avenue?"[131] Running between the two planned central railroad stations, with the Great Hall – 726 feet high, 850 feet across the dome – at its center point, this north–south avenue was to spell out in stone "the political, military, and economic power of Germany." In the center sat the absolute ruler of the Reich, and in his immediate proximity, as the highest expression of his power, was the great domed hall which was to be the dominant structure of the future Berlin."[132] Each time he saw the plans again, he would repeat, "My only wish, Speer, is to see these buildings. In 1950 we'll organize a world's fair."[133]

The plans that bored him extended the City Beautiful principle to the edges of the city, and beyond; Speer, who admired Washington and Burnham's Columbian Exhibition, evidently took to heart Burnham's exhortation to make no little plans.[134] Seventeen radial highways, along which higher buildings were permitted all the way to the periphery, were intersected by four rings, partly built on existing streets, partly new.[135] There were to be big satellite towns to north and south; the bigger, Südstadt, was to have 210,000 people and 100,000 industrial jobs. In it, despite Nazi prejudice in favor of single-family homes, a new version of the familiar Berlin *Mietskaserne* would dominate: a closed apartment block around a big yard.[136] Here as in the center, the plan had a very regular, hard-lined, monumental quality, almost as if it were designed to be seen from the air.[137] In its basic principles – if not in its surface clothing – Speer's plan exhibited conventional

---

[127]   Speer, 1970, 80.
[128]   Speer, 1970, 75–7; Larsson, 1978, 42–3.
[129]   Speer, 1970, 70.
[130]   Speer, 1970, 69.
[131]   Speer, 1970, 79.
[132]   Speer, 1970, 138.
[133]   Speer, 1970, 141.
[134]   Helmer, 1980, 317, 326–7.
[135]   Speer, 1970, 78; Larsson, 1978, 33–6.
[136]   Larsson, 1978, 86–7, 94.
[137]   Larsson, 1978, 95–6.

Figure 6.9 Speer's Berlin. Speer's monumental north–south way leads via the Triumphal Arch to the gigantic domed *Kupferhalle*: a city fit to be capital of the Thousand Year Reich, none of it even started. *Source*: © ullsteinbild/TopFoto.

enough qualities: incompatible land uses were segregated, through traffic was excluded from residential areas, there was plenty of air and light and space; very little, indeed, to which a Congrès Internationaux d'Architecture Moderne member could object, apart from the architectural style.[138]

[138] Larsson, 1978, 112–13.

It was a costly obsession. Speer's own estimate was that the total cost for Berlin alone would have been between 4 and 6 billion marks, perhaps $5–8 billion in today's money.[139] Rearmament brought postponement. Work on producing the east–west processional axis, much of which was already in place, started in 1937 and was partly completed in 1939; almost unbelievably, work was started on the main project in 1941.[140] Finally, all that ever resulted from the whole grandiose vision was the creation of one ceremonial space on the east–west axis, and the replanting of the historic forest ring outside the city with a mixture of deciduous and coniferous trees.[141] With an especially appropriate irony, after the war the Russians completed the east–west axis in their sector, and named it Stalinallee.

It was not an isolated piece of plagiarism. Wolfgang Sonne has pointed out the astonishing continuities of urban design in Berlin's history. The idea of a north–south axis for the government district survived three radically different political systems, from the German Empire through the Weimar Republic to the Third Reich. The axis as significant urban form was also picked up by the German Democratic Republic (GDR) and even played a role in the Western competition for Berlin as capital city in 1958. Only the historical legacy that identified axial planning with Nazism ruled out its employment in the Federal Republic. The public urban square, seen as a stage for a real or imaginary communal spirit, appears as the "Forum des Reiches" for a militaristic Empire, the "Forum der Republik" for the Weimar democracy, the square in front of Hitler's Great Hall, the diverse forums from the Berlin Capital City competition – with their floating space, but nevertheless public squares for democracy – the "Zentraler Harz" of GDR planning, and finally the "Bundesforum" in the Spreebogen for the united Federal Republic.[142]

Nazi Berlin would have been the ultimate City Beautiful. Its sources of inspiration, even down to details – Burnham's domed civic center, Lutyens's domed Viceregal palace – are only too evident.[143] It was also ultimately impossible to build; even in the most favorable circumstances, it would have taken a disproportionate part of the country's available resources. The odd fact was that a far poorer capital under an equally megalomaniac dictator, Joseph Stalin, managed to achieve in a short time much of what Hitler only dreamed of.

The first decade of Soviet planning deserves a book to itself. As in so many other fields, it was a time of wild experiment, of impassioned debate between proponents of equally improbable theories. The urbanists wanted to house everyone in towers; naturally enough, Corbusier was their god and their ally, and so they will be discussed together with him in Chapter 7. The deurbanists, a much wilder bunch, wanted to disperse everyone in mobile homes across the countryside, and eventually demolish Moscow; their spiritual affinity was with Frank Lloyd Wright,

[139] Speer, 1970, 140.
[140] Larsson, 1978, 32–3, 53.
[141] Speer, 1970, 78; Helmer, 1980, 201.
[142] Sonne, 2004, 304.
[143] Larsson, 1978, 116.

and we will encounter them in Chapter 8. (As noted more than once, logic and chronology refuse stubbornly to keep in step.) Both groups consulted foreign experts: May, predictably, suggested satellite towns, Corbusier a completely new high-rise Moscow on a new site.[144] At the Central Committee session in June 1931, their debate came to an abrupt end.[145] The Full Assembly denounced foreign theories of planning, notably those of Corbusier and Wright, and called for a five-year Development Plan for Moscow, to be produced forthwith.[146] Moscow certainly needed a plan. Its population, which had declined sharply in the chaotic years after 1917, had by 1926 climbed just above pre-revolutionary levels, to more than two million; by 1931 it probably exceeded three million.[147] Its physical structure, and its equipment, were simply archaic: it consisted mainly of one- or two-story wooden buildings; the average housing space had been 89 square feet per person in 1926, and there had been a deterioration since then; in 1937, Ernest Simon could report that slums being demolished as unfit for habitation in Manchester – then one of the most slum-ridden cities in England – would provide better accommodation than 90% of Moscow families had.[148] Water, sewerage, and electricity supplies were all woefully short.

Perhaps understandably, after 1931 no more overseas experts were invited. The plan unveiled in July 1935 called for a limit on the city's future growth, coupled with forced modernization. The city was to be developed as a single integral unit; reconstruction was to be based on the "unity and harmony of architectural compositions";[149] the City Beautiful had come to Moscow.

The impetus of course was national pride: in 1937, everybody Simon spoke to "was most emphatic that the old two-story houses must go, that Moscow be a real city with buildings worthy of the capital of the greatest country in the world."[150] To achieve this, Moscow became a construction camp. What escaped the visitors was that all the emphasis was on the most visible and the most prestigious projects: three metro lines with their chandelier-light stations, housing along the main streets, public buildings, stadiums, squares, and parks.[151] Significantly, of all flats under construction in 1939, 52% were along the main thoroughfares.[152] Perhaps this was because the projects of different ministries were never coordinated, while the housing program fell more and more behind schedule;[153] perhaps, more likely, because the planners were trying to impress the public; most likely of all, because they were trying to please their master.

[144]   May, 1961, 181–2; Simon, 1937b, 382.
[145]   Svetlichny, 1960, 214.
[146]   Machler, 1932, 96; Parkins, 1953, 30–1.
[147]   Harris, 1970a, 257; Simon, 1937b, 381.
[148]   Simon, 1937a, 154–5.
[149]   Parkins, 1953, 36.
[150]   Simon, 1937a, 160.
[151]   Ling, 1943, 7; Parkins, 1953, 42, 44–5.
[152]   Berton, 1977, 235.
[153]   Parkins, 1953, 44–5.

And Stalin knew what he liked. "Henceforth, architecture had to be expressive, representational, oratorical. Every building however modest its function, had henceforth to be a monument."[154] He personally approved the plans for major buildings; once, offered two versions, he chose both and the terrified architects followed him, producing a structure in which the left side did not match the right.[155] And Stalin, too, had his own Socialist equivalent of Hitler's giant domed hall: the 1,300-foot Palace of the Soviets, to be crowned by a gigantic statue of Lenin. Actually started, it ran into structural problems and began to sink into the ground; perhaps mercifully, it was abandoned.[156] But all over Moscow, the wedding-cake architecture still recalls Stalin's tastes and whims.

So Moscow in the 1930s was a kind of Potemkin village. Just like Burnham's Washington and Chicago, just indeed like Haussmann's Paris, the new facades alongside the giant highways concealed a mass of ancient slums behind them. Even in the 1960s, the last remnants of that old wooden Moscow were still visible in the back streets. But doubtless the facades pleased the master; and the planners slept a little better at night for it.

Stalin's baleful heritage, which began to erode soon after his death in 1953, exerted itself across his empire. The newly formed GDR, cut off from its ties with the West, determined to build a large iron and steel combine near the town of Fürstenberg an der Oder, on the Polish border, with a new town to house the workers. Stalinist orthodoxy raged against "cosmopolitanism," meaning Bauhaus modernism, in favor of a so-called "national building tradition." Ironically, of course, the Bauhaus was a central part of the national heritage, especially of socialist architecture. But it was conveniently condemned as a "universal art" and "American imperialism."[157] The chief architect of Moscow came to Berlin to view the newly completed Stalinallee and pronounced that it was "typically German."[158]

So Stalinstadt – so it was originally named – was developed according to GDR's Sixteen Principles of Urban Development, thus emphasizing qualities of urbanity. On one point the principles were silent: the city was seen as an ultimate kind of social living, while denying any capacity for social action. The town is defined by the political center; the only actor is the national government.[159] In the plan for Stalinstadt, a planned City Hall was replaced by a "House of the party and municipal administration." "The *Polis* disappeared from the plans. Party, administration and culture had taken its place."[160] And the emphasis on axes, monumentalism, and masses conveniently ignores the fact that these were also the foundations of Nazi town planning.[161]

[154]   Kopp, 1970, 227.
[155]   Berton, 1977, 228–9.
[156]   Berton, 1977, 223–4; Kopp, 1970, 223.
[157]   May, 2003, 54.
[158]   May, 2003, 55.
[159]   May, 2003, 57.
[160]   May, 2003, 72.
[161]   May, 2003, 57.

In the event, Stalin conveniently died and none of the planned major buildings were ever built. The planned axis between the works gate "cathedral" and the city hall tower never came into being. Between the works and the town, there is a broad four-lane thoroughfare. Yet the Central Square remains empty and is today used as a car park.[162]

There was one last Great Dictator, and his megalomaniac dreams exceeded even those of his predecessors. Nicolae Ceauşescu's mission was to rebuild Romanian society and give birth to the "new man." To that end, aided by an earthquake that conveniently took place nearby in March 1977, he would simply obliterate Bucharest's historic center, replacing it by a landscape of wide and straight boulevards, massive high-rise buildings, and monumental urban spaces for political ceremonies and rituals – all designed to celebrate the achievements of the Ceauşescu era.[163] The aim was "the restoration of our Capital-city according to *a new outlook*, based on the assertion of traditional Romanian architectural elements harmoniously blending with the gains of world architecture and structural technique."[164] The aim was to eradicate anything that connected the people of Bucharest with their past culture, historical background, and social values that might be embodied in the diverse building forms inherited from past historical periods.[165]

The great man personally took charge of designing the Victoria Socialismului civic center: "the *historical decision* for building a new centre *belongs to Comrade Nicolae Ceausescu* … Architects, town-planners, engineers and constructors benefit from the permanent and precise instructions of Comrade Nicolae Ceausescu, who dedicates great part of his precious time to personally direct the activity of construction, architecture and systematization in Bucharest."[166] He alone conducted the meetings with architects participating in the competition, making observations that were incorporated as recommendations to be followed in the projects.[167]

Bulevardul Victoria Socialismului, the axis of the new center, 3.5 kilometers long and 92 meters wide, is big enough to assemble half a million people, and is lined with ten-story buildings. There is a central strip of land, 8 meters wide, with 17 fountains; two traffic lanes paved with colored mosaics; two 8.5-meter-wide green areas lined with lime, oak, and fir trees; and two pedestrian promenades 5 meters wide, also paved with decorative mosaics. This is not a boulevard designed for traffic, save occasional excursions by Ceauşescu and his entourage; its purpose was to provide a monumental approach to Casa Republicii,[168] one of the largest political-administrative buildings in the world, 86 meters high with facades 276 meters long, on 6.3 hectares of land, and housing 700 offices, meeting rooms, restaurants,

---

[162]   May, 2003, 69.
[163]   Cavalcanti, 1997, 84.
[164]   Cavalcanti, 1997, 84–5 (emphasis added).
[165]   Cavalcanti, 1997, 85.
[166]   Cavalcanti, 1997, 86 (emphasis added).
[167]   Cavalcanti, 1997, 89.
[168]   Cavalcanti, 1997, 96–8.

libraries, and assembly halls for 1,200 people.[169] As Maria Cavalcanti remarks, it bears an uncanny similarity to schemes earlier conceived by Napoleon III, Stalin, Hitler, and Mussolini in other European capitals.[170]

The odd conclusion is that there is no single easy explanation for the phenomenon of the City Beautiful. It manifested itself, over an 80-year period, in a great variety of different economic, social, political, and cultural circumstances: as a handmaiden of finance capitalism, as an agent of imperialism, as an instrument of personal totalitarianism of both the Right and Left varieties, so far as those labels have meaning. What these manifestations had in common, with some qualifications and exceptions, was a total concentration on the monumental and on the superficial, on architecture as symbol of power; and, correspondingly, an almost complete lack of interest in the wider social purposes of planning. This is planning for display, architecture as theater, design intended to impress. Only the hopefully impressionable objects differ: *nouveaux riches* in search of dissipation and titillation; cowed colonial subjects and haughty rulers of minor principalities; peasant migrants to the great city; depressed or dispossessed bourgeois families recalling past glories. All, with luck, will like the show; for many, rather like the Hollywood of the 1930s, it will take their minds off the grim reality outside. But at least the Hollywood productions were released on schedule; and they did not bankrupt their audiences.

[169]   Cavalcanti, 1997, 98.
[170]   Cavalcanti, 1997, 104.

The City of Towers

Ye towers of Julius, London's lasting shame,
With many a foul and midnight murther fed.

Thomas Grey, *The Bard* (1757)

The simplest solution is flats. If people are going to live in large towns at all they must learn to live on top of one another. But the northern working people do not take kindly to flats; even when flats exist they are contemptuously named "tenements". Almost everyone will tell you that he wants "a house of his own", and apparently a house in the middle of an unbroken block of houses a hundred yards long seems to them more "their own" than a flat situated in mid-air.

George Orwell, *The Road to Wigan Pier* (1937)

… the solution of the housing problem in any great English city does not lie in the provision of High Barbicans or High Paddingtons. They may be physically and theoretically possible but they are completely alien to the habits and tastes of the people who would be expected to live in them.

Harold Macmillan, *Internal Memorandum as Minister of Housing and Local Government* (1954)

Cities of Tomorrow: An Intellectual History of Urban Planning and Design Since 1880,
Fourth Edition. Peter Hall.
© 2014 Peter Hall. Published 2014 by John Wiley & Sons, Ltd.

7

The City of Towers

The Corbusian Radiant City: Paris, Chandigarh, Brasília, London, St Louis, 1920–1970

The evil that Le Corbusier did lives after him; the good is perhaps interred with his books, which are seldom read for the simple reason that most are almost unreadable. (The pictures, it should be said, are sometimes interesting for what they reveal of their draughtsman.) But the effort should be made, because their impact on twentieth-century city planning has been almost incalculably great: obscurity is no barrier to communication, at least of a sort. Ideas, forged in the Parisian intelligentsia of the 1920s, came to be applied to the planning of working-class housing in Sheffield and St Louis, and hundreds of other cities too, in the 1950s and 1960s; the results were at best questionable, at worst catastrophic. How and why this should happen is one of the most intriguing, but also one of the most chastening, stories in the intellectual history of modern planning.

Perhaps the most important facts about Le Corbusier were that he was not French but Swiss; and that this was not his real name. He was born Charles-Edouard Jeanneret at La Chaux-de-Fonds near Neuchâtel in 1885, and lived regularly in Paris only from the age of 31. The Swiss, as the least perceptive visitor has noticed, are an obsessionally well-ordered people: their cities are models of neat self-control, with not a blade of grass or a stray hair out of place. All Corbusier's cities would be like that. The chaos of the old Paris, that Haussmann's reconstruction left intact behind the new facades, must have been anathema to the Calvinist mores of the rising young architect. He devoted his professional life to Genevaizing it, and any other city that had the impertinence to be unruly.

The third significant fact about him is that he came from a family of watchmakers. (The name Le Corbusier was a pseudonym adopted from a maternal grandfather when he began to write, in 1920.) He was to achieve greatest fame for his statement, first made at that time, that a house is a machine to live in.[1] In one book, *Vers une architecture*, he insists that architecture must be totally machine-like and functional,

---

[1] Quoted in Fishman, 1977, 186.

Figure 7.1 Le Corbusier and Unité. A machine for living in, as prescribed by the Supreme Architect. *Source*: Popperfoto/Getty Images.

indeed produced by industrial mass-produced methods.[2] (The later excesses of industrialized housing in the 1960s, it becomes clear, were not merely consequences of political pressures and inadequate preparation; they represented a consistent policy, and their failures need to be judged in that light.) And so it comes as no surprise that, in another work, *Urbanisme*, triumphs of engineering are hailed as great architecture.

That was natural: the tradition, of crowding thousands of minute components into a planned harmony, came out of a long heritage. But people are not escapements, and society cannot be reduced to clockwork order; the attempt was an unhappy one for humanity. There is an anomaly, though: the Jura watchmakers were sturdy guardians of their local liberties, and for this were admired both by Proudhon and Kropotkin. Corbusier soon put that behind him.

If Switzerland gave him his view of the world, Paris provided both his raw material and his vision of an ideal order. Just as Howard cannot be understood save in the context of late nineteenth-century London, or Mumford save in that of the New York of the 1920s, so all Corbusier's ideas need to be seen as a reaction to the city in which he lived and worked from 1916 until shortly before his death in 1965.[3] The history of Paris has been one of constant struggle between the forces of exuberant, chaotic, often sordid everyday life and the forces of centralized, despotic order. In the 1920s and 1930s, it was clear that the former were winning and the latter had been in long retreat. Behind the facades, the city was racked by slums and disease.

---

[2] Le Corbusier, 1998.
[3] Fishman, 1977, 29, 101, 114, 183–4.

Figure 7.2 Louis XIV commands the building of the Invalides. Le Corbusier's favorite vision of the Master Architect at work: "We wish it." Unfortunately he never found his Roi Soleil. *Source*: © RMN-Grand Palais (Château de Versailles)/Franck Raux.

The city authorities of the Third Republic had all but given up the attempt even to complete the last of Haussmann's improvements, let alone take new initiatives like clearing the worst of the slums.[4]

Paris, the young Corbusier concluded, could be saved only by the intervention of *grands seigneurs*, men "without remorse": Louis XIV, Napoleon, Haussmann.[5] Their "grand openings" were for him "a signal example of *creation*, of that spirit which is able to dominate and compel the mob."[6] He concluded his early book *Urbanisme*

4   Sutcliffe, 1970, 240–1, 257; Lavedan, 1975, 492–3, 497–500; Evenson, 1979, 208–16.
5   Fishman, 1977, 210.
6   Le Corbusier, 1929, 293.

with a picture of Louis XIV personally directing the construction of the Invalides, which he captioned

> Homage to a great town planner – This despot conceived immense projects and realized them. Over all the country his noble works still fill us with admiration. He was capable of saying, "We wish it", or "Such is our pleasure."[7]

He searched all his life for a latter-day Roi Soleil, but never found him.

The Corbusian Ideal City

Meanwhile he had to make do with bourgeois patrons. His Plan Voisin of 1925 had nothing to do with neighborhood units, but was the name of an aircraft manufacturer who sponsored it.[8] (This helps explain the planes that fly, with such insouciant disregard of air traffic control, in between these and other Corbusian skyscrapers.) Its 18 uniform 700-foot-high towers would have entailed the demolition of most of historic Paris north of the Seine save for a few monuments, some of which would be moved; the Place Vendôme, which he liked as a symbol of order, would be kept.[9] He was apparently quite unable to understand why the plan aroused such an outcry in the city council, where he was called a barbarian.[10] He always thought that the Gothic cathedral-builders of thirteenth-century Europe, through whose efforts over a mere 100 years "The new world opened up as a flower on the ruins," must likewise have been misunderstood in those first years "when the cathedrals were white."[11]

He was not deterred: "The design of cities was too important to be left to the citizens."[12] He developed his principles of planning most fully in *La Ville Contemporaine* (1922) and *La Ville Radieuse* (1933). The key was the famous paradox: we must decongest the centers of our cities by increasing their density. In addition, we must improve circulation and increase the amount of open space. The paradox could be resolved by building high on a small part of the total ground area.[13] This demanded, as Corbusier put it in characteristic capital letters: "WE MUST BUILD ON A CLEAR SITE! The city of today is dying because it is not constructed geometrically."[14] The needs of traffic also demanded total demolition: "Statistics show us that business is conducted in the centre. This means that wide avenues must be driven through the centres of our towns. *Therefore the existing centres must come down.* To save itself,

---

[7]   Le Corbusier, 1929, 310.
[8]   Fishman, 1977, 211.
[9]   Banham, 1960, 255.
[10] Evenson, 1979, 54.
[11] Le Corbusier, 1937, 4.
[12] Fishman, 1977, 190.
[13] Le Corbusier, 1929, 178.
[14] Le Corbusier, 1929, 232.

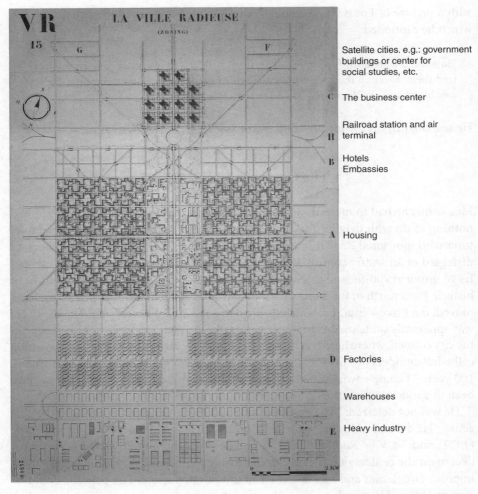

Figure 7.3 *La Ville Radieuse*. The total geometrical vision: massed machines for living and working in. *Source*: © FLC/ADAGP, Paris and DACS, London 2013/Scala, Florence.

every great city must rebuild its centre."[15] This was the first suggestion of its kind; 30 years later, it was to be taken up with a vengeance. But, as Harry A. Anthony has pointed out, there is no recognition anywhere in it of the problem of garaging all these cars, or of the environmental problems that would result from their noise and emissions; they are simply ignored.[16]

The way in which the new structure was to be achieved was, however, not uniform across the entire city: the Contemporary City was to have a clearly differentiated spatial structure. And this was to correspond to a specific, segregated social

[15] Le Corbusier, 1929, 128.
[16] Anthony, 1966, 286.

structure: one's dwelling depended on one's job.[17] At the center were the skyscrapers of the Plan Voisin which, Corbusier emphasized, were intended as offices for the elite *cadres*: industrialists, scientists, and artists (including, presumably, architects and planners); 24 of these towers would provide for between 400,000 and 600,000 top people's jobs at 1,200 to the acre, with 95% of the ground area left open.[18] Outside this zone, the residential areas would be of two types: six-story luxury apartments for these same *cadres*, designed on the so-called step-back principle (in rows) with 85% of ground space left open, and more modest accommodation for the workers, built around courtyards (on a uniform gridiron of streets), with 48% left open.[19]

These apartments would be mass-produced for mass-living. Corbusier had no time for any kind of individual idiosyncrasy; well did he call them "cells":

> We must never, in our studies, lose sight of the perfect human "Cell", the cell which corresponds most perfectly to our physiological and sentimental needs. We must arrive at the "house-machine", which must be both practical and emotionally satisfying and designed for a succession of tenants. The idea of the "old home" disappearing and with it local architecture, etc., for labour will shift about as needed, and must be ready to move, *bag and baggage*.[20]

Not only would the units all be uniform; they would all contain the same standard furniture. Possibly, he admits, "my scheme ... at first might seem to warrant a certain fear and dislike." But variations in layout, and generous tree-planting, would soon overcome this.[21] And not only would the units be mass-produced; for the bourgeois elite, they would also be collectively serviced: "though it will still always be possible to have a maid or a children's nurse of your own, a family servant if you wish," in the Radiant City "the servant problem would be solved":

> If you desired to bring some friend back to supper round about midnight, say after the theatre, a mere telephone call is all that is needed for you to find the table laid and waiting for you – with a servant who is not sulking.[22]

The core of the Contemporary City, clearly, was a middle-class sort of place. And, in the midst of the office center, he created an entertainment and cultural complex to minister to their needs, where the elite would talk and dance in "profound calm 600 feet above the ground."[23]

The blue-collar workers and the clerks would not live like this, of course. Corbusier provided for them in garden apartments within satellite units. Here, too, there would

---

[17] Fishman, 1977, 199.
[18] Le Corbusier, 1929, 215; Fishman, 1977, 195.
[19] Le Corbusier, 1929, 215, 222–3.
[20] Le Corbusier, 1929, 243.
[21] Le Corbusier, 1929, 243, 250–2.
[22] Le Corbusier, 1929, 229.
[23] Quoted in Fishman, 1977, 198.

be plenty of green space, sports facilities, and entertainments – but of a different sort, appropriate for those who worked hard for eight hours a day. Unlike the Paris of the 1920s, where rich and poor tended to live in close juxtaposition, *La Ville Contemporaine* would have been a completely class-segregated city.

By the time of the Radiant City, though the tenets of the Corbusian religion remained unchanged, there were important theological variations. Corbusier had lost his faith in capitalists, probably because in the middle of the Great Depression they had lost the capacity to fund him. Now, he came to believe in the virtue of centralized planning, which would cover not merely city-building but every aspect of life. The way to this would come through syndicalism, but not of the anarchist kind: this would be an ordered, hierarchical system, having some close affinities to the left-wing variety of Italian fascism. Many French syndicalists indeed joined the Vichy regime in 1940; Corbusier himself believed that "France needs a Father. It doesn't matter who."[24] In this system, everything would be determined by the plan, and the plan would be produced "objectively" by experts; the people would have a say only in who was to administer it.

> The harmonious city must first be planned by experts who understand the science of urbanism. They work out their plans in total freedom from partisan pressures and special interests; once their plans are formulated, they must be implemented without opposition.[25]

In 1938 he designed a "National Centre of Collective Festivals for 100,000 People," where the leader could address his people; it is like an open-air version of Hitler's Domed Hall.[26]

But the new syndicalist city is different in one vital respect: now, everyone will be equally collectivized. Now, everyone will live in giant collective apartments called *Units*; every family will be given an apartment not according to the breadwinner's job, but according to rigid space norms; no one will be given anything more or less than the minimum necessary for efficient existence. And now, everyone – not just the lucky elite – will enjoy collective services. Cooking, cleaning, and child care are all taken away from the family.

In the meantime, significantly, Corbusier had been to the Soviet Union. And, in the 1920s, an important group of Soviet architects – the urbanists – had developed ideas very close to his. They wanted to build new cities in open countryside, in which everyone would live in gigantic collective apartment blocks, with individual space reduced to the absolute minimum needed for a bed; there would be no individual or family kitchens and bathrooms. In one version, life would be regulated by the minute, from a 6 a.m. reveille to departure for the mine at 7; another

---

24   Fishman, 1977, 237, 239–40.
25   Fishman, 1977, 239.
26   Fishman, 1977, 241.

urbanist envisaged a unit in which huge orchestras would induce sleep for insomniacs, drowning the snores of the others.[27] The plans by some members of this group – Ivanov, Terekhin, and Smolin in Leningrad, Barshch, Vladimirov, Alexander, and Vesnin in Moscow – are almost identical, down to details, to the *Unité* as developed in the Radiant City and as actually built at Marseille in 1946.[28] But, after 1931, the Soviet regime – like the fascist regime in Italy a few years later – rejected Corbusier's advice.

And, by the 1940s, he had modified his views again – though as usual, only in the details. His ASCORAL (Assemblé de Constructeurs pour une Rénovation Architecturale), founded during the war, argued that *Les Cités radio-concentriques des échanges*, the centers of education and entertainment, still designed in the old Corbusian way, should be joined together by *Les Cités linéaires industrielles*, which would be continuous lines of industrialization along transportation corridors.[29] He had ceased to be optimistic about the big city, believing that the population of Paris should shrink from three to one million.[30] These notions had curious echoes of the Soviet deurbanists of the 1920s, whom Corbusier had so bitterly derided. But there was a crucial difference: his were to be concentrated "green factories" with workers living segregated, immobile lives in vertical garden cities, each having between 1,500 and 2,500 workers, of course with the inevitable collective catering.[31] He remained implacably opposed to the idea of *cités jardins*, which he consistently confused, like most of his fellow French planners, with garden suburbs.[32]

None of this was ever built. The remarkable fact about Corbusier is just how phenomenally unsuccessful he was in practice. He traveled all over Europe, and outside it, producing his grandiose urban visions; page after page of his book *The Radiant City* is filled with them: Algiers, Antwerp, Stockholm, Barcelona, Nemours in North Africa. All remained on paper. In World War Two, with the establishment of the puppet Pétain regime in Vichy, he thought his time at last had come. Invited to head a study commission on housing and planning, he predictably produced a scheme for an elite of town planners heading huge architectural and engineering offices, able to override all interference. At their head was to be a "regulator," an architect-administrator who formulated the entire national plan for building. Modesty for once overcame him; he failed to name his candidate for the post.[33] In fact, he got nowhere with Vichy either. His simple-minded egomania and his total political naiveté made it difficult for him to understand his failure; at the end of the war he was a deeply disillusioned man.

[27] Hamm, 1977, 62–3; Berton, 1977, 210.
[28] Kopp, 1970, 146–7, 169, 171.
[29] Le Corbusier, 1948, 48; 1959, 103, 129.
[30] Sutcliffe, 1977, 221.
[31] Le Corbusier, 1948, 54.
[32] Le Corbusier, 1937, 255, 258; 1948, 68.
[33] Fishman, 1977, 247–8.

The Planning of Chandigarh

Ironically, his only real planning achievement on the ground – apart from the Marseille *Unité*, a single block that was supposed to be the start of a complex but was never completed, plus two reverential copies in France and another in Berlin – came posthumously.

The government of India had decided for political reasons to build a new capital for the Punjab at Chandigarh. They hired a planner, Albert Mayer, who produced a worthy plan in the Unwin–Parker–Stein–Wright tradition.[34] They approved the plan, but decided to bring in a team of the most prestigious modern architects – Corbusier, his own cousin Jeanneret, Maxwell Fry, and Jane Drew – to give expression to it. Fry describes the traumatic first meeting, for which Mayer was late:

> Corbusier held the crayon and was in his element.
> "*Voilà la gare*" he said "*et voici la rue commercial*", and he drew the first road on the new plan of Chandigarh. "*Voici la tête*", he went on, indicating with a smudge the higher ground to the left of Mayer's location, the ill effects of which I had already pointed out to him. "*Et voilà l'estomac, le cité-centre*". Then he delineated the massive sectors measuring each half by three quarters of a mile and filling out the extent of the plain between the river valleys, with extension to the south.
> The plan was well advanced by the time the anxious Albert Mayer joined the group … not in any way was he a match for the enigmatic but determined figure of the prophet.
> We sat around after lunch in a deadly silence broken by Jeanneret's saying to Mayer, "*Vous parlez français, monsieur?*" To which Mayer responded, "*Oui, musheer, je parle*", a polite but ill-fated rejoinder that cut him out of all discussion that followed.
> And so we continued, with minor and marginal suggestions from us and a steady flow of exposition from Corbusier, until the plan as we now know it was completed and never again departed from.[35]

There followed arguments between the architects and the planners, followed by arguments between the architects, with Fry and Jeanneret complaining at the way Corbusier had taken complete charge, including detailed layouts and designs. Rather naively, they said they wanted to work within the spirit of the Congrès Internationaux d'Architecture Moderne (CIAM), that is, collaboratively. The outcome was significant: a division of labor, in which Corbusier was given the brief for the central administrative complex.[36] But what had happened was more fundamental: a shift from a planning style to an architectural style, meaning "a shift towards a preoccupation with visual form, symbolism, imagery and aesthetics rather than the basic problems of the Indian population. By concentrating on providing Indian architecture with forms suited to the Second Machine Age, the existing Indian situation could be more or less totally ignored."[37]

[34]   Evenson, 1966, 13–14.
[35]   Quoted in Sarin, 1982, 44.
[36]   Sarin, 1982, 45.
[37]   Sarin, 1982, 47.

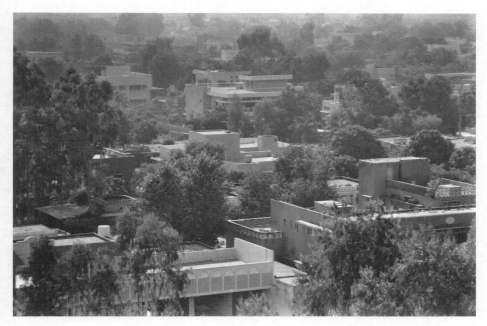

Figure 7.4 Chandigarh. The only realized Corbusian city design: here a residential quarter, functionalist boxes for Punjabi functionaries, from the pen of the master. *Source*: Madhu Sarin.

Figure 7.5 Chandigarh. The reality of the people's city behind the facades; foreground, autonomous housing; left background, tent city. *Source*: Madhu Sarin.

The result was a set of rich multiple ironies. Corbusier found his patron in a post-colonial government steeped in the autocratic traditions of the British Raj. He produced for them an exercise in the City Beautiful decked in the trappings of modern architecture; a latter-day New Delhi. There was a grid of fast traffic roads, already used in plans for Marseille and Bogotá, to cater for a level of car ownership even lower than the Paris of 1925, which was low enough. The relationship between streets and buildings is totally European, and is laid down without regard for the fierce North Indian climate or for Indian ways of life.[38] There is a total failure to produce built forms that could aid social organization or social integration; the sections fail to function as neighborhoods.[39] The city is heavily segregated by income and civil service rank, recalling *La Ville Contemporaine*; there are different densities for different social groups, resulting in a planned class segregation.[40] So the contrasts are stark:

> As one walks around the magnificent campus of the Punjab University … (where most of the classrooms and offices are used for only three hours a day), one can see over the high campus walls thousands of people living in slums, without any electricity or running water.[41]

By the 1970s, 15% of the population were living in squatter or semi-squatter settlements; more than half the traders were operating informally from barrows or stalls.[42] Since they conflicted with the Master Plan's vision of urban order, the authorities made repeated attempts to harass and break them up. The traders responded by a series of public events worthy of an Indian version of an old Ealing comedy. To commemorate the inauguration of a new illegal market at a time when Sikh separatism was very sensitive, they arranged a whole series of sacred Sikh religious events; when the enforcement staff arrived, the Sikh traders announced that they would let themselves be cut to pieces before these would be stopped. Later on the traders stage-managed elaborate funeral ceremonies for the Prime Minister who had just died, thus attracting huge publicity.[43]

All of which is part of the rich pageant of Indian life, and nothing to do with Corbusier. True, most of the problems were only indirectly to be laid at his door; he was by then dead, and in his last years he had been concentrating on the central monumental complex and on the general visual symbolism, the part of the plan that works best.[44] But that was just the point: at the end of the day, like Hitler dreaming his futile dreams in Berlin, what he really cared about was the monumental part. He was the last of the City Beautiful planners. The rest does not work, but in a sense that

---

[38] Evenson, 1966, 92.
[39] Evenson, 1966, 95.
[40] Gupta, 1974, 363; Schmetzer and Wakely, 1974, 352–3.
[41] Gupta, 1974, 368.
[42] Sarin, 1979, 137.
[43] Sarin, 1979. 152.
[44] Evenson, 1966, 39, 94.

is beside the point. At least, in Chandigarh the housing was much better than what the people had known before, and probably better than they could ever have hoped for if the city had never been built. But when Corbusier's disciples finally came to apply their master's precepts in the cities of the West, it was a rather different matter.

Brasília: The Quasi-Corbusian City

There was one other completely new Corbusian city, though he did not design it. Brazil, like many another developing country, had grown around its port city which had willy-nilly become its capital. But by the 1940s, despite partial attempts at reconstruction, Rio de Janeiro was bursting at the seams. There had long been a plan for a new Federal capital in the interior; in 1823 José Bonifácio de Andrada e Silva, "father of his country," had suggested and named it; in 1892 a Commission had already found the site; in 1946 a new democratic commission provided for it; in 1955 another commission rediscovered the site. The same year, Juscelino Kubitschek de Oliveira, a charismatic politician, committed himself to build it during his presidential election campaign, and narrowly won.[45] There was a long Brazilian political tradition of building grandiose public works within impossibly short times; Brasília became its apotheosis.[46] The Rio press were predictably critical: "The limit of insanity! a dictatorship in the desert." Kubitschek was undeterred.[47]

He went to his old friend, the architect Oscar Niemeyer. The Institute of Brazilian Architects protested; there must be a competition. Niemeyer was of course on the jury; it reached its decision after a mere three days' deliberation, awarding one of the biggest city planning exercises of the twentieth century to Lúcio Costa, another pioneer of the modern architectural movement in Brazil. His entry consisted of freehand drawings on five medium-sized cards: not a single population projection, economic analysis, land-use schedule, model, or mechanical drawing.[48] The jury liked its "grandeur"; "It was apparent from the beginning that Brasília was to be an architect's, rather than a planner's, city."[49]

The plan was variously described as an airplane, bird, or dragonfly: the body, or fuselage, was a monumental axis for the principal public buildings and offices, the wings were the residential and other areas. In the first, uniform office blocks were to line a wide central mall leading to the complex of governmental buildings. In the second, uniform apartments were to be built in Corbusian superblocks fronting a huge central traffic spine; precisely following the prescription of *La Ville Radieuse*, everyone, from Permanent Secretary to janitor, was to live in the same blocks in the same kind of apartment.

---

45 Epstein, 1973, 36, 42, 45; Evenson, 1973, 49, 108, 112–13.
46 Epstein, 1973, 36.
47 Evenson, 1973, 114.
48 Epstein, 1973, 49; Evenson, 1973, 145.
49 Evenson, 1973, 117, 142–3.

But, as James Holston argues, Brasília demonstrates that modernism had a very radical social and political intent: to replace capitalism by a new collectivist social order. Though Kubitschek was a Latin American populist, Niemeyer was an avowed communist. The plan, according to Holston, was the ultimate political achievement of the modern movement, "a CIAM city ... the most complete example ever constructed of the architectural and planning tenets put forward in CIAM manifestos";[50] it would achieve the objective for which the pioneers had struggled in vain. Its hidden agenda was to create a totally new built form as a shell for a new society, without reference to history: the past was simply to be abolished. "Brasília," he writes, "was built to be more than the symbol of this new age. Rather, its design and construction were intended as means to *create* it by transforming Brazilian society."[51] It embodies perfectly a key premise of the modern movement, "total decontextualization," in which a utopian future becomes the means to measure the present, without any sense of historical context: a city created on a clean slate, without reference to the past.[52] In this new city the traditional Brazilian society, heavily stratified, would be replaced by a totally egalitarian one: in the uniform apartment blocks, governors and ambassadors would live as neighbors with janitors and laborers. Traditional divisions between public and private space would be abolished; these blocks would be machines for collective public living. And even the traditional street – the age-old essence of the division between public and private life – must disappear; hence Brasília's eight-lane expressways, which act as social divisors rather than social integrators.

The construction of Brasília became a legend even in Brazil, that country of bizarre fable. An American wrote that "It was as if the opening of the west had been delayed a hundred years and then done with bulldozers."[53] Since at all costs the capital must be dedicated on April 24, 1960, at the end of Kubitschek's four-year term, it was decreed that there should be non-stop 24-hour construction for one year. It all "represented a triumph of administration in a country never noted for efficient administration; it represented adherence to a time schedule in a society where schedules are seldom met; and it represented continuous hard work for a people reputedly reluctant to work either hard or continuously."[54] Legends abounded, all doubtless true: the truck drivers who delivered the same load of sand several times a day; typographers hired as topographers, brick-counters as accountants.[55] The last thing anyone considered was the cost. William Holford, a jury member, said that no one knew the size of the bill; the President of NOVACAP (Companhia Urbanizadora da Nova Capital do Brasil), the New Town Corporation, said that

50   Holston, 1990, 31.
51   Holston, 1990, 3.
52   Holston, 1990, 9.
53   Evenson, 1973, 155.
54   Evenson, 1973, 155.
55   Epstein, 1973, 63.

he was not bothered by accounts; Niemeyer told the British architect Max Lock that he had no idea what the Presidential Palace had cost: "How should I know?" he disarmingly asked.[56] Well did Epstein, author of one of the two standard histories of the city, dedicate his book:

> Aos trabalhadores de Brasília, que construíram a nova capital;
> Aos trabalhadores de Brasil, que pagaram.[57]
> (To the workers of Brasília, who built the new capital;
> To the workers of Brazil, who paid for it.)

Unbelievably, 60,000 workers managed to finish it. In one day 2,000 light poles were erected; overnight 722 houses were painted white. On the appointed day, the Presidential Palace, the Executive Palace, the National Congress, the Supreme Court, 11 ministries, a hotel, and 94 apartment blocks were gleaming in the sunlight on the open *campo* of central Brazil. It was of course all a shell; the buildings were unfinished inside; after the ceremony, many of the officials took planes back to Rio. But even after Kubitschek, too much had been invested in the city to turn back; over the following decade, the whole machinery of government did move there.

And it came to work, after a fashion. As car ownership rose, the vast expressways and cloverleaves filled with traffic; since the plan did not attempt to resolve pedestrian–vehicle conflicts, streams of pedestrians cheat death daily as they weave between speeding cars on the central mall. This is a detail; the real failure was that, just as in Chandigarh, an unplanned city grew up beside the planned one. The difference was that here, it was far larger.

The Brazilian *favela*, like its equivalent in every other developing country, is a familiar feature of the urban landscape; one of the best-known swarms very visibly up the hillside behind Rio's famous Copacabana beach. But Brasília, symbol of modernity, was to have none of this; squatting was simply to be abolished there.[58] And so it was, in a sense: it was just pushed out of sight and out of mind. In the construction period, a so-called Free Town had to be created; soon, squatting created the nearby settlement of Taguatinga. After dedication, the authorities tried to destroy it, provoking an agitation; in 1961, to the dismay of the architectural profession, a law was passed permitting it to remain. By the mid-1960s, it was officially estimated that one-third of the population of the Federal District, 100,000 people, lived in "sub-habitations"; soon, the figure was more than one-half.[59] The authorities responded to invasions by trying to lay out minimal site-and-service plots; Epstein's account of the process has a special irony.

Actual assignment of the lots and the laying out of new streets were in the hands of two men, one of them illiterate, under the supervision of a NOVACAP foreman. None of these was formally trained in urban planning, social work or in surveying. They laid out a gridwork of streets crossing each other at right angles.[60]

Such was the end of the dream of creating a classless urban society in a country where rich and poor had always been segregated. The difference, if anything, was that in Brasília they were more ruthlessly separated than in any of the older cities: a *cordon sanitaire* was placed between them and the monumental, symbolic city, so that they might never spoil the view or disturb the image. The servants who remained in the superblocks, ironically, were cooped up in closet spaces far worse than they had enjoyed in traditional apartments. The deep class structures of Brazil, subtly racial in origin, reasserted themselves. Niemeyer himself, by this time, was saying that the plan had been distorted and traduced; only a socialist regime, he felt, could have implemented it.[61] Corbusier suffered from the same feelings much of his life: it is hard to build a City Beautiful amidst the confusion of democracy and the market.

Figure 7.6 Brasília. The vision of a modernized, sanitized capital city, sketched by Lúcio Costa on five index cards.

---

[60] Epstein, 1973, 121–2.
[61] Evenson, 1973, 180.

Figure 7.7   Taguatinga, Brasília. Started as a construction camp, the first of the popular settlements that represent the reality for most of the capital region's people: impossible to suppress, eventually accepted but ignored.

The Corbusians Come to Britain

They did little better in the developed world; though they tried. The means to the end was the influence of CIAM, "the Jesuits of the new faith" founded in 1928 "at the invitation of the Swiss *animateur* Siegfried Giedion":[62] the Swiss connection, again, visible also five years later when Giedion took the initiative in starting the Modern Architecture Research group (MARS) in London.[63] By 1938 Corbusier was haranguing the British faithful:

> The benefits of the new architecture must not be confined to the homes of the few who enjoy the privilege of taste or money. They must be widely diffused so as to brighten the homes, and thus the lives, of millions upon millions of workers … It naturally postulates the most crucial issue of our age: a great campaign for the rational re-equipment of whole countries regarded as indivisible units.[64]

He was preaching to the converted, but there were as yet not many of them. A few, notably those who had attended CIAM II in Frankfurt in 1929, were aware of the work of Ernst May in Frankfurt and his modernistic interpretations of the garden-city idea,[65] but in the 1930s, despite trips abroad, most local authorities regarded

[62]   Esher, 1981, 37.
[63]   Hardy, 2005, 39.
[64]   Quoted in Esher, 1981, 37.
[65]   Ward, 2010, 122–3.

flats as an unfortunate necessity, and only two schemes – one in London, one the famous Quarry Hill flats in Leeds, which originated from a visit of two councilors to Vienna – even broke the five-story barrier.[66] Overseas émigrés – Serge Chermayeff, Ernö Goldfinger, Bernard Lubetkin, Peter Moro, and Nikolaus Pevsner – played key roles in spreading the new gospel from mainland Europe.[67] At the MARS group's exhibition in London in 1938, originally planned in 1935 but repeatedly postponed, suburbia appeared as a *bête noire*: the flat roof represented the way forward.[68]

Seven years later, all was changed. There was a huge, pent-up political force. By the end of the war, a real revolution had already occurred: government in Britain had assumed responsibility for the welfare of the people in a way that would have been unthinkable in the 1930s.[69] Associated with this was an extraordinary sense that Britain must be rebuilt, that the slums must be swept away. At Plymouth, one of the worst-bombed cities, Lord Astor, the lord mayor, and a group of councilors received John Reith, Minister of Works; that evening, Reith witnessed an extraordinary sight:

> Two thousand people were dancing in the open air – an idea of Waldorf Astor's. Below them was spread the awful havoc lately wrought on their city; not far away across the sea the enemy. As they danced the summer evening into night I saw a coastal forces flotilla steam out from their Davenport anchorage in single line ahead; there was business for them to do, and they would probably do it all the better for what they could see on the Hoe.[70]

Astor told him that, as a result of their meeting, all opposition to the idea of planning had disappeared. And with this went a swing of the pendulum, away from traditionalism and in favor of modernism. As John Gold comments, "the task of rebuilding took on something of a mystic aura, a Phoenix-like process in which the very fabric of society would be renewed. Dirty Victorian buildings and mean streets came to characterize the past and … the future could be portrayed in the clean lines and steel, glass and concrete of modernist architecture."[71]

After the war, the CIAM-MARS architects soon found themselves in conflict with the garden-city tradition in the new towns, though modernist architects were appointed to plan many of them: Gibberd at Harlow, Gordon Stephenson and Peter Shepheard at Stevenage, William Holford at Corby, Lubetkin at Peterlee, Lionel Brett (Lord Esher) at Hatfield and later Basildon.[72] But, Maxwell Fry asserted,

[66]   Ravetz, 1974, 133, 140, 144; Daunton, 1984, 140–2.
[67]   Gold, 1997, passim.
[68]   Gold, 1993, 360, 365.
[69]   Titmuss, 1950, 506.
[70]   Reith, 1949, 428.
[71]   Reith, 1949, 428.
[72]   Gold, 1997, 195.

At the beginning of the New Towns we were very much at one with government, as witness the fact that most New Towns were built by MARS group architects. It was not until we realized that they were extended Garden Cities that our enthusiasm waned a little.[73]

In fact, the terms of reference of the program, set by the Reith Committee, made this inevitable;[74] "the idea that New Towns could have escaped from their Garden City origins was probably wishful thinking."[75] At Peterlee, Lubetkin engaged in repeated battles with the National Coal Board over his concentrated high-density design, and when his tenure ended in March 1950 it was not renewed.[76]

Underlying this was an exceedingly strange story: the ideological associations of British modernism with communism. In 1935, the Architectural Association (AA) under its new principal, Eric Rowse, became Britain's first avowedly modernist architecture school. The uncompromising Rowse soon fell foul of the AA governors, but the modernist program survived, providing a home for communist sympathies amongst teachers and students. Many prominent architects and planners who worked or were trained there, including Richard Llewelyn-Davies, Max Lock, Ann MacEwen, and Graeme Shankland, were then communists.[77] A young communist architect-planner, Arthur Ling, visited the Soviet Union in 1939 and became central to British planning's links with it over many years. He was also Secretary of the MARS Group's Town Planning Committee and in 1941 joined the London County Council (LCC) Architect's Department led by John Forshaw. This became an important hub of communist activism in architecture and planning during the 1940s. Ling (with other prominent LCC communists including Kenneth Campbell) played an important role in the 1943 County of London Plan, and appears prominently in the official film of the plan, *Proud City*. In 1945, he became leader of the Town Planning Division of the Architect's Department.[78] At the same time, a new Architecture and Planning section of the Anglo-Soviet Friendship Society was created with Ling as Chairman[79] and a host of significant members including William Holford, Charles Holden, Coventry's Donald Gibson, Graeme Shankland and Ted Hollamby.[80]

Despite these links the communist influence waned, often for overt political reasons as the Cold War intensified. In Peterlee, Lubetkin, encouraged by the prominent LCC communist Monica Felton, who was Chair of the Development Corporation, formulated an essentially Marxist plan to reflect the class solidarity of the Durham miners. Despite moral qualms, Felton used her personal intimacy with Lewis Silkin to gain his support, though this was far from wholehearted. During 1949, Lubetkin's

[73] Quoted in Gold, 1997, 95.
[74] Gold, 1997, 95–6.
[75] Gold, 1997, 96.
[76] Gold, 1997, 198–9.
[77] Ward, 2012a, 505.
[78] Ward, 2012a, 506.
[79] Ward, 2012a, 507.
[80] Ward, 2012a, 508.

proposed high-density urban core was deemed inconsistent with exploiting the underlying coal. When Silkin moved Felton to Stevenage in autumn 1949, Lubetkin was left completely isolated. In 1950, his plan was finally jettisoned for a more conventional low-density layout.[81] Finally, in June 1951, during the Korean War, Silkin's successor Hugh Dalton dismissed Felton as Chairman of Stevenage Development Corporation. Stephen Ward comments that she has been almost completely airbrushed from British planning history.[82]

During 1955, a security service investigation identified six planners involved in planning an international conference (including Ling, Lock, Johnson-Marshall, and Leslie Ginsburg) as current or recent communists or active in friendship organizations. Amid accusations of McCarthyism, the government discouraged civil servant participation.[83] Some "more specific Soviet impacts on British planning," Stephen Ward comments, "were subtle almost to the point of invisibility." Within the LCC architects, the Soviet admirers favored a relatively traditional, softer Swedish form of modernism, rejecting the Corbusian path. Other communists, particularly Shankland and Hollamby, went further, rediscovering the father of British revolutionary socialist design, William Morris.[84] Ironically, as time went on, ardent Soviet admirers became leaders of the profession, joining the mainstream of the British planning establishment, and producing some of its most innovative schemes of the later 1950s: the unbuilt but seminal plan for Hook (Shankland), the "figure of eight" plan for Runcorn (Ling) and the extensible grid plans for Washington and Milton Keynes (Llewelyn-Davies and Bor). They also served an increasingly market-led mixed economy. The ultimate irony came in 1981 when Hollamby's long career culminated as Chief Architect and Planner of the London Docklands Development Corporation, the apotheosis of Thatcherite neoliberal urbanism.[85]

Meanwhile, as postwar reconstruction gained momentum, the original modernist consensus began to wane. Research by planning historians in major cities shows that the original wartime enthusiasm for the plans, the work of a relatively small elite network, began to wane as the job of implementation drew in other much larger groups of actors and interests. In Plymouth, Stephen Essex and Mark Brayshay find that the interactions and tensions among the players in these bigger networks led to significant compromises and, ultimately, there was a mismatch between the original vision and the reality that was delivered.[86] Waldorf Astor, a veteran politician who acted as Plymouth's lord mayor for the duration of the war, knew Lord Reith, the Minister of Works and Planning from 1940 to 1942, George Pepler, the town planning adviser at the Ministry of Health, and Patrick Abercrombie, who he was instrumental in hiring to produce the highly radical Plan for Plymouth in 1943.[87]

[81]   Ward, 2012a, 509.
[82]   Ward, 2012a, 509.
[83]   Ward, 2012a, 511.
[84]   Ward, 2012a, 517.
[85]   Ward, 2012a, 517–18.
[86]   Essex and Brayshay, 2007, 417.
[87]   Essex and Brayshay, 2007, 421.

Abercrombie's appointment was virtually signed and sealed before anyone else had fully considered the matter.[88] The key feature of the plan, a broad avenue from the railway station on the northern edge of the city center to the Hoe in the south (Armada Way), emerged equally instantaneously during the weekend of October 18–19, 1941, later recalled by Astor:

> I well recollect how my wife took him [Abercrombie] for a walk … They had the vision of a view … which for generations had been blotted out by promiscuous buildings. That is how we got the conception of a broad open way from the high ground at North Road station down through the heart of Plymouth and up to the old Eddystone Lighthouse, which has been re-erected as a monument on the Hoe.[89]

Essex and Brayshay comment that for such a tiny group to have made such sweeping – and ultimately irrevocable – decisions, without public consultation or participation, is remarkable. But "Even more remarkable is the skilful manner in which the core network managed to implant the idea of these central elements into the consciousness of the city to a point where they became a 'magna carta' that even the ministry felt obliged to acknowledge as non-negotiable."[90] But the influence of both Astor and Abercrombie waned, particularly after 1944, and, at the implementation stage, powerful new actors began to play an increasingly important role. A dilution of the original blueprint began to occur: city officials, councilors, and retailers sought modifications and the civil servants of the new Ministry of Town and Country Planning exercised their overriding influence, introducing what were seen as more realistic and practicable interpretations, driven by functionalism, economics, and different viewpoints.[91]

Likewise, Phil Hubbard and Lucy Faire show that Donald Gibson's celebrated plan for Coventry, product of the first local authority architect's department in Britain, was marked by endless disputes with the City Engineers, headed by Ernest Ford.[92] Encouraged by Lord Reith, the Town Clerk commissioned them to collaborate on a redevelopment plan for the square mile of the city center, but they were still unable to agree. Two plans were submitted; Gibson's prevailed. It deliberately disregarded existing property ownership in order to create "a shopping centre envisaged as two main blocks flanking a shopping avenue from which only pedestrians would have access to recessed arcades," and a recreation center where "cinemas and theatres would take their place in and contribute to the design as a whole." It also stressed planning for the car and car parking, with suggestions for a system of radial and ring roads intended to decongest the city center, so that "through traffic would remain unhampered by local traffic."[93] Although Gibson and his team did their utmost to

[88]   Essex and Brayshay, 2007, 423.
[89]   Essex and Brayshay, 2007, 424.
[90]   Essex and Brayshay, 2007, 436.
[91]   Essex and Brayshay, 2007, 436.
[92]   Hubbard and Faire, 2003, 380.
[93]   Hubbard and Faire, 2003, 380.

persuade the public, as well as councilors, of the merits of their clean-sweep approach, concerns were raised by both insiders (notably, Ernest Ford) and outsiders (including William Holford, who was concerned about the practicalities). The remaining war years, therefore, witnessed Gibson appeasing opponents of this radical urban vision by tempering the excesses of his scheme – to the extent that he took on board many of Ford's suggestions.[94] An exhibition of the resultant plan, in October 1945, attracted 48,808 visitors over 13 days, but they were, in fact, profoundly ambivalent about the proposals – possibly because they had more important priorities to worry about.[95]

Next door, in Birmingham, David Adams argues that the creation of "Modern" Birmingham, Britain's largest provincial city, in the years immediately following World War Two, involved attempts by planners to impose a particular vision of the city:[96] the vision of Herbert Manzoni, who had joined the City in 1927 and became Chief Surveyor and Engineer in 1935, largely due to his personal determination and the high regard in which he was held by local politicians. It had two elements: a network of ring roads around the city core, early plans for which had been drawn up as long before as 1917–18, and five giant slum-clearance areas, identified by 1941, which were to be systematically demolished and rebuilt in a modernist style.[97] This was no long-term, all-enveloping utopian blueprint for a perfect city, as in so many bombed and un-bombed cities; indeed, no overall official "plan" was ever produced for the city or even the city center. But, as in Plymouth and Coventry, it represented an expert-driven, paternalist approach to planning which has become the only official story.[98] During the 1950s, idealized representations, depicting a seemingly rational allocation of land uses, communicated the idea of a forward-thinking "Modern" Birmingham liberated from the vicissitudes of physical congestion that appeared to characterize some parts of the prewar city. Even in the "unplanned" central core, where the council felt that a reconstruction plan would be restrictive to prospective commercial businesses, "official" visions were based on the creation of spaces for rapid motorized transit, through the construction of the inner ring road, which generally took precedence over pedestrian flow in an attempt to mold pedestrian and motorist behavior rather than to respect existing patterns of circulation.[99]

Over the water in Rotterdam, Cordula Rooijendijk shows that even there, the idea of urban planning as modernist was an oversimplification.[100] In the years immediately after 1945, a conflict developed between traditional urban repairers who tried to rebuild inner cities according to an improved version of their historical form, and modernist urban developers who wanted to build brand new inner cities.[101] The outcome

[94]   Hubbard and Faire, 2003, 381.
[95]   Hubbard and Faire, 2003, 388.
[96]   Adams, 2011, 237.
[97]   Adams, 2011, 244.
[98]   Adams, 2011, 238.
[99]   Adams, 2011, 239.
[100] Rooijendijk, 2005, 177.
[101] Rooijendijk, 2005, 181.

was two plans: the conservative Witteveen plan aimed at rebuilding the old form, and the utopian 1946 Basisplan,[102] which won out because of a new desire to create totally new cities to provide the foundation for a new society. It was one of those comparatively few postwar reconstruction plans that really did break with the past.[103] But, Rooijendijk finds, there is clear evidence that not everyone approved of the Basisplan.[104] The authorities tried to limit public debate by giving the public hardly any chance to react. They repeatedly stressed that there was no time to lose; the final plan was approved just three months after publication. It marked a triumph for the modernist ideal urban image, an image of a highly functional and spatially ordered city with an efficient central business district at its heart. It became an inspirational example for urban planners all over the world; from America, Edmund Bacon and Lewis Mumford both commended it as an ideal example of the modern, future city: "For at least two decades, Rotterdam was regarded as *the* city of tomorrow."[105] But, as the years passed, the modernistic city, which was to replace the inflexible old one, became just as inflexible. And the public spaces, squares, and streets did prove inappropriate for public interaction, exactly as opponents had warned.[106]

In London, Abercrombie and Forshaw opened their County of London Plan with a picture that, decades later, leaps out of the page and sears the eyes: it shows a poor East End street, totally devastated, the pathetic belongings of the people loaded on to a truck. In the foreground, the children stare at the camera, as in mute accusation. Under it is a quotation from Winston Churchill.

> Most painful is the number of small houses inhabited by working folk which has been destroyed … We will rebuild them, more to our credit than some of them were before. London, Liverpool, Manchester, Birmingham may have much more to suffer, but they will rise from their ruins, more healthy, and, I hope, more beautiful … In all my life I have never been treated with so much kindness as by the people who suffered most.[107]

In the City of London, where one-third of the built area had been destroyed, including 20 of the City's ancient churches, 16 of the livery halls, and a large part of Guildhall,[108] Junichi Hasegawa has shown that the wartime Coalition government and its Labour successor forced the City Fathers to abandon their original plan in favor of a new plan from outside consultants, William Holden and Charles Holford, which won wide praise from the media.[109] But, long after that, the first new buildings were severely criticized for their poor aesthetic quality and siting. In 1955, Duncan

---

102 Rooijendijk, 2005, 182.
103 Rooijendijk, 2005, 192.
104 Rooijendijk, 2005, 199.
105 Rooijendijk, 2005, 198–9.
106 Rooijendijk, 2005, 199.
107 Forshaw and Abercrombie, 1943, frontispiece.
108 Hasegawa, 1999, 122.
109 Hasegawa, 1999, 137.

Sandys, the planning minister,[110] specified that a new plan should be prepared for the area around St Paul's, where new buildings of poor architectural quality were going up. The Corporation again called Holford in, and his vision of the area was completed in 1967.[111] But, meanwhile, because of excessive caution, the planning ministry effectively let development proceed, losing a unique chance to provide an ideal environment for the City. This, Hasegawa suggests, was sadly illustrative of the general run of postwar reconstruction in Britain.[112]

The other big problem was the East End. Here plans had been developed, as early as 1935, to sweep away and rebuild a huge area: 700 acres in Stepney, Shoreditch, and Bethnal Green, forming a corridor some one and three-quarter miles long and three quarters of a mile wide between the London Docks and the Regents Canal.[113] On top of the huge slum problem here, bombing of the Docks meant that the East End was very badly damaged: in Stepney 40% of all dwellings were destroyed or severely damaged by November 1940, in Bermondsey 75% were damaged. More went in the raids of 1944–5, and as people began to straggle back the housing problem began to seem less tractable than ever.[114]

Abercrombie and Forshaw showed just how huge the task would be. They recognized that "There is abundant evidence … that for families with children, houses are preferred to flats. They provide a private garden and yard at the same level as the main rooms of the dwelling, and fit the English temperament."[115] But to put everyone in houses would mean that two-thirds or three-quarters of the people would have to move elsewhere. Their preference was for half houses, half flats, at 100 to the net residential acre, but even this would mean too big an overspill problem – too big, they felt, to be balanced by equivalent out-movement of jobs. So they settled on their famous inner-London density of 136 per acre, which – on the basis of the research they did – put one-third of the people in houses, and some 60% in eight- and ten-story flats; about a half of the families with two children would have to go into flats, but even this density meant an overspill of close to four in ten of all the people living in this zone in 1939. To obtain it, the old rigid 80-foot height limit on residential blocks should be replaced by a more flexible system.[116] All this, in due course, was embodied into the statutory development plan of 1951.

A critical role was played by the 1951 Festival of Britain, run by a very tight group of designers, architects, and engineers who all knew each other: Herbert Morrison,

---

[110]   Duncan Sandys (1908–87) was Minister of Housing and Local Government in the then Ministry of Housing and Local Government. This, rather confusingly, was the planning ministry: Conservative governments, then as later, tried to avoid using that word. Sandys achieved later distinction for founding the Civic Trust – and, less heroically if true, as it was claimed in an August 2000 documentary, for being revealed as the "headless man" in the 1963 Profumo scandal.

[111]   Hasegawa, 1999, 137.

[112]   Hasegawa, 1999, 139.

[113]   Yelling, 1989, 293.

[114]   Bullock, 1987, 73–4.

[115]   Forshaw and Abercrombie, 1943, 77.

[116]   Forshaw and Abercrombie, 1943, 79–83, 117–19.

"Lord Festival," used his under-secretary, Max Nicholson, who selected most of the committee, including the director Gerald Barry; the two together chose the others to represent art, science, architecture, industrial design, and film. Hugh Casson himself said that the organization was inbred; it had to be, for speed. "The planners were overwhelmingly middle-class men of the sort Michael Frayn has described as 'do-gooders: the readers of the *News Chronicle*, the *Guardian*, and the *Observer*; the signers of petitions; the backbone of the BBC."[117] The Festival was a showpiece of modern architecture and design,[118] together with the Lansbury Estate which, with the Festival Hall, was the LCC's contribution.[119] On the other hand, when Percy Johnson-Marshall was appointed to head the LCC planning team in 1949, he fought to have the 136-per-acre density at Lansbury reduced, but failed.[120]

A whole generation was waiting for the call: the generation that had flooded from the forces into the British architectural schools, determined at last to create the brave new world. Frederic Osborn wrote to Lewis Mumford in 1952 about the cult of Corbusier at the Architectural Association school, "the young men under his influence are completely impervious to economic or human considerations ... it was just as if I had, in my youth, questioned the divinity of Christ. I had the same impression of animal unreason."[121] There was, as one chronicler wrote, "the tradition of Newness ... a special blend of *avant-garde* eccentricity" which "can be continually traced through the AA. It owes something to its being an international organism just resting on English soil ... The AA has always been open to the incoherent, uncompromising, culturally-lateral musings of foreigners who turn up in London."[122] Into this cultural hothouse,

> Rushing back to qualify as architects, the first post-war generation were full of enthusiasm for technology ... To suggest a better and special world was no arrogance – merely their inheritance ... Soon there were two essential sources of inspiration – Corb and Mies ... the Ville Radieuse and the Unité d'Habitation suggested a model to be applied by good hard socialist principles in good hard modernist materials.[123]

Soon, as perhaps only it could, the AA was out-Corbuing Corbu. By 1954 there was Ronald Jones's Life Structure: a land-ship 2,360 meters long, 560 meters high, and 200 meters wide:

> ... thermal energy tapped from a mantle of molten rock 2900 km deep will release man through an energy spiral to gear him on a fantastic journey on a nuclear earth-ship ... Unit cities will have core, administration, elected government, arts and creative centres,

[117]   Conekin, 1999, 229–30.
[118]   Gold, 1997, 211–12.
[119]   Gold, 1997, 213.
[120]   Gold, 1997, 214.
[121]   Hughes, 1971, 205.
[122]   Cook, 1983, 32.
[123]   Cook, 1983, 33.

Figure 7.8 Bombed London East End street. The frontispiece from Forshaw and Abercrombie's 1943 County of London plan, which says it all.

universities, specialist colleges, institutes, sports and recreation stadia, stereo cinemas, hospitals, hypermarkets, civic shopping centres. Core areas will be linked by horizontal, vertical and diagonal travelators … each metropolitan city and town will be planned to grow to first, second, third and fourth dimensions in response to human ecological need.[124]

Like so much that followed from the basement at Bedford Square, it was good clean juvenile fantasy. The problem – as Cook details, and as the AA's own retrospective catalogue shows – was that before many years passed, as successive waves of students passed out into the real world, the fantasies were turned into reality. Jones's own creation became the Hong Kong and Shanghai Bank (though its architect did not study at the AA); a high-density housing scheme for Paddington (1956) became Parkhill in Sheffield (1961) and Western Rise in Islington (1969); a warehouse (1957) became the Leicester University Engineering Department (1963); housing of 1961 turned up in Milton Keynes in 1975. By that time, further flights of fantasy were still lined up on the Bloomsbury runway: a house built of Sugar Puffs packets, or the 1971 scheme for a "Sand Castle. A brothel for oil miners in the

---

[124]   Cook, 1983, 33–4.

Sahara … constructed from continuous plastic tube, filled with sand *in situ*, and wound up into a series of interconnecting vaults."[125] By then, "comprehensive urbanism" had ceased to be an acceptable subject of conversation – the winds from Europe had changed.[126] But its monuments, from generations of AA graduates, were scattered across the face of urban England.

The *Architectural Review* led the attack as early as 1953 with an editorial from J. M. Richards lambasting the early new towns for their lack of urbanity, which was blamed on too low densities and the evil influence of the Town and Country Planning Association (TCPA).[127] In 1955 it published *Outrage*, the celebrated onslaught by Ian Nairn on the quality of British urban design, which was uniquely influential in the general British intelligentsia; it announced

> … a prophecy of doom: the prophecy that if what is called development is allowed to multiply at the present rate, then by the end of the century Great Britain will consist of isolated oases of preserved monuments in a desert of wire, concrete roads, cosy plots and bungalows. There will be no real distinction between town and country … Upon this new Britain the REVIEW bestows a name in the hope that it will stick: SUBTOPIA.[128]

The conclusion followed inexorably: "The more complicated our industrial system, and the greater our population, the *bigger* and *greener* should be our countryside, the *more* compact and neater should be our towns."[129] Accordingly, two years later the editors launched *Counter-Attack against Subtopia*.[130] Meanwhile, in 1955 the Royal Institute of British Architects had run an influential symposium on high flats, opened by Dame Evelyn Sharp, the Permanent Secretary of the Ministry of Housing and Local Government, who had quoted a poem on their beauty.[131]

There were plenty of allies. The farm lobby went back to the fundamentalism of the Scott Report on Rural Land Use of 1942[132] with its insistence on trying to save every possible last acre for agriculture. The sociologists weighed in with Michael Young and Peter Willmott's enormously influential *Family and Kinship in East London*, which argued that by exporting people from London to overspill estates the planners were destroying a uniquely rich pattern of working-class folk-life.[133] (Surveys showed that the great majority wanted to leave, especially among young families. The only exceptions were poor owner-occupiers.[134]) In vain did the agricultural economist Gerald Wibberley show that the farmland was surplus to national

[125] Cook, 1983, 41.
[126] Cook, 1983, 40.
[127] Richards, 1953, 32.
[128] Nairn, 1955, 365.
[129] Nairn, 1955, 368.
[130] Architectural Review, 1957, passim.
[131] Dunleavy, 1981, 135, 165.
[132] GB Ministry of Works and Planning, 1943.
[133] Young and Willmott, 1957.
[134] Yelling, 1999b, 10.

needs, or Peter Stone calculate the true costs of building high;[135] to no avail did F. J. Osborn tirelessly campaign against subsidies for high flats.[136] The politics were against them; the government wanted urban containment, and an end to the new-towns program, at any cost.

So the crucial question for planning historians has to be, how far was this a commitment of the modernist architects, how far did it arise from other influences? A revisionist school suggests that the answer is complicated. In 1943, at work on the County of London Plan, Abercrombie, the greatest architect-planner of them all, was walking a tightrope, and Osborn certainly thought that he had been completely coopted by the LCC forces (Chapter 5). His 1943 plan solution

> ... cleverly combined and modified two existing influences, both of continental origin, and subsequently reformulated as a British "tradition". The first was a combination of German ideas of three-dimensional compositions in space, including Mendelsohnian "dynamism" and International Modern's rectilinear layouts of differently-dimensioned Zeilenbauten, mixed with Swedish point blocks in wilderness landscaping; on the other, the apparent opposite – a spatial appreciation of towns and streets, of enclosed or interrupted rather than open space, derived from Sitte via Unwin; after the war, these were synthesised under the label of "townscapes."[137]

He may have been walking a tightrope, but he was massively helped by the unusual, even unique, conditions of the time. Wartime emergencies and the suspension of normal democratic processes, including elections, meant that the LCC was able to operate much more independently than ever before. An elaborate structure of consultation on planning proposals, established during the 1930s – the 28 metropolitan borough councils, property, industrial, and commercial bodies, amenity groups – was set aside: Abercrombie was left free, drawing his own academically derived information about London's "inherent" social and community structure.[138] But things did not remain that way for long. The stress on decentralization raised alarm bells among members and officers concerned for electoral strength – the main losses would be felt in inner boroughs with Labour majorities – and financial resources: these areas offered the best potential for commercial development, boosting the LCC's tax base. This financial risk forged an alliance between Labour leaders and LCC officers, especially the Valuer and Comptroller, the chief financial officer. This central dilemma already surfaced in the production of the plan. It accepted the need to reduce densities, but, because of the difficulties of achieving decentralization, reluctantly accepted that high densities as high as 136 persons per acre were inevitable in Stepney: "While we should like to see the lowest density of 100 adopted (which would allow two-thirds houses to one-third flats), we feel that the actual

[135]   Wibberley, 1959; Stone, 1959; 1961.
[136]   Osborn, 1955.
[137]   Horsey, 1988, 168–9.
[138]   Garside, 1997, 21–2.

numbers to be decentralised would be difficult to equate with the amount of industry that could be expected to migrate."[139] "The LCC," Osborn bitterly commented, "is led by middle-class Labour councillors, right out of touch with popular opinion but … terrified of a drop in rateable value or the loss of their slum electorate."[140] In both the selection of large-scale redevelopment areas in London and in the detailed planning proposals drawn up for them, the emphasis was on maximizing government subsidies, minimizing immediate losses of rateable values, and maximizing prospects for future income. In all three objectives the claims of industry were weak and the effect was to promote commercial and high-density residential building in redevelopment at the expense of industry.[141]

There is yet another suspect here: the Dudley Committee, set up under the eponymous peer in 1942. The evidence of people's preferences was clear: overwhelmingly, they wanted houses, not flats. But the committee recommended a range of densities ranging from 30 persons per acre for open developments outside towns, to 100 and even 120 per acre in large concentrated urban areas. They were undoubtedly influenced by the then-emerging Abercrombie–Forshaw analysis; here, the 136-per-acre standard meant over 60% of all dwellings would have to be in tall blocks.[142] But in turn, Bullock argues that the key evidence seems to have come from the National Council of Social Service (NCSS), whose studies on neighborhoods influenced Abercrombie and Forshaw; Wesley Dougill worked on the NCSS team in 1942. A key role was also played by housing reformer Elizabeth Denby, who had visited and admired continental schemes.[143]

As Stephen Ward has shown, there was a battle inside government.[144] Gordon Stephenson, appointed to the research section of the Planning Division in the newly formed Ministry of Town and Country Planning in 1942, reluctantly accepted LCC's arguments but firmly opposed the proposals in the Merseyside Plan for 136 persons per acre in the inner zone and 184 near the riverside. He reiterated the Dudley standard that 100 persons per acre should be the maximum inner density with a few riverside areas at 120. Yet the Ministry of Health controlled housing subsidies, so the matter was not easily settled. Stephenson also doubted the extent of administrative support in his own department. Its formidable Deputy Secretary, Evelyn Sharp, lately transferred from Health, had brought with her that Ministry's thinking about "vertical density." Stephenson directly challenged her in a tetchy three-page memorandum, pointing out what high "vertical densities" actually meant, and citing the poor family living conditions in the five-story-flat schemes recently built in Liverpool. Disputing the common view that they allowed dockers to live close to their work, he argued that the real reasons were political and religious, with density

[139]   Garside, 1997, 31.
[140]   Garside, 1997, 34.
[141]   Garside, 1997, 22.
[142]   Bullock, 1987, 74, 76, 82.
[143]   Bullock, 1987, 78.
[144]   Ward, 2012b, 286.

policies a way of excluding Irish Catholics from suburban council estates. Stephenson also criticized the City Architect, Lancelot Keay, another important voice in the Ministry of Health. The latter's lately acquired professional preference for high-rise flats Stephenson thought too conveniently consistent with his political paymasters' sectarianism. Stephenson felt that flats would become "the new slums, financial and social white elephants." Instead the answer lay in managing outward expansion and embracing more varied but essentially medium densities throughout the city. His fears were justified. In the 1950s, inner city housing policies reverted to the Ministry of Housing line, implemented by a merged successor Ministry of Housing and Local Government, led by Dame Evelyn Sharp.[145]

Inside the LCC the most influential figure was the Valuer and Comptroller. For him, any commitment to ideal densities, as recommended by garden-city advocates, was anathema because of capital costs and the loss of residential rateable values.[146] The key in choosing areas for comprehensive redevelopment was, above all, to rebuild rateable values by limiting population decentralization and introducing commerce into areas previously dominated by residential or industrial uses.[147] Even heavy industry was to be kept as far as possible, so that, as Osborn inimitably put it, the choice would still be between being "a squirrel in a cage or a rat in a drain."[148] The problem is that though the 1947 Act had dealt with the compensation and better-ment problem, it could not deal with the rateable value problem;[149] the opportunity was lost to grapple with *existing* land values, though the Uthwatt report had tried to address it.[150] And there was no central mechanism whereby losses in the cities could be offset by gains in the relocated areas.[151]

The planners in the Architect's Department tended to defend the sanctity of the Plan against the Comptroller and the Valuer, who wanted ever more flats;[152] the architects eventually won.[153] The Treasury subsidy for expensive land was paid only for flats, and the calculations assumed a break-even level at 35 dwellings per acre; only a small exception was made to allow houses on sufficiently developed areas.[154] In practice the Valuer won:[155] between 1945 and October 1951 the LCC built 13,072 flats and only 81 houses, the boroughs 13,374 against 2,630, and 15 of the 24 built only flats.[156] The Valuer continued to argue for higher densities, and he was given responsibility for housing because this was a priority and there were too

[145] Ward, 2012b, 287.
[146] Garside, 1997, 22.
[147] Garside, 1997, 23.
[148] Garside, 1997, 31.
[149] Garside 1997, 32.
[150] Yelling, 1994, 143.
[151] Yelling, 1994, 143.
[152] Yelling, 1994, 146.
[153] Gold, 1997, 221–2.
[154] Yelling, 1994, 146.
[155] Yelling, 1994, 142.
[156] Bullock, 1987, 93–4.

few out-County opportunities.[157] Roehampton was planned at 30 dwellings per acre instead of the 20 originally envisaged, though opposed by the Town Planning chairman.[158]

The Great Rebuild

Thus everything seemed to come together: a private movement among the architects had great significance, because it tweaked sympathetic political chords. In 1955, the Conservative government, in the form of Housing Minister Duncan Sandys, launched a major slum-clearance program that was to run for nearly two decades, and simultaneously encouraged local authorities around the major cities to designate green belts in order to contain urban growth; coupled with a birth rate which started unexpectedly to rise that very year, this soon produced an impossible land-budget arithmetic.[159] Land acquisition costs rose, especially after changes in the law in 1959. The big cities, many of which were not averse to keeping their own people rather than exporting them to new and expanded towns, read all this as a signal to build dense and build high.[160] The big builders were ready to move in, and sold their ability to solve the cities' housing problems fast through package deals.[161] And the government, despite a barrage of protest from Osborn at the TCPA, obligingly gave them the special subsidies they needed for the job: from 1956, three times as much for a flat in a 15-story block as for a house.[162] Dutifully, the proportion of high-rise in the total public housing program rose year by year: units in five-story and more blocks were about 7% of the total in the late 1950s, as much as 26% in the mid-1960s.[163]

In all this, there was considerable schizophrenia, even in individuals. Richard Crossman, who as Sandys's successor nearly a decade later spearheaded the Labour government's accelerated slum-clearance and housing drive, could record in his diary that he did not like the idea of people living in huge blocks of high-rise housing, yet almost simultaneously encourage even bigger programs of destruction and industrialized building:

> In conversation I asked why it was only 750 houses they were building at Oldham; why not rebuild the whole thing? Wouldn't that help Laing, the builders? "Of course it would", said Oliver [Cox], "and it would help Oldham too" ... I drove back to the Ministry ... warmed and excited.[164]

[157]   Yelling, 1994, 147.
[158]   Yelling 1994, 147.
[159]   Hall *et al.*, 1973, II, 56–9; Cooney, 1974, 160.
[160]   Cooney, 1974, 161–2.
[161]   Cooney, 1974, 168; Dunleavy, 1981, 72, 114.
[162]   Dunleavy, 1981, 37; Cooney, 1974, 163.
[163]   Cooney, 1974, 152.
[164]   Crossman, 1975, 81.

Figure 7.9 The Great Rebuild in the East End. A 1965 picture with the job half-complete: the old two-story terraces on the left, LCC tower blocks and nondescript borough slabs on the right.

The LCC's immensely prestigious Architect's Department, under first Robert Matthew, then Leslie Martin, provided a model in the early years; it had an unusually free hand, because the Ministry's ordinary cost sanctions did not apply to it.[165] It first produced "the great Corbusian slabs" which culminated at the end of the 1950s in Alton West, Roehampton, the most complete homage to – and only true realization of – *La Ville Radieuse* in the world; then began "the era of the high towers, slimmer, less oppressive, and of course more highly subsidized":[166] 384 of them, in all, completed between 1964 and 1974. After the reorganization of 1965, the new boroughs made their own distinctive contributions, like Southwark's huge megastructures in North Peckham, later to become some of London's most problematic blocks. The architects were not completely agreed, even inside the LCC:[167] from the early 1950s, there then emerged a division between self-styled Humanist and Formalist factions, symbolized by the distinction between the Scandinavian New Empiricism of Alton East and the Corbusian Alton West; the Corbusians gradually gained the upper hand during the 1950s, as seen by the rectilinear-plan, Zeilenbau mid-1950s landscapes of Loughborough Road and Bentham Road.[168]

[165] Dunleavy, 1981, 170.
[166] Esher, 1981, 129.
[167] Bullock, 1987, 93.
[168] Horsey, 1988, 169; Gold, 1997, 222–3.

Some few among the great British provincial cities tried to compete in prestige. Two AA graduates headed the team that developed Park Hill, the great wall of deck-access flats that juts like a fortress above the center of Sheffield and that, it must in fairness be said, is still highly successful with its tenants. Glasgow hired Basil Spence for the Gorbals and then built huge towers up to the city's edge; here, where the tenants all had a totally un-English tradition of high-density tenement living, there were few consistent problems with the design except for those with children, unsurprising since four in five children lived above the fourth floor.[169] But there were many other places where the architect was uninspired or non-existent, and where tenants found themselves uprooted into hurriedly constructed system-built flats that lacked amenities, environment, community – that lacked, in fact, almost anything except a roof and four walls.

But basically, as Glendinning and Muthesius show in their monumental account, London was quite different from the other cities of England and Scotland. (Wales, oddly, never got the high-rise bug at all.) In London, top architects dominated everything, first in the heyday of the LCC Architect's Department and in some of the smaller LCC-era Metropolitan Boroughs (Finsbury, for instance, where Lubetkin and Tecton followed the trail they had blazed prewar in Highgate's Highpoint), then in a few of the post-1965 boroughs to which some LCC stalwarts decanted themselves. High- rise in London was thus an immensely exciting architectural campaign: to import into Britain the essence of the modern movement, thus turning the country from a backwater to a pacesetter.

From the mid-1950s, there was also something new. Commercial and speculative development, driven by an alliance of financiers, property developers, accountants, and a group of commercially minded architects, became the major force behind the rebuilding of London, especially in the West End and the City, for much of the 1950s and early 1960s. The lifting of building controls by the Conservative government in November 1954 was the starting gun for the most intense phase of a property boom that continued unabated until 1964, when Labour again instituted strict regulations on development throughout the Greater London area. Property millionaires, such as Charles Clore, Jack Cotton, Harry Hyams, and Harold Samuel, loomed large, along with their dedicated architect, Richard Seifert. Around 24 million square feet of new office space was built in central London during the 1950s.[170]

Its symbol, and a battle ground for much of this time, was Piccadilly Circus. "Piazzadilly!" read the headline on the front page of the London *Evening Standard*, on April 12, 1962, celebrating yet another proposal for Piccadilly Circus that promised "comprehensive redevelopment" of the area. Almost all of the familiar Victorian and Edwardian buildings would go, replaced by a new theater and concert hall, roof gardens, tall office blocks, and a "vertical feature," a floodlit steeple, in the words of its planner – the ever-present William Holford – "visible from a distance

---

[169]   Jephcott, 1971, 140.
[170]   Mort, 2004, 121–2.

and marking the Circus as the hub of the West End." Below, the familiar statue of Eros was retained as the centerpiece of a new pedestrian piazza. It never happened: Holford's proposal of 1962 was just one in a series of comprehensive plans for the area between the late 1950s and the early 1970s.[171]

The oddity is what, while all this was not happening, was actually happening: "the spaces of the new youth culture of the period, the boutiques and clubs that transformed London's international reputation were quite precisely *not* those of modern planning and architecture." They happened in the back streets, in hasty and improvised refurbishments of old Victorian buildings. The cityscape imagined by Holford and his generation was castigated by conservatives as a brutalist betrayal of London's heritage, but it could as easily be condemned by a younger generation as the dreary, pleasure-free territory of old-guard modernists. It ended with the campaign against the comprehensive redevelopment of Covent Garden.[172]

But in the provinces and in Scotland, it was all much more prosaic: there, the architects counted for little against the massive accumulated strength of the housing departments, and the aim was to obtain the maximum number of dwelling units (telling phrase) in the minimum possible time.[173] And it was difficult to deny them. For in those cities, housing conditions in the 1950s were unimaginably, primevally awful. In Glasgow, as seen in one macabre diagram, a family of nine could live in a one-room Gorbals slum, 11 feet by 8.[174] When you see that, you know why the politicians and the professionals were engaged in a holy crusade to get rid of the slums, and why a new high-rise apartment represented a one-step jump from the nineteenth century into the twenty-first. That is why Basil Spence's high-rise Gorbals block, spectacularly demolished on TV in 1993, seemed like a new world.

Commercial considerations also entered on a massive scale. After a decade in which the pace of redevelopment outside the South East was glacial, by the early 1960s there was sudden enthusiasm for "comprehensive redevelopment."[175] This was a new model of planning, aimed not at substituting for private developers' schemes, but at inviting and facilitating them. The great midland and northern cities – Liverpool, Newcastle, Leicester – set up planning offices separate from the engineer's department.[176] Planners and architects were no longer leading events; they were responding to them.[177] The "modernist" ambitions of planners eroded in the face of the conservative onslaught, giving way to a "market-driven version" which "meant handing town centres over to developers."[178]

---

[171]   Edwards and Gilbert, 2008, 455–6.
[172]   Edwards and Gilbert, 2008, 474–5.
[173]   Glendinning and Muthesius, 1994, passim.
[174]   Glendinning and Muthesius, 1994, 178.
[175]   Mandler, 1999, 220.
[176]   Mandler, 1999, 220.
[177]   Mandler, 1999, 221.
[178]   Mandler, 1999, 227.

What then went wrong? Glendinning and Muthesius argue that, just like the high-rise enthusiasm itself, the attack on the genre was driven by intellectual fashion: there was as little substance in the counter-attack as in the original myth. More specifically, both were driven and supported by fairly unspecific pop sociology. So we still do not know, for certain, exactly why so many high-rise developments came to be seen as failures. The authors suggest that there was a disastrous self-destructive, self-justifying dynamic: after 1968 there was a sudden housing surplus, problem families were moved in, others moved out, in no time some developments acquired the label of problem estates. Perhaps the most telling passage in the entire book is an account by an Edinburgh tenant of just this process, starting with nice people in nice flats, ending in *Clockwork Orange* horror. Andrew Balderstone, a sheet-metal worker, lived for 20 years in a maisonette in John Russell Court, a 20-story point block in Edinburgh, from 1964, when it was opened, to 1984, when it was emptied and rehabilitated:

> It wasn't anything to do with the block itself, really, it was a change in the kind of people who lived there, and how people behaved. When we first went in, we were introduced to the Caretaker, a retired seaman. He was very enthusiastic about his job. And for the first five or ten years, things were really great, everybody kept the block spotless, you were really proud of having such a nice new house ...
>
> The problems only started after about five or ten years, when they started putting a different kind of tenant in ... This was the idea of the Corporation housing management. "Management" – what a sick joke! They had this crazy idea that by spreading the bad ones out among the normal tenants, you'd bring them up to your level – but what happened, especially in a big block like that, it was the opposite – *they* brought *us* down!
>
> It was like a kind of cancer. At first you tried to keep your standards up, but you soon learnt it was a waste of time ...
>
> Well, the Caretaker couldn't cope with all this, so he left, then more and more of the neighbours got fed up and got out – and all the Housing department could do was fill the vacant flats with single parent families, faster and faster. After they started putting the druggies in, about the late seventies, the vandalism and the break-ins really got going, all-night parties with idiots using the rubbish chutes at 3 a.m., masses of bottles crashing down. That was the time when the craze for throwing things out suddenly started ...
>
> ... It all seems such a terrible waste – they were perfectly good houses, if the Council had only bothered to look after them, rather than using them as a dumping ground![179]

So, the book concludes, do not accept the journalistic stereotype: with good management, the great majority of high-rise blocks are great places to live, well liked by those who live in them.

Glasgow was a very special case. It always had an extraordinarily high proportion of households in rented tenements.[180] Abercrombie's Clyde Valley Plan of 1946 recommended four new towns: two – East Kilbride and Cumbernauld – that would eventually be built, two that would not; even so, they would take only one-third of

---

[179] Glendinning and Muthesius, 1994, 323.
[180] O'Carroll, 1996, 56.

the half-million to be decentralized from Glasgow, while at least half the remaining population would be resettled on the City periphery. But many in the Glasgow Corporation accepted spillover late and reluctantly;[181] they wanted to "do it all in Glasgow, keep the rateable value, and keep yourself as the second city of the Empire"; in the late 1950s, aided by changes in the subsidy regime they won, forcing through a program of unremitting high-rise tenement construction.[182]

The remarkable fact was how long it took for anyone to see that it was wrong. In order to appreciate why, it is necessary to do something that for anyone born after 1960 requires an effort of imagination: to appreciate just how bad were the dense rows of smoke-blackened slums that the towers replaced. The fact that later on the bulldozers started to remove sound and saveable houses may obscure the fact that most were neither. As Lionel Esher says, "even the preservationists saw the great mass of our Victorian 'twilight areas' as expendable. Six years of war had reduced those parts of London and the great provincial cities to a sinister squalor that recalled the darkest passages of *Bleak House*."[183] In Ravetz's words, "For two full decades … any social disbenefits of clean-sweep planning and its transformation of the town passed unremarked other than by cranks, a few people with residual ideals from the 1940s, or those who lamented the passing of the old on artistic grounds."[184] It was not the fact of clean-sweep planning that began to be criticized, but the form that it took.

Accentuated by the media after the disastrous collapse of Ronan Point, an East London system-built tower block, in a gas explosion of 1968, the criticism soon became deafening. In fact, the subsidy system had been recast the previous year, and local authorities were already phasing out their high-rise blocks. Now, everything was suddenly wrong with them: they leaked, they condensed, they blew up, the lifts did not work, the children vandalized them, old ladies lived in fear. All of this had some basis. Kenneth Campbell, in charge of housing design at the LCC and the Greater London Council from 1959 to 1974, listed three failures: the lifts (too few, too small, too slow), the children (too many), the management (too little).[185] Anthony Greenwood's 1968 White Paper *Old Houses into New Homes* marked the big anti-reaction.[186] The resultant 1969 Housing Act effectively moved away from rebuilding to improvement – so much so, that a decade later, when the economics did not add up, it proved impossible ever to return to the bulldozer age.[187]

Even in the modernist heyday of reconstruction, the bulldozer never reigned completely supreme. Peter Larkham has studied several hundred reconstruction plans for cities, both those suffering bomb damage, and those relatively or completely unscathed, and questions the conventional view that they were overtly

[181] Wannop, 1986, 211.
[182] Horsey, 1988, 179–80.
[183] Esher, 1981, 45.
[184] Ravetz, 1980, 89.
[185] Esher, 1981, 129–30.
[186] Yelling, 1999a, 14.
[187] Yelling, 1999a, 16.

modernist. True, few were sensitive to the context of areas and groups of buildings. Yet there is clear evidence in some plans for a broader concept of conservation, two decades before Duncan Sandys's Civic Amenities Act permitted the designation of "conservation areas."[188] Early plans – such as those for Plymouth and Bath, both heavily damaged – were radical. Yet, even there, radical reshaping was largely limited to the areas suffering the most severe damage. Thomas Sharp's early plans – as for Durham, in 1944 – include a very small number of new roads aimed at diverting traffic and thus protecting the town.[189] True, conservation was a very small element, often limited to a small number of key buildings.[190] But, as early as the 1943 Plymouth plan, there is evident concern for area-based conservation – particularly by the most prolific consultants, Abercrombie and Sharp.[191]

But what had happened, in this brief passage of time during the late 1960s, was an intellectual seismic shift. Twenty years earlier, in the historic 1947 Act, a requirement to compile lists of buildings for preservation was injected at the last minute. But the Ministry of Housing and Local Government did not begin to see a relation between conservation and planning until the mid-1960s, when Wayland Kennet became Junior Minister with responsibility for conservation, and established rapport with Crossman. Duncan Sandys, who as Minister had set up the Civic Trust, drew first place in the ballot for Private Members' Bills. Crossman persuaded him to adopt a bill to strengthen powers to prevent demolition of listed buildings, and offered his Department's help.[192] Crossman wrote,

> Kennet is really splendidly energetic. Though he peeves me a little by his desire to take everything over, I am delighted that he is that sort of person. He is going to run the historic buildings as hard as he possibly can and he is going to be helped by Duncan Sandys' Bill as well as by the decision to get working parties going on my five selected towns.[193]

Later he revealed that he had had to battle with his top civil servant, the redoubtable Dame Evelyn Sharp: "She, who counted herself a modern iconoclast, took the extremely – yes, I will say it, – illiterate view that there was a clear-cut conflict between 'modern' planning and 'reactionary' conservation. During my time as Minister, in speech after speech, I tried to break down this false dichotomy and to establish a new and sensible relationship between planning and preservation."[194] He was succeeded in 1966 by Anthony Greenwood, "a weak Minister who some felt took little interest in anything except his personal appearance";[195] he was content to leave most work to junior ministers, and this opened the door to

---

[188] Larkham, 2007, 295, 316.
[189] Larkham, 2007, 316–17.
[190] Larkham, 2007, 318.
[191] Larkham, 2007, 317.
[192] Delafons, 1997, 60, 87, 89, 90, 93.
[193] Delafons, 1997, 93
[194] Delafons 1997, 94.
[195] Delafons, 1997, 94.

Kennet, who stayed on until the 1970 election and made a very positive contribution. Kennet later recorded that in those years public opinion was shifting after "an age of blindness";[196] the Historic Buildings Council had one-seventh of the budget for military bands.[197] But Sandys's bill passed with bipartisan support, and Kennet drove the work energetically forward through a vigorously written circular that encouraged local authorities "to designate first and think later, and this, broadly speaking, is what they did."[198] John Delafons, a planning official who later became a planning historian, commented, "Those who wonder when the floodgates of conservation were opened, need look no further than Circular 53/67."[199] By 1972, Kennet was able to record that some 1,350 conservation areas had been designated by about 130 local authorities; 20 years later that total had risen to over 6,500.[200]

So the great Corbusian rebuild was over. But, in fairness to the Corbusians, some things should be said. First, though some London estates were directly inspired by the master, and some of these proved design disasters, many others up and down Britain were bought off the peg by local authorities too lazy or unimaginative to hire architects and planners of their own. It was Crossman, visiting Wigan as early as 1965, who commented that its "enormous building programme" was of "an appalling dimness and dullness, and I am afraid that they have built a Wigan that in 2000 will look just as bad as the old 1880 Wigan looks in the eyes of the 1960s."[201] Secondly, Corbusier never advocated putting people (as distinct from jobs) in high towers; his proletarian housing would have looked more like Manchester's huge Hulme Estate, the biggest urban renewal project ever carried out in Europe, which consisted of medium-rise blocks but also proved a design disaster. In fact, the architectural fashion that followed the high-rise era, high-density low-rise, had proved a failure in Glasgow immediately after World War Two[202] and would later be criticized just as severely:

> High-density low-rise in practice meant mobs of children in echoing bricky court-yards, and mobs meant vandalism ... They became "hard-to-let", i.e. lettable only to the poorest and most disorderly families, who seldom had cars to occupy the now mandatory basement garages, and whose children wrecked the few they had.[203]

Ironically, this too was a Corbusian solution. All of it missed the real criticism, which was of design solutions laid down on people without regard to their preferences,

---

196   Delafons, 1997, 95.
197   Delafons, 1997, 96.
198   Delafons, 1997, 100.
199   Delafons, 1997, 101.
200   Delafons, 1997, 101.
201   Crossman, 1975, 341.
202   Armstrong and Wilson, 1973.
203   Esher, 1981, 134.

ways of life, or plain idiosyncrasies; laid down, further, by architects who – as the media delighted to discover – themselves invariably lived in charming Victorian villas. When later some actually lived in the places they were designing, as did Ralph Erskine's site architect, Vernon Gracie, in the famous Byker Wall at Newcastle, it was a matter for comment. The main result of this failure, of which Corbusier is as fully culpable as any of his followers, was that the middle-class designers had no real feeling for the way a working-class family lived. In their world,

> Mum isn't isolated at home with the babies, she is out shopping at Harrods. The chil-
> dren, when small, are taken to Kensington Gardens by Nannie. At the age of eight they
> go to a preparatory school and at thirteen to a public school, both residential. And
> during the holidays they are either away in the country, or winter-sporting, sailing and
> so on: golden and brown in the playful wind and summer sun. At any rate they are not
> hanging around on the landing or playing with the dustbin lids.[204]

There is a striking fact about Le Corbusier's celebrated first *Unité*, in Marseilles: it is quite different from its many faithful imitations, less because it was designed by the Master himself, than because it is occupied by a quite different clientele. It is a middle-class professional enclave of people who clearly relish living in one of France's greatest architectural monuments (and who have, in consequence of that fact, received unprecedented sums of public money for its restoration). From elegant foyer to delightful rooftop swimming pool, it more resembles a medium-quality hotel than a British council block of the 1960s (or, if one should seek the explanation in the unique awfulness of the British, a *grand ensemble* in the Paris suburbs). The fact is that from first to last, Corbusier had no understanding of people who were unlike himself.

The rich, then, could always live well at high densities, because they had services; that is why those quotations of Corbusier were so telling. But for ordinary people, as Ward says, the suburbs have great advantages: privacy, freedom from noise, greater freedom to make a noise yourself. To have this at a high density requires expensive treatment, generally not possible in public housing. Above all, the problem is one of children, for "unless they get a chance to play out their childhood, they are certainly going to make a nuisance of themselves when they are older."[205] And this is especially true, as Jephcott concluded in 1971, for families with children that are less well-equipped educationally, living in high-density high-rise: "local authorities should discontinue this form of housing except for a limited range of carefully selected tenants or in cases of extreme pressure."[206] Corbusier, of course, was blissfully unconscious of all this, because he was both middle-class and childless.[207]

[204] Ward, 1976, 51.
[205] Ward, 1976, 54.
[206] Jephcott, 1971, 131.
[207] Anthony, 1966, 286.

Urban Renewal in America

The Americans discovered some of all this even before the British, and it is interesting to ask why. One reason is that they started earlier. Their urban renewal
program began with the Housing Act of 1949 and the amending Act of 1954, and
stems from even earlier origins: the 1937 report of the Urbanism Committee of the
National Resources Planning Board, *Our Cities: Their Role in the National Economy*,
with its stress on urban decay caused by obsolescent land uses, and the very influential short pamphlet of 1941 by Alvin Hansen and Guy Greer, which developed this
argument and argued that federal aid would be needed to buy blighted property, the
cities in return being required to draw up plans for redevelopment.[208] The resulting
1949 Act represented a strange but successful coalition of conservative and radical
interests: federal money could be applied to renewing outworn parts of cities, but
principally residential parts; yet adequate housing tools were not provided.[209]

To understand why, it is necessary to penetrate this unlikely coalition a little
deeper. Congress had passed a landmark public housing measure, the Wagner Act,
as long ago as 1937. This had been the outcome of a bitter and protracted struggle
between powerful interest groups. On one side were liberal housing experts
like Catherine Bauer, lining up with the construction unions. On the other were
the National Association of Real Estate Boards (NAREB) and its research arm, the
Urban Land Institute (ULI). NAREB and ULI were all for federal mortgage insurance, a principle they had won when the Federal Housing Association was established
in 1934. They were all against public housing. The resulting compromise established
public housing as a temporary expedient for the deserving poor, the newly unemployed, who could be expected to buy their own houses as soon as the economy
lifted off again. It would exclude the old poor: the predominantly black, really poor
underclass. The means to discriminate lay in the finances of the act: federal funds
would pay for land acquisition and development, not for running costs, which must
be met from the rent. Really poor families would thus never be able to get in.[210] At
the end of the 1940s, that barrier fell: welfare families began to enter the projects.
But, since the financial arrangements stayed unchanged, the resulting contradictions soon after produced catastrophic consequences.[211]

The 1949 and 1954 Acts represented another triumph of the NAREB–ULI lobby.
Their aim was not cheap housing, but commercial redevelopment of blighted areas at
the edge of downtown, on the model successfully used by Pittsburgh in its Golden
Triangle redevelopment. Though bitterly opposed to NAREB, the public housing
movement went along with the idea of urban renewal in the hope that it too could
achieve its objectives.[212] In fact, though presented as a measure to secure "the realization

---

[208]   Greer and Hansen, 1941, 3–4, 6, 8.
[209]   Salisbury, 1964, 784–7; Lowe, 1967, 31–2; Mollenkopf, 1983, 78; Fox, 1985, 80–100.
[210]   Friedman, 1968, 104–9.
[211]   Meehan, 1977, 15–16, 19.
[212]   Weiss, 1980, 54–9, 62.

as soon as feasible of the goal of a decent home and a suitable living environment for every American family," urban renewal was kept separate from public housing and put in the hands of the Housing and Home Finance Agency, which promptly worked to discourage low-rent housing and to encourage commercial redevelopment; the clause in the 1949 Act, stipulating that the area should be "predominantly redeveloped," was progressively eroded.[213] Using the powers to tear down slums and offer prime land to private developers with government subsidy, cities sought "the blight that's right," as Charles Abrams inimitably put it.[214] In city after city – Philadelphia, Pittsburgh, Hartford, Boston, San Francisco – the areas that were cleared were the low-income, black sections next to the central business district; and the promised alternative housing did not materialize because "Public housing, like the Moor in *Othello*, had done its reverence in justifying urban renewal and could now go."[215]

The agents were "growth coalitions," often consisting of younger businessmen – bankers, developers, construction corporations, realtors, retailers. But they were not just that, because if they had been they probably would have failed; they also included liberal-technocratic mayors (Lee in New Haven, Daley in Chicago) and they were supported by labor councils, construction trade councils, good government groups, professional planners, and others, even the public housing lobby.[216] And they also involved a small but powerful new group of professional urban renewal executives: Robert Moses in New York, Ed Logue in New Haven, Boston, and New York, Justin Herman in San Francisco.[217] As Catherine Bauer Wurster said, "seldom had such a diverse group of would-be angels tried to dance on the same small pin."[218]

As a result, of course, the coalition pulled different ways; and as it did, it often pulled apart. One group, the developers and their allies, wanted large-scale redevelopment in the interests of established downtown firms – but also to attract outside business, which could bring them into conflict with local interests. They also wanted to do so, if possible, through administrative arrangements that bypassed local interests. But increasingly, through the 1950s and especially the 1960s, they fell foul of other groups: local residents conserving and defending their neighborhoods, small businesses threatened by clearance, who could form anti-renewal coalitions.[219] That story replicated itself in city after American city.

New York was special; but, under Robert Moses, New York always was. In his nearly 50 years of multiple office, he became indisputably "America's greatest builder," responsible for public works which, in terms of 1968 dollars, totalled $27 billion.[220] He built parkways, bridges, tunnels, expressways. And, when the urban

[213] Weiss, 1980, 67.
[214] Abrams, 1965, 74, 118; Bellush and Hausknecht, 1967b, 12; Arnold, 1973, 36; Frieden and Kaplan, 1975, 23; Kleniewski, 1984, 205.
[215] Abrams, 1965, 82; Kleniewski, 1984, 210–11.
[216] Mollenkopf, 1978, 135–6; Weiss, 1980, 68–9; Kleniewski, 1984, 212–13.
[217] Mollenkopf, 1978, 134; Hartman, 1984, 18.
[218] Quoted in Mollenkopf, 1983, 5.
[219] Fainstein and Fainstein, 1983b, 255.
[220] Caro, 1974, 9–10.

renewal spigot began to flow, he built public housing. From 1949 to 1957, New York City spent $267 million on urban renewal; all other cities in the United States spent $133 million. When he resigned from the urban-renewal post, in 1960, he had built more, in terms of completed apartments, than all the rest put together.[221] He did it, as he had done all the others before, by a unique combination of two qualities which he had learned in very early professional life: his rooted belief in top-down planning by the incorruptible, public-spirited civil servant, as most finely represented by the British system which he so much admired; and his bitter early discovery that, in the American urban jungle at least, political connections also mattered.[222] From these two foundations he built a system of power, influence, and patronage that made him almost impregnable – finally to mayors, to governors, even to presidents:[223] "Honest graft, endorsements, campaign contributions, Robert Moses provided the machine with everything it needed. And as a result, he bent the machine to his ends, mobilized its power and influence behind his plans."[224]

During World War Two Moses effectively planned Stuyvesant Town, Metropolitan Life's mammoth East Side project which cleared 11,000 working-class tenants to house 8,756 middle-class families; he could not have succeeded without left-wing support in wartime conditions.[225] Predictably, in 1946, new mayor William O'Dwyer named Moses New York City Construction Coordinator.[226] By January 1945, Moses had already drawn up a huge program of state-funded housing projects, almost all based on a refusal to build public housing on vacant land, but instead to concentrate it on the Lower East Side, in East Harlem, and in Brooklyn near the Navy Yard and in Brownsville. In his mind, these were already classified by race: he spoke of "the Bronx colored project."[227]

Title I of the 1949 Housing Act gave him his chance, and the amazing fact was that "the city that led the nation in racial decency would lead it in the final art of 'Negro removal'":[228] within a decade, the city leveled huge areas of Manhattan and the Bronx to build 17 Title I projects, replaced 100,000 low-income people, nearly 40% of them black and Hispanic, replacing them by middle-income professionals, as well as displacing at least 5,000 businesses, mainly mom-and-pop affairs.[229] But Moses was only following a city tradition of abandoning municipal responsibility for tenant relocation, as Title I had stipulated, for in New York even liberals vied for public subsidies for private developers: they agreed that the working classes had no special place in the inner city. Everyone backed him – even Tugwell, who called him "the second or third best thing that ever happened to it (New York)."[230]

[221] Lowe, 1967, 48; Caro, 1974, 12.
[222] Caro, 1974, 52–5, 70–1, 85.
[223] Caro, 1974, 427–31.
[224] Caro, 1974, 740.
[225] Schwartz, 1993, 84.
[226] Schwartz, 1993, 108.
[227] Schwartz, 1993, 113–15.
[228] Schwartz, 1993, xv.
[229] Schwartz, 1993, xv, 295.
[230] Schwartz, 1993, 143, 297, 61.

Ironically, he finally went too far, and that proved his undoing: "Democracy had not solved the problem of building large-scale public works, so Moses solved it by ignoring democracy."[231] True, as throughout his life he took care to build a broad and diverse coalition of interest groups: hospitals and universities in search of land, cultural and business promotion groups, even trade unions interested in cooperative housing, and the always-supportive *New York Times*.[232] He scorned rehabilitation: "They think we should ... fix up with rubber bands, Scotch tape and violins."[233]

But finally, small groups of citizens began to protest; Moses tried to ride rough-shod over them but found that he could not. Among them was a housewife and architectural journalist in West Greenwich Village, Jane Jacobs, who mobilized local opinion after she found that he planned to tear her neighborhood down.[234] She won, and the experience proved the trigger for one of the most influential books in twentieth-century planning history: *The Death and Life of Great American Cities*. By then, Moses was no longer in charge of renewal; and in 1968, stripped of the last of his offices at the age of 79, Robert Moses was the Master Builder no more.[235]

New Haven, the other city that first and most brilliantly exploited the new powers, provides another classic illustration: its mayor, Richard Lee, came from the Catholic working class of the city, but could move easily at different levels of society including the Yale establishment; he was extremely sensitive to shifts in opinion, and was a master of public relations.[236] He formed a close team with Edward C. Logue, his Development Administrator, and Maurice Rotival, his Redevelopment Director, in which it was "only a slight oversimplification to say that it was the mayor's task to get the support of the major political interests in the city, the Development Adminis-trator's to insure the participation of developers, and the Redevelopment Director's to win the consent of the Federal agencies":[237] Lee's coalition embraced Democrat leaders, Republican business, Yale administration and faculty, ethnic groups, and trade unions; the Citizens' Action Committee, a deliberate creation by Lee, "virtually decapitated the opposition."[238] The result was the demolition of a major – an increasingly black – slum area to build downtown offices, aided by the use of federal highway funds to build a downtown distributor.[239]

Pittsburgh, another pioneer – even before 1949, in fact – is the same kind of story. After decades of moribund local leadership, a new business elite determined that the city must take action to prevent economic collapse. As early as 1943 it set up an Allegheny Conference on Regional Development to build a coalition to revitalize the downtown area. The result was an unlikely alliance between a Republican group

---

[231]   Caro, 1974, 848.
[232]   Lowe, 1967, 86–8.
[233]   Lowe, 1967, 92.
[234]   Lowe, 1967, 101–3.
[235]   Caro, 1974, 1144.
[236]   Dahl, 1961, 118–19.
[237]   Dahl, 1961, 129.
[238]   Dahl, 1961, 133.
[239]   Lowe, 1967, 406, 417; Fainstein and Fainstein, 1983a, 40.

of corporate leaders and a Democratic political boss. An Urban Renewal Authority was set up in 1946. It was given unprecedented powers – challenged but established as constitutional – to condemn property for city-planning purposes. Renaissance I, as it came to be called, was fundamentally a private development operation, with the public sector playing a facilitatory role, and with close, overlapping membership of the main agencies: the Allegheny Conference, the Urban Renewal Authority, the Planning Commission. Over the next two decades the plans rebuilt more than a quarter of the so-called Golden Triangle, displacing at least 5,400 low-income, principally black, families, and replacing them principally by offices which have made the whole area a 9-to-5 commuter zone.[240]

San Francisco was yet another classic case. The argument for urban renewal came from organized business through the Bay Area Council, "a private regional government," of 1944, and the Blyth–Zellerbach Committee of 1956. The San Francisco Redevelopment Agency of 1948, a year before the 1949 Act, neatly anticipated its powers; in 1958, it was reshaped under Blyth–Zellerbach impetus. Justin Herman, "St Justin" to the downtown business group, the "White Devil" to the low-income residents of the Western Addition and the South of Market areas next door, became its director in 1959. He stood for the sanitation of these areas, meaning the removal of their inhabitants. As one business supporter eloquently put it, "You certainly can't expect us to erect a 50 million dollar building in an area where dirty old men will be going around exposing themselves to our secretaries."[241]

In fact, Chester Hartman argues, the "skid row" label was a carefully cultivated image to justify renewal. Though the area south of Market Street was a zone of residential hotels overwhelmingly occupied by men, most were simply retired or disabled. They organized, and found a leader in an 80-year-old trade unionist, George Woolf. In an epic legal fight he forced the Renewal Agency in 1970 to agree to build low-rent units. Herman, incensed, called the tenants' lawyer "a clever, well-financed, able, ambulance-chasing lawyer." A year later, he died of a heart attack.

Further lawsuits came and went during the following decade. While that happened, Urban Renewal funds were replaced by Community Development Block Grants, which spread funding across the city; the Renewal Agency lost its independent funding, and the Mayor's Office took greater control. But meanwhile, the office-building boom boomed ever more loudly. By the late 1980s, after three decades of confrontation, the South of Market redevelopment was nearing completion. The citizens of San Francisco, by now highly organized to protect their neighborhoods, belatedly passed a stringent measure to restrict further office growth anywhere in their city.[242]

The astonishing feature of these coalitions in those years, in fact, is just how successful they were in pushing through policies that were clearly against the

[240] Lubove, 1969, 87, 106–11, 127–31, 139–40; Lowe, 1967, 134, 140–1; Stewman and Tarr, 1982, 63–5, 74–6, 103–5.

[241] Quoted in Hartman, 1984, 51.

[242] Fainstein, Fainstein, and Armistead, 1983, 216, 226; Hartman, 1984, 185, 309–11.

interests of voters. Boston's West End, an old-established and extremely well-knit Italian community – an urban village, in Herbert Gans's words – was a classic instance. On the advice of mortgage bankers, the clearance plans were extended to include non-blighted areas. The general population thought the whole area was a slum because the press told it so. The locals believed that it would never happen. The developers wanted the land for high-income housing, and the city went along.[243] Later, Fried found that the West Enders, particularly the traditional working class among them, had been profoundly affected by the experience, rather as if a loved one had died.[244]

But all good things come to an end. By the mid-1960s, the criticism of urban renewal had become deafening. Charles Abrams pointed out that many of the cleared areas – Washington Square South in New York City, Bunker Hill in Los Angeles, Diamond Heights in San Francisco – were, like the West End, "no slum at all in the real estate sense": they were so because officials said so.[245] Martin Anderson calculated that to the end of 1965 renewal would evict one million people, most of whom paid very low rents; three-quarters of these had relocated themselves, nine in ten of them to substandard dwellings at higher rents. Overall, to March 1961 the program had destroyed four times as many units as had been built; typically, land was left vacant, since the average scheme took 12 years to complete. Nearly 40% of the new construction was not for housing; and of the replacement housing units, most were privately built high-rise apartments commanding high rents.[246] Thus, though 85% of all areas certified for assistance in the Act's first 10 years were residential before redevelopment, only 50% were so afterwards.[247] Or, as Scott Greer put it, "At a cost of more than three million dollars the Urban Renewal Agency (URA) has succeeded in materially reducing the supply of low-cost housing in American cities."[248] Chester Hartman concluded that, perversely, the effect of the program had been to make the rich richer and the poor poorer.[249] Gans neatly spelt out the absurdity of it all:

> Suppose that the government decided that jalopies were a menace to public safety and a blight on the beauty of the highways, and therefore took them away from their drivers. Suppose, then, that to replenish the supply of automobiles, it gave these drivers a hundred dollars each to buy a good used car and also made special grants to General Motors, Ford and Chrysler to lower the cost – though not necessarily the price – of Cadillacs, Lincolns and Imperials by a few hundred dollars. Absurd as this may sound, change the jalopies to slum housing, and I have described, with only slight poetic license, the first fifteen years of a federal program called urban renewal.[250]

[243] Gans, 1962, 4, 283–90, 318.
[244] Fried, 1963, 167–8.
[245] Abrams, 1965, 118–22.
[246] Anderson, 1964, 54–67, 73, 93.
[247] Grigsby, 1963, 324.
[248] Greer, 1965, 3.
[249] Hartman, 1964, 278.
[250] Gans, 1967b, 465.

How could this have happened? Several critics underlined the fact that the cynical explanation was not necessarily the right one; though some had profited hugely, "There is something that one can only call civic patriotism" which "blends nicely with financial interests." In the growth coalition, many members had pure motives: "mayors concerned with the central city tax base, civic leaders with a patriotic desire to 'make our city center beautiful', businessmen with deep commitments to downtown real estate, and those who believe that government should innovate in the public interest" had together produced "a program that rewards the strong and punishes the weak."[251] The program could only be implemented locally; and locally, most cities wanted the revival of downtown and the return of the middle class from the suburbs.[252]

Some of the worst excesses of urban renewal were later avoided, true: more areas were rebuilt for housing, there was more low-rent housing, more blacks were rehoused.[253] And clearly, since rehousing was one of the last things that the program actually achieved in its first 15 years of life, most of the ills of American urban renewal could not be laid at Corbusier's door. But the Corbusian and the urban renewal prescriptions did share what Martin Anderson graphically called the Federal Bulldozer approach. What emerges from the American critiques is that it might actually have been better to leave the poor alone. Greer quotes a local official: "So what are we saying? The widow either has to live on $2 a month or she has to have substandard housing by those standards. There's real need for what we call secondary housing, and if we condemned it we'd wipe out the housing the people could afford."[254] Add to this the psychic costs of breaking up old-established neighborhoods, and the case becomes even stronger.

Counter-Attack: Jacobs and Newman

The failure of American urban renewal, and the increasing doubts about its British equivalent, help explain the colossal impact in both countries of Jane Jacobs's *The Death and Life of Great American Cities*, published in America in 1961, which rapidly became one of the most influential books in the short history of city planning. It was one of those classic cases of the right message at the right time. Jacobs hit out at both the great orthodoxies on which city planning had based itself in its first half-century of life. The garden-city movement was attacked on the ground that its "prescription for saving the city was to do the city in," by defining "wholesome housing in terms only of suburban physical qualities and small-town social qualities"; for good measure, it "conceived of planning also as essentially paternalistic, if not authoritarian."[255] The Corbusians were vilified for egotism: "No matter how

251   Greer, 1965, 94, 122.
252   Grigsby, 1963, 323.
253   Sanders, 1980, 106–7, 112.
254   Greer, 1965, 46–7.
255   Jacobs, 1962, 17, 19.

vulgarized or clumsy the design, how dreary and useless the open space, how dull the close-up view, an imitation of Le Corbusier shouts 'Look what I made!' Like a great, visible ego it tells of someone's achievement."[256]

The point, she argued, was that there was nothing wrong with high urban densities of people so long as they did not entail overcrowding in buildings: traditional inner-city neighborhoods like New York's Brooklyn Heights, Philadelphia's Rittenhouse Square, and San Francisco's North Beach were all good areas, though densely populated.[257] A good urban neighborhood, she argued, actually needed 100 dwellings, equivalent perhaps to 200–300 people, per acre – a high density even for New York, and higher than almost anything in post-1945 London. But it could be achieved by cutting out open space:

> To say that cities need high dwelling densities and high net ground coverage, and I am saying they do, is conventionally regarded as lower than taking sides with a man-eating shark.
>
> But things have changed since the days when Ebenezer Howard looked at the slums of London and concluded that to save the people, city life must be abandoned.[258]

The Jacobs prescription amounted to keeping the inner-city neighborhood more or less as it was before the planners had got their hands on it. It should have mixed functions and therefore land uses, to ensure that people were there for different purposes, on different time-schedules, but using many facilities in common. It must have conventional streets on short blocks. It must mix blocks of different age and condition, including a significant share of old ones. And it must have a dense concentration of people, for whatever purpose they are there, including a dense concentration of residents.[259]

It sounded good to her overwhelmingly middle-class readers. The irony, as was pointed out 20 years later, was that the result was the yuppification of the city:

> Urbanism proved as susceptible as modernism to having its egalitarian impulses subordinated to the consumer interests of the upper middle class ... It took over forty years to go from the first Bauhaus manifesto to the Four Seasons; it took only half that time to go from Jane Jacobs's apotheosis of her humble corner grocer to his replacement by Bonjour, Croissant and all that implies.[260]

One middle-class reviewer who was less impressed was Lewis Mumford. He confessed to Osborn that he had held his fire for a year, "But I can't pretend that I didn't enjoy giving her an awful walloping on the soft part of her carcass that she

---

[256] Jacobs, 1962, 23.
[257] Jacobs, 1962, 202–5.
[258] Jacobs, 1962, 218.
[259] Jacobs, 1962, 152, 178, 187, 200.
[260] Muschamp, 1983, 168.

had so carelessly exposed."[261] This, as Leonard Fishman argues, is odd: both shared a vision of freedom, both hated suburban sprawl, but for Jacobs the huge city was the seat of liberation, for him the opposite.[262] By this time, Mumford was an old and deeply disillusioned man; he believed that huge corporate forces had captured America and would destroy the urban texture she sought to preserve. He proved wrong, of course, and the gentrification of Greenwich Village was merely the precursor of a process that has subsequently affected every American city. But, oddly, it has happened in parallel with its precise opposite: a process of white middle-class flight and abandonment.[263] And therein lies the paradox of almost every American city at the beginning of the twenty-first century: vibrant downtowns and gracious middle-class enclaves sit next door to war zones, as if occupying two entirely different cities in different countries, almost different planets. Which, in a terrible sense, they do.

This says something important about Jacobs's thinking. Opposed to any kind of preconceived planning, it was based on a core belief that cities like New York were

> self-organizing. The most properly designed place cannot compete. Everything is provided which is the worst thing we can provide. There's a joke that the father of an old friend used to tell, about a teacher who warns children, "In Hell there will be wailing and weeping and gnashing of teeth". "What if you don't have teeth?" one of the children asks. "Then teeth will be provided", he says sternly. That's it – the spirit of the designed city. Teeth Will Be Provided for You.[264]

The problem with this is that it cannot guarantee the development of good neighborhoods. In fact, it is likely that they would never happen, because citizen opposition would stop them; they prefer things to stay as they are.[265] "Were someone to propose a Beacon Hill, a Georgetown, a South End in Boston, or a Nob Hill in San Francisco it would never get off the ground."[266] So the good places will remain unchangeably good, and likewise with the bad ones. The Jacobs philosophy is ultimately the quintessence of *laissez-faire*.

The Dynamiting of Pruitt–Igoe

Yet, whatever the later implications, urbanism spelt doom for the Federal Bulldozer. But it took more than just that. Though by British standards America had built all-too-little public housing, still it had built some. And some of the biggest and most influential cities had followed a Corbusian model: St Louis, Chicago, Newark, among

---

[261] Fishman, 1996, 4.
[262] Fishman, 1996, 4–5.
[263] Fishman, 1996, 8, 9.
[264] Quoted in Hirt, 2012, 41.
[265] Stockard, 2012, 52.
[266] Stockard, 2012, 52.

others. By the end of the 1970s, they were contemplating their abandonment. Many were 30 or 40% vacant. The classic case was Pruitt–Igoe, an award-winning 1955 project in St Louis, which achieved notoriety by being blown up 17 years after it was built. That day, the demolition preserved for posterity on film, it became an instant symbol of all that was perceived as wrong with urban renewal, not merely in the United States but in the world at large.

When the Captain W. O. Pruitt Homes and the William L. Igoe Apartments were unveiled in 1950, the experimental high-rise design by the distinguished architect Minoru Yamasaki brought together a cluster of design features advocated by modern architects: slab and rowhouse buildings of various heights; wide access-gallery corridors in the apartment slabs meant to function as play areas, porches, laundry drying areas, duplex units with skip-stop elevators, and a river of open space winding through the site, a concept proposed by Harland Bartholomew. The *Architectural Forum* lauded it as the "best high apartment" of 1951. But then, under the 1949 Federal Housing Act, the minimum standards were made maximum, and federal officials insisted all buildings were made a uniform 11 stories.[267] The 33 identical blocks, containing over 2,800 apartments, were completed in 1955–6. They were on a bare site open to transient traffic. To keep within cost limits, huge and arbitrary cuts were made during construction. Space inside the apartments, especially for the large families that came to occupy many of them, "was pared to the bone and beyond to the marrow."[268] Locks and doorknobs broke on first use, sometimes before occupancy. Window panes blew out. One lift failed on opening day. "On the day they were completed, the buildings in Pruitt and Igoe were little more than steel and concrete warrens, poorly designed, badly equipped, inadequate in size, badly located, unventilated, and virtually impossible to maintain."[269] That would have been bad enough. But in addition, the tenants who came were not the ones for whom the blocks had been designed. The design, like that of most public housing down to the 1950s, was for the deserving poor. Most heads of households were employed males. St Louis in 1951 was a segregated city: Pruitt was all-black, but after public housing was desegregated by decision of the Supreme Court, the authority tried to integrate Igoe. To no avail: whites left, and blacks – including many welfare-dependent, female-headed families – moved in. By 1965, more than two-thirds of the inhabitants were minors, 70% of them under 12; there were two and a half times as many women as men; women headed 62% of the families; 38% contained no employed person, and in only 45% was employment the sole source of income.[270]

Rapidly, the development became a byword for disaster. Occupancy rates in Pruitt, 95% in 1956, fell to 81% six years later and to 72% in 1965; Igoe started at less than 70% and stayed at that level. The development began to deteriorate: pipes burst,

267 Mumford, 1995, 34–5.
268 Meehan, 1975, 35.
269 Meehan, 1979, 73.
270 Rainwater, 1970, 13.

Figure 7.10 and **Figure 7.11** Pruitt–Igoe. The world's most notorious high-rise housing project as it was supposed to look – and actually did look for a short while at the start – and at the moment of its demolition in 1972. *Source*: © Bettmann/CORBIS (fig. 7.10) and Time & Life Pictures/Getty Images (fig. 7.11).

there was a gas explosion. By 1966, resident poverty-program workers recorded the scene:

> Glass, rubble and debris litter the streets, the accumulation is astonishing ... abandoned automobiles have been left in parking areas; glass is omnipresent; tin cans are strewn throughout, paper has been rained on and stuck in the cracked, hardened mud. Pruitt–Igoe from without looks like a disaster area. Broken windows are apparent in every building. Street lights are inoperative ... As the visitor nears the entrance to a building, the filth and debris intensify. Abandoned rooms under the building are receptacles for all matter of waste. Mice, roaches, and other vermin thrive in these open areas ...
>
> The infamous skip-stop elevator is a revelation even for those considering themselves prepared for anything. Paint has peeled from the elevator walls. The stench of urine is overwhelming; ventilation in the elevators is nonexistent ... When the visitor emerges from the dark, stench-filled elevator on to one of the building's gallery floors, he enters a grey concrete caricature of an insane asylum. Institutional grey walls give way to institutional grey floors. Rusty institutional-type screens cover windows in which no glass exists. Radiators once used to heat these public galleries have been, in many buildings, stripped from the walls. Incinerators, too small to accommodate the quantity to [sic] refuse placed into them, have spilled over – trash and garbage are heaped on the floors. Lightbulbs and fixtures are out; bare hot wire often dangles from malfunctioning light sockets.[271]

In 1969, there was a nine-month rent strike, the longest in the history of American public housing. At one point, 28 of the 34 elevators were inoperative. By 1970, the project was 65% unoccupied. In 1972, accepting the inevitable, the authority blew it up.

The question, asked by a whole series of academic observers, is how it happened: in just a decade, a design showpiece had become one of the worst urban slums in the United States. And there were as many explanations as observers.

The first culprit, clearly, was the design. As Oscar Newman put it in a celebrated analysis,

> the architect was concerned with each building as a complete, separate, and formal entity, exclusive of any consideration of the functional use of grounds or the relationship of a building to the ground area it might share with other buildings. It is almost as if the architect assumed the role of a sculptor and saw the grounds of the project as nothing more than a surface on which he was endeavoring to arrange a whole series of vertical elements into a compositionally pleasing whole.[272]

Or, as Jacobs would have said, it represented an architect's ego-trip. Specifically, Pruitt–Igoe was designed – as were many similar Corbusian layouts in American

---

[271] Quoted in Montgomery, 1985, 238.
[272] Newman, 1972, 59.

public housing of the early 1950s – on the basis of a superblock of between four and twelve ordinary street blocks of the kind Jane Jacobs commended, within which the high-rise blocks – in the Pruitt–Igoe case, 11-story slabs at an average 50 units to the acre – were freely positioned in the landscape, invariably with entry from the grounds, not from the street.[273] This feature, plus the long high-level access decks, created the maximum possible area of what Newman, in a memorable phrase, called indefensible space: the decks, shown by the architect in his 1951 drawing as full of children, toys, and (white) mothers, soon became vandalized and feared.[274]

The problem, as other observers found, was compounded by the rules of financial management imposed by Washington. Since rents must cover maintenance, and tenants could not pay the rents, the city cut maintenance. And even then tenants could not pay. In 1969, when a quarter of families were paying more than 50% of their incomes for rent, they went on strike.[275] And the irony was that this non-policy of non-maintenance was being applied to apartments that had been extremely expensive to build: at $20,000 each in 1967 values, they were only a little cheaper to build than top-grade luxury apartments.[276]

The root of the problem, Newman found on deeper analysis, was the failure in architectural education to stress the need to learn how well or badly existing buildings worked, and then to improve the designs; "the full extent of this tragedy is best appreciated when we realize that the most recognized of architects are often those who turn out the most dramatic failures."[277] And this, in turn, was because there had been two camps in modern architecture, the "social methodologists" and the "style metaphysicians," but the United States had imported only the second, Corbusian, tradition.[278] This conclusion is supported by the finding that conventional low-rise developments, with similar mixes of tenants, had no such problems.[279]

But Newman was at pains to point out that design was not the only, or even the necessary, culprit. The worst deterioration occurred only after the Department of Housing and Urban Development changed its rules to admit problem families, many from rural backgrounds, into public housing, in 1965: "In the intervening seven years, the high-rise buildings to which they were admitted have been undergoing systematic decimation";[280] not only Pruitt–Igoe, but other similar blocks (Rosen Apartments in Philadelphia, Columbus Homes in Newark) were likewise abandoned. The root cause was that very poor welfare families, with large numbers of children, with a deep fatalism about the power to influence their environment, could not cope with this kind of building, nor it with them. As one sociologist-observer,

273   Newman, 1972, 56.
274   Newman, 1972, 56–8.
275   Meehan, 1979, 83; Montgomery, 1985, 232, 238.
276   Meehan, 1975, 65; Meehan, 1979, 73–4.
277   Newman, 1980, 322–3.
278   Newman, 1980, 294–5.
279   Meehan, 1979, 86.
280   Newman, 1972, 188.

Lee Rainwater, observed, the ideals and aspirations of Pruitt–Igoeans were similar to those of other people, but they could not realize them:

> The realization of these Pruitt–Igoe ideals would produce a life hardly distinguishable from other working-class life, white or black. And it seems likely that the resources necessary to maintain such a family life would require the stability and level of income characteristic of the upper working class, a level of income anywhere from 50 to more than 100 per cent higher than is available to most families in Pruitt–Igoe.[281]

Middle- and upper-income families, with a proportion of families with children that did not exceed 50%, and with superintendents and at least one parent supervising, could live comfortably in such environments, but "while a middle-class family will not perform too differently in one building type versus another, the performance of a welfare family proves to be greatly influenced by the physical environment"; for them, "the high-rise apartment building is to be strictly avoided."[282] Colin Ward's statement, exactly.

There were two places in the world, from the 1960s onward, where the city of towers was realized in its ultimate purity. Both Singapore and Hong Kong had good reason: they were island or peninsular city states, with rapidly growing populations and an acute shortage of available land. But there was another odd similarity, noticed by Manuel Castells, that "one of the most striking paradoxes of urban policy in the world, the two market economies with the highest rates of growth in the last twenty-five years are also those with the largest public housing programs in the capitalist world, in terms of the proportion of the population directly housed by the government."[283] Between 1945 and 1969, Hong Kong built 1.4 million public housing units;[284] Singapore built 15 new towns and 86% of the population live in public-sector housing.[285] In this process, as Robert Home has shown, the public were not involved. Oddly, in Singapore a post-colonial state continued the paternalist policies of the colonial state it replaced. The lively public spaces of the old colonial city were replaced by public housing and planned public spaces; hawkers and market-stall traders were relocated to purpose-built structures.[286] Within one generation, Singaporeans found themselves living in a perfect realization of CIAM mass housing,[287] produced according to an abstract and hugely rational design process, but one lacking any data on the way people had behaved in the old Singapore. The new planned public spaces tended to be hierarchical by size and evenly distributed in location.[288]

---

[281]   Rainwater, 1970, 50.
[282]   Newman, 1972, 193.
[283]   Castells *et al.*, 1990, quoted in Home, 2013, 212.
[284]   Home, 2013, 213.
[285]   Home, 2013, 214.
[286]   Hee and Ooi, 2003, 88.
[287]   Hee and Ooi, 2003, 90.
[288]   Hee and Ooi, 2003, 96.

The Corbusian Legacy

The irony then was that the Corbusian city of towers was perfectly satisfactory for the middle-class inhabitants whom he had imagined living their gracious, elegant, cosmopolitan lives in *La Ville Contemporaine*. It might even work for the solid, tough, traditional tenement-dwellers of Glasgow, for whom the transition from a Gorbals rear-end slum to the twentieth floor seemed like the ascent to paradise. But, for a welfare mother born in a Georgia shack and dumped in St Louis or Detroit with a brood of uncontrollable children, it proved an urban disaster of the first magnitude. The sin of Corbusier and the Corbusians thus lay not in their designs, but in the mindless arrogance whereby they were imposed on people who could not take them and could never, given a modicum of thought, ever have been expected to take them.

The final irony is that, in cities all over the world, this was condemned as the failure of "planning." Planning, in the common-or-garden sense, means an orderly scheme of action to achieve stated objectives in the light of known constraints. Planning is just what this was not. But, as Jon Lang has pointed out, it does belong to a *genre* of urban design: as opposed to an empiricist paradigm, which seeks to work from experience of precedents that have worked well, this is a rationalist paradigm, built on abstract ideas.[289] Unfortunately, these ideas were tested on human guinea-pigs; and therein lies a terrible object lesson for future generations of planners.

[289]	Lang, 2000, 84–5.

The City of Sweat Equity

Art was once the common possession of the whole people; it was the rule in the Middle Ages that the produce of handicraft was beautiful ... today, it is prosperity that is externally ugly ... we sit starving amidst our gold, the Midas of the ages.

William Morris, *Forecasts of the Coming Century* (1897)

The Town Planning Movement is on this side a revolt of the peasant and the gardener, as on the other of the citizen, and these united by the geographer, from their domination by the engineer. Only when the mechanical energies of the Engineer are brought into line with all other aspects of the city, and these reunited in the service of life, can he change from blundering giant into helpful Hercules ...

Patrick Geddes, *Report on the Planning of Dacca* (1917)

... if we are going to reform the world, and make it a better place to live in, the way to do it is not to talk about relationships of a political nature, which are inevitably dualistic, full of subjects and objects and their relationship to one another; or with programmes full of things for other people to do ... The social values are right only if the individual values are right. The place to improve the world is first in one's heart and hands, and then work outward from there. Other people want to talk about how to expand the destiny of mankind. I just want to talk about how to fix a motorcycle. I think that what I have to say has more lasting value.

Robert M. Pirsig, *Zen and the Art of Motorcycle Maintenance* (1974)

Cities of Tomorrow: An Intellectual History of Urban Planning and Design Since 1880,
Fourth Edition. Peter Hall.
© 2014 Peter Hall. Published 2014 by John Wiley & Sons, Ltd.

8

The City of Sweat Equity

The Autonomous Community: Edinburgh, Indore, Lima, Berkeley, Macclesfield, 1890–1987

The reaction against the Corbusian city of towers brought the much-belated triumph of the anarchist strain of planning thought that had so heavily infused the early garden-city movement and its regional planning derivative. So this history has not yet done with Geddes. He, more than anyone, contributed to planning theory the idea that men and women could make their own cities, thus escaping from mass industrialism to a world of craft activity, where once again things would look beautiful because they were made right. That strand is implicit in Kropotkin, explicit and central in the works of William Morris and Edward Carpenter; Unwin in turn based his philosophy on Morris and was an early member of Carpenter's socialist group in Sheffield, where he heard Kropotkin lecture on the union of intellectual and craft work.[1]

But the main line runs through Geddes, whom Unwin met at the cheap cottages exhibition held at Letchworth in 1905.[2] It was Geddes who, as Kropotkin records in a letter of 1886 to Reclus, "has now just got married, leaving his house and taking a very poor flat among the workers. Everywhere, in one form or another, one finds similar things. It is a complete reawakening. What direction will it take?"[3] Geddes himself described it, much later in his life, in a characteristic Geddesian outpouring:

> Social conscience was then stirring throughout the cities, and we had both felt it strongly – and so strengthened each other: so after a single winter of bonnie home … we crossed to the high James Court tenement of the Old Town opposite, with opposite view accordingly, and thus enabling us to endure, by facing and tackling of dirt and overcrowding and disorder of even more infernal slumdom than now exists in

---

[1]   Jackson, F., 1985, 13–14, 17; Creese, 1966, 169–73.
[2]   Jackson, F., 1985, 102–3.
[3]   Boardman, 1978, 87.

Edinburgh; and to begin such changes as might be, thus became problems as scientific, as technical, as had been those of living nature and its science for myself, or of music for my companion.[4]

They began with the basics:

Beginning within our limited range, with flower-boxes for dull windows and colour-washing for even duller walls (than which there is no better, no simpler and no brighter beginnings for city improvements) we soon got to fuller cleanings and repairings, next even to renewals, at length to building as through Lawnmarket, Castle Hill to Ramsay Garden, of course with thanks to growing cooperation alike from students and citizens, increasingly becoming good neighbours.[5]

Their example spread:

One by one, some denizens of the courts began to give their own time to the jobs that Geddes persuaded them to tackle with him, clearing, whitewashing, or gardening; nor could they work beside him, listening to his flow of ideas about the job in hand and the further possibilities, without capturing something of his sanguine spirit. For the first time they began to feel that something could be done to change their surroundings.[6]

James Mavor, a contemporary observer, thought that "Geddes was really on the same track as Morris": furnishing their apartment with good Scots eighteenth-century furniture, he and his wife were providing examples for all to see "of the surroundings of the period before the factory system had divorced the fine arts from production"; but, unlike Morris, he believed all this could be done incrementally.[7]

The result of all this a decade later was described by Israel Zangwill:

Everywhere a litter of building operations, and we trod gingerly many a decadent staircase. Sometimes a double row of houses had already been knocked away, revealing a Close within a Close, eyeless house behind blind alley, and even so the diameter of the Court was still but a few yards ... Those sunless courts, entered by needles' eyes of apertures, congested with hellish, heaven-scaling barracks, reeking with refuse and evil odours, inhabited promiscuously by poverty and prostitution, worse than the worse slums of London itself ... "Do you wonder Edinburgh is renowned for medical schools?" asked the Professor grimly.[8]

Zangwill's comment is revealing: "His own destruction was conservative in character; it was his aim to preserve the ancient note in the architecture, and to make a clean

---

[4] Boardman, 1978, 86.
[5] Boardman, 1978, 86–7.
[6] Mairet, 1957, 52.
[7] Quoted in Boardman, 1978, 89.
[8] Quoted in Boardman, 1978, 146.

old Edinburgh of a dirty."[9] Effectively, know it or not, he was following a tradition: as a founder-member of the Environmental Society in 1884, which soon evolved into the better-known Edinburgh Social Union, with the immediate aim of raising standards without waiting for legislation; he was using methods similar to those of Canon Barnett and Octavia Hill, whom he visited in London around 1886, admiring her work in the Marylebone slums.[10] And Hill had another admirer in Anna Morton, who became Anna Geddes.[11]

Here, in the tenements of the Old Town, Geddes developed his method of civic survey, which drew on his training as a botanist.[12] Based on three-dimensional aerial drawings by Frank C. Mears, who would later become his son-in-law, it allowed Geddes to develop simple logical connections: overcrowding and underhousing, with high rents and high land values, resulted from the restricting defensive walls of the medieval city; the notorious filth was due to its poor water supply, which in turn came from its hill site.[13] He was an inveterate organizer, carrying out social reconstruction through Ruskinian guilds: the Artistic Guild, the Educational Programme, the Entertainment Committee, the Public Open Spaces Committee and the Housing Guild. The Social Union's Housing Guild built up a fund by managing property for owners and organizing rent collection by volunteers. It developed university residence halls.[14]

But all this did not come cheap: in 1896, after years in which he had earned £200 a year as part-time professor, he had acquired properties worth more than £53,000. To save him from bankruptcy and his wife from nervous breakdown, that year his friends formed the "Town and Gown Association, Limited," to take over most of these enterprises and put them at last on a business basis.[15] But years of recrimination followed, as Geddes accused the directors of timidity and conservatism.[16]

Geddes Goes to India

In 1914, already aged 60, he sailed for India, to show his Civic Exhibition – which had first seen life at the great international town-planning meeting in London in 1910 – in Madras. It was a disaster: the boat carrying the exhibits was sunk by a German warship.[17] Yet, undiscouraged, in two months he traveled between two and three thousand miles, consulting on the improvement of Indian cities.[18] Here and in

---

[9]   Quoted in Boardman, 1978, 146.
[10] Meller, 1990, 71–3.
[11] Leonard, 1999, 34.
[12] Leonard 1999, 34.
[13] Leonard, 1999, 38.
[14] Leonard, 1999, 42–4.
[15] Boardman, 1978, 146–7.
[16] Boardman, 1978, 164–6, 232–3.
[17] Boardman, 1978, 253.
[18] Boardman, 1978, 254.

two subsequent visits, he developed his concept of "conservative surgery" – or, in latter-day jargon, urban rehabilitation.[19] The resulting reports – at least 24 of them, perhaps 30, some still awaiting discovery, some existing in unique copies in the India Office library in London, many of them evidently produced at extraordinary speed, a day at a time – include the best work Geddes did in his life.[20]

On that first visit, he was soon railing that

> I have a new fight before me, as with the Housing at Delhi. Here it is to be with the Sanitary Authority of the Madras Government, with its death-dealing Haussmannising and its squalid (Belfast 1858) industrial bye-laws, which it thinks, enacts and enforces as up-to-date planning … From the callous, contemptuous city bureaucrat at Delhi, I have now to tackle here the well-intentioned fanatic of sanitation – perhaps an even tougher proposition.[21]

He carried that battle from city to city. The fact was that, even more than their brethren at home, the British in India had an obsession with drains; at the time of the Mutiny, losses from disease had been far greater than those from battle, and a Royal Commission of 1863 had pronounced that "It is indeed impossible to separate the question of health, as it relates to troops, from the sanitary condition of the native population, especially as regards the occurrence of epidemics." "The habits of the natives," it had warned, "are such that, unless they are closely watched, they cover the whole neighbouring surface with filth."[22]

In fact, Geddes was facing up to a ferociously well-established bureaucracy who believed it knew what was best: "A new breed of sanitary experts emerged in the Eastern empire, attributing high death rates from disease to 'the insanitary and immoral lives of the Asiatic races.'"[23] Following the prescription of Sir William John Ritchie Simpson, first Health Officer for the Calcutta Municipal Administration and then, for 28 years, Professor of Hygiene and Public Health at the University of London, racial segregation became a general rubric of colonial sanitary administration;[24] Lord Lugard, the legendary Nigerian civil servant, wrote in 1919 that

> The first object … is to segregate Europeans, so that they shall not be exposed to the attacks of mosquitoes which have become infected with the germs of malaria and yellow fever, by preying on Natives, and especially Native Children, whose blood so often contains these germs … Finally, it removes the inconvenience felt by Europeans, whose rest is disturbed by drumming and other noises dear to the Native …[25]

---

[19] Mairet, 1957, 180; Boardman, 1978, 264–5.
[20] Tyrwhitt, 1947, 102–3; Geddes, 1965a, vi–vii; Geddes, 1965b, passim.
[21] Mairet, 1957, 161.
[22] Harrison, 1980, 171, 173.
[23] Home, 1997, 43.
[24] Home, 2013, 48.
[25] Lugard, 1919, quoted in Home, 2013, 125.

All this was based on elaborate pseudo-scientific rationales. In Sierra Leone, a team of scientists led by Dr Ronald Ross, at the time with the Liverpool School of Tropical Medicine, pinpointed the anopheles mosquito as the vector for malaria and recommended nocturnal separation of the natives from the Europeans by a minimum of 430 yards, since they could not fly farther. But in India the authorities implemented racial residential segregation policies as far back as 1819.[26]

All this Geddes was to find when he reached India in October 1914, his Exhibition sunk in the following ship together with "Christmas consignments for the Madras shops, motor-cars for a member of council and lesser individuals, the season's supply of wine for Government house."[27] He immediately began to criticize the practice of driving wide roads through traditional quarters, which did not endear him to officialdom.[28] In Bombay, a British Imperial Civil Service official of autocratic style, C. H. Bompas, was appointed chair of the Improvement Trust and "supreme and undisputed master of the situation." With generous grants, it began to clear parts of the densely populated area next to the business quarter, which had 333 people to the acre and only 5% road coverage. Bompas said squatters were merely "temporary immigrants to Calcutta, whose displacement would cause no great hardship."[29]

So for half a century the Sanitary Branch of the Home Department, and the Sanitary Commissioners, had zealously worked to extend drains and build latrines for the congested old Indian cities. And early Indian town-planning education had been largely in the hands of military engineers.[30] But, according to Geddes, they were plain wrong. At Balrampur in 1917, he wrote, "Since drains are for cities, not cities for drains, Town-Planning cannot but reverse the customary procedure for Engineering, and begin with the general problem of City Improvement, though with drainage of course as one of its many factors."[31] The engineer's approach led to absurdities like provision of water closets that cost twice as much as the value of the houses.[32] Against this belief that "individuals and cities are only to be sanitated from behind, or from below upwards" which was "one of the most depressing of our many modern superstitions," he suggested, "Why not a large barrow, regularly and easily removable by hand labour: or in larger places, even a spare cart and this brightly painted, and standing on a cemented platform which can be kept comparatively dust-free in its decently screened yet accessible corner.[33] The moral should be, he suggested, "instead of the nineteenth century European city panacea – of 'Everything to the Sewer!' ... the right maxim for India is the traditional rural one, of 'Everything to the Soil!'"[34] The street sweepers should become gardeners, taking the waste out of

---

26   Njoh, 2009, 311–12.
27   Home, 2013, 155.
28   Home, 2013, 156.
29   Home, 2013, 86.
30   King, 1980b, 215.
31   Geddes, 1917c, 3.
32   Geddes, 1917b, 17.
33   Geddes, 1917c, 37–8.
34   Geddes, 1918, I, 73.

the city to new suburbs, and manuring the space between the houses to create "a verdant and fruitful garden environment."[35]

Of course, it did not endear him to the engineers, and nor did his insistence that their road widenings and clearances were mostly unnecessary. In Lahore, he pronounced himself "completely staggered" by the proposed demolitions in an old area, which recalled "back-streets in Lancashire towns ... as they were laid out by sanitarians and engineers from about 1860 onwards" until the British 1909 Planning Act had stopped that kind of thing; "The existing roads and lanes are the past product of practical life, its movement and experience," therefore they only needed improvement.[36] For a bazaar quarter of Balrampur, similarly, he suggested clearing a few derelict houses, extending open spaces, planting trees: "As these dilapidated and depressed old quarters reopen to one another, the old village life, with its admirable combination of private simplicity and sacred magnificence, will be seen only awaiting renewal."[37] This was to be complemented by a new suburb of houses with gardens and patios, developed by cooperation between the engineer – who would be needed to allocate sites, make roads and drains, and sink wells – and the local community; they would be developed as "a succession of village groups, each with its own centre."[38]

Similarly, for the factory town of Indore he proposed

> antisepsis and conservative surgery – in plainer terms, cleaning up and clearing up ... In this way the old life of the Mohallas and Bazars is substantially left to go on, upon their present lines, without any serious changes ... By our small removals, straightenings, openings, and replannings in detail, a network of clean and decent lanes, of small streets, and open places, and even gardens, is thus formed, which is often pleasant, and I venture to say sometimes beautiful.[39]

His approach, he was at pains to stress, was both much cheaper and also brought immediate returns in dramatic reductions in sickness and in death rates: "It cannot be too clearly affirmed ... that it is we town planners of a later School who are careful to make streets (a) only where they are really needed, and (b) in the directions required, who are the practical men, the real utilitarians, and the economists, both of the City's purse and those of the citizens."[40] In one of his earliest reports, for Tanjore in the Madras Presidency, he estimated that his plan would cost one-sixth the engineers' gridiron plan.[41] But he did admit that

> The conservative method, however, has its difficulties. It requires long and patient study. The work cannot be done in the office with ruler and parallels, for the plan must

[35]   Geddes, 1918, I, 76.
[36]   Geddes, 1965a, 6–7.
[37]   Geddes, 1917c, 41.
[38]   Geddes, 1917c, 34, 77.
[39]   Geddes, 1918, I, 161.
[40]   Geddes, 1965a, 15.
[41]   Tyrwhitt, 1947, 41.

be sketched out on the spot, after wearying hours of perambulation – commonly among sights and odours which neither Brahmin nor Briton has generally schooled himself to endure … This type of work also requires maps of a higher degree of detail and accuracy than those hitherto required by law for municipal or governmental use … Even after a good deal of experience of the game, one constantly finds oneself … tempted, like the impatient chess-player, to sweep a fist through the pieces which stand in the way.[42]

There is a rare irony here; for in India Geddes never carried out any detailed survey work himself, relying wherever possible on available local surveys.[43] In the Bombay Presidency, where he visited six towns, "His reports on all of them were quite sketchy but his message was quite clear."[44] The Lucknow reports, likewise, contain no new ideas and do not even add up to a comprehensive plan for the city; "Geddes was always too busy to carry out any systematic survey work."[45] As usual, he was winging it: "His confidence knew no bounds as his socio-biological approach seemed to suit Indian conditions so well."[46] He was so sure of his ground: the clearance policy was "one of the most disastrous and pernicious policies in the chequered history of sanitation"; the result was to crowd the people into worse housing than they had before.[47]

He wrote,

> The town planner fails unless he can become something of a miracle worker to the people. He must be able to show them signs and wonders, to abate malaria, plague, enteric, child-mortality, and to create wonders of beauty and veritable transformation scenes. Sometimes he can do this in a few weeks, or even a few days, by changing a squalid slum into a pleasant courtyard, bright with colour-wash and gay with old wall-pictures, adorned with flowers and blessed again by its repaired and replanted shrine. Within a few weeks he can change an expanse of rubbish mounds, befouled in every hollow and defiling every home with their germ-laden dust, into a restful and shady open space, where the elders can sit in the evening watching the children at play and watering the new trees they have helped to plant."[48]

"Geddes had the ambitious notion that his kind of town planning could help hold the British Empire together." He was "adamant" that if his work with Unwin in Ireland had not been cut short in 1914, the Easter Rising could have been averted.[49]

Conservative surgery, he explained in his 1918 report for Lahore, as for many other places, would be complemented by the creation of proposed "Garden Villages" around the town, to which industries would move;[50] they would attract thousands of

42   Tyrwhitt, 1947, 44–5.
43   Meller, 1990, 210.
44   Meller, 1990, 243.
45   Meller, 1990, 247.
46   Meller, 1990, 240.
47   Tyrwhitt, 1947, 45.
48   Geddes, Report on Indore 1918, quoted by Tyrwhitt, 1947, 38, in Home, 2013, 149.
49   Home, 2013, 151.
50   Geddes, 1918, I, 40.

people from the old town, "thus the many-seated Latrines would lose their custom" and costly drainage schemes could be obviated.[51] They would be built on the cooperative tenant principle, just as Unwin and Parker had done at Hampstead and Ealing and other places, but here Geddes proposed an adaptation to Indian conditions: the state would provide just the land on easy terms, then "simplifying the building itself, to a reasonable minimum to start with, yet with incentive to improvement";[52] structures would be "kucha" (temporary materials), and "labour can often, at least partly be given by the worker himself"; the state could help by providing the materials.[53] And the whole plan, Geddes stressed, must be realized with the "real and active participation" of the citizens; he warned against the "Dangers of Municipal Government from above" with resultant "detachment from public and popular feeling, and consequently, before long, from public and popular needs and usefulness."[54]

His report on Indore, Geddes concluded significantly, was "the fullest and most detailed of schemes, so far as the writer knows, for any City"; it "has been the best, because fullest, opportunity of my life as a town-planner."[55] The clue lay in the fact that

> Since City Life, like organic and individual life, exists and develops with the harmonious functioning of all its organs, and their adaptation to all its needs, the endeavour has been made to provide, and in growing measure, towards all of these, and so not only to work in, with or for each as a specialism, but also to con-specialise each towards the fuller life of the whole ... It is but in the earlier stage of every scientific and technical education, that we analyse and see and handle things strictly apart: in the needed further phase we again see them as an interacting whole, and so re-adjust them together. It is because minds fix in the first stage, that great dis-specialised schemes – say here past Water and Drainage Schemes – so rapidly pass into failures and extravagance.[56]

He might well say all that. In 1918, he had just anticipated by exactly half a century the planning philosophy of the 1960s. The world was not quite ready. Some of the reports show signs of anguished disagreement with local officials.[57] He was not thanked for it, anywhere in the official hierarchy: Lutyens in 1914 reported that "Hailey, Montmorency, and all from H. E. downwards" were unimpressed, in fact, wildly angry,

> with a certain Professor Geddes who has come out here to lecture on town planning – his exhibits were sunk by the *Emden*. He seems to have talked rot in an insulting way and I hear he is going to tackle me! A crank who don't [sic] know his subject. He talks a lot, gives himself away, and then loses his temper.[58]

---

[51] Geddes, 1918, I, 64.
[52] Geddes, 1918, I, 70.
[53] Geddes, 1918, I, 70.
[54] Geddes, 1918, II, 104.
[55] Geddes, 1918, II, 187, 190.
[56] Geddes, 1918, II, 187.
[57] Geddes, 1965a, 51.
[58] Hussey, 1953, 336.

The sentiment was mutual, Geddes inveighing against the Madras government's "death-dealing Haussmannising and its squalid (Belfast 1858) industrial bye-laws" and promising to battle with "the well-intentioned fanatic of sanitation."[59] But he fared better in Indore, where he was allowed to be "Maharajah for a day," burning the "Giant of Dirt and the Rat of Plague" on a bonfire before fireworks.[60] And the Maharajah of Baroda, a small state, was a particular enthusiast.[61]

More than 10 years after his major reports, a standard manual of Indian planning practice, by one J. M. Linton Bogle (Bachelor of Engineering, Liverpool; Associate Member of the Institution of Civil Engineers, ditto of the Town Planning Institute; Chief Engineer, Lucknow Improvement Trust) was still recommending "a well designed Street Plan" with streets as wide as 100 feet. Patrick Geddes's name, needless to say, was not mentioned.[62] Geddes, or his ghost, would have to wait a while.

But in Lucknow, where Geddes worked with Indian assistants and had an enlightened trust chair, L. M. Jopling, his ideas were carried out.[63]

Arcadia for All at Peacehaven

Meanwhile, people who had never heard of Geddes went on building their own houses, as through the ages they always had. They were doing it all over southern England in the 1920s and 1930s, especially on the coast: on the Isle of Canvey and the Isle of Sheppey, at Peacehaven near Brighton and at Jaywick Sands near Clacton, at Shoreham Beach and Pagham Beach and a score of other places. Mostly, they were poor people using their own hands, with knock-down materials drawn from the scrapyards of industrial civilization; superannuated tramcars were a particular favorite.[64] They built very cheaply, because they had to; one, who started with a borrowed £1 note in 1932, said that she felt sorry for a latter-day generation of young couples, who did not have the chance she had.[65]

The results did not always have that happy vernacular quality that Unwin so admired, and that he tried to capture in all those drawings in *Town Planning in Practice*. They were sometimes garish, and they lacked expensive services that their builders could not afford; in the largest, the plotlands at Laindon in Essex, some three-quarters of the 8,500 houses had no sewers, half no electricity.[66] In the 1930s, they were a principal cause of the cries of woe from architects and others about the despoliation of the countryside, a story already told in Chapter 3. World War Two

[59] Kitchen, 1975, 257.
[60] Home, 2013, 157.
[61] Home, 2013, 158.
[62] Bogle, 1929, 24, 27, 60.
[63] Home, 1997, 173.
[64] Hardy and Ward, 1984, passim.
[65] Hardy and Ward, 1984, 201.
[66] Hardy and Ward, 1984, 204.

helped these critics: the armed forces demolished a lot of them on the ground of defense against invasion. After it, the newly empowered local authority planners followed up with a whole series of legal and quasi-legal harassments: in one place they created a country park, in another a whole private-enterprise new suburb, even – at Laindon – a whole new town.[67] But they could not eliminate them entirely; England's plotlands – and their occupiers – still survive, testimony to an extraordinary era of building by the people for the people.

Some few saw and admired. One, Colin Ward, began in the early 1950s to write in the anarchist magazine *Freedom*, extolling the principles of self-build. And shortly before that, Ward had been briefly involved in a remarkable meeting of minds at the Architectural Association (AA) school in London. In 1948, the AA – better known as the chief originator in Britain of megalomaniac Corbusian fantasies – acted out of character: it invited the Italian anarchist architect Giancarlo de Carlo. De Carlo had been impressed by the appalling conditions in which the Italian poor then lived: conditions, he said, "little different from those of the slaves of the third century B.C. or from those of the plebeians in Imperial Rome."[68] Municipal housing was no solution, for it meant "those squalid barracks which line monotonously the perimeter of our towns."[69] Therefore, he argued, "The housing problem cannot be solved from above. It is a problem of *the people*, and it will not be solved, or even boldly faced, except by the concrete will and action of the people themselves."[70]

Planning could aid this, but only so long as it were conceived "as the manifestation of communal collaboration," whereupon "it becomes the endeavour to liberate the true existence of man, the attempt to establish a harmonious connection between nature, industry and all human activities."[71]

This struck a chord in one of the AA's ex-servicemen students. John Turner, unlike most of his generation, was no admirer of *La Ville Radieuse*. Later he recalled that

> For some minor misdemeanor at the English public school I attended, a prefect made me read and precis a chapter of Lewis Mumford's *The Culture of Cities*. Mumford quoted his own teacher, Patrick Geddes, whose name stuck in my mind. Later, Geddes' work caused me to doubt the value of my professional schooling, and, when I eventually escaped into the real world, his work also guided my reschooling and re-education.[72]

In the army, he had read *Freedom* and had been converted to anarchism. Hence, when de Carlo arrived at the AA, he was preaching to at any rate one semi-converted member of the audience. Turner went back to the Geddesian method, which, "clearly

---

[67] Hardy and Ward, 1984, 211–30.
[68] De Carlo, 1948, 2.
[69] De Carlo, 1948, 2.
[70] De Carlo, 1948, 2.
[71] De Carlo, 1948, 2.
[72] Turner, 1972a, 122.

enough, was to involve himself as closely as possible with all the people involved, especially those who were suffering most from the consequences of urban dysfunctions and blight."[73] But the possibilities for a young professional to do this "in such a thoroughly institutionalized country as the United Kingdom seemed remote," and, when he was given the chance to work in Peru with Eduardo Neira, he jumped at it.[74]

Turner Goes to Peru

From the mid-1950s to the mid-1960s Turner worked in the Lima *barriadas*, which mushroomed from 100,000 to 400,000 people in the six years 1958–64.[75] This was a time when the orthodox view, reinforced by the publication of Oscar Lewis's enormously influential work on the culture of poverty,[76] was that such informal slum settlements were "breeding-grounds for every kind of crime, vice, disease, social and family disorganization."[77] Even in 1967, one distinguished expert, from the Massachusetts Institute of Technology, was writing of them that

> Typically, their children do not go to school, do not find work (other than the most menial and unrewarding), do not become urbane in any significant sense (other than the urbanity of big-city delinquency and crime) … considerable resources must be expended to maintain them even in this miserable condition of life … more police and firemen, more hospitals and schools, more housing and related activities.[78]

This, to be sure, represented a rather massive misunderstanding of what Lewis had actually said; like many another distinguished academic, he seems to have been quoted mainly by those who had not bothered to read him. He had written about "a way of life, remarkably stable and persistent, passed on from generation to generation along family lines."[79] But he had also emphasized, in an early study of Mexican peasants coming to Mexico City, that

> they adapt to city life with far greater ease than do American farm families. There is little evidence of disorganization or breakdown, of culture conflict, or of irreconcilable conflicts between generations … Family cohesiveness and extended family ties increase in the city, fewer cases of separation and divorce occur, no cases of abandoned mothers and children, no cases of persons living alone or of unrelated families living together.[80]

[73]   Turner, 1972a, 124.
[74]   Turner, 1972a, 124.
[75]   Turner, 1965, 152.
[76]   Lewis, 1966, 19–25.
[77]   Ward, P. M., 1976, 89.
[78]   Lerner, 1967, 24–5.
[79]   Lewis, 1961, xxiv.
[80]   Lewis, 1952, 39–41.

Figure 8.1 San Martín de Porres, Lima, 1962. "The notion that the *barriada* is a slum varies between a half-truth and an almost untruth" (John F. C. Turner). *Source*: John F. C. Turner.

And later, he was at pains to emphasize that the phrase, "culture of poverty,"

> is a catch one and is misused with some frequency in the current literature … The culture of poverty is not just a matter of deprivation or disorganization, a term signifying the absence of something. It is a culture in the traditional anthropological sense in that it provides human beings with a design for living, with a ready-made set of solutions for human problems, and so serves a significant adaptive function. In writing about "multiproblem" families the scientists … often stress their instability, their lack of order, direction and organization. Yet, as I have observed them, their behavior seems clearly patterned and reasonably predictable. I am more often struck by the inexorable repetitiousness and the iron entrenchment of their folkways.[81]

Further, he emphasized, by no means all poor people were locked into the culture of poverty; a certain rather special set of conditions had to be met, including a cash economy with high unemployment, lack of any kind of organization for the poor, lack of extended kinship, and a dominant value system that suggested poverty was due to personal inadequacy.[82] Not only this; in his study of poverty and prostitution in Puerto Rico, *La Vida*, his central character experiences acute feelings of withdrawal when persuaded to leave the slum for a peripheral public housing project:

[81] Lewis, 1966, 19.
[82] Lewis, 1966, 21.

The place is dead. It's true what the proverb says, "May God deliver me from quiet places; I can defend myself in the wild ones ..." Here even my saints cry! They look so sad. They think I am punishing them ... Maybe I was better off in La Esmeralda. You certainly have to pay for the comforts you have here! Listen, I'm jittery, really nervous, because if you fail to pay the rent even once here, the following month you're thrown out.[83]

But, though Lewis was saying pretty well the opposite, people believed him to tell them what they wanted to believe: the informal housing area was by definition a slum, there-fore – again by definition – an area of delinquency, breakdown, and general social malaise. In the early 1960s, even as distinguished and as liberal an expert as Charles Abrams – who, having himself grown up in a slum, had fewer misconceptions than most – was doubting the value of self-help, especially in urban areas, on the grounds of difficulties of organization, delays, poor quality construction, lack of mass produc-tion, and the fact that the results generally represented safety and health hazards.[84]

Turner was the first to find what multiple sociological and anthropological research was later to prove: that the truth was almost the reverse of what the conven-tional wisdom was saying. In fact, the invasions that produced the *barriadas* were highly organized, orderly, and peaceful; they were followed by massive investments in housing; employment, wages, literacy, and educational levels were all better there than average, let alone in comparison with city slums.[85]

The majority of the Lima Barriada population are not, by Peruvian and even by Lima standards very poor and the lives they lead in their Barriadas are a considerable improvement on their former condition, whether in the city slums from which they moved to the Barriada or in the villages from which they moved into the city slums.[86]

The notion that the *barriada* (or its equivalents, the Brazilian *favela*, the Mexican *colonia proletaria*, the Venezuelan *rancho*) was a slum "varies between a half-truth and an almost total untruth":[87] the owner had land, part at least of a fairly well-built dwelling, security, status, and a vested interest in social development and political stability;[88] its people were "the (very much poorer) Peruvian equivalent of the Building Society house-buyers of the suburbs of any city of the industrialized world."[89] And these non-material aspects were particularly important, for, though the official world did not recognize it, housing was more than a material product, it also provided people with existential qualities like identity, security, and opportu-nity, which quite transformed the quality of ordinary people's lives:[90]

83   Lewis, 1967, 592–4.
84   Abrams, 1964, 22, 172.
85   Ward, P. M., 1976, 89.
86   Turner, 1965, 152.
87   Turner, 1965, 152.
88   Turner, 1965, 152.
89   Turner, 1968a, 357.
90   Turner, 1972b, 151–2, 165.

That the mass of the urban poor in cities like Lima are able to seek and find improvement through home-ownership (or *de facto* possession) when they are still very poor by modern standards is certainly the main reason for their optimism. If they were trapped in the inner cities, like so many of the North American poor, they too would be burning instead of building.[91]

What he further found was the truth that people knew best what they wanted for themselves: when they first came to the city, unmarried or just-married, they preferred to live in central slums, near jobs and cheap-food markets; then, as children came, they looked for space and security;[92] at that point, if free to act, they preferred to live in large unfinished houses, or even large shacks, rather than in small finished ones: "As Patrick Geddes wrote half a century ago in India: 'I have to remind all concerned (1) that the essential need of a house and family is *room* and (2) that the essential improvement of a house and family is *more room*.'"[93] They put the house – and community services like markets, schools, and police – first, services (save perhaps electricity) second; they knew they could obtain these in time.[94]

The problem was that the official world refused to recognize this. Lima's subdivision codes, dating from 1915, and minimum housing standards, dating from 1935, simply put the majority of all potential house-owners out of the market: in the legal market, people were paying a higher percentage of their incomes for worse housing than their grandfathers in the 1890s.[95] Thus "autonomous urban settlement ... is the product of the difference between the nature of the popular demand for dwellings and those supported by institutionalized society";[96] there was a gap between the values of the governing institutions in the society, and those which the people had developed for themselves, in response to the circumstances of their lives.[97]

In his earliest Peruvian work, in the city of Arequipa, Turner had assumed that the role of the professional was to organize the self-build process. Then he realized that the people knew perfectly well not only what to build, but how to build it: that he had been guilty of the "liberal authoritarian view that all local autonomous organizations tended to be subversive."[98] And, indeed, they were – to the power of the professional elite. Thus he came to his fundamental discovery that

When dwellers control the major decisions and are free to make their own contributions in the design, construction or management of their housing, both this process and the environment produced stimulate individual and social well-being. When

[91] Turner, 1968a, 360.
[92] Mangin and Turner, 1969, 133–4.
[93] Turner, 1970, 2.
[94] Turner, 1970, 8–9.
[95] Turner, 1972b, 149.
[96] Turner, 1969, 511.
[97] Turner, 1971, 72.
[98] Turner, 1972a, 138.

people have no control over nor responsibility for key decisions in the housing process, on the other hand, dwelling environments may instead become a barrier to personal fulfillment and a burden on the economy.[99]

The squatters managed to build their houses for half the amount that a contractor would charge, while creating an investment worth four or five times their annual incomes: twice the usual maximum for conventionally built housing.[100] And, on the contrary, putting people into government housing projects did little to halt the cycle that developed into Lewis's culture of poverty.[101]

What then should be the role of government and of planning? Was it to walk away and leave the people well alone? Not at all, said Turner: planning should aim to provide the framework, within which people should then be left free to get on. Government should cease to be financier and builder; it should instead be promoter and coordinator. People would still need help, for they did not necessarily have the skills to build themselves;[102] it was a myth, he later stressed, that autonomous housing was cheaper because self-built, for the owner rarely contributed more than half the total labor, often very little; rather, the savings came from the fact that the owner was his own contractor.[103] For this reason, government could provide a useful function by aiding small contractors and cooperative organizations to provide materials or specialized services.[104] And government action would be essential to provide land as close as possible to possibilities of employment, to provide advance infrastructure, and to legalize the framework when the settlement was ready.[105]

Even after the settlements were built, Turner and his group recognized that problems were likely to remain; at least, some of these might be reduced during construction. The huge scale of the settlements in many Latin American cities – an estimated three-quarters of Lima's 1990 population of six million, against perhaps 5% of 600,000 in 1940 – meant that many would be paying high costs to get to work, and perhaps for servicing their houses; and the low densities, at which many of the settlements were built, would affect this.[106] And this kind of housing required at least some minimum income, which many – even in Latin America, still more so in Africa – still lacked.[107] If lower-income people squatted at the peripheries of established settlements, then they might frustrate efforts to upgrade them.[108] And the settlers could themselves become locked into land speculation, from which,

99   Fichter, Turner, and Grenell, 1972, 241.
100 Fichter, Turner, and Grenell, 1972, 242.
101 Mangin and Turner, 1969, 136.
102 Turner *et al.*, 1963, 391–3.
103 Turner, 1976, 86.
104 Payne, 1977, 198.
105 Payne, 1977, 188–91, 195, 198.
106 Turner, 1969, 523–4.
107 Turner, 1969, 519.
108 Turner, 1970, 10.

perversely, they would benefit as the value of their houses escalated: a problem that has latterly exercised many experts from the World Bank and elsewhere.[109]

Meanwhile, both academic research and professional experience had confirmed that indeed autonomous housing constituted "slums of hope," in the phrase first used as early as 1962 by Charles Stokes.[110] By now, scores of other studies in other places had suggested that his conclusions were generally applicable. Frieden had reached the same answer for Mexico City in the mid-1960s;[111] Romanos confirmed it for Athens, Epstein for Brazilian cities.[112] And Janice Perlman's celebrated 1976 study of the Rio *favelas*, *The Myth of Marginality*, found

> the prevailing wisdom completely wrong: the favelados and suburbanos do *not* have the attitudes and behavior supposedly associated with marginal groups. Socially, they are well organized and cohesive and make wide use of the urban milieu and its institutions. Culturally, they are highly optimistic and aspire to better education for their children and to improving the condition of their houses ... Economically, they work hard, they consume their share of the products of others ... and they build ... Politically, they are neither apathetic nor radical ... In short, *they have the aspirations of the bourgeoisie, the perseverance of pioneers, and the values of patriots*. What they do not have is an opportunity to fulfill their aspirations.[113]

This conclusion, she suggested, was supported by many other studies. The myth persisted because it was useful: it upheld the status quo and justified any action the state might want to take, including clearance of the *favelas*.[114] In fact, the removal of one such inner-city Rio *favela*, in the early 1970s, had caused great hardship as people were relocated in peripheral housing projects, far from work and lacking all sense of community.[115]

Backed by studies like these, by the 1980s, Turnerite policies had received the ultimate accolade of respectability: they had been embraced by the World Bank. Perhaps predictably, because he was now orthodox, an anti-Turner school of thought had by now developed. It suggested that self-build housing was, in fact, relatively expensive to construct, and that the apparent economy came only from uncosted do-it-yourself work; that it was most profitable to the landowners; and that the occupants could pay a high cost to establish legal tenure.[116] There was a suggestion that though the conclusions might apply to most such places, they did not extend to all: not to the bustees of Calcutta, for instance.[117] (Ironically, at just that time, having at first

[109] Dunkerley *et al.*, 1983.
[110] Stokes, 1962, 189.
[111] Frieden, 1965, 89–90.
[112] Romanos, 1969, 151; Epstein, 1973, 177–8.
[113] Perlman, 1976, 242–3.
[114] Perlman, 1976, 249–50.
[115] Perlman, 1976, 230–3.
[116] Connolly, 1982, 156–63.
[117] Dwyer, 1972, 211–13.

tried to clear the bustees, Calcutta too had realized its futility and was about to start on a huge improvement program.)[118] And of course some, taking their stand on Marxist analysis, argued that the self-builder was still a mere tool of capitalism: "Turner's recommendations represent nothing less than the now traditional attempts of capitalist interests to palliate the housing shortage in ways that do not interfere with the effective operation of these interests."[119]

Turner, fairly obviously just baffled by all this, took his stand on the view that housing can be a lever of social change. In any case, Gilbert and Ward's survey of people in autonomous housing in Mexico City found that – dupes of the system or not – they pronounced themselves well satisfied:

> low-income groups have benefited from the process even if they have suffered from prolonged insecurity of tenure, inadequate services, the loss of leisure time taken up in house building and neighbourhood improvements, and the high cost of paying for land, regularization, taxes and bribes … at the end of the day, residents possess a plot which acts as a hedge against inflation, constitutes solid equity, and can be used to generate income through renting or sharing.[120]

Here and in Bogotá, they suggested, both the capitalist class and the low-income group have gained; the ability of any group to control the system is constrained by the electoral process:[121] "structuralism is capable of explaining both the grinding down of the working class by authoritarian governments and the improvement of conditions for the poor. Since nothing is precluded, nothing is explained."[122] In fact, government planning bureaucracies had helped the poor and also, by stabilizing the society, helped themselves.[123]

China Goes to the Mountains and the Country

On the other side of the third world, in these years, an even more audacious planning experiment was taking place: perhaps, the most radical in the whole history of twentieth-century planning. China, at the time of the communist revolution in 1949, was one of the world's most outstanding examples of what later came to be called uneven development. About nine-tenths of all the country's industrial infra-structure was concentrated in some 100 "treaty ports" along the coast; some one-fifth in Shanghai alone. In these foreign-controlled cities the Chinese found themselves strangers in their own land, humiliated by the grosser trappings of colonialism: in

118   Rosser, 1972a, 189–90.
119   Burgess, 1982, 86.
120   Gilbert and Ward, 1982, 99–100.
121   Gilbert and Ward, 1982, 118.
122   Gilbert and Ward, 1982, 118.
123   Gilbert and Ward, 1982, 120.

one Shanghai park, a notorious notice barred dogs and Chinese.[124] Small wonder that the new communist rulers were ideologically anti-urban: though mostly of urban origin themselves, and dependent for support on an urban proletariat, they had raised the flag of revolution in the countryside and firmly believed that here lay the source of native, non-corrupt Chinese values.[125]

There was another, harder-nosed reason why they should back rural development: there was no option. In the first years after the revolution people flooded from the backward and war-torn countryside into the cities, which could not take the burden.[126] And the true reason for reversing this flow was the need to industrialize the country.[127] The response was the famous policy of *shang shan xia xiang*, educated youth to the mountains and country areas: millions of graduates were shipped from the cities to help provide the leadership for rural development. It happened especially in the late 1950s, the time of the disastrous Great Leap Forward, and in the late 1960s, the period of the Cultural Revolution.[128] It involved two elements. One, not so well publicized but almost certainly more important, was the development of large-scale industry in interior cities like Lanchow and Sinkiang, as a deliberate counterweight to the treaty ports. The other, which the whole world knows, was self-sufficient rural development through land reform, farm improvements, and small-scale rural industry.[129]

It was heroic, and it has become the model of what has come to be called bottom-up planning.[130] The problem is that it was not what it seemed, and that it was a failure. It was never truly bottom-up, because it was always directed from the center even if – by sheer necessity – administered locally.[131] The main elements – provision for basic needs, local control of agricultural and small-scale industrial enterprises, emphasis on local self-reliance – were all secured through a national planning framework, which used tax and pricing policies to favor the rural sector.[132] And it was marked by repeated, sometimes disastrous, failures that arose from the sheer inability of the communes to manage the system, as in the Great Leap Forward.[133] The rural industries, such as the notorious backyard steel furnaces of the 1950s, proved to run at very high cost.[134] The whole structure depended on perhaps as many as 15 million urban professionals, who – disaffected, often in conflict with the peasantry – wanted nothing so much as to return to the cities; they provided a rich source of refugees for Hong Kong, greatly aiding that city's meteoric development.[135]

[124] Murphey, 1980, 27–31; 1984, 197.
[125] Murphey, 1980, 30; Kirkby, 1985, 8–9.
[126] Murphey, 1980, 43; Kirkby, 1985, 38.
[127] Kirkby, 1985, 14.
[128] Kirby, 1978, 39–42; 1985, 10.
[129] Murphey, 1980, 46–7, 49–50, 60–1.
[130] Stöhr, 1981.
[131] Wu and Ip, 1981, 155–6.
[132] Wu and Ip, 1981, 175–7.
[133] Wu and Ip, 1981, 162–3.
[134] Aziz, 1978, 71; Murphey, 1984, 200.
[135] Murphey, 1980, 105–7; 1984, 200.

Under the Deng regime of the late 1970s and 1980s – conservative by classical Maoist standards, radical by others – the policy was largely abandoned. Its results are meagre. The treaty ports are still by far the biggest cities of China and the key to its industrial production; small-scale rural industry employs perhaps 3% of the rural workforce; the cities are still growing; in a quarter-century of communist rule, the overall population distribution is little changed.[136] Yet, in comparison with other third-world countries, it has to be said that the number of big cities is quite small – 25 in all of more than one million people, six of more than two million – and the growth of the cities has been kept in line with that of the population as a whole.[137] So the great experiment achieved something, after all. But whether it really represented the triumph of local, autonomous, bottom-up planning, as some would devoutly like to believe, is another question altogether: one on which the verdict, lacking the real documentary evidence, has still to come in.

Autonomy in the First World: Wright to Alexander

All this had few echoes in the first world; asked to find lessons of third-world informal housing for the United States in 1968, a group of housing experts could find very few.[138] But a few people, over the years, had been thinking about it. The most notable was Frank Lloyd Wright, whom we shall logically consider as a leading exponent of the roadside city in Chapter 9. But Broadacre City was more than that; it was to be a city built by its own inhabitants, using mass-produced components:[139]

> to start building his home he ought to be able to buy the modern, standardized privy, cheap. That civilized "privy" is now a complete bathroom unit manufactured in factories, delivered complete to him as a single unit (his car or refrigerator is one now) ready to use when connected to the city water system and a fifteen-dollar septic tank or a forty-dollar cesspool. Well advised, he plants this first unit wherever it belongs to start his home. Other units similarly cheap and beneficial designed for living purposes may be added soon.[140]

In fact, many of the strands that went into Wright's thinking, whether consciously or not, were shared with the Regional Planning Association of America: anarchism, liberation by technology, naturalism, agrarianism, the homesteading movement. Yet they, like almost everyone else, attacked him;[141] and no one in the urban establishment took heed. By one of those frequent ironies that seem to recur in the history of urbanism, the people who did implement his ideas were the Levitts, a firm of commercial builders, who, just after World War Two, conceived the idea of a cheap

---

[136]   Murphey, 1980, 146; 1984, 198; Wu and Ip, 1981, 160.
[137]   Aziz, 1978, 64; Murphey, 1984, 198.
[138]   Goetze *et al.*, 1968, 354.
[139]   Fishman, 1977, 130.
[140]   Wright, 1945, 86.
[141]   Grabow, 1977, 116–17, 121.

basic house of standard industrial components, which could be extended by the owner at leisure; their triumph will be detailed in Chapter 9. But in American architecture and planning schools, the idea of self-build went strangely underground for another 30 years, until it reappeared at Berkeley, in the writings of Christopher Alexander.

Alexander, Viennese-born, came to Britain as a child and had an extremely eclectic education in the architecture school of the University of Cambridge, from where he emigrated to America. Almost from the start, he became engaged in a personal odyssey to discover what he called "the quality without a name" in buildings, which he described in an interview as

> a building which is like a smile on a person's face, and which has that kind of rightness about it, and which is really like that and not just saying it is like that … at such moments, things are completely orderly and at peace with themselves – not at all in the pretentious sense that we tend to call beautiful, but in an incredibly simple and straight-forward and at the same time deep and mysterious sense.[142]

Searching for this quality, in the 1960s he developed the idea that it could be objectively determined. But he now saw that modern architects actually denied their own natures: their "cardboard-like" architecture came out of a fear of showing emotion. True "organic order," the "quality without a name," could be found in traditional architecture, like the relationship of college buildings in Cambridge, or an English village street; if architects really experienced this quality, then they could not design the kinds of buildings they did.[143]

So far, it seems, he was identifying just those qualities for which Morris and then Unwin and Geddes were searching, though they did not express it that way: Unwin and Parker's best housing at New Earswick or Letchworth has this very quality. But then, about 1972, he saw that it was "not enough to tinker with the zoning ordinances because the exact rules of the ordinances – which govern that process – are themselves produced by the process by which zoning is administered."[144] Instead, he developed the idea that groups of people might change their own environment, partly subsidized from above: the "individual is not only taking care of his own needs, but also … contributing to the needs of the larger group to which he belongs."[145] In the project People Rebuilding Berkeley, he tried to develop the idea of "self-sustaining, self-governing" neighborhoods.[146] It did not work, somehow returning to traditional master-planning.

Disillusioned, he then came to believe that "in order for things to become beautiful and alive, it is necessary for people like myself to be directly involved in the act of construction rather than fiddling around on paper."[147] It also made him feel better.

[142] Grabow, 1983, 21.
[143] Grabow, 1983, 57, 68–9, 83–6, 100.
[144] Grabow, 1983, 139.
[145] Grabow, 1983, 155.
[146] Grabow, 1983, 157.
[147] Grabow, 1983, 222.

So, in a self-build project at Mexicali, he actually became involved in helping the Mexicans create their own environment. The result was a set of very unusual buildings, "a bit more funky than I would have liked," which seem to be well liked by the people who built them.[148]

Berkeley was not the only place where people were returning to ideas of self-help and community participation in the 1970s, but because of Alexander it was probably the most important. In England, Ralph Erskine, the British-born architect who had worked for many years in Sweden, returned to Tyneside to build the remarkable Byker Wall, a redevelopment project which became one of the very few pieces of public housing that was designed in continuous dialogue with the residents. The original suspicions were broken down; "In the end, the quantity and quality of social activity in Byker became a by-word – a local joke – but a triumph."[149] And the result was one of the most extraordinary structures ever created in any city, let alone by a public housing authority: "the great Wall itself, tall, austere and abstract on the cold side, bending, rising, falling, projecting, receding for a full mile and a half, has on its seemingly lower sunny side the intricate, shabby, makeshift, intensively humanized quality of a shantytown in Hong Kong."[150] It is inhabited mainly by old people, who pay it the highest possible compliment: they say that it is like the Costa Brava.[151]

They like it; but they did not build it, and Byker categorically has the air of architectural style, even whimsy, about it. Meanwhile, in 1969 there had appeared a highly iconoclastic manifesto in the pages of the English weekly social science journal, *New Society*. Written jointly by Reyner Banham, Paul Barker, Peter Hall, and Cedric Price, it argued that

> The whole concept of planning (the town-and-country kind at least) has gone cock-eyed ... Somehow, everything must be watched; nothing must be allowed simply to "happen." No house can be allowed to be commonplace in the way that things just *are* commonplace: each project must be weighed, and planned, and approved, and only then built, and only after that discovered to be commonplace after all.[152]

So the group proposed

> a precise and carefully controlled experiment in non-planning ... to seize on a few appropriate zones of the country, which are subject to a characteristic range of pressures, and use them as launchpads for Non-Plan. At the least, one would find out what people want; at the most, one might discover the hidden style of mid-20th century Britain.[153]

---

[148]   Grabow, 1983, 170.
[149]   Esher, 1981, 186.
[150]   Esher, 1981, 187.
[151]   Esher, 1981, 187.
[152]   Banham *et al.*, 1969, 435.
[153]   Banham *et al.*, 1969, 436.

The article proposed three such zones: Nottinghamshire's Sherwood Forest, the corridor up the then-unbuilt M11 motorway from London to Cambridge, the Solent area on the south coast. It ended defiantly:

> ... except for a few conservation areas which we wish to preserve as living museums, physical planners have no right to set their value judgement against yours, or indeed anyone else's. If the Non-Plan experiment works really well, people should be allowed to build what they like.[154]

It was, of course, received in deafening silence; it took another 10 years for a group at the Town and Country Planning Association, led by Colin Ward and David Lock, to try to return to the pure Howard vision with a proposal for a Third Garden City, to be planned – and in part built – by the people who would live in it. Frustrated after long negotiation with the new city of Milton Keynes, they finally began work on a self-build community at Lightmoor in Telford new town in 1984.[155]

There was a parallel movement in the United States. In fact, Jane Jacobs can be said to have started it as early as 1961 with her plague-on-both-your-houses attack on both the Corbusians and the garden-city planners, and her appeal for a return to the density and mixed land uses of the traditional unplanned city.[156] In 1970, Richard Sennett weighed in with his *Uses of Disorder*, contrasting "a life in which the institutions of the affluent city are used to lock men into adolescence even when physically adult" with "the possibility that affluence and the structures of a dense, disorganized city could encourage men to become more sensitive to each other as they become fully grown"; he argued that this was "not a utopian ideal; it is a better arrangement of social materials, which as organized today are suffocating people."[157] In an imaginary account of the life of a young girl in such a city, he suggested how this might happen:

> She lives, perhaps, on a city square, with restaurants and stores mixed among the homes of her neighbors. When she and the other children go out to play, they do not go to clean and empty lawns; they go into the midst of people who are working, shopping, or are in the neighborhood for other reasons that have nothing to do with her. Her parents, too, are involved with their neighbors in ways that do not directly center on her and the other children of the neighborhood. There are neighborhood meetings where disruptive issues, like a noisy bar people want controlled, have to be fought out ... her parents are out a great deal merely to find out who their neighbors are and see what kind of accommodations can be reached where conflicts arise.[158]

[154]   Banham *et al.*, 1969, 443.
[155]   Gibson, 1985; see also Hughes and Sadler, 2000.
[156]   Jacobs, 1962, passim.
[157]   Sennett, 1971, 189.
[158]   Sennett, 1971, 190.

The paradox, he concluded, was "that in extricating the city from preplanned control, men will become more in control of themselves and more aware of each
other."[159]

The Great War against Urban Renewal

Jacobs and Sennett were alike in illustrating a general disillusionment with the
results of planning-from-above in American cities, symbolized for many by the live
television coverage of the demolition of the Pruitt–Igoe project in St Louis, described
in Chapter 7.[160] That disillusionment, to be sure, did not take the form of a naive
desire to start reconstructing cities with hammers and nails. Rather, it expressed itself
in the demand that local communities should have greater say in the shaping – and
especially the reshaping – of their own neighborhoods; it was a demand that
expressed itself forcibly in the reformulation of American urban renewal policy after
1964, and in some epic conflicts over urban reconstruction projects in the hearts of
European cities in the late 1960s and early 1970s.

By 1964, with Johnson in the White House and campaigning for re-election, the
criticisms of urban renewal had reached deafening levels (Chapter 7). And that
summer, riots broke out in the black ghetto areas of a whole series of cities, focusing
the Presidential mind on the political need to be seen to do something fast.[161] The
Model Cities program, centerpiece of Johnson urban policy, was designed to meet
these criticisms head-on. It would attack hard-core slums; it would increase, not
reduce, the supply of low-cost housing; it would help the poor; it would do so by
upgrading a whole neighborhood at a time.[162]

And it would work in a novel way: it would harness the anger and energy of the
poor for constructive purposes, by involving the local community in the process of
change. In each targeted area, there was to be a Community Development Agency
(CDA) to draw the widest possible citizen participation and local initiative.[163]
True, by the time the legislation was passed by Congress in 1966, the Johnson
administration had learned some bitter lessons from the experience of its earlier
"War on Poverty," enshrined in the Economic Opportunity Act of 1964, with its
famous – soon notorious – requirement that the program be administered by
community action agencies "with maximum feasible participation of the residents
of the areas and the members of the groups served." That phrase, later pilloried as
"maximum feasible misunderstanding," had become a byword for conflict between
local activists and City Hall; Model Cities deftly sidestepped that, by ensuring that
the CDAs would be firmly under the control of the mayors.

[159]   Sennett, 1971, 198.
[160]   Fishman, 1980, 246.
[161]   Haar, 1975, 4–5.
[162]   Frieden and Kaplan, 1975, 45, 52–3.
[163]   Fox, 1985, 201.

The original idea, put forward by Leonard Duhl and Antonia Chayes in an appendix to the 1964 report of Johnson's Task Force, suggested only three such "demonstration" projects; the Congressional pork-barrel process inexorably drove the number up, until three became 66, then 150, and the jam was spread ever more thinly on the bread.[164] As the money came down from Washington, despite the stage-management, all kinds of conflict and confusion broke out. The cities resented sharing powers with community activists, or – as in some cities – being bypassed altogether.[165] The guidelines from Washington were naive and obscure, written in language that was "more appropriate to a college classroom than a mayor's office or a residents' meeting."[166] It proved difficult to coordinate the different federal agencies, partly because they resented the infant Department of Housing and Urban Development and did not want to be coordinated; so complex were the Washington negotiations that one task-force member was gripped by a fantasy that after death he might be reincarnated as a member.[167] The interminable federal review process, coupled with local disagreements, meant that cities spent barely half of their thin entitlement.[168] And, as the threat of riot receded, the program lost some of its political urgency, and lacked a national, even a local, consensus;[169] Nixon tried to kill it in 1968, though it survived by the skin of its teeth.[170] Charles Haar, evaluating it after a decade of life, felt that it had not delivered on "its own high-flown promises."[171]

The irony, Haar pointed out, was that having aimed at local participation, it had actually achieved "the high point of technicians' dominance": the processes included "All the buzzwords of the planning profession" – sequential, rational, coordination, innovation, goals, and objectives – and "the effort began to resemble a restructuring of a planning curriculum rather than an effort to guide city actions."[172] It thus represented a failure of traditional planning, rather than the success of a new approach: extreme centralization, wrapped in the trappings of local community participation. But perhaps, truth to tell, that was the intention all along.

Small wonder that some reacted, preferring a style where the professional achieved true humility, acting merely as the agent of the people's will. That was the spirit of the first recorded exercise in community design: the Architectural Renewal Committee of Harlem in New York, founded in 1963 to fight a proposed Robert Moses freeway. It was also the spirit of the advocacy planning movement of the time. Both were reacting against the tradition of top-down planning, based on narrow technical performance criteria, so well represented in the urban renewal and freeway schemes of the time. They were invariably reacting against some product or other of that

164   Frieden and Kaplan, 1975, 47–9, 215–7; Haar, 1975, 218.
165   Frieden and Kaplan, 1975, 88–9; Haar, 1975, 175.
166   Frieden and Kaplan, 1975, 139.
167   Frieden and Kaplan, 1975, 232, 236.
168   Frieden and Kaplan, 1975, 229.
169   Frieden and Kaplan, 1975, 257; Haar, 1975, 254–6.
170   Frieden and Kaplan, 1975, 203–12.
171   Haar, 1975, 194.
172   Haar, 1975, 205.

approach: the Cooper Square renewal scheme in New York City and the Yerba Buena scheme in San Francisco were classic battlegrounds, in which idealistic young professionals joined forces with local communities. But often, the result was a disaster: the people were incoherent, the professionals took charge, no one really knew how to achieve anything, little was produced.[173]

So, during the 1970s, the focus of community design shifted. The professionals became harder-nosed, more entrepreneurial, more single-mindedly obsessed with sticking to a job and finishing it. They also became more concerned about earning a living; now, they served small community organizations and related small businesses needing architectural services, and – subsidized by federal or state governments – able therefore to pay a fee. Nevertheless, the style was very different from anything known before: it stressed the needs of the client rather than the nature of the product, and used a variety of methods to tailor the solution to those needs. In the process, it achieved more solid results and gave both client and professional the feeling that they could succeed.[174]

Meanwhile, perhaps in reflection, the emphasis of the urban renewal program was changing steadily, away from bulldozer clearance, toward rehabilitation and small-scale spot clearances. While Boston's notorious West End project (Chapter 7) involved total clearance and an almost complete shift from low-rent to middle- or high-rent residence, the later Downtown Waterfront scheme only cleared 24% of the area and achieved a net housing gain – admittedly, most in the form of luxury apartments.[175] Cynics might say that the development industry had decided that city-center sites were more profitable and rehabilitation cheaper. But that would be less than fair: nationally, between 1964 and 1970 the residential component in renewal rose sharply.[176] So did the share of rehabilitation, in some cases dramatically: from 22 to 68% in Philadelphia, from 34 to 50% in Minneapolis, from 15 to 24% in Baltimore.[177]

That in itself says nothing about who was doing the rehabilitation. While in some cities it came from local residents with or without city aid, in others it was done by higher-status, young-urban-professional gentrifiers, most of them coming not from the suburbs but from other parts of the inner city.[178] Those displaced, according to a Department of Housing and Urban Development study, were primarily the elderly, the minorities, the renters, and the working class.[179] In many cases, the shift to rehabilitation actually gave a fillip to the gentrification process: "sweat equity" – the term that Baltimore used to describe its "homesteading" and "shopsteading" programs, where blighted structures were virtually given away to would-be renovators – may prove to be something that accumulates, like most

[173]   Comerio, 1984, 230–4.
[174]   Comerio 1984, 234–40.
[175]   Sanders, 1980, 109.
[176]   Sanders, 1980, 110–11.
[177]   Sanders, 1980, 113.
[178]   Cicin-Sain, 1980, 53–4.
[179]   Cicin-Sain, 1980, 71.

forms of equity, in middle-class savings banks. But, to be fair, few of the gentrifiees reported much sense of loss or displacement; it might just be that, by giving the blighted city back to energetic yuppies, policy was achieving some kind of Pareto-optimal solution, whereby no one lost but many gained. And, in an odd way, these gentrifiers strangely resembled those indefatigable improvers of the Rio *favelas* and the Lima *barriadas*.

The War Comes to Europe

Meanwhile, at the same time in the capitals of Europe, a strange new phenomenon was visible: local community activists were beginning to do battle with their own City Halls over proposals for large-scale city-center renewal. What was new about their conflicts was that they were fighting the very idea of the bulldozer approach. Down to the mid-1960s, the prevailing ethos – shared by planner and planned alike – was that comprehensive development of large areas was a thoroughly good thing: it swept away old and outmoded buildings, it aided traffic circulation, it could above all be used to separate pedestrians from traffic. Indeed, one of the most celebrated and longest-running early controversies, over Piccadilly Circus in London, started because the objectors were *demanding* comprehensive replanning; ironically, after 13 years of dithering, the London planning machine returned to its point of departure, piecemeal rebuilding.[180]

While all this was happening, an even bigger drama was being fought out a mile away. Covent Garden had been London's fruit and vegetable market, as well as one of its theater centers, since the seventeenth century; but, as in other cities, it had long become an inefficient, congestion-generating anomaly, and in 1962 a New Covent Garden Market Authority took over to prepare the move to another site, which duly happened in 1974. In 1965, a consortium of local authorities began work on a redevelopment plan for the market and a much wider area around, covering no less than 96 acres and including some 3,300 residents and 1,700 firms, many of them small. Their plan, which emerged in draft in 1968 and in final form in 1971, involved a combination of conservation, especially in the historic core around the market itself, and large-scale redevelopment – partly to carry the profitable development to help pay for the scheme, partly to ease traffic flow – on the edges.[181]

Meanwhile, the deputy leader of the team, a Merseysider of radical inclinations called Brian Anson, was wrestling with his conscience. At the exhibition of the plans in 1968, 3,500 people turned up and a mere 350 commented; of those, a mere 14 were local residents, and 14 of those were against the scheme – most of them in vituperative terms. Anson became convinced that the real beneficiaries and instigators

---

[180]   Cherry and Penny, 1986, 176–91.
[181]   Christensen, 1979, 10, 20–9.

of the plan were property developers. Expressing his doubts to local community leaders, he was abruptly removed from his post by his employers, the Greater London Council. His removal became a *cause célèbre* in the media.[182]

At the public inquiry in 1971, it was opposed by everyone: the local Covent Garden Community Association, the Society for Protection of Ancient Buildings, the Georgian Group, the Victorian Society, the Civic Trust, the Town and Country Planning Association. The community group's star witness was Brian Anson:[183] "London now had its own version of the People's Park in Berkeley … a conveniently accessible battleground for AA and LSE students, 'advocacy planners' and assorted activists from all over."[184] The uproar was such that, although the inquiry inspector found in favor of the plan, the Minister made huge changes that effectively invalidated it.[185] A revised plan, produced in 1976 after huge tensions between the local community group and the forum set up by the Greater London Council, in effect conceded most of the community's points though they continued to criticize it.[186]

In this saga, there were two extraordinary features. One was that, in the words of the bruised leader of the official planning team, around 1968 there was "a national nervous breakdown":

> The whole of Great Britain was at that time involved in saving something. In the 1960s, change was considered a good thing because it improved the city, providing new facilities, open space, new housing, all the kinds of things people wanted and then profits could be made to pay for these things. Almost overnight this became a bad thing. From insensitive development to don't touch a thing … The whole thing went lunatic.[187]

The other point was that, even so, the community lost. As Esher put it, "planning here becomes estate management: making the best of what one has got."[188] But that could be very good indeed: already by 1979, the property developers had discovered that the cost of renovation was less than half that of redevelopment, but could yield almost the same rents. Local shops were being replaced by boutiques and craft shops, and Covent Garden was becoming the fashionable shopping and tourist area that almost the whole world knows today.[189] Anson, writing the story years after, commented that

> a working-class shop or housing block could be destroyed by other things than a bulldozer … The local baker's becomes a professional studio, the cheap cafe a chic restaurant, the dartboard is removed from the pub and gradually many more gins and tonics are sold.[190]

182   Anson, 1981.
183   Anson, 1981, 37–8.
184   Esher, 1981, 142.
185   Esher, 1981, 46–8.
186   Esher, 1981, 53–72.
187   Quoted in Christensen, 1979, 96.
188   Esher, 1981, 146.
189   Esher, 1981, 86, 133–4.
190   Anson, 1981, 103.

Perhaps it was poetically right that this story should have happened in a country experiencing a national nervous breakdown. But, less publicized, almost the same drama was being enacted in staid Stockholm. And there, the controversy ranged over no less than the hallowed plan of 1945–6 by Sven Markelius, which had become the world's favorite textbook example of enlightened social democratic planning. Its aim had been deliberately to concentrate the city's central business functions into a relatively small area of Lower Norrmalm, around a subway station that would be the focus of the city's planned new network. For 20 years all went ahead according to plan, Swedish-fashion; in the mid-1950s the saying was that "it is impossible to visit Stockholm now as the town is closed for repairs."[191] The subway lines were built; the road system was reconstructed at enormous cost around a new circus, with pedestrians circulating at lower level directly into the subway station; five uniformly massed office towers and a new pedestrian shopping mall were built.[192] All this was based quite openly on providing more space for headquarters of banks, insurance, and industrial concerns, as well as department stores, hotels, and entertainment.[193]

Then, in 1962, the City published a plan for the remaining area. It was not really new; really, it was a synthesis of earlier proposals that had gone through the council on the nod. It was immediately attacked in the journal *Arkitektur* by three young architects, written as "a protest against the form which is being given to our towns,"[194] on the ground that it was too business-oriented and failed to give sufficient protection to residents. The attack was taken up by two leading newspapers; but the plan failed to become an issue at the local elections, and late in 1963 the council approved it. In 1967 the City produced a detailed plan for the area, based on a competition-winning design, and in 1968 approved it.[195]

At that point, just as in London, all hell broke loose. Just as there, a diverse opposition formed. It happened that a centerpiece of the plan was an Intercontinental Hotel; at the height of the Vietnam War, this became a flashpoint for anti-American feeling, then running high in Sweden. The company pulled out, leaving a huge hole in the ground. Finally, with redevelopment coming to a standstill, in 1975 the city agreed a compromise plan. Big road widenings and parking garages went; the hotel became an enclosed shopping mall; many existing buildings were preserved.[196]

Conventional urban-political analysis, especially of the Marxist kind, does not much help in these cases. In London, most of the actors agreed that the difference was not one of party politics.[197] In Stockholm, it was the Social Democrats who were committed to a scheme that displaced local residents, reduced employment opportunities, and replaced local business and small shops by big retailing, banking,

---

[191]   William-Olsson, 1961, 80.
[192]   Sidenbladh, 1965, 109–10; Stockholm, 1972, 92–4; Hall, T., 1979, 188–93.
[193]   Markelius, 1962, xxxvi.
[194]   Edblom, Strömdahl, and Westerman, 1962, xvi.
[195]   Hall, T., 1979, 194–202.
[196]   Hall, T., 1979, 204–6; Berg, 1979, 162–3.
[197]   Christensen, 1979, 101.

financial services, and consultancy.[198] Just as in London, the planners were clearly surprised and injured by the force of the attacks; they defended themselves on the ground that in order to attract developers, they must maintain the continuity of the planning process and must provide the kinds of large new buildings these developers were alleged to want.[199] What seems to have happened is that the all-powerful technical planners made mistakes and the politicians, obsessed by the idea that a bigger city meant more tax revenues, weakly went along.[200] In the event, the big organizations did not even occupy the available office space.[201]

The Battle of Paris was a more colorful affair, with a plot of enormous length and complexity, and a huge cast of characters; everyone who mattered in France, it seemed, had to get in on the act. In 1960, the central government proposed that the historic wholesale food market, Les Halles, should move out of the center; two years after that, a decree confirmed it; in 1963, the City Council set up an organization, SEAH (Société Civile d'Études pour l'Aménagement du Quartier des Halles), to plan the reconstruction of the area, and an architect was charged to prepare a renewal plan for a huge 470-hectare strip of central Paris; four years later, another organization, SEMAH (Société d'Économie Mixte d'Aménagement des Halles), was entrusted with carrying out the project.

This same year, 1967, the City Council invited several architects to prepare plans for a much more modest 32-hectare site around the market itself; a year later it turned them all down, one commissioner asking "Are we, twenty years later, ourselves to execute Hitler's orders?"[202] But in 1967 another body, APUR (Atelier Parisien d'Urbanisme), had approved a new central interchange station, to form the focus of the entire RER (Réseau Express Régional); and in July 1969, a few months after Baltard's historic glass market pavilions had become empty, the Council accepted APUR's design for a huge underground commercial center and a world trade center on the site, entailing their demolition. The following year, despite a proposal by the Minister of Construction to keep them, the Council voted to raze them, and – during the summer of 1971, when nearly all Paris was on vacation – despite battles between conservationists and police, it did so.[203]

The future of Les Halles now became the kind of national scandal that all French politicians love. In 1973, the Council gave a permit for the world trade center, and work started. The next year, Valéry Giscard d'Estaing became President and immediately annulled the permit, involving demolition of the part-completed structure; much later, a commission determined the damages at 65 million francs. The site became a park; the government announced a new consultation with architects. In 1975, three projects were displayed at the town hall; the public having indicated a

198   Hall, T., 1979, 215, 220.
199   Westman, 1967, 421.
200   Hall, T., 1979, 217, 220, 223.
201   Hall, T., 1979, 223.
202   Anon, 1979a, 12.
203   Anon, 1979a, 12; Anon, 1979b, 7–8.

pronounced preference for one, the two others – including that by the Catalonian post-modern architect Ricardo Bofill – were chosen. After many subsidiary sub-plots, in 1977 Bofill's plan for part of the area was exhibited, causing the President of the Syndicat des Architectes de Paris to launch an immediate campaign against it. Jacques Chirac, elected mayor in 1976, joined the campaign, referring in an unusual fit of absent-mindedness to "Lofill? Fillbo? Ah oui! Bofill." A few months later he dismissed Bofill, declaring "L'architecte en chef de l'opération des Halles, c'est moi," a job he would undertake "tranquillement et sans complexes." Bofill's architecture, "greco-egyptian with Buddhist tendencies," did not appeal to Chirac. "It has been questioned and it is questionable."[204] "These architectural Olympics," he suggested, "have gone on long enough. Ten years is enough." The Centre Pompidou "was a sufficient landmark of the architectural fantasy of the end of the twentieth century."

His decision was immediately protested by every international architect of any consequence: Johnson, Venturi, Niemeyer, Stirling, Kroll, and many others. The magazine *L'Architecture d'aujourd'hui*, however, supported him, possibly out of exhaustion. Bofill sued for seven million francs. In 10 years, at least 70 projects had come and gone: the project had shrunk from 32 hectares, including huge skyscrapers and highways, to 15 hectares, mainly a park; Corbusier was truly dead, and Giscard and Chirac now began a deadly battle about whether the park should be "French" or "Italian" in character.[205]

Meanwhile, life went on. And the really significant point about Les Halles is that exactly the same process occurred to it as to Covent Garden: it was gentrified. People moved out; so did local shops; boutiques and restaurants took their place. And the city did not intervene in the process. Certainly, the Battle of Les Halles did not represent any kind of triumph on the part of the local community. Indeed, it was quin-tessentially French in that it turned on a battle between those two traditional enemies, the French state and the city of Paris. Still less, clearly, did it represent some movement of the Paris *artisanat*, determined to take the rebuilding of the city into its own hands. In such a context, the battle was fought on different issues. But it did, like the Battles of Covent Garden and Lower Norrmalm, represent a turning-point in attitudes to large-scale urban renewal. Community activists now felt that they could fight the urban bulldozer, and win.

Community Architecture Arrives in Britain

This was nowhere more evident than in Britain. Here, the entrepreneurial approach to community architecture was certainly visible from the start. In 1971, Rod Hackney, a young architect just writing a PhD at Manchester University and short of money, paid £1,000 to buy 222 Black Road – a small 155-year-old terrace house lacking basic amenities – in Macclesfield, a small English industrial town south

204 Quoted in Dhuys, 1983, 9.
205 Anon, 1979c, 11–12; Anon, 1979d, 7–10; Anon, 1979e, 4; Anon, 1979f, 1; Anon, 1979 g, 8.

Figure 8.2   Lightmoor, Telford New Town. The people get down to work in the project that eventually won the accolade from Prince Charles. On the right, Tony Gibson, Lightmoor's John Turner. *Source*: Town and Country Planning Archive.

of Manchester. When he applied for a grant to improve it, he discovered that it and its 300 neighbors were scheduled for demolition. He organized his neighbors into a campaign and in 1973 persuaded the local town council to change its mind: 34 of the houses would be made a General Improvement Area, meaning that the owners could receive grants to improve the houses. Hackney, who used skills he had learned designing houses for squatters in Tripoli, could later claim that the resulting improvement was completed in one-third of the time, and at one-third of the cost, of the demolition and replacement scheme. In 1975, it won a Good Design in Housing Award from the Department of the Environment.[206]

That was just the start. Hackney soon found himself, still working from an office in Black Road, doing similar schemes all over the country. The 1974 Housing Act, which switched funds into rehabilitation, was influenced by his work. By the early 1980s he was employing more than 30 people from eight area offices. Hackney gave his own views of the community architecture movement:

> Community architecture means attempting to understand the needs of a small group
> of residents and then working with them and under their instructions and guidance, in
> order to articulate their case and present it to the various organisations that hold either
> the purse strings or the approval/rejection powers … We, the architects, got it terribly

[206]   Knevitt, 1975; 1977.

wrong in the 1960s. Community architecture will help us to bring back the integrity of the architectural profession by getting it right in this decade and subsequent decades.[207]

It was heady stuff. The media loved it because it gave them David versus Goliath stories and because Hackney, traveling from one job to another – first in his Saab, later a customized Range Rover, complete with car telephone when no one else had one – was an endless source of pithy one-liners. Younger architects loved it too, because it cocked a snook at the dreary official architecture they hated and offered them a chance of interesting private work.

They, and their clients, had some spectacular successes. In Liverpool, a city dominated by the insensitive slum-clearance housing built in the 1950s by the council – 25,000 of which, one-third of the total, were officially hard-to-let by the 1980s – a Liberal council decided to encourage the community design approach. The tenants were not asked to participate in the design; they were put in total control. They chose the architects, the site, the layout, the floor plans, the elevations, the brick color, and the landscaping; when it was all built, they ran the scheme. Their first concern, the architects soon found, was that their houses should not look like "Corpy" housing: "Council housing is the worst housing ever," said the 34-year-old unemployed bricklayer chairman of one cooperative, "It's boring, pathetic, inhuman – like someone went into the architect's department and said, 'I want 400 houses – get the drawings in by half-three.' They're not houses for *people*."[208] What emerged were small brick houses around courts, simple and almost utilitarian in style. The architects said it was hard work, but the most rewarding work they had ever done; the residents named the scheme Weller Court, after the city engineer who had been a thorn in their side.[209]

The movement gained strength. Its members founded a Community Architecture Group within the Royal Institute of British Architects (RIBA), which came into increasingly bitter confrontation with the leadership. In May 1984, Prince Charles, addressing the RIBA 150th anniversary conference in Hampton Court Palace, stunned the Institute's leadership by lashing out publicly at the low quality of architectural design: the proposed extension to the National Gallery, he said, was like a monstrous carbuncle on the face of a friend. Community architecture, he declared – mentioning Hackney by name – was the answer. The architectural establishment was bitterly offended. Two and a half years later, Hackney – by then running a £4 million a year business with 20 regional offices and a staff of 200 – defeated the official candidate to become President of the RIBA: community architecture had officially arrived. It would, he confidently declared, become "the political architecture of a post-industrial age."

In June 1987, Hackney – just installed as President – sat on the platform at the Royal Institute of British Architects' London headquarters with Prince Charles, who presented the year's awards for outstanding community architecture. The top prize

[207] Quoted in Wates, 1982a, 43.
[208] Wates, 1982b, 52.
[209] Wates, 1982b, 52.

went to the Town and Country Planning Association's Lightmoor project at Telford New Town. In his speech, the prince delivered yet another of his memorable quotes for the assembled media: he spoke of the need to overcome the "spaghetti bolognese of red tape" that held up the efforts of ordinary people to create their own environment. As one television program after another followed the battles of the community-builders with the entrenched bureaucracies, it seemed that Howard, Geddes, Turner, and the anarchist tradition in planning had achieved ultimate respectability at last.

Few, seemingly, noticed the irony: that the accolade had come under a radical right-wing government, which now – as in Liverpool – made common cause with the anarchists against the spirit of bureaucratic socialism. That autumn, Mrs Thatcher unveiled the centerpiece of her continuing revolution of the Right: following the sale of a million public housing units to their tenants, the government would now seek to turn over the remainder to tenant cooperative management, thus finally removing the dead hand of the bureaucracy. Geddes, that pupil of Bakunin and Kropotkin, who had fought so long before against its colonial manifestation, would certainly have appreciated this strange twist of history.

The City on the Highway

This segregation of motor traffic is probably a matter that may begin even in the present decade … And the quiet English citizen will, no doubt, while these things are still quite exceptional and experimental in his own land, read one day in the violently illustrated popular magazines of 1910, that there are now so many thousand miles of these roads already established in America and Germany and elsewhere. And thereupon, after some patriotic meditations, he may pull himself together.

H. G. Wells, *Anticipations of the Reaction of Mechanical and Scientific Progress upon Human Life and Thought* (1901)

Las Vegas takes what in other American towns is but a quixotic inflammation of the senses for some poor salary mule in the brief interval between the flagstone rambler and the automatic elevator downtown and magnifies it, foliates it, embellishes it into an institution. For example, Las Vegas is the only town in the world where the landscape is made up neither of buildings, like New York, nor of trees, like Wilbraham, Massachusetts, but signs. One can look at Las Vegas from a mile away on Route 91 and see no buildings, no trees, only signs. But such signs! They tower, they revolve, they oscillate, they soar in shapes before which the existing vocabulary of art is helpless.

Tom Wolfe, *The Kandy Kolored Tangerine Flake Streamline Baby* (1966)

Cities of Tomorrow: An Intellectual History of Urban Planning and Design Since 1880,
Fourth Edition. Peter Hall.
© 2014 Peter Hall. Published 2014 by John Wiley & Sons, Ltd.

9

The City on the Highway

The Automobile Suburb: Long Island, Wisconsin, Los Angeles, Paris, 1930–1987

"Suburbia," a suburban child of the turn of the century later recalled, "was a railway state … a state of existence within a few minutes' walk of the railway station, a few minutes' walk of the shops, and a few minutes' walk of the fields."[1] It was the outward extension of that railway state that – as seen in Chapter 3 – brought about the growth of early twentieth-century London, and with it the call for urban containment. And the same was true of the United States, where the classic early suburbs – Llewellyn Park in New Jersey, Lake Forest, and Riverside outside Chicago, Forest Hills Gardens in New York – were planned around railway stations.[2] That reflected stark reality: though the motor car became a technological reality around 1900, its price restricted its ownership to a tiny minority. Only with the revolution wrought by Henry Ford, on the magneto line at his Highland Park works in 1913, did mass-production techniques – all developed by others elsewhere, but here brought together – make possible a car for the masses.[3] And even then, the car's primitive technology, and the even more primitive state of the roads on which it ran, severely circumscribed its use. For its first decade of life, the Model T was what Ford had conceived it to be: a farmer's car, successor to the family horse and buggy.[4]

A Wellsian Prophecy is Fulfilled

But one visionary had seen the future. Already, in *The Sleeper Awakes* (1899), H. G. Wells was thinking railways – but twenty-first-century ones. The world would be laced with a network of rapid transit railways, with trains traveling at speeds of 200

---

[1] Kenward, 1955, 74.
[2] Stern and Massingale, 1981, 23–34; Stern, 1986, 129–35.
[3] Nevins, 1954, 471; Flink, 1975, 71–6.
[4] Flink, 1975, 80.

or 300 miles per hour, as well equipped and comfortable "as a good club." In *A Modern Utopia* (1905) his fictional explorers travel from Switzerland by a high-speed train, through a Channel tunnel, to London.[5]

Then, in *Anticipations*, first published in 1901, Wells had speculated on the possibility that "the motor omnibus companies competing against the suburban railways will find themselves hampered in the speed of their longer runs by the slower horse traffic on their routes," and that they therefore would "secure the power to form private roads of a new sort, upon which their vehicles will be free to travel up to the very limit of their possible speed." Though Wells was wrong in many pre-dictions in this book, this was one he got uncannily right. He said that "Almost insensibly, certainly highly profitable longer routes will be joined up," though the Americans and Germans would move much faster than the staid English. He pre-dicted that "they will be used only by soft-tired conveyances; the battering horse-shoes, the perpetual filth of horse traffic, and the clumsy wheels of laden carts will never wear them"; that "They will have to be very wide" and that "Their traffic in opposite directions will probably be strictly segregated"; that "where their ways branch the streams of traffic will cross not at a level but by bridges," and that "once they exist it will be possible to experiment with vehicles of a size and power quite beyond the dimensions prescribed by our ordinary roads – roads whose width has been entirely determined by the size of a cart a horse can pull."[6]

Wells's remarkable prescience did not end there. For he predicted not merely the age of the motorway, but also its effect. In a chapter on "The Probable Diffusion of Great Cities," he predicted that "Practically, by a process of confluence, the whole of Great Britain south of the Highlands seems destined to become … an urban region, laced all together not only by the railway and telegraph, but by novel roads such as we forecast" as well as "a dense network of telephones, parcels delivery tubes, and the like nervous and arterial connections." The result, he suggested, would be

> a curious and varied region, far less monotonous than our present English world, still in its thinner regions, at any rate, wooded, perhaps rather more abundantly wooded, breaking continually into park and garden, and with everywhere a scattering of houses … Through the varied country the new wide roads will run, here cutting through a crest and there running like some colossal aqueduct across a valley, swarming always with a multi-tudinous traffic of bright, swift (and not necessarily ugly) mechanisms; and everywhere amidst the fields and trees linking wires will stretch from pole to pole.[7]

As on other occasions, Wells proved over-sanguine as to the pace of technological change. But he was uncannily right about its location. The pioneer, as he predicted, was America. That was because down to 1950, thanks to the revolution Ford had wrought, America was the only country in the world that could boast mass car

---

[5]   Hardy, 2005, 37.
[6]   Wells, 1902, 17–19.
[7]   Wells, 1902, 61–2.

ownership. By 1927, building 85% of the world's cars, it could already boast one car for every five Americans: a car ownership level of one to approximately two families.[8] Thereafter, world slump and world war kept the level pegged down for more than two decades: not until the early 1950s did car ownership exceed the level of the late 1920s.

As a result, mass motorization had already begun to impinge on American cities by the mid-1920s, in a way the rest of the world would not know until the 1950s and 1960s. By 1923, traffic congestion in some cities was already so bad that there was talk of barring cars from downtown streets; by 1926, Thomas E. Pitts had closed his cigar store and soft drink bar at a major intersection in the center of Atlanta because congestion made it impossible to operate.[9] In the same decade, Sears, Roebuck, and then Montgomery Ward planned their first automobile-oriented suburban stores.[10] When the Lynds came to make their classic sociological study of "Middletown" (actually, Muncie in Indiana), at the end of the 1920s, they found that already car ownership was allowing the ordinary worker to live farther from his work.[11] And, by that time, already in some cities – Washington, Kansas City, St Louis – downtown commuters by automobile outnumbered those coming by transit. Unsurprisingly, then, the 1920s were the first decade when the Census-takers noticed that the suburbs were growing much faster than the central cities: by 39%, more than four million people, as against 19% or five million in the cities. In some cities the suburbanization trend was even more marked: the relative rates of growth in New York City were 67 against 23%, in Cleveland 126 against 12%, in St Louis 107 against 5%.[12]

The remarkable fact was that some American planners, at any rate, greeted this trend with equanimity, even with enthusiasm. At the National Conference of City Planners in 1924, Gordon Whitnall, a Los Angeles planner, proudly declared that western planners had learned from eastern mistakes, and would now lead the way to the horizontal city of the future. During the 1920s, as transit systems for the first time reported falling ridership and loss of profits, Detroit and Los Angeles considered large-scale support for transit investment in order to support their downtown areas, but found that voters would not support it.[13]

This ever-growing volume of car traffic for the most part traveled on ordinary city streets, widened and upgraded to cope with the flood. By the end of the 1920s there were very few examples even of simple underpasses or overpasses on American highways.[14] The outstanding exception was New York, which during the 1920s followed a distinctive path, deriving directly from an older tradition already noticed in Chapter 4: the parkway. First used by Olmsted in his design for New York's Central Park in 1858, the parkway had been widely employed by landscape architects in the

---

[8] Flink, 1975, 142–3; Jackson, K., 1973, 212.
[9] Flink, 1975, 163, 178.
[10] Dolce, 1976, 28.
[11] Dolce, 1976, 157.
[12] Tobin, 1976, 103–4.
[13] Foster, 1981, 80–5, 88–9.
[14] Hubbard and Hubbard, 1929, 208.

planning of parks and new residential areas in cities as diverse as Boston, Kansas City, and Chicago.[15] But, beginning with William K. Vanderbilt's Long Island Motor Parkway (1906–11), which can claim to be the world's first limited-access motor highway, and the 16-mile Bronx River Parkway (1906–23), followed by the Hutchinson River Parkway of 1928 and the Saw Mill Parkway of 1929, this distinctively American innovation was rapidly adapted to a new function: extended continuously for 10 or 20 miles into open countryside – and sometimes, as in the Bronx Parkway, used to clear up urban blight – it now gave rapid access from the congested central city both to new suburbs and to rural and coastal recreation areas.[16]

The moving spirit was New York's master-builder, Robert Moses. Using a State Act of 1924, which he had personally drafted to give him unprecedented (and, to the hapless legislators, unappreciated) powers to appropriate land, he proceeded to drive his parkways across the cherished estates of the Long Island millionaires – the Phipps, the Whitneys, the Morgans, the Winthrops – to give New Yorkers access to the ocean beaches. It was done, like most other things Moses did, for the highest public-spirited motives; and it established the base of his unprecedented public support, which he then skilfully extended through his management of the Triborough Bridge and Tunnel Authority, tying his parkway system together and linking it to the teeming tenements of Manhattan and the Bronx.[17]

But there were limits to public spirit: deliberately, Moses built the parkway bridges too low not only for trucks, but also for buses. The magnificent bathing beaches that he built at the ends of the parkways would thus be strictly reserved for middle-class car owners; the remaining two-thirds of the population could continue to ride the subway to Coney Island. And, when in the 1930s Moses extended his system down the west side of Manhattan Island to create the Henry Hudson Parkway, the world's first true urban motorway, the same applied: Moses was now consciously planning a system for car commuters.[18]

The point about Moses's gigantic public works of these years was indeed precisely this: whatever their ostensible original purpose, once linked by the Triborough Bridge they constituted a vast network of urban expressways, making it possible to commute to Manhattan offices from distances up to 20, even 30 miles: three or four times the effective radius of the subway system. There was an immediate effect: the population of Westchester and Nassau counties, served by the new roads, increased by 350,000 during the 1920s.[19] But the full implications would emerge only in the suburban building boom after World War Two. It was no accident that the most celebrated of all the resulting developments, the one that came almost to symbolize the whole process, was located where it was: the original Levittown stands just off an interchange on Moses's Wantagh State Parkway, built nearly 20 years earlier as one of the approaches to Jones Beach State Park.

[15] Scott, 1969, 13–15, 22, 38–9; Dal Co, 1979, 177.
[16] Rae, 1971, 71–2; Dolce, 1976, 19; Jackson, K., 1985, 166; Gregg, 1986, 38–42.
[17] Caro, 1974, 143–57, 174–7, 184–5, 208–10, 386–8.
[18] Caro, 1974, 318, 546–7.
[19] Dolce, 1976, 25.

(a)   (b)

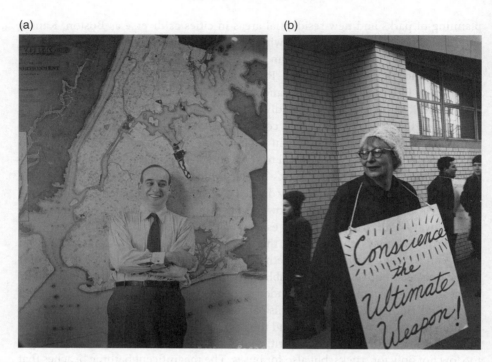

Figure 9.1   Robert Moses and Jane Jacobs: New York's all-conquering master-builder and the Greenwich Village housewife who finally brought him down. *Sources*: (a) © Bettmann/ CORBIS; (b) Fred W. McDarrah/Getty Images.

Some planners, even then, embraced the idea of new roads as the basis of a new urban form. One of the founding fathers of the Regional Planning Association of America (RPAA), Benton MacKaye, had – as seen in Chapter 5 – developed the idea of a townless highway, or "motorway." Seizing upon the plan of Radburn – developed by two other RPAA stalwarts, Clarence Stein and Henry Wright – he argued for its extension to the regional scale.

> The townless highway is a motorway, in which the adjoining towns would be in the same relationship to the road as the residential cul-de-sacs in Radburn are to the main traffic avenues. What Radburn does in the local community, the townless highway would do for the community at large … Instead of a single roadtown slum, congealing between our big cities, the townless highway would encourage the building of real communities at definite and favorable points *off* the main road.[20]

The concept was clear and consistent:

> the abolition of approaches to the main highway except at certain points; public ownership, or effective public control through rigorous zoning, of the foreground along

[20]   MacKaye, 1930, 94.

Figure 9.2 Jones Beach. One of the great Moses projects of the 1920s: recreation for the motorized masses, but the bridges on the parkways are built deliberately too low for buses. *Source*: Getty Images.

the right-of-way ... proper landscape development of the foreground, including the culture of shade trees and the strict regulation of telephone and electric-light lines; and finally, strict control of highway service station development.[21]

All that, of course, came to pass – but first in other places, and only long afterwards in the United States. And the other part of the prescription, the ultimate RPAA dream – "To stimulate the growth of the distinct community, compactly planned and limited in size, like the old New England village or the modern Radburn"[22] – was to remain unrealized in the land of its origin.

Everywhere but in the United States, the automobile revolution had yet to come. That was undoubtedly true in Europe, where down to World War Two only a tiny minority – at most 10% – of families owned cars. The first assembly line in Britain, at the Morris works in 1934, came more than 20 years after Ford's pioneering effort in Detroit.[23] And it was particularly true of the other highway-building pioneer, Germany; for Adolf Hitler's promised People's Car, which began production at the huge Wolfsburg plant in 1937, was diverted into war service and became a reality in the people's garages only long after World War Two. Yet Germany can dispute with

21 MacKaye, 1930, 95.
22 MacKaye, 1930, 95.
23 Flink, 1975, 32.

America the claim to have built the world's first true motorway: the AVUS (*Automobil-Verkehrs- und Übungsstrasse*), a 6-mile combined racing track and suburban commuter route, built through the Grunewald in Berlin between 1913 and 1921. Though a private company produced a plan for nearly 15,000 miles of motorways in Germany as early as 1924, and though by the end of the 1920s another company was well advanced on a plan for a 550-mile highway connecting Hamburg, Frankfurt, and Basel, only one other short inter-urban motorway, connecting Cologne and Bonn, was built before Hitler seized power in 1933.

Originally opposed to all the plans of the Weimar Republic, the Nazis hastily reversed their position; the *Autobahnen* promised quick unemployment relief, and they had critical military importance. So they simply took over the existing plans and, using a special subsidiary of the German State Railways, turned them into concrete at epic speed. Dr Todt, Inspector-General of the *Reichsautobahnen Gesellschaft*, finished the first stretch from Frankfurt to Darmstadt in the summer of 1935; his name proved only too symbolic, as there was a fatal accident that very day. Thence, with a construction force that reached 250,000 workers by 1934, the completion rate was dizzying: more than 600 miles by 1936, 1,900 miles by 1938, 2,400 miles by the start of World War Two.[24]

The pace showed. By later engineering standards, these early *Autobahnen* – seldom now to be seen, since a reunified Germany tore up the infrastructural archaeology bequeathed by the old communist régime – were strikingly primitive: they ran like a roller-coaster over every undulation in the landscape, almost devoid of cut-and-fill techniques; acceleration and deceleration lanes, ill-understood and probably unnecessary for the cars of those days, were conspicuous by their absence; on- and off-ramps were too tightly engineered. But, primitive though they might be, the *Autobahnen* created a new highway landscape that would later be faithfully imitated in almost every other country in the world. And, ironically, it was precisely the landscape that MacKaye – the archetypal liberal social democrat – had imagined in that paper of 1930: the separated carriageways, the grade-separated interchanges, the impeccably designed and landscaped service stations, even the huge blue signs with their distinctive lower-case lettering, that became part of a new global visual symbolism. The historic irony was this: independently conceived in Weimar Germany and Coolidgean America, they were indeed part of that movement that embraced Ernst May and Benton MacKaye, Martin Wagner and Henry Wright. It was the identity of the midwife that proved so disturbingly incongruous.

For in such long-distance interurban highway building, during the Depression decade of the 1930s the United States lagged. Though the lawyer-planner Edward M. Bassett had coined the term "freeway" in a *New York Times* article of 1928, the notion remained on paper.[25] Apart from a longer-distance extension of the New York Parkway system into the neighboring state of Connecticut – the Merritt and Wilbur Cross Parkways – which were toll roads, restricted to private motor traffic – America's

---

[24] GB Admiralty, 1945, 468–70; Anon, 1979a, 13–15; Petsch, 1976, 141–3.
[25] Foster, 1981, 110.

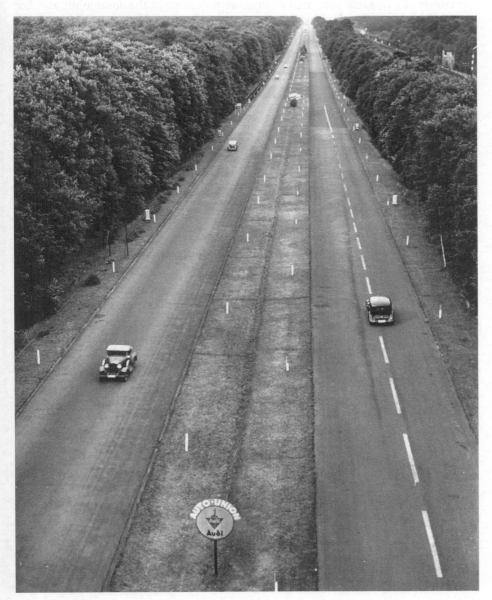

Figure 9.3 AVUS. The Automobil-Verkehrs- und Übungsstrasse, built through Berlin's Grunewald and completed in 1921, can claim to be the world's first true motorway. *Source*: © ullsteinbild/TopFoto.

first true inter-city motorway, the Pennsylvania Turnpike through the Appalachians from Carlisle near Harrisburg to Irwin near Pittsburgh, opened only in 1940.[26] December of that same year marked another milestone in the automobile age: Los Angeles completed its Arroyo Seco Parkway, now part of the Pasadena Freeway. Like the early *Autobahnen*, it was under-designed; in an extraordinary rerun of the opening of the first *Autobahn*, the opening ceremony was marked by a multiple shunt collision involving three car-loads of dignitaries.[27]

Los Angeles Shows the Way[28]

Los Angeles was a rehearsal, a laboratory, for the late twentieth-century urban future: what architectural historian Richard Longstreth calls "a seminal proving ground" for attempts by planners and architects to accommodate the car.[29] In 1915, Los Angeles already had one car for every eight residents, compared with a national average of one per 43 people; by 1920, one to 3.6 against one to 13.1; by 1930, one to 1.5 against one to 5.3.[30] So from 1920 Los Angeles began to experience the impact of mass car ownership, in a way that would remain unknown in other American cities until the 1950s, and in European cities until the 1980s.

It was an unusual American city: the people who poured into it were not, like immigrants into New York or Chicago or other cities, poor peasants from Europe; they were Americans from farms and small towns, and many were already car-dependent. They were free to follow Ford's aphorism: they would solve the city problem by leaving the city.[31] They demanded freedom: freedom to live where they liked and to travel when and how they liked. Their Los Angeles would be a city of suburbs, a city where everyone could live in a city yet not be part of a city, a city where individualism and privacy would be untempered by the old urban constraints of collective living and collective movement.

But, even before they came, the scene was already set. In 1900, dotted around the Los Angeles basin, from coast to mountains, was a series of small and still for the most part sleepy towns, many of them little more than villages, separated by fields and orchards: some farm communities, some resorts, some railroad commercial centers, some purely speculative ventures. The important point was that, whether agricultural or not, they were separate small settlements: the polycentric tradition of Southern California began early, as did its anti-urban bias.

Both were now massively reinforced: what really controlled the development of Southern California, giving it a polycentric and suburban form even before its

[26]   Rae, 1971, 79–81.
[27]   Jackson, K., 1985, 167.
[28]   This section is based on Hall, 1998, Ch. 26, where a fuller account is given.
[29]   Longstreth, 1992, 142.
[30]   Different authors' estimates are not easy to reconcile; Bottles, 1987, 93, 170; Flink, 1970, 76, 78; Foster, 1981, 118; Longstreth, 1992, 142.
[31]   Brodsly, 1981, 79–80; Flink, 1988, 139; Nelson, 1959, 95.

conquest by the car, was the electric light railway system that came to link up all these small places: the interurbans. As the historian of the Los Angeles system has put it, "in Southern California, the interurban was the pioneer. After its arrival, the population followed."[32] Henry E. Huntingdon was the real builder of this system, and thereby the real builder of Los Angeles; but he is little known, even to the thousands who visit the galleries or library that bear his name. Between 1901 and 1911, Huntingdon merged, organized, consolidated, and extended no less than 72 separate light rail systems into what became the Pacific Electric Railway: the largest electric interurban system in the United States, serving 56 communities within a 100-mile radius of Los Angeles.[33] At its peak, in the mid-1920s, Pacific Electric tracks stretched for 1,164 miles, from San Fernando to Redlands, and from Mount Lowe to the Pacific Ocean, and the Big Red Cars carried over 109 million passengers in a single year. Eight hundred passenger cars ran 6,000 scheduled trips daily. From the Pacific Electric Building at Sixth and Main Streets in Los Angeles to Long Beach took 50 minutes; to Pasadena or Glendale, 45 minutes; to Santa Monica, about an hour; the downtown commuter was still the basis of the system.[34]

His genius was to use the rails as a means of massively promoting real estate development.

> Pacific Electric extended its interurban tracks, throughout the county, Huntington Land purchased adjacent ranches in the San Gabriel Valley, and Valley Water developed a domestic water system. His holdings connected with the transportation and provided with water, Huntington waited for an advance in the residential real estate market. Huntington Land then subdivided its acreage into suburban tracts, paid deposits to utility companies for electric, gas, and telephone service, and employed outside organizations to publicise and sell the lots. Indeed, Huntington integrated his undertaking so effectively that while Pacific Electric lost millions and Valley Water thousands, Huntington Land's earnings justified the entire investment.[35]

But, with the rise of car ownership, the pattern of development changed. Before 1914, developers would rarely dare to build houses more than four blocks away from a streetcar line; but by the 1920s, new housing was being built in the interstitial areas, inaccessible by rail. They now spread more than 30 miles from the center of the city: outside the range of Hollywood's pistol shots, as a local wag said. This was decentralization on a scale quite inconceivable before the age of mass car ownership – that is, only 15 or 20 years earlier.[36] By 1930, Los Angeles City had 93.9% single-family homes, an extraordinarily higher proportion than older eastern or midwestern cities; in comparison the figure for New York was 52.8, for Chicago 52.0, for Boston 49.5.[37]

---

[32] Crump, 1962, 18.
[33] Flink, 1988, 141–2.
[34] Crump, 1962, 156–7, 159.
[35] Fogelson, 1967, 104.
[36] Bottles, 1987, 183; Foster, 1981, 48, 101.
[37] Fogelson, 1967, 143–6.

This, as Robert Fogelson observes, was unique:

> Nowhere else in the United States did suburbs extend so far into the countryside and downtown decline so drastically as the center of commerce and industry. This process, which reflected the newcomers' preferences, the subdividers' practices, and the businessmen's inclinations, was also self-perpetuating. Dispersal devastated the central business district, and decentralization spurred outlying subdivision. Given additional urbanization, moreover, nothing but the mountains and the sea inhibited the sprawl of the metropolis – a prospect which, whatever the attendant problems, including the failure of the electric railways, the people of Los Angeles saw as their consummate achievement.[38]

By the late 1930s, the traffic showed a pattern never before seen in any city: one of multiple origins and multiple destinations and multiple travel corridors, the product but also the generator of an automobile-dependent economy and society. Now, as increasing volumes of crosstown traffic tried to move on a street system that still radiated from the city center, there was a threat of total breakdown. And, portent of what was to come, congestion also increased in outlying business districts.[39] During the 1920s, the central area's share of retail trade plummeted from 75 to 25%. By 1934, there was no doubt that the commercial future lay on Miracle Mile: the city made a new cut through Westlake (now MacArthur) Park, joining Wilshire to Grand Avenue in downtown, and "A sixteen-mile boulevard, itself a new form of horizontal downtown, now connected downtown Los Angeles to the sea. Wilshire Boulevard had become the central thoroughfare of the City of the Angels."[40]

Now, the trend was unstoppable: by the mid-1930s, 88% of new retail stores were opening in the suburbs. As late as 1929, three-quarters of all department store sales in Los Angeles County were in the central business district (CBD); only 10 years later, the figure had sunk to 54%; the growth was happening not only along Wilshire, but in the San Fernando Valley, Westwood, and Hollywood. The CBD lost $25 million in assessed value between 1934 and 1939.[41] As E. E. East commented in 1941, "The so-called central business center is rapidly becoming just another center, with few notable characteristics to differentiate it from others."[42]

With the decline of Downtown went the decline and finally the demise of the Los Angeles light rail system. The Big Red Cars carried 315,000 passengers to the downtown area in 1923; by 1931, the total was down to 250,000, a 24% decline, with big losses in off-peak and weekend service.[43] Then, passenger traffic declined from 107,180,838 in 1929 to 67,695,532 in 1934, or by one-third.[44]

---

[38] Fogelson, 1967, 161.
[39] Bottles, 1987, 206, 213.
[40] Starr, 1990, 83.
[41] Bottles, 1987, 194–5, 214.
[42] Bottles, 1987, 195; this was written in 1941: 284, note 7.
[43] Bottles, 1987, 56; Crump, 1962, 146–7, 172, 189, 195; Fogelson, 1967, 179–80.
[44] Crump, 1962, 195.

   This did not happen through carelessness: Los Angeles consciously abandoned its huge public transport system. For the sudden collapse of the Pacific Electric in the mid-1920s provoked a huge debate in the city, which raged for years in the public prints and through the polling booths. In essence the issue was simple and stark: whether the city should seek to bolster the threatened system by massive public subsidy and new investment, or effectively let it go to the wall. It was significant because Los Angeles was at that point unique; as in so many other respects, the city was conducting a dress rehearsal for a play that was to run in every other city, the world over, for the following half-century and more.

   There can have been few more significant debates in the history of twentieth-century urbanism. In particular, some of the debaters had a very clear vision of a new kind of city, quite unlike any traditional city of the past. They understood that the city was starting to decentralize in a way never before witnessed anywhere; and they rejoiced in the fact. One such was no less than the city's planning director, G. Gordon Whitnall, who was already calling for "Not another New York, but a new Los Angeles. Not a great homogeneous mass with a pyramiding of population and squalor in a single center, but a federation of communities co-ordinated into a metropolis of sunlight and air."[45] That argument was even more decisively stated by Clarence Dykstra, Efficiency Director of the city's Department of Water and Power, in a brief article published in 1926, "Congestion Deluxe – Do We Want It?":

> Is it inevitable or basically sound or desirable that larger and larger crowds be brought into the city's center; do we want to stimulate housing congestion along subway lines and develop an intensive rather than an extensive city; will rapid transit spread the population anywhere except along the new right of way; is it ultimately desirable to have an area of abnormally high land values with its consequent demand for the removal of building restrictions; must all large business, professional and financial operations be conducted in a restricted area; must the worker be transported through the heart of the city to get to his work; as a matter of fact are not all of these assumptions, which were controlling in the past generation, being severely arraigned by thoughtful students?[46]

Everywhere, he argued, businesses – banks, factories, theaters, stores – were decentralizing.[47] He commended the alternative vision of the Los Angeles City Club, that "the city of the future ought to be an harmoniously developed community of local centers and garden cities in which the need for rapid transportation over long distances will be reduced to a minimum."[48]

   The answer then was to recognize the fact of dispersion, and to plan around it. In an article published in 1941, E. E. East, chief engineer of the Southern California Automobile Club and one of the founding fathers of the Los Angeles freeways,

---

[45]   Quoted in Fogelson, 1967, 163.
[46]   Dykstra, 1926, 397.
[47]   Dykstra, 1926, 397.
[48]   Dykstra, 1926, 397.

outlined a vision of the future which was essentially the same one as Whitnall and Dykstra had voiced in the mid-1920s.

> The Los Angeles area probably more than any other area of the United States is a product of the motor vehicle age. Here, out of the confusion of present day metropolitan transportation is emerging a new city pattern. Will it become the accepted pattern of tomorrow's cities, or have we built upon a foundation of sand? From an economic and engineering view the answer is clear. The city of tomorrow, built upon a motor vehicle foundation, will be a better and more efficient city in which to live and work than are the cities of today.[49]

East described the life of a typical Los Angeles family, the Joneses; they lived in Beverly Hills and he worked in East Los Angeles, commuting by car; so did his two student children who drive to college:

> Each morning the maid motors over from Pasadena, the gardener from Inglewood and the laundress from Van Nuys. The milkman, the postman, the paper boy, the butcher, and the baker each come and go in his own private conveyance. During the day the wife shops along Wilshire Boulevard, in downtown Los Angeles and Pasadena, and possibly plays bridge in Long Beach. She travels in her own automobile.[50]

The result was "A million automobiles moving in a million different directions, with their paths of travel conflicting at a million intersections, a million times a day."[51] And this pattern of conflict was progressively spreading outward.[52] There was only one way out of the impasse, East argued:

> The solution of the transportation and land use problem for the Los Angeles metropolitan district, assuming it is the desire of the inhabitants to continue to use individual transportation, is from an engineering and financing standpoint a simple problem. It consists of developing over a period of years a network of motorways designed to serve transportation rather than land … Passing through built-up business districts, these new facilities could be carried into and through specially designed motorway buildings located in the centers of the blocks with connecting bridges over the cross streets.[53]

At least 80% of all trips were by automobile.[54] This both stemmed from, and in turn reinforced, the dispersed pattern of homes and jobs:

> The 1937 survey discloses a distinct change in the directional movement of traffic. A rectangular traffic movement has been super-imposed upon the original and greatly

49   East, 1941, 91.
50   East, 1941, 95.
51   East, 1941, 96.
52   East, 1941, 97.
53   East, 1941, 98.
54   Automobile Club, 1937, 12.

augmented radial movement, resulting in a crisscrossing of traffic and a street and highway congestion and hazard without parallel.[55]

The only way to provide for such a pattern of movement, the authors argued, was by a radically new system.

> The solution of the problem of providing adequate facilities for through traffic will be found in providing a network of traffic routes for the exclusive use of motor vehicles over which there shall be no crossing at grade and along which there shall be no inter-ference from land use activities … It is recommended that a network of motorways be constructed to serve the entire metropolitan area of Los Angeles as defined in this report … These motorways should be developed upon a right-of-way of not less than 360 feet in width through residential territory and not less than 100 feet in width through established business districts.[56]

But little could be done at first. In 1930, two of the most celebrated planning consul-tancies of the era, the Olmsted Brothers and Harlan Bartholomew and Associates, had jointly produced a report, *Parks, Playgrounds and Beaches for the Los Angeles Region*, proposing an extensive system of playgrounds and parks, linked to outlying natural "reservations" by a series of regional "parkways."[57] It was environmentally unambitious: it did not seek to protect watersheds and wetlands as unique ecosystems, but simply to preserve and create scenic vistas, recreational spaces, and verdant parkways as part of a package of managed or planned commercial development. Scenery had cultural, economic, and social value, rather than ecological and environmental significance.[58]

Olmsted went so far as to stipulate specific park and parkway design principles for the automobile, advocating that planners favor routes with "broad sweeping views" and designated viewing areas. But his vision went beyond the purely technical management of weekend traffic: "It is vital to the nervous health of the people and the maintenance of what makes life worth living," he explained, "to provide town-strained men and women such measure as can be provided within their reach of the kind of refreshment obtainable in no other way than in beautiful and spacious, open 'natural' scenery, contrasting to the utmost with the scenery of streets and build-ings."[59] It was the same vision as animated advocates of the Westchester County Parkway system: conveniently, scenic parkways provided a landscape resource that increased real estate values and promoted community growth while creating and preserving scenic beauty and increasing access to recreational pursuits.[60]

It spurred action – but on a minuscule scale. Construction of the Arroyo Seco Parkway started in 1938 and was finished in 1940; a 1-mile stretch of what was to

---

[55]   Automobile Club, 1937, 21.
[56]   Automobile Club, 1937, 30–1.
[57]   Shaffer, 2001, 357, 359–60.
[58]   Shaffer, 2001, 359.
[59]   Shaffer, 2001, 374–5.
[60]   Shaffer, 2001, 375.

become the Hollywood Freeway, through the Cahuenga Pass north of Hollywood, was constructed during the same period.[61] Local, state, and some federal money was cobbled together for the Arroyo Seco, and for a couple of wartime projects; but by 1945, only 11 miles of freeways had been opened in Los Angeles, followed by 4.3 miles during 1945–50.[62] The big changes came after the war, with a huge program of new building: total freeway mileage was increased four and a half times from 1950 to 1955, including large parts of the Hollywood–Santa Ana and San Bernardino freeways. The huge four-level downtown interchange, the "stack," was completed in 1953. When the act was passed, California had a mere 19 miles of freeway; within 10 years it had 300 miles more, mainly around Los Angeles and San Francisco where congestion was worst.[63]

But perhaps what gave Los Angeles its mythical reputation was not the extent of its freeway network – the New York metropolitan area, with the head start Moses gave it, could always win on that score – but the total dependence of its citizens on it, revealed by the rarity of public transportation and by that telling phrase of Angelenos who talk of "going surface" as if it were an eccentric undertaking. It was also the distinctive lifestyle that ensued: a style exemplified by the heroine of Joan Didion's novel *Play It as It Lays*, who, deserted by her husband, "turns to the freeways for sustenance," and was finally initiated:

> Again and again she returned to an intricate stretch just south of the interchange where a successful passage from the Hollywood onto the Harbor required a diagonal move across four lanes of traffic. On the afternoon when she finally did it without once braking or once losing the beat on the radio she was exhilarated, and that night slept dreamlessly.[64]

It was also the resulting pattern of urban growth. The opening of the Arroyo Seco was followed almost immediately by higher land values in Pasadena. Thence, wherever the freeways went, the developers followed. And, unlike Moses's network in New York, this system was not radial – or at most, only partially so; it rather formed a loose trapezoidal grid, giving roughly equal accessibility from anywhere to anywhere. True, this had also been a feature of the old Big Red Cars, whose routes the freeways almost invariably followed.[65]

So Wells had proved right; but it all took longer than he had imagined, and its impacts were seen on Long Island and in the Los Angeles basin long before they were observable in the English shires. The first stretch of motorway in Britain, 8 miles round Preston in Lancashire, opened in December 1958, nearly 40 years after its first German equivalent and 50 years after its first American one.[66] And only

---

[61]   Brodsly, 1981, 97–8; Los Angeles County Regional Planning Commission, 1943, 8.
[62]   Brodsly, 1981, 112.
[63]   Brodsly, 1981, 116; Rae, 1971, 184.
[64]   Quoted in Brodsly, 1981, 56.
[65]   Fogelson, 1967, 92, 175–85; Rae, 1971, 243; Warner, 1972, 138–41; Brodsly, 1981, 4; Foster, 1981, 17; Wachs, 1984, 303; Jackson, K., 1985, 122.
[66]   Starkie, 1982, 1.

in the 1960s did the car begin fundamentally to affect the ways of life, and the settlement forms, of the English countryside.

Frank Lloyd Wright and the Soviet Deurbanists

In America, long before that, automobile-oriented suburbs were being consciously planned, even on a large scale. Thus in Kansas City, George E. Kessler's great city parks plan of 1893–1910, which included recreational parkways, provided a basis for the developer Jesse Clyde Nichols's Country Club District begun in 1907–8; influenced both by the City Beautiful movement and by a bicycle tour of European garden cities, designed by Kessler to integrate with his parks, it was the first garden suburb specifically based on the automobile. Nichols deliberately bought cheap land outside the range of the city's streetcar system, allowing him to build at low density – first at six houses per acre, then even less; at the center, the brilliant Country Club Plaza (originated by the architect Edward Buhler Delle in 1923–5) was the world's first car-based shopping center.[67] In Los Angeles both Beverly Hills (1914) and Palos Verdes Estates (1923) followed similar planning principles; though the first was originally based on a Pacific Electric Railway station, both soon became classic early automobile suburbs.[68]

All these were private speculative developments pure and simple. They were designed to make money and they did. They owed their outstanding success to the quality of their design and to the use of private covenants to guarantee that this quality would be maintained. But there was also a highly idealized version of the automobile city, and a rationale for it. Appropriately enough, the most complete formulation of it came from America's outstanding native architect, Frank Lloyd Wright. But another, uncannily similar version came from a source as unlikely as could be imagined: the Soviet Union.

The Soviet deurbanists of the 1920s, led by Moisei Ginsburg and Mikhail Okhitovich, argued – like Wright, and perhaps influenced by him – that electricity and new transportation technologies, above all the car, would allow cities to empty out.[69] They too were essentially individualistic and anti-bureaucratic; they similarly argued for new kinds of built form based on factory-produced materials, with individual lightweight transportable homes located in natural countryside, thus creating a "townless, fully decentralized, and evenly populated country";[70] they even envisaged the eventual razing of the cities to form huge parks and urban museums.[71] But these were Soviet planners, and their version of individualism was curiously collective: all activities, save sleeping and repose, would be communal.[72] The

[67] Stern and Massingale, 1981, 76; Jackson, K., 1985, 177–8, 258.
[68] Stern and Massingale, 1981, 78; Jackson, K., 1985, 179–80.
[69] Parkins, 1953, 24; Frampton, 1968, 238; Bliznakov, 1976, 250–1; Starr, 1977, 90–1; Thomas, 1978, 275.
[70] Bliznakov, 1976, 250.
[71] Thomas, 1978, 275.
[72] Bliznakov, 1976, 251.

technological imperative was identical to that of Frank Lloyd Wright; the moral
order was – at least superficially – quite different.

In the event, given material conditions in the Soviet Union at the time, it was all
quite fantastic. There were hardly any cars, and not much electricity. Well might
Corbusier, who was of course allied to the opposite urbanist camp, parody the
deurbanist vision:

> The cities will be part of the country; I shall live 30 miles from my office in one
> direction, under a pine tree; my secretary will live 30 miles away from it too, in the
> other direction, under another pine tree. We shall both have our own car. We shall use
> up tires, wear out road surfaces and gears, consume oil and gasoline. All of which will
> necessitate a great deal of work ... enough for all.[73]

Perhaps, such a vision was all conceivable in America; even in the Depression-
ridden America of the early 1930s. But in the Soviet Union, even given the appalling
condition of Moscow's housing and infrastructure at the time, it was not. The historic 1931 Party Congress determined that anyone who denied the socialist character
of existing cities was a saboteur; from 1933, a decree laid it down that city centers
should be rebuilt to express "socialist greatness."[74] Stalin had spoken; the great Soviet
urban debate was stilled for a generation.

Frank Lloyd Wright's vision, in contrast, was perfectly attuned not only to its
author's personal philosophy but also to the conditions of its time. It was, indeed,
the distillation of almost everything that he felt and had expressed about the theory
of built form. In the process, it managed in a rather extraordinary way to weave
together almost every significant strain of American urban – more precisely,
anti-urban – thinking.

Wright began to conceive of Broadacre City as early as 1924, and soon afterwards coined the title in a lecture at Princeton University.[75] The conception shares
many philosophical affinities with the ideas of the RPAA, and some of these with
Ebenezer Howard. There is the same rejection of the big city – specifically, New
York – as a cancer, a "fibrous tumour"; the same populist antipathy to finance
capital and landlordism; the same anarchist rejection of big government; the same
reliance on the liberating effects of new technologies; the same belief in the homesteading principle and the return to the land; there is even that distinctively
American transcendentalism that derives from writers like Emerson, Thoreau,
and Whitman.[76]

But there are also differences, particularly in comparison with Howard (as indeed
with the Soviet deurbanists): Wright claimed to liberate men and women not in
order to join in cooperation, but to live as free individuals; he desired not to marry

[73] Le Corbusier, 1967, 74.
[74] Bliznakov, 1976, 252–4.
[75] Wright, 1945, 138.
[76] White and White, 1962, 193; Grabow, 1977, 116–17; Fishman, 1977, 124–7; Ciucci, 1979, 296–300,
Muschamp, 1983, 75.

Figure 9.4 Broadacre City. Frank Lloyd Wright's "Usonian Vision" of the low-density marriage of suburb and countryside; every citizen simultaneously an urbanite and a farmer. Something perilously like it happened all over the US in the 1950s, but stripped of its social and economic message. *Source*: Scottsdale (AZ), The Frank Lloyd Wright Foundation. Photo by Skot Weidemann © 2013. The Frank Lloyd Wright Fdn, AZ/Art Resource, NY/ Scala, Florence.

town and country, but to merge them.[77] Above all, there is the notion that the new technological forces could recreate in America a nation of free independent farmers and proprietors: "Edison and Ford would resurrect Jefferson."[78] In this regard, the similarity is rather with the Greenbelt communities of Rexford Tugwell; but Tugwell shared with Mumford, Stein, and Chase a belief in community planning, hard to trace in Wright. Rather, Wright shares with the RPAA a common background of experience: the slow decay of rural America, ground down between the soul-destroying drudgery of the pre-electric farm and the welcoming bright lights of the city, as poignantly recorded by Hamlin Garland in his autobiographical *A Son of the Middle Border*:

> In those few days, I perceived life without its glamor. I no longer looked upon these toiling women with the thoughtless eyes of youth. I saw no humor in the bent forms and graying hair of the men. I began to understand that my own mother had trod a

---

[77] Fishman, 1977, 92–4.
[78] Fishman, 1977, 123.

similar slavish round with never a full day of leisure, with scarcely an hour of escape from the tugging hands of children, and the need of mending and washing clothes.[79]

Liberated at last by World War One and the automobile, they left the farms "in rattle-trap automobiles, their fenders tied with springs, and curtains flapping in the breeze ... with no funds and no prospects."[80] And then, the migration turned into sheer necessity, as depression brought farm foreclosures and the forced conversion of proprietors into sharecroppers.[81] Yet, as Charles Abrams put it at the time, "Not only is the frontier closed, but the city is closed"; the farmer had nowhere to go.[82] Hence the Resettlement Administration's Greenbelt towns, described in Chapter 4; hence Broadacre City.

But Broadacre would be different. The new technologies, as Kropotkin had argued more than three decades earlier, were transforming, even abolishing, the tyranny of geography. "Given electrification, distances are all but eliminated as far as communication goes ... Given the steamship, airship, and the automobile, our human sphere of movement immeasurably widens by many mechanical modes, by wheel or air."[83] Now, "not only thought but speech and movement are volatile: the telegraph, telephone, mobilization, radio. Soon, television and safe flight."[84] Modern mobility was available even for the poor man, "By means of a bus or a model A Ford."[85]

Coupled with this, new building materials – high-pressure concrete, glass, and "innumerable broad, thin, cheap sheets of wood, metal or plastics" – made a new kind of building possible: "buildings may be made by machinery going to the building instead of the building going to machinery."[86] And at the same time, "machine-shop fabrication" made water, gas, and electricity cheaply "available in quantity for all instead of still more questionable luxuries for the few."[87] So "The congested verticality of any city is now utterly inartistic and *unscientific!*"[88]

Out of these technological ingredients, Wright constructed what he called his "Usonian Vision":

> Imagine, now, spacious, well-landscaped highways, grade crossings eliminated by a new kind of integrated by-passing or over- or under-passing all traffic in cultivated or living areas ... Giant roads, themselves great architecture, pass public service stations no longer eyesores but expanded as good architecture to include all kinds of roadside service for the traveler, charm and comfort throughout. These great roads unite and separate, separate and unite, in endless series of diversified units passing by farm units, roadside markets, garden schools, dwelling places, each on its acres of individually

[79]   Garland, 1917, 366.
[80]   Fogelson, 1967, 74.
[81]   Abrams, 1939, 68.
[82]   Abrams, 1939, 68.
[83]   Wright, 1945, 34.
[84]   Wright, 1945, 36.
[85]   Wright, 1945, 86.
[86]   Wright, 1945, 37.
[87]   Wright, 1945, 37.
[88]   Wright, 1945, 34.

adorned and cultivated ground, developed homes all places for pleasure in work or leisure. And imagine man-units so arranged that every citizen as he chooses may have all forms of production, distribution, self-improvement, enjoyment within the radius of, say, ten to twenty miles of his own home. And speedily available by means of his private car or public conveyance. This integrated distribution of living related to ground composes the great city that I see embracing this country. This would be the Broadacre City of tomorrow that is the nation. Democracy realized.[89]

Broadacre, of course, would be a city of individuals. Its houses would be designed "not only in harmony with greenery and ground but intimate with the pattern of the personal life of the individual on the ground. No two homes, no two gardens, none of the farm units on one – to two, three – to ten acres or more; no two farm-steads or factory buildings need be alike ... Strong but light and appropriate houses, spacious convenient workplaces to which all would be tributary, each item would be solidly and sympathetically built out of materials native to Time, Place, and Man."[90]

All this was the physical shell. But for Wright, just as for Mumford or for Howard, the built forms were merely the appropriate expression of a new kind of society. The skyscraper city, for him, represented "the end of an epoch! The end of the plutocratic republic of America."[91] Through another mass migration, as huge and as momen-tous as the original homesteading of America, the new pioneer would replace the plutocracy of the landlords and the giant corporations by "a more simple, natural-basis right to live by and enough to live upon according to his better self."[92] The vision is almost identical to Howard's:

> Emancipated from rent, were good ground made available to him, he – the machine worker rented by wages – paying toll to the exaggerated city in order that the city give him work to do – why should not he, the poor wage-slave, go forward, not backward, to his native birthright? Go to the good ground and grow his family in a free city?[93]

There, he would rediscover the quintessential American democracy: "Democracy is the ideal of reintegrated decentralization ... many free units developing strength as they learn by function and grow together in spacious mutual freedom."[94] It was the vision of his Wisconsin boyhood, recaptured through the new technology.

No one liked it. For his pains, he was attacked by almost everyone: for naiveté, for architectural determinism, for encouraging suburbanization, for wasteful use of resources, for lack of urbanity, above all for being insufficiently collective in his

[89]   Wright, 1945, 65–6.
[90]   Wright, 1945, 66.
[91]   Wright, 1945, 120.
[92]   Wright, 1945, 121.
[93]   Wright, 1945, 86.
[94]   Wright, 1945, 45–6.

philosophy.[95] He developed no movement to realize his ideas, received no commissions from Tugwell's Resettlement Administration, and had no moral support at all from the other powerful figures – above all the leaders of the RPAA – who were working in favor of planned decentralization.[96]

And, as Herbert Muschamp has eloquently argued, there was finally a contradiction in the whole vision – the free commonwealth of individuals would live in houses designed by the master-architect:

> When all the Whitmanesque windbag rhetoric extolling the pioneer spirit is swept away, what remains is a society constructed upon the strict hierarchical principle of Wright's own Taliesin Fellowship: a government of architecture, a society in which the architect is granted ultimate executive power ... It is easy, therefore, to view Broadacre as proof that within every self-styled individualist is a dictator longing to break free.[97]

The heart of the contradiction, for Muschamp, lay in the belief that the architect could control the whole process. In fact, by the early 1950s, the American actuality "threatened to liquidate his own Romantic dream in a vista of carports, split-levels, lawn sprinklers washing away the Usonian dream to make way for the weekend barbecue."[98] The final irony came at the end of the 1950s: Wright unsuccessfully sued the local county to remove the pylons that disfigured the view from Taliesin III, erected to carry power to new Phoenix suburbanites. Yet, in the same decade, driving Alvar Aalto around the Boston suburbs, he could claim that he had made all this possible. Muschamp comments,

> Didn't the Adventurer in Wright want to roar with laughter at the thought that the greatest architect of all time had made possible the conversion of America's natural paradise to an asphalt continent of Holiday Inns, Tastee-Freeze stands, automobile graveyards, billboards, smog, tract housing, mortgaged and franchised coast to coast?[99]

Perhaps. There was a contradiction, to be sure: Wright wanted it all architect-designed, sanitized, in uniform good taste; it came out anything but. Perhaps he did have more in common with the Soviet deurbanists than either would have admitted; they were all architects, after all. Yet Broadacre City is significant for the nature of its vision. It probably could not have occurred in just that way, when it did, in any other country. It seized the American future, and embodied it in a vision. The remarkable fact is just how visionary it proved to be.

[95]   Grabow, 1977, 119–22.
[96]   Fishman, 1977, 146–8.
[97]   Muschamp, 1983, 79–80.
[98]   Muschamp, 1983, 93.
[99]   Muschamp, 1983, 185.

"The Suburbs Are Coming!"

This then was the ironic outcome: after World War Two a suburban building boom created a kind of Broadacre City all over America, but entirely divorced from the economic basis or the social order Wright had so steadfastly affirmed. In the late 1940s and the 1950s, thousands of square miles of American farmland disappeared under it; one *New Yorker* cartoon showed a traditional farm family sitting on their porch with a bulldozer rearing over the brow of the nearby hill, as the wife shouts "Pa, get your gun! The suburbs are coming." But the people who moved into the new tract homes typically owed their living to those very mammoth corporations which Wright assailed; their homes were mortgaged to giant financial institutions; and in no sense did they constitute a society of sturdy self-sufficient proprietors. Americans had the shell without the substance.

There were four main foundations for the suburban boom. They were new roads, to open up land outside the reach of the old trolley and commuter rail routes; zoning of land uses, to produce uniform residential tracts with stable property values; government-guaranteed mortgages, to make possible long-repayment low-interest mortgages that were affordable by families of modest incomes; and a baby boom, to produce a sudden surge in demand for family homes where young children could be raised. The first three of these were already in place, though sometimes only in embryonic form, a decade before the boom began. The fourth triggered it.

The roads were embryonic. As already seen, they were there in one or two places: New York from the 1920s, Los Angeles from the 1940s. But, remarkably, developers do not seem to have appreciated their potential for a decade or more after they were in place. Still, in the 1930s, a majority of New Yorkers did not own cars. And many of those who did happened to work in Manhattan, to which car commuting was almost impossible; suburbanization must await the outward movement of jobs to places where the car was more convenient than the subway – which began to happen on any scale only in the 1950s. And in any event, generally the roads were not there. The Depression and wartime years had brought a halt to the rise in car ownership; not until 1949 did registrations again exceed the level of 1929.[100] And road-building, too, had stagnated.

It was the 1956 Interstate and Defense Highways Act that marked the real beginning of freeway suburbanization. But at the beginning, it does not seem to have been meant that way at all. True, Roosevelt in 1941 had appointed Rexford Tugwell, Frederic Delano, and Harland Bartholomew – all known supporters of planned decentralization of people and jobs – to an Inter-Regional Highways Committee under the chairmanship of Bibb Graves of Alabama, and served by Thomas H. MacDonald, Commissioner of Public Roads – whom MacKaye had commended, in that paper of 1930, for his "far-seeing" approach to "broad-gauged regional and Inter-regional planning."[101] It called for a 32,000-mile Interstate system,

---

[100] Tobin, 1976, 104.
[101] MacKaye, 1930, 95.

and Congress duly passed the Federal Aid Highway Act of 1944. But that was to be a strictly interurban system, bypassing the cities; and, before it could be built, political splits emerged: between engineers who just wanted to pour concrete and city planners (like the veteran Harland Bartholomew) who wanted to use new roads to cure urban blight, between those who wanted self-financing toll roads and those who wanted federal subsidy. Truman in 1949 and Eisenhower in 1954 signed Urban Renewal Acts but kept highways out of them.

Finally, Eisenhower – who believed that he had won the war on the German *Autobahnen* – accepted the argument that new roads were not only vital for national defense in an era of Cold War, but could also generate an economic boom. He called on a retired General, Lucius Clay, to head a committee of inquiry; most of the evidence came from the pro-roads side – including Robert Moses, who used the roads-fight-blight argument. But the fight over paying for them, which was essentially between fiscal conservatives and the highways lobby, almost killed the resulting bill. Finally, a compromise version, providing for the new roads to be built by a special fund through a tax on gasoline, oil, buses, and trucks, was passed in June 1956; in the House of Representatives it went through without dissent, in the Senate one solitary vote was recorded against it.[102] The greatest public works program in the history of the world – $41 billion for 41,000 miles of new roads – was under way.

The critical question, still, was what sort of road system it should be. Congress in 1944 had endorsed the principle that it should bypass the cities. Planners like Bartholomew and Moses argued on the contrary that it should penetrate into their hearts, thus removing blighted areas and improving accessibility from the suburbs to downtown offices and shops. In practice, given the strength of the urban renewal lobby in the 1950s and 1960s, there was little doubt about the outcome: the system would be used to create new corridors of accessibility from city centers to potential suburbs, as Moses had tried to do 30 years earlier.[103] When the program began in earnest, its chief, Bertram D. Tallamy, said that the new highways were built on principles that Moses had taught him as long ago as 1926;[104] at that time, and for long after, Moses was, after all, the only really experienced urban-highway builder in the United States.

The second requirement, zoning, had originated as early as 1880 in Modesto, California, where it had been used to remove Chinese laundries: a particularly apt beginning, since thereafter one of its principal functions was to safeguard property values by excluding undesirable land uses and undesirable neighbors.[105] And the city that took the lead in the zoning movement from 1913 on, New York City, was impelled to do so by the complaints of mid-town retailers who, complaining that industrial incursions were threatening their profits, appealed loudly to "every financial interest" and "every man who owns a home or rents an apartment."[106] The city's Commission on Building Heights accepted their argument that zoning secured "greater safety and

[102]   Davies, 1975, 13–23; Rose, 1979, 19, 26, 62–4, 70–99.
[103]   Leavitt, 1970, 28–35.
[104]   Caro, 1974, 11.
[105]   Marcuse, 1980, 32–3.
[106]   Scott, 1969, 154–5.

Figure 9.5 Kansas City, Country Club District. J. C. Nichols's Country Club Plaza (1922), equally, can lay claim to be the first out-of-town shopping center. *Source*: J. C. Nichols Company Scrapbooks (K0054), Wilborn & Associates Photographers.

security in investment."[107] And when, in 1926, an historic Supreme Court decision, *Village of Euclid et al v. Ambler Realty Co.*, confirmed the general validity of zoning, the great planner-lawyer Alfred Bettman – whose brief, submitted late in the hearing, may well have proved crucial – argued that the "public welfare" served by zoning was the enhancement of the community's property values.[108] The point at issue, significantly, was whether land should be zoned as industrial or residential (Chapter 3).[109]

Because it was meticulously designed as part of a general police power to safeguard "public welfare" and "public health, safety, morals and convenience," thus to avoid all suggestion of compulsory purchase with claims for compensation, New York's comprehensive zoning resolution of 1916 deliberately avoided long-term plans; Edward Bassett, the attorney in charge, proudly declared that "We have gone at it block by block," invariably confirming the status quo.[110] And most of America followed suit. Thus arose a paradox: land-use control in the United States, in sharp contrast to much of Europe, came to be divorced from any kind of land-use planning; it could not be used to raise the level of design, which had to be secured – on the model of Kansas City's Country Club District and its imitators – through private restrictive covenants.[111]

[107]   Glaab and Brown, 1976, 266.
[108]   Quoted in Fluck, 1986, 333.
[109]   Fluck, 1986, 328; Bettman, 1946, 54.
[110]   Scott, 1969, 154–6.
[111]   Lubove, 1967, 14.

The third precondition for the suburban boom was cheap long-term housing finance. In this regard, as already noticed in Chapter 3, America lagged strangely behind Britain. There, the permanent building societies had developed from the turn of the century, offering 20- or 25-year mortgages with low down payments, and powerfully fueling the great suburban spread around London in the 1920s and 1930s. In contrast, until the 1930s the typical American mortgage was only for five or ten years at 6 or 7% interest: a ruinously high burden for the average family.[112] It was an early New Deal experiment – the Home Owners Loan Corporation (HOLC), introduced as an emergency measure of April 1933 to stem farm foreclosures – that introduced into America the long-term, self-amortizing mortgage. The next year, the National Housing Act established the Federal Housing Authority (FHA), with powers to insure longer-term mortgage loans by private lenders for home construction and sale, with a down payment as low as 10% and a period of 25 or 30 years at only 2 or 3%.[113] Between 1938 and 1941, it was insuring some 35% of all home loans in the United States.[114]

From 1934, then, the most powerful constraint to suburban home-building had been removed. For the FHA took over from the HOLC the notion of appraising whole neighborhoods, and thereby redlining those deemed to be undesirable; in practice, this meant the whole of America's inner cities. Further, the "FHA exhorted racial segregation and endorsed it as a public policy"; as late as 1966, it had not insured a single mortgage in Paterson or Camden in New Jersey, two predominantly black cities.[115] The central objective of the FHA was identical with that of zoning: it was to guarantee the security of residential real-estate values. And both worked through exclusion, to divert investment massively into new suburban house-building at the expense of the central city.

Some of the consequences could already be glimpsed later in that decade. The National Resources Planning Board report *Our Cities*, published in 1937 (and already discussed in Chapter 5), drew attention to the fact that even between 1920 and 1930, suburbs had grown twice as fast as central cities: "the urbanite is rapidly becoming the suburbanite," as families fulfilled "the urge to escape the obnoxious aspects of urban life without at the same time losing access to its economic and cultural advantages."[116] During that decade, some suburbs had grown at dizzy speed: Beverly Hills by 2,500%, Shaker Heights outside Cleveland by 1,000%.[117] But then, the Depression drastically cut new housing starts – by as much as 95% between 1928 and 1933 – and brought a huge crop of mortgage foreclosures.[118] Not until after World War Two did the industry completely recover.

---

[112]   Tunnard and Reed, 1955, 239–40; Jackson, K., 1985, 196.
[113]   Jackson, K., 1985, 196, 205.
[114]   Glaab and Brown, 1976, 275.
[115]   Jackson, K., 1985, 213.
[116]   US National Resources Planning Board, 1937, 35.
[117]   Wright, 1981, 195.
[118]   Glaab and Brown, 1976, 273.

Given an almost complete moratorium on new construction – save for essential war-related building – between 1941 and 1945, the result at war's end was a huge accumulated shortage: an estimated 2.75–4.4 million families sharing, and another half-million in non-family quarters.[119] On top of that came the baby boom, as the servicemen returned and the delayed crop of wartime babies coincided with the regular cohorts. The industry spectacularly responded: as against a mere 515,000 starts in 1939, there were 1,466,000 by 1949, 1,554,000 by 1959.[120] And in the 1949 Housing Act – as well as initiating the urban renewal process, chronicled in Chapter 7 – Congress massively increased the FHA's lending powers.[121]

As before, this money went into the suburbs. By 1950, the suburbs were found to be growing at 10 times the rate of the central cities; by 1954, it was estimated that in the previous decade nine million people had moved into the suburbs.[122] The 1950s, as the 1960 Census showed, was the decade of the greatest suburban growth in American history: while the central cities grew by six million or 11.6%, the suburbs grew by a dizzy 19 million, or by 45.9%. And ominously, for the first time, some of the nation's greatest cities recorded actual population decline: Boston and St Louis each lost 13% of their population.[123]

This huge migration was made possible by a new breed of builder: large-scale, economy- and efficiency-conscious, capable of building houses like refrigerators or cars. The archetypal firm, which became a legend in its own time, had been founded in 1929 by Abraham Levitt and his sons William and Alfred, as a small family firm on Long Island outside New York City. During World War Two they learned how to build workers' housing fast, and rapidly waxed larger. In the town of Hempstead on Long Island, 23 miles from midtown Manhattan, they began in 1948 a suburb based on the techniques they had learned: flow production, division of labor, standardized designs and parts, new materials and tools, maximum use of prefabricated components, easy credit, good marketing. The people came and queued in long lines for hours to buy their houses; when the Levitts had finished, they had completed more than 17,000 homes housing some 82,000 people: the largest single housing development in history.[124] They went on to develop similar Levittowns in Pennsylvania and New Jersey.

In an afternoon peregrination down Long Island, the earnest student of planning history can progressively view Stein and Wright's pioneering Sunnyside Gardens of 1924, Attlebury's earlier model suburb at Forest Hills Gardens of 1912, and finally Levittown. The result, taken in that order, is anticlimactic. For Levittown is simply dull. It is not that there is anything wrong with it, considered simply as a piece of

[119] Checkoway, 1984, 154.
[120] Checkoway, 1984, 154.
[121] Checkoway, 1984, 161.
[122] Jackson, K., 1985, 238.
[123] Tobin, 1976, 106.
[124] Checkoway, 1984, 158; Jackson, K., 1985, 234–5.

Figure 9.6 Levittown, Long Island. The Levitts' standard Cape Cod design, modified in a thousand different ways by its owners; pleasant enough but ultimately bland, an *ersatz* version of the great suburbs of the American past.

residential real estate. The Levitts' basic Cape Cod design, repeated in a limited number of variants, has since been modified by its owners in a thousand different ways, as the Levitts always intended it should. (And, if it is not sacrilegious to say, Richard Norman Shaw used a similar limited range of house types in his model London suburb at Bedford Park.) The trees have grown almost to maturity, softening the harshness of the original townscape as it appears in the old pictures.

But the residential streets are slightly too long and slightly too wide and slightly too straight, so – despite the variations – the overall result is monotonous and vapid. And the shopping center – developed as a commercial strip along the Hempstead Turnpike that bisects the development – is a logistical and aesthetic disaster. The commuters have insufficient road access on to the main highway, so their cars back up; and once there, they come in conflict with the commercial traffic. The visual quality is the worst kind of 1950s American roadside goop; the whole area cries out for the kind of planned commercial mall that in the 1960s and 1970s the Americans did so often and so successfully. So as a piece of planning Levittown is for the most part inoffensive, only occasionally plain bad. What it lacks is any kind of imagination or visual delight, such as the best planned suburbs in their different ways all offered. It is not bad, but it could be better.

It was and is also rigidly segregated by age, income, and race. Those who came here were overwhelmingly young married couples in the lower-middle income range, and without exception they were white: as late as 1960, Levittown had not a single black, and in the mid-1980s it did not have conspicuously many. As the elder

Levitt put it, "We can solve a housing problem, or we can try to solve a racial problem. But we cannot combine the two."[125] So Levittown and all its countless imitators were homogeneous places: like lived with like. And, as places like St Louis eloquently showed, a large part of the suburban flight from the city was white flight: here, as elsewhere, the blacks were coming from the countryside to the city, the whites were simultaneously leaving the city for the suburbs.[126]

The question will be asked and should be asked: what has all this to do with planning? Does a place like Levittown belong in a history of city planning at all? Insofar as Long Island had both planners and plans, then – at least in a formal sense – it does. But Gottdiener's exhaustive analysis suggests that in practice Long Island's planners had little power: "The decisions made by the politicians, speculators and housing developers lead to the same land-use pattern," he concludes, "as would result from no planning or zoning."[127] This leads him to ask, "if planners do not implement land-use decisions nor guide directly social growth in our society, we are left with the intriguing question – what, then, do planners do?"[128] His answer is that they produce plans: "The planning process, as it is usually practiced in the society, makes planners advisory bystanders to decisions that are being carried out elsewhere – by political leaders and private businessmen";[129] their ideas – whether on physical matters, or on social – find little favor among the majority of white middle-class suburban residents, who would like yet more low-density suburban sprawl. Which, after all, is hardly surprising.

Suburbia: The Great Debate

But – here, or elsewhere – the planners had some vocal people on their side; while those who built the suburbs, and those who lived in them, were either too preoccupied or too non-voluble to defend them. So, as it burgeoned, American suburbia came to be almost universally vilified in the public prints. What condemned it was the fact that it failed to conform to traditional – that is to say, European – notions of urbanity. Here are three representative critiques:

> In every department, form disintegrated: except in its heritage from the past, the city vanished as an embodiment of collective art and technics. And where, as in North America, the loss was not alleviated by the continued presence of great monuments from the past and persistent habits of social living, the result was a raw, dissolute environment and a narrow, constricted, and baffled social life.[130]

> Sprawl is bad aesthetics; it is bad economics. Five acres are being made to do the work of one, and do it very poorly. This is bad for the farmers, it is bad for communities, it is

[125] Quoted in Jackson, K., 1985, 241.
[126] Montgomery, 1985, 236.
[127] Gottdiener, 1977, 111.
[128] Gottdiener, 1977, 116.
[129] Gottdiener, 1977, 143.
[130] Mumford, 1938, 8.

bad for industry, it is bad for utilities, it is bad for the railroads, it is bad for the recreation groups, it is bad even for the developers.[131]

The question is, shall we have "slurbs," or shall we plan to have attractive communities which can grow in an orderly way while showing the utmost respect for the beauty and fertility of our landscape? If present trends continue, we shall have slurbs.[132]

Many points of attack recur here: waste of land, increased commute times, higher service costs, lack of parkland. But the central criticism is that the suburbs lack *form*. As usual, Mumford puts it best, in his appreciation of the garden-city alternative:

A modern city, no less than a medieval town ... must have a definite size, form, boundary. It was no longer to be a mere sprawl of houses along an indeterminate avenue that moved towards infinity and ended suddenly in a swamp.[133]

Ian Nairn, similarly, criticized the suburban landscape for the fact that "Each building is treated in isolation, nothing binds it to the next one," for "togetherness in the landscape or townscape, like the coexistence of opposites, is essential."[134]

The interesting fact is that the intellectual counter-attack, when it finally came, originated from the American West. James E. Vance, a Berkeley geographer, argued for the San Francisco Bay Area that

It is fashionable, if extremely trite, to refer to the urban area as a shapeless sprawl, as a cancer, as an unrelieved evil ... The erroneous notion that no such structure exists must result from a failure to study the dynamics of urban growth, or possibly from the desire to put forward a doctrine of what is "right" or "good" in urban growth.[135]

And Robert Riley similarly defended the "new" cities of the American Southwest, like Houston, Dallas, and Phoenix:

The new city has been damned simply because it is different ... The planning proposals made for these cities – and, largely, too, for Eastern megalopolises – are based on nothing more or less than channeling growth back into a form that we recognize as the only true city – the traditional city.[136]

Taking up the case for the defense, Melvin Webber of Berkeley argued,

I contend that we have been searching for the wrong grail, that the values associated with the desired urban structure do not reside in the spatial structure per se. One pattern and its internal land use form is superior to another only as it better serves to

[131]   Whyte, 1958, 117.
[132]   Wood and Heller, 1962, 13.
[133]   Mumford, 1938, 397.
[134]   Nairn, 1965, 13.
[135]   Vance, 1964, 68–9.
[136]   Riley, 1967, 21.

Figure 9.7   The Las Vegas Strip. The ultimate highway strip city; the signs are the true town-scape; the buildings are reduced to decorated sheds surrounded by the vast spaces of the parking lots. *Source*: © Peter Horree/Alamy.

accommodate ongoing spatial processes and to further the nonspatial ends of the political community. I am flatly rejecting the contention that there is an overriding universal spatial or physical aesthetic of urban form.[137]

New communications technologies, he argued, had broken down the age-old connection between community and propinquity: the urban place was being replaced by the nonplace urban realm.[138] Later in the decade, Reyner Banham wrote his appreciative essay on Los Angeles;[139] three years after that, Robert Venturi and Denise Scott Brown published their celebrated exercise in architectural iconoclasm, boldly proclaiming across its dust jacket, "A Significance for A&P Parking Lots, or *Learning from Las Vegas* ... Billboards are Almost All Right."[140] The battle lines could not be more clearly drawn: the West Coast had at last reasserted itself against the traditions of Europe.

The defection of Venturi, one of America's most distinguished architects, was especially significant. For he and his colleagues were passionately arguing that the roadside civilization of American suburbia, most exuberantly exemplified by the

---

[137]   Webber, 1963, 52.
[138]   Webber, 1964b, passim.
[139]   Banham, 1971.
[140]   Venturi *et al.*, 1972.

great neon-lit Strip at Las Vegas, should no longer be judged by the functionalist criteria that had ruled ever since the triumph of the international style in the 1930s. "Learning from the existing landscape," they began, "is a way of being revolutionary for an architect. Not the obvious way, which is to tear down Paris and begin again, as Corbusier suggested in the 1920s, but another, more tolerant way; that is, to question how we look at things."[141] They studied Las Vegas "as a phenomenon of architectural communication";[142] because people now moved in cars at high speeds and often in complex patterns, a whole new architecture of signs had arisen to guide and to persuade: "the graphic sign in space has become the architecture of this landscape,"[143] while the building itself is set back, half hidden – like most of the environment – by parked cars:

> The A&P parking lot is a current phase in the evolution of vast space since Versailles. The space that divides high-speed highway and low, sparse buildings produces no enclosure and little direction. To move through a piazza is to move through high enclosing forms. To move through this landscape is to move over vast expansive texture: the megastructure of the commercial landscape … Because the spatial relationships are made by symbols more than by forms, architecture in this landscape becomes symbol in space rather than form in space. Architecture defines very little. The big sign and the little building is the rule of Route 66.[144]

This analysis, notice, represents the perfect analogue at the micro- or urban-design scale of the Berkeley geographer-planners' argument at the wider urban-structural scale: the new landscape is not worse, it is different; it cannot be appreciated and should not be judged by the traditional rules, but by its own.

The result, for international architecture, was cataclysmic: *Learning from Vas Vegas* is one of the distinct breakpoints that mark the end of the modern architectural movement and its displacement by postmodernism, with its new stress on architecture as symbolic communication.[145] For the student of urbanism, it likewise marked a revolution: henceforth, the artifacts of roadside civilization were worthy of study for their own sake. So, by the mid-1980s, a scholarly treatise could trace the evolution of the 1920s motor court into the 1930s motel and finally into the 1950s motor hotel; this last mutation represented by the historic first Holiday Inn, developed by Kemmons Wilson and the prefabricated home-builder Wallace E. Johnson in Memphis, Tennessee, in 1952.[146] Or it could analyze the evolution of the fast-food outlet from the White Castle chain started by Edgar Ingram and Walter Anderson at Kansas City in 1921, via Howard Johnson's pioneering efforts in Massachusetts in 1929–30 and the historic McDonalds drive-in outlet at San Bernardino, California,

[141] Venturi *et al.*, 1972, 0 [*sic*].
[142] Venturi *et al.*, 1972, 0 [*sic*].
[143] Venturi *et al.*, 1972, 9.
[144] Venturi *et al.*, 1972, 10.
[145] Jencks, 1981, 45.
[146] Liebs, 1985, 182–5.

Figure 9.8 The first Holiday Inn. Memphis, Tennessee, 1952: the birth of the roadside chain. Three years later came the first standardized, franchised McDonalds outlet, in Des Plaines, Illinois. *Source*: Holiday Inn/IHG.

in 1948, to their standard design of 1952, first marketed nationally by Ray Kroc at Des Plaines, Illinois, in 1955.[147] Such work revealed just how long and rich this tradition of roadside architecture had been, making it the more remarkable that previously no one had possessed the sensibility or the energy to see or to analyze the landscape in front of them.

But in many ways, at least initially, the revolution failed to happen in the place where it might most logically be expected to happen: Los Angeles commercial design was conservative in the way it adapted to the car and the highway. The cover photograph of Longstreth's history of Los Angeles commercial architecture, *City Center to Regional Mall*, shows West Seventh Street in downtown, in 1926. The sidewalks are crowded with shoppers and the trolleys share the street comfortably enough with the cars, controlled by a solitary policeman. Still, downtown dominated retailing and other business.[148] But already congestion and parking were

---

[147] Liebs, 1985, 185, 202, 206–8, 212–13; Schlosser, 2001, 34.
[148] Longstreth, 1997, 32, 34.

bringing problems. The first big change came with the Dyas department store in Hollywood of 1927–8 and, almost simultaneously, the transformation of Wilshire, with Bullock's.[149] By the end of World War Two, it was already clear that downtown played a minor role: even in 1948, against 30% of regional sales in 1929, it had a mere 11%. And in the retail sales boom that followed – a 50% rise, the fastest in the nation, to 1954 – it could just not adapt.[150]

But at first, this dispersed shopping took a very traditional linear form, bringing congestion to the suburbs; even the supermarket, universal by the mid-1930s, was built away from existing centers, but with a traditional street front and with parking treated as a residue, tucked away at the side. On Miracle Mile, as in the classic case of Bullock's Wilshire, developers and boosters preferred a "metropolitan" image, simultaneously skyscraper and dispersed linear city; it presented a shop front to the street, to retain the "metropolitan illusion" from the car, while parking was relegated to the rear.[151] It provided the model for countless more modest suburban retail precincts of the 1930s and 1940s, in which street facades were emphasized: "On the whole, merchants showed a persistent reluctance to abandon their traditional sidewalk orientation."[152]

It was the fast-food merchandisers, not the retailers, who set the pace. Slowly, from the 1930s, merchants began to set back buildings behind parking lots, or even to put the buildings right at the rear of the lots. They created what Chester H. Liebs has called "Architecture for Speed-Reading": buildings that conveyed instant imagery to the passing motorist, through huge glass walls and self-advertising vertical pylons. In the coffee shops and filling stations of the late 1940s came "exaggerated modern," with huge areas of glazing, to draw attention inside, but also with exaggerated "airplane" or "parabolic" roofs. And thus developed the classic Los Angeles roadside forms, a new landscape of cantilevered plate-glass walls and golden arches.[153] As the critic Alan Hess describes it:

> The mobile car and the immobile building had slowly been woven into one seamless landscape. Bob's Big Boy gave you a picture window of the strip; Henry's gave you a patio on the strip; Biff's brought the car almost smack into the middle of the restaurant.[154]

In this form, "the car and the architecture of the car culture constituted a popular aesthetic of kinetics, symbols, structure, forms and experiment, and a new urban space that flowed freely from the driver's seat to the coffee shop counter."[155] The cars of the late 1950s, with their flowing lines, are of the same ilk as the coffee shops and

[149]   Longstreth, 1997, 43, 58–9, 86–9, 112–27.
[150]   Longstreth, 1997, 214–15, 218, 223.
[151]   Longstreth, 1992, 142–3, 150–2.
[152]   Longstreth, 1992, 152.
[153]   Langdon, 1986, 61–2, 66, 84–5, 115; Liebs, 1985, 14–15, 39, 44, 61–2.
[154]   Hess, 1992, 173.
[155]   Hess, 1992, 167.

hamburger stands: huge areas of glass turn round corners, above which the roof floats in space.[156]

But until the late 1940s, this revolution had little impact on Los Angeles retailing. The great breakthrough was the Crenshaw Center of 1947 on Crenshaw Boulevard, independent and with ground-level parking for 2,500 cars, although still transitional in having both a street and a parking lot frontage.[157] The next turning-point was Lakewood Center (1950–3) near Long Beach, one of the earliest regional shopping centers in the United States, offering 12,000 parking spaces.[158] Los Angeles was of course not unique in developing the new form, but it flourished here.[159] The regional mall became the ultimate expression of the revolution in retailing: it balanced the needs of parking against the needs of shoppers, with the aim of distancing the shoppers from their cars and making the mall a world in itself.[160] Southern California became one of the great testing-grounds for the new form.[161]

Yet, even then, the innate conservatism of the local business community frustrated innovation. Clarence Stein was a great advocate, though ironically his design for Los Angeles was never built. Victor Gruen was more successful nationally, and can be credited with the cluster form around a dominant department store, but he never built a major scheme here either. Department stores were the key players, establishing anchor stores of the new malls, which for the first time were quite dissociated from residential areas: the very obverse of the true community centers that Stein or Gruen had envisaged.[162] Along the boulevards that the subdividers had created in the 1920s and 1930s, there came a basic change in urban form:

> The boulevard … became, as it were, the commercial strip, a much more loosely organized panoply in which open space tended to dominate and free-standing signs often assumed a more important role than buildings as the means by which the motorist's attention was secured.[163]

But as the commercial architects stood traditional urban forms and designs on their heads, the great intellectual reversal had begun with a whole series of studies from American social scientists, fundamentally questioning many of the basic assumptions that had underlain the previous criticisms of the suburbs and the suburban way of life. Particularly important were those from the sociologists. During the 1950s, several classic works of mainstream American urban sociology – Riesman's *The Lonely Crowd*, Whyte's *The Organization Man* – had reinforced the stereotype of the suburb as a place of boring homogeneity, in which all individuality was

[156]   Hess, 1992, 167, 172.
[157]   Longstreth, 1997, 230–3.
[158]   Longstreth, 1992, 152.
[159]   Longstreth, 1997, 271.
[160]   Longstreth, 1997, 308.
[161]   Longstreth, 1997, 312.
[162]   Longstreth, 1997, 313, 320–31, 349–50.
[163]   Longstreth, 1992, 152.

progressively eroded away and rich human interaction was lacking; suburbanization, the inference clearly ran, would eventually destroy most of what was valuable
in the culture of cities.[164] To test these assumptions, Herbert Gans went to live in
Levittown, New Jersey, for an extended period. His book, which appeared in 1967,
predictably triggered critical reviews in East Coast papers. For Gans discovered that
the conventional wisdom was a myth:

> The findings ... suggest that the distinction between urban and suburban ways of
> living postulated by the critics (and by some sociologists as well) is more imaginary
> than real. Few changes can be traced to the suburban qualities of Levittown, and the
> sources that did cause change, like the house, the population mix, and newness, are not
> distinctively suburban. Moreover ... when suburbs are compared to the large urban
> residential areas beyond the downtown and inner districts, culture and social structure
> are virtually the same among people of similar age and class. Young lower middle class
> people in these areas live much like their peers in the suburbs, but quite unlike older,
> upper middle class ones, in either urban or suburban neighborhoods.[165]

The Levittowners, Gans found, refused to fit the labels that earlier sociologists had
tried to pin on them:

> Levittowners are not really members of the national society, or for that matter, of a
> mass society. They are not apathetic conformists ripe for takeover by a totalitarian elite
> or corporate merchandiser; they are not conspicuous consumers and slaves to sudden
> whims of fashion, they are not even organization men or particularly other-directed
> personalities ... Their culture may be less subtle and sophisticated than that of the
> intellectual, their family life less healthy than that advocated by psychiatrists, and their
> politics less thoughtful and democratic than the political philosophers' – yet all these
> are superior to what prevailed among the working and lower middle classes of past
> generations.[166]

Gans's conclusions massively reinforced those of another sociologist, Bennett Berger,
of blue-collar workers in a California suburb. He too had found that these typical
suburbanites did not behave as earlier investigations of suburbia had suggested they
should: they were not socially or geographically mobile, they were not joiners or
belongers, and their neighbors were people like themselves.[167] The fact was that
these other studies had analyzed relatively unusual upper-middle-class communities, or had overstressed upper-middle-class features in mixed communities.
Typical suburbanites, those who inhabited the new mass-produced suburbs, simply
did not share the same concerns; they would be living much the same lives, with
much the same patterns of social relationships, whether they lived in areas labeled as

164   Riesman, 1950, 132–4; Whyte, 1956, 46–7.
165   Gans, 1967a, 288.
166   Gans, 1967a, 417.
167   Berger, 1960, 15–25, 58–9, 65.

urban or in areas labeled as suburban. Thus, sociologist-planners had hopelessly exaggerated the effect of the physical character of the urban milieu upon people's lifestyles. In Gans's conclusion:

> The planner has only limited influence over social relationships. Although the site planner can create propinquity, he can only determine which houses are to be adjacent. He can thus affect visual contacts and initial social contacts among their occupants, but he cannot determine the intensity or quality of the relationships. This depends on the characteristics of the people involved.[168]

True, the character of an area – its social homogeneity, or otherwise – could be affected by planning. But only within very narrow limits; in a society like the American one, the market will be the main determinant and the customers will register their own preferences there. Above all, planners must beware of trying to impose their own value systems upon people with quite different ones: particularly, if they believed that long commuter trips and traffic congestion are to be avoided at all costs, and that higher densities would be better because they would cut commuter times and save land and increase urbanity, they must be aware that most suburbanites will just not agree.[169] In other words, in attacking the essential features of post-1945 American suburbia, they were simply expressing their own class prejudices.

Thus spoke the sociologist. A few years later, one of America's most distinguished land economists, Marion Clawson, made his own investigation of the costs of suburban sprawl. He gave his verdict:

> It is impossible to judge suburban land conversion simply and unequivocally – to say that it is "good" or "bad" or describe it by using some other single and unqualified term. The process is much too complicated for that.[170]

On the plus side, it had been a process of extraordinary vitality, producing millions of new homes and hundreds of shopping districts, and thus contributing to national economic growth; it had produced a lot of rather good housing and of rather pleasant neighborhoods; and the dispersed nature of the whole decision-making process had avoided big blunders.[171] On the negative side, the costs of scatteration had made house prices needlessly high; much land had simply gone to waste, needlessly, and might remain thus for a long time; and the results had been less aesthetically pleasing than many buyers might have liked, for they had little or no choice.[172] But the most serious criticism, according to Clawson, was that the whole package had proved too expensive for a full half of the population: thus the urban population had

[168] Gans, 1961a, 139.
[169] Gans, 1961b, 293.
[170] Clawson, 1971, 317.
[171] Clawson, 1971, 319.
[172] Clawson, 1971, 319–20.

become increasingly stratified by race, income, and occupation. Of course, Clawson was quick to admit, some of this segregation arose from deeper social and economic forces; but the suburban development process had certainly contributed.[173]

Thus Clawson's economic verdict put a marginal gloss on Berger's and Gans's sociological one: yes, Americans did make their free choices in the marketplace, and thus obtained approximately what they wanted, more effectively and efficiently than via a centrally planned system; but no, the process was not completely efficient in doing this, and could be improved so as to generate a slightly better housing package at a slightly lower cost. There was a more-than-marginal point too: half of all Americans were shut off from the process altogether because they were too poor (and, in some cases, because they were black, which amounted to being poor). But one could well retort that, at bottom, this was a problem outside the province of the urban planner: the problem of the poor was that they lacked money. If they had it, Clawson affirmed, they would go and get exactly what the more fortunate half of the population had: a stake in suburbia. Planning and related forms of public intervention, then, could improve the process somewhat; but fundamentally, it gave the mass of people what they wanted.

Controlling Suburban Growth in Europe

That conclusion was of more than strictly American interest. For, in varying degrees, European governments after World War Two had succeeded in controlling and regulating the suburban tide to a degree that would have been unthinkable in the United States. By the mid-1960s, that was even evident to transatlantic air travellers from their vantage point 7 miles up: traveling west, they would be bemused by the scale of the development, by the apparently endless sprawl of the suburbs in the east-coast megalopolis, by the vast network of freeways that linked them; traveling east, they would be equally surprised by the relative puniness of the development, by its toy-town-like quality, by the planned precision of the almost geometrical break between town and country, by the apparent absence of agricultural decay in the fringe areas around the suburbs. And all this would be true, with slight variations, in Britain, the Netherlands, the Federal Republic of Germany, or Scandinavia.[174]

The question, of course, was what costs and what benefits these tighter, neater systems had conferred on the people who lived under them. For the perpetrators of the conventional planning wisdom, of course, the answer was self-evident; but in the light of the American questioning of that wisdom, it was a question worth investigating. There was no better comparison to make than America versus Britain. For, ever since 1947, Britain had operated an extremely close control over new development: the historic Town and Country Planning Act of that year (Chapter 4) had effectively nationalized the right to develop land, and thereafter the local

---

[173] Clawson, 1971, 321.
[174] Hall, 1968, 100.

planning authorities had used the new powers to contain suburban growth around the cities, employing green-belt restrictions to divert the pressures into more distant small and medium-sized towns. So, in parallel with the Clawson study, a British team worked to analyze the operation and the impacts of this containment policy.

Their results, published in 1973, cast yet more doubt on the conventional, comfortable picture. Land-use planning in postwar England, they concluded, had produced three main effects. The first was *containment*: the amount of land converted from rural to urban uses had been minimized and also compacted. A second, somewhat perverse, result was what the authors called *suburbanization*: the growing spatial separation of the new residential areas from the main employment centers. A third impact was even more perverse, in that it was totally undesired by anyone except perhaps a small body of speculators: it was *the inflation of land and property values*, on a scale never previously witnessed.[175]

Containment, the first effect, worked in various ways. Green belts around the conurbations and the larger freestanding towns had effectively stopped their further peripheral growth; beyond these green belts, development had been concentrated in small towns and villages, especially in the least attractive parts of each county; typically, densities had been kept up; the conurbation authorities had responded by building public housing that was dense and high, at any rate in comparison with the kinds of housing they had built before the 1939–45 war.[176] The leapfrogging pattern of urban development, so clearly evident in Clawson's American study, had been avoided.

Suburbanization had meant that the new residential developments were nearly all farther from employment opportunities than equivalent developments of the 1930s or any earlier decade; similarly, they were more distant from the higher-level shopping, entertainment, educational, and cultural facilities. So journeys, especially commuter trips, had become longer. This in part reflected the preference of planners for maintaining a traditional, centralized urban structure, in part the desire of city politicians to maintain the strongest possible economic base. But sociological study showed that the new suburbanites were well satisfied with their lifestyle and particularly with the long commuter trips that this involved; their main desire, indeed, was to move out farther into the country.[177]

The rise in land values had been far in excess of the general salary or price level, and this undoubtedly had made new housing more expensive in real terms than in the 1930s. The developers had adjusted by using smaller sites, building at higher densities – particularly for cheaper housing – and reducing the quality of the houses below the levels that had become mandatory in the public sector. Since many builders also responded by switching into the higher-priced end of the market, which the planning authorities preferred to see anyway, the result was less housing choice at the lower end. In this respect, the research concluded, British policies had

[175]   Hall *et al.*, 1973, II, 393–4.
[176]   Hall *et al.*, 1973, II, 394–7.
[177]   Hall *et al.*, 1973, II, 397–9.

been far less successful than American ones in accommodating the demands of a more affluent, more space-using lifestyle.[178]

The interesting point, as always, was who gained and who lost. The ruralites, especially the well-heeled ones, were the clear gainers: planning, by establishing a polite English version of apartheid, simply preserved the status quo and thus their comfortable lifestyle. The more affluent new suburbanites did well enough, though at a cost; the less affluent ones did much more badly, in terms of cramped space and relatively high costs. Since they were more likely to be one-car families, the burden of commuting might also be greater for them – though on that score, the research recorded few complaints.[179]

The group that had done worst, in the view of the team, was the people left in the cities. Those who had moved into public-sector housing had good-quality homes, better equipped than the poorer owner-occupiers; but they were often forced to live at high densities and in high-rise blocks, which many did not like, in comparison with their equivalents of 30 and 40 years earlier. And the low-income private tenant, living in substandard accommodation, had done worst of all. Thus the overall effect of the policies, in income terms, had been perversely regressive: those with the most had gained the most, and vice versa.[180] The team's analysis concluded:

> None of this was in the minds of the founding fathers of the planning system. They cared very much for the preservation and the conservation of rural England, to be sure. But that was only part of a total package of policies, to be enforced in the interests of all by beneficent central planning. It was certainly not the intention of the founders that people should lead cramped lives in homes destined for premature slumdom, far from urban services or jobs; or that city dwellers should live in blank cliffs of flats, far from the ground, without access to playspace for their children. Somewhere along the way, a great ideal was lost, a system distorted and the great mass of the people betrayed.[181]

When the British and American researchers compared their results, they concluded that both planning systems had produced inconsistent and perverse outcomes. The tighter British system and the looser American system had both produced urban structures which few people had actually chosen, and few would have wanted if given the choice.[182] In both countries, the rich had done well out of urban development while the poor had done badly;[183] in both, the poor were condemned to inferior housing in the older inner cities. But for the great middle group, the verdict for the two countries was almost the opposite: in Britain they were housed too densely, in small houses almost certainly destined to become slums; in America they were housed too sprawlingly, with wasted land that benefitted no one, and with

---

[178]   Hall *et al.*, 1973, II, 399–405.
[179]   Hall *et al.*, 1973, II, 406–7.
[180]   Hall *et al.*, 1973, II, 407–8.
[181]   Hall *et al.*, 1973, II, 433.
[182]   Clawson and Hall, 1973, 260.
[183]   Clawson and Hall, 1973, 266–7.

consequently higher servicing costs.[184] In both countries, however, land-use controls had made land for suburban development artificially scarce and had therefore aided the land speculator. So, in both countries, ordinary people would have benefitted either from a much looser land-use planning regime, or from a much tighter one; what was not satisfactory was the halfway house.[185]

Which country then did worse? Was it better to live in Britain with its rather elaborate system of urban planning, which had produced results different from those its sponsors intended, or in the United States, where city planning never really promised much, and never delivered much? The answer, the study concluded, depended on your values. If you put a high value on giving a large section of the population the material goods they want through market mechanisms, then you must conclude that American suburbia, for all its inefficiency and its occasional ugliness, is greatly superior to the cramped and costly British equivalent. If you put a greater value on protection by society of its land and the natural resources that go with it, you will probably elect for the British system of effective land-use planning. The American policy had been populist, the British policy more elitist.[186]

Since that conclusion, and especially during the 1980s, the British system has moved steadily in the direction of the American: the stress there too is increasingly on setting the land market free. But the paradox remains, and is bound to do so in any advanced country where different social and income groups obtained bundles of goods and bads from collective political action. Many people in Britain are still deeply committed to the preservation of the countryside and the containment of the cities, and they continue to be well organized in their rural shires and districts. Thus, even on the right wing of the political spectrum, there is a continuing built-in contradiction between the desire to let the developer serve market needs, and the need to palliate deep-held local fears and prejudices; a contradiction well seen in the 1986 statement by Nicholas Ridley, Secretary of State for the Environment and a leading Tory free-marketeer, that the green belt was sacrosanct in his hands. In the United States this balance is different; but there, too, nothing is clearer than the rise of the anti-growth movement in certain regions such as California, with results – in higher land and property prices – very similar to those observed in Britain.[187] So, perhaps, both countries were moving slowly and hesitantly towards each other.

Squaring the Circle: Planning the European Metropolis

Long before all that, of course – as already seen in Chapter 5 – European planners had grappled with the problem of reconciling the car and the city. Over the years from 1943 to 1965, several of Europe's capital cities produced plans that, in their

---

184 Clawson and Hall, 1973, 269.
185 Clawson and Hall, 1973, 269.
186 Clawson and Hall, 1973, 271.
187 Dowall, 1984, 132–3, 168–70.

different ways, suggested radical alternatives to America's city on the highway. Given the very different background of the European urban experience, that perhaps was not remarkable. What was more remarkable was that the plans were actually implemented.

Already, in his London plans of 1943 and 1944, Abercrombie had sought to use new urban highways not merely to alleviate congestion, but to help define the identity of the neighborhoods of the giant metropolis; here, he had drawn freely on the ideas of a Scotland Yard Assistant Commissioner, Alker Tripp, who had developed the idea of the residential precinct from which extraneous through traffic – not, at that stage, all traffic – would be excluded.[188] Already, too, he had boldly used the Howard–Unwin vision of the garden-city to plan new towns where the conflict between car and city would be less pervasive. For him, and for other planners of that generation, the conflict was evident, but was capable of effective and even elegant resolution.

The Stockholm Alternative[189]

Stockholm in 1950 still looked and felt like a small city: a metropolitan area, including suburbs, of only about one million people,[190] in which a 20-minute walk from the center would bring a visitor to greenery, and a 20-minute tram ride would reach a terminus at the edge of birch woods and lakes. Yet it had some of the worst housing conditions in Europe.[191] It had built English-style garden cities at Enskede (1908) and Äppelviken (1913), and followed with further garden cities, like Enskede Gård; but they had become white-collar communities. To provide more affordable housing, in 1926 the city had started a self-build housing program. The resulting areas, built by ordinary working Stockholmers – Olovsund, Norra Ängby, and Tallkrogen – still have a special charm.[192] And, side by side with the self-build scheme, the city developed a public housing program: long three-story *lamella* blocks. They were designed for maximum sun exposure, but architects criticized them for their tedium and lack of community facilities.[193]

Then, in major national decisions – in 1942, in 1945–7, and in 1958 – the Social Democrats determined to develop a very deliberate public housing policy, creating "the largest state-controlled, more or less self-contained economic sector in any Western country."[194] It would also win voters, of course.[195] Legislation in 1947, 1953,

188   Tripp, 1938; 1942; Forshaw and Abercrombie, 1943, 50–2.
189   This section is based on Hall, 1998, Ch. 26.
190   Anon, 1989, 12; Chandler and Fox, 1974, 337–8, 377.
191   Headey, 1978, 50; Holm, 1957, 61; Jenkins, 1969, 65; Johansson, 1975, 44; Milner, 1990, 196–7; Popenoe, 1977, 36.
192   Childs, 1936, 94–5; Johansson, 1975, 44–5; Pass, 1973, 33; Sidenbladh, 1981, 6.
193   Hall, 1991b, 211; Pass, 1973, 32, 34; Sjöström, 1975, 106.
194   Headey, 1978, 44.
195   Headey, 1978, 92; Heclo and Madsen, 1987, 220–2.

and 1967 essentially stopped private development save of individual houses, and gave municipalities a right of first refusal on all land sales.[196] Housing would be primarily provided by local government, supplemented by cooperatives.[197] From 1945 to the mid-1970s, 45% of new housing in Sweden was built by public authorities, usually by non-profit housing corporations, 20% by cooperatives, and only 35% was privately built. By 1970, 35% of all units were owner-occupied, 30% privately rented, 14% cooperative, and 21% public housing.[198]

At the start, the basic fact was sheer basic shortage of housing. On top of the accumulated deficiencies of the past, people were pouring into the cities: city-dwellers formed 55% of the total Swedish population in 1940, 65% in 1950, 73% in 1960, and 81% in 1970, one of the most rapid urbanization processes in all Europe.[199] So the government adopted extraordinarily high building targets: 650,000 units for 1956–65, and the so-called Million Programme for 1965–74: 1,005,578 dwellings were completed, 37% by the Municipal Housing Corporations, whose share of multi-family housing production rose from 53 to 68%. The program stressed large apartment complexes, generally in high-rise blocks, in outlying satellite towns catering for mixed classes and incomes.[200]

Central here was the fact that, from 1904 on, the city of Stockholm had begun to buy large tracts of land towards the city limits and even beyond them: eventually, it owned about 70% of all the land within its own limits, and large tracts outside. In the late 1970s, 27% of the 1.6 million acres of Stockholm County were in public ownership, the largest land bank of any metropolitan area in Western Europe.[201] Critically, in 1912 it bought land at Farsta, and in 1927 and 1931 at Vällingby; they were later brought within the city limits, as part of a series of annexations – in 1913, 1916, 1948, and 1961.[202]

Within the city administration, a key role was played by Yngve Larsson: a longtime local politician, not of the Social Democratic Party but of the Liberal Party, who took responsibility for City Planning in 1940. In 1944 he replaced the existing city planner, Albert Lilienberg, by Sven Markelius; he later said he wanted "a prominent architect, trained in planning and thoroughly abreast of the latest ideas."[203] In 1954, Markelius's deputy, Göran Sidenbladh, took over as City Planner and also became City Architect, the two posts being combined.[204]

---

[196] Åström, 1967, 61; Elander and Strömberg, 1992, 11; Esping-Andersen, 1985, 189; Sidenbladh, 1968, 77; Strong, 1979, 65; 1971, 24, 58.
[197] Esping-Andersen, 1985, 189; Headey, 1978, 45; Strong, 1971, 24, 26; Tilton, 1991, 121.
[198] Elander, 1989, 3; Headey, 1978, 45; Jenkins, 1969, 65; Lundqvist, 1984, 216; Strong, 1971, 26, 35; Tilton, 1991, 121.
[199] Esping-Andersen, 1985, 187; Headey, 1978, 47; Heclo and Madsen, 1987, 214.
[200] Esping-Andersen, 1985, 188; Headey, 1978, 82; Lundqvist, 1984, 228.
[201] Pass, 1973, 32; Strong, 1979, 43.
[202] Childs, 1936, 93; Larsson, 1977, 630; Pass, 1973, 29, 62; Popenoe, 1977, 38; Sidenbladh, 1968, 76; Strong, 1979, 47–50; 1971, 41; Stockholm Information Board, 1972, 22; Goldfield, 1979, 148–9.
[203] Pass, 1973, 111, 115; Sidenbladh, 1981, 562.
[204] Pass, 1973, 40–1, 64, 115, 118.

Central to the planning of the city was a 1928 proposal to reconstruct the city's central business district, at the southern end of the northern mainland, immediately behind the parliament building. In a 1946 revision, it included five uniform high-rise office towers, Hötorgs City, which eventually became as familiar a part of the Stockholm skyline as Ragnar Östberg's City Hall. The city politicians wanted to ensure that the city center would maintain its dominant role in the commerce of the city and indeed of the nation; there was a need to provide for larger retail units, and to cope with traffic congestion. A special *Lex Norrmalm*, passed in 1953, aided the process. This was the high-water mark of modernist planning: few protests were raised when, from 1951 to the end of the 1980s, more than 400 buildings, many in good condition, were demolished and replaced by about 100 new ones.[205]

On that basis, over seven long years, Markelius's team produced the 1952 General Plan for Stockholm. It was based on a projection that the population, then just under one million, could reach two million by the end of the century. It proposed new sub-urban satellites, each for 10,000–15,000 inhabitants, strung like beads along the lines of a new subway system. Within them, apartment blocks were to be built within 500 yards of the stations; single-family houses, constituting no more than 10–15% of housing units in each district, were to be built within 1,000 yards but no further. There would be traffic-free neighborhoods, on the Radburn principle. A group of suburban districts, serving 50,000–100,000 residents, would offer virtually a full range of urban services appropriate to a medium-sized town: theaters, restaurants, business offices, medical centers, libraries. Thus there would be a hierarchy of facilities and services: area centers for 50,000–100,000 people, district centers for 8,000–15,000 (later increased to 25,000 to improve service provision), and neighborhood centers for 4,000–7,000.[206]

The critical decision to build high-density apartment clusters was crucially influenced by the prior decision, in 1944, to build a full-scale subway, the *Tunnelbana*, rather than a light rail system. The first two lines, to Farsta and Vällingby, were completed and connected by 1957.[207] Each station on the subway was to generate enough traffic to make it self-supporting. That meant that the satellites were designed with high-density concentrations of flats for 10,000–15,000 people within 500 meters (1,650 feet) of each station, and medium-density areas of terrace houses, villas, and small cottages within 900 meters (3,000 feet), avoiding the need for expensive bus connections.[208] Markelius thought that single-family houses would be needed for families with children and, indeed, for those who wanted them:[209] multi-story housing was for

> a clientele, small families and bachelor households, less interested in those installations requiring space in planning than the advantages gained by building concentration – proximity to station, comfortable access to shops, restaurant, cinema, theater and other spare-time activities and to various kinds of collective household services.[210]

[205] Hall, 1991b, 232–3; Sidenbladh, 1981, 567; Stockholm, 1947.
[206] Pass, 1973, 65, 115; Popenoe, 1977, 37; Sidenbladh, 1968, 83, 86; Strong, 1971, 45.
[207] Sidenbladh, 1981, 565; 1968, 85; Stockholm, 1952, 303; Strong, 1971, 43, 63–4.
[208] Markelius, 1957, 25.
[209] Markelius, 1957, 26.
[210] Markelius, 1957, 26.

Thus, of Stockholm's investment in the subways – over one billion kronor, $200 million, down to the end of the 1960s – four-fifths was met by revenues, one-fifth from taxes.[211] But also relevant was that at the first satellite, Vällingby, the Stockholm Retail Trade Federation had a 3,300-square-meter shopping area raised to 20,000, and successfully argued for 20,000–25,000 residents to be housed within walking distance.[212]

It made sense at the time. In 1945, there were only 9 cars per 1,000 inhabitants in Stockholm; by the end of 1964 the figure was 190 per 1,000, and ownership was by then rising by 12% a year. Even so, in 1970, 45% of Stockholm's households had no car; only 7% had two or more cars. In 1971, 60% of all journeys to and from work in Greater Stockholm, 70% in the city, were by public transport.[213] For the others, there would be a high-capacity highway network, designed especially to provide for circumferential trips.[214]

The plan was also based on decentralizing employment. Each satellite was to be an "ABC community" with *Arbete, Bostad, Centrum* (workplace, dwelling, center): not merely a dormitory town, but an employment and community center. The inspiration was the London new towns. But Markelius recognized that his satellites had to be different:

> I studied the New Towns, of course, and with great interest, but the solution in Stockholm had to satisfy the special conditions of Stockholm. I have no feeling that Vällingby is copied from the New Towns, even though they were planned at about the same time and there are some general ideas they have in common.[215]

His answer, appropriately, was the same as that of May in Frankfurt, a city of similar size, in the 1920s: satellite towns. Markelius's outer suburban units – Vällingby of 1950–4, Farsta of 1953–61, Skärholmen of 1961–8, Tensta-Rinkeby of 1964–70 – are often inaccurately called new towns; they are not, if by that is meant the pure self-contained Howardian vision. They are part-commuter towns. But, by providing some jobs in the satellites, even if filled by commuters, Markelius argued that there would be a benefit because reverse commuters would balance the load on the subway.[216] In practice it did not work like that. The assumption was a rule of halves: half the working inhabitants would commute out of them, half the workforce were to be drawn in from elsewhere. But by 1965, only 24% of Vällingby residents worked locally; 76% commuted out. Most jobs were fueled by in-commuters, while the residents went out. Farsta did even worse: in 1965, only 15% of residents worked locally, 85% commuted out.[217]

By 1961, the Vällingby and Farsta satellites had been substantially completed on the ABC principle: the 13 units within them varied in population from 8,000 to

211   Popenoe, 1977, 44; Sidenbladh, 1968, 85; Strong, 1971, 42–3.
212   Ågren, 1975, 135; Hall, 1991b, 217; Pass, 1973, 123.
213   Popenoe, 1977, 39–40; Sidenbladh, 1968, 83–6.
214   Sidenbladh, 1965, 114–16; Stockholm Information Board, 1972, 35, 51–72.
215   Pass, 1973, 116.
216   Markelius, 1957, 24–5, 27.
217   Pass, 1973, 19, 25, 58; Sidenbladh, 1968, 84.

Figure 9.9 and **Figure 9.10**   Vällingby and Farsta, Stockholm's first two "B" level satellite town centers to be developed, with their inevitable standard features: pedestrian shopping mall, Tunnelbana (metro) station, high-density high-rise apartment blocks close by.

16,000. Nearly one-third of the dwellings were built by public housing corporations, almost one-third by cooperatives and similar non-profit-makers, a little less than one-third by private builders, and the remaining one-tenth consisted of one-family houses. About 95% of all dwellings were financed with public aid; and of course there was no upper income level for families housed there.[218]

Visited today, the satellites show variations on a theme, as their planners tried to learn from experience, but also as they compromised to meet the demands of the Million Programme. Vällingby's nine- to twelve-story point-blocks around the center, or the very long three- to six-story slab-blocks farther out,[219] are far from oppressive, as Thomas Hall argues; this first satellite

> differs from suburbs built ten years or so later, in that the houses are not yet so big or the production methods so rationalized as to disallow this freedom in forms and orientations. Vällingby also maintains a pleasant balance between built and open spaces: the houses are sufficiently close to one another to create spatial coherence and a certain atmosphere of "town", and yet they are scattered enough to retain something of the original topography and natural landscape.[220]

Vällingby took the form that was to be repeated in every subsequent case: a central, high-level shopping and service center, roughly equal to that found in one of Abercrombie's London new towns and serving 80,000–100,000 people, was supplemented by local district centers; all were connected by the subway; residential densities were highest around the major center, high around the local centers, progressively lower away from these centers, so as to bring the maximum number of people within walking distance of shops and services, implying that nearly everyone would be housed in apartment blocks. This standard prescription varied only slightly through the developments that followed, reflecting experience and changes in fashion: very high high-rises around an open pedestrian mall at Farsta, with three times the car-parking that had been provided at Vällingby; a tighter, more enclosed pedestrian mall and low-rise high-density apartments at Skärholmen with a further expansion of parking into a vast multi-story garage for 3,000 cars, the biggest in Scandinavia; an enclosed mall, with direct access into the subway station, at Mörby.[221]

The question that was becoming critical even by the late 1940s, reaching crisis point in the late 1950s, was where the city would find building land outside its boundaries. Stockholm reached its maximum population, 808,000, in 1960; thence it rapidly began to empty out, declining to only 661,000 by 1976. The suburbs rejected the pressures, leading by mid-1950 to deep rifts.[222] Finally, in 1959, city and county acceded to the *Lex Bollmora*: Stockholm could build outside its borders, but only when invited to do so. Over a few years, 10 agreements were reached between

[218]   Strong, 1971, 45.
[219]   Strong, 1971, 46.
[220]   Hall, 1991b, 220.
[221]   Stockholm Information Board, 1972, 52–71.
[222]   Anton, 1975, 40–5; Larsson, 1977, 636.

the city and eight suburban municipalities for 31,000 new units, 70% of which would be at the disposal of the city; suburban Social Democratic politicians accepted this because it gave them public housing.[223]

But these new suburbs – Tyresö, Huddinge, Järfälla – created new problems of disjointed transport. In December 1964, agreement was reached on a Greater Stockholm Traffic Association (Storstockholms Lokal-Trafikförbund, SL) and a private operating company to take over all services. Then, in June 1966, city and county agreed to establish the Greater Stockholm County Council; coming into existence in January 1971, it took over the responsibility for building and operating the *Tunnelbana*.[224]

The resulting developments were part of the Million Programme, under which 100,000 homes would be built each year for 10 years, an impressive goal considering that the total Swedish housing stock at that time was barely three million dwellings. Standardization and prefabrication were boosted by state support, which also assisted local authorities' land provision. The people in charge were ultimately well-meaning: as Thomas Hall concludes, they built what they thought people ought to have and could afford, without taking much interest in what they actually wanted. All the surveys showed that most people wanted to live in small houses, but this was largely ignored. Shortage of available land, and of municipal planning and development resources, combined with theoretical calculations of housing demand, simply failed to provide for single-family houses.[225]

Then, around 1970, the world that the Swedish Social Democrats had built began almost to fall apart: the economy, the welfare state, the housing and planning programs all quite suddenly and simultaneously began to show signs of system failure. And curiously, though the crises were indirectly linked, they had quite independent causes.

One crucial part was a housing and a planning crisis: the system, geared to maximum production, suddenly found itself overproducing in quantity and massively underproducing in quality; there was a completely unpredicted surplus of unlettable dwellings, and, worse, a problem of unlettable problem estates. In the newest satellites, built mainly on land acquired by the city outside its boundaries, the housing was completed at top speed, with little attention to the quality of the surrounding environment; much of it was industrialized, highly monotonous, and built at too high a density; services like transport were not ready; rents were high; occupants had no choice. Around 1970 came a quite sudden reaction against these newest satellites: first against Skärholmen, then against Tensta, part of the huge Järvafältet scheme, finally against the planning system itself.[226] Tensta in particular was a huge mistake: a vast apartment complex of concrete blocks, very monotonous, without adequate public transport and therefore difficult to commute from, with few social

---

[223]   Anton, 1975, 72, 74–5, 77, 86, 92, 95; Headey, 1978, 81.
[224]   Anton, 1975, 98–9, 101, 103, 105–9, 116–18, 121, 135.
[225]   Hall and Vidén, 2005, 323.
[226]   Anton, 1975, 204; Headey, 1978, 48; Karyd and Södersten, 1990, 174; Sjöström, 1975, 122.

services or commercial facilities. It presented a singularly unattractive image, and the vacant flats confirmed it.[227] Thomas Hall, the Swedish planning historian, has summed it up:

> As these standardized giants were assembled largely from prefabricated panels, all design considerations were abandoned. The overriding goal was development in large units and quick rational construction. The design of the setting in which these houses appeared was determined not by the needs of the future residents, but by the requirements of the cranes and lorries shuttling back and forth as building proceeded.[228]

They proved unattractive not merely to the critics, but to their prospective residents: they had high vacancy rates and a very high turnover. Their image continued to deteriorate: most long-stay residents were immigrants and problem families.

The result was market saturation and unlet housing: by 1975, there were 25,000 vacant units, most of them in the new developments; vacancies in public housing rose suddenly from 1.6% in 1970 to 13.4% in 1974, and there was much criticism of "megalomaniac" estates. At the end of 1978, the average vacancy rate on some estates reached 17%.[229] As one observer described it, "The problem families met the problem areas":[230] places like Tensta and Skärholmen became stigmatized as examples of "planning over people's heads."[231]

The mood of the mid-1970s is well described by Thomas Hall:

> There was a widespread belief that the age of the planner and developer was over. Modern Sweden had been built, and all that remained to do was maintenance, a certain amount of clearance and a little additional building.[232]

In consequence, even in this holy temple of city planning, the professionals' omniscience came to be challenged. The main drama focused on the redevelopment of the central business district of Lower Norrmalm. With a failure of growth and a change in public opinion, rebuilding came to a juddering halt. A 1975 city plan marked an almost complete stop to the idea of comprehensive redevelopment. But, in the process, many buildings were blighted.[233] The battle now extended to urban renewal in the older residential districts close to the center, where city officials fought a running battle with squatters.

But the criticism also came to extend to the satellites themselves; a new generation of architects and planners attacked them for being built too quickly, for sacrificing quality to quantity, for producing new slums. The volume of complaints from all

[227]   Goldfield, 1979, 150; Heclo and Madsen, 1987, 216.
[228]   Hall, 1991b, 225.
[229]   Daun, 1985, 3; Esping-Andersen, 1985, 188; Hall, 1991b, 225; Lundqvist, 1984, 222, 229; Strong, 1979, 80.
[230]   Sjöström, 1975, 122.
[231]   Sjöström, 1975, 122.
[232]   Hall, 1991b, 238.
[233]   Hall, 1991b, 234–6.

sides, reported in the media, grew deafening: "inhuman environments"; "brutal destroyers of the landscape"; "social disaster areas"; "architectural monstrosities"; "concrete jungles."[234] Especially, the satellite of Tensta – built in a hurry by industrialized building techniques – was execrated in the media as *en stora planering katastrof*: a great planning disaster.[235] The question, in the title of one article, became: How could it go so wrong?[236] Laying down how people ought to live, by central edict of the planning office, came to be seen as a form of liberal totalitarianism.

The politicians and the planners tried to learn from their mistakes. But the basic question was how collectivist ideology could respond to the varied and individual demands of an affluent society.[237] For, offered the choice, most Swedes overwhelmingly wanted to be owner-occupiers of single-family homes. And now they began to get them. Often the new suburbs were monotonous, reminiscent of the worst kind of American suburbia; but the demand was huge, and they sold easily.[238] Meanwhile, the surplus rental units went to anyone who would take them: to people with social problems, such as alcoholism[239]; and to immigrants from Yugoslavia, Greece, Turkey, and South America. Native Swedes felt uncomfortable; if they could, they migrated away to the new suburbs. As the new suburbs became marred by vandalism, graffiti, and signs of social breakdown, Swedes began to question their own model. It seemed as if an entire social experiment had suddenly soured.[240]

But one point, interestingly, the critics found it harder to make. All over the world, the ecological movement was then at its height. Indeed, a central point of conflict between the city and its critics, which in 1971 became a national *cause célèbre*, concerned the fate of a small bunch of elm trees in Kungsträdgården, a central Stockholm square.[241] In the aftermath of the energy crisis, here as elsewhere, the entire automobile culture was under attack; one early ecological movement – *Alternativ Stad*, founded in 1965 – campaigned for banning cars from the city altogether.[242] But Markelius had anticipated this conflict of affluence 30 years earlier, building a superb public transport system in advance of the advent of mass car ownership. In this respect, his grand design has stood the test of time: despite the critics, Stockholm works better, and has more effectively reconciled the conflict between car and urban environment for a longer period, than most other cities.

And the pilgrims still come in their reverent thousands to see them, and are duly impressed: by the standards of most other places, everything seems to work, everything is in place, everything is in the best of good taste; on the last subway line to be

---

[234]   Popenoe, 1977, 217–21.
[235]   Höjer *et al.*, 1977, 19.
[236]   Lindström, 1977, 203.
[237]   Goldfield, 1979, 152; Heclo and Madsen, 1987, 217.
[238]   Daun, 1985, 3; Goldfield, 1979, 153; Hall, 1991b, 229; Heclo and Madsen, 1987, 215, 225; Lundqvist, 1984, 228.
[239]   Daun, 1985, 4.
[240]   Daun, 1985, 4–5, 7.
[241]   Berg, 1979, 171–2.
[242]   Herlitz, 1977, 219–20.

finished, they even had a separate artist to decorate each station.[243] And, a visiting American sociologist found, in Vällingby most people seemed well content: as compared with American suburbanites in Levittown, the men had more time with their children, the women and teenagers found it easier to get around without a car, the children had better-planned open space and special services. Even then, polled, most said that they would prefer a house to an apartment: a conclusion that the sociologist, clearly moonstruck by the quality of Stockholm life, felt must reflect a fault in the poll.[244]

But then, in Sweden it is easy for visitors to become moonstruck; it sometimes seems as if all things vulgar and tawdry have been proscribed by Act of Parliament. Yet, on closer look, paradise is not quite gained: on the subway platforms, graffiti deface the exquisite artists' designs; on the subway trains, drunken Saturday-night gangs terrorize the passengers; press reports tell of anomie and alienation in the satellite towns, where – especially on those last to be finished, such as Tensta and Rinkeby – vast numbers of immigrant workers are concentrated. Older Stockholmers say sadly that it was not like that once; back in the 1950s, in developments like Vällingby, they believed in the possibility of a secular millennium, where liberal enlightenment and social harmony would henceforth reign for ever; but somewhere, the worm entered the bud.

And the returning pilgrim finds startling changes too. At Skärholmen, there is the ultimate in coordinated Social Democratic planning: high-density apartments around a central commercial megastructure, in turn centered upon the *Tunnelbana* station. But the lowest level of the multi-story garage is permanently converted into a flea market; the approaches to the center are hung with gaudy home-made posters; the center itself, rebuilt with a roof after it started to go downhill commercially, is a riot of commercial advertising, which shouts its contradictory messages as insistently as if this were Bangkok or New Delhi. And the reason for this desperation is soon found if one climbs to the top level of the garage: for, immediately spread out on the horizon, is a rival shopping center developed within the neighboring municipality of Huddinge after the collapse of an agreement with Stockholm. A three-minute drive takes the visitor across an invisible Iron Curtain: here is an equally standardized world, the nonplace world of the 1990s shopping center, totally car-based, with the familiar icons: Toys 'R' Us, McDonalds, and – the Swedish contribution to the genre – Ikea.

It encapsulates the change that came over Sweden during the 1980s, as the long-held Social Democratic consensus unraveled. It is repeated on a far larger scale north of Stockholm, where the visitor passes from Kista – the last of the great satellite developments, completed only at the end of the 1970s – into another world, the creation of the 1980s and 1990s: a vast linear Edge City of business parks and hotels and out-of-town shopping centers, stretching along the E4 highway, for 20 kilometers and more towards the Arlanda airport. It is almost indistinguishable from its

[243] Berg, 1979, 187–202.
[244] Popenoe, 1977, 177–201, 236.

counterparts in California or Texas. And, more poignantly than any other such sight, it underlines the fact that the Social Democratic consensus itself is now a piece of history, to be analyzed and explained.

One other place in Scandinavia acquired a legendary reputation equal to the Stockholm satellites: Tapiola and Vantaanpuisto in the Helsinki metropolitan region. In 1967, the American Institute of Architects' R. S. Reynolds memorial award for community architecture went jointly to the Stockholm satellites and to Tapiola and Cumbernauld.[245] As early as 1947, a Helsinki Regional Planning Association had been established; the concept of a Helsinki metropolitan area became common parlance.[246] Then, in 1951, the Housing Foundation was founded by several Finnish public utility organizations, specifically to build a new residential suburb just outside Helsinki.[247] It promoted Tapiola aggressively as a "Garden City" or "New Town"[248] – pedantically not quite correct, but a common enough misinterpretation almost everywhere outside the United Kingdom. The resulting plan combined four basic modern international planning principles: the Anglo-American neighborhood-unit system of Clarence Perry, adapted for Tapiola by Otto-Iivari Meurman; Congrès Internationaux d'Architecture Moderne urbanism, interpreted by Aarne Ervi (1910–77), one of Finland's leading architects of the 1950s and 1960s; zoning, applied, notably, by using forest and park zones between the neighborhoods; and traffic segregation of pedestrians and car traffic in the shopping centers, with through traffic separated from local traffic in the housing neighborhoods.[249]

Paris: Haussmann Revisited

Europe's other grand historic attempt to plan a metropolis around a new transit system came a full two decades after Markelius. It came about in a very strange way. In the early 1960s Paris had been trying to limit its own growth and had been manifestly failing. Official policy reflected the thesis of Jean-François Gravier, a geographer and an official in the Ministry of Urban Planning and Reconstruction, who had written his book *Paris et le désert français* during the quasi-fascist Vichy regime (1940–4), but published it only in 1947.[250] The central target of his polemic was Paris, which for a century – he argued – had devoured the substance of the nation, sterilizing the economy of provincial France. Paris, he wrote, had appropriated for itself all the leading activities, leaving only subordinate ones to the rest of France: a quasi-colonial regime.[251] Further, he borrowed from Rousseau: urban

---

[245] Lahti, 2008, 158.
[246] Lahti, 2008, 152.
[247] Lahti, 2008, 153.
[248] Lahti, 2008, 157.
[249] Lahti, 2008, 156.
[250] Marchand and Cavin, 2007, 30–1.
[251] Quoted in Marchand and Cavin, 2007, 31.

life was sterile and harmful to humankind, causing men and women to lose all their morality[252] – an argument uncannily close to that of Nazi Germany urbanists of the time.

Yet, despite these strange origins and affiliations, Gravier's book rapidly became the Bible of French spatial planning. Even Paul Delouvrier, who would later challenge and overthrow it, confessed that he too initially believed it: "We were all fans of Gravier, that is, more or less convinced that Paris, particularly during the nineteenth century, had devoured the rest of France."[253] It took until 1995 for the French Ministry of Finances, in a document requested by the European Commission, to reveal the truth: three urban regions subsidized all the others. Alsace (Strasbourg) paid 300 million euros more than it received, Rhône-Alpes (Lyon, the second city) paid 650 million more than it received, and the Île-de-France (the Paris region) contributed an epic 18 billion euros more than it received from the national budget: 1,600 euros per capita each year, including babies and retired people.[254]

Meanwhile, back in the early 1960s, France was seeing its own baby boom for the first time in centuries; the young people were pouring off the land and heading for the bright lights of the metropolis. In 1961, de Gaulle, who believed that Paris should fulfill its historic destiny as the physical symbol of the glories of France, called in an official who had come to his attention in the agonizing withdrawal from Algeria, and asked him to head a team to produce a new plan. The 1965 *Schéma-Directeur* for the Région Île-de-France was the latter-day equivalent of Haussmann's grand design for Paris, now logically extended to cover the entire Parisian region; de Gaulle's hand-picked Haussmann, at first entitled Délégué Général au District de la Région de Paris, then – from 1966 – Préfet de la Région Parisienne, was Paul Delouvrier. He was appointed at the age of 47, three years older than Haussmann had been on his own appointment. When Delouvrier died in 1995, the *Cahiers* of the Institut d'Aménagement d'Urbanisme de la Région d'Île-de-France, the journal of the institute he established to provide the basis for the plan, recalled that in 1961 de Gaulle had toured the region by helicopter, demanding that someone "put a little order into all that," meaning the vast unplanned structure of the suburbs below.[255] Delouvrier did just that: as he later said, Haussmann had 17 years to change Paris, he had only seven.

They ran the numbers and concluded that even if the national planning system were successful in building up the biggest provincial cities as effective *métropoles d'équilibre*, the Paris region would grow from 9 to between 14 and 16 million by the end of the century. Early in 1962, apparently, Delouvrier convinced de Gaulle in a personal interview that this picture of a dynamic Paris, "bursting at the seams," was correct.[256] Considering alternatives – conventional annular growth, counter-magnets 60 or more miles different, Abercrombie-style new towns, a "second Paris" –

---

[252] Marchand and Cavin, 2007, 33.
[253] Marchand and Cavin, 2007, 48–9.
[254] Marchand and Cavin, 2007, 49.
[255] Anon, 1995, no pagination.
[256] Alduy, 1983, 75.

Figure 9.11   Marne-la-Vallée. The Stockholm model applied on a far larger spatial scale in the new towns for Paris under the 1965 plan. The express transit system, RER (Réseau Express Régional), runs directly under the town center deck.

they rejected them all: the magnetism of Paris was such that the people wanted to be there, not some other place, yet if it grew as it had been growing the city would throttle.[257]

So they effectively adopted a Stockholm plan on a mega scale, appropriate to a metropolis 10 times Stockholm's size. Paris would have new towns; yet these would be towns not on the Howard–Abercrombie model, but rather satellites in the May–Markelius mold. Since Paris was huge, the satellites would be correspondingly so: against 10,000–20,000 in the Frankfurt of the 1920s, or 80,000–100,000 in the Stockholm of the 1940s, the Paris of the 1960s demanded eight units of between 300,000 and 1,000,000 each.[258] As in Stockholm, they were to be linked with the center, and with each other, not only by circumferential highways but by a new transit system; but again with a difference. Unlike the Stockholm *Tunnelbana*, unlike the London Underground on which it had been based, unlike the existing Paris Métro or indeed any of the subway systems of the 1890–1910 era, this was to be an express transit system: having the characteristics of a commuter rail service, it could move people long distances in short times. Its only near equivalent, then still on the drawing board, was the Bay Area Rapid Transit (BART) system planned for San Francisco.

But BART was never seen as the agent of a coherent regional plan; presented as a solution to threatened chaos on the region's highways, in fact it promoted further

257   Hall, 1984, 72–6.
258   Rubenstein, 1978, 107.

suburbanization and transferred the gridlock there. The 160-mile Réseau Express Régional (RER), in contrast, was planned – as in Stockholm 20 years earlier – integrally with the new satellites. These would be arrayed on two "preferential axes," one on the north side of the existing agglomeration, one on the south; to link them, the RER would take the form of a letter "H" placed sideways, with a main east–west line branching out at each end. But thus it would link not only the planned satellites, but also new inner-urban centers which would act as catalysts for urban renewal in the shabby middle ring of the Paris region and would provide badly needed services there. The largest such center, at La Défense immediately outside the inner city to the west, had already started when the plan was being prepared, and thus represented a kind of commercial *fait accompli* which the planners took in their stride.

If audacity is a criterion for merit in urban planning, then the Paris *Schéma Directeur* of 1965 must surely belong in some category by itself. Nothing so grandiose was ever attempted in the history of urban civilization. The total bill to the French exchequer was mind-boggling: the 12-year plan, drawn up at the same time as the *Schéma Directeur*, called for a total of 29 billion francs on highways and nine billion for public transport, not to mention 140,000 new dwellings a year.[259] Only a country led by a figure with a Messianic belief in his own destiny, only one in the middle of an economic boom almost unprecedented in history, only one with a centuries-old tradition of top-down public intervention, could even have contemplated it; maybe not even then.

It was the ultimate plan. All kinds of academic theorist, in historical retrospect, can prove anything they like from it. Marxists can represent it as a supreme instance of large-scale capital manipulating the state in its own interests, particularly to provide the social investments necessary to ensure the reproduction of labor power; not for nothing were modern urban Marxist studies born in Paris between 1965 and 1972. Believers in the resilience of national culture, contrariwise, will see in it the long tradition represented by Louis XIV and by Haussmann: Delouvrier, ironically, achieved the kind of planning to which Corbusier long aspired in vain. For theorists of the state, on the other hand, it is the classic example of a central bureaucracy entrenching its independent power. Paul Alduy – who, as a key official during its preparation and implementation, has written the definitive account of it as a conspiracy against democracy – gives them their evidence: "it involved new methods of state intervention, that of a central State acting as an arbiter above party and their elected representatives."[260] More than that: as he shows, large parts of the existing bureaucratic machine, and their political heads, were simply ignored in the plan's preparation: "The purpose was obviously, not to negotiate with anybody but, above all, to develop a propaganda operation aimed at presenting a new image of the State, a new mode of intervention and furthermore, a new relationship between the State and local authorities."[261]

Somehow, it survived and, in a fashion, was achieved. Not, of course, without modification, or without pain: in 1969, economic crisis and demographic changes brought a rewrite, in which three of the eight *villes nouvelles* were dropped and others reduced in scale.[262] But the others were pressed ahead; and some, indeed, proved a magnet for private construction capital which built offices, shopping centers, and homes for sale on a huge scale. That perhaps is the final moral of the Parisian story: as French planners had always argued, public plans can provide a set of clear signals to the private sector, thus enabling it in turn to make its own phased investment programs. Delouvrier did for the suburbs of Paris what Haussmann had done 100 years earlier for the city; the polycentric structure of the region at the millennium – its five new towns, its three circumferential motorways, its five RER lines – is the worthy lineal successor to Haussmann's works. Together de Gaulle and Delouvrier awoke Paris from the long sleep that had descended on it after the departure of Louis-Napoleon and Haussmann. Audacity can work.

The Great Freeway Revolt and After

But the critical point remains: neither Stockholm in 1945, nor Paris in 1965, succeeded in weaning Europeans from their cars. The years from 1945 to 1975, indeed, were the ones in which Europe supplanted America as the main car-builder of the world; all that had happened was that the automobile revolution came to Europe 40 years later.[263] In the process, it began profoundly to affect both traditional lifestyles and traditional urban structures. In Sweden, single-family homes zoomed from 32% of new housing construction in 1970 to 55% in 1974 and to over 70% by the late 1970s, responding to individual preferences that showed as many as 90% of Swedes preferring houses to flats.[264] In the Paris *villes nouvelles*, similarly, single-family homes made up the overwhelming majority of the housing completions, the supermarkets were full of barbecues and garden furniture, and – most significant sign of all – there were few restaurants to be found, let alone good ones.

So the car in Europe, as in its first homeland, was an agent of suburbanization. Which came first, the suburban chicken or the automotive egg, is impossible to say; as already noted for Los Angeles, and as earlier noted (in Chapter 3) for London, suburban sprawl pre-dated mass car ownership, but in turn the automobile allowed the suburbs to sprawl more freely, and farther, than mass transit could ever have done. What was true everywhere was that in the process, the problem of the car in the historic city became an acute one. American cities, facing the conflict from the 1920s onwards, reacted by loosening and weakening their earlier tight urban structures. European city fathers were less reluctant to see this happen. The crunch came over the massive construction evidently needed to accommodate the age of universal automobility in the cities.

---

262   Rubenstein, 1978, 107.
263   Roos and Altshuler, 1984, 18–22.
264   Popenoe, 1977, 222; Goldfield, 1979, 152–3.

For more than a decade from the mid-1950s onwards, a new generation of urban traffic analysts came to dominate city planning, first in the United States, then – as they exported themselves and their techniques – in Europe also. Their computer models appeared to demonstrate the inexorable necessity to build vast networks of new urban highways in order to grapple with the rising curve of traffic. For a time, they met no resistance. In Britain at the end of 1963, the Minister of Transport published a report on *Traffic in Towns*, produced by a technical group directed by a then unknown planner-engineer, Colin Buchanan.[265] It proved a bestseller; Buchanan became a public figure overnight. Buchanan's argument was a subtle one, derived from Alker Tripp's philosophy of precinctual planning a quarter-century previously: it was that the planner should set fixed standards for the urban environment, whereupon more traffic could be accommodated only through massive reconstruction; if the community were unwilling or unable to foot this bill, then it must restrain the traffic. Hardly anyone grasped the message; the public, bemused by the media pictures of vast multi-level reconstruction, became convinced that Buchanan was calling for the bulldozing of urban Britain. At first, they seemed to receive this with equanimity, even enthusiasm; this was the era of the great rebuilding of Britain, when comprehensive redevelopment was everywhere still seen as a thoroughly good thing. Behind Buchanan came the traffic engineers with their plans for urban motorways: hundreds of miles for London, similarly vast networks for every provincial city.

But Buchanan did like motorways. In 1937, a British official delegation – 224 people, including representatives of motoring organizations, politicians, local government highways engineers, and others including the veteran Thomas Adams (but lacking anyone from the Ministry of Transport where the minister, Leslie Hore-Belisha, was Jewish) – went to study the German *Autobahn* system then under construction.[266] But the young Buchanan had made his own private tour a few weeks earlier, and never lost his first flush of enthusiasm for the technical and aesthetic qualities of German transport planning.[267] Small wonder therefore that *Traffic in Towns* offered a mixture of American and European – mainly German – solutions for British cities. Big new urban motorway systems could be combined with areas of traffic restraint and even exclusion, which he called "environmental areas." In city centers, these areas would increasingly be pedestrianized.[268] Twenty years after that, Carmen Hass-Klau, an Anglo-German urban transport planning expert, played an important role introducing another German import: traffic calming (*Verkehrsberuhigung*) in the form of engineering measures like speed humps, tables, chicanes and other physical restrictions, many closely based on existing German examples. Missing, however, were the more strategic German approaches, using a variety of integrated methods to reduce and slow motor traffic so as to make it less unpleasant for those who lived in cities and moved around them in ways other than by car.[269]

[265] GB Minister of Transport, 1963.
[266] Ward, 2010, 124.
[267] Ward, 2010, 125.
[268] Ward, 2010, 128.
[269] Ward, 2010, 130–1.

Meanwhile, in California, as usual the harbinger, the tide had already turned. San Francisco, that most European of American cities – and, therefore, the city most determined to be unlike its arch-rival Los Angeles – awoke to a plan to drive an elevated double-deck freeway along its historic waterfront, past the famous Fisherman's Wharf. In the world's first freeway revolt, the Embarcadero Freeway was stopped in its tracks. Then, dizzy with triumph, the city stopped building freeways altogether; everywhere, the bemused visitor could see elevated structures that stopped suddenly, in mid-air. It commissioned a consultants' report of 1956, and a subsequent one from the same source in 1962, calling for a $900-million new transit system, deliberately engineered to preserve San Francisco as a European-style, strong-center city. San Franciscans voted two to one in favor; suburbanites were less enthusiastic, but the proposal scraped home and the state-of-the-art BART system started construction.[270]

The revolt spread across North America; Toronto stopped its Spadina Expressway, and later turned the right-of-way into a subway. It spawned imitators in Europe: one morning in April 1973, the incoming Labour administration at the Greater London Council (GLC), fulfilling an election promise, tore up the whole of the GLC motorway plans. It was all part of the new *Zeitgeist*, in which all the popular planning slogans were suddenly stood on their heads: this was the time of the Club of Rome report, the belief that small was beautiful, the emphasis on planning for the disadvantaged, and the great Organization of the Petroleum Exporting Countries energy crisis. But the revolt against the freeways came before that crisis, which merely seemed to reinforce the rightness of the policy reversal.

In Britain, as elsewhere, central government policy went into reverse. The aim was no longer to reshape cities to fit projected demands for car travel, but to encourage the use of public transport. Though partially undermined by the Thatcher governments of the 1980s,[271] the new trend reasserted itself at the beginning of the 1990s. First, there was a basic challenge to the "predict and provide" ideology, principally from increasing evidence that road construction induced demand for road travel. And secondly, there was growing awareness of the ecological damage caused by motor traffic, often coming to a head in marginal constituencies in the early 1990s, exposing a basic contradiction between two traditional Conservative policy aims of promoting economic competitiveness and protecting the countryside.[272] And this contradiction remained: there were many more votes for local politicians in espousing such policies than in restricting the freedom of motorists. "The more recent notion that reducing road space can, in many instances, actually cut traffic," Geoff Vigar concludes, "requires a further leap of faith on the part of politicians and practitioners"; possibly a leap too far.[273]

The logical result – not merely in Britain, but much more wholeheartedly in more affluent European economies like France and West Germany – was a massive shift of

[270]   Zwerling, 1974, 22–3, 27; Hall, 1980, 114–15.
[271]   Vigar, 2001, 277.
[272]   Vigar, 2001, 279.
[273]   Vigar, 2001, 286.

investment into urban mass transit. Now, other cities followed the pioneer trail beaten by pioneers like Stockholm and Paris. In Germany, by the early 1980s, virtually every major city was building a new or reconstructed rail transit system.[274] The European suburb, too, was a city on the highway; but it was also a city on the subway. Its inhabitants, in particular those among them with less access to cars, were given a choice.

America, too, began to move in the European direction: by the mid-1980s, over 40 major American cities had rail transit systems either operating or building or in the planning stages, some on the BART long-distance model, some more modest light-rail systems.[275] Yet it was a question not just of investing in transit, but also of structuring the suburbs around them. And that was something that American cities – driven by the market mechanism, equipped with only minimal planning powers – would be unwilling or unable to do. So the conclusion for many of these systems was likely to be the drastic one reached by Melvin Webber for BART in 1977: failure, because they simply did not fit the dispersed land-use patterns and so did not offer an attractive alternative to the car.[276]

That could be changed only if Americans were suddenly willing to live like Europeans; and that would require that they accept European systems of land-use regulation. In places, to be sure, there was evidence by the 1970s that some Americans were willing to be more regulated. Californian communities like Petaluma, faced with the outwash of suburbia from the San Francisco Bay, fought bitter battles to regulate their own growth. After huge fights between the construction lobby and the environmental lobby, the California legislature, in 1972, passed a comprehensive law that effectively stopped all development along the coastline. Such measures did affect the shape of the suburban flood: effectively, the San Francisco Bay Area is surrounded by a green belt almost as effectively protected as London's, and the result – according to David Dowall – has been the same as that reported for London: housing land scarcity and higher housing land prices.[277] But it has not affected the general fact: beyond the green belt, in the corridor followed by Interstate Highway 680 from Concord to Fremont, 20 and more miles from downtown San Francisco, the suburbs continue to sprawl and the jobs are moving out too. The result, according to Dowall's colleague Robert Cervero, is that the Suburban Squeeze is followed by Suburban Gridlock: the highway system is overwhelmed by the volume of suburb-to-suburb commuter journeys, which the BART system – indeed, any conventional radial transit system – is quite unfitted to serve.[278]

Not only then were Americans failing to adopt European urban lifestyles; the evidence seemed to be, if anything, that progressively just the opposite was happening. The energy crisis did not suddenly reverse, or even stem, the tide of out-migration from the cities; during the 1970s, following a pattern long familiar in the United States, more and more European countries began to report losses in their central-city

[274]   Hall and Hass-Klau, 1985.
[275]   McClendon, 1984, 22–3; Anon, 1985, 42–3.
[276]   Webber, 1976, 34; Hall, 1980, 122–3.
[277]   Dowall, 1984.
[278]   Cervero, 1986.

populations.[279] And, though some of the European transit systems were successful in attracting passengers, they were invariably – like their American equivalents – heavily subsidized ones. On both sides of the Atlantic, it seemed, the City on the Highway was winning out over the traditionally structured transit city. The people were voting for it with their wheels; more precisely, those that had them were voting thus, and more had them every year. Wells's prophecy was coming truer every year that passed.

But the great Californian freeway bonanza ended in the 1970s, as inflation eroded the value of the gasoline tax, and as construction costs rose at two and a half times the rate of the consumer price index. The Nimby – Not In My Back Yard – factor made itself felt: local opposition to several freeways, particularly the Beverly Hills and Century freeways, became more vociferous, and all attempts to increase highway user taxes were defeated. Caltrans, the California Department of Transportation, which superseded the old Division of Highways in 1973, was left with the job of keeping the existing system running; little new construction was planned, and every project involved huge difficulties. It took seven years of litigation and controversy to start the 15.5-mile Century freeway, in spite of the fact that it had 92% federal funding.[280]

Now, as population and car ownership rose and construction stalled, the freeway system gradually moved towards gridlock: by the 1980s peak-hour delays currently extended to four hours twice a day, and small incidents could cause paralysis of the system. There were inevitably growing demands for an alternative approach. Further freeway construction was seen as self-defeating; a powerful coalition developed, devoted to the principle that Los Angeles should again have a rail system. In 1980, Los Angeles County voters approved Proposition A, a measure which would lower bus fares from 85c. to 50c. for three years, provide discretionary local transport funds, and – critically – build a county-wide system of new rail rapid transit lines.[281]

On July 14, 1990, the new 22-mile (35-kilometer) $900 million Blue Line light rail system began service between downtown Los Angeles and Long Beach. Ironically, it occupied almost precisely the same right-of-way as the old Pacific Electric line, which had been the last to cease service, in 1961. It was followed in 1993 by the first short downtown stretch of an even more ambitious heavy rail metro, the Red Line; and in 1994 by another light rail project, the Green Line running in the median strip of the new Century Freeway.[282] It had taken less than 30 years to bring the interurbans back to Los Angeles. Critics – and there were many – shared the view of John Kain of Harvard University: "My overall impression is that your transportation planners are trying to impose a 19th century technology on a 20th or 21st century city."[283] The twenty-first century will tell whether they will succeed in reversing the direction of urban history, or are pursuing a will-o'-the-wisp.

[279] Hall and Hay, 1980; Cheshire and Hay, 1987.
[280] Brodsly, 1981, 120, 126.
[281] Richmond, 2005, 33.
[282] Read, 1993, 43, 45; Richmond, 2005, 33–6.
[283] Quoted in Richmond, 2005, 38.

The City of Theory

Grau, teurer Freund, ist alle Theorie
Und grün das Lebens goldner Baum.
Johann Wolfgang von Goethe, *Faust*, I (1808)

Read no history; nothing but biography, for that is life without theory.
Benjamin Disraeli, *Contarini Fleming* (1832)

He who can, does. He who cannot, teaches.
George Bernard Shaw, *Maxims for Revolutionists*
(*Man and Superman*) (1903)

All professions are conspiracies against the laity.
George Bernard Shaw, *The Doctor's Dilemma* (1913)

Cities of Tomorrow: An Intellectual History of Urban Planning and Design Since 1880,
Fourth Edition. Peter Hall.
© 2014 Peter Hall. Published 2014 by John Wiley & Sons, Ltd.

10

The City of Theory

Planning and the Academy: Philadelphia, Manchester, California, Paris, 1955–1987

The chapter title might suggest total superfluity: for this book has been about nothing else than cities of theory, and attempts to bring them to actuality. And, down to about 1955, that adequately describes the main current of twentieth-century planning history; such has been the central thesis. But from then on, it will not do. Hence the need for this chapter, and the title.

The reason is paradoxical: at that point, city planning at last became legitimate; but in doing so, it began to sow the seeds of its own destruction. All too quickly, it split into two separate camps: the one, in the schools of planning, increasingly and exclusively obsessed with the theory of the subject; the other, in the offices of local authorities and consultants, concerned only with the everyday business of planning in the real world. That division was not at first evident; indeed, during the late 1950s and most of the 1960s, it seemed that at last a complete and satisfactory link had been forged between the world of theory and the world of practice. But all too soon, illusion was stripped aside: honeymoon was followed in quick succession during the 1970s by tiffs and temporary reconciliations, in the 1980s by divorce. And, in the process, planning lost much of its new-found legitimacy.

The Prehistory of Academic City Planning: 1930–1955

It was not that planning was innocent of academic influence before the 1950s. On the contrary: in virtually every urbanized nation, universities and polytechnics had created courses for the professional education of planners; professional bodies had come into existence to define and protect standards, and had forged links with the academic departments. Britain took an early lead when in 1909 – as already detailed in Chapter 5 – the soap magnate William Hesketh Lever, founder of Port Sunlight, won a libel action against a newspaper and used the proceeds to endow his local University of Liverpool with a Department of Civic Design. Stanley Adshead, the

Figure 10.1 Patrick Abercrombie. Photographed outside the Palace after receiving his knighthood in 1945, Abercrombie celebrates his two great plans for London and 30 years as a leader of British planning education. *Source*: Getty Images.

first professor, almost immediately created a new journal, the *Town Planning Review*, in which theory and good practice were to be firmly joined; its first editor was a young faculty recruit, Patrick Abercrombie, who was later to succeed Adshead in the chair first at Liverpool, then at Britain's second school of planning: University College, London, founded in 1914. The Town Planning Institute (TPI) – the Royal accolade was conferred only in 1959 – was founded in 1914 on the joint initiative of the Royal Institute of British Architects, the Institution of Civil Engineers, and the Royal Institution of Chartered Surveyors; by the end of the 1930s, it had recognized seven schools whose examinations provided an entry to membership.[1]

The United States was slower: though Harvard had established a planning course in 1909, neck-and-neck with Liverpool, it had no separate department until 1929. Nevertheless, by the 1930s America had schools also at the Massachusetts Institute of Technology (MIT), Cornell, Columbia, and Illinois, as well as courses taught in other departments at a great many universities across the country.[2] And the American City Planning Institute, founded in 1917 as a breakaway from the National Conference on City Planning, 10 years later became – mainly through the insistence

[1] Cherry, 1974, 54, 56–60, 169, 218–22.
[2] Scott, 1969, 101, 266–7, 365–6; Wilson, 1974, 138–9.

of Thomas Adams – a full-fledged professional body on TPI lines, a status it retained when in 1938 it broadened to include regional planning and renamed itself the American Institute of Planners.[3]

The important point about these, and other, initiatives was this: stemming as they did from professional needs, often through spinoffs from related professions like architecture and engineering, they were from the start heavily suffused with the professional styles of these design-based professions. The job of the planners was to make plans, to develop codes to enforce these plans, and then to enforce those codes; relevant planning knowledge was what was needed for that job; planning education existed to convey that knowledge together with the necessary design skills. So, by 1950, the utopian age of planning – main theme of this book – was over; planning was now institutionalized into comprehensive land-use planning.[4] All this was strongly reflected in the curricula of the planning schools down to the mid-1950s and, often, for years after that; and these in turn were reflected in the books and articles that academic planners wrote. Land-use planning, Keeble told his British audience in 1959 and Kent reminded the American counterpart in 1964, was a distinct and tightly bounded subject, quite different from social or economic planning.[5] And these texts reflected the fact that "City planners early adopted the thoughtways and the analytical methods that engineers developed for the design of public works, and they then applied them to the design of cities."[6]

The result, as Michael Batty has put it, was a subject that for the ordinary citizen was "somewhat mystical" or arcane, as law or medicine were, but that was – in sharp contrast to education for these older professions – not based on any consistent body of theory; rather, in it, "scatterings of social science bolstered the traditional architectural determinism."[7] Planners acquired a synthetic ability not through abstract thinking, but by doing real jobs; in them, they used first creative intuition, then reflection. Though they might draw on bits and pieces of theory about the city – the Chicago school's sociological differentiation of the city, the land economists' theory of urban land rent differentials, the geographers' concepts of the natural region – these were employed simply as snippets of useful knowledge;[8] in the important distinction later made by a number of writers,[9] there was some theory *in* planning but there was no theory *of* planning. The whole process was very direct, based on a single-shot approach: survey (the Geddesian approach) was followed by analysis (an implicit learning approach), followed immediately by design.

True, as Abercrombie's classic text of 1933 argued, the making of the plan was only half the planner's job; the other half consisted of planning, that is implementation;[10]

---

3   Scott, 1969, 163; Birch, 1980a, 26, 28, 31–2; Simpson, 1985, 126–7.
4   Galloway and Mahayni, 1977, 65.
5   Keeble, 1959, 1:2; Kent, 1964, 101.
6   Webber, 1968/9, 192–3.
7   Batty, 1979, 29.
8   Keeble, 1959, 2:2.
9   Hightower, 1969, 326; Faludi, 1985, 27.
10   Abercrombie, 1933, 139.

Figure 10.2 Thomas Adams. The ultimate transatlantic planner, Adams worked at Letchworth and became the Town Planning Institute's first president before moving to direct the New York Regional Plan, a job he combined with a flourishing regional planning practice in England. *Source*: © Garden City Collection, Letchworth Garden City Heritage Foundation.

but it was nowhere assumed that some kind of continuous learning process was needed. True, too, the 1947 Act provided for plans – and the surveys on which they were based – to be quinquennially updated; the assumption was still that the result would be a fixed land-use plan. And, a decade after that, though Keeble's equally classic text referred to the planning process,[11] by this he simply meant the need for a spatial hierarchy of related plans from the regional to the local, and the need at each scale for survey before plan; nowhere is found a discussion of implementation or updating. Thus – apart from extremely generalized statements like Abercrombie's famous triad of "beauty, health and convenience"[12] – the goals were left implicit; the planner would develop them intuitively from his own values, which by definition were "expert" and apolitical.

[11]   Keeble, 1959, 2:1.
[12]   Abercrombie, 1933, 104.

So, in the classic British land-use planning system created by the 1947 Town and Country Planning Act, no repeated learning process was involved, since the planner would get it right first time[13]:

> The process was therefore not characterised by explicit feedback as the search "homed in" on the best plan, for the notion that the planner had to learn about the nature of the problem was in direct conflict with his assumed infallibility as an expert, a professional ... The assumed certainty of the process was such that possible links back to the reality in the form of new surveys were rarely if ever considered ... This certainty, based on the infallibility of the expert, reinforced the apolitical, technical nature of the process. The political environment was regarded as totally passive, indeed subservient to the "advice" of the planners and in practice, this was largely the case.[14]

It was, as Batty calls it, planning's golden age: the planner, free from political interference, serenely sure of his technical capacities, was left to get on with the job. And this was appropriate to the world outside, with which planning had to deal: a world of glacially slow change – stagnant population, depressed economy – in which major planning interventions would come only seldom and for a short time, as after a major war. Abercrombie, in the plan for the West Midlands he produced with Herbert Jackson in 1948, actually wrote that a major objective of the plan should be to slow down the rate of urban change, thus reducing the rate at which built structures became obsolescent – the ideal city would be a static, stable city:

> Let us assume ... that a maximum population has been decided for a town, arrived at after consideration of all the factors appearing to be relevant ... Allowance has been made for proper space for all conceivable purposes in the light of present facts and the town planner's experience and imagination.
>
>   Accordingly, an envelope or green belt has been prescribed, outside which the land uses will be those involving little in the way of resident population. The town planner is now in the happy position for the first time of knowing the limits of his problem. He is able to address himself to the design of the whole and the parts in the light of a basic overall figure for population. The process will be difficult enough in itself, but at least he starts with one figure to reassure him.[15]

Interestingly, American planning was never quite like that. Kent's text of 1964 on the urban general plan, though it deals with the same kind of land-use planning, reminds its students of "end-directions which are continually adjusted as time passes."[16] And, because the planner's basic understanding of the interrelationship between socio-

---

[13]   Batty, 1979, 29–31.
[14]   Batty, 1979, 30–1.
[15]   Abercrombie and Jackson, 1948, para. 4.1.
[16]   Kent, 1964, 98.

Figure 10.3 T. J. Kent, Jr. Three waves of planning theory at the University of California, Berkeley. (1) Kent, the school's founder, wrote the classic 1962 text on the urban general plan.

economic forces and the physical environment was largely intuitive and speculative, Kent warned his student readers that

> in most cases it is not possible to know with any certainty what physical-design measures should be taken to bring about a given social or economic objective, or what social and economic consequences will result from a given physical-design proposal. Therefore, the city council and the city-planning commission, rather than professional city planners, should make the final value judgements upon which the plan is based.[17]

But even Kent was certain that, despite all this, it was still possible for the planner to produce some kind of optimal land-use plan; the problem of objectives was just shunted off.

---

[17] Kent, 1964, 104.

The Systems Revolution

It was a happy, almost dream-like, world. But increasingly, during the 1950s, it did not correspond to reality. Everything began to get out of hand. In every industrial country, there was an unexpected baby boom, to which the demographers reacted with surprise, the planners with alarm; only its timing varied from one country to another, and everywhere it created instant demands for maternity wards and child-care clinics, only slightly delayed needs for schools and playgrounds. In every one, almost simultaneously, the great postwar economic boom got under way, bringing pressures for new investment in factories and offices. And, as boom generated afflu-ence, these countries soon passed into the realms of high mass-consumption soci-eties, with unprecedented demands for durable consumer goods: most notable among these, land-hungry homes and cars. The result everywhere – in America, in Britain, in the whole of Western Europe – was that the pace of urban development and urban change began to accelerate to an almost superheated level; the old planning system, geared to a static world, was overwhelmed.

These demands in themselves would force the system to change; but, almost coin-cidentally, there were changes on the supply side too. In the mid-1950s there occurred an intellectual revolution in the whole cluster of urban and regional social studies, which provided planners with much of their borrowed intellectual baggage. A few geographers and industrial economists discovered the works of German theorists of location, such as Johann Heinrich von Thünen (1826) on agriculture, Alfred Weber (1909) on industry, Walter Christaller (1933) on central places, and August Lösch (1940) on the general theory of location; they began to summarize and analyze these works, and where necessary to translate them.[18] In the United States, academics com-ing from a variety of disciplines began to find regularities in many distributions, including spatial ones.[19] Geographers, beginning to espouse the tenets of logical pos-itivism, suggested that their subject should cease to be concerned with descriptions of the detailed differentiation of the earth's surface, and should instead begin to develop general hypotheses about spatial distributions, which could then be rigorously tested against reality: the very approach which these German pioneers of location theory had adopted. These ideas, together with the relevant literature, were brilliantly syn-thesized by an American economist, Walter Isard, in a text that became immediately influential.[20] Between 1953 and 1957, there occurred an almost instant revolution in human geography[21] and the creation, by Isard, of a new academic discipline uniting the new geography with the German tradition of locational economics. And, with official blessing – as in the important report of Britain's Schuster Committee of 1950, which recommended a greater social science content in planning education – the new locational analysis began to enter the curricula of the planning schools.[22]

[18]   Thünen, 1966; Weber, 1929; Christaller, 1966; Lösch, 1954.
[19]   Zipf, 1949; Stewart, 1947; 1956; Carrothers, 1956; Stewart and Warntz, 1958; Garrison, 1959/60.
[20]   Isard, 1960.
[21]   Johnston, 1979.
[22]   GB Committee, 1950.

The consequences for planning were momentous: with only a short time lag, "The discipline of physical planning changed more in the 10 years from 1960 to 1970, than in the previous 100, possibly even 1,000 years."[23] The subject changed from a kind of craft, based on personal knowledge of a rudimentary collection of concepts about the city, into an apparently scientific activity, in which vast amounts of precise information were garnered and processed in such a way that the planner could devise very sensitive systems of guidance and control, the effects of which could be monitored and if necessary modified. More precisely, cities and regions were viewed as complex systems – they were, indeed, only a particular spatially based subset of a whole general class of systems – while planning was seen as a continuous process of control and monitoring of these systems, derived from the then new science of cybernetics developed by Norbert Wiener.[24]

This shift was based on two different foci: systems planning was based on the view that the *object* of town planning was the urban or regional system, whereas rational planning concerned the *process*. "But both views, taken together, represented a departure from the prevailing design-based view of town planning."[25] There were four elements, as Nigel Taylor explains: "First, an essentially physical or morphological view of towns was replaced with a view of towns as systems of inter-related activities in an almost constant state of flux."[26] Secondly, a physical and aesthetic view of towns was replaced by a socio-economic view.[27] Thirdly, this implied replacement of "end state" planning by a "process" view.[28] Fourthly, this implied "scientific" skills: "planning was a science, not an art."[29]

A very early pioneer was Liverpool, where Gordon Stephenson, appointed in 1948 to follow William Holford in the chair of civic design, had been influenced by the "MIT model" he had known as a student in the 1930s, providing a general model for American planning education: courses were at graduate level, covered the social sciences as well as design, were open to students from a range of backgrounds, and were intended to produce "general practitioners in planning rather than planning specialists." In his evidence to the Schuster committee, he echoed the American view that planning was a postgraduate subject. Like its MIT counterpart, the Liverpool course was designed for well-qualified graduates in any subject, on the basis that the great majority of students would consist of three classes of graduates: social sciences like geography, economics, and statistics; creative design subjects like architecture, engineering, and landscape architecture; and administrative subjects like general arts, law, and estate management.[30]

But elsewhere, change came exceedingly slowly. Schuster recommended that the "right preparation" for planning was a degree course in one of the old-established

23 Batty, 1979, 18.
24 Wiener, 1948; Hall, J. M., 1982, 276.
25 Taylor, 1998, 159.
26 Taylor, 1998, 159.
27 Taylor, 1998, 159–60.
28 Taylor, 1998, 160.
29 Taylor, 1998, 160.
30 Batey, 2012, 146–7.

subjects followed by a postgraduate course in planning, to avoid the creation of "specialist in blinkers." But "in practice, neither the intellectual challenge nor the educational pattern of the Schuster model was taken up." The debate on generalist versus specialist did not go away and indeed was heightened so far that in 1974 Gordon Cherry[31] referred to it as the "war of the 1960s." Nor was Schuster's intellectual proposition, aiming to transform planning from a design-based to a social science-based discipline, adopted. It took the Royal Town Planning Institute (RTPI) another 20 years to change the syllabus and 30 years before introducing social scientific thought into planning education, and even then not without a fight.[32]

However slowly and grudgingly, there was thus, in the language later used in the celebrated work of Thomas Kuhn (1962), a paradigm shift. It affected city planning as it affected many other related areas of planning and design. Particularly, its main early applications – already in the mid-1950s – concerned defense and aerospace; for these were the Cold War years, when the United States was engaging in a crash program to build new and complex electronically controlled middle systems. Soon, from that field span off another application. Already in 1954, Robert Mitchell and Chester Rapkin – colleagues of Isard at the University of Pennsylvania – had published a book suggesting that urban traffic patterns were a direct and measurable function of the pattern of activities – and thus land uses – that generated them.[33] Coupled with earlier work on spatial interaction patterns, and using for the first time the data-processing powers of the computer, this produced a new science of urban transportation planning, which for the first time claimed to be able scientifically to predict future urban traffic patterns. First applied in the historic Detroit Metropolitan Area transportation study of 1955, further developed in the Chicago study of 1956, it soon became a standardized methodology employed in literally hundreds of such studies, first across the United States, then across the world.[34]

Heavily engineering-based in its approach, it adopted a fairly standardized sequence. First, explicit goals and objectives were set for the performance of the system. Then, inventories were taken of the existing state of the system: both the traffic flows, and the activities that gave rise to them. From this, models were derived which sought to establish these relationships in precise mathematical form. Then, forecasts were made of the future state of the system, based on the relationships obtained from the models. From this, alternative solutions could be designed and evaluated in order to choose a preferred option. Finally, once implemented, the network would be continually monitored and the system modified as necessary.[35]

At first, these relationships were seen as operating in one direction: activities and land uses were given; from these, the traffic patterns were derived. So the resulting methodology and techniques were part of a new field, transportation planning,

[31]   Cherry, 1974, 202.
[32]   Davoudi and Pendlebury, 2010, 623.
[33]   Mitchell and Rapkin, 1954.
[34]   Bruton, 1975, 17.
[35]   Bruton, 1975, 27–42.

which came to exist on one side of traditional city planning. Soon, however, American regional scientists suggested a crucial modification: the locational patterns of activities – commercial, industrial, residential – were in turn influenced by the available transportation opportunities; these relationships, too, could be precisely modeled and used for prediction; therefore the relationship was two-way, and there was a need to develop an interactive system of land-use–transportation planning for entire metropolitan or sub-regional areas. Now, for the first time, the engineering-based approach invaded the professional territory of the traditional land-use planner. Spatial interaction models, especially the Garin–Lowry model – which, given basic data about employment and transportation links, could generate a resulting pattern of activities and land uses – became part of the planner's stock in trade.[36] As put in one of the classic systems texts:

> In this general process of planning we particularise in order to deal with more specific issues: that is, a specific real world system or subsystem must be represented by a specific conceptual system or subsystem within the general conceptual system. Such a particular representation of a system is called a *model* ... The use of models is a means whereby the high variety of the real world is reduced to a level of variety appropriate to the channel capacities of the human being.[37]

This involved more than a knowledge of computer applications – novel as that seemed to the average planner of the 1960s. It meant also a fundamentally different concept of planning. Instead of the old master-plan or blueprint approach, which assumed that the objectives were fixed from the start, the new concept was of planning as a *process*, "whereby programmes are adapted during their implementation as and when incoming information requires such changes."[38] And this planning process was independent of the thing that was planned;[39] as Melvin Webber put it, it was "a special way of deciding and acting," which involved a constantly recycled series of logical steps: goal-setting, forecasting of change in the outside world, assessment of chains of consequences of alternative courses of action, appraisal of costs and benefits as a basis for action strategies, and continuous monitoring.[40] This was the approach of the new British textbooks of systems planning, which started to emerge at the end of the 1960s, and which were particularly associated with a group of younger British graduates.[41] It was also the approach of a whole generation of sub-regional studies, made for fast-growing metropolitan areas in Britain during that heroic period of growth and change, 1965–75: Leicester–Leicestershire, Nottinghamshire–Derbyshire, Coventry–Warwickshire– Solihull, South Hampshire. All were heavily suffused with the new approach and the new techniques; in several,

[36] Lowry, 1964; 1965; Batty, 1976.
[37] Chadwick, 1971, 63–4, 70.
[38] Faludi, 1973, 132.
[39] Galloway and Mahayni, 1977, 68.
[40] Webber, 1968/9, 278.
[41] McLoughlin, 1969; Chadwick, 1971.

Figure 10.4   Melvin M. Webber. Three waves of Berkeley planning theory continued. (2) In the 1960s Webber developed radical ideas about the nonplace urban realm and argued that planning had failed to develop a distinctive methodology.

the same key individuals – McLoughlin in Leicester, Batty in Notts–Derby – played a directing or a crucial consulting role.

But the revolution was less complete – at least, in its early stages – than its supporters liked to argue: many of these "systems" plans had a distinctly blueprint tint, in that they soon resulted in all-too-concrete proposals for fixed investments like freeway systems.[42] Underlying this, furthermore, were some curious metaphysical assumptions, which the new systems planners shared with their blueprint elders: the planning system was seen as active, the city system as purely passive; the political system was regarded as benign and receptive to the planner's expert advice.[43] In practice, the systems planner was involved in two very different kinds of activity: as a social scientist, he or she was passively observing and analyzing reality; as a designer, the same planner was acting on reality to change it – an activity inherently less certain, and also inherently subject to objectives that could only be set through a complex, often messy, set of dealings between professionals, politicians, and public.

[42]   Faludi, 1973, 146.
[43]   Batty, 1979, 21.

The core of this problem was a logical paradox: despite the claims of the systems planners,[44] the urban planning system was different from (say) a weapons system. In this latter kind of system, to which the "systems approach" had originally and successfully been applied, the controls were inside the system; but here, the urban–regional system was inside its own system of control.[45] Related to this were other crucial differences: in urban planning, there was not just one problem and one overriding objective, but many, perhaps contradictory; it was difficult to move from general goals to specific operational ones;[46] not all were fully perceived; the systems to be analyzed did not self-evidently exist, but had to be synthesized; most aspects were not deterministic, but probabilistic; costs and benefits were difficult to quantify. So the claims of the systems school to scientific objectivity could not readily be fulfilled. Increasingly, members of the school came to admit that in such "open" systems, systematic analysis would need to play a subsidiary role to intuition and judgment; in other words, the traditional approach.[47] By 1975, Britton Harris, perhaps the most celebrated of all the systems planners, could write that he no longer believed that the more difficult problems of planning could be solved by optimizing methods.[48]

The Search for a New Paradigm

All this, in the late 1960s, came to focus in an attack from two very different directions, which together blew the ship of systems planning at least half out of the water. From the philosophical Right came a series of theoretical and empirical studies from American political scientists, arguing that – at least in the United States – crucial urban decisions were made within a pluralist political structure in which no one individual or group had total knowledge or power, and in which, consequently, the decision-making process could best be described as "disjointed incrementalism" or "muddling through." Meyerson and Banfield's classic analysis of the Chicago Housing Authority concluded that it engaged in little real planning, and failed because it did not correctly identify the real power structure in the city; its elitist view of the public interest was totally opposed to the populist view of the ward politicians, which finally prevailed. Downs theorized about such a structure, suggesting that politicians buy votes by offering bundles of policies, rather as in a market. Lindblom contrasted the whole rational-comprehensive model of planning with what he found to be the actual process of policy development, which was characterized by a mixture of values and analysis, a confusion of ends and means, a failure to analyze alternatives, and an avoidance of theory. Altshuler's analysis of Minneapolis–St Paul suggested that the professional

---

[44]   Chadwick, 1971, 81.
[45]   Batty, 1979, 18–21.
[46]   Altshuler, 1965a, 20; Catanese and Steiss, 1970, 8.
[47]   Catanese and Steiss, 1970, 17, 21.
[48]   Harris, 1975, 42.

planner carried no clout against the political machine, which backed the highway-building engineers against him; they won by stressing expertise and concentrating on narrow goals, but theirs was a political game; the conclusion was that planners should recognize their own weakness, and devise strategies appropriate to that fact.[49]

All these analyses arose from study of American urban politics, which is traditionally more populist, more pluralist, than most; even there, Rabinowitz's study of New Jersey cities suggested that they varied greatly in style, from the highly fragmented to the very cohesive;[50] while Etzioni, criticizing Lindblom, suggested that recent United States history showed several important examples of non-incremental decision-making, especially in defense.[51] But, these reservations taken, the studies did at least suggest that planning in actuality was a very long way indeed from the cool, rational, Olympian style envisaged in the systems texts. Perhaps it might have been better if it had been closer; perhaps not. The worrisome point was that in practice, local democracy proved to be an infinitely messier business than the theory would have liked. Some theorists accordingly concluded that if this was the way planning was, this was the way it should be encouraged to be: partial, experimental, incremental, working on problems as they arose.[52]

That emerged even more clearly, because – as so often seems to happen – in America the left-wing criticism was reaching closely similar conclusions. By the late 1960s, fueled by the civil rights movement and the war on poverty, the protests against the Vietnam War and the campus free-speech movement, it was this wing that was making all the running. Underlying the general current of protest were three key themes, which proved fatal to the legitimacy of the systems planners. One was a widespread distrust of expert, top-down planning generally – whether for problems of peace and war, or for problems of the cities. Another, much more specific, was an increasing paranoia about the systems approach, which in its military applications was seen as employing pseudo-science and incomprehensible jargon to create a smokescreen, behind which ethically reprehensible policies could be pursued. And a third was triggered by the riots that tore through American cities starting with Paterson, New Jersey, in 1964 and ending with Watts, Los Angeles, in 1967. They seemed to prove the point: systems planning had done nothing to ameliorate the condition of the cities; rather, by assisting or at least conniving in the dismemberment of inner-city communities, it might actually have contributed to aggravating it. By 1967, one critic, Richard Bolan, could argue that systems planning was old-fashioned comprehensive planning, dressed up in fancier garb; both, alike, ignored political reality.[53]

The immediate left-wing reaction was to call on the planners themselves to turn the tables, and to practice bottom-up planning by becoming advocate-planners.[54]

[49]   Meyerson and Banfield, 1955; Downs, 1957; Lindblom, 1959; Altshuler, 1965b.
[50]   Rabinowitz, 1969, passim.
[51]   Etzioni, 1968, passim.
[52]   Bolan, 1967, 239–40.
[53]   Bolan, 1967, 241.
[54]   Davidoff, 1965.

Particularly, in this way they would make explicit the debate about the setting of goals and objectives, which both the blueprint and systems approaches had bypassed by means of their comfortable shared assumption that this was the professional planner's job. Advocacy planners would intervene in a variety of ways, in a variety of groups; diversity should be their keynote. They would help inform the public of alternatives; force public planning agencies to compete for support; help critics to generate plans that were superior to official ones; compel considerations of underlying values. The resulting structure was highly American: democratic, locally grounded, pluralistic, but also legalistic in being based on institutionalized conflict. But, interestingly, while demoting the planner in one respect, it enormously advanced his or her power in another: the planner was to take many of the functions that the locally elected official had previously exercised. And, in practice, it was not entirely clear how it would all work; particularly, how the process would resolve the very real conflicts of interest that could arise within communities, or how it could avoid the risk that the planners, once again, would become manipulators.[55]

At any rate, there is more than a passing resemblance between the planner as a disjointed incrementalist, and the planner-advocate; and, indeed, between either of these and a third model set out in Bolan's 1967 paper, the planner as informal coordinator and catalyst, which in turn shades into a fourth: Melvin Webber's probabilistic planner, who uses new information systems to facilitate debate and improve decision-making. All are assumed to work within a pluralist world, with very many different competing groups and interests, where the planner has at most (and, further, should have) only limited power or influence; all are based, at least implicitly, on continued acceptance of logical positivism. As Webber put it, at the conclusion of his long two-part paper of 1968–9,

> The burden of my argument is that city planning failed to adopt the planning method, choosing instead to impose input bundles, including regulatory constraints, on the basis of ideologically defined images of goodness. I am urging, as an alternative, that planning tries out the planning idea and the planning method.[56]

In turn, Webber's view of planning – which flatly denies the possibility of a stable predictable future or agreed goals – provides some of the philosophical underpinnings of the Social Learning or New Humanist approach of the 1970s, which stressed the importance of learning systems in helping cope with a turbulent environment.[57] But finally, this approach divorced itself from logical positivism, returning to a reliance on personal knowledge which was strangely akin to old-style blueprint planning; and, as developed by John Friedmann of the University of California at Los Angeles, it finally resulted in a demand for all political activity to be

---

[55]   Peattie, 1968, 85.
[56]   Webber, 1968/9, 294–5.
[57]   Schon, 1971; Friedmann, 1973.

decomposed into decision by minute political groups: a return to the anarchist roots of planning, with a vengeance.

So these different approaches diverged, sometimes in detailed emphasis, sometimes more fundamentally. What they shared was the belief that – at any rate in the American political system – the planner did not have much power and did not deserve to have much either; within a decade, from 1965 to 1975, these approaches together neatly stripped the planner of whatever priestly clothing, and consequent mystique, she or he may have possessed. Needless to say, this view powerfully communicated itself to the professionals themselves. Even in countries with more centralized, top-down political systems, such as Great Britain, young graduating planners increasingly saw their roles as rather like barefoot doctors, helping the poor down on the streets of the inner city, working either for a politically acceptable local authority, or, failing that, for community organizations battling against a politically objectionable one.

Several historical factors, in addition to the demolition job on planning by the American theorists, contributed to this change: planners and politicians belatedly discovered the continued deprivation of the inner-city poor; then, it was seen that the areas where these people lived were suffering depopulation and deindustrialization; in consequence, planners progressively moved away from the merely physical, and into the social and the economic. The change can be caricatured thus: in 1955, the typical newly graduated planner was at the drawing board, producing a diagram of desired land uses; in 1965, she or he was analyzing computer output of traffic patterns; in 1975, the same person was talking late into the night with community groups, in the attempt to organize against hostile forces in the world outside.

It was a remarkable inversion of roles. For what was wholly or partly lost, in that decade, was the claim to any unique and useful expertise, such as was possessed by the doctor or the lawyer. True, the planner could still offer specialized knowledge on planning laws and procedures, or on how to achieve a particular design solution; though often, given the nature of the context and the changed character of planning education, she or he might not have enough of either of these skills to be particularly useful. And, some critics were beginning to argue, this was because planning had extended so thinly over so wide an area that it was almost meaningless; in the title of Aaron Wildavsky's celebrated paper, If Planning Is Everything, Maybe It's Nothing.[58]

The fact was that planning, as an academic discipline, had theorized about its own role to such extent that it was denying its own claim to legitimacy. Planning, Faludi pointed out in his text of 1973, could be merely *functional*, in that the goals and objectives are taken as given; or *normative*, in that they are themselves the object of rational choice.[59] The problem was whether planning was really capable of doing that latter job. As a result, by the mid-1970s planning had reached the stage of a "paradigm crisis";[60] it had been theoretically useful to distinguish the planning

---

[58]   Wildavsky, 1973, 130.
[59]   Faludi, 1973, 175.
[60]   Galloway and Mahayni, 1977, 66.

process as something separate from what is planned, yet this had meant a neglect of substantive theory, pushing it to the periphery of the whole subject. "Consequently, new theory is needed which attempts to bridge current planning strategies and the urban physical and social systems to which strategies are applied."[61]

The Marxist Ascendancy

That became ever clearer in the following decade, when the logical positivists retreated from the intellectual field of battle and the Marxists took possession. As the whole world knows, the 1970s saw a remarkable resurgence – indeed a veritable explosion – of Marxist studies. This could not fail to affect the closely related worlds of urban geography, sociology, economics, and planning. True, like the early neo-classical economists, Marx had been remarkably uninterested in questions of spatial location – even though Engels had made illuminating comments on the spatial distribution of classes in mid-Victorian Manchester. The disciples now reverently sought to extract from the holy texts, drop by drop, a distillation that could be used to brew the missing theoretical potion. At last, by the mid-1970s, it was ready; then came a flood of new work. It originated in various places and in various disciplines: in England, the geographers David Harvey and Doreen Massey helped explain urban growth and change in terms of the circulation of capital; in Paris, Manuel Castells and Henri Lefebvre developed sociologically based theories.[62]

In the endless debates that followed among the Marxists themselves, a critical question concerned the role of the state.[63] In France, Lokjine and others argued that it was mainly concerned, through such devices as macro-economic planning and related infrastructure investment, directly to underpin and aid the direct productive investments of private capital. Castells, in contrast, argued that its main function had been to provide collective consumption – as in public housing, or schools, or transportation – to help guarantee the reproduction of the labor force and to dampen class conflict, essential for the maintenance of the system.[64] Clearly, planning might play a very large role in both these state functions; hence, by the mid-1970s French Marxist urbanists were engaging in major studies of this role in the industrialization of such major industrial areas as Dieppe.[65]

At the same time, a specifically Marxian view of planning emerged in the English-speaking world. To describe it adequately would require a course in Marxist theory. But, in inadequate summary, it states that the structure of the capitalist city itself, including its land use and activity patterns, is the result of

[61] Galloway and Mahayni, 1977, 68.
[62] Harvey, 1973; 1982; 1985a; 1985b; Castells, 1977; 1978; Lefebvre, 1968; 1972; Massey and Meegan, 1982; Massey, 1984.
[63] Carnoy, 1984.
[64] Lokjine, 1977; Castells, 1977, 276–323; 1978, 15–36.
[65] Castells, 1978, 62–92.

Figure 10.5 Manuel Castells. Three waves of Berkeley planning theory continued. (3) Castells came in 1979 from Paris, where his *Urban Question*, a Marxist analysis of planning's role within the capitalist state, had become an instant international classic.

capital in pursuit of profit. Because capitalism is doomed to recurrent crises, which deepen in the current stage of late capitalism, capital calls upon the state, as its agent, to assist it by remedying disorganization in commodity production, and by aiding the reproduction of the labor force. It thus tries to achieve certain necessary objectives: to facilitate continued capital accumulation, by ensuring rational allocation of resources; by assisting the reproduction of the labor force through the provision of social services, thus maintaining a delicate balance between labor and capital and preventing social disintegration; and by guaranteeing and legitimating capitalist social and property relations. As Dear and Scott put it, "in summary, planning is an historically-specific and socially-necessary response to the self-disorganizing tendencies of *privatized* capitalist social and property relations as these appear in urban space."[66] In particular, it seeks to guarantee collective provision of necessary infrastructure and certain basic urban services,

---

[66]   Dear and Scott, 1981, 13.

and to reduce negative externalities whereby certain activities of capital cause losses to other parts of the system.[67]

But, since capitalism also wishes to circumscribe state planning as far as possible, there is an inbuilt contradiction: planning, because of this inherent inadequacy, always solves one problem only by creating another.[68] Thus, say the Marxists, nineteenth-century clearances in Paris created a working-class housing problem; American zoning limited the powers of industrialists to locate at the most profitable locations.[69] And planning can never do more than modify some parameters of the land development process; it cannot change its intrinsic logic, and so cannot remove the contradiction between private accumulation and collective action.[70] Further, the capitalist class is by no means homogeneous; different fractions of capital may have divergent, even contradictory interests, and complex alliances may be formed in consequence; thus, latter-day Marxist explanations come close to being pluralist, albeit with a strong structural element.[71] But in the process,

> the more that the State intervenes in the urban system, the greater is the likelihood that different social groups and fractions will contest the legitimacy of its decisions. *Urban life as a whole becomes progressively invaded by political controversies and dilemmas.*[72]

Because traditional non-Marxian planning theory has ignored this essential basis of planning, so Marxian commentators argue, it is by definition vacuous: it seeks to define what planning ideally ought to be, devoid of all context; its function has been to depoliticize planning as an activity, and thus to legitimate it.[73] It seeks to achieve this by representing itself as the force that produces the various facets of real-world planning. But in fact, its various claims – to develop abstract concepts that rationally represent real-world processes, to legitimate its own activity, to explain material processes as the outcome of ideas, to present planning goals as derived from generally shared values, and to abstract planning activity in terms of metaphors drawn from other fields like engineering – are both very large and quite unjustified.[74] The reality, Marxists argue, is precisely the opposite: viewed objectively, planning theory is nothing other than a creation of the social forces that bring planning into existence.[75]

It makes up a disturbing body of coherent criticism: yes, of course, planning cannot simply be an independent self-legitimating activity, as scientific inquiry may claim to be; yes, of course, it is a phenomenon that – like all phenomena – represents the circumstances of its time. As Scott and Roweis put it,

[67] Dear and Scott, 1981, 11.
[68] Dear and Scott, 1981, 14–15.
[69] Scott and Roweis, 1977, 1108.
[70] Scott and Roweiss, 1977, 1107.
[71] Mollenkopf, 1983.
[72] Dear and Scott, 1981, 16.
[73] Scott and Roweis, 1977, 1098.
[74] Cooke, 1983, 106–8.
[75] Scott and Roweis, 1977, 1099.

there is a definite mismatch between the world of current planning theory, on the one hand, and the real world of practical planning intervention on the other hand. The one is the quintessence of order and reason in relation to the other which is full of disorder and unreason. Conventional theorists then set about resolving this mismatch between theory and reality by introducing the notion that planning theory is in any case not so much an attempt to explain the world as it *is* but as it *ought* to be. Planning theory then sets itself the task of rationalizing irrationalities, and seeks to materialize itself in social and historical reality (like Hegel's World Spirit) by bringing to bear upon the world a set of abstract, independent, and transcendent norms.[76]

It was powerful criticism. But it left in turn a glaringly open question, both for the unfortunate planner – whose legitimacy is now totally torn from him, like the epaulette from the shoulder of a disgraced officer – and, equally, for the Marxist critic: what, then, is planning theory about? Has it any normative or prescriptive content whatsoever? The answer, logically, would appear to be no. One of the critics, Philip Cooke, is uncompromising:

> The main criticism that tends to have been made, justifiably, of planning is that it has remained stubbornly normative … in this book it will be argued that (planning theorists) should identify mechanisms which cause changes in the nature of planning to be brought about, rather than assuming such changes to be either the creative idealizations of individual minds, or mere regularities in observable events.[77]

This is at least consistent: planning theory should avoid all prescription; it should stand right outside the planning process, and seek to analyze the subject – including traditional theory – for what it is, the reflection of historical forces. Scott and Roweis, a decade earlier, seem to be saying exactly the same thing: planning theory cannot be normative, it cannot assume "transcendent operational norms."[78] But then, they stand their logic on its own head, saying, "a viable theory of urban planning should not only tell us what planning is, but also what we can, and must, do as progressive planners."[79] This, of course, is sheer rhetoric. But it nicely displays the agony of the dilemma. Either theory is about unraveling the historical logic of capitalism, or it is about prescription for action. Since the planner-theorist – however sophisticated – could never hope to divert the course of capitalist evolution by more than a millimeter or a millisecond, the logic would seem to demand that she or he sticks firmly to the first and abjures the second. In other words, the Marxian logic is strangely quietist: it suggests that the planner retreats from planning altogether into the academic ivory tower.

Some were acutely conscious of the dilemma. John Forester tried to resolve it by basing a whole theory of planning action on the work of Jürgen Habermas. Habermas, perhaps the leading German social theorist of the post-World War Two

[76]   Scott and Rowis, 1977, 1116.
[77]   Cooke, 1983, 25, 27.
[78]   Scott and Roweiss, 1977, 1099.
[79]   Scott and Roweiss, 1977, 1099.

era, had argued that latter-day capitalism justified its own legitimacy by spinning around itself a complex set of distortions in communication, designed to obscure and prevent any rational understanding of its own workings.[80] Thus, he argued, individuals became powerless to understand how and why they act, and so were excluded from all power to influence their own lives

> as they are harangued, pacified, mislead [*sic*], and ultimately persuaded that inequality, poverty, and ill-health are either problems for which the victim is responsible or problems so "political" and "complex" that they can have nothing to say about them. Habermas argues that democratic politics or planning requires the consent that grows from processes of collective criticism, not from silence or a party line.[81]

But, Forester argues, Habermas's own proposals for communicative action provide a way for planners to improve their own practice:

> By recognizing planning practice as normatively role-structured communicative action which distorts, covers up, or reveals to the public the prospects and possibilities they face, a critical theory of planning aids us practically and ethically as well. This is the contribution of critical theory to planning: pragmatics with vision – to reveal true alternatives, to correct false expectations, to counter cynicism, to foster inquiry, to spread political responsibility, engagement, and action. Critical planning practice, technically skilled and politically sensitive, is an organizing and democratizing practice.[82]

Fine. The problem is that – stripped of its Germanic philosophical basis, which is necessarily a huge oversimplification of a very dense analysis – the practical prescription all comes out as good old-fashioned democratic common sense, no more and no less than Davidoff's advocacy planning of 15 years before: cultivate community networks, listen carefully to the people, involve the less-organized groups, educate the citizens in how to join in, supply information and make sure people know how to access it, develop skills in working with groups in conflict situations, emphasize the need to participate, compensate for external pressures. As Nigel Taylor puts it, "by the early 1990s, a whole new theory of planning came to be articulated around the idea of planning as a process of communication and negotiation."[83] This came about partly because planners wanted to find a more effective way of doing things, but mainly because "these planning theorists were also motivated by the ideal of a democratic, participatory style of planning which incorporated all groups who stood to be affected by environmental change, not just those powerful actors who were in a position to carry out – or 'implement' – major development and environmental change."[84] True, if in all this planners can sense that they have

---

[80] Bernstein, 1976; 1985; Held, 1980; McCarthy, 1978; Thompson and Held, 1982.
[81] Forester, 1980, 277.
[82] Forester, 1980, 283.
[83] Taylor, 1998, 122.
[84] Taylor, 1998, 123.

penetrated the mask of capitalism, that may help them to help others to act to change their environment and their lives; and, given the clear philosophical impasse of the late 1970s, such a massive metaphysical underpinning may be necessary.

What was interesting about the new emphasis was its relationship to what came before. Teaching planners that they should try to "get to yes" by working effectively to mediate between different groups and interests,[85] it demanded that the planner understand how the system works, and in that sense it has something in common with the radical political economy theory of the 1970s. But there was a key difference: the political economists did not want to make the system work, but to aid its replacement; in contrast, the new theory wanted to work with the market.[86] By the 1990s, radical theorists like Leonie Sandercock were urging less control of urban space, so that people could negotiate their own lives; in a strange reflection of Thatcherite libertarian logic, they rejected the welfare state with its standard operating procedures, its vertical chains of command, and its standardized services.[87]

Sandercock argued that virtually all previous planning history told an "official story," the story of the modernist planning project, the representation of planning as the voice of reason in modern society, the carrier of the Enlightenment mission of material progress through scientific rationality: "Planning itself is the real hero, battling foes from left and right, slaying the dragons of greed and irrationality and, if not always triumphing, at least always noble, always on the side of the angels."[88] This is the story of planning by and through the state, part of a tradition of city and nation building. But, she countered, alternative traditions of planning had always existed outside the state, sometimes in opposition to it. These she called *insurgent planning histories*, arguing that they "challenge our very definition of what constitutes planning."[89]

In particular, these alternative histories featured new actors. In the official story, only "professionals" were seen as relevant players. The result was a narrative about the ideas and actions of white middle-class men, since women and people of color were – throughout most of planning history – systematically excluded from the profession because they lacked access to higher education. And in parallel, Sandercock's new history would tell about different actions: no longer state-led, but that "whole realm of community-driven and community-based planning (sometimes in opposition to the state) which arguably has a significantly longer history than that of the profession."[90]

In a second book, Sandercock went further, arguing that new socio-cultural forces – the "age of migration," a new politics of "multi-cultural citizenship," the age of post-colonialism, a politics of reclaiming urban and regional space by indigenous and formerly colonized peoples, and the age of women and other so-called "minorities" – were

---

[85]   Taylor, 1998, 226.
[86]   Taylor, 1998, 127.
[87]   Fischler, 2000, 150; Sandercock, 1998a, 212.
[88]   Sandercock, 1998a, 4.
[89]   Sandercock, 1998a, 1–2.
[90]   Sandercock, 1998a, 7.

combining to transform cities and planning.[91] Her book, she argued, "is the first to give systematic attention to the crumbling pillars of modernist planning, and to suggest a way out of the impasse, a way of advancing a progressive planning practice into the twenty-first century, based on the insights of feminist, postmodern and postcolonial thinking."[92]

How justified were her claims, viewed over a decade later? Ward, Freestone, and Silver conclude that she had then – and to a lesser extent still had – a point. But, even in 1998, workers from other disciplines – social, political, and cultural historians – had always been more inclined to see planning (and especially planners) as only part of their subject.[93] More generally, recent work had seen more explorations of alternative explanations to conventional wisdom, studies of conflict, utilization of popular media to supplement official sources, and acknowledgement of planning's "darker side."[94]

Sandercock could – and doubtless would – claim that she helped kick-start the process. But there are two further problems with her thesis. The first, simply, is that by redefining planning as something else, something entirely different from anything that went before, she robs the word of all meaning: as in *Alice in Wonderland*, "When *I* use a word," Humpty Dumpty said, in rather a scornful tone, "it means just what I choose it to mean – neither more nor less." This is postmodernism with a vengeance. The other is that by hinting darkly at planning's *noir* side – a concept fashionable at the time at the University of California, Los Angeles, and almost inevitably borrowed from Hollywood – she manages to imply that all official planning has a secret underlying significance, and further that this is always malign. In other words, real estate interests practicing exclusionary zoning in the America of the 1920s can be equated with Social Democratic politicians and professional planners in the Sweden of the 1960s. Taken to this level of paranoia, of course, all human action is finally irrational and finally meaningless. And this reflects the bizarre influence of the ultimate cult of the 1990s: postmodernism.

The Continuing Divorce of Theory and Practice: Postmodern Theory Exits from the World as We Know It[95]

By then, the radical academic coterie, who might have been most active on the barricades against any kind of cooperation with "the system," were themselves in intellectual retreat. And it took a strange form: as if anticipating the collapse of the Soviet Union and the Eastern European People's Democracies, already by the late 1980s they were withdrawing ever farther from the high ground of socio-economic debate,

---

91   Sandercock, 1998b, 2–3.
92   Sandercock, 1998b, 4.
93   Ward *et al.*, 2011, 247.
94   Ward *et al.*, 2011, 248.
95   This section is based in part on Hall, 1998, Ch. 1.

into the muddied thickets of cultural discourse. Deriving from the Frankfurt school of sociology of the 1920s, and its exile in New York in the 1950s and 1960s, this gave us the theory of postmodernity. And this became a strange intellectual bandwagon on which almost anyone could climb: it embraced all kinds of intellectual positions, which do not comfortably sit together and may even contradict each other. Often, in the writings of French theorists like Jean Baudrillard and Jean-François Lyotard, it achieved a deliberate and profound obscurity. But Anthony Giddens has encapsulated its key tenets: nothing can be known with certainty; "history" has no teleology, so that "progress" is impossible; and that, with new ecological concerns and perhaps new social movements, there is a new social and political agenda – though exactly what this is, we are not quite certain.[96] Partly this is because postmodernists seem to think that reality is no longer very real.[97] It is obsessed with art forms that reflect a transitory, flimsy, unstable notion of reality; at the extreme, in the work of Jean Baudrillard, everything is reduced to a world of signs, in which distinctions between real and unreal disappear.[98] Similarly, the French situationist Guy Debord argues that we have entered a world of "alienated consumption," in which people are only connected to the world by images created by someone else.[99]

So these new-style radical intelligentsia engaged in endless debates on the significance of postmodernism: in architecture, in the cinema, in television, in anything that would support a paper or a conference contribution. The contributions themselves were written as if by central *Diktat* in a strange hermetically sealed style, clearly directed at a small coterie of fellow cognoscenti, and characterized by odd private linguistic tricks like the placement of qualifying syllables in brackets, as in (un)inspiring or (un)original. It doubtless reflected the emergence on the market of a flood of recent graduates in architecture and media studies, for whom this represented a sole source of gainful employment; it did not produce much insight or enlightenment. And it left some older-generation, still politically committed Marxists in a state of near-apoplexy on the sidelines.[100]

Small wonder; for what was never quite clear about this flood of literature was what exactly it was all about, even as an intellectual activity, still less as a political project: intellectually, the much-quoted (but perhaps little-read) model was the long-dead Berlin critic Walter Benjamin, celebrator of the *flâneur* or fly-on-the-café-wall; politically, it amounted at most to polysyllabic mutterings about deconstructing the hegemonic projects of capitalism. The problem, as Anthony Giddens well pointed out, is that the postmodernists were all responding – in their highly oblique ways – to developments in contemporary capitalism, and in this sense they were simply following a long radical tradition.[101] But their theory lacks explanation: there is a vague

[96]   Berman, 1982, 29–32; Best and Kellner, 1991, 16, 26, 29; Giddens, 1990, 46; Lyotard, 1984, xxiii–xxv.
[97]   Lash, 1990, 12.
[98]   Baudrillard, 1988, 76; Best and Kellner, 1991, 119, 121; Kellner, 1987, 132–4; Lash, 1990, 192–3.
[99]   Debord, 1970, para. 42; 1990, 27; cf. Sussman, 1989, 3–4; Wollen, 1989, 30, 34.
[100]   Harvey, 1989.
[101]   Best and Kellner, 1991, 15; Giddens, 1990, 46.

sense that we have entered a new era in which all previous theories have been rendered obsolete, but because the new theory denies meta-theory, it proves incapable of explaining complex socio-economic-political relationships.[102]

Perhaps postmodernism was just a 1980s fad, arising from the frustration of French intellectuals in the wake of the failed 1960s revolution and their fears that they were being sidelined.[103] All, perhaps, a useful way of keeping unemployed graduates off the streets in warm well-lit seminar rooms; but of little more significance. It was a rum old world, this world of urban discourse in the mid-1990s: but that perhaps reflected a situation long familiar in the cafés of continental Europe, where the universities had a longer tradition of producing permanent students. Of course, occasionally they might emerge on to the streets to engage in real *événements*; but this time there did not seem to be much of a political project to which they might attach themselves.

And they are deliberately, rather infuriatingly aspatial: they are entirely uninterested in the question of what happens where, and why. David Harvey, who – like many critics – doubts that postmodernism means much, suggests that in the field of architecture and urban design, it broadly signifies a break with "large-scale, metropolitan-wide, technologically rational and efficient urban *plans*, backed by no-frills modern architecture …"[104] in favor of "Fiction, fragmentation, collage, and eclecticism, all suffused with a sense of ephemerality and chaos."[105] This, for a traditional Marxist like Harvey, arises from a changed regime of accumulation and mode of regulation,[106] which is characterized by "voodoo economics … political image construction and deployment, and … new social class formation."[107] So there is a significance; but exactly what is unclear.

Jane Jacobs, already considered in Chapter 9, plays a curious role in the postmodernist tradition. Modernism's faith in reason – what Habermas called the "project" of modernity – and science had its roots in eighteenth-century Enlightenment, and planning was an intrinsic part of this process.[108] Thus the radical nature of Jacobs's critique lay in "her implicit questioning of whether cities could be made better places by rational planning at all."[109] Ultimately, this led to Anthony Giddens's critique: that, if anyone were to hold such a view, "they could scarcely write a book about it. The only possibility would be to repudiate intellectual activity altogether."[110] And that, of course, might serve as a verdict on postmodernism generally.

Early in the new millennium, in a magisterial study, Michael Storper reviewed the entire development of late twentieth-century intellectual radicalism. There is a utopian impulse, he pointed out, behind radical social science: "we have great difficulty in

102   Best and Kellner, 1991, 260–1.
103   Best and Kellner, 1991, 297.
104   Harvey, 1989, 66.
105   Harvey, 1989, 98.
106   Harvey, 1989, 121.
107   Harvey, 1989, 336.
108   Taylor, 1998, 164.
109   Taylor, 1998, 164.
110   Quoted in Taylor, 1998, 165.

separating our analysis of what is from what we want it to be."[111] As Marxism went out of fashion, so the utopian impulse moved to postmodernism on the theory side, and to multiculturalism and "cultural politics" in political practice. Marxism suffered because it lacked the ability to link micro-analysis to the macro-analysis of capitalist development that it did so well.[112] Maybe for that reason, maybe because of some obscurer cause, there occurred a major shift, a "cultural turn":

> In certain social sciences in the Anglo-American world, radicalism has come to be closely associated with what is known as the "cultural turn" consisting of theory and research based on the overall notion that the keys to understanding contemporary society and to transforming it lie in the ways that culture orients our behaviors and shapes what we are able to know about the world. The keystone to the cultural turn is that knowledge and practice are relativistic, because culturally determined. The cultural turn variously blends postmodernist philosophy, cultural theories of society, and poststructuralist philosophy. These literatures explicitly disavow what they term "metanarratives". These ideas are associated by intellectuals with certain social movements; the "race/gender/culture/sexuality" liberation nexus, as well as community-based organizations of all types, environmentalism and postcolonialist politics.[113]

Storper dissects what he calls "the cultural turn's intellectual solipsism."[114] Its theory of society is based on relationships not between individuals (as for liberals) or between classes (as for Marxists), but between culturally different groups. This has helped illuminate many important issues, hitherto little explored. But, says Storper, many postmodernists and cultural-turn scholars attack not just the record of modern societies, but the very cornerstone of modernism, the rule of reason. In an extreme form, they come to celebrate difference for its own sake. And this, Storper might have added (but does not), can lead to a form of intellectual fascism. Or, at very least, to a kind of gung-ho localism which either disdains state-oriented collective solutions to problems, or promotes the replacement of statism by localism and voluntarism. Thus, "Decentralization of all sorts has been transformed into a good in and of itself,"[115] becoming "an ideological legitimization – perhaps unwilling – of retreat of the state from its desirable role in capitalist societies. And in many cases this localism aids and abets reactionary policies."[116]

All this has had an influence on urban planning: "advocacy planning" has become "radical democracy," the taking of power from below: in both, "planners set themselves up not as counselors to the prince, but counselors to the downtrodden."[117] And this becomes an end in and for itself, leading to mutual antagonisms, and

---

[111]   Storper, 2001, 156.
[112]   Storper, 2001, 156, 158.
[113]   Storper, 2001, 16.
[114]   Storper, 2001, 161.
[115]   Storper, 2001, 170.
[116]   Storper, 2001, 170.
[117]   Storper, 2001, 168.

ironically relegitimating the pursuit of group interests for ethnic minorities.[118] One expression, of course, is communicative planning theory, based on the notion that "if different groups – all presumed to have legitimate claims – can be brought to the negotiating table, the resulting communication, if handled with contemporary consensus-resolution techniques, will somehow prove beneficial in identifying the best possible solutions for all concerned."[119] But, as many planners now admit, it can run up against powerful interests, and communication may not be so clear or under-standing as we would like.[120]

How significant were these shifts? Nigel Taylor argues that none of them – first the shift from urban design to systems and rational planning, in the 1960s, secondly the development of "communicative planning" from the 1970s, even the "cultural turn" towards postmodernism in the 1990s – was a true "paradigm shift." After the first, planners still judged proposals on design grounds, even though the design tradition was marginalized, so that in the United Kingdom the 1973 Essex Design Guide had a major impact on planning practice; the real impact was to distinguish more clearly between strategic and local planning styles. The second in effect polarized two views, one insisting that the planner still had special skills, the other claiming that planning was essentially political and value-laden. The most important result was a greater con-cern with implementation, from which came the stress on effective communication and facilitative skills – though perhaps implying that the planner could still profess some special degree of expertise. And the final shift, towards "postmodernism," has moved planners towards a total relativism, a denial of any kind of norms; but expo-nents like Sandercock have retreated from such a stance, and have accepted the need for some kind of state planning.[121] It is doubtful, Nigel Taylor argues, whether any of these shifts really involved a Kuhnian shift in views of the world.[122] The shifts in town-planning thought over a 50-year period can be seen as developmental rather than as ruptures between incompatible paradigms; they have "filled out," and thereby enriched, the rather primitive conception of planning that prevailed in the immediate postwar years, developing sophistication as we have learned more about the greater complexity of urban environments and the diverse values of different communities.[123]

The World Outside the Tower: Practice Retreats from Theory

In any case, there was one thing with which most of this theory – with the exception of communicative planning – had categorically nothing to do, and that was the bor-ing job of planning real places. As in the 1970s and 1980s, but even more so, the

---

[118] Storper, 2001, 168–9.
[119] Storper, 2001, 169.
[120] Storper, 2001, 169.
[121] Taylor, 1999, 333–40.
[122] Taylor, 1999, 341.
[123] Taylor, 1999, 341–2.

worlds of urban studies and urban planning had become steadily more uncoupled. The only good news, perhaps, was that in the process academic planners were becoming more concerned with real-life issues. And in some fields – particularly in analyzing the role of different discourses in public participation – they did actually manage to make some tenuous connections between the two worlds: a small but respectable positive point.

Meanwhile, if the theorists were retreating in one direction, the practitioners were certainly reciprocating. Whether baffled or bored by the increasingly scholastic character of the academic debate, they lapsed into an increasingly untheoretical, unreflective, pragmatic, even visceral style of planning. As Mark Tewdwr-Jones has put it,

> planning has been reduced to a bureaucratic regulatory process in which the political has been downplayed in the interests of organisational efficiency. The "vision thing", the concept that gave birth to town planning as a professional activity in the early years of the twentieth century, has been lost, partly as a consequence of legislative fiat, a New Right determination to standardise and commodify planning as a public service, and individual planners' recalcitrance. Town planning is no longer a political and professional activity; it is rampant technocracy, shared between the public and private sectors.[124]

Conservative governments in the 1980s and early 1990s, having tried to eliminate planning, were content to reduce it to a codified, bureaucratized activity, the "New Proceduralism," which it has remained. The profession failed to contest its negative image; the RTPI "could be accused of an intellectual abdication."[125] In the land of its birth, planning was slipping into insignificance, not because it was wrong or misplaced, but because it lacked the intellectual wherewithal to defend itself.

That was not entirely new: planning had come under a cloud before, as during the 1950s, and had soon reappeared in a clear blue sky. What was new, strange, and seemingly unique about the 1980s and the 1990s was the divorce of the Marxist and post-Marxist theoreticians of academe – essentially academic spectators, taking grandstand seats at what they saw either as one of capitalism's last games, or as constructs of an unreal reality – from the anti-theoretical, anti-strategic, anti-intellectual style of the players on the field down below. The 1950s were never like that; then, the academics were the coaches, down there with the team.

It was not entirely like that. Many academics did still try to teach real-life planning. The RTPI enjoined them to become ever more practice-minded. The practitioners had not all shut their eyes and ears to the academy; some even returned for refresher courses. And if this was true in Britain, it was even more so of America, where the divorce had never been so evident. Yet there was a clear and unmistakable trend; and it was likely to be more than cyclical.

The reason is simple: as professional education of any kind becomes more fully absorbed by the academy, as its teachers become more thoroughly socialized within

---

[124] Tewdwr-Jones, 1999, 139.
[125] Tewdwr-Jones, 1999, 144.

it, as careers are seen to depend on academic peer judgments, then its norms and values – theoretical, intellectual, detached – will become ever more pervasive; and the gap between teaching and practice will progressively widen. One key illustration: of the huge output of books and papers from the planning schools in the 1980s, there were many – often, those most highly regarded within the academic community – that were simply irrelevant, even completely incomprehensible, to the average practitioner.

Perhaps, it might be argued, that was the practitioner's fault; perhaps too, we need fundamental science, with no apparent payoff, if we are later to enjoy its technological applications. The difficulty with that argument was to find convincing evidence that – not merely here, but in the social sciences generally – such payoff eventually comes. Hence the low esteem into which the social sciences had everywhere fallen, not least in Britain and the United States; hence too the diminished level of support for them, which – at any rate in Britain – had directly redounded on the planning schools. The relationship between planning and the academy had gone sour, and that is the major unresolved question that must now be addressed.

The City of Enterprise

It is not from the benevolence of the butcher, the brewer, or the baker that we expect our dinner, but from their regard to their own interest. We address ourselves, not to their humanity but to their self-love, and never talk to them of our own necessities but of their advantages. Nobody but a beggar chooses to depend chiefly upon the benevolence of his fellow-citizens.

Adam Smith, The Wealth of Nations (1776)

But beware! The time for all this is not yet. For at least another hundred years we must pretend to ourselves and to everyone that fair is foul and foul is fair; for foul is useful and fair is not. Avarice and usury and precaution must be our gods for a little longer still. For only they can lead us out of the tunnel of economic necessity into daylight.

John Maynard Keynes, "Economic Possibilities for our Grandchildren"
(Essays in Persuasion) (1930)

It is of the utmost importance to the argument of this book for the reader to keep in mind that the planning against which all our criticism is directed is solely the planning against competition – the planning that is to be substituted for competition ... But as in current usage "planning" has become synonymous with the former kind of planning, it will sometimes be inevitable for the sake of brevity to refer to it simply as planning, even though this means leaving to our opponents a very good word meriting a better fate.

Friedrich von Hayek, The Road to Serfdom (1944)

Cities of Tomorrow: An Intellectual History of Urban Planning and Design Since 1880,
Fourth Edition. Peter Hall.
© 2014 Peter Hall. Published 2014 by John Wiley & Sons, Ltd.

11

The City of Enterprise

Planning Turned Upside Down: Baltimore, Hong Kong, London, 1975–2000

Sometime during the 1970s, the city planning movement began to turn upside down and inside out; during the 1980s, it seemed at times almost on the point of self-destruction. Conventional planning, the use of plans and regulations to guide the use of land, seemed more and more discredited. Instead, planning turned from regulating urban growth, to encouraging it by any and every possible means. Cities, the new message rang loud and clear, were machines for wealth creation; the first and chief aim of planning must be to oil the machinery. The planner increasingly identified with his traditional adversary, the developer; the gamekeeper turned poacher.

Nowhere was this more clearly seen than in Britain; it was poetic justice, perhaps, that the land that gave birth to the movement should also be the scene of its apparent death-throes. But the origin of the whole reversal lay in the United States, where regulatory planning had never been as strong and the habit of development, the tradition of enterprise, had always been uppermost.

The root cause was economic. Conventional land-use planning had flourished in the great boom of the 1950s and 1960s, perhaps the greatest sustained period of growth the capitalist economy had ever known. That was because it had served as a means of guiding and controlling explosive physical growth. The great recession of the 1970s and 1980s was bound to change the nature of the basic perceived problem with which planning had to deal, and thus to threaten its very legitimacy. It hit the British with especial force, exposing deep structural weaknesses: a large part of the country's manufacturing base disappeared, bringing a loss of two million factory jobs between 1971 and 1981 alone.[1] A new geography emerged, with a contrast between the decaying inner cities – which now included not only old problem cases like Glasgow and Liverpool but once-proud seats of manufacture like London

---

[1]   Massey and Meegan, 1982; Massey, 1984; Hudson and Williams, 1986; Hausner, 1987.

and Birmingham – and the still-expanding high-tech corridors of southern England.[2] In these select places, conventional regulatory planning still commanded grassroots political support. But, over wide areas of the country, the call was no longer for the control and guidance of growth; it was for the generation of growth-promoting activities by almost any means.

There was a parallel development in the United States. There, too, the traditional industrial regions – New England, the Mid-Atlantic, and above all the Midwest – were attacked by the same virus of overseas competition, falling profits, and restructuring. The nation's manufacturing belt found itself given a new media epithet: the Rustbowl. Barry Bluestone and Bennett Harrison, in their book dramatically titled *The Deindustrialization of America*, estimated that during the 1970s the combined effect of runaway plants, shutdowns, and permanent physical cutbacks may have cost the country as many as 38 million jobs. And, of an estimated 35 million lost jobs between 1969 and 1976, more than half were in the so-called Frostbelt: in other words, the industrial heartland.[3]

It took planners, and their urban political leaders, by surprise. They had forgotten their history. As told in Chapter 5, Clarence Stein, that visionary founder of the Regional Planning Association of America and designer of Radburn, had predicted the decay of the urban economy in a remarkable article in May 1925, entitled *Dinosaur Cities*.[4] Colin Clark, that equally perspicacious economist, had correctly forecast the general contraction of manufacturing employment in his book *The Conditions of Economic Progress*, in 1940.[5] Neither had been much heeded. They had the misfortune to be too far ahead of their fellows.

Yet there was more to it than that. During the 1970s, in both Britain and the United States, neo-conservative think tanks – the British Centre for Policy Studies, the American Heritage Foundation – began to challenge the whole cozy consensus which had produced Keynesian economic policy and welfare state social policy. Following the early arguments of classics in the genre, now elevated to the status of sacred texts – like Hayek's 30-year-old *Road to Serfdom* – planning itself became a central part of the bundle of policies under assault. It had – so the radical right alleged – distorted and inhibited the operation of market forces, forcing industrialists to take sub-optimal location decisions and even throttling entrepreneurship. It was at least partly responsible for the failure of lagging cities and regions to generate new growth industries to replace declining ones. Regional planning was especially objectionable in this respect; but – despite Hayek's own reservations as to the scope of his attack – land-use planning did not escape censure.

But the first warnings came long before this fundamental critique; they were sounded in the late 1960s. In the United States, the Johnson administration redoubled its urban anti-poverty programs after the riots of 1964–7. The Model

[2]   Boddy *et al.*, 1986; Hall *et al.*, 1987.
[3]   Bluestone and Harrison, 1982, 26, 30.
[4]   Stein, 1925.
[5]   Clark, 1940.

Figure 11.1 Liverpool. Giles Gilbert Scott's massively dignified Anglican cathedral rises high over abandoned streets. *Source*: © Richard Baker/In Pictures/CORBIS.

Cities Program and associated Community Development Program (Chapter 8) were the results. Over in Britain, a series of reports – Milner Holland (1965) on London housing, Plowden (1967) on primary schools, Seebohm (1968) on social services – marked the official rediscovery of poverty by the British establishment. Perceptive academic commentators like David Eversley – brought out of academia to head strategic planning for London – began to point to the ominous decline of London's economic base.[6] Enoch Powell's notorious April 1968 speech on the problem of racial tension in the cities, in which he recalled the Tiber flowing with blood, brought an immediate panic political response from the then Wilson Labour government: an urban program, which was to give special aid to areas with high concentrations of immigrants – or, as the official euphemism had it, areas of special need.[7] The Community Development Projects (CDP) of 1969, a carbon-copy of the American program, aimed to raise the consciousness of deprived local communities; some of the project teams, full of youthful Marxist verve, set about their task so enthusiastically that they clashed head-on with local bureaucracies, and in 1976 the whole experiment came to an abrupt end.[8]

[6]   Greater London Council, 1969; Donnison and Eversley, 1973.
[7]   Edwards and Batley, 1978, 46.
[8]   McKay and Cox, 1979, 244–5; Hall, 1981, Ch. 5.

But there was a rare historical irony. The message from the CDP teams was that the problem – of places like Saltley in Birmingham, of Benwell in Newcastle upon Tyne – was "structural": a new vogue word from academia had entered the language of planning. Major forces in the latter-day capitalist economy – in particular, the increasing concentration of capital in ever fewer monopolistic hands – were transferring control of firms and industries out of local hands and into the boardrooms of ever more distant multinational enterprises. It was that conclusion, with its implication that the solution was not to be found within the confines of the capitalist system, that made the message so unacceptable to the then political leadership of the cities or to the British Home Office. The first irony was that a decade later, a new generation of politicians in the Town Halls would have warmly agreed. The second was that even before this happened the notion of structural decline had become part of received establishment thinking.

The vehicle was in some ways an unlikely one. In 1972, Peter Walker, Secretary of State for the Environment in the then Tory administration, had appointed three of Britain's most senior consultancies to investigate in depth the problems of three deprived inner-city areas. Their final reports, which were published simultaneously in the summer of 1977, underlined the same conclusion: deprivation was no longer a matter of individuals or households falling below the poverty line; rather, it had become a matter of the failure of entire urban economies.[9] The government of the day, now a Labour one, took the message: in a White Paper of 1977,[10] and in the Inner Urban Areas Act of 1978, it switched the emphasis of inner-city policy massively to economic revival. Henceforth, inner cities would be given high priority for new industrial development; central government resources were to be switched from new towns to help the cities; the urban program would be massively expanded; and central–local government partnerships would be introduced for some of the hardest-hit areas in some of the major cities.

At first, the full extent of the shift was not apparent. Existing bureaucracies dusted down existing programs that had been gathering dust in drawers, and these reflected traditional responsibilities and preoccupations: a leisure center here, a piece of landscaping there. But, as the 1970s gave way to the 1980s and the inner-city economies continued to hemorrhage, the emphasis shifted. Almost all authorities by then had economic development offices under various names, staffed by a new breed of local government officer.[11] Planners sometimes took these jobs, but they then found that they must reverse their traditional roles. The guidance and control of growth, traditional concern of the British statutory planning system since 1947, had quite suddenly been replaced by an obsession with encouraging growth at almost any cost; the political issue began to center on how best this should be done.

---

[9]   GB Department of the Environment, 1977a; 1977b; 1977c; 1977d.
[10] GB Secretary of State for Environment, 1977.
[11] Young and Mason, 1983.

The Rousification of America

At that point, some British planners and politicians began to look across the Atlantic. For the message, coming loudly from the other side in these late-1970s years, was that American cities had found a magic formula. At a typical high-level Anglo-American gathering, the glum British would show slides of the barren desolation of inner Liverpool; the exuberant Americans would arrive with pictures of a vibrant downtown Boston, full of life and color and excitement – plus, almost needless to say, booming sales and expanding jobs.[12] The magic recipe for urban revitalization – the American buzzword that began to circulate at such gatherings – seemed to consist in a new kind of creative partnership, a word used incessantly by the Americans, between the city government and the private sector. It would be seasoned by judicious funding from Washington, to which – in contrast with Whitehall's aid to British cities – relatively few strings were attached.

It also seemed to consist in a frank realization that the days of the urban manufacturing economy were over, and that success consisted in finding and creating a new service-sector role for the central city. Bored suburbanites would come in droves to a restored city that offered them a quality of life they could never find in the shopping mall. Yuppies, or Young Urban Professionals – the word began to circulate in the early 1980s – would gentrify the blighted Victorian residential areas close to downtown, and inject their dollars into restored boutiques, bars, and restaurants. Finally, the restored city would actually become a major attraction to tourists, providing a new economic base to the city.

The concept of the festival marketplace had started as early as 1964 with San Francisco's Ghiradelli Square, an old chocolate factory conveniently located near the popular Fisherman's Wharf that became a series of small shops, restaurants, and craft vendors around a large open space where people could linger and wander and entertainers could perform. In 1976, James Rouse's Faneuil Hall in Boston, comprising three historic warehouses close to downtown Boston, became the quintessential festival marketplace – and in fact gave birth to the title. An attractive destination to office workers during their lunch hour and to Boston's many tourists, its success rapidly led to imitations in Baltimore, St Louis, Milwaukee, and Minneapolis. The secret lay in new kinds of outlet for new markets: locally owned small shops selling unusual speciality items, not national chain stores, food and entertainment as anchors rather than large department stores, serving a specialized market of young, well-educated, affluent adults, both tourists and locals.[13]

This was the formula that had already revived the Boston waterfront and was just then transforming the Inner Harbor of Baltimore – the two great showcases of urban revitalization in its first phase. Viewed more closely, it was of course more complex. Both cities, which began to experience urban decline as early as the 1950s, had been working on the problem since then – two decades before their British equivalents.

[12] Hall, 1978, 33–4.
[13] Roberston, 1997, 389.

Both, in the 1960s, had first gone for fairly conventional headquarters-type office development: a formula somewhat easier for them than for their British equivalents, since both were old-established commercial centers and Boston was a major home for financial institutions. Both had then grafted on large-scale waterfront redevelopments of their derelict inner port areas, involving the then novel combination of restored warehouse and market buildings, boutique shopping, bars, restaurants, and hotels, and restoration of old residential areas.

And, in both cities, the same key agent was at work. James Rouse was already celebrated, in the late 1960s, as a Baltimore developer who had built Columbia, one of the most ambitious of the private-enterprise new towns that were developed in the United States at that time. Through his leading role in the Greater Baltimore Committee, a business elite group founded in 1956, he had also been involved in the revitalization of downtown Baltimore from its earliest stage: the 33-acre Charles Center, a complex of offices, shop, hotels, and apartments developed from the late 1950s. This, interestingly, was developed under the Urban Renewal legislation of 1949 and 1954, and in almost every respect followed the model set by Pittsburgh and Philadelphia (Chapter 7): a new, radical business elite effectively took over the city, leading a pro-growth coalition which skilfully marshaled public support and combined federal and private funds to promote large-scale commercial redevelopment.[14]

There was nothing very new about that; dozens of cities were doing it, or trying to do it. But Rouse's role in the Baltimore Inner Harbor, and in the equivalent Quincy Market and Boston Waterfront schemes, marked something different. These schemes were bigger – 250 acres in Baltimore – and they incorporated a new combination of activities: recreation, culture, shopping, mixed-income housing. They also were based on the then new concept of adaptive reuse: the rehabilitation and recycling of old physical structures to new uses.[15] They involved a relatively much bigger public role and a bigger federal commitment: $180 million in the Baltimore case, against $58 million from the city and only $22 million from the private sector. So federal grantsmanship, coupled with a new view of public-sector investment in speculative enterprise, and the cooperation of public- and private-sector entrepreneurs, were critical elements of the new formula.[16] Significantly, in both cities they were carried through by shrewd and well-established Democratic mayors who had good links with the neighborhoods – Kevin White in Boston, William Donald Schaefer in Baltimore.

The resulting developments have much in common with London's Covent Garden, which was being recycled at much the same time (Chapter 7). They are unashamedly tourist-based: Baltimore attracts 22 million visitors a year, of whom 7 million are tourists, a figure comparable with Disneyland. And this provides a critical clue to the revolutionary nature of these developments:

Figure 11.2 Boston, Quincy Market. *Source*: Peter Hall.

Figure 11.3 Baltimore, Inner Harbor. The two showpieces of American inner-city regeneration through public–private partnership, both through the Rouse Corporation: "Rousification" enters the planner's vocabulary.

the process of creating successful places is only incidentally about property development. It is much more like running a theatre, with continually changing attractions to draw people in and keep them entertained. It is no surprise that perhaps the most successful model of all, the 28,000 acre Walt Disney World in Florida, is run by a company which has divisions concerned with "Imagineering" and "Attractions". It does not seem to be surveyors and planners who have the qualities needed to create major theatres, even though they may be very useful as actors or playwrights.[17]

The Rousification of Boston and Baltimore – a process to be repeated in a score of older American industrial cities – thus involved the deliberate creation of the city-as-stage. Like theater, it resembles real life, but it is not urban life as it ever actually was: the model is the Main Street America exhibit which greets entering visitors at the California Disneyland, sanitized for your protection (as the phrase goes), wholesome, undangerous, and seven-eighths real size. Around it, the charmingly restored streets – all yuppified with a massive injection of Department of Housing and Urban Development funds – have exactly the same quality: they manage to look like a Disney movie lot of an imagined urban America, but they happen incongruously to be real.

But, despite early successes, it soon became evident that the festival marketplace worked well only in a special type of city with a large regional population to serve as a visitor base, an historical waterfront, warehouse, and/or industrial district within close walking distance of downtown, and a strong tourist base. Many mid-size cities with only modest tourist appeal – Flint, Michigan; Norfolk, Virginia; Toledo, Ohio – experienced disappointment. Even in places where it worked, oversaturation could happen – as in Minneapolis–St Paul, which had no fewer than five in the late 1980s. Thus, steadily, the special character of the early marketplaces has become much more commonplace. As one observer commented, "if every city in America wants a festival market because it's a unique and attractive resource, it's quite natural to wonder what exactly is unique about a concept that's being repeated again and again."[18]

The same fate befell pedestrian malls – outdoor pedestrianized streets which appeared in American downtowns as a direct counter-response to the early suburban shopping malls. First tried in Kalamazoo (Michigan) in 1959, it was followed by over 200 American cities, mostly during the 1960s and early 1970s. More than three decades later, it has become clear that they work only close to the office/financial cores of large cities (Denver, Boston, Portland, Minneapolis) or in university towns with dense pedestrian traffic (Boulder, Colorado; Burlington, Vermont; Madison, Wisconsin). Most have failed to rejuvenate downtown retailing, and very few new ones (save the highly regarded 16th Street Mall in Denver) have been built since the late 1970s; in fact, several places – New London, Connecticut; Providence, Rhode Island; Norfolk, Virginia; St Cloud, Minnesota – have given up and put the traffic back.[19]

[17]   Falk, 1986, 150.
[18]   Robertson, 1997, 391.
[19]   Robertson, 1997, 389.

But in any case, Boston and Baltimore came to seem more and more interesting. For, all over the advanced western world, old dockland areas were becoming a principal focus, perhaps the principal focus, of large-scale urban regeneration. During the 1970s, in city after city, these areas went quite suddenly from prosperity to dereliction, victims of a complex conjunction of global economic recession, technical change (containerization), and shifts in world trade patterns. During the 1980s, these same areas underwent intensive regeneration for offices, retailing, housing, entertainment, culture, and leisure. Some – the Inner Harbor in Baltimore, London Docklands – became almost obligatory items on any urban planner's international tourist circuit. Almost all exhibit a remarkable redevelopment partnership between the public and the private sectors, sometimes involving the city administration, sometimes an urban development corporation, sometimes a hybrid form.[20]

The Great Enterprise Zone Debate

Here, one particular notion came to play a role never imagined by its author. In an address to the Royal Town Planning Institute's conference at Chester in 1977, Peter Hall – joint author of the iconoclastic Nonplan manifesto of 1970 (Chapter 8) – addressed the emerging problem of urban decline: "The biggest urban areas have seen their growth slow down, stop and then reverse. They are losing people and jobs." Reviewing possible ways of rebuilding these cities' economic bases, he came to the possibility that "none of these recipes can really perform the miracle for some areas." Here, he suggested,

> the best may be the enemy of the good. If we really want to help inner cities, and cities generally, we may have to use highly unorthodox remedies: ... a final possible remedy, which I would call the Freeport solution. Small, selected areas of inner cities would be simply thrown open to all kinds of initiative, with minimal control. In other words, we would aim to recreate the Hong Kong of the 1950s and 1960s inside inner Liverpool or inner Glasgow.[21]

This would involve three elements. Each area would be completely open to immigration of entrepreneurs and capital – meaning no immigration controls. It "would be based on fairly shameless free enterprise"; "Bureaucracy would be kept to the absolute minimum." And residence would be based on choice, since the area would effectively be outside the United Kingdom's normal legislation and controls. Hall concluded, "Such an area would not conform at all to modern British conventions of the welfare state. But it could be economically vigorous on the Hong Kong model. Since it would represent an extremely drastic last-ditch

[20]   Hoyle *et al.*, 1988, passim.
[21]   Hall, 1977, 5.

solution to urban problems, it could be tried only on a very small scale." He ended
with a disclaimer that in the event proved ironic:

> I do not expect the British government to act on this solution immediately, and I want
> to emphasise that I am not recommending it as a solution for our urban ills. I am
> saying that it is a model, and an extreme one, of a possible solution.[22]

In some ways, as emerged from later and closer analysis, his evocation of Hong Kong
was an odd one. For, in terms of Turner's campaign against third-world housing
bureaucracies, Hong Kong was an outstanding example of ultimate conservatism:
throughout the 1960s and 1970s, contrary to its outside-world mythical image, it
had maintained what was in relative terms the largest public housing program in the
non-communist world.[23] Jonathan Schiffer was later to suggest an ingenious explanation: the program, by keeping the costs of mass housing to a guaranteed minimum,
greatly dampened demands for wage increases and kept Hong Kong's labor costs
among the lowest in the developed world.[24] Further, though by conventional British
standards Hong Kong did not have a very restrictive or comprehensive British-style
land-use planning system,[25] by the standards of many developing countries there
was a good deal of planning intervention. Nonetheless, Hall could defend his basic
point: however indirectly subsidized in this and other ways, Hong Kong had proved
one of the world's most successful examples of how to move rapidly into new entrepreneurial lines in response to the state of the world market, mainly through the
extraordinary adaptability of its dominant small-business sector.[26]

All this, however, was part of a rather obscure academic debate. The odd point is
that, despite Hall's total skepticism as to the possibilities of action, he did not have to
wait long. In 1980 the new Conservative government in Britain introduced provision for Enterprise Zones, and the Chancellor of the Exchequer specifically cited
him as the author of the scheme. During 1980–1, 15 zones were designated – one of
them, the Isle of Dogs, in the heart of the London Docklands. The whole notion, and
its hapless author, were duly attacked by radical academics from both sides of the
Atlantic.[27]

In practice, as introduced in Howe's 1980 budget, it turned out much tamer: the
benefits were now based on direct financial subsidy rather than deregulation.
Companies moving into an Enterprise Zone could receive 100% capital allowances
and de-rating on industrial and commercial buildings, as well as exemption from
development land tax and many of the usual planning and other regulatory constraints. As emerged later, private investment was attracted into the zones mainly by
the Treasury subsidy in the form of capital allowances and rates exemptions, which

---

[22]   Hall, 1977, 5.
[23]   Choi and Chan, 1979, 187.
[24]   Schiffer, 1984, passim.
[25]   Bristow, 1984.
[26]   Sit, 1978, 92.
[27]   Harrison, 1982; Massey, 1982; Goldsmith, 1982.

amounted to more than £150 million by 1985.[28] Most of the other elements – the free migration of labor, the encouragement of immigrant entrepreneurs, the general freedom from mainstream legislation – were conspicuously missing: a particularly poignant example of the way that, especially in Britain, radical ideas are taken on board by the establishment, only to be sanitized into something completely harmless. What was conspicuously lacking, despite the title, was any mechanism for encouraging innovation, in the sense enunciated by Joseph Schumpeter, as a way of providing alternative industrial traditions for areas where the traditional industrial base had disappeared.[29]

One good point about the Enterprise Zones is that the government paid to have them independently evaluated. The definitive exercise, in 1987, found that over the period 1981/2 to 1985/6, the 23 zones were estimated to have cost some £297 million. This money had attracted just over 2,800 firms, employing about 63,300 people. But some 23% of them had been there previously; 37% were transfers; 14% were branches; just over 25% were new start-ups. And, of the transfers, 58% came from the local area immediately around the zone, 80% from the local region. Of the 63,300 jobs, the consultants found, only about 35,000 were a direct result of Enterprise Zone policy; most were local transfers, but some were new. Subtracting the losses that had occurred to local areas immediately outside the zone, and adding indirect benefits to these areas (such as linkages and construction jobs), the consultants concluded that the total net job creation in the zone and in the local area was just under 13,000. Each of these jobs had cost £8,500; the cost of each additional job in the wider local area (including the Enterprise Zones) was between £23,000 and £30,000.[30]

Three in four Enterprise Zone companies thought they had benefited from the Enterprise Zone being there; but no less than 94% thought that exemption from rates was the most important incentive. The effect of relaxing planning controls was difficult to judge because many planning authorities owned the land anyway, and had sought to maintain some broad pattern of land use while liberalizing restrictions where possible.[31]

The Battle for Docklands[32]

All this was highly relevant to the British debate. And inevitably, given the scale and the nature of the problem, that debate became politicized. For, by the late 1970s, in all the great British cities, a new phenomenon was manifest: huge tracts of vacant or semi-vacant land, marked by the gaunt ruins of derelict industrial or warehouse buildings, awaited redevelopment. Invariably, most of this land was in public or

[28] Brindley *et al.*, 1989, 107; Johnson, 1991, 196; Lawless, 1986, 263.
[29] Hall, 1982b, 419.
[30] GB Department of the Environment, 1987, 2, 10–12, 18, 21, 25, 30, 52–3.
[31] GB Department of the Environment, 1987, 30, 57, 70, 85.
[32] This account is based on Hall, 1998, Ch. 28.

quasi-public ownership: it belonged either to the local municipalities, who had acquired it for housing or road-building schemes that were now threatened by expenditure cuts (or, with the roads, public opposition), or to public corporations like docks authorities, British Gas, or British Rail, which had taken their operations elsewhere.

The most spectacular case, by far, was the London Docklands: a huge tract, some 8.5 square miles in extent, beginning at the very edge of the City of London's famous square mile and stretching downstream for some 8 miles on both sides of the Thames. There was surely no more telling contrast, anywhere in the urban world, than between the square mile of the City of London, and the London Docklands beginning at Tower Bridge next door. They had grown together: trade in the port had fathered commerce in the City, making it a "central switchboard" of the world economy, in Anthony King's words: the world's first true global city.[33] But now their fortunes had spectacularly diverged.

The docks had developed during the nineteenth and early twentieth century, as the growth of trade caused massive congestion on the river below London Bridge: the first, the West India Dock, opened in 1802–6, the last, the George V Dock, in 1921.[34] By then, London was the world's busiest port in value and volume of trade, and around the docks grew industries – above all, noxious industries located outside the bounds of the old London County Council, like the huge Beckton Gas Works. This was heavy manual work, much of it casual in nature, resulting in solidly working-class communities all around; labor relations were monumentally bad, and the workers were very active politically.[35]

Casualization in the docks ended in 1967; ironically, the East India Dock shut its gates that same year.[36] Thence, the docks closed down even more rapidly than they had opened. The last group – the Royal Docks, which had once served 100 ships a day – shut in 1981.[37] Containerization was the basic reason, favoring estuary ports near the sea like Harwich and Felixstowe, where labor costs were far lower, or the Port of London's Tilbury base, 20 miles downstream outside London altogether. Of 30,000 London dockers, a mere 3,000 were left to handle 50 million tonnes of goods per year at Tilbury.[38] On top, the gasworks at Beckton and then at Greenwich closed; port-based industries began to contract. By 1981, unemployment in Docklands reached 18.6%.[39]

All this took the planners by surprise. Very soon, with the closure of the old inner docks, the 5,000-acre Docklands site suddenly emerged as London's greatest development opportunity since the Great Fire of 1666. But local communities remained deeply suspicious. Two groups, the Docklands Forum and the Joint

[33] King, 1990, 74.
[34] Al Naib, 1990, 1–3; Brownill, 1990, 16–17; Hardy, 1983a, 5; King, 1990, 74; Ogden, 1992a, 4.
[35] Hardy, 1983a, 6–7; Brownill, 1990, 18; Hardy, 1983b, 9, 11; Ledgerwood, 1985, 42–3.
[36] Al Naib, 1990, 3; Hardy, 1983b, 10.
[37] Al Naib, 1990, 3; Ogden, 1992a, 4.
[38] Al Naib, 1990, 3; Hardy, 1983a, 12; Newman and Mayo, 1981, 534–5.
[39] Brindley *et al.*, 1989, 99; Falk, 1981, 67; Ledgerwood, 1985, 59.

Figure 11.4 and **Figure 11.5**   London Docklands: before and after. The transformation of the London Docklands during the 1980s represented the biggest piece of urban revitalization in Europe, if not the world. For some, it was a shining example of how to do it; for others, of how not to. *Source*: Shutterstock/R.Nagy (fig. 11.5).

Dockland Action Group, emerged in the mid-1970s as quasi-official spokesmen for local community interests.[40] When a Conservative government commissioned a report from consultants Travers Morgan in 1973, setting out five alternative futures – one building on the area's traditional character, the others representing radically new approaches – it was savaged both by local community groups and by the local boroughs, and was abandoned by a new minister; soon after, Labour came back to power in Whitehall.[41]

Now, in the mid-1970s, the entire concept of large-scale, top-down, profession-ally oriented planning was replaced by its radical opposite: bottom-up planning through local community groups, in which the planner was the servant of the public. This entailed a delicate, even tentative, negotiated style of planning, through a Docklands Joint Committee plus a Docklands Forum to represent the public, notably the militant community groups.[42] The result, the London Docklands Strategic Plan of 1976, aimed to preserve and reinforce the status quo – assuming, of course, that there was a status quo to preserve.[43] The general response, as Grant Ledgerwood puts it, was one of "melancholic bemusement." *The Times* commented, "The characteristic East End approach to the matter is a paradoxical one – 'We want whatever other parts of London have, and to stay as we are.'"[44]

But in 1977 there was a major financial crisis and government money was unforth-coming; by the time funds were again available, in 1978, the country was heading for a general election.[45] In any case, the Inner Areas Act of 1978 provided no funding for land purchase, which was crucial. The Docklands Joint Committee achieved virtually nothing, and meanwhile the local economy was collapsing. As Nicholas Falk pointed out, the local communities were locked into a fantasy of their own making.[46]

In May 1979, Margaret Thatcher appointed Michael Heseltine as her Secretary of State for the Environment. He recalled flying over Docklands in 1973,

> pressing close against the clamour of the City's square mile lay the emptiness and hopelessness of hundreds of acres of deserted docks, wharves and warehouses ... There were all kinds of committees, reports, discussions, but beneath me stretched this appalling proof that no one was doing anything effective ... Everyone was involved. No one was in charge.[47]

[40]   Falk, 1981, 66; Hardy, 1983a, 8; Ledgerwood, 1985, 68–73, 75.
[41]   Brindley *et al.*, 1989, 100; Ledgerwood, 1985, 87, 91–4, 99–100.
[42]   Brindley *et al.*, 1989, 100; Ledgerwood, 1985, 95–9, 101–3.
[43]   Docklands Joint Committee, 1976, 8; Hall *et al.*, 1976, 274; Ledgerwood, 1985, 115, 118–21, 129.
[44]   Quoted in Ledgerwood, 1985, 123.
[45]   Brindley *et al.*, 1989, 101; Brownill, 1990, 26–7, 29; Ledgerwood, 1985, 116, 122.
[46]   Brownill, 1990, 27, 29; Hardy, 1983a, 16; Brindley *et al.*, 1989, 29–30, 101; Savitch, 1988, 225–6; Falk, 1981, 78.
[47]   Heseltine, 1987, 133.

He immediately asked the Department of Environment's Permanent Secretary, Sir John Garlick, to write legislation. The Local Government, Planning and Land Act of 1980 duly created powers to establish Enterprise Zones and Urban Development Corporations (UDCs).[48]

The UDCs, as Heseltine freely admitted, were modeled on the successful New Town corporations, a Labour government initiative of 1946; the intention, in his own words, was to "create new towns in old cities."[49] But there were significant differences. Most importantly, they would replace local authorities as development control authorities, and were given powers to have land "vested" in them without appeal. The *Daily Telegraph* rightly observed, in 1987, that "the Corporation … is more of a socialist concept than a child of a Tory administration."[50] The essential notion was American: leverage. Public investment, kick-starting the process, plus the new powers, would create the right conditions to bring in a much bigger volume of private funds.[51] Heseltine was quite specific about bypassing the local planners:

> We took their powers away from them because they were making such a mess of it. They are the people who have got it all wrong. They had advisory committees, planning committees, inter-relating committees and even discussion committees – but nothing happened … UDCs do things. More to the point they can be seen to do things and they are free from the inevitable delays of the democratic process.[52]

To run the London Docklands Development Corporation (LDDC) Heseltine chose Nigel Broackes, chairman of Trafalgar House, a businessman and property specialist, as chair and Reginald Ward, a veteran local government administrator, as CEO. LDDC deliberately did little planning; it used consultants to draw up broad development frameworks, which provided guidance but were completely flexible and above all demand-led. The boroughs nursed their wounds, and Southwark even tried to draw up its own plan before it was quashed in court; the community groups could not even agree among themselves.[53]

Underlying these clashes were different constituencies, as Richard Batley's analysis shows: as Heseltine had emphasized from the start, the boroughs served their local communities, the LDDC the national interest in future development.[54] Over the decade, the LDDC developed very different relationships with the boroughs: non-cooperating and confrontational in the case of "new urban left" Southwark, cooperating with Tower Hamlets, negotiating commercial deals with Newham.[55]

[48]   Heseltine, 1987, 133, 135–6; Imrie and Thomas, 1993, 8; Lawless, 1991, 25; Meadows, 1985, 162.
[49]   Heseltine, 1987, 157.
[50]   Brindley *et al.*, 1989, 115.
[51]   Letwin, 1992, 181.
[52]   Thornley, 1991, 181.
[53]   Brownill, 1990, 111; Ledgerwood, 1985, 158; Hall, 1992, 22; Thornley, 1991, 175–7, 179.
[54]   Batley, 1989, 171–5, 180.
[55]   Batley, 1989, 178; Brownill, 1990, 121.

By the end of the 1980s, it was all over; Thatcher had won. By March 1991, the LDDC had bought 2,109 acres (40% of the total area of Docklands, 20% of it being water): 401 acres were to remain as water, 483 acres were earmarked for infrastructure, 1,225 acres were for development, of which 661 acres had been sold to the private sector by 1990, and 564 acres (mainly the Royals) were being reclaimed or awaiting development.[56] The LDDC profited from a huge increase in land values brought about by its own activities: prices in the Enterprise Zone rose from £80,000 an acre (£198,000 per hectare) in 1981, to £4 million per acre (£10 million per hectare) in 1988, by which time residential land prices were comparable to West London riverside sites. The sales paid for major infrastructure works, such as the Beckton extension of the Docklands Light Railway (DLR). Overall, from 1981 to 1989, the LDDC spent £790 million; land acquisition accounted for 16%, works 17%, land reclamation 11%, and transport 21%.[57]

Transport was a special problem, much more so than foreseen at the start. The DLR's first phase from Docklands Gateway to Tower Gardens and Stratford, opened in 1987, was cheap at £77 million, but the Beckton extension cost £276 million, the Bank extension and the rebuilding of Canary Wharf station £282 million. The first phase brought huge increases in land values, but was quite inadequate for the resulting scale of activity, requiring an expensive rebuild; in 1989 the system broke down, on average, 10 times a month. That year, agreement was reached to extend the existing Jubilee Line into Docklands with the developers Olympia & York contributing one-third of the estimated cost, which would later escalate threefold.[58]

How successful was the LDDC in leveraging these huge public funds? The government told a House of Commons Committee that by 1987 it was achieving a 12.5:1 ratio. But this excluded substantial public expenditures such as housing, the DLR, trunk roads, and rate and tax allowances in the Enterprise Zone. Even so, the LDDC was the most prominent example of leverage planning in the 1980s, and its apparent success became a model for the regeneration of other inner-city areas.[59]

A related question must be how much expenditure the LDDC recouped by land sales. By 1988–9, sales amounted to 50% of total income; the LDDC was allowed to keep all of it. But, after the property crash of 1989, this positive cash flow dried up.[60] Two-thirds of the land vested by the LDDC had been earmarked by the local authorities for housing. Much of it went to housing, but not of the same kind: some 80% went for owner-occupiership. The new residents had distinctly higher income than the average local resident, and by the end of the 1980s only 5% of sales were in the

[56]   Brindley *et al.*, 1989, 104; Brownill, 1990, 42–3; Church, 1992, 43.

[57]   Brownill, 1990, 40, 47–8, 74, 91.

[58]   Association of London Authorities, Docklands Consultative Committee, 1991, 10; Brownill, 1990, 137–8.

[59]   Association of London Authorities, Docklands Consultative Committee, 1991, 3–4; Batley, 1989, 177; Brindley *et al.*, 1989, 104, 114; Brownill, 1990, 46.

[60]   Association of London Authorities, Docklands Consultative Committee, 1991, 3–4; Brownill, 1990, 44–5, 90–1; Imrie and Thomas, 1993, 17–18.

Figure 11.6 Paul Reichmann. The Toronto developer with Canary Wharf: the summit of his ambition, lost and then regained. *Source*: PA/PA Archive/Press Association Images.

"affordable" category, while local authority and housing association programs were truncated.[61]

The Isle of Dogs Enterprise Zone, in the heart of the LDDC area, was designated in 1982. But, down to 1985, low-rise high-tech tin sheds and newspapers were the effective limit.[62] Then, in the mid-1980s property boom fueled by the deregulation of financial services, the LDDC shifted its market strategy to the City: by the end of 1986 there was intense competition for commercial space, stimulated by the incentives and by land prices kept deliberately below market value.[63]

Then came Docklands' *pièce de résistance*, unveiled in 1985: Canary Wharf. Originally a warehouse in the West India Docks for bananas and sugar cane from the West Indies and fruit from the Canary Islands, it was now to become an 8.8 million square foot office development, estimated to create more than 40,000 jobs. The journalists called it "Kowloon-on-Thames." Planning permission was granted without a public inquiry: as Labour MP Nigel Spearing put it, the largest development in Europe was approved with less scrutiny than "a planning application for an

[61] Association of London Authorities, Docklands Consultative Committee, 1991, 11; Brindley *et al.*, 1989, 119; Brownill, 1990, 68, 71, 76–81.
[62] Church, 1992, 46.
[63] Brindley *et al.*, 1989, 108–9; Brownill, 1990, 90; Church, 1992, 49.

illuminated sign on a fish and chip shop in the East India Dock Road"; LDDC minutes said that "political considerations" favored the scheme.[64]

The original promoters were a consortium of three American banks, Financière Credit Suisse–First Boston, Morgan Stanley, and First Boston Docklands Associates, plus a colorful developer from Texas named G. Ware Travelstead, soon to be nick-named G. Whizz; they attracted capital allowances against tax of about £470 million. On top, the LDDC agreed to extend the DLR to the Bank, and to provide £250 million for roads, notably the tunneled and expensive Limehouse Link.[65] But in mid-1987, Travelstead withdrew; after desperate attempts to find an alternative developer, an agreement was reached with the Toronto-based developers Olympia & York (O&Y).[66]

It was the creation of Paul, Albert, and Ralph Reichmann: three of six children of Jewish refugees from Vienna into Toronto; educated in yeshivas and lacking professional or technical education, in the mid-1950s they started a building supply company, supplying luxury bathrooms. In 1965, Albert and Paul founded York Developments; it was incorporated, in 1969, as Olympia & York Developments.[67] Their downtown retail and office developments, based on financial wizardry, boomed. They specialized in massive public–private partnerships like the World Financial Center in New York: they provided the financing, a government provided cheap land, and together they created new urban centers. They had a reputation for taking over tricky projects and making them work: Canary Wharf, where the initial consortium of US and UK banks had failed to finance or start, looked just right for them.[68]

At Canary Wharf they used the same methods they had so successfully used in New York: they bought out leases to entice companies out of central London: they persuaded American Express to move from Broadgate, the *Daily Telegraph* to move from South Quay. Canary Wharf would become an extension of the City, just as the World Financial Center had become an appendage of Wall Street; acute shortages of City space were forcing up rents on the fringes; both City rents and Docklands rents were rising. Even Black Monday, October 19, 1987, seemed a blip on the chart.[69]

But in London, the City was a separate planning authority. Michael Cassidy, the City planning chair, was determined to preserve the City as a financial center to counter the Docklands threat. He tore up the development plan and substituted another: drastic modifications – decking over London Wall and Upper Thames Street, redeveloping Cannon Street – would increase floorspace by 25%. Between 1985 and 1987, the City approved five times as much office floorspace as during 1982–4; by 1992, great swathes of redevelopment appeared on the City fringe, at Ludgate Hill and London Wall.[70]

[64] Brindley *et al.*, 1989, 108; Brownill, 1990, 55–6; Fainstein, 1994, 197.
[65] Brownill, 1990, 15, 54–5; Fainstein, 1994, 199.
[66] Brownill, 1990, 56; Fainstein, 1994, 197, 199.
[67] Fainstein, 1994, 172.
[68] Fainstein, 1994, 172–4, 176–7, 189; Zukin, 1992, 215.
[69] Fainstein, 1994, 201; Zukin, 1992, 238.
[70] Fainstein, 1994, 40, 103; King, 1990, 98–9; Thornley, 1991, 130–1; Williams, 1992, 252.

Developers reacted in their usual Pavlovian way: between 1985 and 1989, Docklands added 2.6 million square feet of office space; the City added 16.5 million square feet, more than six times as much.[71] In 1991, office completions were approaching 620,000 square meters; there was a whole ring of them around the City fringe: Broadgate, Ropemaker Place, Little Britain, Alban Gate, and Royal Mint Court were completed; London Bridge City, Spitalfields, and Bishopsgate were in the pipeline. But now came the slump. Jobs in financial and business services fell by 90,000 between 1990 and 1992, wiping out all the gains of the preceding five years. One-sixth of all office space in the City and its fringes was already empty; a number of American banks and other firms had withdrawn parts of their operations from London. By April 1992, the vacancy rate for offices in Central London and Docklands was 18%; in Docklands, the vacancy rate was about 50%; in Canary Wharf, over 40%. Here, many developments went bankrupt, including Burrells Wharf, South Quay Plaza, Tobacco Dock, Baltic Wharf, and Butlers Wharf. Development in the Royals virtually collapsed.[72]

But the most spectacular of all the bankruptcies was Olympia & York. O&Y had become New York City's largest office property owner, with nearly 22 million square feet. They owed more than $18 billion: more than the debts of most third-world nations. All construction loans are short-term, and are refinanced through long-term mortgages when construction is finished; but banks panicked, and refused these loans. O&Y were especially vulnerable, for they had issued short-term bonds backed by occupied buildings as collateral to finance further growth. Now, they tried to use their older New York buildings as collateral to finance their equity contribution to London's Canary Wharf, but they could not secure funds. In summer 1992, four million square feet of Canary Wharf was complete, but 53% of the office space and almost all the retail space remained unlet; the large committed tenants – American Express, Crédit Suisse, First Boston, Morgan Stanley, Bear Stearns, and Texaco – were all American, some closely associated with the development.[73]

In Canada, O&Y filed for bankruptcy on May 14; in London, as banks refused new funds for their contribution to the Jubilee line, they went into administration on May 27. Canary Wharf, which had cost £1.4 billion including bank borrowings of £1.1 million, was now in the hands of a consortium of banks; one mid-1992 estimate of its value was as little as £150–200 million.[74] O&Y had made the last and largest of a series of audacious gambles, but this time they had lost. The odds were stacked against success: the size of the investment was too big, the cycles in the property market too short, the developers too dependent on short-term money which could dry up as lenders lost confidence. One developer was quoted in the *Independent*: "North Americans have no sense of place, or of history. He didn't realise that British people and business are tied by invisible threads to places: to the Bank of England or just to

[71] Fainstein, 1994, 39, 41.
[72] Budd and Whimster, 1992, 239–40; Church, 1992, 49–50; Fainstein, 1994, 51; Lee, 1992, 13.
[73] Fainstein, 1994, 61, 201–2.
[74] Fainstein, 1994, 203–4; Lee, 1992, 8.

a set of streets, some shops, a restaurant."[75] Finally, as one business associate put it, "The key to everything is the psychology of Paul Reichmann. He is a deal junkie. Deal-making is what he lives and breathes for, the obsessive need to go on making bigger and better deals."[76] Some said that meeting Thatcher had turned his head.

As Susan Fainstein says, the failure "indicates the limits on turning to the private sector for achieving public ends."[77] But this was compounded by urban policies, or the lack of them. The French government restricted development in Paris to help the La Défense project, but the British government did nothing to stop the City of London wrecking Canary Wharf.[78]

What can be the verdict on the Docklands saga? Strictly as an exercise in regeneration, it has to be judged a modest success. Between 1981 and 1990 Docklands lost 20,532 old jobs but gained 41,421 new ones: 24,559 by transfers from other places – chiefly other parts of London – and 16,862 new jobs.[79] But the lost jobs were very different from the new ones: port jobs disappeared, manufacturing stayed almost static, while the big gains were in advanced services, above all banking, insurance, and finance; service employment rose from 32 to 60% of the total.[80] And very few jobs – no more than a quarter, probably far fewer – went to local people. Overall, from 1981 to 1989 unemployment rates in the three core boroughs – Newham, Southwark, Tower Hamlets – declined, albeit slightly less than in Greater London as a whole. But in 1991, unemployment across Docklands was nearly two and a half times the London average.[81] One good explanation for the low take-up of new jobs by residents is that educational achievements in Docklands were often very low. In 1988, the average proportion staying on at school after 16 was 33% in all inner London schools, 25% in Tower Hamlets, and 12% in Southwark.[82]

Without doubt, as John Hall concluded in his independent evaluation, the LDDC has vindicated Michael Heseltine's view: it showed that it could deliver. The environment has been transformed, the population has grown, there are new jobs, road and rail construction continue at a frenetic pace; London Docklands has become almost a symbol of a certain style of development, culture, and politics in the 1980s and 1990s.[83] But Susan Fainstein's verdict, reached on the basis of deep analysis of the London and New York property markets in the 1980s, is more sobering:

[75]   Quoted in Fainstein, 1994, 202.
[76]   Fainstein, 1994, 207.
[77]   Fainstein, 1994, 209.
[78]   Fainstein, 1994, 204, 211.
[79]   Hansard, May 8, 1991.
[80]   Association of London Authorities, Docklands Consultative Committee, 1991, 6; Brownill, 1990, 93; Docklands Forum, 1990, 5.
[81]   Association of London Authorities, Docklands Consultative Committee, 1991, 5, 7; Brindley *et al.*, 1989, 109; Brownill, 1990, 98–9.
[82]   Brindley *et al.*, 1989, 109; Docklands Forum, 1990, 61–2.
[83]   Hall, 1992, 24.

The whole Docklands experience exposes the fatal weakness of relying heavily on property development to stimulate regeneration – government-supplied incentives to the development industry inevitably beget oversupply if not accompanied by other measures to restrict production.[84]

Margaret Thatcher and Michael Heseltine might reply with the immortal response of the sometime Chancellor of the Exchequer, Norman Lamont: "That's capitalism." There was simply no other economy on which to rely, no other base on which to build the whole program. And perhaps, as the global capitalist economy shifts from goods-handling to information-handling, it will everywhere depend more and more on such speculative development. A style of regeneration harnessed to the property cycle must expect to go through more than one period of boom and bust before it is over, and – given what we know about the timing of such a cycle – it may need a long wait and much patience. So the final verdict on Docklands might take a while yet: urban regeneration, like ancient Rome, will not be built in a day.

Ironically, in October 1995 Paul Reichmann, backed by Saudi money, bought his own development back from the consortium of banks that had been administering it. And Citibank, whose principal shareholder happened to be the Saudi prince who was backing Reichmann, announced that Canary Wharf could be a suitable location for its new headquarters – thus launching the long-delayed second phase of the development. The final irony was that by 2001, after one of the longest booms in British history, Canary Wharf was nearing completion, and developers were already considering a vast extension: Millennium Quarter.

Dozens of other places regenerated their waterfronts, of course; and not all, even in Britain, called in Development Corporations. In Greater Manchester, next to the Trafford Development Corporation and Enterprise Zone, the City of Salford itself successfully turned its docks around, culminating in 2000–2001 with a spectacular arts and museum complex incorporating a new gallery for the city's most famous artist, L. S. Lowry, and a northern branch of the Imperial War Museum designed by Daniel Libeskind. Rotterdam too did the job itself. And, though there are obviously similarities – with Baltimore, which seem to have provided a model, and London Docklands – Rotterdam has been distinctive because throughout it sought to incorporate a social concern, including a lot of public and cooperative housing, and a serious attempt to employ local people in the huge Kop van Zuid extension to the city center. But, despite these efforts, unemployment in the city has remained stubbornly above national average levels; in the Netherlands, as in Britain, the big cities have been making painful economic adjustments, and Rotterdam's is perhaps the most painful of all.[85]

---

[84] Fainstein, 1994, 213.
[85] McCarthy, 1999, 303–6.

Regeneration in Action: Manchester and Rotterdam

Manchester's Castlefield dates back to Roman times. But its restoration depended on more recent history: the heritage of the early industrial revolution, the Bridgewater Canal, the world's first modern cut canal, of 1764, and Liverpool Road Station, the world's first passenger railway station, of 1830, which generated a landscape of warehouses, canals, locks, viaducts, railway lines, and good sheds, many of them listed as of architectural or historical importance.[86] All around, though, between 1961 and 1983 Manchester lost over 150,000 manufacturing jobs, resulting in levels of unemployment in inner city Manchester that averaged 30%, and leaving dead space at the heart of the center. Railway arches housed car maintenance and repair premises, the wastelands were littered with scrap yards, and disused buildings became resting places for the city's marginal population;[87] Castlefield during the 1970s was described as a "den of thieves and vice"; entering the area was to "take your life into your hands." In a very short time, it went from the birthplace to the "grave of the industrial revolution."[88]

Slowly, with huge efforts, the area began to regenerate. First, from 1967 to 1983 came a concerted effort by the voluntary sector and then the County Council to improve the awareness of the area and its historic significance. Secondly, from 1984 to 1988 the City Council picked up the baton. Finally, from 1989 to 1996 a Development Corporation modeled on London Docklands brought streamlined powers, fast-tracked planning opportunities, and further resources into the area to reconceptualize the urban space to fit the local, national, and European agenda, and to further diversify the range of regeneration.[89] Already, by 1980, of £290 million generated by tourism in the North West, £58 million came from Greater Manchester. The Air and Space Museum housed in the former Upper and Lower Campfield Markets adjacent to Liverpool Road Station, an exhibition space for the Science and Industry Museum located in the 1830 warehouse, an annual Castlefield Carnival, the national boat and canal rally, a visitor and heritage center, guided tours of the area, and improved signposting each contributed to a greater awareness of the area and its potential, culturally and commercially.[90]

Repopulating the city center and restoring its tax base was a key task for the City Council. The inner six wards, including Castlefield, were responsible for 75% of the total population loss of the city during 1951–1991; in the 1980s the city center population was estimated to be as low as 250, and establishing a residential base with tax revenue potential was seen as vital for long-term regeneration.[91] Accordingly, the

[86]	Madgin, 2010, 32–3.
[87]	Madgin, 2010, 32–3.
[88]	Madgin, 2010, 34.
[89]	Madgin, 2010, 35–6.
[90]	Madgin, 2010, 39.
[91]	Madgin, 2010, 40.

Local Plan (1984) focused on creating more housing units; it stressed that "the listed riverside warehouses may have potential for conversion to housing," illustrating the potential of the historic buildings to attract a resident population which would boost tax revenues.[92]

Ironically, soon afterwards it was displaced by the Central Manchester Development Corporation (CMDC), deliberately intended to take over its role. Despite City opposition, the CMDC started work in 1988. But pragmatically, a set of criteria was put in place to secure a harmonious working relationship. The City Council retained its development control powers; it had three seats on the CMDC board; the Development Corporation used the existing City-created Local Plan; and the two partners mutually acknowledged their cooperation. The Development Corporation was able to access different types of funding to lever in private investment and was also able to fast-track planning.[93] Effectively, the City Council allowed the Development Corporation to regenerate Castlefield even though they did not hold equal weight in the partnership.[94] Castlefield was reconceptualized as a cosmopolitan, mixed-use, urban idyll, frequented by entrepreneurs, young professionals, and service-sector workers seeking to enjoy an urban lifestyle,[95] a process paralleled in other British and continental European cities.[96] The Development Corporation's grant-aiding and pump-priming powers allowed it to spend £8 million in Castlefield, attracting more than £100 million in private investment. From the outset, one of CMDC's priorities was to "ensure the transformation of Manchester into a twenty-first century city on a par with the great provincial cities of Europe."[97]

Rotterdam provides an interesting parallel. There, the Dutch government's 1990 Fourth Report for Planning (Extra) aimed to boost the country's competitive advantage, with an emphasis on "city marketing" intensified by the emergence in 1992 of the Single European Market. "Key projects" were designated in cities, with Rotterdam playing a particularly important role as a point of access and competitive location for international business uses.[98] The report also emphasized the need to improve the range and quality of cultural facilities in the cities so as to enhance their international image.

The 1985 Inner City Plan for Rotterdam had already built on the maritime legacy of the "Waterstad," created between 1600 and 1620, by providing a series of new cultural and entertainment uses clustered around new maritime tourism facilities.[99] Then, the 1993–2000 Inner City Plan extended the idea of city center uses to the underused Kop van Zuid area, directly south of the river from the city's central area, which had been used for port-related purposes that had recently become obsolete.

[92] Madgin, 2010, 41.
[93] Madgin, 2010, 42.
[94] Madgin, 2010, 42.
[95] Madgin, 2010, 43.
[96] Madgin, 2010, 43.
[97] Madgin, 2010, 43.
[98] McCarthy, 1999, 292–3.
[99] McCarthy, 1999, 299–300.

The scheme was designed to provide a mix of uses including 60,000 square meters of new office space, together with 5,500 dwelling units, 60,000 square meters of retail space, hotels, and a convention center.[100] Designated as a "key project" for its national significance, it applied the government's "compact city" policy by encouraging people to live in the central area.[101] An early element was the Erasmus Bridge connecting the city center to the area, opened in September 1995. Controversial locally, Ben van Berkel's design, incorporating a 139-meter-high pylon, was well received internationally.[102] In addition, a new metro station was opened, providing a link to the international rail network, and new roads were proposed to connect the area to surrounding residential neighborhoods as well as to the city's ring road.[103]

The Enterprise Zone Goes Abroad

Despite the travails of the Enterprise Zone in its homeland, the idea was in turn warmly espoused by the Reagan administration in the United States, where, interestingly, it also tended to win support from left-liberal inner-city politicians.[104] Despite this, it failed to gain enactment into federal law. The States stepped in: 26 legislatures adopted legislation, creating more than 1,400 local enterprise zones in 680 localities. A small sample of only 10, studied by the United States Department of Housing and Urban Development in 1986, showed that 263 firms had invested over $147 million to create or keep over 7,000 jobs.[105]

The Reagan administration, however, did in an important sense implement the original notion in another way: by openly failing to police the border with Mexico, it condoned a huge illegal immigration into Sunbelt cities like Houston or Los Angeles, which – administration officials would openly boast in private – constituted working models of the pure enterprise zone idea. For the working results, of course, they were roundly condemned by left-radical urban analysts.[106]

The Docklands development had followed the American models in one critical respect. This was the concept of using relatively modest public funds to generate – or, to use the quaintly ungrammatical American verb, to *leverage* – a much larger amount of private investment. In Boston, for instance, $2.7 million of federal preservation grant from the Department of Housing and Urban Development attracted private investment of more than six times that amount.[107] The Carter administration, in 1977, had enshrined this principle in legislation. The Urban Development Action Grant (UDAG) was posited on the notion of leveraging between 4.5 and 6.5 units of

[100]   McCarthy, 1999, 300.
[101]   McCarthy, 1999, 300–1.
[102]   McCarthy, 1999, 301.
[103]   McCarthy, 1999, 301.
[104]   Hall, 1982, 419.
[105]   US Department of Housing and Urban Development, 1986.
[106]   Soja *et al.*, 1983.
[107]   Hart, 1983, 20.

private investment for every one of public investment. A community could apply for a UDAG if it met standards of physical and economic distress or had a pocket of poverty. It had to show that it would attract at least 2.5 times as much private as public funding, and that the project could be funded no other way.

Down to the end of 1983, 929 communities had attracted over 1,900 projects and $3 billion of UDAG funds, with a median leverage ratio of 3.9; unsurprisingly, the lion's share of the funds had gone to the stricken bigger cities of the manufacturing belt, and New York City and Baltimore each had over 50 schemes. The program had generated an expected total of some 411,000 new permanent jobs – 56% of them, significantly, in commercial projects, and 55% for low- or moderate-income people.[108] It was small wonder that the UDAG scheme was widely regarded as one of the few real success stories of urban regeneration policy; small wonder, either, that in 1983 the British government's Urban Development Grant scheme paid it the sincerest form of flattery.

There were, inevitably, some criticisms. Some said that too much of the money had gone on hotel projects (to which the retort was that hotels generate a lot of low-skill employment, suitable for unemployed inner-city residents). Others posed the standard question about each and every such device: how many of the jobs would have been there anyway, scheme or no scheme? Yet others pointed out that UDAGs could never restore lost manufacturing jobs, or even replace as many jobs as had been lost.[109] But that was part of a wider debate about the march through the sectors to the service economy. Many economists, following the pioneer analyses of A. G. B. Fisher and Colin Clark half a century before, argued that the decline in manufacturing jobs was an inevitable development of the latter-day capitalist economy, and that the only intelligent policy was to accept and anticipate it. Others argued that the service economy mainly generated low-wage fast-food type jobs, and that – in the words of one major piece of academic polemic – Manufacturing Matters.[110]

The Attack on Planning

The point is that the real debate on both sides of the Atlantic was still all about economic development. And meanwhile, in other more traditional parts of the British planning system, during the 1980s the history increasingly resembled a movie run backwards. Progressively, after 1979, the Thatcher government dismembered the strategic planning system that had been painfully built up by successive governments during the 1960s and maintained during the 1970s. The Regional Economic Planning Councils were the first element to go, in 1979. The next year, when the government had to update the 1970 Strategic Plan for the South East – a plan which consisted of a main report and five large research volumes – it did so

---

[108] Hart, 1983, 25; Gatons and Brintnall, 1984, 116–17, 124, 130.
[109] Hart, 1983, 26–7.
[110] Cohen and Zysman, 1987.

through two and a half pages of typescript; in 1986, repeating the exercise, it extended to six. The 1980 Planning Act effected a significant shift of powers from the counties to the districts, making the county structure plans less effective; a Green Paper of 1986 proposed doing away with them altogether, in effect removing the county level of planning. In the major urban areas, an Act of 1986 did away with the Greater London Council and the six metropolitan counties, England's unique experiment in metropolitan government.[111]

All this marked a significant change in planning style. The 1983 White Paper, which presaged the abolition of metropolitan government, declared flatly that there was no longer the same need as in the 1960s for strategic planning; the clear sugges- tion was that all that was needed was a residual land-use planning activity, pro- ceeding on a case-by-case basis.[112] Local government took the hint. One county – Berkshire, one of the fastest-growing in all of England – abolished its planning department, merging it with the surveyor's department. Within the profession, there was a distinct weakening of the links with the university and polytechnic schools. There was a sharp reduction in the demand for planners, exacerbated by the sudden arrival on the job market of hundreds of displaced metropolitan and county planners. Simultaneously, funding organizations cut student support, precipitating the closure of several planning schools.

Perhaps, after all, in the long historical perspective it was just another turn of the cyclical screw. Planning in Britain had been rather like this in the relatively stagnant early 1950s, when – under an earlier Conservative government – it had come under a cloud; yet after that, during the high-growth era of the 1960s, it had bounced back to register one of the most successful periods of its short life. That, in a sense, is pure grist to the academic Marxists' mill: planning changes shape as it is required to face new challenges, or old challenges come back again. What was new, as already seen in Chapter 10, was the increasing detachment of the academic commentators from the whole process.

Will planning die away, then? Not entirely. Planning will survive, because in every advanced country it has a large – and in the long run, increasing – political constit- uency. Good environment, as the economists would say, is an income-elastic good: as people, and societies generally, become richer, they demand proportionately ever more of it. And, apart from building private estates with walls around them, the only way they are going to obtain it is through public action. The fact that people are wil- ling and even anxious to spend more and more of their precious time in defending their own environment, through membership of all kinds of voluntary organizations and through attendance at public inquiries, is testimony to that fact – as also to the fact that, not seldom, my good environment is my neighbor's bad one. So, in very advanced post-industrial societies – South East England, the San Francisco Bay Area – the politics of planning become ever more complex, ever more protracted, ever more bitter.[113]

[111]   Breheny and Hall, 1984.
[112]   GB Department of the Environment, 1983; Breheny and Hall, 1984.
[113]   Frieden, 1979; Blowers, 1980; Hall, 1980.

That, ironically, became plain during the course of the 1980s. The first Thatcher government of 1979 had been clearly determined to remove the shackles of planning from the developer. In 1983, Michael Heseltine – then Secretary of State for the Environment – shocked true-blue Tory central Berkshire by modifying the county's structure plan, allowing 4,000 extra houses to be built on green fields. There was impassioned opposition. The local district council refused to write the provision into its own district plan. Ironically, Heseltine himself had weakened the structure planners' power to control the lower-level district plans in an act of 1980; he, or shortly after his successor, was hoist with his own petard.[114]

Meanwhile, the private sector was girding its loins. Consortium Developments Ltd (CDL) was established in 1983 to develop up to 15 new country towns around London, where housing demand was high but local planning very restrictive. Each would comprise around 5,000 dwellings with social and physical infrastructure largely provided by CDL.[115] Curiously the initiative came from those in charge of the new towns, who had begun to make strenuous efforts to attract the major private house builders. The leader was Fred Lloyd Roche, general manager of the largest new town, Milton Keynes, who took a central part in discussions with the Volume House Builders' Study Group, formed in 1975 as a breakaway from the main house builders' lobby group, the House Builders Federation. An association of Britain's biggest speculative house builders, its members were building roughly a third of new British housing by the early 1980s, averaging *ca.* 5,000 dwellings each per annum. Working in the new towns, these builders learned the advantages of building within a properly planned development.[116] Their driving force – and later of CDL – was Tom Baron, the head of Christian Salvesen (Properties), then a major house builder.[117] He stated his view forcibly:

> To keep expanding existing settlements, you're going to get political outcry because the "haves" are going to object to the green fields going. It's better to have one big row and solve it by dropping it in an area surrounded by cows, because moos don't vote.[118]

In 1980, Roche had left Milton Keynes, taking several other staff including David Lock and Lee Shostak, joining the well-known retail and design entrepreneur Terence Conran to form the architectural practice of Conran Roche. Lock and Shostak wrote an (unpublished) two-volume report, *The Need for New Villages*.[119] It brilliantly linked the volume builders' crude need for land to build big housing estates with British planning's most potent tradition, the garden cities and new towns. There were, though, two key differences. First, the volume builders were normal profit-seeking companies;[120] secondly, they lacked compulsory purchase powers.

114   Short *et al.*, 1986, 240–7; Hall *et al.*, 1987, 154.
115   Quoted in Ward, 2005, 329.
116   Ward, 2005, 335.
117   Ward, 2005, 334–5.
118   Quoted in Ward, 2005, 329.
119   Ward, 2005, 337.
120   Ward, 2005, 338.

They had first to secure options to purchase, actually buying the land only if approval was secured. The "new village" concept thus became an attempt to adapt the garden-city/new-town tradition to the realities of Thatcherism.[121]

The first foray came in 1985, when they announced that the first village would be built on a green-belt site at Tillingham Hall in Essex.[122] The inquiry became one of those *causes célèbres* of planning history in which the English delight. The developers lost; doubtless to their great surprise, for a whole series of well-publicized official statements, with titles like *Lifting the Burden*, had clearly led them (and almost everyone else) to believe that the government would back them.[123] Then, in 1987 – admittedly, in the run-up to a general election – the government was forced to backtrack on a relatively minor policy change, which would remove the need to monitor agricultural considerations in the case of development proposals on poorer-quality farmland. The radical Right government, here as elsewhere, was proving that its bark was a good deal more significant than its bite.

Ultimately they failed, and this reveals a significant fact about planning in the Thatcher years.[124] Their style had the effect of intensifying opposition, partly because they always made their local intentions into much more than just a local issue. "In the collective imagination of the Conservative grassroots of England's outer southeast, CDL too readily filled the role of the evil specter that would prevail if free enterprise Thatcherism really did manage to deregulate local planning."[125] Essentially, they lost because they took Thatcherism at face value. Here, at least, Thatcherism faltered and restrictive planning survived and prospered.[126]

No, planning will not go away; no, it will never again be depoliticized, as some once hoped. Like the Abbé Sieyès in an earlier revolution, it lives. But in the 1990s traditional land-use planning came under more basic attack in its country of birth than ever in its 80 years of existence. It became determinedly reactive, artisan, and anti-intellectual, while planning in the academy retreated ever higher up its ivory tower. Meanwhile, it faced a new range of problems, with which its practitioners were never equipped by education (and perhaps by inclination) to tackle: the problem of structural economic decline of whole urban economies and of rebuilding a new economy on the ruins of the old.

---

[121]   Ward, 2005, 338.
[122]   Shostak and Lock, 1984, 9–13; Consortium Developments, 1985.
[123]   GB Minister without Portfolio, 1985.
[124]   Ward, 2005, 352.
[125]   Ward, 2005, 352–3.
[126]   Ward, 2005, 353.

The City of the Tarnished
Belle Époque

Yet identity is becoming the main, and sometimes the only, source of meaning in an historical period characterized by widespread destructuring of organizations, delegitimation of institutions, fading away of major social movements, and ephemeral cultural expressions. People increasingly organize their meaning not around what they do but on the basis of what they are, or believe they are ... *Our societies are increasingly structured around a bipolar opposition between the Net and the Self.*

Manuel Castells, *The Information Age: Economy, Society, and Culture,*
volume I, *The Rise of the Network Society* (1996)

Cities of Tomorrow: An Intellectual History of Urban Planning and Design Since 1880,
Fourth Edition. Peter Hall.
© 2014 Peter Hall. Published 2014 by John Wiley & Sons, Ltd.

12

The City of the Tarnished
Belle Époque

Infocities and Informationless Ghettos: New York, London, Tokyo, 1990–2010

The 1980s were thus a time of a new kind of planning, some would say anti-planning: anti-strategic, opportunistic, project-based, regeneration-focused. Two decades later, and over a decade into a new century, the question is what is new and different? The answer is not much; rather, much more of the same. But so much more, that it throws into even starker relief the history told in the previous chapter; and it poses the even more disturbing question of what story a future planning historian might tell. For the fact is that everywhere the city of enterprise has boomed and busted and then boomed and busted again, as have global economies all around it; partly in consequence, the fates of its citizens have diverged.

The Global-Informational City: Symbolic Analysts and No-Hopers

In the late 1980s and early 1990s, major books – refreshing exceptions to the general trend – began to examine in detail and in depth the forces driving the contemporary city. To Manuel Castells we owe the insight that, emerging in the late twentieth century, there is "a new, informational mode of development: on the basis of the convergence through interaction of information technologies and information-processing activities into an articulated techno-organizational system."[1] Such a mode of development, for Castells, is not simply technology driven: "Modes of development evolve according to their own logic."[2] This does not imply that capitalism is being superseded[3] – a remarkable shift in position for Castells, once the *doyen* of French Marxist urbanism. On the contrary: information technology has powerfully boosted

---

[1] Castells, 1989, 19.
[2] Castells, 1989, 11.
[3] Castells, 1989, 16.

the system, contributing to increasing rates of profit, accelerating internationalization, and engendering a new policy agenda on the part of governments, to foster capital accumulation at the expense of social redistribution.[4]

The resulting regional and urban geography is characterized by sharp spatial divisions of labor, with the decentralization of production functions, often with extreme flexibility in location, but with informational industries remaining highly concentrated in innovative urban milieux.[5] For Castells, these milieux of innovation – places like Silicon Valley, but also older urban places like Munich, Paris, and Boston – continue to command the crucial productive chains; they are the powerhouses of the contemporary capitalist economy.[6] Thus there is a contrast: high-level decision-making is increasingly centralized; other activities are decentralized either locally within major metropolitan areas, or more widely throughout national economies and indeed the world.[7]

Castells concludes that the restructuring process has deliberately aimed at "The supersession of places by a network of information flows," outside human control. He fears the outcome: "the ushering in of an era characterized by the uneasy coexistence of extraordinary human achievements and the disintegration of large segments of society, along with the widespread prevalence of senseless violence."[8]

Saskia Sassen poses a similar dichotomy: manufacturing disperses out of old industrial centers; office work decentralizes locally,[9] but international financial activity and service transactions, which grew hugely during the 1980s, are increasingly concentrated in a few countries and cities.[10] And these contrary trends are actually two sides of the same coin: the geographical dispersal of factories, offices, and service outlets and the reorganization of the financial services industry have created a need for centralized management and regulation in a few major cities. Here are found both traditional banks and corporate headquarters, but also a host of corporate service firms and non-bank financial institutions. And such cities have emerged as key locations for the production of innovative services.[11] Thus,

> to a considerable extent, the weight of economic activity over the last fifteen years has shifted from production places, such as Detroit and Manchester, to centers of finance and highly specialized services. While the dispersion of plants speeds the decline in old manufacturing centers, the associated need for centralized management and control feeds growth in servicing centers. Similarly, the ascendance of the advanced services in economic activity generally has shifted tasks out of the shop floor and into the design room and has changed management from what was once an activity focused on production to one that is finance focused today.[12]

[4]   Castells, 1989, 23–32.
[5]   Castells, 1989, 74.
[6]   Castells, 1989, 124; cf. Castells and Hall, 1994, Ch. 7.
[7]   Castells, 1989, 169.
[8]   Castells, 1989, 350.
[9]   Sassen, 1991, 25–7.
[10] Sassen, 1991, 87.
[11] Sassen, 1991, 126.
[12] Sassen, 1991, 325.

In the global cities, clustered around the major banks and headquarters offices, is a huge array of service industries: advertising, accounting, legal services, business services, certain types of banking, engineering and architectural services, which increasingly work for firms engaged in international transactions. However, Sassen stresses that during the 1980s there was a major shift: a growing sector of the financial services industry became in effect a commodity sector, in which the buying and selling of instruments became an end in itself. New York, London, and Tokyo emerged as the leading centers in this new industry; they effectively functioned as a single transnational marketplace.[13]

In other words, a new division of labor has emerged on a global scale: a division based not on product (Lancashire cotton, Sheffield steel) but on process (London and New York global finance, Berkshire and Westchester back offices, Leeds and Omaha direct telephone sales). Insofar as an activity can be decentralized to a lower-cost location, it will be; and, while manufacturing moves out from the advanced economies to Thailand and China, so services now move out to suburban or provincial locations, limited so far by linguistic and cultural barriers, but doubtless soon overleaping those too. What remains, and what grows, is a cluster of highly specialized activities based on access to privileged, esoteric information: financial services of the most speculative kind, specialized business services depending on face-to-face encounter, media services and the like.

This is often described as globalization; and globalization, the lowering or removing of barriers to the free movement of goods and services, is part of it. But it works rather differently for services than for goods. As sophisticated telecommunications services have grown, costs have fallen and the old barriers of distance have eroded, allowing information to be moved around the world instantaneously and effortlessly. The exponential spread in the mid-1990s of the Internet and the World Wide Web, with their zero charges for distance, were merely the logical conclusion of this century-long process. But, as this has occurred, it has paradoxically increased the attraction of the few key cities where special information is exchanged and shared.

The Digitalization of the World

For the future, the major question was what would ever drive urban economies up again. Most experts seemed to concur that the 1980s would not repeat themselves: financial services would not prove the fundamental force next time around; instead, that role might be played by new sectors, such as the arts, culture, entertainment, educational and health services, and tourism. In particular, the prospect was that high technology would fuse with the creative sectors, to create new industries: multimedia, new combinations of education and entertainment, virtual reality, all made possible by the total digitalization of information and the consequent fusion of formerly separate technologies – broadcasting, computing, telecommunications – into one. By the late

[13]   Sassen, 1991, 326.

1990s the bookstores were flooded with new books, almost without exception American, by devotees of the new gospel: Bill Gates's *The Way Ahead* and *Business @ the Speed of Thought*, certainly the best-publicized, and three contributions from professors at the Massachusetts Institute of Technology, William J. Mitchell's *City of Bits* and *e-topia*, and Nicholas Negroponte's *Being Digital*.[14] They described a world in which digitalized information of all kinds would flow effortlessly and in unlimited quantities, down the cable and through the ether, to miniaturized apparatus which would receive and process and exchange it. It all seemed a world removed from the clunky realities of the Internet in 1996, but the authors stressed that they were describing a vision 10, 20, even 50 years hence.

The critical question for planners concerned the impact on cities. One, very fashionable, view was that the flow of information would lead to the "Death of Distance"[15] and thus at last remove the need for cities: anyone could perform any activity anywhere, only so long as the right digital connections were available. Distance learning could replace traditional universities, trading on the screen could replace the Stock Exchange floor, and surgeons could even perform operations from home on patients thousands of miles away.

But the actual empirical evidence, limited as it was, suggested rather different conclusions: though these new industrial sectors might develop anywhere, in the mid-1990s the evidence was that they were growing in traditional urban places: in Los Angeles, in a belt between the old Hollywood studios and the high-technology Aerospace Alley; in the San Francisco Bay Area, within Silicon Valley and the San Francisco downtown, in the East Bay and in suburban Marin County; in New York City, in SoHo and Tribeca between Downtown and Midtown; in London, likewise, in Soho and Fitzrovia between the City and West End.[16] The reason was clear enough: like all creative activities, they depended on interaction, on networking, on a certain amount of buzz and fizz, which was more likely to be found in such places than anywhere else. Further, they related to other more traditional live performing arts which had always been here; and these in turn related to urban tourism, one of the great growth industries of the 1980s and 1990s, itself a reflection of the new globalized economy. In other words, there was a paradox: these new activities were supposed to substitute for face-to-face communication, but actually they depended on it, and in turn fortified the need for it: viewing electronic entertainment was likely to bolster the demand for the real thing, and similarly for electronic education, electronic consultancy, electronic anything.[17] A telling graph in Graham and Marvin's book *Telecommunications and the City* showed telecommunications and personal traffic in France over a 150-year period since the birth of the railway and the electric telegraph: the two curves marched upwards together, hardly deviating from each other.[18]

---

[14]   Gates, 1995; 1999; Mitchell, 1995; 1999; Negroponte, 1995.
[15]   Cairncross, 1997.
[16]   Hall, 1998, Ch. 30.
[17]   Hall, 1998, 963–4.
[18]   Graham and Marvin, 1996, 262.

Beyond this, the new multimedia industries needed low rents for start-up companies, which could be found in the urban interstices between the high-rise tower
clusters of the central business district. And, finally, they interacted with a variety of
specialized business services, in the fields of design, which had a quite separate
existence from the financial service industries that traditionally clustered around
banking quarters like Wall Street and the City of London and Otemachi.[19] So the
evidence, fragmentary and anecdotal as much of it still was, suggested that the city
as a place of congregation and interaction was far from dead: in these emerging
fields, as in finance, access to privileged information was all-important. And this,
interestingly, was the reluctant conclusion of one of the high priests of the cyber-
revolution, William Mitchell:

> Does development of national and international information infrastructures, and the
> consequent shift of social and economic activity to cyberspace, mean that existing cit-
> ies will simply fragment and collapse? Or does Paris have something that telepresence
> cannot match? Does Rome have an answer to *Neuromancer*? Most of us would bet our
> bottom bits that the reserves of resilience and adaptability that have allowed great cities
> to survive (in changed form) the challenges of industrialization and the automobile
> will similarly enable them to adapt to the bitsphere.[20]

However, the disturbing implication remained: all these were very much informational industries, and so they depended on the ability to access and to use information,
which meant education and sophisticated kinds of knowledge; thus, they might
prove to be the agents of yet further and yet more fundamental polarization of the
economy, of society, of the city. Optimistic observers found comforting anecdotal
evidence, suggesting that some artistic activities – music, visual design – could
employ informal, intuitive, artistic talents that other sectors could not, and so might
prove an integrative rather than a divisive force; pessimists noted that the new
artistic activities like multimedia were actually at the very frontier of technological
sophistication. The verdict is not in; and a whole urban future might depend on it.

Planning and Urban Policy: Codification versus Urban Entrepreneurship

For the fear is that polarization might remain the heart of the contemporary urban
problem, and thus of the world that urban planning has to deal with. The question
is what, in fact, planning has done about it; and the answer is not much. In fact, during the 1990s urban planning and urban policy moved in rather strangely opposite
directions, to become increasingly divorced from one another. British planning, traditionally flexible in response to changing circumstances, moved in the direction of

[19]   GB Government Office for London, 1996.
[20]   Mitchell, 1995, 169.

codification and legalization: Section 54A of the 1990 Town Planning Act stated that, in judging appeals against refusal of planning permission, the chief material consideration would be conformity to the plan. But urban policies increasingly stressed a highly competitive, innovative approach to urban regeneration: in the United Kingdom, the City Challenge scheme and its successor, the Single Regeneration Budget, both abandoned fixed allocations in favor of open competition between cities for funds. There could be no doubt that this new approach had advantages: it engendered much enthusiasm among local authorities, it brought forth some high-quality schemes (albeit very design-based in most cases), and it allowed big funds to be diverted into important schemes. But critics, who tended to be on the opposite side of the political fence, argued that, in fact, it was a colorful device for masking cuts in funds to the mainline regeneration programs.

What this meant in practice, though perhaps it was not fully appreciated, was that urban regeneration became separated from the mainstream planning process: mainstream planning dealt with codified incremental change, regeneration was about entrepreneurial response to new development opportunities and must therefore avoid rigidity. The quintessential example of this approach was the logical and the geographical sequel to the London Docklands project: Thames Gateway.

Thames Gateway: The last 1980s Regeneration Project?

Thames Gateway was likewise the brainchild of Michael Heseltine, on his return to the Department of the Environment in 1990. As seen in Chapter 11, by 1995, sufficient confidence had returned to see the first stage of the project substantially let; and Paul Reichmann of Olympia & York, the original developer, returned to ownership with the aid of Saudi Arabian money. But, undeterred by the gathering Docklands storm, in March 1991 Heseltine announced what was without doubt the largest piece of urban regeneration and development ever proposed in any city in the world: the East Thames Corridor, later rechristened Thames Gateway, a scheme extending more than 50 miles down the Lower Thames from Docklands to the estuary, and following the rerouted line of the planned high-speed rail link from central London to the Channel Tunnel. The underlying notion was that, just as the decision in 1943 to develop Heathrow airport had engendered growth along the corridor leading from London to the west, so now the direction of development could be dramatically reversed, regenerating the depressed areas east of London and taking pressure off the overheated West. But now, the Urban Development Corporation – favorite Heseltine device of the 1980s, and used first in Docklands, then in a dozen regeneration schemes in almost all the major cities of Britain – was eschewed in favor of a more sober and pragmatic approach: advance government provision of infrastructure in the form of road and rail improvements; clearance and preparation of land by what was in effect a roving English Development Corporation, English Partnerships; and a strong hint of favorable treatment in the annual Single Regeneration Budget (SRB) competition.

Figure 12.1   Thames Gateway. The United Kingdom's attempt to outdo the French in mega-strategic-planning, a 50-mile development corridor down the river, based on the new Channel Tunnel high-speed rail link; here, a computer simulation of the proposed development – so far awaiting implementation – around the Ebbsfleet train station. *Source*: Reproduced by permission of Land Securities.

Work proceeded steadily, first on a survey of the corridor's development potential, then on producing a strategic framework – not a strategic plan, significantly; that word must be avoided at all cost – for development, published in mid-1995; in parallel, the government refined the route of the new rail line and opened up a competition to build and operate it, finally announcing the winner in February 1996.[21]

A decade into the new century, and two decades after Heseltine's announcement, Thames Gateway was – all too slowly – appearing on the ground: in the Royal Docks at the eastern end of Docklands and the western end of the corridor, a huge new exhibition and conference center, an urban village, and a new campus for the local University of East London; at Barking Reach, a small start to a New Town Intown for some 20,000 people; at Bluewater Park in Dartford, the biggest retail park in Europe. The rail link, delayed by a financial crisis which hit the winning company, finally opened in 2007 with domestic services to the Kent Coast two years afterwards, and with two new stations which would provide the basis for major developments, at Stratford in East London and close to Bluewater in Kent. At Stratford, development received a totally unpredictable boost from the decision in 2005 to locate the 2012 Olympic Games there, largely on the basis of its contribution to regenerating the area; the Games were a public relations triumph for London, a year later the Olympic Village was being transformed into a new residential area, with plans for five further neighborhoods, to be developed by a Mayoral Development Corporation, around it: a veritable New Town Intown, on what had been London's greatest urban wasteland. Elsewhere, at Barking Riverside and Ebbsfleet, progress had been slower, even glacial: there had been problems in paying for the necessary transport infrastructure, compounded after 2008 by the global financial crisis and resulting collapse in house-building. So the pragmatic approach seemed to be working, more slowly and more patchily than anyone had ever hoped or expected at first, but happening nonetheless; but it would take another decade, or even two, before the success of the scheme could properly be judged.

Thames Gateway was a 1990s mega-version of the 1980s mega-project, launched with counter-cyclical courage at an unpropitious time (but so, of course, was London Docklands in 1981); it came at a moment when, worldwide, the urban property bubble had burst, leaving the usual tale of destruction in all the major cities. Generally, it was clear that the development cycle had taken its all-too-predictable form; developers, full of animal spirits, had all-too-predictably overreached themselves; and the development industry was in the doldrums. That might mean that it might go slowly in early years; but, given that it was a long-term project anyway, that might not matter save to the politicians, who would doubtless like it to show results not later than the next election. It did pose the question of whether any strategy so dependent on property regeneration, which was the fundamental approach not merely in London but in every great global city during the 1980s, could yield results save during brief bursts of optimism, which might occur at intervals of 20 years or more. But to that there was the obvious retort: what other kind of strategy was there? In a world in which service industries were the economic driver, most development would inevitably be commercially speculative, mimicking and amplifying the market signals in the underlying fundamental economy. So perhaps this was the only game in town: any town.

The Mega-Project: An Eastern Asian Art Form?

In other parts of the world, governments engaged with commercial capital even more enthusiastically, even maniacally – so much so, that the mega-project became almost an eastern Asian art form.[22] The most extraordinary case of all was the People's Republic of China, which engaged in two mega-projects to end all

22 Olds, 1995.

mega-projects, one in the Pudong district of Shanghai, the other in the Special Economic Zone of Shenzhen next to the Hong Kong border. Shenzhen's self-proclaimed goal is "Environment like Singapore with Efficiency of Hong Kong." By the year 2001, within a 17-year construction period, it had emerged from effectively nothing into a 30-kilometer linear city with a population of four million, most likely even more, all arrayed along a Los Angeles-style urban boulevard, and paralleled a couple of kilometers away by a Los Angeles urban freeway. The freeway is lined with Singapore-style landscaping, to create a continuous urban parkway; the boulevard is lined with Hong Kong-style skyscrapers (built speculatively, with Hong Kong capital); the whole complex is crowned by a whole cluster of theme parks (one containing a miniature Eiffel Tower) in between the skyscrapers.

There cannot be anything quite like Shenzhen in the world, just as there cannot be anything like Pudong, of which the Executive Vice-Chairman of the Shanghai Foreign Investment Commission, Ye Longfei, memorably said,

> we will not only use the method employed in Shenzhen of, "building nests to attract birds" (meaning building infrastructure facilities and standard factory buildings ourselves), but also try the method of Yangpu of Hainan Province of "alluring birds to build nests" (meaning let foreign businessmen invest in the development of whole lots of land), and also the stratagem being used in Xiamen of "having birds come and bring nests with them" (meaning inviting foreign businessmen to invest in the development of land and bring with them their investment partners).[23]

But, in many respects, Shenzhen's Special Economic Zone was a disappointment. True, it quickly developed from a farm town into a city of 350,000, with no unemployment, a sharp increase in the standard of living, and rapid infrastructure construction and industrial development. But it did not bring in the advanced technology that China expected. Instead of building up China's reserves, it turned into an import-processing zone for Hong Kong, by providing cheap land and labor, thus draining hard currency. And the quasi-market system gave opportunities for corruption and profiteering, by the "maggots of the Special Zone," the government officials who abused their position of power for personal gain.[24]

So Pudong, formally unveiled by the government in April 1990, was going to be different. No less a figure than Deng Xiaoping declared in 1991 that "Finance is the heart of modern economy, Shanghai will be the most important city to win for China its world position in this field." And, that same year, Li Peng laid down that "The construction of Pudong will be the focus of China's development for the next decade." Covering an area of 522 square kilometers, projected to run to the year 2030 with a total estimated cost of $80 billion, the Pudong New Area was to be by far the largest construction site in the world, designed to become "Asia's financial center of the 21st century."[25]

23   MacPherson, 1994, 78.
24   Wu, 1998, 146.
25   Wu, 1998, 133.

Figure 12.2   Pudong. Shanghai's amazing new central business district, created on former rice fields in an astonishingly short time.

Pudong was more even than that: it was emblematic of China's ideological transformation. The leadership not only wants to transform its economic system, it also wants to become a major world economic power in an amazingly short period of time. Its reforms are often experimental in nature, with the potential to unleash unforeseen results. This predilection for the grandiose amidst waves of controversy fits with China's recent and past history.[26]

But the decision to develop it was taken in dramatic political circumstances – not only the dismissal of Hu Yaobang and Zhao Ziyang, but the rise of Shanghai's former mayor, Jiang Zemin, to Chinese Communist Party (CCP) General Secretary, a move undertaken to reassure the world of Beijing's commitment to reform. Less than a year later, Zhu Rongji, then mayor of Shanghai, was promoted to Vice-Premier of the State Council, and commenced the push to develop Pudong.[27] The reality was that, in the aftermath of Tiananmen and the collapse of the Soviet Communist Party, the CCP realized that it was their last chance: Deng and his supporters knew that their legitimacy depended on their capacity to deliver the economic goods. In Deng's much publicized Southern Tour of Wuchang, Shenzhen, Zhuhai, and Shanghai in early 1992, he expressed his backing for rapid growth and an open economy, with

---

[26]   Wu, 1998, 134.
[27]   Wu, 1998, 141.

construction as the main focus. It became the keynote of the Third Plenary Session of the CCP's Fourteenth Central Committee in November 1993, often called "the Decision."[28] Pudong was in many respects a manifestation of "the Decision," carrying with it the same feeling of charging boldly ahead, but yet, with caution. With the fading of the original Special Economic Zones as models for development, Pudong became the new model for the next decade – if not the next half-century. China had adopted the East Asian model of development, as represented by Singapore, where government control would underpin economic growth.[29] Central planners allocated $36 billion to Pudong for the second phase (1996–2000) of Pudong, four times more than for the first five-year phase – and more even than for the Three Gorges Dam.[30] The message to the world was clear: China was serious about reform, and Pudong would exemplify China's current and future economic strength.[31]

But even mega-projects like Pudong represent only part of a much larger phenomenon, which has appeared in the late twentieth century in eastern Asia: the mega-city, a vast complex of networked cities housing up to 30 or 40 million people, and extending over a vast space of thousands of square kilometers. The archetype is the Pearl River delta between Hong Kong and Guangzhou, with Shenzhen at its very core. Such complexes represent the ultimate in urban organization; the significant fact is that they represent parts, albeit the most advanced parts, of poor countries embarked on the steep upward curve of development. The Asian Development Bank's annual report, published in April 1997, forecast that by the year 2025 Asia will have 20 cities with populations of more than 10 million; double the number in 1997. Currently there are nine mega-cities with more than 10 million inhabitants in the region: Beijing, Bombay, Calcutta, Jakarta, Osaka, Seoul, Shanghai, Tianjin, and Tokyo. They will shortly be joined by Bangkok, Dhaka, Karachi, and Manila. By 2025 even Rangoon will be included, as well as Lahore, Hyderabad, Bangalore, and Madras in India, and Shenyang in China.[32]

The Campaign for Urban Quality

There was another emerging theme in the 1990s, but in a sense it was a reassertion and a reinterpretation of a 1980s theme: it was a new emphasis on quality in the urban environment, a theme that became almost a personal crusade on the part of the British Secretary of State for the Environment, John Gummer, in 1993–6. It was an approach that saw the city largely in design terms, and it accorded well with another theme of the 1980s and 1990s: the stress on competition between cities, on marketing them like cars or kitchens, which was part and parcel of globalization in an era where

[28] Wu, 1998, 142.
[29] Wu, 1998, 143.
[30] Wu, 1998, 144.
[31] Wu, 1998, 145.
[32] Anon, 1997, 23; Hall, 1999, passim.

Figure 12.3 La Défense. The ultimate French *grand projet*, 40 years in the making; the total integration of everything, all aligned on the historic *grand axe* of Paris, looking back at the *Arc de Triomphe*.

the old locational advantages had blown away.[33] It marked a strong re-entry of the architectural profession into the planning arena, recalling a very similar trend in the 1930s, and for the same crude reason: the architects, reeling under the worst development slump since that time, were short of work. They could do worse, at least, than dream urban dreams and publicize them; someone might respond. And in Britain the runaway success of the National Lottery, which produced a flow of funds for Parisian-style (or eastern-Asian style) *grands projets* – another clear case of competitive emulation – helped restore their flagging creative spirits.

In Britain, from 1974 to 1994 there was a loss of 3.6 million jobs, 45%,[34] heavily concentrated in the country's great cities. "By the late twentieth century, none of these cities could any longer be regarded as industrial."[35] Birmingham in 1991 had less than a quarter of its workforce in manufacturing, Sheffield and Leeds just under one-fifth; Manchester, Liverpool, Bristol, and Glasgow just over 15%, Newcastle 12.9%, inner London 8.76%.[36] The central feature was an employment structure dominated by services, especially in their central areas and adjacent waterfront areas.[37] Sooner or later, all realized that their futures lay in reinventing themselves as post-industrial service centers.[38]

[33] Gold and Ward, 1994; Ward, 1998.
[34] Ward, 1998, 187.
[35] Ward, 1998, 187.
[36] Ward, 1998, 187.
[37] Ward, 1998, 189–90.
[38] Ward, 1998, 187.

They followed American cities into the unfamiliar territory of city marketing. New York had invented "I ♥ New York" in 1977, at almost the same time as Mayor Kevin White of Boston initiated its claim to be the post-industrial city.[39] Glasgow followed in 1983 with "Glasgow's Miles Better," developed by the Lord Provost Michael Kelly, who was very impressed by the New York campaign, and the advertising agent John Struthers.[40] "Claimed as Scotland's most successful ever advertising campaign, 'Miles Better' caught the public imagination in Britain as no place selling campaign had done since 'Skegness is So Bracing.'"[41]

But, as Steven Ward points out, "marketing, narrowly defined, is not enough; behind the fine words and images there has to be at least some physical activity of buildings, public spaces and activities that give at least some genuine promise of a re-invented city," partial as this may be; "… never before had urban design and planning been used in quite such a systematically calculating way to re-image and sell places."[42]

In this process, "The magic word was 'partnership.'"[43] The private and public sectors had to come together.[44] Pioneered in Boston (Chapter 11), it came to Britain much later:[45] "the hopes of the Thatcher government were based on exaggerated assumptions about what had actually been happening in the United States"[46] and radical Left Labour local governments were not interested.[47] Ward comments, "There was, therefore, no spontaneous emergence of local, American-style business-led partnerships in British cities. Much of what did happen involved Thatcherite centrally-stimulated initiatives such as Urban Development Corporations and Enterprise Zones."[48] The London Docklands Development Corporation spent between 1 and 4% of total expenditure on publicity, and the Central Manchester Development Corporation (CMDC) in 1992–3 spent £1.1 million out of £17.2 million.[49]

But, in fact, the Thatcherite property-led regeneration of the late 1980s, based upon a purely physical planning process which effectively excluded the wider community, had run its course by the mid-1990s. Even before the 1997 election and the arrival of New Labour, it was abandoned in a "turn to community." The City Challenge program and its successor, the Single Regeneration Budget, ushered in partnership-based and community-centerd approaches to regeneration and renewal. They provided the foundations for New Labour's wide-ranging urban regeneration

[39]   Ward, 1998, 191.
[40]   Ward, 1998, 191–2.
[41]   Ward, 1998, 192.
[42]   Ward, 1998, 193.
[43]   Ward, 1998, 194.
[44]   Ward, 1998, 194.
[45]   Ward, 1998, 195.
[46]   Ward, 1998, 196.
[47]   Ward, 1998, 196.
[48]   Ward, 1998, 197.
[49]   Ward, 1998, 198.

program, with its emphasis on combating social exclusion, renewing neighbor-hoods, and involving communities.[50]

Sustainable Urbanism in Practice: The United Kingdom's Urban Task Force and After

All these dilemmas, and more, culminated in the report of the United Kingdom's Urban Task Force in June 1999.[51] Essentially, it was a response to two quite separate but related questions that were vexing British planners and policy-makers in the mid-1990s: what to do about urban decay, and what to do about development in the South East.

The problem of urban decay was evident in outline when the Task Force began its work, but became dramatically clear towards its end, when one member, Anne Power, published the results of her work on Manchester and Newcastle.[52] Whole areas of these cities, she showed, had entered into an American-style cycle of esca-lating physical decay and social collapse: people were abandoning their homes, selling them for anything they could get; whole streets of houses were progressively being abandoned and boarded up. The causes were extremely complex, but they included the long-term structural decline of the economy – these typically were the cities' old industrial areas, which had suffered most drastically from the long deindustrialization of the 1970s and 1980s – leading in turn to long-term unemployment among old and young alike, poor-performing school systems that perpetuated the problem from one generation to another, family collapse, drink and drug problems, the growth of a criminal economy based on drugs, and gang warfare. So, by the late 1990s, parts of East Manchester and West Newcastle were beginning to look ominously reminiscent of North Philadelphia and South Chicago. And the further paradoxical parallel with these places was that – as Professor Brian Robson commented in a report in 2001 – the city centers were thriving as centers of the new 24-hour economy, attracting not merely tourists and night-time visitors but also new residents who were colonizing converted warehouses and new apartment blocks: urban renaissance and urban collapse were standing side by side, sometimes as little as a mile apart.

That was what could be called the northern urban agenda. It was quite different from the southern one, which was indeed almost its reverse. There, London was booming: its population was increasing again for the first time in 50 years, and was predicted to rise again to its 1939 peak by the year 2016. True, as with the northern cities, people were still leaving for the surrounding smaller towns; but just as many people were flowing in from abroad, comprising a huge social spectrum from inter-national bankers to asylum seekers, while new Londoners were being born in larger

[50]   Shaw and Robinson, 2010, 125.
[51]   GB Urban Task Force, 1999.
[52]   Power and Mumford, 1999; Rogers and Power, 2000.

and larger numbers, a product in large measure of the capital's high concentrations of young ethnic minorities. So London, with a few exceptions, was almost full up, and the problem was to shoehorn more and more people in while preserving a reasonably decent quality of urban life. Yet, even if this were done, the problem would still be the net outflow, which was politically explosive; the people in the surrounding shire counties, many of whom had themselves moved out not so many years before, now wanted to pull up the drawbridge and preserve what they saw as their rural quality of life. And the torch to light the explosion came in 1996 with new population projections, showing an expected 4.4 million additional households in England over a 25-year period.

All this was confusingly tangled up with a debate about the future of foxhunting, and led in early 1998 to a huge march of enraged countrysiders in their Barbour coats and green wellies on the heart of the capital. It sounded a huge political alarm: to try to defuse the situation, the government appointed a task force under the leadership of the architect and Labour politician Richard Rogers. In response, the task force in June 1998 produced a single vision to suit all cities: a vision based on urban renaissance, of a continental European-style urban life which would offer a real alternative to a 200-year English history of suburbanization. There was an impeccable logic here: since those household projections had shown, quite remarkably, that close on four in five of the new households would consist of only one person living alone, many of them could be presumed to be well content with an apartment life in the big cities. The task force produced no less than 105 recommendations designed to bring the urban renaissance about, many of them concerning fiscal incentives to make it more attractive to build in the cities and to live in them.

Barcelona, considered below, was a model – indeed, *the* model. Whatever its rights or wrongs, planning under New Labour had a new mission: to create a spectacular urban landscape and an intense, high-quality lifestyle experience for a select group, to create a "buzz." As John Prescott, Deputy Prime Minister, put it in a favorite phrase, "By getting architects, town planners and developers to work together we have created a new 'wow' factor in the North."[53]

Place shaping was all about creating a composite package of housing, workplace, and lifestyle "offers," carefully shaped and marketed to attract a narrowly defined class of creative/knowledge workers.[54] Urban places became little more than fashion or lifestyle accessories:

> Similar to the fashion catwalk, cities now contend with each other by parading made-up images of different areas of the city which advertise these spaces as favourable and appealing environments for business and leisure. Cities proudly display their new styles and designed environments on the global catwalk.[55]

53   Prescott, 2003.
54   Allen and Crookes, 2009, 458.
55   Degen, 2008, 27, quoted in Allen and Crookes, 2009, 459.

The Urban White Paper thus departed fundamentally from a long tradition of "anti-urbanism" in English urban policy. Cities were no longer the problem; they were the solution.[56] Suddenly, there was a new "Urban Idyll." As Gareth Hoskyns and Andrew Tallon describe it:

> Imagine strolling through a dockland area digesting Friday's lunch one summer's after-noon. You cross paved walkways punctuated with illuminated water features and hear the liquid patter of a fountain's droplets overlaying the hum of a not-too-distant business district winding down for the week; you negotiate the clutter of plastic art planted sporadically in the concrete and circle a twelve-foot anchor drenched in treacle-like gloss paint; you approach an arcade and hear people conversing around brushed steel tables of coffee houses whose interiors invoke an impression of Latin-American Moderne. Drinking espresso, soy latte, or the finest bottled Belgian beer, these people are part of the new British metropolitan bohemia and while your cynicism compels its condescension you secretly fancy yourself as a member.[57]

This borrows associations from rural life – the "local community," "nature," "heritage," the "village" – to recreate a vision of civilized urban living: the urban village. Its inhabitants are exclusively young urban professionals, single or childless, with a high disposable income and high social, educational, and cultural capital.[58] In reality, however, areas that have thus been rapidly regenerated and gentrified, such as parts of London's East End, reveal a quasi-complete separation between the refurbished loft apartments and newly built secured developments on Hoxton Square and Kingsland Road and the social housing estates a few blocks away: a mosaic of "utopian and dystopian spaces," "physically proximate but institutionally estranged."[59] Maybe, as Rowland Atkinson suggested, this was a price worth paying for attracting the middle class back into the inner city, promoting public spaces and increasing the quality of life of most city-dwellers.[60] But the radical critics were not satisfied: "We have Rogers on the 'urban', the Social Exclusion Unit on 'poor neighbourhoods' and the local government White Paper on local 'governance'. The consequence of this is to provide one set of policies for the urban middle classes, one for the urban poor and another for the partial reform of the political establishment governing both."[61]

Faced with the new challenges of transforming their economies, rebuilding their structures, and changing their images, the leading English core cities adopted very different strategies – and with very different outcomes, as emerges from the verdicts of local academic experts in a symposium edited by John Punter. Manchester was famously entrepreneurial, opportunistic, and market-oriented, building a very strong reputation as a good city to do business with. Unconstrained by statutory

56   Gordon, 2004, 374, quoted in Colomb, 2007, 4.
57   Hoskins and Tallon, 2004, 25, quoted in Colomb, 2007, 6.
58   MacLeod and Ward, 2002, and Lees, 2003, quoted in Colomb, 2007, 7.
59   MacLeod and Ward, 2002, 154, quoted in Colomb, 2007, 10.
60   Atkinson, 2003, quoted in Colomb, 2007, 18.
61   Shaw and Robinson, 2010, 130, quoted in Amin, *et al.*, 2000, 7.

planning and politically unchallenged, its Local Development Framework "is as noncommittal as it can be about building density, height or land use, allowing hope values to roam freely and the city to negotiate developments case by case" – yet it takes urban design seriously and hires world-class consultants to provide it.[62] Leeds was less successful: "a whirlwind of development control activity with policy struggling to keep up, let alone firmly controlling the nature, location, amount and style of development of various kinds, while prioritising sustainable development." It seemed to oscillate between adopting a boldness and timidity; it aimed to become a truly European city, but the reality fell short.[63] Sheffield successfully transformed its city center through innovative approaches. Like other cities, it has promoted a vision of an urban "Mediterranean" lifestyle revolving around a "cafe culture." But it also created covered public spaces like the Winter Gardens and Millennium Galleries.[64] It put huge effort into creating a route from the railway station to the town hall, suggesting that it was obsessed with image creation for visitors.

In Liverpool a frenetic decade brought a real impact, led by the new administration's council leader and chief executive who set up Liverpool Vision and secured the role of Grosvenor in the new shopping center of Liverpool One, setting a benchmark for open street systems and a more urbane form of comprehensive development, whilst establishing a new market confidence for development in the city center. Liverpool led the way in the United Kingdom in embracing its outstanding cultural institutions[65] and developing a good public realm. It emphasized mixed-use development, and the city center residential population soared. But much of this success was concentrated in the city center.[66] Bristol provides a sad contrast, with mediocre development. Perhaps it did not need an "urban renaissance" because, unlike post-industrial cities such as Birmingham, Glasgow, and Manchester, it was never in any real danger of "dying." For many, Bristol remains a good place to live and work despite the limited achievements of its planners, developers, and regeneration initiatives.[67] Newcastle noticeably improved the physical and economic quality of its city center. Some find the new spaces and images corporate and elitist, not responsive enough to the local character and needs, and not sufficiently subtle or coherent.[68] Nottingham prepared strategic master-plans for the remaining major redevelopment areas on the fringe of the city core – Waterside, Southside, and Eastside – creating a coherent framework for this regeneration process while striving to link deprived inner-city communities back to the prosperous city center and reunite the city with the River Trent. It successfully transformed itself from a manufacturing to a service- and knowledge-based economy, through a consistent and long-term strategy. It rightly insisted on combining planning, urban design, and

[62]   Hebbert, 2010, 66.
[63]   Unsworth and Smales, 2010, 83.
[64]   Booth, 2010, 98.
[65]   Biddulph, 2010, 113.
[66]   Biddulph, 2010, 114.
[67]   Shaftoe and Tallon, 2010, 131.
[68]   Madanipour, 2010, 146.

transportation under one coordinating section, using a design-led approach to planning and transportation, with detailed planning briefs for all key sites and the promotion of three-dimensional design briefs for particularly important development opportunities.[69]

John Punter, reflecting on these varied histories, concludes that they reflect less the outcomes of deliberate urban renaissance policy than the impact of the 1993–2007 property boom, which gave cities a long-awaited opportunity to repopulate their central areas, to remove dereliction, to reinforce service employment, particularly in the high gross-value-added financial service sector;[70] to expand their shopping centers and widen their catchments; and to expand their appeal as cultural, party, entertainment or "city break" destinations. Most city councils developed explicit competitiveness agendas and entrepreneurial strategies to attract investment and deliver major regeneration projects and public realm improvements. Business and property interests loomed large in the scale and variety of their public–private partnerships, in the influence of major investor-developers on local strategic (or transport) partnerships, and in the ways in which councils managed major development projects.[71]

Most importantly, in all the cities the most dramatic physical impacts of the urban renaissance were concentrated in the city centers and their immediate fringes. The typical combination, Punter found, was greatly expanded central retail, hotel, leisure, and eating/drinking sectors, a reflection of the growth in consumerism, and dramatic increases in the number of apartments in areas around the commercial core. The city center was everywhere the "engine of growth," and the scale of redevelopment was unprecedented in modern times; at the height of the boom in 2006, several cities reported 15–20% of their central area under development. A key objective was to repopulate and extend the city center, increase its critical mass, diversify its character, and revitalize areas immediately beyond it. High-rise, high-density apartment investment was concentrated in declining commercial areas on the edges of city centers or in former industrial/warehouse areas, along waterfronts and other areas of higher amenity.[72] Between 1998 and 2006, some 5,000–9,000 apartments were built in the fringes of the city centers of Manchester, Leeds, Birmingham, Liverpool, Cardiff, and Bristol. Now accounting for more than half of all local housing production, these apartments became the focus of severe design criticism, but the repopulation of the city centers has brought major benefits in terms of increased urban vitality, and met the housing demands of many small households.

Overall, Punter concluded, there had been an appreciable improvement in the quality of the built environment and the public realm in the centers, with new "quarters" providing more choice for businesses, residents, consumers, and citizens. But, beyond these enlarged city centers, there was only sporadic evidence of renaissance.

[69]   Heath, 2010, 162.
[70]   Punter, 2010a, 325.
[71]   Punter, 2010a, 326.
[72]   Punter, 2010a, 328–9.

In many cities, there remained an all-too-evident break point at which high-level refurbishment and maintenance for well-heeled consumers and the tourists ends and the minimal expenditure for the residents begins.[73]

It all accorded rather well with the new emphasis: on entrepreneurial regeneration through a series of spectacular projects which would transform the image of a rundown urban area. And it marked a sharp shift in emphasis: away from growth-oriented strategies to house people, so typical of the 1960s and 1970s, and towards strategies that depended on the renewal of brownfield areas much closer to the city centers. It would be possible to dismiss this as a purely political shift, peculiar to the United Kingdom; but it occurred simultaneously in socialist France, where the 1994 *Schéma Directeur* for the Île-de-France sharply contrasted with its predecessors on this point. The fact was that the planning movement had become decoupled from the housing movement, which had provided the essential fuel to sustain it over much of its twentieth-century life; the new name of the game was regeneration, and in this planning was reduced to a secondary role.

There was another feature, which was that the entire enterprise strangely echoed the City Beautiful movement: as nearly a century before, architect-planners almost exclusively emphasized appearance, the decorative side of cities; they showed a marked bias toward the treatment of great central public spaces, at the expense of the places where ordinary city dwellers lived and worked; thus, they relegated into deep background the deeper and less tractable social issues, like structural unemployment and the emergence of an urban underclass. It was all uncannily reminiscent of Burnham's Chicago. Perhaps it was involuntary: one should not expect architects to act as social engineers, a job for which they had seldom demonstrated much enthusiasm. But the shift of emphasis was itself significant; one could dismiss it as simply a political agenda, but it surely went deeper than that.

The odd thing was that it was all happening at just the point when the new projections, all over Europe, showed an almost unprecedented demand for new housing. These projections began to appear in the mid-1990s, and it inevitably took time for their implications to permeate fully; it seemed certain that they would engender a passionate debate, for they struck at the heart of Nimby desires to keep the green enclaves green.

The Search for Sustainability

There was another major theme for planners by the early 1990s, which was the search for what emerged as almost a Holy Grail: sustainable urban development. The problem was that though everyone was in favor of it, nobody knew exactly what it meant. To be precise: though they could all quote by heart the definition of sustainability, from the Brundtland Report of 1987 – "development which meets present needs without compromising the ability of future generations to achieve their

---

[73] Punter, 2010a, 330.

own needs and aspirations" – it was not at all clear how this mapped into actual everyday decisions in everyday urban contexts. The general objectives were easy enough: we should develop building forms that conserve energy and minimize emissions of pollutants; we should encourage accessibility without mobility, or specifically without the need for mechanized transportation (particularly, by providing for places to be reachable on foot and by bicycle); we should therefore develop public transport and discourage single-user driving, develop new forms of propulsion that are less polluting and more economical of energy than the internal combustion engine, and develop centers of activity around public transport nodes. The difficult part was the next step: to translate these objectives into actual contexts. Consequently and quite predictably, everyone defined them to suit themselves: Nimbys – Not In My Back Yarders from posh exurban counties – interpreted them to mean pulling up the drawbridge to stop anyone else entering their well-heeled enclaves (save perhaps a few select people like themselves, whom it would be fun to have to drinks on Sundays); developers interpreted them to mean fashionable urban villages on otherwise difficult-to-sell sites in the cities, or perhaps equally fashionable downtown loft conversions.

Simin Davoudi argues that the problem goes deeper: the concept of sustainability is itself inherently ambivalent. Modern planning arose out of a vision of an alternative society, a utopia.[74] But, as the interventionist state of the postwar period gave way to the enabling state of the 1970s, "classical town planning" lost its force. "The golden age of planning" – when planners free from political interference and confident of their technical capacity were left to get on with the job – came to an end.[75] The social purposes that once shaped its original foundation were renounced. Planning has become a bureaucratic routine and a technical exercise which has little in common with reform.[76]

The hope therefore was that a new vision could emerge from sustainability. But, Davoudi argues, two different discourses of sustainability have emerged, providing fundamentally distinctive development paths for the planning system. One, "ecological modernization," reinforces the technical and regulatory face of the system; the other, the "risk society" approach, calls for a resurgence of its ideological and proactive face.[77] These two alternative concepts of sustainability reflect the underlying conflicts between those who believe that society can achieve sustainability without seriously impeding economic growth, and those who argue that society cannot achieve sustainability unless alternative modes of production are pursued.[78] The "professional" definition of planning, as conceptualized by government and adopted in practice, neatly accords with the ecological modernization approach.[79]

[74]   Davoudi, 2000, 124.
[75]   Davoudi, 2000, 124.
[76]   Davoudi, 2000, 127.
[77]   Davoudi, 2000, 123.
[78]   Davoudi, 2000, 127–8.
[79]   Davoudi, 2000, 130.

In the middle of all this, some sincere people, mainly of an academic cast of mind, were trying to puzzle out what sustainability might mean in practice. It all started with a publication by two Australian planners, Peter Newman and Jeffrey Kenworthy, in 1989: this showed that the inhabitants of American cities consumed much more energy for transport than urban Australians, and they in turn used more than Europeans. The main difference, they found, was that Europeans in particular used more public transport, and this could be explained by the fact that their cities were denser. So the key, they concluded, was to create cities that were denser and more compact.

Needless to say, not all their fellow academics agreed; they never do. In particular, two of them – Harry Richardson and Peter Gordon of the University of Southern California – produced evidence that California-style spread cities were actually energy-efficient, because jobs moved out with people, so that average journeys were short.[80] Apart from this major difference, most academics found themselves in a remarkable – even unusual – degree of agreement: that development should be based on fairly small neighborhood units, each combining homes, job opportunities, and services, not to guarantee that everyone would minimize travel but to give them at least the opportunity if they wished; these should be clustered into roughly rectangular groups for up to 250,000 people, along public transportation spines.[81] In California, the architect-planner Peter Calthorpe was trying to give physical expression to such ideas through his concept of the pedestrian pocket, which has been used in the city of San Jose and has become the basis for the urban master-plan for the state capital of Sacramento.[82] And, over on the other side of the continent at Seaside in Florida, Andres Duany and Elizabeth Plater-Zyberk provided a very similar model of a sustainable community.[83]

These American reinventions were with rare exceptions (Seaside, Celebration) garden suburbs, not self-contained garden cities. But in this they merely followed Radburn and the Greenbelt cities, nearly a century earlier: Clarence Stein had written that "Radburn had to accept the role of a suburb."[84] What Mumford memorably called the "Radburn idea" provided the basis for virtually every American new town from then to 1980, including the green-belt towns, Reston and Columbia, the federal new communities of the 1960s and 1970s, and Californian "master-planned communities" like Irvine, Valencia, and Westlake Village.[85] The New Urbanists were traditionalists to the core: they married Jane Jacobs's advocacy of traditional neighborhood design – houses facing the street, a grid system ensuring busy pedestrian sidewalks – with the equally traditional neighborhood unit

---

[80]   Gordon *et al.*, 1989a; 1989b; 1989c; Gordon and Richardson, 1996; Gordon *et al.*, 1991.

[81]   Banister, 1992; 1993; Banister and Banister, 1995; Banister and Button, 1993b; Breheny, 1991; 1992a; 1995a; 1995b; 1995c; Breheny *et al.*, 1993; Breheny and Hall, 1996; Breheny and Rookwood, 1993; Owens, 1984; 1986; 1990; 1992a; 1992b; Owens and Cope, 1992; Rickaby, 1987; 1991; Rickaby *et al.*, 1992.

[82]   Kelbaugh *et al.*, 1989; Calthorpe, 1993; Calthorpe and Fulton, 2001.

[83]   Duany *et al.*, 2000.

[84]   Fulton 2002, 162.

[85]   Fulton 2002, 163.

Figure 12.4 Sustainable development. Two concepts from 1993, one British (Michael Breheny and Ralph Rookwood, for the Town and Country Planning Association), one American (Peter Calthorpe): independently conceived, almost identical in form. *Sources*: (a) M. Breheny and R. Rockwood, from A. Blowers (ed.): *Planning for a Sustainable Environment – A Report by the Town and Country Planning Association* © 1993 Earthscan. Reproduced by permission of Taylor and Francis Books, UK. (b) Calthorpe Associates.

principle: Andrés Duany wrote an introduction to a new edition of Unwin's *Town Planning in Practice*, and Walter Creese pointed out in 1992 that Seaside was based on the ideas of Raymond Unwin and his American disciple John Nolen.[86] The New Urbanists were divided among themselves,[87] some declaring that they were anti-Stein but pro-Nolen. As William Fulton observes, "such a dichotomy is rich with irony"[88] because both Nolen and Stein combined the formal and the informal:[89] "the formal and the informal fit together more successfully than many New Urbanists are willing to admit. The formal and the informal are the ying and yang of garden city design."[90]

The New Urbanists were much influenced by the evident success, from the mid-1960s onward, of Historic Districts, themselves tidied-up, idealized versions of their pasts, much influenced by ideas of what constitutes good city form[91] – notably Kevin Lynch's *The Image of the City*. New Urbanism too evokes an idealized past, a past that never was, a modern-day creation arising out of the same processes as Historic Districts.[92] Writers like Camillo Sitte and Raymond Unwin, much quoted by the New Urbanists, were never pure preservationists: their message was that we must grasp the underlying intuitive notions that shaped the cities of the past but have been obscured by bureaucratic procedures.[93]

Yet one of the most influential New Urbanists was not American. He was Léon Krier, a Luxembourger who worked and had most influence in the United Kingdom.[94] He rejected modern architecture and postmodern clichés with equal vehemence, refusing "to accept any of the basic premises of the modern industrial state and its consumer-oriented mentality."[95] He was a crucial foundation member of the Urban Villages Group, set up in 1989 as a result of a challenge from the Prince of Wales, providing a conceptual basis for their model. They triumphed when the urban village model was incorporated in the government's planning policy guidance notes, PPG1.[96] On the other side of the Atlantic, Krier also claims credit for the idea of the Congress for the New Urbanism as an alternative planning movement to Congrès Internationaux d'Architecture Moderne; Andres Duany identifies Krier as one of his most important mentors,[97] as master-planner for Poundbury, an urban extension for 5,000 people on a 158-hectare site owned by the Duchy of Cornwall on the western edge of Dorchester.[98]

---

[86] Fulton, 2002, 164–5.
[87] Fulton, 2002, 165–6.
[88] Fulton, 2002, 166.
[89] Fulton, 2002, 166.
[90] Fulton, 2002, 170.
[91] Hamer, 2000, 107, 112.
[92] Hamer, 2000, 113.
[93] Hamer, 2000, 117.
[94] Thompson-Fawcett, 1998, 170–1.
[95] Thompson-Fawcett, 1998, 172.
[96] Thompson-Fawcett, 1998, 177–8.
[97] Thompson-Fawcett, 1998, 179.
[98] Thompson-Fawcett, 1998, 180.

The odd fact was that the resulting prescription sounded and looked uncannily like Ebenezer Howard's Social City of 1898; or, for that matter, Sven Markelius's and Göran Sidenbladh's Stockholm General Plan of 1952. American planners, it seemed, had reinvented the wheel. One could say that it was a good wheel, worth reinventing. But one could also notice that in practice the Stockholm satellites never worked quite as their creators had imagined: as seen in Chapter 7, many more people commuted out of them and into them, especially after acquiring their first Volvo.[99] And doubtless the same would be even more true in the 1990s, with two-earner households leaving their front doors in opposite directions each day, traveling to multiple job opportunities in distant places. In fact, the so-called New Urbanism[100] has not worked quite like its advocates have suggested: one of the models, Kentlands in Maryland, is an automobile-dependent suburb beyond the end of the Washington, DC, metro; Laguna West in California is unconnected to the Sacramento light rail system and depends on a handful of peak-hour buses a day. Further, transport experts – first in North America, then in Europe – began to notice that the great majority of trips by car were no longer to work, but to other places for other purposes; and these were extremely difficult to manage through land-use policies alone. Straight fiscal policies, like higher fuel tax or parking charges, were the only way to get results – or so they suggested; all the different urban forms in the world might not make that much difference.

Still, planners should do what they could to make people virtuous. And besides, land-use policies would be only part of a package that might include other disincentives to use the car and incentives to use other ways of moving around: higher fuel taxes, road pricing, parking charges, physical curbs on traffic. In the Netherlands' Fourth Plan, EXTRA of 1991, and in the United Kingdom's PPG-13 of 1993, these joint land-use–transport packages were eagerly employed, at least in principle; and, implementing the Rio accords of 1991, governments actually began to implement policies such as higher fuel taxes. But within limits: save for Scandinavia, which experimented gingerly and partially with the notion, no country was prepared to follow Singapore with its bold electronic road pricing scheme, implemented on schedule (like everything in Singapore) in 1998. There were limits, it seemed, to the politically possible: like St Augustine, voters and their elected representatives desired to be virtuous, but not yet.

New Models for Planning Pilgrims

Meanwhile, something odd and interesting had been happening in other places: in a few cities on the European mainland, and in others far distant. During the first decade of the new millennium, they became places of pilgrimage for planners who wanted to understand how they had achieved their success.

---

[99]   Hall, 1998, Ch. 27.
[100]   Katz, 1994.

Barcelona. Barcelona, at the end of the 1990s, was the first: the emblematic city for the Urban Task Force and particularly for its chairman Richard Rogers.[101] The Urban Task Force report commended it for two closely associated types of planning intervention: small operations on small urban spaces, followed by "strategic" projects.[102] Within Barcelona, during the 1980s, approximately 150 operations of creating or recovering public space were realized, bringing international attention and awards.[103] Pasqual Maragall, former mayor of Barcelona (1982–97), wrote the foreword with the critical prescription: "The trick in Barcelona was quality first, quantity after."[104]

The Barcelona phenomenon, Francisco Javier Monclús explains, was strongly influenced by two architectural-urban discourses and their corresponding slogans over the 1970s and early 1980s: the "architecture of the city," stemming from the book by Aldo Rossi (1966) which was particularly influential in Italy, France, and Spain – especially in Barcelona – and the "reconstruction of the European city," with a renewed interest in the existing city. Critically, also, it reflected the growing importance of the "urban project," an architect-led alternative to the generalist strategic planning characteristic of the years of high urban growth in the 1950s and 1960s. This thread runs through events in Barcelona and also in the *grands projets* in Paris, or above all, the Internationale Bauausstellung (IBA) in Berlin. These shared common elements: a new appreciation of the "historic" city (especially that of the nineteenth and early part of the twentieth centuries), the reclaiming of traditional public spaces (streets, squares, and parks), the integration of urban planning and architecture as a reaction to abstract strategic planning. A central focus was to tackle urban problems through specific projects, especially the regeneration of public space and community facilities.[105] The opportunity arose because of the growing obsolescence and abandonment of large central city areas – former industrial zones, port and railway facilities – a general process across Europe, already chronicled in Chapter 11.[106] Urban projects, backed by "urban marketing" and image creation, became a means to "relaunch" cities, as part of their economic conversion from an industrial- into a service-based one, aiding their ranking in the "international urban league," particularly attractive to social democratic local governments.[107] But Barcelona was also, of course, unique in its recent recovery of democracy and the importance of its neighborhood associations, as well as the special role played by the architects.[108]

In parallel to coastal and waterfront projects directly associated with the 1994 Olympic Games, another series of large projects benefited from special planning conditions to attract new types of management and tertiary uses in the services and facilities sectors, in spaces with obsolete uses but with good accessibility. In parallel

---

[101] Monclús, 2003, 401.
[102] Monclús, 2003, 401.
[103] Monclús, 2003, 407.
[104] Monclús, 2003, 402.
[105] Monclús, 2003, 403.
[106] Monclús, 2003, 404.
[107] Monclús, 2003, 408.
[108] Monclús, 2003, 406.

there would be operations associated with the remodeling of the port, the transport hub in the Delta del Llobregat, the airport, the high-speed train and the Sagrera area, and the "Diagonal Mar" operation.[109]

Barcelona thus became a "winning city" in the new international economic and urban order.[110] But, as Monclús observes, entirely missing from the Urban Task Force report is the fact that over these 20 years of transformation, the "real city," to which Maragall often refers, became a metropolitan region ever more dispersed and less "Mediterranean."[111] By 2010, the much-vaunted "compact city" of Barcelona was merely the core of Metropolitan Barcelona, a vast agglomeration of more than four million inhabitants, sprawling across a territory of more than 3,000 square kilometers within a radius of 30–45 kilometers. And during the triumph of the "Barcelona model," the city lost almost 250,000 people, declining from 1.75 million in 1981 to 1.51 million in 1996, and losing significant economic activities. Some critics have even suggested that Barcelona was exporting its problems to the periphery.[112]

Curitiba.[113] Curitiba has one supreme qualification as a place of urban pilgrimage: like Lourdes or Santiago de Compostela, it is a long way from anywhere else. Not only is Brazil at the other end of the world from Europe; Curitiba is another hour's flight from Rio or São Paulo. When the pilgrim finally arrives, he or she immediately notices two things: first, the airport looks like a mini-Zürich; secondly, appropriately, everybody else suddenly dons a sweater from their hand baggage. Curitiba – a cool 15 °C, all year round – is no Copacabana. In more senses than one, it is Cool Brazil.

This provides the clue: Paraná, the province of which Curitiba is capital, was settled by Germans, Poles, and Ukranians. In one of its happiest (and neatly politically correct) inspirations, in its different new parks the city has created a shrine to each of its great immigrant streams; the Polish one, a village complete with chapel dedicated to the famous Black Madonna of Częstochowa, was blessed by the Pope when he passed this way. And, arriving in the Rua de XV Novembro, the vast pedestrian main drag in the city center, you might well feel overcome: surely this is Kraków, or Munich, or any city center between the Rhine and the Vistula. The crowds look Germano-Polish. And there is a general lack of the outdoor pavement cafés that characterize the Portuguese-Italian culture of other Brazilian cities.

The weather has something to do with it, of course. But Jaime Lerner, the fabled mayor who put Curitiba on the map and is now state governor, comes from Polish stock. Lerner is also an architect by training. Put a Polish architect in charge of a Brazilian city, which is what happened here 30 years ago, and the result was an explosion of creativity that rocked the world.

---

[109] Monclús, 2003, 410.
[110] Monclús, 2003, 412–13.
[111] Monclús, 2003, 402.
[112] Monclús, 2003, 414.
[113] Hall, 2000. This section borrows largely from this source.

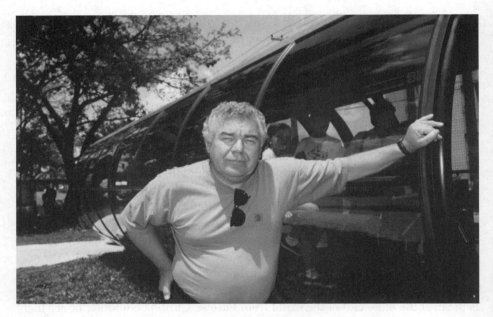

Figure 12.5   Jaime Lerner. The legendary Brazilian architect-planner, Mayor of Curitiba and then Governor of the state of Paraná, photographed against one of his iconic bus shelters. *Source*: © HerveCollart/Sygma/CORBIS.

Lerner's achievement, which must make him the twentieth century's outstanding municipal politician, was to develop initiatives that brilliantly did several things all at once. Gathering around him a team of extraordinarily creative professionals – one of them, who guided me round, told me that people flock from all over this vast country for the chance to work here – he developed a set of solutions to the city's problems that were extraordinarily lateral-thinking, extremely cost-effective, visual in a symbolic way, and above all politically astute.

The best of all, which has established the city's image wherever urbanists gather, is the buses. Thirty years ago, Rio and São Paulo were planning metro systems. Needless to say, Brazil being Brazil, they set new standards for elegance of design. But Curitiba, then a smallish half-million kind of a place, couldn't justify building one. So Lerner simply decided that his city would have a bus metro instead, for a fraction of the price.

The clue was that on three of the main corridors leading into the city center, there was what the Curitiba planners call a trinary road system: a rather broad boulevard bordered on either side by two narrower streets. And it would be easy to build the boulevards out as the city extended. So Lerner's engineers turned the two bordering streets into one-way arteries, with a green wave traffic light system that allowed traffic to flow, and then took over the boulevard. They took the entire center strip as a reserved busway, and gave the buses priority at peak hours. Cars, moving or parked, had the rest, but weren't exactly encouraged. At intervals along these arteries, they built bus stations – 20 in the city, plus another five in the wider metro area – where the express buses interchange with local services coming from the neighborhoods, and with orbital buses. Each kind of bus has its own color: red for the busway routes, silver for other express buses, green for the orbitals (*interbairros*) and yellow for the thousands of local buses, labeled *convencionais*, some of which serve as feeders (*alimentador*) to the expresses.

But transport was only half the story: Lerner's team integrated it with land use. The city zoned the land: it specified high-density high-rise along the main axes and nowhere else. Further, it encouraged new supermarkets and banks and other services next to the bus stops. The developers responded, as developers will when they are given clear signals. From the city's telecommunications tower, the sightseer views these astonishing walls of high-rise radiating out from the center.

As the traffic built up and the system expanded – the main axes now extend over 43 miles – the problem was capacity. Curitiba solved it in two ways: first, it coupled the express buses together into *expresso articulado* units and then, more recently, *expresso biarticulado* units which carry an astonishing 270 people at peak hours. Then, it speeded up the buses at the stops by designing the famous Curitiba shelter: a glass tube, which you enter through a turnstile by means of a token that you can buy at any newsstand. As a result, it is actually quite difficult to film one of these extraordinary buses in action: in a trice, they empty, fill up, and are gone.

The entire system, which now extends outside the city into 12 adjacent suburbs, operates on a single flat fare with one permitted transfer. And, rather amazingly, like London's it is privatized. The city is divided into 10 "pizza slices," each franchized to one company, with another 16 in the wider metro area, and the revenues are pooled.

The results speak for themselves. Curitiba is one of the most prosperous cities in Brazil, with high car ownership. But the system's 1,700 buses carry nearly two million passengers each day, and a quarter of car owners use the buses. The main north–south axis, where the buses have a peak capacity of 14,000 passengers an hour (comparable to London's Docklands Light Railway) carries 300,000 people a day, a figure many rail system managers would kill to achieve.

The point is that the bus system is a phenomenal bargain. They are just rebuilding the east–west corridor to accommodate the new *biarticulados*: it will cost them about £17 million, of which £7.5 million will go on the busway itself. This is a tiny fraction of a typical investment in light rail, let alone a new metro line.

It is the same story with the recycling: brilliant flair coupled with total cost-conscious canniness. In all the poor neighborhoods in the city (which, by the way, feature medium-density low-rise public housing; no *favelas* here), on one day every week two green municipal trucks arrive together, carrying the slogan *O lixo que não é lixo* (The rubbish that isn't rubbish). Almost immediately, there is an almost surreal sight: hundreds of people, young and old, come out with sacks full of recyclable material, bottles, cans, paper, all pre-sorted. Arriving at truck number one, they present their sacks and receive vouchers. Walking to truck number two, they exchange these for bags of fresh food, bought from local farm surpluses.

Finally, the ultimate gesture of the mayor-architect: Curitiba was full of old worked-out quarries, the by-product of the city's mushroom growth over the last 30 years. Filled with water, they were a challenge and a menace to the city's children. The conventional answer was to tip landfill into them. Lerner's answer was to turn each of them into a city park, adorned by a brilliant building. One has the Open University of the Environment: a magical tree structure, reached on ladders, to which thousands of city children come each week to be taught about the environment of the planet and their role in protecting it. Watching one of these classes, sitting on the ground spellbound in front of a Zen-style lake, inspired by a brilliant actor-teacher, was a magical, heart-rending sight.

In other restored quarries, the city has hired architects to produce startling buildings to support a permanent festival of the arts. The most extraordinary of all, the wire palace, is a Crystal Palace-style opera house which houses a huge range of dramatic and musical performances, reached via a bridge over water. Here, as elsewhere, the real genius of this city emerges: it is to develop a unique solution to a problem, a solution that turns the problem into a positive inspiration (*the problem that isn't a problem*, you could say), and then to embody it in a brilliant physical solution. Each structure that confronts the visitor around every corner of this amazing place carries its message: this is a symbol of this city.

Lerner's constant admonition to his planning team was "You can do it! You can!" – a phrase that was later adapted, to great effect, by another master politician. Lerner's inspired term for it, which he subsequently exported as a consultant to countless other cities across the world, is *urban acupuncture*: small-scale interventions, costing trifling amounts of money, that transform a whole area of the city and also enhance the city's image as a whole. It is very similar to the concept in Barcelona, which he has visited and where he addressed a notable session of the city's memorable 2004 Forum – its intellectual sequel, a decade later, to the Olympic Games.

Freiburg. During the first decade of the new century, Freiburg rapidly became the reference point for planners everywhere, above all in Britain. "Better than Freiburg! Better than Vauban!" became the slogan of the Communities and Local Government's Eco-Towns Challenge Panel. It was not just a slogan: the Panel felt that Freiburg represented some kind of yardstick, some universally applicable measure, of what a sustainable twenty-first-century community should be.[114]

Other places, like Hammarby Sjöstad in Stockholm or HafenCity in Hamburg, might have an equal claim as representative models for the rest of the world to follow. But Freiburg was somehow in a class of its own. First, though Vauban is the exemplar neighborhood to which all visitors flock, it is only part of a concept that animates everything the city does, from power generation to building codes. And, though some other European cities can also claim to be trying to do the same, Freiburg was doing it for longer, with single-minded consistency, than any other city anywhere. Hence all those eco-pilgrims – who, visitors soon find, are now so numerous that they are beginning to represent some kind of a problem for the city and its people.

---

[114]   Hall, 2008, 444. This section borrows directly from this source.

A city of 200,000 people in the far southwest corner of Germany, a stone's throw from the French border and a mere half-hour train ride from the Swiss city of Basel, Freiburg enjoys an idyllic location where the Black Forest meets the flat Rhine valley plain. The sunniest city in Germany, it has a wonderful climate, cool and crisp in winter, warm and balmy in summer. An ancient city, founded in 1120 by the local duke as a free market town (Freiburg: Free Borough), it also boasts one of Germany's oldest universities, dating back to 1457. That background is significant, because the city is a magnet for in-migration and the university has 32,000 students – making it larger than almost any British university and a major player in the city and its politics. Freiburg is part of the *Land* (state) of Baden-Württemberg, a major industrial powerhouse of Germany – Mercedes-Benz is based in the state capital of Stuttgart – but is not itself a manufacturing city: it is an archetypal example of the twenty-first-century knowledge economy. But it is also relevant to realize that Baden-Württemberg in general, and Freiburg in particular, are among the most successful and affluent places in Germany – and, by the same token, the world. This makes the place interesting: rather like California, but in a distinctively European way, it shows the way that other places may go as they graduate into affluence.

Or rather, the way that they might go if their politics took the same direction. Germany has also been the country that in the past – during the Weimar republic in the 1920s – took a world lead in developing radical new approaches to almost everything, including urban planning and design (Chapter 4). It has long had an exceptionally strong environmentalist movement, which you can trace back to naturalist movements a century and more ago. This began to play a major part in the 1970s, when a tiny collection of Freiburgers fought a proposal for a nuclear power station. Forced to develop an alternative solution, they began to think furiously about renewable energy. It is rather as if some Oxford or Cambridge students had formed a tiny environmentalist cell that gradually took over the city. Progressively, as the greens won more seats on the council, the city initiated greener and greener policies, years in advance of almost anywhere else in Germany – and therefore, by definition, in the world.

In 1992, the city council decided that it would only permit construction of low-energy buildings on land it owned, and that all new buildings must comply with certain "low energy" specifications: as well as solar panels and collectors on the roof, providing electricity and hot water, passive features use the sun's energy to regulate the temperature of the rooms. It implemented transport policies that reversed long and deep trends: Freiburgers travel less by car, more by public transport, than 30 years ago. Finally, Freiburg became the only major German city with a green mayor: Dieter Salomon, born in Australia but brought up in Bavaria, came to the university and gained his PhD in 1991, becoming a student activist in the process, and was elected mayor in 2001 with over 64% of the vote on a second ballot.

But in parallel, equally significant, in the early 1980s the city appointed a young planning officer, Wulf Daseking, who was continuously in post for 26 years until his retirement in 2012. Anywhere else, that might be a recipe for tired and mediocre leadership. Instead, Daseking – who, in fact, holds the position of *Oberbaudirektor*, head of

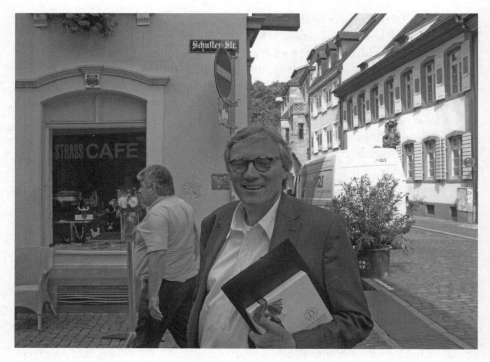

Figure 12.6 Wulf Daseking. Freiburg's legendary city planner over a quarter-century, whose team created the "Freiburg model" of "the city of short distances." *Source*: Peter Hall.

planning and building – has steadily developed his eco-vision for the city, attracting in the process one of the most talented and dedicated teams of planners of any city in the world. That vision is important, because in Freiburg everything – building policies, planning policies, energy policies, waste policies – fits together as parts of a wider whole. The only apt comparison is with Curitiba in Brazil, already considered. It underlines the banal but profound point: people make the difference. Salomon–Daseking are not global household names, even in the world of planning. But they represent something special, which is long-term vision allied to sustained delivery.

Applied to planning, at one level the vision is astonishingly simple. The strategic plan aims to keep the city compact, by redeveloping brownfield land rather than invading greenfield – which in any case would be difficult, because the city is surrounded on three sides by the Black Forest, which is effectively a national park. But this policy has been aided by the fortunate accident of two brownfield windfalls on the urban periphery: an old sewage farm, Rieselfeld to the west, and an old French army barracks, Vauban, to the southwest. Both have become new urban extensions, within a short (15-minute) tram ride of the city center. And, because Freiburg followed many other German cities in keeping its trams in the 1950s when British cities were scrapping theirs, it proved relatively simple and economic to build the short extensions that were needed.

Figure 12.7   Rieselfeld. Interior of a residential area in a Freiburg urban extension, with natural drainage for ecological conservation and children's playspace. *Source*: Peter Hall.

Given that, Daseking's policy was disarmingly simple. There would be no tall buildings: the maximum height, 12.5 meters, basically accommodates four-story structures. Inside the new neighborhoods, the design couldn't be simpler, almost boring: rectangular grids of streets and green public places, with the buildings – some town houses, others apartments – either parallel to the main street carrying the tramway or at right angles to it. There are some small local shops: Daseking doesn't like chain stores, and has even kept them out of the city center (though there is a large *Kaufhof* department store there). Schools and kindergarten are set in the residential areas. In Rieselfeld, which is twice as big as Vauban (Rieselfeld: 72 hectares, 12,000 people; Vauban: 42 hectares, 5,000 people) there is a large Mediothek, a Tower Hamlets Idea Store-style library. In Vauban, there is a flourishing community center where people can hold meetings or organize entertainments or just drop in for a casual drink or meal.

But there was another key idea: within a quite rigid overall master-plan, the city encourages maximum local bottom-up implementation. This is most evident in Vauban, where during the 1990s – after the French abandoned their barracks following the end of the Cold War – there was a running battle between a group of *Fundis* – fundamentalist eco-freaks – who squatted the site, and the city, eventually resolved by years of painstaking mediation; even today, the visitor is greeted by defiant slogans from a small residual group, still holed up in their army surplus vehicles behind a wire fence. In the process, Freiburg developed a remarkable idea, albeit one derived from the community architecture movement of the 1970s: each individual piece of the development, consisting of a superblock of buildings around a semi-public open space, would be undertaken by a local Building Group (*Baugruppe*) working together with their own architect. In consequence, Vauban – and much of Rieselfeld, similarly developed – have an extraordinary built quality: there's a uniform background of height and massing, and a universal devotion to modernist architecture (significantly, a street name commemorates Walter Gropius) that produces a modernist version of Georgian London squares, but within this each superblock contains huge detailed variation, both within individual terraces and even more so between one complex and another.

And this richness of detail is multiplied in the semi-public spaces enclosed by the blocks, where imagination – especially in treatment of children's play areas – has run riot. Truly, this is a children's paradise – as visitors on sunny summer days testify: alas, it rained during our visit. These are magical places where, as Colin Ward once memorably said, children can play out their childhood. And that includes the spirit of adventure. Perhaps the most chastening point was when, in Rieselfeld, we saw a wonderful space with a pond in the center, fed naturally by drainage. No local authority in England would ever dare do that, someone said: contrary to health and safety. It seemed to say it all.

But this mode of development vitally depends on one precondition: the city acquires the land and builds the necessary infrastructure before development takes place, using investment funds through a trust. The city's investment is then recovered through selling off sites to builders and individuals. This has worked triumphantly, because good location and brilliant design have generated huge demand, effectively allowing the process to self-fund. And, by engaging the future residents in the design process from the start, many of the development risks are simply removed, generating strong built-in neighborhood feelings and accumulated social capital as soon as the first residents move in. Further, there are some tough social control policies in operation here: there's a strong emphasis on creating mixed communities, but social housing tenants are rigorously checked out to exclude problematic neighbors.

The contrast with the usual UK development process could not be more striking. Asked in 2008 by a British visiting group for final words of wisdom to take back, Wulf Daseking replied, "Don't let the developers near. They won't develop." A radical message, indeed. But Daseking was far from averse to harnessing the desire for private profit where it could help. He explained how, in one scheme, he persuaded private developers to pay for major social facilities through a kind of mega Section 106 agreement. Deals like this not only generate developments like leisure centers that benefit everyone, but also enhance the overall design quality by injecting high-quality open space: everywhere you go in these districts, the impression is how literally green they are. Rieselfeld for instance is bordered on its outer edge by a huge nature park which stretches out towards the hills, forming a wonderful recreational space as well as an educational asset.

What are the lessons for other places? Four critical points emerged.

First, cities must be given the freedom to make their own policies, including their own mistakes, and the money to go with that freedom. British cities cannot go on being regarded as handmaidens of Whitehall. That could include allowing them to set their own standards in many areas that are now legislated centrally.

Secondly, central policies are needed that do the things central policies should be doing: creating systems of incentives and disincentives to encourage places and people to do more right things and fewer wrong ones. The Federal German law of 2000, which introduced the feed-in tariff allowing households to generate their own energy and sell it to the national grid, is widely regarded by German environmentalists as the best law passed by any German government in a century. They may exaggerate, but they have a point.

Thirdly, with direct relevance to the UK eco-towns program, should we ask the private sector to shoulder a burden that really belongs to the public sector? The 28 new towns in the 30 years after World War Two were built the German way, by giving the initiative to public bodies which could then – as in Milton Keynes in the 1980s – involve the private sector on their own terms. As the private house-building sector collapsed after the 2007 crisis, leaving major developments half-finished or unstarted, that is an important lesson.

Fourth, the eco-towns returned back to the 1898 Ebenezer Howard vision of small, isolated garden cities set in the countryside. But in Freiburg, as in the great German garden cities of the 1920s, they have created urban extensions, close to city centers, and linked to them by excellent public transport.

Emscherpark. The fourth model, the IBA Emscherpark in the Ruhr area of Germany, was the brainchild of Johannes Rau, then the Minister for Urban Development, Transport, and Housing in the *Land* government of Nordrhein Westfalen, and his team. Invited at the end of the 1980s by the organizers of IBA exhibitions to suggest ideas, they came up with two: within 10 years (1989–99), they would convert derelict industrial sites for cultural uses and maintain the old structures as historical relics; and a badly degraded natural environment would be restored for new, ecologically beneficial uses. Within the whole area, an Emscherpark "exhibition area" would cover an area of about 800 square kilometers of abandoned industrial land, including 17 towns and cities with five million inhabitants. The very badly polluted river Emscher, running through the northern border of the area, provided the name *Emscherpark*.

This was a massive undertaking, beyond anything that had ever been undertaken anywhere in the world at that time. It proved a winner. Over the following 10 years, the Emscher Landscape Park was designed. The Emscher system was turned from a regional waste water canal and ecologically restored. The gigantic gas container at Oberhausen was reinvented as a regional landmark, its huge internal space open for exhibitions. Slag heaps were greened and made accessible as public parks, with new artistic landmarks. The area's biggest coal mine, built in the 1920s in the modern style of the time, was listed by UNESCO as a world heritage site. These activities and many more contributed to the special new identity fostered within the region, which is rooted in sensitivity to its past. A regional green-belt system, developed by the planner Robert Schmidt in the 1920s (Chapter 6), was preserved and enhanced. Regional ministries and local institutions, especially local universities founded in the 1970s (Duisburg, Essen, Bochum, Dortmund, Wuppertal, and the Open University at Hagen) worked on plans together and linked up with local communities.[115]

Less known, especially outside Germany, is that conserving the industrial heritage was an overwhelmingly bottom-up movement, led by students, many of them the children of miners or factory workers, the first in their families to attend university. They were the children of 1968, a new and rebellious generation determined to transform the world. Students and faculty at the new University of Dortmund conducted a huge campaign to save the classic local workers' garden village Am Sommerberg/Am Winterberg, built between 1914 and 1924, from redevelopment; in 1971, demolition was prohibited, and in 1975, the settlement was listed.[116]

Beyond this, there was a huge set of problems in preserving and reusing the old mines and industrial structures. These were incredibly large buildings and structures – a gas storage tank, the rusty giant of a blast furnace, or the simmering mountain of a spoil heap – with an overwhelming amount of internal and external machinery, conveyor belts, railroad tracks, and wastelands, to be handled.[117] IBA's director, Professor Dr Karl Ganser, was determined: "although certain building types may be difficult to preserve, it is necessary to do so in order to retain the spatial identity, to give points of orientation, and to explain the history of the region, as well as to give the next generation the opportunity to interpret their heritage for themselves." He succeeded in winning time by securing a stay on demolition: "Give things time," he said, "First let everything stay."[118] IBA developed a flexible approach: fine to protect entire sites, to conserve everything pedantically, but in practice it was impossible – particularly since it also recognized that conservation should not be limited to a few obvious cases, but involved the entire historic landscape.[119] One of its biggest triumphs was the huge Thyssen-Meiderich steelworks in Duisburg, which closed in 1985. The city of Duisburg, backed by local residents, proposed to include it in IBA's planned Emscher Landscape Park.[120] Even they were taken aback: it has become the most-visited place in Nordrhein-Westfalen after Cologne Cathedral.[121]

Ganser has been hailed as "the most effective preservationist of the 20th century." After IBA was succeeded by *Projekt Ruhr GmbH*, also fully owned by the *Land*

[115]   Petz, 2010, 380–1.
[116]   Raines, 2011, 186–7.
[117]   Raines, 2011, 194–5.
[118]   Raines, 2011, 195.
[119]   Raines, 2011, 195.
[120]   Raines, 2011, 195.
[121]   Raines, 2011, 195–6.

government, there was a new slogan: "time to take things seriously." But sustainable, local, participatory projects have been succeeded by separate "flagship developments," "urban entertainment," and "waterfront development," often with substantial backing from foreign investors.[122] The original driving vision was lost.

In any case, there was a basic problem which emerged with startling clarity in the mid-1990s: a striking increase, across Europe, in the projected numbers of new households – a result not of population growth, as in the 1950s and 1960s, but rather of the splitting up of a population into more and more, smaller and smaller, households. Everywhere the really big growth was in single-person households, people literally living alone: a product of young people leaving home early for college or career, of increasing separations and divorces, and of older people living ever longer and being widowed. In Great Britain in 1995, the projections suggested that by 2016 there might be no fewer than 4.4 million new household units.[123] Projections of that order implied that there was no practicable way of squeezing all the extra households into high-density living in the cities: whatever the possibilities for young single-person households who might value accessibility and conviviality above suburban space and peace, there was simply not the space for everyone on the brownfield sites and in the urban regeneration areas. So there was going to be a need for fairly massive building in greenfield areas; the question was whether at least some of these developments, and the people in them, could be weaned from dependence on the private car.

After a year and a half of frantic activity, the government produced its response in the form of an Urban White Paper:[124] it accepted some of the recommendations, postponed action on many others. This left a huge question as to whether this would be enough to achieve its own objectives. For the key objective had been to defuse the countryside debate by setting a target of 60% of all new development on previously developed brownfield land. The Urban Task Force had reported that it could – but only if its recommendations were accepted and implemented. And buried deep in Chapter 7 of its report was a table showing that in the South East outside London, even that would not be achievable; there, the figures suggested that only 39% of development could go on brownfield – or, with the new policies in place, perhaps 3 or 4% more.

All this was soon churned into the real hurly-burly of local policies. For the local planning authorities in the South East had been invited by the Secretary of State for Environment in the new 1997 Labour government to produce their own Strategic Planning Guidance for the region: "ownership" of regional planning, Prescott proudly announced, was being handed back to the regions. But before long, it landed like a boomerang back on his desk. For the local authorities produced a house-building target of only some 33,000 houses a year – a figure which, scrutinized at a public examination by the retired chief planning inspector, was condemned in no uncertain words as completely wide of the mark: 54,000 was the new recommended figure. Predictably,

[122]   Raines, 2011, 201.
[123]   GB Department of the Environment, 1995; Breheny and Hall, 1996.
[124]   GB Deputy Prime Minister, 2000.

the balloon went up: the planning authorities were outraged; the government first split the difference, at 43,000, then, after further howls of protest, came down to 39,000.

This of course was not planning; it was politics of a particularly crude and unpleasant kind. Underlying it was a definite arithmetic, but not one that had the slightest to do with housing needs or housing supply; it concerned the number of marginal seats in rural southern England that the government had wrested from the Conservatives in 1997, and planned to retain at the next election in 2001. Meanwhile, the government's resolution of its own problem proposed to concentrate a significant part of the growth in three areas: around the 1960s new town of Milton Keynes, at Ashford next to the Channel Tunnel in Kent, and along the M11 motorway connecting East London with Stansted Airport and Cambridge.[125] Still unresolved was the thorniest question of all: how to satisfy the demands in the frenetically booming wedge of territory west of London, including Heathrow airport and the concentrations of high-tech industry leading out from it.

Planning Gain and Social Equity

It was odd, in a way, because there were critically important policy questions to which members of the academic world might have powerfully contributed, had more of them cared to do so. Not least among these were the vexed questions of planning gain, impact fees, and development conditions, which together made up a perplexing policy package in the late 1980s and 1990s.

The central issue was a simple one, which had concerned planners in Britain almost from the start. (In America it had not, because there planning derived from the general concept of police power, and – as seen in Chapter 3 – its legitimacy had been established in the landmark Supreme Court decision on land-use zoning, *Village of Euclid et al v. Ambler Realty Co.*, in 1926.) In Britain, the state in 1947 nationalized the right to develop land, and declared that it would compensate land-owners for their lost rights of development. That having happened, logic suggested that all subsequent development gains should accrue to the community. But it proved politically too drastic: the market stopped operating, and the Conservatives in 1954 effectively rescinded these provisions. Twice afterwards, in 1967 and 1975, a Labour government devised alternative ways of clawing back at least some of the development value; twice, a subsequent Conservative government canceled the provision. And there the matter rested – except that in 1971, a Conservative administration passed a Town and Country Planning Act which provided that a developer could *voluntarily* agree with a planning authority to make a financial contribution as a condition of being granted permission. The idea was that the development might require some public action – a new connecting road, for instance – to which the developer might be both willing and able to contribute. In California, a very similar measure was enacted in 1980.

---

[125]   GB Government Office for the South East *et al.*, 2000.

These measures proved enormously useful and popular during the great development boom of the 1980s, when beleaguered local communities and their Nimby-minded electorates found it possible to wring quite large sums of money out of developers desperate to proceed with their schemes. Meanwhile, in the United States local communities had increasingly resorted to an alternative method, which was to impose an actual money fee – an impact fee – on developers to pay for public improvements that were held to be needed as a result of the development. But these devices ran into legal roadblocks on both sides of the Atlantic. And they concerned the same point: what American lawyers call nexus. In 1987, the US Supreme Court found that the California Coastal Commission had no right to demand a public right of beach access in front of a house as a condition of allowing it to be rebuilt; there was no direct connection, or nexus, between the permission and the grant of access. Similarly, in 1995, the English High Court found that the local district council of Witney in Oxfordshire had no right to require a superstore chain to construct a new road as a condition on the grant of planning permission for a new outlet, even though the company was perfectly willing; the connection was not direct enough – though oddly, in this case, it transpired that the authority could have required the company to pay money to it to build the road.

In any event, the entire planning agreement/impact fee cornucopia abruptly emptied in the late 1980s recession. By the 1990s, there was almost nothing to be had; developers had to be wooed to attempt anything at all. But few doubted that one day the good times would roll again, and that when they did the entire issue would again loom large. In the United Kingdom, it appeared that it would loom on the political agenda, doubtless proving as controversial as it ever had during its tempestuous history.

One reason lay in the renewed interest in the household projections. For they must mean increasing pressure on greenfield sites in the countryside, which the planning system, and local electorates, saw it as their sacred duty to keep green. However, the uncomfortable fact was that the real losers could be the less-well-heeled locals: the farm workers and the performers of other kinds of low-skill but essential work. Land shortages would without doubt mean escalating land and house prices, and as the newcomers poured in, these locals would find themselves ever more excluded from the chance of finding affordable housing, whether for sale or to rent.

The logic was to allow local authorities to incorporate provision for affordable housing into their local plans. In the United Kingdom that was a matter for administrative discretion, and the government actually encouraged it, so that it was becoming a widespread practice by the mid-1990s. In the United States, as so often, it all had to be fought out in the courts: the scene of the battle was the small New Jersey community of Mount Laurel, a municipality outside the city of Camden with 22 square miles and a population of 11,000, where two decisions by the State Supreme Court, in 1975 and 1983, established the remarkable principle that local communities *must* provide housing areas for low-income existing residents. Mount Laurel had zoned itself for half-acre developments for the wealthy; Ethel Lawrence, a black

American woman whose family had lived here for seven generations, led a group in an action to build low-income units, and won.[126] As the great American commentator on planning law, Charles M. Haar, put it,

> the New Jersey Supreme Court undertook the boldest and most innovative judicial intervention ever to countermand exclusionary zoning: in the landmark Mount Laurel trilogy of cases, the court identified and enunciated a constitutional right for all people – rich or poor, black or white – to live in the suburbs.[127]

The law had been used to promote exclusion, by giving localities the sovereign power to regulate land as they saw fit: "Law has become a surrogate for physical walls."[128] The decision thus went against local rights, and the question was: Who upholds the welfare of the wider metropolitan community? In Haar's words,

> the upshot is that towns may not refuse to confront the future by building moats around themselves and pulling up the drawbridge through prohibitory land-use controls ... No longer is it our prime task to tend our own gardens – unless we take a more expansive view of the garden's extent.[129]

The problem was whether of course such provisions could be made effective. For first-time buyers or renters, perhaps; but what would happen when they in turn moved on? Would they be able freely to dispose of their home, or would it continue to be subject to special rules? There was a widespread inclination to prefer the latter; but it could be extremely difficult to manage and to police.

Growth, Equity, and Environment

One central thesis of this book is that perhaps we came back full circle: at the end of nearly a century of modern planning, the problems of cities remained much as they had been at the start. Not precisely so, of course, because in the course of that century all advanced economies had become immeasurably richer; and that had two principal consequences. First, most people and most households belonged essentially to a large and heterogeneous middle class, within which sub-groups were defined by demographic and lifestyle characteristics rather than by income. And secondly, this society was able to afford provision for the less fortunate on a scale inconceivable a century earlier. True, there was a clear ideological move away from the Keynesian welfare state of the 1950s and 1960s, most enthusiastically in the United Kingdom and United States, but noticeable almost everywhere; but

---

[126]   Haar, 1996, 17–18.
[127]   Haar, 1996, 3.
[128]   Haar, 1996, 8.
[129]   Haar, 1996, 9, 193.

nonetheless, social expenditures remained high, if only because economic recession made it difficult to shrink them.

This has meant that while the underlying policy priorities and conflicts are the same as before, they are expressed in different ways. Very large majorities in most advanced countries enjoy a high standard of living, but they owe it to a combination of private effort and public action. Whereas the pioneers of 1900 were concerned with the "standard" of life, their successors in 2000 were talking about "quality" of life; material conditions were so significantly better that higher-order wants had arrived on the political agenda.[130] Key elements of this quality of life demand strong social controls, among which planning is critical; that is why the attempts of Thatcher governments to erode the planning system, in Britain during the mid-1980s, got absolutely nowhere and were followed by ignominious reversal. People care about their jobs and the incomes they generate, especially so in a recession-ridden era when jobs are less secure than they ever have been since the 1930s; but for the most part they consume their wealth in different places from the ones where they make it, and their first priority at home is to defend the quality of their own immediate environment.

To this has been added a new set of environmental imperatives: to reduce pollution, to avoid consuming non-renewable resources, and to avoid actions that could trigger irreversible planetary damage. But very often these wider concerns can be mapped down in ways that serve individual and sectional interest: let private motoring be restricted, especially other people's; stop burying green fields under bricks and mortar, especially in front of my house.

So the phenomenon of environmentally conscious Nimbyism looms ever larger, as well seen in the case of the South East of England; and it is very difficult to combine it with any concept of social equity, whether for the less fortunate in the local community, or still more for the less fortunate in other places, or for younger generations, or for generations still unborn. It is likely in practice to mean pulling up the drawbridge against newcomers, especially if they lack the right income or the right accents. And that will be even truer, if it emerges that the demands are coming from young people who left home early because they could not get on with parents or step-parents, or from poor single mothers with young children; the first are likely to get very short shrift on the ground that they brought their fate upon themselves, the second to receive residual aid on the Victorian principle of less eligibility.

Thus, the less fortunate groups are likely to be increasingly dammed up in the cities, where they will perhaps be housed after a fashion, all in the name of sustainable urban development. The good news, if any, is that the cities will be where some of the more exciting new economic developments are taking place. The bad news is that these groups may not be playing much of a role in them. Rather, they may find themselves in but not of the city, divorced from its new mainstream informational economy, and subsisting on a mélange of odd jobs, welfare cheques, and the black economy. It is a fate not too far removed from that of the dockers and match girls of

---

[130]   Fischler, 2000, 140.

London's East End, or the sweatshop laborers of New York's East Side, 100 years earlier; save that for these their descendants, the way out may paradoxically be even harder, because other kinds of jobs no longer exist.

It is a parody picture, perhaps: the educational system provides a way out, and is immeasurably richer than its nineteenth-century equivalent. But not enough of a parody to leave anyone feeling comfortable: too many of the young people of the city – whether that city is London or Paris or Amsterdam, New York or Chicago or Los Angeles – are alienated from the educational process and are effectively withdrawn both from it, and thus from the informational economy to which it provides the one essential key. Of them, it is no exaggeration to say that they remain in the City of Dreadful Night; and the night is the deeper for being bordered, all around, by the City of Enlightenment. Thus planners face a nightmarish return of the oldest of urban problems, which more than any other originally brought it into being and gave it its legitimacy: the problem of the urban underclass, waiting as a sullen and disaffected mass outside the gates.

For the title of his book on the coming of the informational economy and society, Barry Jones, the Australian academic-cum-politician, borrowed a title from a Bach Cantata: *Sleepers, Wake!*[131] Indeed, the watchman on the heights is calling; but his message could spell doom to the city, unless the day rises also on the city of darkness just outside the gate. There is a riddle here, so far unanswerable by the wit of planners, or indeed that of any other kind of social engineer; and, as a new millennium opens, it casts a deep pre-dawn chill.

[131]   Jones, 1982.

The City of the Permanent Underclass

The reactive mass of the industrial reserve army increases therefore with the potential energy of wealth. But the greater this reserve army in relation to the active labour-army, the greater is the mass of consolidated surplus-population, whose misery is in inverse proportion to its torment of labour. The more extensive, finally, the lazarus-layers of the working class, and the industrial reserve army, the greater is official pauperism. *This is the absolute general law of capitalist accumulation.*

Karl Marx, Capital, I (1867)

> If you catch me stealin', I don't mean no harm,
> If you catch me stealin', I don't mean no harm;
> It's a mark in my family and it must be carried on.
>
> I got nineteen men and I want one mo',
> I got nineteen men and I want one mo';
> If I get that one more, I'll let that nineteen go.
>
> Bessie Smith, Sorrowful Blues (1924)

> I'm bound for Black Mountain, me and my razor and my gun,
> Lawd, I'm bound for Black Mountain, me and my razor and my gun;
> I'm gonna shoot him if he stands still, and shoot him if he run.
> ...
> There's a devil in my soul, and I'm full of bad booze,
> There's a devil in my soul, and I'm full of bad booze;
> I'm out here for trouble. I've got the Black Mountain Blues.
>
> Bessie Smith, Black Mountain Blues (1930)

Cities of Tomorrow: An Intellectual History of Urban Planning and Design Since 1880,
Fourth Edition. Peter Hall.
© 2014 Peter Hall. Published 2014 by John Wiley & Sons, Ltd.

13

The City of the Permanent Underclass

The Enduring Slum: Chicago, St Louis, London, 1920–2011

There is thus one outstanding enigma: for any urbanist, the greatest and least answerable of all. It was the one posed by the 87-year-old Lewis Mumford, at the start of the first volume of his autobiography, in 1982. It was the "breakdown of law and order at the very peak of metropolitan power and prosperity," which formed for Mumford "one of the chronic puzzles of history."[1] Comparing the New York City of the 1980s with that of his childhood, Mumford chillingly reflected on

> the more ominous spread of violence and lawlessness, which, in the city of my youth, used to be confined, like a carbuncle, to certain self-enclosed areas, like the Bowery or Hell's Kitchen. Such quarters had not yet poured their infection into the whole bloodstream of the city … For one thing, it was possible for men, women and children, even when alone, to walk over a great part of the city, and certainly to walk through Central Park or alongside Riverside Drive at any time of the day or evening without fear of being molested or assaulted.[2]

"There was," he continued, "a kind of moral stability and security in the city of my youth that has now vanished even in such urban models of law and order as London."[3] And he confessed that more than once, latter-day New York had reminded him of Petrarch's fourteenth-century comparison of "the desolate, wolfish, robber-infested Provence of his maturity, in the wake of the Black Plague, with the safe, prosperous region of his youth."[4]

Statistics, notoriously, can lie; none more so than social statistics, and none among these more so than statistics of crime. Every novice undergraduate is familiar with the multiple caveats: who reports what and when, who writes what down in the

[1] Mumford, 1982, 5.
[2] Mumford, 1982, 5.
[3] Mumford, 1982, 5.
[4] Mumford, 1982, 5.

record book, who decided to prosecute and why. But no conceivable stream of qualifications and reservations will wash away the mountain of urban crime, and above
all violent urban crime, which in the late twentieth century rose almost visibly, like
some erupting volcano, to threaten the fabric of social life in every major city of the
world. It was, indeed, a twentieth-century plague. And its causes were as mysterious
to the afflicted, as those of the Black Death to the hapless citizenry of fourteenth-
century London, Paris, or Constantinople.

If not to explain it, at least to understand it, some historical perspective is needed.
We must go back full circle, to the origins of this story, and come forward again to
the present. And, in doing so through this long chapter, somewhat whimsically,
planning – the subject of the tale – will seem to disappear from view. The point,
finally, must be to ask why. For neither urban crime, nor the fear of the average
urban citizen of it, is new; as Mumford reminds us, only their pervasiveness is.
Indeed, twentieth-century city planning came out of the complex emotional reaction –
part pity, part terror, part loathing – of the late-Victorian middle class to their discovery of the urban underclass. That reaction, as seen in Chapter 2, took the form of
a secular Last Judgement: the virtuous poor would be assisted to go directly via the
settlement house or the municipal housing project to the garden-city heaven; the
vicious would remain perpetually repressed in their own urban hell, or go to peni-
tential labor colonies where they might at last see the light. And, in those European
countries where the city planning movement waxed strongest, that approximately is
what came to pass. Half a century later, in the welfare state era of the 1950s and
1960s, came the triumph of liberal theology: now, all – even the urban underclass – were
instantly perfectible; all might gain immediate access by the strait gate to the
Corbusian city of towers.

But in the United States, it was not like that at all. The established religion, whether
Protestant, Catholic, or Jewish, was heavily supportive of free enterprise: God helped
those who helped themselves, Horatio Alger-fashion, out of the slum and into the
ranks of the entrepreneurs. The main task, for public enterprise and voluntary organization alike, was therefore to socialize the immigrant and his children into
knowledge of American folkways and acceptance of American values, thus to put
the first foot on the ladder leading to success in the new land. Only those who stayed
truly down in the pit, far out of reach of the bottom rung, might be given the
equivalent of poorhouse relief, in the form of public housing that carried automatic
social stigma.

Chicago Discovers the Underclass

This helps explain one significant fact: in the early twentieth century, not only
American social experimentation, but also American social investigation, were
dominated by the central perceived problem of the immigrant and his socialization. Since – especially after the effective closure of the frontier in 1890 – the immigrants went overwhelmingly to the cities, it was there that both experimentation

Figure 13.1   Chicago slum, *ca.* 1900. An unidentified alley at the time of the Chicago Tenement House Survey: for hundreds of thousands of immigrants from Europe home in America meant this. Source: Chicago History Museum, ICHi-00808.

and research focused; for there, as already observed in Chapter 2, was the middle-class fear of submergence and mob rule most acutely felt. And there was a certain historic justice in the fact that both activities should flower in Chicago, the quintes-sential immigrant city. Here, in 1889, Jane Addams founded her settlement house; here, from 1914, developed the world's first true school of urban sociology.

That last is a large claim. Booth and his collaborators, as seen in Chapter 2, had pioneered modern techniques of mass social observation in London in the 1880s, and had produced a still-unequaled masterpiece of empirical urban sociology. The Germans had created theoretical sociology at about that time, and Robert E. Park, one of the founders of the Chicago school, had studied under Georg Simmel in

Figure 13.2 Dr Robert E. Park. Founder of the Chicago school of sociology, whose studies in the 1920s first pinpointed the roots of social disintegration in the city's slums. *Source*: © Bettmann/CORBIS.

Berlin. But only in Chicago, during the 1920s, did Park, Burgess, McKenzie, and Worth join these two traditions, thus to work towards a total understanding – based on theory, tested by observation – of the social structure of a great city. In 1925, they published their classic collection of essays on the sociology of the city.[5] And in his opening essay, which laid out the school's research agenda, Park already made clear its central bundle of concerns.

The "simplest and most elementary form of association" in the city, Park argued, was the local neighborhood. So:

> It is important to know what are the forces which tend to break up the tensions, interests and sentiments which give neighborhoods their individual character. In general these may be said to be anything and everything that tends to render the population unstable, to divide and concentrate attentions upon widely separated objects of interest.[6]

But "certain urban neighborhoods suffer from isolation"; here, "to reconstruct and quicken the life of city neighborhoods and to bring them in touch with the larger

[5] Park *et al.*, 1925.
[6] Park, 1925a, 8.

interests of the community," the social settlement movement had in part sprung up.[7] And, in American cities,

> the attempt has been made to renovate evil neighborhoods by the construction of playgrounds and the introduction of supervised sports of various kinds, including municipal dances in municipal dance halls. These and other devices which are intended primarily to elevate the moral tone of the segregated populations of great cities should be studied in connection with the investigation of the neighborhood in general.[8]

But the neighborhood essentially represented the old pre-industrial social order: industrial competition, coupled with the division of labor, was replacing it by an alternative organization of the city, based on differentiation by vocation and thus by class.[9] Through the medium of money, "values have been rationalized and sentiments have been replaced by interests."[10] The resulting organization, "composed of competing individuals and of competing groups of individuals,"[11] meant that

> cities, and particularly the great cities, are in unstable equilibrium. The result is that the vast casual and mobile aggregations which constitute our urban populations are in a state of perpetual agitation, swept by every new wind of doctrine, subject to constant alarms, and in consequence the community is in a chronic condition of crisis.[12]

This suggested "the importance of a more detailed and fundamental study of collective behaviour," focusing on "the psychology of crisis," including the extent to which "the parliamentary system, including the electoral system, [may] be regarded as an attempt to regularize revolution and to meet and control crises."[13]

Park went on to speculate, "It is probably the breaking down of local attachments and the weakening of the restraints and inhibitions of the primary group, under the influence of the urban environment, which are largely responsible for the increase of vice and crime in great cities."[14] "In the immigrant colonies which are now well established in every large city," foreign populations lived isolated lives, but each with an independent and vigorous political and social organization of its own:[15]

---

[7]   Park, 1925a, 8.
[8]   Park, 1925a, 9.
[9]   Park, 1925a, 14.
[10] Park, 1925a, 16.
[11] Park, 1925a, 17.
[12] Park, 1925a, 22.
[13] Park, 1925a, 22.
[14] Park, 1925a, 23.
[15] Park, 1925a, 23.

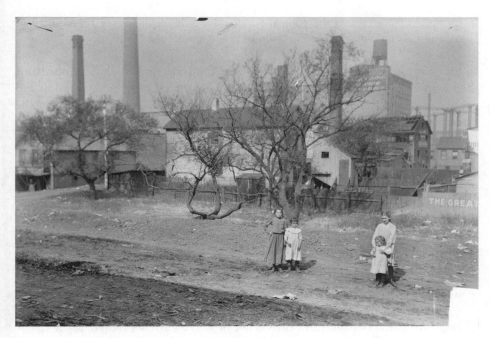

Figure 13.3 Chicago's "Little Hell," 1902. One of the city's Italian enclaves, which became notorious as a seat of vice and crime. *Source*: Chicago History Museum, DN-0000208, *Chicago Daily News*.

Under these conditions the social ritual and the moral order which these immigrants brought with them from their native countries have succeeded in maintaining themselves for a considerable time under the influences of the American environment. Social control, based on the home mores, breaks down, however, in the second generation.[16]

Parallel to this erosion of primary relationships, the old informal controls, based on these family mores, were replaced by formal legal mechanisms.[17]

Part of this new and distinctive urban social organization, Park argued, was the "moral region": "the population tends to segregate itself, not merely in accordance with its interests, but in accordance with its tastes or its temperaments," producing "detached milieus in which vagrant and suppressed impulses, passions, and ideals emancipate themselves from the dominant moral order."[18] Hence "the segregation of the poor, the vicious, the criminal, and exceptional persons generally," wherein

Association with others of their own ilk provides ... not merely a stimulus, but a moral support for the traits they have in common which they would not find in a less select

[16] Park, 1925a, 27.
[17] Park, 1925a, 28.
[18] Park, 1925a, 43.

society. In the great city the poor, the vicious, and the delinquent, crushed in an unhealthful and contagious intimacy, breed in and in, soul and body.[19]

In an essay on juvenile delinquency, later in the collection, Park developed this theme further. "We are living," he argued, "in … a period of individualization and social disorganization. Everything is in a state of agitation – everything seems to be undergoing a change. Society is, apparently, not much more than a congeries and constellation of social atoms."[20] The automobile, the newspaper, and the motion picture had contributed powerfully to this change. And

> the mere movement of the population from one part of the country to another – the present migration of the Negroes northward, for example – is a disturbing influence. Such a movement may assume, from the point of view of the migrants themselves, the character of an emancipation, opening to them new economic and cultural opportunities, but it is none the less disorganizing to the communities they have left behind and to the communities into which they are now moving. It is at the same time demoralizing to the migrating people themselves, and particularly, I might add, to the younger generation.
>
> The enormous amount of delinquency, juvenile and adult, that exists today in the Negro communities in northern cities is due in part, though not entirely, to the fact that migrants are not able to accommodate themselves at once to a new and relatively strange environment. The same thing can be said of the immigrants from Europe, or of the younger generation of women who are just now entering in such larger numbers into the newer occupations and the freer life which the great cities offer them.[21]

As to explanation, let alone remedy, Park finally offered none: "The thing of which we still know least is the business of carrying on an associated life."[22] "I have a feeling that this paper lacks a moral," he confessed, "and I know that every paper on a social topic should have a moral"; the fact was that "the problem of juvenile delinquency seems to have its sources in conditions over which, in our present knowledge, we have very little control."[23] Doubtless, were Park to return to the Chicago South Side of the early twenty-first century, he would be an even more puzzled and worried man.

In a series of studies, seeking to answer the questions which Park threw out, members of the Chicago school grappled with the raw facts of social disintegration and delinquency so evident on the city's streets. Thrasher's monograph on *The Gang*, published the year after, confirmed that it was especially a phenomenon of what Burgess, in his classic social geography of the city,[24] had called the "Zone in Transition" around the city center:

[19] Park, 1925a, 45.
[20] Park, 1925b, 107.
[21] Park, 1925b, 108.
[22] Park, 1925b, 110.
[23] Park, 1925b, 110.
[24] Burgess, 1925, 51, 55.

It is in these regions that we find deteriorating neighborhoods, great mobility, areas of immigrant first settlement, corrupt ward politics, vice, crime, and general disorder. The basic reason, however, for the development of gangs in these areas is the failure of customary social institutions to function in such a way as to organize the life of the boy.[25]

And this was a function of immigration: three-quarters of the people of Chicago, at that time, were "foreign-born peoples and their immediate progeny":

Chicago is a mosaic of foreign colonies with conflicting social heritages. There has not yet been time for adjustment among these diverse elements and for the development of a consistent and self-controlled social order. The gang is one symptom of this "cultural lag."[26]

His research showed that the great majority of gang members were immigrant children whose parents, mainly rural peasants, could no longer control them because of their inadequate English and the lack of any community code of conduct: "the children of immigrants tend to become quickly and superficially Americanized, becoming assimilated to the more racy and more vicious aspects of American life which they encounter in the disorganized and mobile areas in which they live."[27]

That had been the pattern of Chicago society as long as anyone had been looking at it: "The entire history of Chicago from its birth to the First World War was characterized by the struggle, sometimes violent, of the first-comers and native whites against the later immigrants – the 'foreigners.'"[28] At the time of Hull House, a settlement worker sadly observed, "The lofty disdain with which the *Dago* regards the *Sheeny* cannot be measured except by the scornful contempt with which the *Sheeny* scans the *Dago*."[29] In this pecking-order someone had to be at the bottom, and at the end of the 1920s it seemed to be the Sicilians on the North Side, where – so the Chicago newspapers told their readers – murder and mayhem were the daily rule. As one of the Chicago sociologists discovered in 1929, this Little Sicily – or Little Hell, home to 15,000 unskilled ex-peasant Sicilians – was indeed the city's main center of bootlegging, of hi-jacking, of criminal gangs.[30] And in such a society, "there is an increasing amount of personal disorganization among the American-born. The second generation finds itself trying to live in two social worlds."[31] "Hence it is that the slum, particularly the foreign slum, is gangland. For gangland is but the result of the boy's creation of a social world in which he can live and find satisfaction for his wishes."[32]

---

[25] Thrasher, 1926, 3.
[26] Thrasher, 1926, 4.
[27] Thrasher, 1926, 4.
[28] Drake and Cayton, 1945, 17.
[29] Philpott, 1978, 68.
[30] Zorbaugh, 1929, 14.
[31] Zorbaugh, 1929, 176.
[32] Zorbaugh, 1929, 155.

More extended work from another member of the school, published that same year, confirmed that the geographical patterns of truancy, juvenile delinquency, and adult crime were closely related. All were highly concentrated in the zone of transition, marked by physical deterioration and declining population, immediately around the city's central business district, occupied by European immigrants and Southern blacks:

> All of them come from cultural backgrounds which differ widely from the situations in the city. In the conflict of the old with the new the former social and cultural controls in these groups tend to break down. This, together with the fact that there are few constructive community forces at work to re-establish a conventional order, makes for continued social disintegration.[33]

And, in the mid-1940s, when Shaw extended this work to a wide range of other cities, he found the same patterns: in some low-income areas, delinquency was a "social tradition."[34]

Generalizing from the first round of Chicago studies at the end of the 1920s, Park produced a phrase that was to echo around the halls of sociology, with increasing discordance, for decades after. Migration into the cities, he argued, following the line of his earlier papers, produced a "changed type of personality … Energies that were formerly controlled by custom and tradition are released. The individual is free for new adventures, but he is more or less without direction and control."[35] The result was "a cultural hybrid, a man living and sharing intimately in the cultural life and tradition of two different peoples … a man on the margin of two cultures and two societies, which never completely interpenetrated and fused,"[36] whose characteristics were "spiritual instability, intensified self-awareness, restlessness and malaise."[37] Such a person, Park suggested, could be called the "Marginal Man."

Some who later inveighed against the concept of "marginality" (Chapter 8) might usefully have referred back to this original source: Park's chosen archetype of Marginal Man was the culturally cosmopolitan emancipated Jew. But, in the universal manner, the phrase proved so memorable that it became detached from its author's original meaning: increasingly, it came to refer to the disaffected member of Park's urban underclass, imperfectly acculturated into urban society, and sunk in what later, in another equally memorable and misunderstood phrase, Oscar Lewis was to call the culture of poverty.

---

[33]   Shaw *et al.*, 1929, 205.
[34]   Shaw and McKay, 1942, 437.
[35]   Park, 1928, 887.
[36]   Park, 1928, 892.
[37]   Park, 1928, 893.

The Sociologists Invade the Ghetto

Most of the delinquents who came under the Chicago school's microscope were white. That reflected the fact that in the 1920s, the children of white ethnic parents were the main inhabitants of the zone of transition and the main victims of imperfect transition from the old to the new society. It may also have reflected the difficulty that white middle-class sociologists would have experienced in penetrating Chicago's newest ghetto. They did not even recognize it by that now-familiar name: in Burgess's classic typology, the "Ghetto" was Jewish, one of a number of ethnic slums – Little Sicily, Greektown, Chinatown – where Old World traditions mixed with American adaptations; the Black Belt, "with its free and disorderly life," was something quite different.[38]

But it already existed; and, labeled or not, it was already the only true ghetto in the city. Here, the founding fathers of urban sociology made one of their few mistakes. Park, Burgess, and Louis Wirth taught a generation of students that all ethnic neighborhoods were temporary ghettos; in them, voluntary segregation would eventually break down as acculturation brought assimilation. Their own research seemed to show that the black ghetto was no more ghettoized than any other. But, half a century later, researchers re-analyzed their basic data to show that they had been wrong. At the level of small census tracts, no European group, at the Census of 1930, was more than 61% ghettoized – and, in these so-called ghettos, the so-called ghetto population never made up more than 54% of the total. But already, close on 93% of the city's black population lived in ghettos; and there, they made up over 81% of the total population.[39]

This segregation, other later researchers found, had come about during World War One. In 1910, no tract had been predominantly black; by 1920, 10 recorded a black percentage of 75% and more.[40] Between 1916 and 1918 Chicago had received 65,000 blacks from the rural areas of the Mississippi Valley, most of whom poured into the city's industries.[41] Despite efforts by black community organizations and newspapers, they found it difficult to adjust to the pressures of city life; a quarter-century later, older blacks were still heard to bemoan the arrival of the newcomers, which they claimed had disrupted racial integration and harmony in the city, and had "made it hard for all of us."[42]

When white servicemen returned from the war, there were pressures in the workplace too; for, among the city's white ethnic working class, the blacks had a reputation – inherited from the great stockyard strike of 1904 – as strikebreakers.[43] Gangs of white working-class youths from the Stockyards district, styling themselves

---

[38]   Burgess, 1925, 56.

[39]   Philpott, 1978, 141.

[40]   Spear, 1967, 146.

[41]   Chicago Commission, 1922, 602.

[42]   Drake and Cayton, 1945, 73; Tuttle, 1970, 169.

[43]   Tuttle, 1970, 117, 126.

as "athletic clubs" and supported by a local ward politician, began to intimidate their black counterparts on the streets.[44]

Finally, on July 27, 1919, an incident involving white and black youths on a crowded bathing beach brought an open urban riot: not the first such – East St Louis, in July 1917, had claimed that title – but one of the bloodiest in American history. When the militia at last brought order five days later, 38 people – 15 white, 23 black – were dead, and 537 injured.[45] As the Commission of Inquiry concluded – though it did not use the term – this was what later sociologists called a "community riot," marked mainly by violence on the part of whites against blacks, whom they saw as invading their neighborhoods and their jobs. And the Commission painted a graphic picture of the black ghetto of that time: over 40% lived in grossly deteriorated housing; 90% were living next to the city's segregated vice districts where children were daily exposed to vice and crime; in over a fifth of the homes children were out of control; many of the children were backward at school because they had been poorly educated in the South.[46]

Still, despite this lead, by and large the Chicago sociologists of the 1920s stayed outside the ghetto. But, by a remarkable chance – remarkable, considering the chances of black advancement in those days – two of the greatest of America's early sociologists happened to be black. And, even more remarkable, one of the founding white fathers of American sociology also devoted his early life to a study of black urban society. Each of these three contributed major empirical studies, which give us a unique historical picture of late nineteenth- and early twentieth-century black American urban society.

What they tell us, unmistakably, is that many of the features that so much concern students of social policy today have long antecedents. In 1899, W. E. B. Du Bois used the methods of Booth's London survey to classify the black population of Philadelphia's Seventh Ward. There was, he told his overwhelmingly white readers, "no surer way of misunderstanding the Negro or being misunderstood by him than by ignoring manifest differences of condition and power in the 40,000 black people of Philadelphia."[47] He classified each family in his survey into one of four grades. The first, the "very poor and semi-criminal," depending on casual labor and living in the slums, made up just under 9% of the total population of the Seventh Ward; the "poor", or "the inefficient, unfortunate and improvident," just under 10%.[48] The biggest single group, numbering nearly 48%, were the "great hard-working laboring class"; they were "honest and good-natured" and lived in houses of three to six rooms, generally well-furnished.[49] Above them were the 25% described as "comfortable," the 4% in "good circumstances," and the 4% who were "well-to-do."

[44]   Chicago Commission, 1922, 12; Spear, 1967, 212; Tuttle, 1970, 199.
[45]   Chicago Commission, 1922, 595–8.
[46]   Chicago Commission, 1922, 192, 264–5, 622.
[47]   Du Bois, 1899, 310.
[48]   Du Bois, 1899, 171–4.
[49]   Du Bois, 1899, 175.

So the great majority of the blacks of Philadelphia were certainly not the degenerate, criminal, slum-dwelling underclass of the rumor mill:

> Nothing more exasperates the better class of Negroes than this tendency to ignore utterly their existence. The law-abiding, hard-working inhabitants of the Thirtieth Ward are aroused to righteous indignation when they see that the word Negro carries most Philadelphians' minds to the alleys of the Fifth Ward or the police courts.[50]

The problem was that the rumor mill focused on a real enough problem: "the increasing number of bold and daring crimes" committed by blacks in the previous decade.[51] Blacks accounted for only 4% of the Philadelphia population but for 9% of the arrests.[52] The fact was that "the illiterate fifth of the Negro population furnished a third of the worst criminals";[53] "the more serious and revolting the crime the larger part does ignorance play as a cause."[54] In particular, "A crime for which Negroes of a certain class have become notorious is that of snatching pocketbooks on the streets"; and "from pocketbook snatching to highway robbery is but a step."[55] Du Bois concluded,

> From this study we may conclude that young men are the perpetrators of serious crime among Negroes; that this crime consists mainly of stealing and assault; that ignorance, and immigration to the temptations of city life, are responsible for much of this crime but not for all; that deep social causes underlie this prevalence of crime and they have so worked as to form among Negroes since 1864 a distinct class of habitual criminals; that to this criminal class and not to the great mass of Negroes the bulk of the serious crime perpetrated by this race should be charged.[56]

When Du Bois turned to "Conjugal Condition," he found a striking anomaly:

> there is a large proportion of single men – more than in Great Britain, France or Germany; the number of married women, too, is small, while the large number of widowed and separated indicates widespread and early breaking up of family life. The number of single women is probably lessened by unfortunate girls, and increased somewhat by deserted wives who report themselves as single. The number of deserted wives, however, allowing for false reports, is astoundingly large and presents many intricate problems. A very large part of the charity given to Negroes is asked for this reason. The causes of desertion are partly laxity in morals and partly the difficulty of supporting a family ... The result of this large number of homes without husbands is to increase the burden of charity and benevolence, and also on account of their poor home-life to increase crime. Here is a wide field for social regeneration.[57]

50 Du Bois, 1899, 310.
51 Du Bois, 1899, 241.
52 Du Bois, 1899, 239.
53 Du Bois, 1899, 254.
54 Du Bois, 1899, 258.
55 Du Bois, 1899, 262, 263.
56 Du Bois, 1899, 259.
57 Du Bois, 1899, 67–8.

Du Bois's conclusions on this point are significant, since they confirm those of Howard Odum, the Southern white sociologist who became the founding father of the Southern Regionalist school of the 1930s and 1940s (Chapter 5). Odum's first published work was a detailed investigation of the lives of blacks in the towns of the South, conducted in the first decade of the twentieth century. So scathing are many of Odum's observations, that 80 years later they are almost unpublishable; were it not for his long and sympathetic subsequent record of work on black culture, it would be easy simply to dismiss him as a racist. He anticipates the criticism: "while there is much unpleasantness and dissatisfaction in criticizing as a 'stranger' the habitations of these people, it is necessary for all concerned to paint the picture from life, to see things as they are," he warned.[58]

On family structure, he confirmed Du Bois's findings: "The proportion of parents without legitimate children is large, in general from fifteen to twenty per cent of the families," "there being some ten per cent of the total number of families with a woman at the head."[59] The average family had four persons, in two rooms: "In such crowded quarters – not infrequently in one room – must exist the entire family with living apparatus."[60] And, said Odum, "With such crowded conditions habits of uncleanliness naturally grow. A glance inside the average negro cottage is most discouraging."[61]

Additionally, since much work was done at home, and the woman of the family must go out to work,

> throughout the day the negro home is full of haste and disorder. The mother who cooks for a white family is up and off early in the morning, leaving the children uncared-for at home; the man soon leaves also for his work. The children thus have no care and attention … In the meantime the household is kept together as best it may be.[62]

As a result, "The children rarely feel kindly towards their parents. So it is that after they have grown up the family is not united in purpose, spirit, or physical presence … The one desire of the younger negroes – and it seems to be a natural one – appears to be freedom from work and parental control."[63]

The result, concluded Odum the moralist, was

> immorality and crime, on the one hand, and disease on the other … The indiscriminate mixing in the home leads to bad personal habits; the utter lack of restraint deadens any moral sensibilities that might be present. Nowhere in the home is there restraint; the contact and conduct of its members belong to the lowest classification. There is little knowledge of the sanctity of home or marital relations; consequently little regard for them. The open cohabitation of the sexes related by no ties of marriage is a very

---

[58]   Odum, 1910, 151.
[59]   Odum, 1910, 153.
[60]   Odum, 1910, 153.
[61]   Odum, 1910, 154.
[62]   Odum, 1910, 155.
[63]   Odum, 1910, 162.

common practice; little is thought of it as it relates to the race; there is apparently no conscience in the matter.[64]

Worse:

> Too often every home is considered a place of debauchery; the negroes know full well the numerous houses to which they are invited and to which they go. The "creeper", the "rounder-shaker", and the "eastman" are too well known to elicit surprise among the negroes. Every home is liable to their criminal influence, when every man and every woman becomes common property.[65]

And still worse, "Perhaps nowhere in negro life does the problem of immorality appear more stupendous than among the children ... The amount of knowledge of evil and evil practices possessed by small children is unthinkable. Their practices are no less appalling."[66] "With the life of immorality comes its celebration in story and song ... The prevailing theme of this class of songs is that of sexual relations, and there is no restraint in its expression."[67]

When it is all coupled with fears that venereal disease may compromise "the purity of the white race," it is all too easily dismissible. All too evidently, the young Odum lacked all standard of sociological comparison; he had no comprehension that almost exactly the same results could be reported for the white underclass of Victorian London. Nor did he have much sense of historic relativity: for good or ill, much of the child behavior he reports sounds uncannily like that of white middle-class suburban American teenagers of the 1960s – including the songs, which the Rolling Stones borrowed from his sources. It might even be said, in historical perspective, that Odum's unthinkable nightmare came true: the norms of the black Southern underclass finally conquered the respectable white world. There is something eerily prophetic about his report that "the habit of using cocaine has constantly grown, and among the better classes, with its evil results. Its extensive use in the cities brings the inevitable influence to the smaller communities."[68]

But there is something more: something he shared with Du Bois, founder of the National Association for the Advancement of Colored People. It was a sense that finally, the collapse of family structure among a section of the black community was attended by appalling consequences, which transmitted themselves from generation to generation. When Odum wrote that "The Negro is becoming less efficient as a workman, not because of ability, but because of indisposition toward work and his persistency in idleness," he was guilty of the worst racial stereotyping. When he wrote that "the criminal ranks are increasing rather than decreasing because of these worthless negroes. From idleness to recklessness and theft, the negro easily develops from the vagrant, the bum,

[64]   Odum, 1910, 163.
[65]   Odum, 1910, 165.
[66]   Odum, 1910, 165.
[67]   Odum, 1910, 166.
[68]   Odum, 1910, 173.

Figure 13.4 Murder in Chicago race riot, 1919. Unlike later riots in American cities, this was a true interracial conflict, prompted by white resentment at black invasions of the city's housing and job markets. *Source*: Chicago History Museum, ICHi-22430, Jon Fujita.

the hobo, the bully boy, the eastman, the rounder, the creeper, to the 'bad man' and the criminal"[69] he was describing a tendency among a small black underclass that – as Du Bois also too well appreciated – was a major potential problem. What both lacked was a clear theoretical explanation of why this might be so. The Chicago school provided one: it was the result of the sudden transition from a rural, traditional society, based on primary family and neighborhood relationships, to the complexities of the city. And it developed in the second generation: the first urban-born children.

That was, in the language of a later generation, the prevailing Chicago paradigm when an African American sociologist, E. Franklin Frazier, arrived there to work on his PhD in 1927. The resulting work marks a milestone in the sociology of the black family. Frazier starts by reviewing a vast volume of literature, from Du Bois onward, on "The Demoralization of the Negro family." He concludes,

> we find that opinions extending over a long period had been unanimous concerning the widespread demoralization of Negro family life. These opinions arose from observers and students with diverse interests and were supported by statistics from many sources, For all except one or two of these observers this widespread demoralization of family life was a sign of the inability of the Negro to measure up to the sex standards of Western civilization and to a few it portended the ultimate extinction of the race.[70]

Frazier's achievement was to start with the fact, and carefully to dissect the causes. He discounted the view that there were either physical or African – that is, racial – origins. Instead, he posited a double historical breakdown: first, emancipation, which had

---

[69] Odum, 1910, 221.
[70] Frazier, 1932, 245.

Figure 13.5 Dr E. Franklin Frazier. The great black sociologist of the Chicago school, whose work in the 1920s and 1930s meticulously detailed the breakdown of black family structures in the northern cities. *Source*: Moorland-Spingarn Research Center, Howard University.

caused instant collapse of the Negro slave family and social organization, but which was followed by a return to a modified form of plantation life as a sharecropping family; secondly, urbanization, which had again led to a collapse of social structures and social control. (Much later, the fundamental research by Fogel on the structure of the black family under slavery was to throw doubt on that part of the explanation; the slaveowners, it emerged, had every interest in preserving stable family structures.)[71] And, just as Park had postulated, this was most evident in the inner city where

> Negro family life tended to disappear. This was the area of crime and vice and free relations ... the high rate of dependency was accompanied by high rates of family desertion, illegitimacy, and juvenile delinquency. The youth of the unmarried mothers indicated, as in the case of juvenile delinquency, the breakdown of family discipline as well as community organization.[72]

[71] Fogel and Engermann, 1974.
[72] Frazier, 1932, 250–1.

But these critical indices of disorganization decreased as one moved out from the "Zone in Transition," coinciding with "the progressive selection of the moral stable elements in the Negro population."[73] So Frazier's work confirmed the Chicago paradigm: the "customary and sympathetic bonds that had held families together in the rural communities of the South were dissolved when they were no longer supported by the neighborhood organization and institutions of the rural southern communities."[74] Thus "The widespread disorganization of Negro family life must be regarded as an aspect of the civilizational process in the Negro group":

> As the Negro is brought into contact with a larger world through increasing communication and mobility, disorganization is a natural result. The extent of the disorganization will depend on the fund of social tradition which will become the basis for the reorganization of life on a more intellectual and more efficient basis.[75]

So time might help; preserving the "social fund" would help even more. The question was how.

From the 1930s, as Professor at Howard University, Frazier extended his work into a monumental study of black social and family structure. He confirmed the pioneer work of Du Bois in Philadelphia, Daniels in Boston, and others: as many as two-thirds of the entire black population of the northern cities was "lower class," distinguished not merely by their low-skill occupations, family disorganization, illiteracy, and poverty, but also by "shiftlessness and irresponsibility ... due partly to their lack of education and partly to the lack of economic opportunity for the great masses of Negro men."[76] In 1930, in the larger northern cities (100,000 and more people), 30% of households were female-headed; in equivalent Southern cities, between one-fifth and one-third.[77] And this was only the most obvious aspect of "the disorganized family life and unregulated sex behavior of these newcomers to the city."[78]

Examining the causes in greater historical detail, Frazier confirmed the analysis in his dissertation. The phenomenon was of long standing: Frazier was able to show that in Washington, DC, one-fifth of black births had been illegitimate in 1881, the same rate as in 1939; most illegitimate births in northern cities were to young mothers, who were newcomers to the city, and few of whom had themselves known ordinary family life.[79] This pattern of "fathers on leave," which was "one of the inevitable consequences of the urbanization of the Negro population," had its origins in the matriarchal structure of the slave society. In the rural South, too, more than one-fifth of households were female-headed; early pregnancy outside marriage was simply commonplace and accepted, for it was associated with a matricentric family in which the grandmother

73   Frazier, 1932, 251.
74   Frazier, 1932, 251.
75   Frazier, 1932, 251.
76   Frazier, 1957, 303.
77   Frazier, 1939, 326.
78   Frazier, 1939, 331.
79   Frazier, 1939, 326, 343, 346–9.

was the key figure. But in the cities, while the female-headed household persisted, this extended family structure disintegrated; illegitimacy, not a problem in the rural areas, became one only when stripped of this supporting structure of the extended family, neighbors, and institutions.[80] Thus, in Frazier's words,

> social and welfare agencies have been unable to stem the tide of family disorganiza-
> tion that has followed as a natural consequence of the impact of modern civilization
> upon the folkways and mores of a simple peasant folk … When one views in
> retrospect the waste of human life, the immorality, delinquency, desertions, and
> broken homes which have been involved in the development of Negro family life in
> the United States, they appear to have been the inevitable consequences of the
> attempt of a preliterate people, stripped of their cultural heritage, to adjust them-
> selves to civilization.[81]

For the children, the consequences were dire. As Frazier went on to show, black juvenile delinquency rates were several times higher than those for whites: three times in New York City, more than four times in Baltimore, for instance, during the 1920s.[82] But in these and other cities, delinquency was heavily concentrated in just those inner-city zones of community disorganization, where lower-class blacks, because of their poverty and cultural backwardness, were forced to live.[83] Thus it was clear that black crime rates – for adults as for children – were high; but the cause, formerly thought to represent physical or moral deficiency, was now generally ascribed to poverty, ignorance, and urbanization.

Five years after Frazier's masterly 1939 work on the black family, another great social scientist wrote another: Gunnar Myrdal's monumental study of the American black was published in 1944. Unsurprisingly, it reached conclusions identical to Frazier's:

> the important thing is that the Negro lower classes, especially in the rural South, have
> built up a type of family organization conducive to social health, even though the
> practices are outside the American tradition. When these practices come into contact
> with white norms, as occurs when Negroes go to the cities, they tend to break down
> partially and to cause the demoralization of some individuals.[84]

Frazier had warned that "the travail of civilization is not yet ended"; yet more blacks would join the road to the city, bringing with them yet new waves of disintegration. And, in the posthumously published final revision of his master-piece a quarter-century later, he could report that he had proved right: "World War 2 did not cause the Negro family to face new problems; it caused new strata of

---

[80] Frazier, 1939, 481–4.
[81] Frazier, 1939, 485, 487.
[82] Frazier, 1939, 358–9.
[83] Frazier, 1939, 374.
[84] Myrdal, 1944, 935.

the Negro population to face the same problems of family adjustment which had been faced by former migrants to the city."[85]

The evidence for that had been assembled on Frazier's own Chicago turf by two black sociologists who followed in his steps, St Clair Drake and Horace Cayton, in 1945. They found that as blacks had continued to pour into the ghetto, it had not expanded; it had grown ever more crowded.[86] Their contribution was to dissect its class structure, a structure that had undoubtedly existed at the time of Frazier's own work and which went back to the arrival of the new migrants in World War One:[87]

> Everybody in Bronzeville recognizes the existence of social classes, whether called that or not. People with small education, small incomes and few of the social graces are always referring to the more affluent and successful as "dicties," "stuck-ups," "muckti-mucks," "high-toned folks," "tony people" ... People at the top of the various pyramids that we have described are apt to characterize people below them as "low-class," "trash," "riff-raff," "shiftless."[88]

When these upper- and middle-class blacks spoke of "advancing the Race," they meant the creation of conditions under which lower-class traits would disappear and something approaching the middle-class way of life would prevail.[89]

Within this structure, the professional and managerial middle class made up a scant 5% of the population. About one-third constituted "an amorphous, sandwich-like" middle class. "Trying with difficulty to maintain respectability, they are caught between the class above into which they (or at least their children) wish to rise and the group below into which they do not wish to fall." But 65% of Chicago's black population fell into the manual working class. The crucial point is that this majority fell into two unequal halves.

> A part of this working class constitutes the backbone of Bronzeville's "middle" *social* class, identified by its emphasis on the symbols of "respectability" and "success". The largest part of this working class is in a "lower" *social* position, however, characterized by less restraint and without a consuming desire for the symbols of higher social prestige. Desertion and illegitimacy, juvenile delinquency, and fighting and roistering are common in lower-class circles ... the lower social class in Bronzeville have their being in a world apart from both white people and other Negroes.[90]

The crucial dividing line was economic. More than one out of every three Chicago blacks, in 1940, was unemployed or on Emergency Work Projects.[91] "Many of these families were actually mutual-aid societies, originated and maintained by economic

[85] Frazier, 1966, 364.
[86] Drake and Cayton, 1945, 174.
[87] Drake and Cayton, 1945, 73.
[88] Drake and Cayton, 1945, 521.
[89] Drake and Cayton, 1945, 710.
[90] Drake and Cayton, 1945, 523.
[91] Drake and Cayton, 1945, 214.

necessity";[92] maintaining any kind of home life was difficult, because of low and fluctuating income and poor housing. "Sometimes families came into being in order that the partners could qualify for more relief. Even illegitimate babies were an asset when confronting a case-worker … In the parlance of the sociologist, Bronzeville was suffering from social disorganization."[93] The result was the familiar pattern, recorded by other sociological studies from Du Bois and Odum onwards. The "lack of economic opportunity, coupled with denial of access to even a grade-school education, resulted very early in a peculiar pattern of restless wandering on the part of Negro men," which had been "an important factor, during the eighty years since slavery, in preventing the formation of stable, conventional family units," and had thus "shifted the responsibility of the maintenance of household units to the women of the lower class," so that "Lower-class men are thus in a weak economic position *vis-à-vis* their women and children. Male control loosened, the woman becomes the dominant figure."[94] Thus,

> an old southern pattern is intensified and strengthened in Bronzeville. Unstable common-law marriages of relatively short duration alternate with periods of bitter disillusionment on the woman's part. The end result is often a "widow" and her children, caused either by a husband's desertion or by a wife's impetuous dismissal of him.[95]

The inevitable results were juvenile delinquency and illegitimacy. In 1930, some 20% of juvenile court appearances were blacks; the Depression made things worse, and "Purse-snatching became general in lower-class areas and even on main thoroughfares." And, for every one arrested, there were "thousands of lower-class young men … who skirted the borderline of crime. These were the 'cats' who, clad in 'zoot-suits,' stood around and 'jived' the women."[96] Between 1928 and 1933, about one in nine of black births was illegitimate, the majority to young lower-class women who had recently come to the city; they were perpetrating an old rural trait, whereby a child is regarded as a welcome gift to help with the farm work, and no stigma attached to the fact.[97]

During the 20 years that followed that study, Chicago's black population grew mightily. Ten times as many blacks lived in the city in 1966 as in 1920; they increased from 4 to 30% of the population. The ghetto itself had hugely expanded; its major business artery shifted 2 miles to the south.[98] It did so only after a serious of riots between 1947 and 1957, in which the retreating whites – as in 1919 – had defended their turf, but with far less bloodshed.[99]

92 Drake and Cayton, 1945, 581.
93 Drake and Cayton, 1945, 582.
94 Drake and Cayton, 1945, 583.
95 Drake and Cayton, 1945, 584.
96 Drake and Cayton, 1945, 589.
97 Drake and Cayton, 1945, 590.
98 Hirsch, 1983, 3.
99 Hirsch, 1983, 68–71.

But in the process, it had also changed character: it was taken over by the Chicago Housing Authority (CHA). The resulting political battle tore the city apart and almost destroyed the Authority itself. The CHA's plan of 1949, for 40,000 additional units over six years, involved putting large numbers of blacks into white areas; as it tried to do so, there were continued riots; the city's ward politicians panicked; finally, CHA's director, Elizabeth Wood, was dismissed.[100] The attempt to integrate was abandoned; the CHA, in a deal with the city's political leaders, became involved in an immense scheme of *de jure* segregation.

Of 33 CHA projects approved between 1950 and the mid-1960s, only one when completed was in an area less than 84% black; all but seven were in tracts at least 95% black; more than 98% of the apartments were in all-black neighborhoods. The CHA, as critics later charged, was building almost a solid corridor of low-rent housing along State Street and nearby streets from 22nd Street to 51st Street.[101] As it did so, the whites moved out: of 688,000 new homes built between 1945 and 1960, more than 77% were built in the suburbs, where hardly any blacks were found.[102] By 1969, a judge found that CHA family housing was 99% black-occupied, and that 99.5% of its units were in black or transitional areas.[103] The city's "second ghetto," several times larger than the first had been during the city's disastrous 1919 race riot, was also more isolated; its older, northern end was now almost solidly frozen in institutional concrete.[104]

The heart and symbol of the new ghetto was the Robert Taylor Homes, the largest public housing project in the world: more than 43,000 units on a 95-acre site, 2 miles by a quarter-mile in extent, with 28 identical 16-story buildings. Of the original 27,000 residents, 20,000 were children. Almost all were black; all were poor; more than half were on public assistance. There were, in the whole project, 2,600 men: it was the equivalent of a town of more than 25,000 people, more than 90% of whom were women and children.[105] One resident said, "We live stacked on top of one another with little elbow room. Danger is all around. There's little privacy or peace and no quiet. And the world looks on all of us like project rats, living on a reservation like untouchables."[106] A private slum had become a public one. Otherwise, in 20 years, nothing had changed.

Visiting the Robert Taylor Homes, in the early 1990s, was a sociological revelation. A young child started in wonderment, "You police?" (we were white males, *therefore* we were police). A colleague, somewhat foolhardily, tried to snap a passerby; his immediate reaction was to cover up his face. We were white males with a camera, *therefore* we were police, about to arrest him. Around the corner came some of the explanation: a vast compound, almost an armed camp, full of police cars. A quarter-mile away, thousands of white commuters passed by on the Illinois

100   Bowly, 1978, 76–84.
101   Bowly, 1978, 112; Hirsch, 1983, 243.
102   Hirsch, 1983, 27.
103   Hirsch, 1983, 265.
104   Hirsch, 1983, 265.
105   Bowly, 1978, 124, 128.
106   Bowly, 1978, 124.

Central Railroad or on Interstate 90; they might have lived and worked in a different country, as in a sense they did. Not many years after that, they began to tear the Robert Taylor Homes down.

In another midwestern public housing ghetto, at about the same time, yet another team of sociologists was undertaking yet another investigation. This one was special, because the subject was the notorious Pruitt–Igoe development in St Louis, the life and death of which have been retold in Chapter 7. What they found was virtually a carbon copy of the Robert Taylor Homes. Of the 9,952 people in the project, well over two-thirds were minors and over two-thirds of them were under 12; women headed 62% of the families; in only 45% was employment the sole source of income.[107] So the story, unsurprisingly, had all the familiar ingredients of family disorganization, male marginality, delinquency, and social disintegration; here, it was merely more extreme and more spectacular. Pruitt–Igoeans lived in a nightmare world in which, since moving into the project, 41% had experienced theft, 35% personal injury, 20% serious physical assault.[108] What was significant, in Rainwater's finding, was that nevertheless the values of the people were mainstream, almost middle-class ones: the problem was that to maintain them would have required a stability and level of income enjoyed by the upper working class, meaning 50 to 100% higher than was available to most of them.[109] The result was

> the belief that respectability, conventional life, is a tenuous and unstable achievement, and that in the lower class ghetto world, the individual who is conforming to conventional expectations may fail at any time. Closely entwined with this generalized judgment about respectability is a basic distrust of other persons, no matter how close they may be by blood or affection. This distrust has two focuses: others may seek to exploit a person and, more subtle but equally important, even without trying to exploit him, others may simply fail one if he depends on them. Relationships may just not work out, whether between lovers, spouses, relatives, or friends.[110]

Thus, "Pruitt–Igoeans perceive a tremendous disjunction between actual behavior in their world and their norms about what behavior should be": a disjuncture that manifested itself in low self-esteem, which was a way of coping with exploitation.[111] Thus the matrifocal family, the marginal male, and the communal disintegration, were accepted as facts of life; "men are just like that," "naturally" irresponsible; no one could depend on anyone, even his or her spouse:[112]

> The relatively higher rate of marital disruption can be seen as a result both of the greater stress placed on the marriage by the highly developed subversion of the family

[107] Rainwater, 1970, 13.
[108] Rainwater, 1970, 104.
[109] Rainwater, 1970, 50.
[110] Rainwater, 1970, 55.
[111] Rainwater, 1970, 61, 75.
[112] Rainwater, 1970, 165–8.

by the street system and the less cohesion within the marriage resulting from the wife's lower incentive to retain her husband.[113]

And from this stemmed other curious consequences: the lack of a strong set of family attachments, or of deep psychological concern on the part of mothers for their children, which in turn appeared to contribute to a disturbingly high level of retarded behavior on the part of the children.[114] As children entered the school years, the difficulties multiplied:

> Pruitt–Igoeans' deep pessimism about human nature, the bedrock conviction that most people will do ill when it is in their interest, that doing ill is more natural than doing good, interacts with the normal contingencies of life that make doing good very difficult. Parents feel that luck more than anything else determines whether their children grow up conforming to their ideas of goodness.[115]

The child in turn learns that he cannot depend on his family, and that unless very lucky his life will not be very different from that of the elders around him; consequently, he might as well start coping with life as it is. In adolescence, his peer group tells him that success will come not from conventional performance in school or employment, but through becoming "the complete hustler, who gets what he wants by working on people's minds, who can produce rewards with a minimum of effort and a maximum of style."[116]

The root causes of this tangled skein of syndromes, in Rainwater's view, are economic marginality and racial oppression. Lower-class blacks cannot find a secure niche in the economic system; racism entrenches this, while ensuring that they receive poorer and dearer services, including housing and education:

> This inability to be like everyone else robs the lower-class Negro of a sense of personal meaningfulness and efficacy which is the accustomed and expected patrimony of the ordinary individual in the simpler, more "primitive tribes" in the underdeveloped parts of the world ... constrained to live among others who are equally marginal in economic terms, and in the community that grows up in this situation, a premium is placed on the exploitation and manipulation of peers.[117]

And the root lay in the poor economic prospects and status of the man, which gave him little status in his wife's eyes, and forced him into a self-protective role of "going for oneself," relying on the responses of others to measure success: "If one is successful in creating a dramatic self, a kind of security has been gained because that self can neither be taken away nor spent (at least in the short run)."[118]

[113]   Rainwater, 1970, 174.
[114]   Rainwater, 1970, 218–20.
[115]   Rainwater, 1970, 222–3.
[116]   Rainwater, 1970, 286.
[117]   Rainwater, 1970, 371.
[118]   Rainwater, 1970, 379.

The importance of this analysis lay in its policy implications: simply trying to intervene from outside, in order to teach middle-class values and aspirations through the educational system, would be foredoomed to failure, because it would not alter the life situations, within which the lower class developed their own view of the world and of their position in it. And conventional anti-poverty programs would fail, because they required the poor to change their behavior without the resources that would allow them to do so. Brutally, the first essential was to give the poor money.[119]

In 1965, more than 25 years after Frazier's classic and more than 20 after Myrdal's, yet another distinguished social scientist made his contribution. Essentially, it underlined their conclusions, confirming that the problem had not gone away. But unlike their work, it caused an unprecedented political storm. The reasons were two. First, Daniel Patrick Moynihan was an academic who had entered politics as a United States senator. And secondly, his report, *The Negro Family: The Case for National Action*, came in the immediate wake of the most turbulent decade in American black history, exceeding even the era of emancipation, which had begun with the historic Supreme Court ruling on *Brown v. Board of Education of Topeka* in 1954, and had culminated in President Johnson's enactment of the Civil Rights Bill in 1964.

Moynihan began as he was to go on, bluntly: "The most difficult fact for white Americans to understand is that … the circumstances of the Negro American community in recent years has [*sic*] been getting *worse, not better*."[120] "The fundamental problem," he continued, echoing Frazier and Myrdal, "is that of family structure":

> The evidence – not final, but powerfully persuasive – is that the Negro family in the urban ghettos is crumbling. A middle-class group has managed to save itself, but for vast numbers of the unskilled, poorly educated city working class the fabric of conventional social relationships has all but disintegrated … So long as this situation persists, the cycle of poverty and disadvantage will continue to repeat itself.[121]

The report gave the all-too-familiar evidence of family disintegration, but now the indices were much worse: nearly one-quarter of black marriages were dissolved; nearly one-quarter of black births, eight times the white rate, were illegitimate; almost one-quarter of black families were female-headed; 14% of black children, against 2% of white, depended on welfare.[122] So, Moynihan concluded, "the family structure of lower class Negroes is highly unstable, and in many urban centers is approaching complete breakdown."[123] The explanations too were identical to Frazier's: slavery, reconstruction, urbanization:

> In essence, the Negro community has been forced into a matriarchal structure which, because it is so out of line with the rest of American society, seriously retards the

---

[119]   Rainwater, 1970, 401–3.
[120]   Moynihan, 1965, n.p.
[121]   Moynihan, 1965, n.p.
[122]   Moynihan, 1965, 7–9, 12.
[123]   Moynihan, 1965, 5.

progress of the group as a whole, and imposes a crushing burden on the Negro male and, in consequence, on a great many Negro women as well.[124]

In particular, he asserted, matriarchal homes contributed to a psychological inability to defer gratification, and thus to a pattern of immature, neurotic behavior in adolescent and adult life.[125]

The consequences were also familiar, at least to any reader of the earlier literature; Moynihan's report merely confirmed that there had been no change. Unemployment among blacks had "continued at disaster levels for 35 years," with the sole exception of a few wartime years.[126] And "The combined impact of poverty, failure, and isolation among the Negro youth," Moynihan continued, "has had the predictable outcome in a disastrous delinquency and crime rate": it was possible that a majority of crimes against the person (rape, murder, aggravated assault) were committed by blacks, the overwhelming majority of them against other blacks.[127] Educationally, too, black youth was seriously disadvantaged: 56% failed the standardized Armed Forces mental test, a basic measure of ability, and "A grown young man who cannot pass this test is in trouble."[128]

Moynihan concluded by saying that the object of his study had been to define the problem, not propose solutions: he merely urged that "a national effort towards the problem of Negro Americans must be directed towards the question of family structure. The object should be to strengthen the Negro family so as to enable it to raise and support its members as do other families."[129] Frazier, he reminded his readers, had said the same thing in 1950, but "Matters were left to take care of themselves, and as matters will, grew worse not better."[130] This time, he believed, there was a crucial difference: the President backed the effort.

If he did, he soon walked away from it; the reason being not so much the subsequent controversy, but the escalating costs of the Vietnam War.[131] The controversy itself put no one in a good light, Moynihan perhaps excepted. The report was prepared for internal government circulation, but it was leaked, forcing publication. Fellow social scientists were embarrassed by Moynihan's open recital of uncomfortable facts; the Washington welfare establishment wanted to maintain a stance of being "color blind."[132] So everyone had an interest in repudiating the report, which they duly did. When the White House called a conference eight months after publication, as one participant put it, the basic assumption was that "no such person as Daniel Patrick Moynihan exists";[133] on the basis

---

124   Moynihan, 1965, 29.
125   Moynihan, 1965, 39.
126   Moynihan, 1965, 20.
127   Moynihan, 1965, 38–9.
128   Moynihan, 1965, 40.
129   Moynihan, 1965, 47.
130   Moynihan, 1965, 48.
131   Rainwater and Yancey, 1967, 294.
132   Rainwater and Yancey, 1967, 299, 304–5, 310.
133   Rainwater and Yancey, 1967, 248.

of critiques, one at least of which had been written without reading the report, an attempt was actually made to stop the conference even discussing family structure.[134]

The Impact of the Ghetto Riots

One of the reasons for this immense controversy, without doubt, was the changed perception on the part of Americans – and above all the American media – of the black American community. But another, more important, reason was that the report came in the middle of the riots that swept through black ghettos in more than a score of American cities, starting in Birmingham, Alabama, in 1963 and culminating in Detroit in 1967.[135] In particular, its publication in March 1965 was followed the same August by the major riot in the Watts district of Los Angeles, in which 34 people were killed and \$35 million of damage was inflicted;[136] the Moynihan report, the media suggested, "explained" the Watts riot.[137]

In fact, later analysis suggested that perhaps it did not. The exhaustive report of the Kerner Commission, appointed by President Johnson in the wake of the 1967 riots, did not look at Watts; but it concentrated on essentially similar riots that had taken place that summer in seven cities including Atlanta, Newark, and Detroit. There, it concluded,

the typical rioter in the summer of 1967 was a Negro, unmarried male between the ages of 15 and 24 in many ways different from the stereotypes. He was not a migrant. He was born in the state and was a life-long resident of the city in which the riot took place. Economically his position was about the same as his Negro neighbors who did not actively participate in the riot.

Although he had not, usually, graduated from high school he was somewhat better educated than the average inner-city Negro, having at least attended high school for a time.

Nevertheless, he was more likely to be working in a menial or low status job as an unskilled laborer. If he was employed, he was not working full time and his employment was frequently interrupted by periods of unemployment.

He feels strongly that he deserves a better job and that he is barred from achieving it, not because of lack of training, ability, or ambition, but because of discrimination by employers.

He rejects the white bigot's stereotype of the Negro as ignorant and shiftless. He takes great pride in his race and believes that in some respects Negroes are superior to whites. He is extremely hostile to whites, but his hostility is more likely to be a product of social and economic class than of race; he is almost equally hostile to middle-class Negroes.[138]

---

[134]　Rainwater and Yancey, 1967, 195, 233.
[135]　US National Advisory Committee, 1968, 25–108.
[136]　US National Advisory Committee, 1968, 37–8.
[137]　Rainwater and Yancey, 1967, 139–40.
[138]　US National Advisory Committee, 1968, 128–9.

In fact, this picture was not so far from the stereotype as the Commission claimed. Put another way, the typical rioter was a second-generation city dweller, a high-school drop-out with no educational qualifications, who nevertheless believed that this was not the reason for his relative failure in the job market; he was extremely hostile to mainstream American society, white or black. Between two-thirds and nine-tenths of the rioters were young adults, one-half to three-quarters were unskilled, one-third to two-thirds were migrants to the city, one-fifth to two-fifths were unemployed and between one-third and nine-tenths had criminal records.[139] Unlike middle-class blacks, they had made little progress in jobs, housing, or educa-tion. In other words, the typical rioter, if he existed, was also a fairly typical member of the underclass as Frazier had described it; the only gloss was that he belonged to the more intelligent and ambitious stratum of that underclass. And, if he did belong, he was more likely than in earlier generations to be out on the streets, especially in order to loot.[140]

Elsewhere, the Commission's report repeated the now familiar litany of the cycle of unemployment, family disintegration, and social disorganization; in ascribing family breakdown to unemployment, it in fact followed the analysis in the Moynihan report. Between 2 and 2.5 million people, 16–20% of the black populations of the cities, lived in squalor and depression in racial ghettos. They suffered unemployment rates more than double those for whites, and black men were three times as likely as white men to be in low-paying unskilled or service jobs; more than 40% of the black population, in 1966, was below the poverty line. And another potent cause of poverty was the familiar fact that nearly 24% of black families, against 9% of white, were female-headed. They concluded, predictably enough,

> The culture of poverty that results from unemployment and family disorganization generates a system of ruthless, exploitative relationships within the ghetto. Prostitution, dope addiction, casual sexual affairs and crime create an environmental jungle characterized by personal insecurity and tension … 1.2 million nonwhite children under 16 lived in central city families headed by women under 65. The great majority of these children were growing up in poverty under conditions that make them better candidates for crime and civil disorder than for jobs providing an entry into American society.[141]

This suggested a key feature of the 1960s riots that was later underlined by Morris Janowitz: unlike the *communal riot* as in East St Louis in 1917 or Chicago in 1919, which was an interracial clash at the boundaries of expanding black ghettos, this was a *commodity riot* within the ghetto, directed at white property and based on large-scale looting.[142] White residences, and white people, were not the objects of attack; the key feature of the riots was "shopping for free." Edward C. Banfield, a Harvard sociologist, wrote a book about the riots: "This book," he opened, "will probably strike many

---

[139]   Fogelson, 1971, 43, 114.
[140]   Janowitz, 1969, 325; Meier and Rudwick, 1969, 312.
[141]   Meier and Rudwick, 1969, 262–3.
[142]   Janowitz, 1969, 317.

readers as the work of an ill-tempered and mean-spirited fellow."[143] Many readers of *The Unheavenly City* vehemently agreed, particularly regarding its most notorious chapter, "Rioting Mainly for Fun and Profit." Students heckled and disrupted his classes. Banfield, by all accounts a disputatious fellow, loved it.

His thesis was that American – and by extension all modern – society has divided into four classes: upper, middle, working, and lower. The first three share common social norms. The lower class doesn't. Its members are what he called present-oriented: chronically unable to think ahead or plan their own future, living only for immediate action, and suffering from deep feelings of self-contempt and inadequacy. He thus invented the concept that lower-class "culture" was the immediate cause of the riots.

In that notorious chapter, he argued that the riots were hardly ever a form of political rebellion; they represented "outbursts of animal spirits and stealing by slum dwellers, mostly boys and young men and mostly negro," exacerbated by what he called "accelerating causes," notably "sensational television coverage." He claimed that images of the Newark riots, showing the police doing nothing, acted as an incentive to looting.

For liberal-minded readers, that was bad enough. But he further infuriated them by concluding there were no answers. Possible solutions – compulsory contraception, intensive stop-and-search, shutting down television coverage – were unenforceable or unacceptable, or both. And, as the lower class was multiplying faster than the rest of the population, it would probably get worse.

Forty years later, after peaking, crime has fallen in America's big cities. Whether or not that was due to intensive policing, Bill Bratton style, or to underlying demographic changes will be endlessly debated here. But, love Banfield's argument or hate it, there is one disturbing element: though his lower class was present in cities through the centuries, today's competitive and affluent society distinguishes this class ever more sharply from the rest of us. To change that would need a sharp turn back to Scandinavian society of the 1950s. And is society – American society, British society, even Swedish society – any longer willing?[144]

Whether you see the riots, like Banfield, as "Rioting mainly for fun and profit," or as "a matter of pride to many, a means of joining a national rebellion and heightening its intensity," as Kenneth Fox later did, is a matter of interpretation.[145] It raised the question for the Kerner Commission that for many Americans was uppermost: why then had blacks failed to follow the typical immigrant path to upward mobility? The Commission's main answer was timing. Blacks arrived in large numbers in the cities just as entry-level unskilled jobs were disappearing. Insofar as they still existed, they carried a stigma not present for earlier generations, when they constituted most jobs. Discrimination against blacks was fiercer than against earlier, white, immigrants. And the political system was no longer adjusted to serving immigrant needs.[146]

---

[143] Banfield, 1970, vii.
[144] Hall, 2011a.
[145] Banfield, 1970, 185–209; Fox, 1985, 160.
[146] US National Advisory Committee, 1968, 278–82.

Finally, then, the Kerner Commission focused its basic explanation not on the disintegration of the black family, but on what it saw as "white racism" which, it argued, was "essentially responsible for the explosive mixture which has been accumulating in our cities since the end of World War Two."[147] Among its main features were pervasive discrimination and segregation in housing, which resulted in black ghettos; black in-migration and white exodus from the cities; and the resultant development of a ghetto culture in which "Crime, drug addiction, dependency on welfare, and bitterness and resentment against society in general and white society in particular are the result."[148]

Thus the Kerner Commission analysis did not unearth much that was new. What was interesting, and significant, was how it made the causal connections, and thus how it placed responsibility for the riots. For Kerner, the riots were the fault of white racism. The whites were thus to blame for the fact that the blacks had rioted. A preponderantly white and conservative group had emerged with an explanation that – after 30 years of study – Frazier, the black Marxist radical, had never remotely suggested. It was an intriguing paradox; a sign of the times.

After the Riots

The Kerner report went on to recommend a series of measures aiming at "the creation of a new union – a single society and a single American identity."[149] Through job creation and the removal of job discrimination, better education and the removal of *de facto* discrimination in the school system, better and more uniform welfare standards, and an attack on substandard housing, it aimed to break down the invisible walls of the ghetto and finally integrate the black underclass into the mainstream of American life.

It did not of course succeed. There have subsequently been at least two major studies of black American progress: by William J. Wilson (1978) and by Reynolds Farley (1984). They appear to disagree, but many of their conclusions are disturbingly similar. Wilson's book is called *The Declining Significance of Race*: his thesis is that "class has become more important than race in determining black access to privilege and power."[150] Thus talented and educated blacks had been entering the professions as fast as, or faster than, whites with comparable qualifications; they had especially benefited from the expansion of government jobs, especially those concerned with distributing welfare.[151] So there had been a huge growth in the black middle class, from 16.4% of black males in 1950 to 35.3% in 1970; conversely, the lower class had fallen from 50.7 to 36.4%.[152]

[147] US National Advisory Committee, 1968, 10.
[148] US National Advisory Committee, 1968, 10.
[149] US National Advisory Committee, 1968, 23.
[150] Wilson, 1978, 2.
[151] Wilson, 1978, 103.
[152] Wilson, 1978, 129.

Yet, despite these encouraging signs, "the black underclass is in a state of hopeless stagnation, falling further behind the rest of society."[153] The reason, Wilson suggested, was a factor called "twist" in the demand for labor, identified by the economist Charles C. Killingworth in a 1968 study: there had been a long-term decline in the demand for low-skill, poorly educated labor, which had been faster than the decline in the supply of such labor.[154] True, such jobs still existed; but the qualifications had been raised, they were somewhat insecure, and many blacks would no longer do them because they felt that they would lose their self-respect.[155] Besides, for members of the underclass, illegal activities were more interesting and profitable; Wilson quotes a 1966 survey of residents of Harlem, where 20% were so engaged.[156]

Similarly, Wilson argued, the phenomenon of the female-headed household was by then a class-based, not a race-based, phenomenon. In 1974, only 18% of children in black families earning less than $4,000 lived with both parents; yet among those earning $15,000 or more, 90% did.[157] The fact was that "The situation of marginality and redundancy created by the modern industrial society deleteriously affects all the poor, regardless of race"; blacks were disproportionately represented in the underclass, and one-third of them were still there, but that was a legacy of past oppression, not of current discrimination.[158]

On that last point, Wilson's analysis agrees with Stephen Steinberg's account in his book *The Ethnic Myth*, three years later. Steinberg too confirms the divergence between a substantial black middle class and "the sheer existence of a vast black underclass," which to him provides "prima facie evidence of institutionalized racism."[159] But it turns out that what Steinberg means by this is racism in long-past generations. He argues – and in this he essentially follows Park's analysis of the 1920s – that the critical variable in the successful adaptation of different ethnic immigrant groups is whether they had previous experience of urban life. Thus the Jews, who were almost exclusively urban before they came, had been outstandingly successful; the rural southern Italians less so.[160] But the blacks, despite being one of America's oldest immigrant groups, had been deliberately kept out of the northern cities after emancipation, because of a tacit conspiracy between Southern plantation owners and northern industrialists.[161] So, when they belatedly arrived, they were totally unprepared for the transition.

Farley's analysis shows much the same divergence between rich and poor blacks: the gap, he suggests, has remained about the same in a relative sense, but has markedly increased in terms of absolute incomes.[162] What he does show, on the basis of

153 Wilson, 1978, 2.
154 Wilson, 1978, 95–8; Killingworth, 1968.
155 Wilson, 1978, 104–6.
156 Wilson, 1978, 108.
157 Wilson, 1978, 132.
158 Wilson, 1978, 154.
159 Steinberg, 1981, 209.
160 Steinberg, 1981, 94–8.
161 Steinberg, 1981, 173–4, 201–2, 221.
162 Farley, 1984, 181–3.

more recent figures than Wilson's, is an ominous reversal in the trend of black progress: the proportion of black Americans who are poor, which declined from over 50% in 1950 to a low point of 30% in 1974, subsequently edged upwards again to 36% in 1982.

Farley argues that his explanation contradicts Wilson: sex, not class, is now the main key to membership of the underclass. But really, his evidence does not clash with Wilson's: both demonstrate the so-called feminization of poverty, which is the product of the rapid rise in female-headed households. And here a major difference has opened up between blacks and whites: whereas in 1960 90% of white children, but only 66% of black ones, lived with both parents, by 1982 these figures had fallen to 81 and 42%.[163] And this in turn is due to a huge rise in black illegitimacy: in 1950, the rates were 2% for whites, 17% for nonwhites; in the late 1960s, 6 and 32%; in 1980, 10 and 55%.[164] Now it is true that the rise in white illegitimacy has been faster; what is disturbing about the black figure is the absolute scale of the problem. Far from improving over time, as most observers expected and hoped, it has got spectacularly worse.

The consequences have been dire. While 19% of black husband–wife families were below the official poverty line in 1982, for female-headed households the figure was 59%.[165] Put another way: while in 1959 two-thirds of poor black households consisted of husband–wife families, by 1980 three in five were female-headed.[166] All this strongly supports Farley's conclusion: "changing living arrangements help to explain persistence of high rates of poverty in the 1970s."[167] Or, as someone has put it, poverty is no longer a matter so much of what you do, as of whom you live with.

The problem, as always, is what caused what. Farley's explanation is that higher welfare payments to families with dependent children – which rose 28% in constant dollars between 1960 and 1980 – may have actually encouraged family breakup; and, in the late 1970s, some 44% of recipients were black.[168] If this were so, Farley points out, it would interestingly contradict Moynihan's thesis of 1965, which was that by creating more jobs for black men, families would be encouraged to stay together; in fact, many such jobs have been created, but it has not had the expected effect. Farley, rather, argued that the changes are the product of deep-seated social changes, which may well be followed by the white community.[169]

That proved prophetic. Black illegitimacy in America climbed ever higher: to 56% of all births by the early 1980s, almost 40% of these to teenagers; almost one in four black teenagers had illegitimate children before the age of 18; 47% of all black families were female-headed.[170] And the basic cause appeared to be an extraordinary

[163]   Farley, 1984, 141.
[164]   Farley, 1984, 138.
[165]   Farley, 1984, 158.
[166]   Farley, 1984, 161.
[167]   Farley, 1984, 160.
[168]   Farley, 1984, 170.
[169]   Farley, 1984, 169–70.
[170]   Hulbert, 1984, 15.

drop in marriage rates, by 45% in the 1970s: by the early 1980s, 86% of black teenage mothers were single.[171] Further, Farley seemed to be right on another trend: a third of white teenage births, too, were by then illegitimate. The differences, though, were still startling: among unmarried girls aged 17 and younger, the black birth rate was eight times the white.[172]

And all the time, the plight of the black underclass seemed to be getting worse. A study by Richard P. Nathan, published early in 1987, concluded that between 1970 and 1980, while the total population of the top 50 American cities fell by 5%, the numbers of those in poverty rose nearly 12%. Yet within this total, the number of poor whites fell by 18%, from 3.2 to 2.6 million; the number of poor blacks rose by 18%, from 2.6 to 3.1 million. Further, 84% of these poor blacks lived in concentrated poverty areas. And, though data were few, indications were that these trends had continued after 1980.[173]

Something quite extraordinary was happening here; but it was not quite clear why. It could not be, as Frazier had suggested long ago, that new waves of imperfectly acculturated rural black girls were descending on the cities; during the 1970s the tide of black migration slowed and even reversed. It might be, as some suggested, that recession and unemployment were making black men reluctant to marry; but that hardly explains the virtual collapse of the institution, or the extraordinary rise in illegitimacy that accompanied it. Nor does the modest rise in welfare levels seem to provide a remotely adequate reason. The disturbing prospect was that America was seeing yet another strange socio-cultural trend among a section of the young.

But at least, in contradistinction to the original furore over Moynihan, the issue of "Children having Children" was being openly aired by black community leaders, who saw in it the seeds of a real future tragedy. "For too long, we may have been too defensive, seeing public discussion of counterproductive tendencies in our community's structure as an attack on black people," said the President of the National Urban League, John Jacob; "In many cases it was that. But the facts must still concern us."[174] Indeed, as the specter loomed of these millions of fatherless children growing up to adulthood on city streets, they did: the fire next time might beggar previous recollections.

Moynihan, it seemed, was at last rehabilitated. In January 1987, he launched a major drive to replace the American welfare program by a completely new system, which would put first emphasis on earned income. Significantly, it won all-party support, from President Reagan downwards. And, a month later, Democrat and Republican state governors likewise approved a resolution demanding that the system of welfare payments be immediately turned into a "workfare" program. They cited in support a background paper, drawing attention to

171 Hulbert, 1984, 16.
172 Hulbert, 1984, 16.
173 Herbers, 1987a.
174 Quoted in Herbers, 1987a, 16.

deep and troubling changes in the fabric of American society: huge numbers of young women and children in poverty, high rates of welfare dependency, a dramatic rise in the number of single-parent households and latchkey children, millions of adults who are functionally illiterate, a growing problem with alcohol and drug abuse, teen-agers who are bearing their second and third child, and many others who have dropped out of school.[175]

The prose was slightly purple; but not much so. Small wonder that the governors expressed widespread confidence that the administration, and Congress, would accept their proposal.

Underlying this, though, were deep shifts in the economy of America and of other advanced nations. As described in Chapter 12, manufacturing was rapidly going the way of agricultural employment; more and more, these nations and their cities existed to handle and trade information. But this change has created a set of multiple polarizations, both between and within cities. As Sassen puts it, the Londons and New Yorks are the gainers; the Birminghams and the Detroits are the losers, unless – as in Birmingham's case – a municipal administration is canny enough to reorient a city away from manufacturing and into informational service niches. By the 1990s America's great industrial cities, like Britain's, had become museum places, shadow landscapes full of empty factories and vast spaces where factories once stood; the houses too had emptied, so that a strange gap-toothed urban landscape had emerged. Within these almost surreal urban places – North Philadelphia, South Chicago, East Manchester, West Newcastle – people still lived, though fewer and fewer of them worked. But even within the highest-order global cities, like New York or London, a massive set of polarities had developed and intensified, between an information-rich majority and an information-poor minority, between what Robert Reich[176] calls the symbolic analysts and the casualized service workers; and these multiply, as the information-poor – who also happen to be the money-poor – are concentrated into public housing estates where local schools take underprivileged children and, in all too many cases, make them more underprivileged still. The result is the kind of city represented in Tom Wolfe's parable *The Bonfire of the Vanities*, where the security-dealing Masters of the Universe come face to face with the urban underclass: it happens to be New York, but it might as well be London, Paris, or Amsterdam. The evidence was accumulating in the 1990s that the underclass phenomenon, once thought a product of the Anglo-American deregulated economies, was appearing also in very different kinds of society and kinds of city: large public housing projects in Paris and Amsterdam were increasingly populated by the structurally unemployed and their children, and – just as in their New York and London equivalents – violence was simmering just below the surface.

There were many rich ironies in this. The underperforming children were too often boys, while the girls pulled ahead of them: the premium paid for brawn and

[175]   Herbers, 1987b.
[176]   Reich, 1991.

muscle, for generations since the beginning of the human race, was now effectively zero (and one might say negative, since surplus testosterone was expended in rape and mayhem); the rent payable on intelligence and self-organization was increasing, and in this poor women seemed to perform better than poor men. Men whose sole asset was their superior physical strength were no longer good prospects either on the labor market or (in consequence) on the marriage market; one result was the breakup of the lower-class family, seen dramatically – but not uniquely – in the low-income Afro-American populations of American cities.

William J. Wilson caused a sensation with this thesis in his book *The Truly Disadvantaged*, published in 1987.[177] Developing his earlier thesis, he described a world in which the Afro-American population had polarized: half of them elevated into the middle class, too often administering welfare programs for the other half; the other living in a world, virtually without jobs and without prospects, in the low-income ghettos. Further, the system was self-reinforcing through the school system. In 1996, Wilson went on to document this phenomenon in detail on the basis of interviews with hundreds of ghetto residents[178] who told him about a world, in the words of the book's title, when work disappears. Massive loss of industrial jobs in America's major cities had thrown countless numbers of lower-skill workers into permanent unemployment or dependence on casual, minimum-pay work. As this happened, the work ethic eroded, leaving entire neighborhoods where hardly anyone worked and where the alternatives – dealing in drugs, early pregnancy and life on welfare checks – came to seem a more attractive alternative. As one 28-year-old welfare mother graphically put it:

> Shit, turn tricks, sell drugs, anything – and everything. Mind you, everyone is not a stick-up man, you know, but any and everything. Me myself have sold marijuana, I'm not a drug pusher, but I'm just trying to make ends – I'm tryin' to keep bread on the table – I have two babies.[179]

In this world marriage becomes increasingly an anomaly, as does regular work. And, as the regular family structure disappears, so does the socialization of children: no one knows anyone with the experience of work or social relations, in other words the normal experience of most people in most societies; crime and drug-hustling come to seem almost the norm.

Wilson's books engendered a huge volume of research both in the United States and elsewhere; in Europe, it emerged that the underclass was by no means co-terminous with urban ethnic minorities, though some of those minorities might well suffer disproportionate rates of unemployment and other poverty syndromes. Essentially, the phenomenon occurred wherever traditional male job opportunities had disappeared and where in consequence large numbers of young men were left without prospects, gradually descending into a life of petty crime and

---

[177]   Wilson, 1987.
[178]   Wilson, 1996.
[179]   Wilson, 1996, 58.

drug or alcohol dependence. It could happen in all sorts of places: in the terraces behind the former shipyards of Tyneside, in the old coal valleys of South Wales, in the traditional industrial areas of East London or Tyneside or northern France. But it was typically urban; and in the great cities it was part of the general polarization of income and living standards, evident throughout society in the most enthusiastic exponents of free-market capitalism like Reagan's America or Thatcher's Britain, but most exaggeratedly evident in global cities like London and New York and Los Angeles.

Here, it came to interact with another disturbing phenomenon, a strange aspect of the globalization of the world: the development of a huge worldwide industry in the cultivation, exchange, and distribution of drugs. The 1994 United Nations Conference on global organized crime estimated that global trade in drugs amounted to about US$500 billion a year – larger than the global trade in oil; the year before, the Organisation for Economic Co-operation and Development reported that at least $85 billion a year of drug money was laundered in the world's financial system; other estimates were even higher.[180] And increasingly, this system extended its tentacles into poor city neighborhoods, where it found both ready markets and a ready supply of potential dealers.

Planning, as such, seemed to have few answers to all this. Some physical determinists, following the line taken by the American architect Oscar Newman in the early 1970s, argued that you could improve the condition of the most problematic urban housing projects by redesigning them so as to excise indefensible space and maximize defensible space; the English geographer Alice Coleman was taken very seriously on this point, and British local authorities enthusiastically Colemanized their worst estates. In one of the most celebrated schemes, on the Mozart estate in the far northwest corner of the City of Westminster, the housing authority removed overhead decks, fenced blocks to separate them, and modified entrances to staircases. But in 1995 a study from the Joseph Rowntree Foundation suggested that the benefits had been short-lived: the changes had reduced burglaries for five months, but then they rose again, as did assaults and street robberies. On another notorious problem estate, Kingsmead in the London borough of Hackney, the authority got tough: it used injunctions and repossession orders to eject persistent criminals, and then developed a program of community activities for young people. In one year, burglaries fell from 340 to 50. The moral was that physical changes alone would not help: they might just shift the crime somewhere else (as Newman had suggested 20 years before) or shift the balance from one kind of crime to another. But design changes could work if they were accompanied by better housing management and by youth and community initiatives. The underlying problem was that local actions like these could not cut long-term youth unemployment, which had a major effect on crime. Design thus could do something, but by itself it was insufficient; the answer lay beyond the boundaries of any one housing authority, and maybe beyond anyone's capacity to provide.

---

[180] Castells, 1998, 168.

The Underclass in Britain

Many, having reached this point in the account, might legitimately ask what it had to do with a history of planning. For planning, in any sense in which it has been used in this book, seems to have been conspicuously absent from the entire American story. There are two justifications for its inclusion. One is that a history of planning cannot be divorced from a history of the problems that give rise to planning; the relevance of the American history is precisely that, almost unbelievably, questions of city planning hardly entered into it. This suggests that in contradistinction to what might have happened in almost any other comparable country, Americans are capable of separating problems of social pathology from any discussion of design solutions. The way to the solution of the problem of the ghetto, if it existed, was by a bundle of policies – in employment, education, housing – that had very little to do with city planning, at least as Americans then understood it. This is even odder when we remember, from Chapter 10, that it was just at the time of the riots that American planning theorists became convinced that planning was an approach that could be applied, suitably modified, to any problem whatsoever.

The other answer, more directly, is that other countries did not make this divorce. In particular Britain, which was also experiencing immigration of ethnic minorities into its inner cities in the 1950s and 1960s, and which in the mid-1960s also began to experience rather similar urban problems, then adopted a battery of solutions – some, such as community development, clearly borrowed from American experience – but combined them with large-scale physical renewal of its cities. And unlike its American equivalent, which had carried the epithet of "Negro removal" (Chapter 7), this had consciously sought to provide public housing for a wide spectrum of the population, including the poorest – which, by definition, came to include many members of the minorities. By the mid-1980s, large numbers of what the Americans call blacks – that is, British people mainly of Caribbean origin – lived in public housing projects, especially in London, where in 1991 43% of all British blacks lived.

The research on them is far less rich than that on their American equivalents. Insofar as it exists, it seems to show that in some few respects the British did better. The welfare state provided a much more generous floor, especially in housing. There were lower illegitimacy rates, probably because of more effective contraception and abortion services; but figures are very hard to come by, because the British statistical services insist on being color-blind, so this could be wrong. But Britain had been much more backward on questions of discrimination in employment, especially in affirmative action (or positive discrimination) programs.

Further, Britain had probably done at least as badly in education, where the schools seemed to have produced proportionately large numbers of unqualified black school leavers, even when the figures were controlled for social class.[181] Thus, emerging from school with lower levels of qualification and skill, black British teenagers found it hard to get jobs: particularly in boroughs with high concentrations

[181] Tomlinson, 1983, 62; Jeffcoate, 1984, 57–64.

of blacks, black youth unemployment was much higher than white – though this is true only of males; black girls did about as well, or as badly, as their white sisters.[182]

It looks then as if, overall, the British story is the same or worse. British blacks, like American blacks, have remained heavily concentrated in the inner and middle rings of the big cities. Relatively few have entered the ranks of the middle class. Their British-born children tend to be poorly qualified and they find it very difficult to get jobs. Though hard figures are difficult to find – those color-blind statistics, again – the evidence suggests that they have high levels of recorded crime, or at any rate of recorded conviction.

Finally, the evident fact is that the British ghettos too have rioted. In London's Brixton, Liverpool's Toxteth, and Manchester's Moss Side in 1981, in Birmingham's Handsworth and London's Broadwater Farm in 1985, violence, looting, and widespread damage occurred. Thanks to the detailed official inquiry by Lord Justice Scarman into the Brixton riot, we have a detailed anatomy.[183] It sounds like an uncanny rerun of the Kerner report: the same pre-history of mounting, barely controllable tension among the young ghetto blacks as they spar with police; the same small triggering incident of an arrest, followed by the spreading of rumor like wildfire; the same almost immediate conflagration.

Scarman concluded that this was not a race riot:[184] it was a clash of cultures, exacerbated by the fact that the black subculture was built on deprivation and disadvantage. And the story has some parallels with the regular outbursts of football-related violence in British cities, which stem largely from young whites. However labeled, the British riots – like their American equivalents – were the product of relatively poor, relatively under-privileged young men who had been encouraged, if not pressured, into developing an elaborate, segregated subculture very different from the mainstream society's.[185] For whatever cause, they were deeply alienated from that society. A high rate of male violence, like a high rate of female teenage illegitimate births, may be simply an expression of that profound alienation: at bottom, their hatred for society reflects self-detestation.

The worst of these British riots, which resulted in the hacking of a policeman to death with a knife by a group of youths, took place in October 1985 at Broadwater Farm in Tottenham, Northeast London. A prizewinning urban renewal project of 1970, it had proved a case study in indefensible space (Chapter 7); its medium-rise blocks, rising from a pedestrian deck above ground-level parking, provided a laboratory culture for vandalism and crime. It degenerated into a hard-to-let estate, with large numbers of problem tenants – particularly, young unmarried black mothers and their children; by 1980, the project was more than half black. A virtual no-go area for the police, it was brought back to life through a remarkable community effort led by one of the black tenants, who developed social facilities

[182] GB Manpower Services Commission, 1981, 8, D5, E5.
[183] GB Home Office, 1981.
[184] GB Home Office, 1981, 45.
[185] GB Home Office, 1981, 11.

Figure 13.6 Broadwater Farm riot, Tottenham, London, 1985. The police restore uneasy order to the indefensible spaces of the concrete jungle: a final comment on the failure of 1960s-style urban renewal. *Source*: Julian Herbert/Getty Images.

Figure 13.7 Riot in Tottenham High Road, London, 2011. Not far from Broadwater Farm, like the equivalent riots of the 1960s in American cities, this was a "commodity riot" triggered by tensions between young blacks and police. *Source*: © Richard Rowland/Demotix/CORBIS.

for the many unemployed teenagers. Then, her absence, and that of other key leaders, helped precipitate a new wave of crime and thus, indirectly, the triggering of the riot.

That same year, a group appointed by the Archbishop of Canterbury published their report *Faith in the City*, triggering an immense political furore. They might have had Broadwater in mind:

> There is a danger of many outer estates, in particular, becoming areas which have a quite different social and economic system, operating almost at a subsistence level, dependent entirely on the public sector, where the opportunities for improvement either through self-help or through outside intervention are minimal ... the degenera-tion of many such areas has now gone so far that they are in effect "separate territories" outside the mainstream of our social and economic life.[186]

The group's prose picture uncannily resembles those descriptions of Pruitt–Igoe before its end: "the architect-designed system-built slums of our post-war era"; "poor design, defects in construction, poor upkeep of public areas, no 'defensible space'"; "packs of dogs roaming around, filth in the stairwells, one or two shuttered shops, and main shopping centers a 20-minute expensive bus journey away"; "unemployment rates are typically 30–40%, and rising"; "Bored out-of-work young people turn to vandalism, drugs, and crime – the estate takes the brunt, and the spiral of decline is given a further twist."[187]

The clerics and their lay brethren were in no doubt as to the root cause: "*It is the national decline in the number of manual jobs, and the concentration of manual workers in the UPAs that lies at the heart of the problem,*" they underlined.[188] But, given that, what astonished and depressed them was the resulting sense of fatalism. They stressed again: "*We believe that at present too much emphasis is being given to individualism, and not enough to collective obligation.*"[189] They roundly attacked the policies of the Thatcher government – on support to local authorities, on welfare – and the attitudes that underlay them:

> It is the poor who have borne the brunt of the recession, both the unemployed and the working poor. Yet it is the poor who are seen by some as "social security scroungers", or a burden on the country, preventing economic recovery. This is a cruel example of blaming the victim.[190]

They ended with an open challenge – effectively, over the heads of the government: "The crucial issue to be faced is whether there is any serious political will to set in motion a process which will enable those who are at present in poverty and power-

---

[186]   Archbishop of Canterbury, 1985, 175.
[187]   Archbishop of Canterbury, 1985, 176.
[188]   Archbishop of Canterbury, 1985, 202.
[189]   Archbishop of Canterbury, 1985, 202.
[190]   Archbishop of Canterbury, 1985, 197.

lessness to rejoin the life of the nation."[191] They were calling others to join them, to "stand more closely alongside the risen Christ with those who are poor and powerless."[192]

It was powerful and passionate; it was far removed from the traditional parody of the Church of England as the Tory party at prayer. But it did curiously echo the righteous anger of Mearns and those countless other clergy, who a century before had railed against the cruelties of the Victorian slum.[193] Here then is the final irony: in the mid-1980s the problem of the urban underclass was still as stubbornly rooted in the world's cities, and in the consciousness of its more sensitive citizens, as in the mid-1880s, when it provided the vital stimulus to the birth of modern city planning.

Fifteen Years Later: The Attack on Social Exclusion

Fifteen years on, towards the end of the century, a new British government threw itself with unparalleled zeal into the task of reducing the plight of poor families and above all poor children. A Social Exclusion Unit was established in the heart of the Prime Minister's office; it was soon able to show that poverty was concentrated to an extraordinary degree in the hearts of the cities. It found that 44 local authority districts had the highest concentrations of deprivation in England: they had for instance nearly two-thirds more unemployment, almost half as many again lone parent households and underage pregnancies, more children on income support and without basic educational qualifications, and mortality rates that were 30% higher. Worse, these authorities contained 85% of the most deprived wards; and here, the concentrations of deprivation were often extraordinary.[194]

On that basis, the Unit began to map out a strategy which culminated, just over two years later, in its strategy for neighborhood renewal,[195] which began,

> Over the past twenty years, hundreds of poor neighbourhoods have seen their basic quality of life become increasingly detached from the rest of society. People living just streets apart become separated by a gulf in prosperity and opportunity.
>
> There are places where more than two in five people rely on means-tested benefits, where three-quarters of young children fail to get five good GCSEs, and where, across England as a whole, a million homes are empty or hard to fill.
>
> Many neighbourhoods have been stuck in a spiral of decline. Areas with high crime and unemployment rates acquired poor reputations, so people, shops and employers left. As people moved out, high turnover and empty houses created more opportunities for crime, vandalism and drug dealing.[196]

[191]   Archbishop of Canterbury, 1985, 360.
[192]   Archbishop of Canterbury, 1985, 360.
[193]   Mearns, 1883.
[194]   GB Social Exclusion Unit, 1998, 15–20.
[195]   GB Social Exclusion Unit, 2001.
[196]   GB Social Exclusion Unit, 2001, 7.

Such neighborhoods, the report stressed, "exist right across the country, north and south, rural and urban."[197] But they were overwhelmingly urban: the highest concentrations of poor neighborhoods were in the North East, the North West, London, Yorkshire, and Humberside, all urban regions, where they constituted between 19 and 36% of the entire populations. Most were in urban areas, one-industry or no-industry towns, and former coal-mining areas.[198] These areas had pulled steadily behind the rest of the country in the 1980s and 1990s:

> Over this period, communities became less mixed and more vulnerable with poor people more likely to be concentrated in the same places. Places that started with the highest unemployment often also saw the greatest rise in unemployment. Health inequalities widened. The proportion of people living in relatively low-income households more than doubled between the end of the 1970s and the beginning of the 1990s. Child poverty more than doubled between 1979 and 1995–6.[199]

And new problems had arisen, such as the phenomenon of housing for which there was little or no demand, as revealed by Anne Power and described in Chapter 12.

The report chronicled the root failures in government policy: failure to address the problems of local economies, failure to promote safe and stable communities, poor core public services, failure to involve communities, lack of leadership and joint working, insufficient information and poor use of it. It set out a whole raft of policies, resulting from the work of 18 Policy Action Teams. It showed in detail how extra resources would be focused on the key problems, to achieve specific targets for improvement: jobs, crime, education, health, housing, and environment. It was an inspired exercise in the Blair government's proud specialism: joined-up government. And the rest of the urban world, which was beginning to take a great deal of notice of it, held its collective breath to see if this country, the oldest urban-industrial country, could at last break the cumulative cycle of deprivation.

But just how intractable the problem might be, came almost immediately in another report from the same government: in spring 2001, the UK Cabinet Office produced a major review that tried to answer the question: Was Britain becoming a more socially mobile country?[200] Almost predictably, it found no easy answer. Social mobility, it concluded, actually appeared to have declined: over the last quarter of the twentieth century it had become more difficult for a person to reach higher income brackets than in the preceding quarter-century from 1950 to 1975. And this was associated with the fact that it seemed to have become more difficult to move from blue-collar to white-collar jobs; the way to the top, it appeared, was increasingly through education. So it was important also to look at mobility between generations. Here, many children were upwardly mobile for the simple reason that there were more top jobs than there used to be; but ominously, the

---

[197]   GB Social Exclusion Unit, 2001, 7.
[198]   GB Social Exclusion Unit, 2001, 13.
[199]   GB Social Exclusion Unit, 2001, 16.
[200]   GB Performance and Innovation Unit, 2001.

trend seemed to have halted in the late twentieth century. Relative mobility – your chances of making it upwards – seemed to have been fairly stable, mainly because of the simple fact that if your parents were in the top group, they would do their best to see that you were too. Education played a vital role here, but it did not explain everything, and it might even be playing a less important role than it did: parents could do other things for their children, for instance by providing them with money or contacts or information early in life.

The hard core of this report concerned poor children. They were more likely to become unemployed, and to earn less even when they were working, even when controlling for the fact that they often had a poorer education than the rest. And this penalty, it seems, had actually increased over the last three decades of the twentieth century. Better-off families could help their children in all kinds of ways; poor families could not, and this disadvantage could be intensifying over time.

So the report discussed possible policies: to remove barriers to mobility, either upward or downward, and to positively promote it. It concluded that not much was known about their efficacy. But some evidence suggested that it would cost a great deal, for instance in spending on education, to remove the barriers that poor children encountered. For instance, recent American work suggested that to equalize race differences there, it would be necessary to spend at least 10 times as much on each black child, on average, as on each white one: probably much more. The accumulated evidence, not just from Britain but across the world, suggested that social mobility had changed very little during the twentieth century; the unstated implication was that it might change very little in the twenty-first.

Postscript: August 2011

In August 2011, unexpectedly, riots flared again in London and other British cities. The trigger was the killing of a suspect by police in pursuit in Tottenham, North London. The police were slow to react to community anger. Almost instantaneously, riots and looting broke out in several parts of London, and then in provincial cities. The official figures are more disturbing than anyone in Britain had before realized. For they paint a picture of an alienated criminal sub-class, detached from mainstream society.

Consider the most basic statistic, earlier revealed by Kenneth Clark: 76% of defendants who came before the courts – 80% of adults, 62% of juveniles – had a previous caution or conviction. They had committed an astonishing total of nearly 20,000 previous offences, an average of 11 apiece. The adult males among them, 90% of the total, were two and a half times more likely to have a conviction than the adult male population as a whole.

This goes along with a drearily consistent life history: of the juvenile offenders, 66% had a special educational need (compared to 21% of all pupils in maintained secondary schools) and 36% had been excluded from school at least once during the previous year (compared to 6% of all Year 11 pupils). Predictably, at age 11, their

English and Maths results had been around two-thirds of the national average. Put crudely, they were the dropouts whom the education system had failed. Or, you could say, the other way round.

There is one other startling feature, on which right-wing media seized: 46% were from a black or mixed black background, 42% white, and only 7% were from an Asian or mixed Asian background. In Haringey, a London borough that includes riot-torn Tottenham as well as leafy Highgate and Muswell Hill, 55% of defendants were black or mixed black, as against 17% of all young people under 40. But this was not a universal pattern: in Salford, 94% of defendants were white, almost the same proportion as in the whole population.

The ethnic classification may differ. These figures signify the emergence of an urban underclass without qualifications, without prospects, and profoundly excluded from all the rest of us: a profoundly disturbing phenomenon.[201]

In this great ongoing debate, where was planning? In the century just passed, despite its numerous errors and aberrations, city planning helped millions of relatively poor and decent people to live far better and more dignified lives than they otherwise might; for this it should be much praised in retrospect, and supported for the future. In the process, society has changed shape: it is no longer a pyramid, with few at the top and many at the bottom, but has become rather like an old-fashioned spinning-top, with a big bulge in the middle. The problem is no longer the first Fabians posed over a hundred years earlier, *Why are the many Poor?* but rather *Why are the few Poor?* Social progress – which is no myth – has left behind, as stubbornly evident as ever, a problem of what the Victorians and their American equivalents called the vicious and degenerate and semi-criminal classes, and which the more enlightened (or mealy-mouthed) early twenty-first century calls the disadvantaged and the underprivileged. Planning, and the whole modern apparatus of the welfare state, has failed to dislodge it, or even satisfactorily to explain it; as then, so now, some blame the system, others original sin.

There is this small comfort: though it is beyond precise social measurement, the locus of the problem has shifted. It is, by definition, the problem of the bottom of the social heap. A hundred years ago, contemporaries located it among the most desperate of those who had been driven into the slums of the giant city, and who had been least successful there in finding a foothold on the socio-economic ladder. A century later, they find it among the same groups. Meanwhile, countless numbers of the great-grandchildren of that first group have climbed out of the underclass. Doubtless, numberless progeny of the second will prove to do the same. The abiding problem is why, despite all the massive intervening economic and social improvement, the underclass should appear so steadily to recruit new members to replace those lost to it. To that question, research as yet provides no answer. Here this story ended in 1988; here it still ends.

[201] Hall, 2011b.

Bibliography

This bibliography contains all works consulted in preparing the book. By no means all of them are actually cited in the text.

Aalen, F. H. A. 1989: Lord Meath, City Improvement and Social Imperialism. *Planning Perspectives*, 4, 127–52.

Aalen, F. H. A. 1992: English Origins. In: Ward, S. V. (ed.) *The Garden City: Past, Present and Future*, 28–51. London: Spon.

Abercrombie, P. 1910a: Modern Town Planning in England: A Comparative Review of "Garden City" Schemes in England. *Town Planning Review*, 1, 18–38, 111–28.

Abercrombie, P. 1910b: Some Notes on German Garden Villages. *Town Planning Review*, 1, 246–50.

Abercrombie, P. 1911: Town Planning in Greater London: The Necessity for Cooperation. *Town Planning Review*, 2, 261–80.

Abercrombie, P. 1914: Berlin: Its Growth and Present State. *Town Planning Review*, 4, 219–33, 302–11.

Abercrombie, P. 1926: *The Preservation of Rural England*. Liverpool and London: University of Liverpool Press; Hodder and Stoughton.

Abercrombie, P. 1933: *Town and Country Planning*. London: Thornton Butterworth.

Abercrombie, P. 1945: *Greater London Plan 1944*. London: HMSO.

Abercrombie, P. and Jackson, H. 1948: *West Midlands Plan*. Interim confidential edition. 5 vols. London: Ministry of Town and Country Planning.

Abrams, C. 1939: *Revolution in Land*. New York and London: Harper and Brothers.

Abrams, C. 1964: *Man's Struggle for Shelter in an Urbanizing World*. Cambridge, MA: MIT Press.

Abrams, C. 1965: *The City Is the Frontier*. New York: Harper and Row.

Abrams, C. 1971: *The Language of Cities: A Glossary of Terms*. New York: Viking.

Abu-Lughod, J. L. 1971: *Cairo: 1001 Years of the City Victorious.* Princeton: Princeton University Press.

Adams, D. 2011: Everyday Experiences of the Modern City: Remembering the Post-War Reconstruction of Birmingham. *Planning Perspectives*, 26, 237–60.

Adams, D. and Tiesdell, S. 2013: *Shaping Places: Urban Design and Development.* Abingdon: Routledge.

Adams, T. 1930: The Need for a Broader Conception of Town Planning and Decentralisation. In: Warren, H. and Davidge, W. R. (eds.) *Decentralisation of Population and Industry: A New Principle of Town Planning*, 135–49. London: P. S. King.

Adams, T. 1935: *Outline of Town and City Planning.* New York: Russell Sage Foundation.

Addams, J. 1910: *Twenty Years at Hull-House: With Autobiographical Notes.* New York: Macmillan.

Addams, J. 1929: A Decade of Prohibition. *The Survey*, 63, 5–10, 54–5.

Addams, J. 1965: *The Social Thought of Jane Addams.* Edited by Christopher Lasch. Indianapolis: Bobbs-Merrill.

Adebisi, B. 1974: The Politics of Development Control in a Nigerian City: Ibadan. *Nigerian Journal of Economics and Social Studies*, 16, 311–24.

Adejuyigbe, O. 1970: The Case for a New Federal Capital in Nigeria. *Journal of Modern African Studies*, 8, 301–6.

Adshead, S. D. 1910: The Town Planning Conference of the Royal Institute of British Architects. *Town Planning Review*, 1, 181.

Adshead, S. D. 1923: *Town Planning and Town Development.* London: Methuen and Co.

Agnew, J., Mercer, J., and Sopher, D. E. (eds.) 1984: *The City in Cultural Context.* Boston: Allen and Unwin.

Ågren, I. 1975: Thinking in Terms of Service. In: Heineman, H. -E. (ed.) *New Towns for Old: Housing and Services in Sweden*, 128–73. Stockholm: The Swedish Institute.

Al Naib, S. K. 1990: *London Docklands Past Present and Future: An Illustrated Guide to Glorious History, Splendid Heritage and Dramatic Regeneration in East London.* London: Ashmead.

Albers, G. 1974: Ideologie und Utopie im Städtebau. In: Pehnt, R. (ed.) *Die Stadt in der Bundesrepublik Deutschland*, 453–76. Stuttgart: Philipp Reclam.

Albers, G. 1975: *Entwicklungslinien im Städtebau: Ideen, Thesen, Aussagen 1875–1945.* Berlin: Bertelesmann Fachverlag.

Albers, G. 1986: Changes in German Town Planning: A Review of the Last Fifty Years. *Town Planning Review*, 57, 17–34.

Albrecht, C. *et al.* (eds.) 1930: *Handwörterbuch des Wohnungswesens.* Jena: G. Fischer.

Albrecht, G. 1930: Gartenstadtbewegung. In: Albrecht, C. *et al.* (eds.) *Handwörterbuch des Wohnungswesens*, 262–6. Jena: G. Fischer.

Aldridge, H. R. 1915: *The Case for Town Planning: A Practical Manual for Councillors, Officers, And Others Engaged in the Preparation of Town Planning Schemes.* London: National Housing and Town Planning Council.

Alduy, J. -P. 1983: 40 Ans de Planification en Region Île-de-France. *Cahiers de l'Institut d'Aménagement et d'Urbanisme de la Région Île-de-France*, 70, 11–85.

Alexander, L. A. 1981: *Winning Downtown Projects: A Photographic Case Study of Outstanding Urban Developments.* New York: Downtown Research and Development Center.

Allardice, C. and Trapnell, E. R. 1974: *The Atomic Energy Commission.* New York: Praeger.

Allen, C. and Crookes, L. 2009: Fables of the Reconstruction: A Phenomenology of "Place Shaping" in the North of England. *Town Planning Review*, 80, 455–80.

Allen, I. L. (ed.) 1977: *New Towns and the Suburban Dream: Ideology and Utopia in Planning and Development*. Port Washington: Kennikat.

Allinson, G. T. 1984: Japanese Urban Society and its Cultural Context. In: Agnew, J., Mercer, J., and Sopher, D. E. (eds.) *The City in Cultural Context*, 163–85. Boston: Allen and Unwin.

Allmendinger, P. and Chapman, M. (eds.) 1999: *Planning Beyond 2000*. Chichester: John Wiley & Sons, Ltd.

Alonso, W. 1963: Cities and City Planners. *Daedalus*, 92, 824–39.

Alonso, W. 1966. Cities, Planners and Urban Renewal. In: Wilson, J. Q. (ed.) *Urban Renewal: The Record and the Controversy*, 437–53. Cambridge, MA: MIT Press.

Altes, W. K. K. 2006: Towards Regional Development Planning in the Netherlands. *Planning Practice & Research*, 21, 309–21.

Altshuler, A. A. 1965a: The Goals of Comprehensive Planning. *Journal of the American Institute of Planners*, 31, 186–97.

Altshuler, A. A. 1965b: *The City Planning Process*. Ithaca: Cornell University Press.

Altshuler, A. A. 1983: The Intercity Freeway. In: Krueckeberg, D. A. (ed.) *Introduction to Planning History in the United States*, 190–234. New Brunswick, NJ: Rutgers University, Center for Urban Policy Research.

Amati, M. and Freestone, R. 2009: "Saint Patrick": Sir Patrick Abercrombie's Australian Tour 1948. *Town Planning Review*, 80, 597–626.

Amin, A., Massey, D. and Thrift, N. 2000: *Cities for All the People Not the Few*. Bristol: Policy Press.

Anderson, M. 1964: *The Federal Bulldozer: A Critical Analysis of Urban Renewal, 1949–1962*. Cambridge, MA: MIT Press.

Anderson, M. 1966: The Federal Bulldozer. In: Wilson, J. Q. (ed.) *Urban Renewal: The Record and the Controversy*, 491–509. Cambridge, MA: MIT Press.

Andrews, H. F. 1986: The Early Life of Paul Vidal de la Blache and the Makings of Modern Geography. *Institute of British Geographers, Transactions*, NS 11, 174–82.

Anon. 1897: *Forecasts of the Coming Century, by a Decade of Writers*. Manchester: Labour Press.

Anon. (ed.) 1918: *Problems of Reconstruction: Lectures and Addresses Delivered at the Summer Meeting at the Hampstead Garden Suburb, August 1917*. With an Introduction by the Marquess of Crewe, K. G. London: T. Fisher Unwin.

Anon. 1925: The Regional Community. *The Survey*, 54, 129.

Anon. 1937a: Prime Minister's Support for Garden Cities. *Town and Country Planning*, 5, 117.

Anon. 1937b: London Regional Planning: Notes of First Meeting of New Standing Conference. *Journal of the Town Planning Institute*, 24, 15–16.

Anon. 1970: *Siedlungsverband Ruhrkohlenbezirk 1920–1970, 29. Schriftenreihe Siedlungs verband Ruhrkohlenbezirk*. Essen: SVR.

Anon. 1979a: *Autobahnen in Deutschland*. Bonn: Kirschbaum.

Anon. 1979b: Kvaliteten i vart bostadsbyggande. *Plan*, 33, 1–6 (and comments, 7–19).

Anon. 1979c: Jeu de l'Oie des Halles de Paris. *Macadam*, 8/9, 12–13.

Anon. 1979d: News item. *Architecture*, 1, 7–10.

Anon. 1979e: News item. *Building News*, 437, 4.

Anon. 1979f: News item. *Building News*, 438, 1.

Anon. 1979g: News item. *Building News*, 456, 8.

Anon. 1985: The Shape of North American Rail Transit. *Railway Gazette International*, 141, 42–3.

Anon. 1989: *The Development of Stockholm*. Stockholm: City of Stockholm.

Anon. 1995: Paul Delouvrier 1914–1995: Le Grand Aménageur de l'Île-de-France. *Cahiers de l'Institut d'Aménagement et d'Urbanisme de la Région Île-de-France*, 108, special supplement.

Anon. 1997: Special Theme: The Development and Management of Asian Megacities. *Asian Development Bank, Annual Report 1996*, 23–51. Manila: ADB.

Anson, B. 1981: *I'll Fight You for It! Behind the Struggle for Covent Garden*. London: Cape.

Anthony, H. A. 1966: Le Corbusier: His Ideas for Cities. *Journal of the American Institute of Planners*, 32, 279–88.

Anton, T. J. 1975: *Governing Greater Stockholm: A Study of Policy Development and System Change*. Berkeley: University of California Press.

Applebaum, R. P. 1978: *Size, Growth, and US Cities*. New York: Praeger.

Archbishop of Canterbury's Commission on Urban Priority Areas 1985: *Faith in the City: A Call for Action by Church and Nation*. London: Church House Publishing.

Architectural Review 1957: Counter-Attack: The Next Stage in the Fight against Subtopia. *Architectural Review*, 121, 405–7.

Armstrong, G. and Wilson, M. 1973: Delinquency and some Aspects of Housing. In: Ward, C. (ed.) *Vandalism, 64–84*. London: Architectural Press.

Arnold, J. L. 1971: *The New Deal in the Suburbs: A History of the Greenbelt Town Program 1935–1954*. Columbus, Ohio: Ohio State University Press.

Arnold, J. L. 1973: City Planning in America. In: Mohl, R. A. and Richardson, J. F. (eds.) *The Urban Experience: Themes in American History*, 14–43. Belmont, CA: Wadsworth.

Arnold, J. L. 1983: Greenbelt, Maryland, 1936–1984. *Built Environment*, 9, 198–209.

Ashworth, W. 1954: *The Genesis of British Town Planning: A Study in Economic and Social History of the Nineteenth and Twentieth Centuries*. London: Routledge and Kegan Paul.

Association of London Authorities, Docklands Consultative Committee 1991: *Ten Years of Docklands: How the Cake Was Cut*. London: ALA.

Åström, K. 1967: *City Planning in Sweden*. Stockholm: Swedish Institute.

Atkinson, R. 2003: Domestication by Cappuccino or a Revenge on Urban Space? *Urban Studies*, 40, 1829–43.

Atkinson, R. 2004: The Evidence on the Impact of Gentrification: New Lessons for the Urban Renaissance? *European Journal of Housing Policy*, 4, 107–31.

Automobile Club of Southern California, Engineering Department 1937: *Traffic Survey, Los Angeles Metropolitan Area, 1937*. Los Angeles: The Club.

Aziz, S. 1978: *Rural Development: Learning from China*. New York: Holmes and Meier.

Baker, H. 1944: *Architecture and Personalities*. London: Country Life.

Baker, P. H. 1974: *Urbanization and Political Change: The Politics of Lagos, 1917–1967*. Berkeley and Los Angeles: University of California Press.

Baldwin, R. N. 1971 (1927): *Kropotkin's Revolutionary Pamphlets: A Collection of Writings by Peter Kropotkin*. New York: Vanguard Press. (Repr. 1971: New York: Dover Publications.)

Ballhatchet, K. and Harrison, J. 1980: *The City in South Asia: Pre-Modern and Modern*. London: Curzon Press.

Banfield, E. C. 1965: *Big City Politics: A Comparative Guide to the Political Systems of Atlanta, Boston, Detroit, El Paso, Los Angeles, Miami, Philadelphia, St Louis, Seattle.* New York: Random House.

Banfield, E. C. 1970: *The Unheavenly City: The Nature and Future of Our Urban Crisis.* Boston: Little, Brown.

Bangert, W. 1936: *Baupolitik und Stadtgestaltung in Frankfurt am Main.* Würzburg: K. Triltsch.

Banham, R. 1960: *Theory and Design in the First Machine Age.* London: Architectural Press.

Banham, R. 1971: *Los Angeles: The Architecture of Four Ecologies.* London: Allen Lane.

Banham, R., Barker, P., Hall, P., and Price, C. 1969: Non-Plan: An Experiment in Freedom. *New Society*, 26, 435–43.

Banister, D. 1992: Energy Use, Transportation and Settlement Patterns. In: Breheny, M. J. (ed.) *Sustainable Development and Urban Form* (*European Research in Regional Science, 2*), 160–81. London: Pion.

Banister, D. 1993: Policy Responses in the UK. In: Banister, D. and Button, K. (eds.) *Transport, the Environment and Sustainable Development*, 53–78. London: E. and F. Spon.

Banister, D. and Banister, C. 1995: Energy Consumption in Transport in Great Britain: Macro Level Estimates. *Transportation Research Part A: Policy and Practice*, 29, 21–32.

Banister, D. and Button, K. (eds.) 1993a: *Transport, the Environment and Sustainable Development.* London: E. and F. Spon.

Banister, D. and Button, K. 1993b: Environmental Policy and Transport: An Overview. In: Banister, D. and Button, K. (eds.) *Transport, the Environment and Sustainable Development*, 1–15. London: E. and F. Spon.

Bannon, M. J. 1999: Dublin Town Planning Competition: Ashbee and Chettle's "New Dublin – A Study in Civics." *Planning Perspectives*, 14, 145–62.

Banton, M. 1971: Urbanization and the Colour Line in Africa. In: Turner, V. (ed.) *Colonialism in Africa 1870–1960*, vol. 3. *Profiles of Change: African Society and Colonial Rule*, 256–85. Cambridge: Cambridge University Press.

Barber, W. J. 1967: Urbanisation and Economic Growth: The Cases of Two White Settler Territories. In: Miner, H. (ed.) *The City in Modern Africa*, 91–125. London: Pall Mall Press.

Barker, T. and Sutcliffe, A. (eds.) 1993: *Megalopolis: The Giant City in History.* Basingstoke: Macmillan.

Barker, T. C. and Robbins, M. 1974: *A History of London Transport*, vol. II, *The Twentieth Century to 1970*. London: George Allen and Unwin.

Barkin, W. 1978: Confronting the Separation of Town and Country in Cuba. In: Tabb, W. K. and Sawers, L. (eds.) *Marxism and the Metropolis: New Perspectives in Urban Political Economy*, 317–37. New York: Oxford University Press.

Barman, C. 1979: *The Man Who Built London Transport: A Biography of Frank Pick.* Newton Abbot: David and Charles.

Barnett, H. 1918: The Garden Suburb: Its Past and Plans. In: Anon. (ed.) *Problems of Reconstruction: Lectures and Addresses delivered at the Summer Meeting at the Hampstead Garden Suburb, August 1917*, 198–207. With an Introduction by the Marquess of Crewe, K. G. London: T. Fisher Unwin.

Barrett, B. 1971: *The Inner Suburbs: The Evolution of an Industrial Area.* Melbourne: Melbourne University Press.

Barth, G. 1980: *City People: The Rise of Modern City Culture in Nineteenth-Century America.* Oxford: Oxford University Press.

Bassett, E. M. 1936: *Zoning: The Law, Administration, and Court Decisions during the First Twenty Years*. New York: Russell Sage Foundation.

Bassett, E. M. 1938: *The Master Plan: With a Discussion of the Theory of Community Land Planning Legislation*. New York: Russell Sage Foundation.

Bassett, E. M. 1939: *Autobiography of Edward M. Bassett*. New York: Harbor Press.

Bastié, J. 1964: *La Croissance de la Banlieue Parisienne*. Paris: Presses Universitaires de France.

Batchelor, P. 1969: The Origin of the Garden City Concept of Urban Form. *Journal of the Society of Architectural Historians*, 28, 184–200.

Bater, J. H. 1979: *The Legacy of Autocracy: Environmental Quality in St Petersburg*. In: French, R. A. and Hamilton, F. E. I. *The Socialist City: Spatial Structure and Urban Policy*, 23–48. Chichester: John Wiley & Sons, Ltd.

Bater, J. H. 1984: The Soviet City: Continuity and Change in Privilege and Place. In: Agnew, J., Mercer, J., and Sopher, D. E. (eds.) *The City in Cultural Context*, 134–62. Boston: Allen and Unwin.

Batey, P. 2012: Gordon Stephenson's Reform of the Planning Curriculum: How Liverpool Came to Have the MCD. *Town Planning Review*, 83, 135–63.

Batley, R. 1989: London Docklands: An Analysis of Power Relations between UDCs and Local Government. *Public Administration*, 67, 167–87.

Batty, M. 1976: *Urban Modelling: Algorithms, Calibrations, Predictions*. Cambridge: Cambridge University Press.

Batty, M. 1979: On Planning Processes. In: Goodall, B. and Kirby, A. (eds.) *Resources and Planning*, 17–50. Oxford: Pergamon.

Baudrillard, J. 1988: *America*. London: Verso.

Bauer, C. 1934: *Modern Housing*. Boston and New York: Houghton Mifflin.

Bauman, J. F. 1980: Housing the Urban Poor. *Journal of Urban History*, 6, 211–20.

Bauman, J. F. 1983: Visions of a Post-War Nation: A Perspective on Urban Planning in Philadelphia and the Nation, 1942–1945. In: Krueckeberg, D. A. (ed.) *Introduction to Planning History in the United States*, 170–89. New Brunswick, NJ: Rutgers University, Center for Urban Policy Research.

Bayliss, D. 2001: Revisiting the Cottage Council Estates: England, 1919–39. *Planning Perspectives*, 16, 169–200.

Beaufoy, H. 1997: "Order Out of Chaos": The London Society and the Planning of London 1912–1920. *Planning Perspectives*, 12, 135–64.

Beaufoy, S. G. 1933: Regional Planning, I. The Regional Planning of South East England. *Town Planning Review*, 15, 83–104, 188–214.

Beaujeu-Garnier, J. *et al.* 1978: *La France des villes*, vol. 1, *Le Bassin parisien*. Paris: La Documentation Française.

Beauregard, R. A. 1976: The Occupation of Planning: A View from the Census. *Journal of the American Institute of Planners*, 42, 187–92.

Beckinsale, R. P. and Houston, J. M. (eds.) 1968: *Urbanization and its Problems: Essays in Honour of E. W. Gilbert*. Oxford: Blackwell.

Beevers, R. 1987: *The Garden City Utopia: A Critical Biography of Ebenezer Howard*. London: Macmillan.

Bell, C. and Bell, R. 1969: *City Fathers: The Early History of Town Planning in Britain*. London: Cresset Press.

Bellamy, E. 1888: *Looking Backward*. New York: Ticknor.

Bellush, J. and Hausknecht, M. (eds.) 1967a: *Urban Renewal: People, Politics and Planning.* Garden City: Anchor.

Bellush, J. and Hausknecht, M. 1967b: Urban Renewal: An Historical Overview. In: Bellush, J. and Hausknecht, M. (eds.) *Urban Renewal: People, Politics and Planning,* 3–16. Garden City: Anchor.

Bellush, J. and Hausknecht, M. 1967c: Public Housing: The Contexts of Failure. In: Bellush, J. and Hausknecht, M. (eds.) *Urban Renewal: People, Politics and Planning,* 451–64. Garden City: Anchor.

Benoît-Lévy, G. 1904: *La Cité-Jardin.* Paris: Jouve.

Berg, E. 1979: *Stockholm Town Trails: From the Old Town to the New "City."* Stockholm: Akademilitteratur.

Berger, B. 1960: *Working Class Suburb: A Study of Auto Workers in Suburbia.* Berkeley and Los Angeles: University of California Press.

Berger, H. 1968: *Ostafrikanische Studien: Ernst Weigt zum 60. Geburtstag.* Nürnberg: Friedrich-Alexander-Universität, Wirtschafts- und Sozialgeographische Institut.

Berger-Thimme, D. 1976: *Wohnungsfrage und Sozialstaat: Untersuchen zu den Anfängen staatlicher Wohnungspolitik in Deutschland (1873–1918).* Frankfurt: Peter Lang.

Bergmann, K. 1970: *Agrarromantik und Grossstadtfeindschaft* (Marburger Abhandlungen zur Politischen Wissenschaft, 20). Melsenheim: Verlag Anton Heim.

Berkowitz, B. L. 1984: Economic Development Really Works: Baltimore, Maryland. In: Bingham, R. D. and Blair, J. P. (eds.) *Urban Economic Development (Urban Affairs Annual Reviews,* 27), 201–21. Beverly Hills: Sage.

Berman, D. S. 1969: *Urban Renewal: Bonanza of the Real Estate Business.* Englewood Cliffs, NJ: Prentice Hall.

Berman, M. 1982: *All that Is Solid Melts into Air: The Experience of Modernity.* New York: Simon and Schuster.

Bernstein, R. J. 1976: *The Restructuring of Social and Political Theory.* New York: Harcourt Brace Jovanovich.

Bernstein, R. J. 1985: *Habermas and Modernity.* Cambridge, MA: MIT Press.

Berton, K. 1977: *Moscow: An Architectural History.* London: Studio Vista.

Best, S. and Kellner, D. 1991: *Postmodern Theory: Critical Interrogations.* Basingstoke: Macmillan.

Betjeman, J. 1978: *The Best of Betjeman.* London: J. Murray.

Bettman, A. 1946: *City and Regional Planning Papers.* Edited by Arthur C. Comey. Cambridge, MA: Harvard University Press.

Betts, R. F. 1985: Dakar: Ville Imperiale (1857–1960). In: Ross, R. and Telkamp, G. J. (eds.) *Colonial Cities: Essays on Urbanism in a Colonial Context (Comparative Studies in Colonial History,* vol. 5), 193–206. Dordrecht: Martinus Nijhof.

Biles, R. 1998: New Towns for the Great Society: A Case Study in Politics and Planning. *Planning Perspectives,* 13, 113–32.

Biddulph, M. 2010: Liverpool 2008: Liverpool's Vision and the Decade of Cranes. In: Punter, J. (ed.) *Urban Design and the British Urban Renaissance,* 100–114. Abingdon: Routledge.

Bing, A. M. 1925: Can We Have Garden Cities in America? *The Survey,* 54, 172–3.

Bingham, R. D. 1975: *Public Housing and Urban Renewal: An Analysis of Federal–Local Relations.* New York: Praeger.

Bingham, R. D. and Blair, J. P. (eds.) 1984: Urban Economic Development. *Urban Affairs Annual Reviews,* 27. Beverly Hills: Sage.

Birch, A. and Macmillan, D. A. (eds.) 1962: *The Sydney Scene: 1788–1960*. Melbourne: Melbourne University Press.

Birch, E. I. 2002: Five Generations of the Garden City: Tracing Howard's Legacy in Twentieth-Century Residential Planning. In: Parsons, K. C. and Schuyler, D. (eds.) *From Garden City to Green City: The Legacy of Ebenezer Howard*, 171–200. Baltimore and London: Johns Hopkins University Press.

Birch, E. L. 1980a: Advancing the Art and Science of Planning. *Journal of the American Planning Association*, 46, 22–49.

Birch, E. L. 1980b: Radburn and the American Planning Movement: The Persistence of an Idea. *Journal of the American Planning Association*, 46, 424–39. Repr. 1983: Radburn and the American Planning Movement: The Persistence of an Idea. In: Krueckeberg, D. A. (ed.), 1983c: *Introduction to Planning History in the United States*, 122–51. New Brunswick, NJ: Rutgers University, Center for Urban Policy Research.

Birchall, J. 1995: Co-Partnership Housing and the Garden City Movement. *Planning Perspectives*, 10, 329–58.

Black, J. T., Howland, L. and Rogel, S. L. 1983: *Downtown Retail Development: Conditions for Success and Project Profiles*. Washington: Urban Land Institute.

Blackwell, W. L. 1976: Modernization and Urbanization in Russia: A Comparative View. In: Hamm, M. F. (ed.) *The City in Russian History*, 291–330. Lexington: University of Kentucky Press.

Bliznakov, M. 1976: Urban Planning in the USSR: Integration Theories. In: Hamm, M. F. (ed.) *The City in Russian History*, 243–56. Lexington: University of Kentucky Press.

Blowers, A. 1980: *The Limits of Power: The Politics of Local Planning Policy*. Oxford: Pergamon.

Blowers, A. (ed.) 1993: *Planning for a Sustainable Environment*. London: Earthscan.

Bluestone, B. and Harrison, B. 1982: *The Deindustrialization of America: Plant Closures, Community Abandonment, and the Dismantling of Basic Industry*. New York: Basic Books.

Bluestone, B. and Harrison, B. 1987: The Grim Truth about the Job "Miracle." *The New York Times*, February 1.

Boardman, P. 1944: *Patrick Geddes: Maker of the Future*. Chapel Hill: University of North Carolina Press.

Boardman, P. 1978: *The Worlds of Patrick Geddes: Biologist, Town Planner, Re-educator, Peace Warrior*. London: Routledge and Kegan Paul.

Boddy, M. 1980: *The Building Societies*. London: Macmillan.

Boddy, M., Lovering, J. and Bassett, K. 1986: *Sunbelt City: A Study of Economic Change in Britain's M4 Growth Corridor*. Oxford: Oxford University Press.

Bogle, J. M. L. 1929: *Town Planning: India* (India of Today, vol. IX). Bombay: Oxford University Press.

Boisier, S. 1981: Chile: Continuity and Change – Variations of Centre-Down Strategies under Different Political Regimes. In: Stöhr, W. B. and Taylor, D. R. F. (eds.) *Development from Above or Below? The Dialectics of Regional Planning in Developing Countries*, 401–26. Chichester: John Wiley & Sons, Ltd.

Bolan, R. S. 1967: Emerging Views of Planning. *Journal of the American Institute of Planners*, 33, 233–45.

Bole, A. 1970: *Urbanization in India: An Inventory of Source Materials*. Bombay and New Delhi: Academic Books.

Boneparth, E. (ed.) 1982: *Women Power and Policy*. New York: Pergamon.

Booth, C. 1887: The Inhabitants of Tower Hamlets (School Board Division), their Condition and Occupations. *Journal of the Royal Statistical Society*, 50, 326–91.

Booth, C. 1888: Conditions and Occupations of the People in East London and Hackney, 1887. *Journal of the Royal Statistical Society*, 51, 276–331.

Booth, C. (ed.) 1892: *Life and Labour of the People in London*, vol. I, *East, Central and South London*. London: Macmillan.

Booth, C. 1901: *Improved Means of Locomotion as a First Step towards the Cure of the Housing Difficulties of London*. London: Macmillan.

Booth "General" W. 1890: *In Darkest England and the Way Out*. London: Salvation Army.

Booth, P. 1999: From Regulation to Discretion: The Evolution of Development Control in the British Planning System 1909–1947. *Planning Perspectives*, 14, 277–89.

Booth, P. 2010: Sheffield: Miserable Disappointment No More? In: Punter, J. (ed.) *Urban Design and the British Urban Renaissance*, 85–99. Abingdon: Routledge.

Borchert, J. 1980: *Alley Life in Washington: Family, Community, Religion, and Folklife in the City, 1850–1970*. Urbana: University of Illinois Press.

Borchert, J. R. 1962: The Soviet City. In: Holt, R. T. and Turner, J. E. *Soviet Union: Paradox and Change*, 35–61. New York: Holt, Rinehart, Winston.

Bose, A. 1973: *Studies in India's Urbanization 1901–1971*. Bombay and New Delhi: Tata McGraw Hill.

Bottles, S. L. 1987: *Los Angeles and the Automobile: The Making of the Modern City*. Berkeley and Los Angeles: University of California Press.

Bournville Village Trust 1941: *When We Build Again: A Study Based on Research into Conditions of Living and Working in Birmingham*. London: George Allen and Unwin.

Bowden, P. 1979: *North Rhine Westphalia: North England: Regional Development in Action*. London: Anglo-German Foundation for the Study of Industrial Society.

Bowley, M. 1945: *Housing and the State, 1919–1944*. London: George Allen and Unwin.

Bowly, D., Jr 1978: *The Poorhouse: Subsidized Housing in Chicago, 1895–1976*. Carbondale: Southern Illinois University Press.

Boyd, R. 1952: *Australia's Home: Its Origins, Builders and Occupiers*. Melbourne: Melbourne University Press.

Boyd, R. 1960: *The Australian Ugliness*. Melbourne: Cheshire.

Boyer, M. C. 1983: *Dreaming the Rational City: The Myth of American City Planning*. Cambridge, MA: MIT Press.

Boyer, P. S. 1978: *Urban Masses and Moral Order in America, 1820–1920*. Cambridge, MA: Harvard University Press.

Bradley, K. 2009: "Growing up with a City": Exploring Settlement Youth Work in London and Chicago, c.1880–1940. *The London Journal*, 34, 285–298.

Brand, R. R. 1976: The Urban Housing Challenge. In: Knight, C. G. and Newman, J. L. (eds.) *Contemporary Africa: Geography and Change*, 321–35. Englewood Cliffs: Prentice Hall.

Brandenburg, A. and Materna, J. 1980: Zum Aufbruch in die Fabrikgesellschaft: Arbeiterkolonien. *Archiv für die Geschichte des Widerstandes und der Arbeit*, 1, 35–48.

Branford, V. 1914: *Interpretations and Forecasts: A Study of Survivals and Tendencies in Contemporary Society*. New York and London: Mitchell Kennerley.

Branford, V. and Geddes, P. 1917: *The Coming Polity: A Study in Reconstruction*. (The Making of the Future.) London: Williams and Norgate.

Branford, V. and Geddes, P. 1919: *Our Social Inheritance*. London: Williams and Norgate.

Breese, G. (ed.) 1969: *The City in Newly Developing Countries: Readings on Urbanism and Urbanization*. Englewood Cliffs: Prentice Hall.

Breheny, M. 1991: Contradictions of the Compact City. *Town and Country Planning*, 60, 21.

Breheny, M. 1992a: The Contradictions of the Compact City: A Review. In: Breheny, M. J. (ed.) *Sustainable Development and Urban Form* (*European Research in Regional Science, 2*), 138–59. London: Pion.

Breheny, M. J. (ed.) 1992b: *Sustainable Development and Urban Form* (*European Research in Regional Science, 2*). London: Pion.

Breheny, M. 1995a: Counter-Urbanisation and Sustainable Urban Forms. In: Brotchie, J. F., Batty, M., Blakely, E., Hall, P., and Newton, P. (eds.) *Cities in Competition*, 402–29. Melbourne: Longman Australia.

Breheny, M. 1995b: The Compact City and Transport Energy Consumption. *Transactions of the Institute of British Geographers*, 20, 81–101.

Breheny, M. 1995c: Transport Planning, Energy and Development: Improving our Understanding of the Basic Relationships. In: Banister, D. (ed.) *Transport and Urban Development*, 89–95. London: Spon.

Breheny, M. and Button, K. (eds.) 1993: *Transport, the Environment and Sustainable Development*. London: Spon.

Breheny, M., Gent, T., and Lock, D. 1993: *Alternative Development Patterns: New Settlements*. London: HMSO.

Breheny, M. and Hall, P. 1984: The Strange Death of Strategic Planning and the Victory of the Know-Nothing School. *Built Environment*, 10, 95–9.

Breheny, M. and Hall, P. 1996: Four Million Households – Where Will They Go? *Town and Country Planning*, 65, 39–41.

Breheny, M. and Hooper, A. (eds.) 1985: *Rationality in Planning: Critical Essays on the Role of Rationality in Urban and Regional Planning*. London: Pion.

Breheny, M. and Rookwood, R. 1993: Planning the Sustainable City Region. In: Blowers, A. (ed.) *Planning for a Sustainable Environment*, 150–89. London: Earthscan.

Brindley, T., Rydin, Y., and Stoker, G. 1989: *Remaking Planning: The Politics of Urban Change in the Thatcher Years*. London: Unwin Hyman.

Bristow, R. 1984: *Land-Use Planning in Hong Kong: History, Policies and Procedures*. Hong Kong: Oxford University Press.

Brodsly, D. 1981: *L. A. Freeway: An Appreciative Essay*. Berkeley and Los Angeles: University of California Press.

Bromley, R. and Gerry, C. (eds.), 1979: *Casual Work and Poverty in Third World Cities*. Chichester: John Wiley & Sons, Ltd.

Brotchie, J. F., Batty, M., Blakely, E., Hall, P., and Newton, P. (eds.) 1995: *Cities in Competition*. Melbourne: Longman Australia.

Brotchie, J. F., Newton, P., Hall, P., and Dickey, J. (eds.) 1999: *East West Perspectives on 21ˢᵗ Century Urban Development: Sustainable Eastern and Western Cities in the New Millennium*. Aldershot: Ashgate.

Brown, K. D. 1977: *John Burns*. London: Royal Historical Society.

Brownell, B. A. 1980: Urban Planning, The Planning Profession, and the Motor Vehicle in early Twentieth-Century America. In: Cherry, G. E. (ed.) *Shaping an Urban World*, 59–77. London: Mansell.

Brownill, S. 1990: *Developing London's Docklands: Another Great Planning Disaster?* London: Paul Chapman.

Brush, J. E. 1962: The Morphology of Indian Cities. In: Turner, R. (ed.) *India's Urban Future*, 57–70. Berkeley: University of California Press.

Brush, J. E. 1968: Spatial Patterns of Population in Indian Cities. *Geographical Review*, 58, 362–91.

Bruton, M. 1975: *Introduction to Transportation Planning*. Second edition. London: Hutchinson.

Bryson, L. and Thompson, F. 1972: *An Australian Newtown: Life and Leadership in a Working-Class Suburb*. Harmondsworth: Penguin.

Budd, L. and Whimster, S. 1992: *Global Finance and Urban Living: A Study of Metropolitan Change*. London: Routledge.

Buder, S. 1990: *Visionaries and Planners: The Garden City Movement and the Modern Community*. New York: Oxford University Press.

Bull, W. J. 1901: A Green Girdle round London. *The Sphere*, 5, 128–9.

Bullock, N. 1978: Housing in Frankfurt 1925 to 1931 and the New Wohnkultur. *Architectural Review*, 113, 335–42.

Bullock, N. 1987: Plans for Post-War Housing in the UK: The Case for Mixed Development and the Flat. *Planning Perspectives*, 2, 71–98.

Bunker, R. 1988: Systematic Colonization and Town Planning in Australia and New Zealand. *Planning Perspectives*, 3, 59–80.

Bunker, R. 1998: Process and Product in the Foundation and Laying Out of Adelaide. *Planning Perspectives*, 13, 243–55.

Bunker, R. 2002: In the Shadow of the City: The Fringe Around the Australian Metropolis in the 1950s. *Planning Perspectives*, 17, 61–82.

Bunker, R. 2008: Why and How Did Adelaide Come About? *Planning Perspectives*, 23, 233–40.

Burgess, E. W. 1925: The Growth of the City: An Introduction to a Research Project. In: Park, R. E., Burgess, E. W., and McKenzie, R. D. *The City*, 47–62. Chicago: University of Chicago Press.

Burgess, R. 1978: Petty Commodity Housing or Dweller Control? A Critique of John Turner's Views on Housing Policy. *World Development*, 6, 1105–34.

Burgess, R. 1982: Self-Help Housing Advocacy: A Curious Form of Radicalism. A Critique of the Work of J. F. C. Turner. In: Ward, P. M. (ed.) *Self-Help Housing: A Critique*, 56–97. London: Mansell.

Burnett, J. 1978: *A Social History of Housing 1815–1970*. Newton Abbot: David and Charles.

Burnham, D. H. and Bennett, E. H. 1970 (1909): *Plan of Chicago*. New York: Da Capo Press.

Burnham, D. H. and Bennett, E. H. 1971 (1905): *Report on a Plan for San Francisco*. San Francisco: Sunset Press. (Repr. 1971, with introduction by James R. McCarthy. Berkeley: Urban Books.)

Burnham, D. H., Jr and Kingery, R. 1956: *Planning the Region of Chicago*. Chicago: Chicago Regional Planning Association.

Burnley, I. H. (ed.) 1974: *Urbanization in Australia: The Post-War Experience*. London: Cambridge University Press.

Burns, J. 1908: Speech on Housing, Town Planning, etc., Bill. *Commons Hansard*, Fourth series, 188, 947–68.

Butcher, G., Collis, P., Glen, A., and Sills, P. 1980: *Community Groups in Action: Case Studies and Analysis*. London: Routledge and Kegan Paul.

Butler, C. *et al*. 1933: The Planned Community. *Architectural Forum*, 58, 253–74.

Butler, S. M. 1981: *Enterprise Zones: Greenlining the Inner Cities*. New York: Universe Books.

Cadbury, G., Jr 1915: *Town Planning: With Special Reference to the Birmingham Schemes*. London: Longmans, Green.

Cairncross, F. 1997: *The Death of Distance: How the Communications Revolution Will Change our Lives*. London: Orion.

Calabi, D. 1984: Italy. In: Wynn, M. (ed.) *Planning and Urban Growth in Southern Europe*, 37–69. London: Mansell.

Calabi, D. 1996: Marcel Poëte: Pioneer of "l'Urbanisme" and Defender of "l'Histoire des Villes." *Planning Perspectives*, 11, 413–36.

Caldenby, C. and Rundberg, E. 1982: Katalog Backström & Reinius. *Arkitektur*, 82/6, 10–32.

Callow, A. B. 1969: *American Urban History: An Interpretative Reader with Commentaries*. New York: Oxford University Press.

Calthorpe, P. 1993: *The Next American Metropolis: Ecology, Community, and the American Dream*. Princeton: Princeton Architectural Press.

Calthorpe, P. and Fulton, W. 2001: *The Regional City: Planning for the End of Sprawl*. Washington: Island Press.

Carnoy, M. 1984: *The State and Political Theory*. Princeton: Princeton University Press.

Caro, R. A. 1974: *The Power Broker: Robert Moses and the Fall of New York*. New York: Alfred A. Knopf.

Carr, M. C. 1982: The Development and Character of a Metropolitan Suburb: Bexley, Kent. In: Thompson, F. M. L. (ed.) *The Rise of Suburbia*, 212–67. Leicester: Leicester University Press.

Carrothers, G. A. P. 1956: An Historical Review of the Gravity and Potential Concepts of Human Interaction. *Journal of the American Institute of Planners*, 22, 94–102.

Carver, H. 1962: *Cities in the Suburbs*. Toronto: University of Toronto Press.

Cassidy, R. 1980: *Livable Cities: A Grass-Roots Guide to Rebuilding Urban America*. New York: Holt, Rinehart and Winston.

Castells, M. 1977: *The Urban Question: A Marxist Approach*. London: Edward Arnold.

Castells, M. 1978: *City, Class and Power*. London: Macmillan.

Castells, M. 1983: *The City and the Grassroots: A Cross-Cultural Theory of Urban Social Movements*. London: Edward Arnold.

Castells, M. 1989: *The Informational City: Information Technology, Economic Restructuring and the Urban–Regional Process*. Oxford: Basil Blackwell.

Castells, M. 1996: *The Information Age: Economy, Society, and Culture*, vol. I, *The Rise of the Network Society*. Oxford: Blackwell.

Castells, M. 1997: *The Information Age: Economy, Society, and Culture*, vol. II, *The Power of Identity*. Oxford: Blackwell.

Castells, M. 1998: *The Information Age: Economy, Society, and Culture*, vol. III, *End of Millennium*. Oxford: Blackwell.

Castells, M. and Hall, P. 1994: *Technopoles of the World: The Making of 21st-Century Industrial Complexes*. London: Routledge.

Castells, M., Goh, L., and Kwok, R. Y. -W. 1990: *The Shep Kip Mei Syndrome: Economic Development and Public Housing in Hong Kong and Singapore*. London: Pion.

Catanese, A. J. and Steiss, A. W. 1970: *Systemic Planning: Theory and Application*. Lexington: D. C. Heath.

Cavalcanti, M. de B. U. 1997: Urban Reconstruction and Autocratic Regimes: Ceausescu's Bucharest in its Historic Context. *Planning Perspectives*, 12, 71–109.

Cederna, A. 1981: *Mussolini Urbanista: Lo sventramento di Roma negli anni del Consenso.* Roma: Laterza.

Cerillo, A., Jr 1977: The Impact of Reform Democracy: Early Twentieth Century Municipal Government in New York City. In: Ebner, M. E. and Tobin, E. M. *The Age of Urban Reform: New Perspectives on the Progressive Era*, 68–85. Port Washington, NY: Kennikat.

Cervero, R. 1986: *Suburban Gridlock*. New Brunswick: Center for Urban Policy Studies.

Chadwick, G. 1971: *A Systems View of Planning: Towards a Theory of the Urban and Regional Planning Process*. Oxford: Pergamon.

Chandler, T. and Fox, G. 1974: *3000 Years of Urban Growth*. London: Academic Press.

Chapman, S. D. (ed.) 1971: *The History of Working-Class Housing*. Newton Abbot: David and Charles.

Chase, S. 1925: Coals to Newcastle. *The Survey*, 54, 143–6.

Chase, S. 1929: *Men and Machines*. New York: Macmillan.

Chase, S. 1931: *The Nemesis of American Business and Other Essays*. New York: Macmillan.

Chase, S. 1932: *A New Deal*. New York: The Macmillan Company.

Chase, S. 1934: *The Economy of Abundance*. New York: Macmillan.

Chase, S. 1936: *Rich Land Poor Land: A Study of Waste in the Natural Resources of America*. New York and London: Whittlesey House.

Cheape, C. W. 1980: *Moving the Masses: Urban Public Transit in New York, Boston, and Philadelphia, 1880–1912*. Cambridge, MA: Harvard University Press.

Checkoway, B. 1984: Large Builders, Federal Housing Programs, and Postwar Suburbanization. In: Tabb, W. K. and Sawers, L. (eds.) *Marxism and the Metropolis: New Perspectives in Urban Political Economy*, 152–73. New York: Oxford University Press.

Checkoway, B. and Patton, C. V. (eds.) 1985: *The Metropolitan Midwest: Policy Problems and Prospects for Change*. Urbana: University of Illinois Press.

Cherry, G. E. 1972: *Urban Change and Planning: A History of Urban Development in Britain since 1750*. Henley: Foulis.

Cherry, G. E. 1974: *The Evolution of British Town Planning*. London: Leonard Hill.

Cherry, G. E. (ed.) 1980a: *Shaping an Urban World*. London: Mansell.

Cherry, G. E. 1980b: The Place of Neville Chamberlain in British Town Planning. In: Cherry, G. E. (ed.) *Shaping an Urban World*, 161–79. London: Mansell.

Cherry, G. E. 1988: *Cities and Plans: The Shaping of Urban Britain in the Nineteenth and Twentieth Centuries*. London and New York: E. Arnold.

Cherry, G. E. 1994: *Birmingham: A Study in Geography, History and Planning*. Chichester: John Wiley & Sons, Ltd.

Cherry, G. E. 1996: *Town Planning in Britain since 1900: The Rise and Fall of the Planning Ideal*. Oxford: Blackwell.

Cherry, G. E. and Penny, L. 1986: *Holford: A Study in Architecture, Planning and Civic Design*. London: Mansell.

Cherry, G. E. and Rogers, A. 1996: *Rural Change and Planning: England and Wales in the Twentieth Century*. London: Spon.

Cheshire, P. and Hay, D. 1987: *Urban Problems in Europe*. London: Allen and Unwin.

Chicago Commission on Race Relations 1922: *The Negro in Chicago: A Study of Race Relations and a Race Riot*. Chicago: University of Chicago Press.

Childs, M. W. 1936: *Sweden: The Middle Way*. London: Faber and Faber.

Choi, C. Y. and Chan, Y. K. 1979: Housing Development and Housing Policy in Hong Kong. In: Lin, T. -B., Lee, R. P. L., and Simonis, U. -E. (eds.) *Hong Kong: Economic, Social and Political Studies in Development,* 183–202. Folkestone: Dawson.

Choudhuri, K., 1973: *Calcutta: Story of its Government.* New Delhi: Orient-Longman.

Christaller, W. 1966 (1933): *Central Places in Southern Germany.* Translated by C. W. Baskin. Englewood Cliffs: Prentice Hall.

Christensen, T. 1979: *Neighbourhood Survival.* Dorchester: Prism Press.

Christopher, A. J. 1977: Early Settlement and the Cadastral Framework. In: Kay, G. and Smout, M. A. H. (eds.) *Salisbury: A Geographical Survey of the Capital of Rhodesia,* 14–25. London: Hodder and Stoughton.

Chudacoff, H. P. 1975: *The Evolution of American Urban Society.* Englewood Cliffs: Prentice Hall.

Church, A. 1992: Land and Property: The Pattern and Process of Development from 1981. In: Ogden, P. (ed.) *London Docklands: The Challenge of Development,* 43–51. Cambridge: Cambridge University Press.

Churchill, H. 1983: Henry Wright: 1878–1936. In: Krueckeberg, D. A. (ed.) *Introduction to Planning History in the United States,* 208–24. New Brunswick, NJ: Rutgers University, Center for Urban Policy Research.

Cicin-Sain, B. 1980: The Costs and Benefits of Neighborhood Revitalization. In: Rosenthal, D. B. (ed.) *Urban Revitalization* (*Urban Affairs Annual Reviews,* no. 18), 49–75. Beverly Hills: Sage.

Ciucci, G. 1979: The City in Agrarian Ideology and Frank Lloyd Wright: Origins and Development of Broadacres. In: Ciucci, G., Dal Co, F., Manieri-Elia, M., and Tafuri, M. *The American City: From the Civil War to the New Deal,* 293–387. Cambridge, MA: MIT Press.

Ciucci, G., Dal Co, F., Manieri-Elia, M., and Tafuri, M., 1979: *The American City: From the Civil War to the New Deal.* Cambridge, MA: MIT Press.

Clapson, M. 1998: *Invincible Green Suburbs, Brave New Towns: Social Change and Urban Dispersal in Postwar England.* Manchester: Manchester University Press.

Clapson, M. 2002: Suburban Paradox? Planners' Intentions and Residents' Preferences in Two New Towns of the 1960s: Reston, Virginia and Milton Keynes, England. *Planning Perspectives,* 17, 145–62.

Clark, C. 1940: *The Conditions of Economic Progress.* London: Macmillan.

Clavel, P. 1986: *The Progressive City: Planning and Participation, 1969–1984.* New Brunswick: Rutgers University Press.

Clavel, P. 2002: Ebenezer Howard and Patrick Geddes: Two Approaches to City Development. In: Parsons, K. C. and Schuyler, D. (eds.) *From Garden City to Green City: The Legacy of Ebenezer Howard,* 38–57. Baltimore and London: Johns Hopkins University Press.

Clavel, P., Forester, J., and Goldsmith, W. W. (eds.) 1980: *Urban and Regional Planning in an Age of Austerity.* New York: Pergamon.

Clawson, M. 1971: *Suburban Land Conversion in the United States: An Economic and Governmental Process.* Baltimore: Johns Hopkins University Press.

Clawson, M. 1981: *New Deal Planning: The National Resources Planning Board.* Baltimore: Johns Hopkins University Press.

Clawson, M. and Hall, P. 1973: *Planning and Urban Growth: An Anglo-American Comparison.* Baltimore: Johns Hopkins University Press.

Cloher, D. U. 1975: A Perspective on Australian Urbanization. In: Powell, J. M. and Williams, M. *Australian Space, Australian Time: Geographical Perspectives,* 104–49. Melbourne: Oxford University Press.

Cohen, S. S. and Zysman, J. 1987: *Manufacturing Matters: The Myth of the Post-Industrial Economy*. New York: Basic Books.

Coleman, A. 1985: *Utopia on Trial: Vision and Reality in Planned Housing*. London: Hilary Shipman.

Coleman, B. I. (ed.) 1973: *The Idea of the City in Nineteenth-Century Britain*. London: Routledge and Kegan Paul.

Collings, T. (ed.) 1987: *Stevenage 1946–1986: Images of the first New Town*. Stevenage: SPA Books.

Collins, J. 1969: *Lusaka: The Myth of the Garden City*. University of Zambia Institute of Social Research. (*Zambian Urban Studies*, no. 2.)

Collins, J. 1980: Lusaka: Urban Planning in a British Colony, 1931–64. In: Cherry, G. E. (ed.) *Shaping an Urban World*, 227–52. London: Mansell.

Collins, M. 1994: Land-Use Planning since 1947. In: Simmie, J. (ed.) *Planning London*, 90–140. London: UCL Press.

Colomb, C. 2007: Unpacking New Labour's "Urban Renaissance" Agenda: Towards a Socially Sustainable Reurbanization of British cities? *Planning Practice & Research*, 22, 1–24.

Colomb, C. 2011: Culture in the City, Culture for the City? The Political Construction of the Trickle-Down in Cultural Regeneration Strategies in Roubaix, France. *Town Planning Review*, 82, 77–98.

Comer, J. P. 1969: The Dynamics of Black and White Violence. In: Graham, H. D. and Gurr, T. R. (eds.) *Violence in America: Historical and Comparative Perspectives*, 341–54. 2 vols. Washington, DC: Government Printing Office.

Comerio, M. C. 1984: Community Design: Idealism and Entrepreneurship. *Journal of Architectural and Planning Research*, 1, 227–43.

Comhaire, J. 1961: Leopoldville and Lagos: Comparative Survey of Urban Condition in 1960. *Economic Bulletin for Africa*, 1/2, 50–65.

Commonwealth of Australia Department of Home Affairs 1913: *The Federal Capital: Report Explanatory of the Preliminary General Plan*. (C. 9681.) Melbourne: Albert J. Mullett, Government Printer.

Condit, C. W. 1973: *Chicago, 1910–29: Building, Planning, and Urban Technology*. Chicago and London: Chicago University Press.

Condit, C. W. 1974: *Chicago, 1930–1970: Building, Planning, and Urban Technology*. Chicago and London: Chicago University Press.

Conekin, B. 1999: "Here is the Modern World Itself": The Festival of Britain's Representations of the Future. In: Conekin, B., Mort, F., and Waters, C. (eds.) *Moments of Modernity: Reconstructing Britain 1945–1964*, 228–46. London and New York: Rivers Oram Press.

Conkin, P. K. 1959: *Tomorrow a New World: The New Deal Community Program*. Ithaca: Cornell University Press.

Conkin, P. K. 1983: Intellectual and Political Roots. In: Hargrove, E. C. and Conkin, P. K. (eds.) *TVA: Fifty Years of Grass-Roots Bureaucracy*, 3–34. Urbana: University of Illinois Press.

Connolly, P. 1982: Uncontrolled Settlements and Self-Build: What Kind of Solution? The Mexico City Case. In: Ward, P. M. (ed.) *Self-Help Housing: A Critique*, 141–74. London: Mansell.

Consortium Developments 1985: *Tillingham Hall Outline Plan*. London: Consortium Developments.

Cook, A., Gittell, M., and Mack, H. (eds.) 1973: *City Life, 1865–1900: Views of Urban America*. New York: Praeger.

Cook, P. 1983: Cook's Grand Tour. *Architectural Review*, 174/10, 32–42.

Cooke, C. 1977: Activities of the Garden City Movement in Russia. *Transactions of the Martin Centre for Architectural and Urban Studies*, 1, 225–49.

Cooke, C. 1978: Russian Responses to the Garden City Idea. *Architectural Review*, 163, 354–63.

Cooke, P. 1990: *Back to the Future: Modernity, Postmodernity and Locality*. London: Unwin Hyman.

Cooke, P. N. 1983: *Theories of Planning and Spatial Development*. London: Hutchinson.

Cooley, C. H. 1909: *Social Organization: A Study of the Larger Mind*. New York: Charles Scribner's Sons.

Cooley, C. H. 1918: *Social Process*. New York: Charles Scribner's Sons.

Cooney, E. W. 1974: High Flats in Local Authority Housing in England and Wales since 1945. In: Sutcliffe, A. (ed.) *Multi-Storey Living: The British Working-Class Experience*, 151–80. London: Croon Helm.

Co-Partnership Tenants' Housing Council 1906: *Garden Suburbs, Villages and Homes: All about Co-Partnership Houses*. London: The Council.

Coppock, J. T. and Prince, H. (eds.), 1964: *Greater London*. London: Faber and Faber.

Council for the Preservation of Rural England: "Penn Country" Branch 1933: *The Penn Country of Buckinghamshire*. London: CPRE.

Council for the Preservation of Rural England: Thames Valley Branch 1929: *The Thames Valley from Cricklade to Staines*. Prepared by the Earl of Mayo, S. D. Adshead and Patrick Abercrombie. London: University of London Press.

Creese, W. L. 1966: *The Search for Environment: The Garden City Before and After*. New Haven: Yale University Press.

Creese, W. L. (ed.) 1967: *The Legacy of Raymond Unwin: A Human Pattern for Planning*. Cambridge, MA: MIT Press.

Creese, W. L. 1990: *TVA's Public Planning: The Vision, The Reality*. Knoxville: University of Tennessee Press.

Creese, W. L. 1992: *The Search for Environment: The Garden City Before and After*. Second edition. Baltimore and London: Johns Hopkins University Press.

Crossman, R. H. S. 1975: *The Diaries of a Cabinet Minister*, vol. 1, *Minister of Housing 1964–66*. London: Hamish Hamilton and Jonathan Cape.

Crow, A. 1911: Town Planning in Old and Congested Areas, with Special Reference to London. In: Royal Institute of British Architects *Town Planning Conference – Transactions*, 407–26. London: RIBA.

Crow, S. 1996: Development Control: The Child that Grew Up in the Cold. *Planning Perspectives*, 11, 399–411.

Crump, S. 1962: *Ride the Big Red Cars: How Trolleys Helped Build Southern California*. Los Angeles: Crest Publications.

Cullen, G. 1953: Prairie Planning in the New Towns. *Architectural Review*, 114, 33–6.

Cullingworth, J. B. 1979: *Environmental Planning* (Peacetime History), vol. III, *New Towns Policy*. London: HMSO.

Cullingworth, J. B. 1993: *The Political Economy of Planning: American Land Use Planning in Comparative Perspective*. New York and London: Routledge.

Cullingworth, J. B. 1997: *Planning in the USA: Policies, Issues and Processes*. London: Routledge.

Cullingworth, J. B. (ed.) 1999: *British Planning: Fifty Years of Urban and Regional Policy*. London: Athlone.

Culpin, E. G. 1913: *The Garden City Movement Up-To-Date*. London: Garden Cities and Town Planning Association.

Cunningham, S. M. 1980: Brazilian Cities Old and New: Growth and Planning Experiences. In: Cherry, G. E. (ed.) *Shaping an Urban World*, 181–202. London: Mansell.

Curl, J. S. 1970: *European Cities and Society: A Study of the Influence of Political Change on Town Design*. London: Leonard Hill.

Dahl, R. A. 1961: *Who Governs? Democracy and Power in an American City*. New Haven and London: Yale University Press.

Dakhil, F. H., Ural, O., and Tewfik, M. F. 1979: *Housing Problems in Developing Countries*. (Proceedings IAHS International Conference 1978.) 2 vols. Chichester: John Wiley & Sons, Ltd.

Dal Co, F. 1979: From Parks to the Region: Progressive Ideology and the Reform of the American City. In: Ciucci, G., Dal Co, F., Manieri-Elia, M., and Tafuri, M. *The American City: From the Civil War to the New Deal*, 143–291. Cambridge, MA: MIT Press.

Dannell, G. 1981: Planering viden skiljeväg. *Plan*, 35, 52–6.

Darley, G. 1975: *Villages of Vision*. London: Architectural Press.

Daun, Å. 1985: *Setbacks and Advances in the Swedish Housing Market*. (*Current Sweden*, 331.) Stockholm: Swedish Institute.

Daunton, M. J. 1983: *House and Home in the Victorian City: Working-Class Housing 1850–1914*. London: Edward Arnold.

Daunton, M. J. (ed.) 1984: *Councillors and Tenants: Local Authority Housing in English Cities, 1919–1939*. Leicester: Leicester University Press.

Davidoff, P. 1965: Advocacy and Pluralism in Planning. *Journal of the American Institute of Planners*, 31, 186–97.

Davies, J. C. 1969: The J-Curve of Rising and Declining Satisfactions as a Cause of Some Great Revolutions and a Contained Rebellion. In: Graham, H. D. and Gurr, T. R. (eds.) *Violence in America: Historical and Comparative Perspectives*, 547–76. 2 vols. Washington, DC: Government Printing Office.

Davies, R. O. 1975: *The Age of Asphalt: The Automobile, the Freeway, and the Condition of Metropolitan America*. Philadelphia: J. B. Lippincott.

Davis, A. F. 1967: *Spearheads for Reform: The Social Settlements and the Progressive Movement, 1890–1914*. New York: Oxford University Press.

Davis, A. F. 1983: Playgrounds, Housing, and City Planning. In: Krueckeberg, D. A. (ed.) *Introduction to Planning History in the United States*, 73–87. New Brunswick, NJ: Rutgers University, Center for Urban Policy Research.

Davis, D. H. 1969: *Lusaka, Zambia: Some Town Planning Problems in an African City at Independence*. University of Zambia, Institute of Social Research. (*Zambian Urban Studies*, no. 1.)

Davis, M. 1990: *City of Quartz: Excavating the Future in Los Angeles*. London: Verso.

Davison, G. 1979: Australian Urban History: A Progress Report. *Urban History Yearbook 1979*. Leicester: Leicester University Press, 100–9.

Davoudi, S. 2000: Sustainability: A New Vision for the British Planning System. *Planning Perspectives*, 15, 123–37.

Davoudi, S. 2005: Understanding Territorial Cohesion. *Planning Practice & Research*, 20, 433–41.

Davoudi, S. and Pendlebury, J. 2010: The Evolution of Planning as an Academic Discipline. *Town Planning Review*, 81, 613–45.

Day, A. F. 1916: *John C. F. S. Day: His Forbears and Himself: A Biographical Study by One of his Sons*. London: Heath, Cranton.

De Carlo, G. 1948: The Housing Problem in Italy. *Freedom*, 9/12, 2, and 9/13, 2.

De Carlo, G. 1980: An Architecture of Participation. *Perspecta*, 17, 74–9.

Deakin, D. (ed.) 1989: *Wythenshawe: The Story of a Garden City*. Chichester: Phillimore.

Dear, S. and Allen, M. J. 1981: Towards a Framework for Analysis. In: Dear, M. S. and Scott, A. J. (eds.) *Urbanization and Urban Planning in Capitalist Society*, 3–16. London: Methuen.

Dear, M. S. and Scott, A. J. (eds.), 1981: *Urbanization and Urban Planning in Capitalist Society*. London: Methuen.

Debord, G. 1970: *Society of the Spectacle*. Detroit: Black & Red. (A Black & Red Unauthorized Translation.)

Debord, G. 1990: *Comments on the Society of the Spectacle*. London: Verso.

DeForest, R. W. and Veiller, L. (eds.) 1903: *The Tenement House Problem: Including the Report of the New York State Tenement House Commission of 1900*. 2 vols. New York: Macmillan.

Defries, A. 1927: *The Interpreter Geddes: The Man and his Gospel*. London: George Routledge and Sons.

Degen, M. 2008: *Sensing Cities: Regenerating Public Life in Barcelona and Manchester*. Abingdon: Routledge.

Dehaene, M. 2004: Urban Lessons for the Modern Planner: Patrick Abercrombie and the Study of Urban Development. *Town Planning Review*, 75, 1–30.

Delafons, J. 1997: *Politics and Preservation: A Policy History of the Built Heritage 1882–1996*. London: Spon.

Delafons, J. 1998: Reforming the British Planning System 1964–5: The Planning Advisory Group and the Genesis of the Planning Act of 1968. *Planning Perspectives*, 13, 373–87.

Delouvrier, P. 1972: Paris. In: Robson, W. A. and Regan, D. E., (eds.) *Great Cities of the World*, II, 731–71. London: George Allen and Unwin.

Dennis, N. 1968: The Popularity of the Neighbourhood Community Idea. In: Pahl, R. E. (ed.) *Readings in Urban Sociology*, 74–92. Oxford: Pergamon.

Dennis, R. 2008: *Cities in Modernity: Representations and Productions of Metropolitan Space, 1840–1930*. Cambridge: Cambridge University Press.

Derthick, M. 1972: *New Towns In-Town: Why a Federal Program Failed*. Washington, DC: The Urban Institute.

Dhuys, J. -F. 1983: Et si M. Chirac avait raison? *Macadam*, 4, 9.

Diamond, S. and Burke, F. G. 1966: *The Transformation of East Africa: Studies in Political Anthropology*. New York: Basic Books.

Didion, J. 1970: *Play It as It Lays*. New York: Farrar, Strauss and Giroux.

Dietrich, R. 1960: *Berlin: Neun Kapitel seiner Geschichte*. Berlin: Walter de Gruyter.

Dimaio, A. J. 1974: *Soviet Urban Housing: Problems and Politics*. New York: Praeger.

Dix, G. 1978: Little Plans and Noble Diagrams. *Town Planning Review*, 49, 329–52.

Dobby, E. H. G. 1940: Singapore: Town and Country. *Geographical Review*, 30, 84–109.

Dobriner, W. M. 1977: The Suburban Evangel. In: Allen, I. L. (ed.) *New Towns and the Suburban Dream: Ideology and Utopia in Planning and Development*, 121–40. Port Washington: Kennikat.

Docklands Forum, Birkbeck College 1990: *Employment in Docklands*. London: Docklands Forum.

Docklands Joint Committee 1976: *London Docklands Strategic Plan*. London: Docklands Development Team.

Dodd, K. S. 1933: Planning in the USSR. *Journal of the Town Planning Institute*, 20, 34–53.

Dolce, P. C. (ed.) 1976: *Suburbia: The American Dream and Dilemma*. Garden City, NY: Anchor.

Donnison, D. V. and Eversley, D. 1973: *London: Urban Patterns, Problems, and Policies*. London: Heinemann.

Dorsett, L. W. 1968: *The Challenge of the City, 1860–1910*. Lexington: D. C. Heath.

Dove, D. 1976: *Preserving the Urban Environment: How to Stop Destroying Cities*. Philadelphia: Dorrance and Co.

Dowall, D. 1984: *The Suburban Squeeze: Land Conversion and Regulation in the San Francisco Bay Area*. Berkeley: University of California Press.

Downs, A. 1957: *An Economic Theory of Democracy*. New York: Harper and Brothers.

Drake, S. and Cayton, H. R. 1945: *Black Metropolis: A Study of Negro Life in a Northern City*. New York: Harcourt Brace.

Draper, J. E. 1982: *Edward H. Bennett: Architect and City Planner, 1874–1954*. Chicago: Art Institute of Chicago.

Dreiser, T. 1947: *The Stoic*. Garden City: Doubleday.

Du Bois, W. E. B. 1899: *The Philadelphia Negro: A Social Study*. Publications of the University of Pennsylvania: Series in Political Economy and Public Law. Philadelphia: The University.

Du Bois, W. E. B. 1920: *Darkwater: Voices from within the Veil*. London: Constable.

Duany, A., Plater-Zyberk, E., and Speck, J. 2000: *Suburban Nation: The Rise of Sprawl and the Decline of the American Dream*. New York: North Point Press.

Dubech, I. and D'Espezel, P. 1931: *Histoire de Paris*. 2 vols. Paris: Les Éditions Pittoresques.

Duhl, L. J. (ed.) 1963: *The Urban Condition: People and Policy in the Metropolis*. New York: Basic Books.

Dulffer, J., Thies, J., and Henke, J. 1978: *Hitlers Städte: Baupolitik im Dritten Reich*. Köln: Bohlau.

Duncan, J. D. and Duncan, N. G. 1984: A Cultural Analysis of Urban Residential Landscapes in North America: The Case of the Anglophile Elite. In: Agnew, J., Mercer, J., and Sopher, D. E. (eds.) *The City in Cultural Context*, 255–76. Boston: Allen and Unwin.

Dunkerley, H. *et al.* 1983: *Urban Land Policy: Issues and Opportunities*. New York: Oxford University Press.

Dunleavy, P. 1981: *The Politics of Mass Housing in Britain, 1945–1975: A Study of Corporate Power and Professional Influence in the Welfare State*. Oxford: Clarendon Press.

Duquesne, J. 1966: *Vivre à Sarcelles? Le Grand Ensemble et ses problèmes*. Paris: Édition Cujas.

Durant, R. 1939: *Watling: A Survey of Social Life on a New Housing Estate*. London: P. S. King.

Dwyer, D. J. (ed.) 1971: *Asian Urbanization: A Hong Kong Casebook*. Hong Kong: Hong Kong University Press.

Dwyer, D. J. (ed.) 1972: *The City as a Centre of Change in Asia*. Hong Kong: Hong Kong University Press.

Dwyer, D. J. (ed.) 1974a: *The City in the Third World*. London: Macmillan.

Dwyer, D. J. 1974b: Attitudes towards Spontaneous Development in Third World Cities. In: Dwyer, D. J., (ed.) *The City in the Third World*, 204–18. London: Macmillan.

Dyckman, J. W. 1970: Social Planning in the American Democracy. In: Erber, E. (ed.) *Urban Planning in Transition*, 27–44. New York: Grossman.

Dykstra, C. A. 1926: Congestion Deluxe – Do We Want It? *National Municipal Review*, 15, 394–8.

East, E. E. 1941: Streets: The Circulation System. In: Robbins, G. W. and Tilton, L. D. (eds.) *Los Angeles: A Preface to a Master Plan,* 7–100. Los Angeles: The Pacific Southwest Academy.

Eberstadt, R. 1911: Town Planning in Germany: The Greater Berlin Competition. In: Royal Institute of British Architects *Town Planning Conference – Transactions,* 313–33. London: RIBA.

Eberstadt, R. 1917 (1909): *Handbuch des Wohnungswesens und der Wohnungsfrage.* Jena: Gustav Fischer.

Ebner, M. E. and Tobin, E. M. 1977: *The Age of Urban Reform: New Perspectives on the Progressive Era.* Port Washington, NY: Kennikat.

Eckstein, S. 1977: *The Poverty of Revolution: The State and the Urban Poor in Mexico.* Princeton: Princeton University Press.

Edblom, M., Strömdahl, J., and Westerman, A. 1962: Mot en ny Miljö. *Arkitektur,* 62, 205–24.

Editors of *Fortune* (eds.), 1958: *The Exploding Metropolis.* Garden City, NY: Doubleday Anchor.

Edwards, A. M. 1981: *The Design of Suburbia: A Critical Study in Environmental History.* London: Pembridge Press.

Edwards, B. and Gilbert, D. 2008: 'Piazzadilly!': The Re-imagining of Piccadilly Circus (1957–72). *Planning Perspectives,* 23, 455–78

Edwards, G. 1966: Comment: The Greenbelt Towns of the American New Towns. *Journal of the American Institute of Planners,* 32, 225–8.

Edwards, J. and Batley, R. 1978: *The Politics of Positive Discrimination: An Evaluation of the Urban Programme 1967–77.* London: Tavistock.

Edwards, S. (ed.) 1969: *Selected Writings of Pierre-Joseph Proudhon.* Garden City, NY: Anchor (Doubleday).

Eels, R. and Walton, C. 1968: *Man in the City of the Future: A Symposium of Urban Philosophers.* New York: Arkville Press.

Egli, E. 1959–67: *Geschichte des Städtebaus.* 3 vols. Zürich: Rentsch.

Ehrlich, H. 1933: *Die Berliner Bauordnungen, ihre wichtigsten Bauvorschriften und deren Einfluss auf den Wohnhausbau der Stadt Berlin.* Jena: G. Neuenhahn.

Elander, I. 1989: *New Trends in Social Housing: The Case of Sweden.* Örebro: University, Centre for Housing and Urban Research.

Elander, I. and Strömberg, T. 1992: Whatever Happened to Social Democracy and Planning? The Case of Local Land and Housing Policy in Sweden. In: Lundqvist, L. J. (ed.) *Policy, Organization, Tenure: A Comparative History of Housing in Small Welfare States.* Oslo: Scandinavian University Press.

Elazar, D. J. 1967: Urban Problems and the Federal Government: A Historical Inquiry. *Political Science Quarterly,* 82, 505–25.

Ensor, R. 1936: *England 1870–1914.* Oxford: Oxford University Press.

Epstein, D. G. 1973: *Brasília, Plan and Reality: A Study of Planned and Spontaneous Urban Development.* Berkeley: University of California Press.

Erber, E. (ed.) 1970: *Urban Planning in Transition.* New York: Grossman.

Esher, L. 1981: *A Broken Wave: The Rebuilding of England 1940–1980.* London: Allen Lane.

Esping-Andersen, G. 1985: *Politics against Markets: The Social Democratic Road to Power.* Princeton: Princeton University Press.

Essex, S. and Brayshay, M. 2007: Vision, Vested Interest and Pragmatism: Who Re-made Britain's Blitzed Cities? *Planning Perspectives,* 22, 417–41.

Estall, R. C. 1977: Regional Planning in the United States: An Evaluation of Experience under the 1965 Economic Development Act. *Town Planning Review*, 48, 341–64.

Etzioni, A. 1968: *The Active Society*. London: Collier-Macmillan.

Evenson, N. 1966: *Chandigarh*. Berkeley and Los Angeles: University of California Press.

Evenson, N. 1973: *Two Brazilian Capitals: Architecture and Urbanism in Rio de Janeiro and Brasília*. New Haven: Yale University Press.

Evenson, N. 1979: *Paris: A Century of Change, 1878–1978*. New Haven: Yale University Press.

Evenson, N. 1984: Paris, 1890–1940. In: Sutcliffe, A. (ed.) *Metropolis 1890–1940*, 259–88. London: Mansell.

Evers, H. -D. 1976: Urban Expansion and Land Ownership in Underdeveloped Societies. In: Walton, A. and Masotti, L. H. (eds.) *The City in Comparative Perspective*, 67–79. New York: John Wiley & Sons, Inc.

Fabian Society 1884a: *Why Are the Many Poor?* (*Fabian Tracts*, no. 1). London: George Standring.

Fabian Society 1884b: *A Manifesto* (*Fabian Tracts*, no. 2). London: George Standring.

Fabian Society 1886: *What Socialism Is* (*Fabian Tracts*, no. 4). London: George Standring.

Fabian Society 1887: *Facts for Socialists: From the Political Economists and Statisticians* (*Fabian Tracts*, no. 5). London: Fabian Society.

Fabian Society 1889: *Facts for Londoners* (*Fabian Tracts*, no. 8). London: Fabian Society.

Fabos, J. G., Milde, G. T., and Weinmayr, V. M. 1968: *Frederick Law Olmsted, Sr.: Founder of Landscape Architecture in America*. Amhurst: University of Massachusetts Press.

Fainstein, N. I. and Fainstein, S. S. 1983a: New Haven: The Limits of the Local State. In: Fainstein, S. S., Fainstein, N. I., Hill, R. C., Judd, D. R., and Smith, M. P. *Restructuring the City: The Political Economy of Redevelopment*, 27–79. New York: Longman.

Fainstein, N. I. and Fainstein, S. S. 1983b: Regime Strategies, Communal Resistance, and Economic Forces. In: Fainstein, S. S., Fainstein, N. I., Hill, R. C., Judd, D. R., and Smith, M. P. *Restructuring the City: The Political Economy of Redevelopment*, 245–82. New York: Longman.

Fainstein, S. S. 1994: *The City Builders: Property, Politics, and Planning in London and New York*. Oxford: Blackwell.

Fainstein, S. S., Fainstein, N. I., and Armistead, P. J. 1983: San Francisco: Urban Transformation and the Local State. In: Fainstein, S. S., Fainstein, N. I., Hill, R. C., Judd, D. R., and Smith, M. P. *Restructuring the City: The Political Economy of Redevelopment*, 202–44. New York: Longman.

Fainstein, S. S., Fainstein, N. I., Hill, R. C., Judd, D. R., and Smith, M. P. 1983: *Restructuring the City: The Political Economy of Redevelopment*. New York: Longman.

Fairfield, J. D. 1993: *The Mysteries of the Great City: The Politics of Urban Design, 1877–1937*. Columbus, OH: Ohio State University Press.

Falk, N. 1981: London's Docklands: A Tale of Two Cities. *London Journal*, 7, 65–80.

Falk, N. 1986: Baltimore and Lowell: Two American Approaches. *Built Environment*, 12, 145–52.

Faludi, A. 1973: *Planning Theory*. Oxford: Pergamon.

Faludi, A. 1985: The Return of Rationality. In: Breheny, M. and Hooper, A. (eds.) *Rationality in Planning: Critical Essays on the Role of Rationality in Urban and Regional Planning*, 27–47. London: Pion.

Faludi, A. and van der Valk, A. 1994: *Rule and Order: Dutch Planning Doctrine in the Twentieth Century*. Dordrecht: Kluwer.

Farina, M. B. 1980: Urbanization, Deurbanization and Class Struggle in China 1949–79. *International Journal of Urban and Regional Research*, 4, 485–502.

Farley, R. 1984: *Blacks and Whites? Narrowing the Gap*. Cambridge, MA: Harvard University Press.

Fassbinder, H. 1975: *Berliner Arbeiterviertel, 1800–1918*. Berlin: Verlag für das Studium der Arbeiterbewegung.

Fava, S. F. 1956: Suburbanism as a Way of Life. *American Sociological Review*, 21, 34–8.

Fava, S. F. 1975: Beyond Suburbia. *The Annals of the American Academy of Political and Social Sciences*, 422, 10–24.

Fehl, G. 1983: The Niddatal Project – The Unfinished Satellite Town on the Outskirts of Frankfurt. *Built Environment*, 9, 185–97.

Fehl, G. 1987: From the Berlin Building-Block to the Frankfurt Terrace and Back: A Belated Effort to Trace Ernst May's Urban Design Historiography. *Planning Perspectives*, 2, 194–210.

Fehl, G. 1992: The Nazi Garden City. In: Ward, S. V. (ed.) *The Garden City: Past, Present and Future*, 88–106. London: Spon.

Feibel, C. and Walters, A. A. 1980: *Ownership and Efficiency in Urban Buses* (World Bank Staff Working Paper no. 371). Washington, DC: The World Bank.

Fein, A. 1967: *Landscape into Cityscape: Frederick Law Olmsted's Plans for a Greater New York City*. Ithaca: Cornell University Press.

Fein, A. 1972: *Frederick Law Olmsted and the American Environmental Tradition*. New York: Braziller.

Fichter, R., Turner, J. F. C., and Grenell, P. 1972: The Meaning of Autonomy. In: Turner, J. F. C. and Fichter, R. (eds.) *Freedom to Build: Dweller Control of the Housing Process*, 241–54. New York: Macmillan.

Field, S. *et al.* 1981: *Ethnic Minorities in Britain: A Study of Trends in their Position since 1961*. (Home Office Research Study, 68.) London: HMSO.

Findlay, J. M. 1992: *Magic Lands: Western Cityspaces and American Culture after 1940*. Berkeley: University of California Press.

Fischler, R. 2000: Planning for Social Betterment: From Standard of Living to Quality of Life. In: Freestone, R. (ed.) *Urban Planning in a Changing World: The Twentieth Century Experience*, 139–57. London: Spon.

Fishman, R. 1977: *Urban Utopias in the Twentieth Century: Ebenezer Howard, Frank Lloyd Wright and Le Corbusier*. New York: Basic Books.

Fishman, R. 1980: The Anti-Planners: The Contemporary Revolt against Planning and its significance for Planning History. In: Cherry, G. E. (ed.) *Shaping an Urban World*, 243–52. London: Mansell.

Fishman, R. 1992: The American Garden City: Still Relevant? In: Ward, S. V. (ed.) *The Garden City: Past, Present and Future*, 146–64. London: Spon.

Fishman, R. 1996: The Mumford–Jacobs Debate. *Planning History Studies*, 10/1–2, 3–12.

Fishman, R. 2002: The Bounded City. In: Parsons, K. C. and Schuyler, D. (eds.) *From Garden City to Green City: The Legacy of Ebenezer Howard*, 58–66. Baltimore and London: Johns Hopkins University Press.

Flink, J. J. 1970: *America Adopts the Automobile, 1895–1910*. Cambridge, MA: MIT Press.

Flink, J. J. 1975: *The Car Culture*. Cambridge: MA: MIT Press.

Flink, J. J. 1988: *The Automobile Age*. Cambridge, MA: MIT Press.

Fluck, T. A. 1986: Euclid v. Ambler: A Retrospective. *Journal of the American Planning Association*, 52, 326–37.

Fogel, R. W. and Engermann, S. L. 1974: *Time on the Cross: The Economics of American Negro Slavery.* 2 vols. London: Wildwood House.

Fogelson, R. M. 1967: *The Fragmented Metropolis: Los Angeles 1850–1930.* Cambridge, MA: Harvard University Press.

Fogelson, R. M. 1971: *Violence as Protest: A Study of Riots and Ghettos.* Garden City, NY: Anchor.

Foley, D. L. 1963: *Controlling London's Growth; Planning the Great Wen, 1940–1960.* Berkeley: University of California Press.

Fonseca, R. 1969: The Walled City of Old Delhi. In: Oliver, P. (ed.) *Shelter and Society*, 103–15. London: Barrie Rokliff: The Cresset Press.

Ford, C. and Harrison, B. 1983: *A Hundred Years Ago: Britain in the 1880s in Words and Photographs.* London: Allen Lane.

Ford, J. 1936: *Slums and Housing, with Special Reference to New York City: History, Conditions, Policy.* 2 vols. Cambridge, MA: Harvard University Press.

Forester, J. 1980: Critical Theory and Planning Practice. *Journal of the American Planning Association*, 46, 275–86.

Forshaw, J. H. and Abercrombie, P. 1943: *County of London Plan.* London: Macmillan.

Fosler, R. S. and Berger, R. A. (eds.), 1982: *Public–Private Partnership in American Cities: Seven Case Studies.* Lexington, MA: Lexington Books.

Foster, M. S. 1981: *From Streetcar to Superhighway: American City Planners and Urban Transportation, 1900–1940.* Philadelphia: Temple University Press.

Fox, K. 1985: *Metropolitan America: Urban Life and Urban Policy in the United States, 1940–1980.* London: Macmillan.

Frampton, K. 1968: Notes on Soviet Urbanism, 1917–32. *Architects' Yearbook*, 12, 238–52.

Frampton, K. 1980: *Modern Architecture: A Critical History.* London: Thames and Hudson.

Frazier, E. F. 1932: *The Negro Family in Chicago.* Chicago: University of Chicago Press.

Frazier, E. F. 1939: *The Negro Family in the United States.* Chicago: University of Chicago Press.

Frazier, E. F. 1957: *The Negro in the United States.* New York: Macmillan.

Frazier, E. F. 1966: *The Negro Family in the United States.* Revised and abridged edition. Chicago: University of Chicago Press.

Freestone, R. (ed.) 2000a: *Urban Planning in a Changing World: The Twentieth Century Experience.* London: Spon.

Freestone, R. 2000b: Master Plans and Planning Commissions in the 1920s: The Australian Experience. *Planning Perspectives*, 15, 301–22.

Freestone, R. 2002: Greenbelts in City and Regional Planning. In: Parsons, K. C. and Schuyler, D. (eds.) *From Garden City to Green City: The Legacy of Ebenezer Howard*, 67–98. Baltimore and London: Johns Hopkins University Press.

Freestone, R. 2008: The Adelaide Wars: An Introduction. *Planning Perspectives*, 23, 221–24.

Freestone, R. 2012: Shaping "The Finest City Region in the World": Gordon Stephenson and Canberra's National Capital Development Commission 1960–73. *Town Planning Review*, 83, 355–75.

French, R. A. and Hamilton, F. E. I. 1979a: *The Socialist City: Spatial Structure and Urban Policy.* Chichester: John Wiley & Sons, Ltd.

French, R. A. and Hamilton, F. E. I. 1979b: Is There a Socialist City? In: French, R. A. and Hamilton, F. E. I. *The Socialist City: Spatial Structure and Urban Policy*, 1–22. Chichester: John Wiley & Sons, Ltd.

Fried, M. 1963: Grieving for a Lost Home. In: Duhl, L. J. (ed.) *The Urban Condition: People and Policy in the Metropolis*, 151–71. New York: Basic Books.

Fried, M. 1966: Grieving for a Lost Home: Psychological Costs of Relocation. In: Wilson, J. Q. (ed.) *Urban Renewal: The Record and the Controversy*, 359–79. Cambridge, MA: MIT Press.

Fried, R. C. 1973: *Planning the Eternal City: Roman Politics and Planning since World War II*. New Haven and London: Yale University Press.

Frieden, B. J. 1964: *The Future of Old Neighborhoods: Rebuilding for a Changing Population*. Cambridge, MA: MIT Press.

Frieden, B. J. 1965: The Search for Housing Policy in Mexico City. *Town Planning Review*, 36, 75–94.

Frieden, B. J. 1979: *The Environmental Protection Hustle*. Cambridge, MA: MIT Press.

Frieden, B. J. and Kaplan, M. 1975: *The Politics of Neglect: Urban Aid from Model Cities to Revenue Sharing*. Cambridge, MA: MIT Press.

Friedman, L. M. 1968: *Government and Slum Housing: A Century of Frustration*. Chicago: Rand McNally.

Friedmann, J. 1955: *The Spatial Structure of Economic Development in the Tennessee Valley: A Study in Regional Planning*. Chicago: University of Chicago Press (Department of Geography, Research paper no. 39).

Friedmann, J. 1973: *Retracking America: A Theory of Transactive Planning*. Garden City: Doubleday.

Friedmann, J. and Hudson, B. 1974: Knowledge and Action: A Guide to Planning Theory. *Journal of the American Institute of Planners*, 40, 1–16.

Friedmann, J. and Weaver, C. 1979: *Territory and Function: The Evolution of Regional Planning*. London: Edward Arnold.

Friedmann, J. and Wulff, R. 1976: *The Urban Transition: Comparative Studies of Newly Industrializing Societies*. London: Edward Arnold.

Frisby, D. 2001: *Cityscapes of Modernity: Critical Explorations*. Cambridge: Polity Press.

Fritsch, T. 1912 (1896): *Die Stadt der Zukunft*. Leipzig: Hammer Verlag.

Frolic, B. M. 1964: The Soviet City. *Town Planning Review*, 34, 285–306.

Frolic, B. M. 1975: Moscow: The Socialist Alternative. In: Eldredge, H. W. (ed.) *World Capitals: Toward Guided Urbanization*. New York: Anchor Press/Doubleday.

Fry, E. C. 1972: Growth of an Australian Metropolis. In: Parker, R. S. and Troy, P. N. (eds.) *The Politics of Urban Growth*, 1–23. Canberra: ANU Press.

Fuchs, C. J. (ed.) 1918: *Die Wohnungs- und Siedlungsfrage nach dem Kriege: Ein Programm des Kleinwohnungs- und Siedlungswesens*. Stuttgart: Wilhelm Mener-Ilschen.

Fulton, W. 2002: The Garden Suburb and the New Urbanism. In: Parsons, K. C. and Schuyler, D. (eds.) *From Garden City to Green City: The Legacy of Ebenezer Howard*, 159–70. Baltimore and London: Johns Hopkins University Press.

Funigiello, P. A. 1983: City Planning in World War II: The Experience of the National Resources Planning Board. In: Krueckeberg, D. A. (ed.) *Introduction to Planning History in the United States*, 152–69. New Brunswick, NJ: Rutgers University, Center for Urban Policy Research.

GB Admiralty 1945: *Geographical Handbook: Germany*. Vol. IV, *Ports and Communications*. London: Naval Intelligence Division.

GB Commission for Racial Equality 1980: *Ethnic Minorities and New or Expanding Towns*. London: The Commission.

GB Committee … Circumstances Connected with the Disturbances at Featherstone 1893: *Report*. (C. 7234). London: HMSO. (*BPP*, 1893–4, 17).

GB Committee … Origin and Character of the Disturbances in the Metropolis 1886: *Report*. (C. 4665). London: HMSO. (*BPP*, 1886, 34).

GB Committee on the Qualifications of Planners 1950: *Report*. (C. 8059). London: HMSO. (*BPP*, 1950, 14).

GB Department of the Environment 1977a: *Unequal City: Final Report of the Birmingham Inner Area Study*. London: HMSO.

GB Department of the Environment 1977b: *Inner London: Proposals for Dispersal and Balance: Final Report of the Lambeth Inner Area Study*. London: HMSO.

GB Department of the Environment 1977c: *Change or Decay: Final Report of the Liverpool Inner Area Study*. London: HMSO.

GB Department of the Environment 1977d: *Inner Area Studies: Liverpool, Birmingham and Lambeth: Summaries of Consultants' Final Reports*. London: HMSO.

GB Department of the Environment 1983: *Streamlining the Cities: Government Proposals for Reorganising Local Government in Greater London and the Metropolitan Counties*. (C. 0062). London: HMSO.

GB Department of the Environment 1987: *An Evaluation of the Enterprise Zone Experiment*. By PA Cambridge Economic Consultants. London: HMSO.

GB Department of the Environment 1993: *East Thames Corridor: A Study of Developmental Capacity and Potential*. By Llewelyn-Davies, Roger Tym and Partners, TecnEcon and Environmental Resources Ltd. London: Department of the Environment.

GB Department of the Environment 1995: *Projections of Households in England to 2016*. London: HMSO.

GB Deputy Prime Minister and Secretary of State for the Environment, Transport and the Regions 2000: *Our Towns and Cities: The Future: Delivering an Urban Renaissance*. (C. 4911). London: Stationery Office.

GB Government Office for London 1996: *Four World Cities: A Comparative Study of London, Paris, New York and Tokyo*. London: Llewelyn Davies Planning.

GB Government Office for the South East, Government Office for East of England, Government Office for London 2000: *Revised Regional Guidance for the South East*. (RPG 9). Guildford: Government Office for the South East.

GB Home Office 1981: *The Brixton Disorders, 10–12 April 1981: Report of an Inquiry by the Rt. Hon. The Lord Scarman, OBE*. (C. 8427). London: HMSO. (*BPP*, 1981–2, C. 8427).

GB Local Government Boards for England and Wales, and Scotland 1918: *Report of the Committee Appointed by the President of the Local Government Board and the Secretary for Scotland to Consider Questions of Building Construction in Connection with the Provision of Dwellings for the Working Classes in England and Wales, and Scotland, and Report upon Methods of Securing Economy and Despatch in the Provision of Such Dwellings*. (C. 9191.) London: HMSO. (*BPP*, 1918, 7).

GB Manpower Services Commission. London Regional Manpower Intelligence Unit 1981: *Ethnic Minority Employment in London*. 2 parts. (Briefing Note no. 5). London: HMSO.

GB Minister of Transport, Steering Group and Working Group 1963: *Traffic in Towns: A Study of the Long Term Problems of Traffic in Urban Areas*. London: HMSO.

GB Minister without Portfolio 1985: *Lifting the Burden*. (C. 9571). London: HMSO.

GB Ministry of Health 1920a: *Type Plans and Elevations of Houses Designed by the Ministry of Health in Connection with State-Aided Housing Schemes*. London: HMSO.

GB Ministry of Health 1920b: *Interim Report of the Committee Appointed by the Minister of Health to Consider and Advise on the Principles to be Followed in Dealing with Unhealthy Areas.* London: HMSO.

GB Ministry of Health 1921: *Second and Final Report of the Committee Appointed by the Minister of Health to Consider and Advise on the Principles to be Followed in Dealing with Unhealthy Areas.* London: HMSO.

GB Ministry of Reconstruction Advisory Council. Women's Housing Sub-Committee 1918: *First Interim Report.* (C. 9166). London: HMSO (*BPP*, 1918, 10).

GB Ministry of Town and Country Planning 1946: *Interim Report of the New Towns Committee.* (C. 6759). London: HMSO. (*BPP*, 1945–46, 14).

GB Ministry of Works and Planning 1943: *Report of the Committee on Land Utilization in Rural Areas.* (C. 6378). London: HMSO.

GB Performance and Innovation Unit 2001: *Social Mobility: A Discussion Paper.*

GB Royal Commission into the Depression of Trade and Industry 1886: *Final Report.* (C. 4893). London: HMSO. (*BPP*, 1886, 23).

GB Royal Commission on the Distribution of the Industrial Population 1940: *Report.* (C. 6153). London: HMSO. (*BPP*, 1939–40, 4).

GB Royal Commission on the Geographical Distribution of the Industrial Population 1937–9: *Minutes of Evidence*, June 16, 1938, paras 59, 66, 69. London: HMSO.

GB Royal Commission on the Housing of the Working Classes. 1885: vol. I. *First Report*, vol. II. *Minutes of Evidence and Appendices.* (C. 4402). London: Eyre and Spottiswoode (*BPP*, 1884–5, 30).

GB Runnymede Trust 1982: *Ethnic Minorities in Britain: A Select Bibliography.* London: The Trust.

GB Secretary of State for the Environment 1977: *Policy for the Inner Cities.* (C. 6845). London: HMSO.

GB Select Committee on Emigration and Immigration (Foreigners) 1889: *Report.* (H. C. 311). London: Henry Hansard. (*BPP*, 1889, 10).

GB Social Exclusion Unit 1998: *Bringing Britain Together: A National Strategy for Neighbourhood Renewal.* (C. 4045). London: Stationery Office.

GB Social Exclusion Unit 1999: *Bridging the Gap: New Opportunities for 16–18 Year Olds Not in Education, Employment or Training.* (C. 4405). London: Stationery Office.

GB Social Exclusion Unit 2001: *A New Commitment to Neighbourhood Renewal: National Strategy Action Plan.* London: Social Exclusion Unit.

GB Thames Gateway Task Force 1995: *The Thames Gateway Planning Framework.* (RPG 9a). London: Department of the Environment.

GB Urban Task Force 1999: *Towards an Urban Renaissance.* London: Spon.

Gallion, A. B. and Eisner, S. 1963: *The Urban Pattern.* Princeton: D. van Nostrand.

Galloway, T. D. and Mahayni, R. G. 1977: Planning Theory in Retrospect: The Process of Paradigm Change. *Journal of the American Institute of Planners*, 43, 62–71.

Gans, H. J. 1961a: Planning and Social Life: An Evaluation of Friendship and Neighborhood Patterns in Suburban Communities. *Journal of the American Institute of Planners*, 27, 134–40.

Gans, H. J. 1961b: The Balanced Community: Homogeneity or Heterogeneity in Residential Areas. *Journal of the American Institute of Planners*, 27, 176–84.

Gans, H. J. 1962: *The Urban Villagers: Group and Class in the Life of Italian-Americans.* New York: The Free Press.

Gans, H. J. 1967a: *The Levittowners: Ways of Life and Politics in a New Suburban Community*. London: Allen Lane.

Gans, H. J. 1967b: The Failure of Urban Renewal: A Critique and Some Proposals. In: Bellush, J. and Hausknecht, M. (eds.) *Urban Renewal: People, Politics and Planning*, 465–84. Garden City, NY: Anchor.

Gardiner, J. 1970: *Some Aspects of the Establishment of Towns in Zambia during the Nineteen Twenties and Thirties*. Lusaka: University of Zambia, Institute for African Studies (formerly Social Research). (*Zambian Urban Studies*, no. 3.)

Gardner, J. 1971: Educated Youth and Urban–Rural Inequalities, 1958–66. In: Lewis, J. W. (ed.) *The City in Communist China*, 235–86. Stanford, CA: Stanford University Press.

Garland, H. 1917: *A Son of the Middle Border*. London: John Lane – The Bodley Head.

Garnaut, C. 2000: Towards Metropolitan Organisation: Town Planning and the Garden City Idea. In: Hamnett, S. and Freestone, R. (eds.) *The Australian Metropolis: A Planning History*, 46–64. Sydney: Allen and Unwin.

Garnaut, C. and Hutchings, A. 2003: The Colonel Light Gardens Garden Suburb Commission: Building a Planned Community. *Planning Perspectives*, 18, 277–93.

Garreau, J. 1991: *Edge City: Life on the New Frontier*. New York: Doubleday.

Garrison, W. 1959/60: Spatial Structure of the Economy. *Annals of the Association of American Geographers*, 49, 238–9, 471–82; 50, 357–73.

Garside, P. L. 1984: West End, East End: London, 1890–1940. In: Sutcliffe, A. (ed.) *Metropolis 1890–1940*, 221–58. London: Mansell.

Garside, P. L. 1988: "Unhealthy Areas": Town Planning, Eugenics and the Slums, 1890–1945. *Planning Perspectives*, 3, 24–46.

Garside, P. L. 1997: The Significance of Post-War London Reconstruction Plans for East End Industry. *Planning Perspectives*, 12, 19–36.

Gates, W. 1995: *The Road Ahead*. London: Viking.

Gates, W. 1999: *Business @ the Speed of Thought: Succeeding in the Digital Economy*. London: Penguin.

Gatons, P. K. and Brintnall, M. 1984: Competitive Grants: The UDAG Approach. In: Bingham, R. D. and Blair, J. P. (eds.) *Urban Economic Development* (*Urban Affairs Annual Reviews*, 27), 115–40. Beverly Hills: Sage.

Gaudin, J. P. 1992: The French Garden City. In: Ward, S. V. (ed.) *The Garden City: Past, Present and Future*, 52–68. London: Spon.

Gauldie, E. 1974: *Cruel Habitations: A History of Working-Class Housing 1780–1918*. London: George Allen and Unwin.

Gawler, J. 1963: *A Roof Over My Head*. Melbourne: Lothian.

Geddes, P. 1904: *City Development: A Study of Parks, Gardens and Culture Institutes*. Edinburgh: Geddes and Co.

Geddes, P. 1905: Civics: As Applied Sociology. *Sociological Papers*, 1, 101–44.

Geddes, P. 1912: The Twofold Aspect of the Industrial Age: Palaeotechnic and Neotechnic. *Town Planning Review*, 31, 176–87.

Geddes, P. 1915: *Cities in Evolution*. London: Williams and Norgate.

Geddes, P. 1917a: *Town Planning in Lahore: A Report to the Municipal Council*. Lahore: Commercial Printing Works. (Repr. as Geddes 1965a).

Geddes, P. 1917b: *Report on Town Planning, Dacca*. Calcutta: Bengal Secretariat Book Depot.

Geddes, P. 1917c: *Town Planning in Balrampur: A Report to the Hon'ble the Maharaja Bahadur*. Lucknow: Murray's Printing Press.

Geddes, P. 1918: *Town Planning towards City Development: A Report to the Durbar of Indore*. Indore: Holkore State Printing Press.

Geddes, P. 1925a: A Schoolboy's Bag and a City's Pageant. *The Survey*, 53, 525–9, 553.

Geddes, P. 1925b: Cities, and the Soils they Grow from. *The Survey*, 54, 40–4.

Geddes, P. 1925c: The Valley Plan of Civilization. *The Survey*, 54, 288–90, 322–5.

Geddes, P. 1925d: The Valley in the Town. *The Survey*, 54, 396–400, 415–16.

Geddes, P. 1925e: Our City of Thought. *The Survey*, 54, 487–90, 504–7.

Geddes, P. 1925f: The Education of Two Boys. *The Survey*, 54, 571–5, 587–91.

Geddes, P. 1965a: *Urban Improvements: A Strategy for Urban Works (Pt. 2: Town Planning in Lahore)*. Government of Pakistan, Planning Commission, Physical Planning and Town Planning Section.

Geddes, P. 1965b: *Reports on Re-Planning of Six Towns in Bombay Presidency, 1915*. Bombay: Government Printing and Stationery, Maharashtra State.

Geen, E., Lowe, J. R., and Walker, K. 1963: *Man and the Modern City*. Pittsburgh: University of Pittsburgh Press.

Gelfand, M. I. 1975: *A Nation of Cities: The Federal Government and Urban America, 1933–1965*. New York: Oxford University Press.

Gelman, T. 1924: The Planning of Moscow. *Town Planning Review*, 11, 13–16.

George, H. 1898a: *The Complete Works of Henry George*. New York: Doubleday and McClure.

George, H. 1898b (1968): City and Country. In: George H. *The Complete Works of Henry George*, 234–40. New York: Doubleday and McClure. (Repr. in Dorsett, L. W. *The Challenge of the City, 1860–1910*, 4–7. Lexington: D. C. Heath.)

Gerckens, L. A. 1983: Bettmann and Cincinnati. In: Krueckeberg, D. A. (ed.) *The American Planner: Biographies and Recollections*, 120–48. New York and London: Methuen.

Ghirardo, D. 1989: *Building New Communities: New Deal America and Fascist Italy*. Princeton: Princeton University Press.

Ghosh, M., Dutta, A. K., and Ray, B. 1972: *Calcutta: A Study in Urban Growth Dynamics*. Calcutta: Firma K. L. Mukhopadhyay.

Gibb, A. 1983: *Glasgow: The Making of a City*. London: Croom Helm.

Gibberd, F. 1953: *Town Design*. London: Architectural Press.

Gibson, A. 1979: *People Power: Community and Work Groups in Action*. Harmondsworth: Penguin.

Gibson, A. 1985: Lightmoor Gives Hope for Wasted Resources. *Town and Country Planning*, 54, 290–1.

Giddens, A. 1990: *The Consequences of Modernity*. Cambridge: Polity.

Gilbert, A. (ed.) 1976: *Development Planning and Spatial Structure*. Chichester: John Wiley & Sons, Ltd.

Gilbert, A. (ed.) 1982: *Urbanization in Contemporary Latin America: Critical Approaches to the Analysis of Urban Issues*. Chichester: John Wiley & Sons, Ltd.

Gilbert, A. and Gigler, J. 1982: *Cities, Poverty and Development: Urbanization in the Third World*. New York: Oxford University Press.

Gilbert, A. and Ward, P. 1982: Low-Income Housing and the State. In: Gilbert, A. (ed.) *Urbanization in Contemporary Latin America: Critical Approaches to the Analysis of Urban Issues*, 79–127. Chichester: John Wiley & Sons, Ltd.

Gilbert, N. and Specht, H. 1977: *Dynamics of Community Planning*. Cambridge, MA: Ballinger.

Gist, J. R. 1980: Urban Development Action Grants: Design and Implementation. In: Rosenthal, D. B. (ed.) *Urban Revitalization* (*Urban Affairs Annual Reviews*, no. 18), 237–52. Beverly Hills: Sage.

Glaab, C. N. and Brown, A. T. 1976: *A History of Urban America*. Second edition. New York: Macmillan.

Glass, R. 1955: Urban Sociology in Great Britain: A Trend Report. *Current Sociology*, 4/4, 5–19.

Glazer, N. 1968: Slums and Ethnicity. In: Sherrard, T. D. (ed.) *Social Welfare and Social Problems*, 84–112. New York: Columbia University Press.

Glazer, N. 1983: *Ethnic Dilemmas 1964–1982*. Cambridge, MA: Harvard University Press.

Glazer, N. and Young, K. (eds.) 1983: *Ethnic Pluralism and Public Policy: Achieving Equality in the United States and Great Britain*. London: Heinemann Education.

Glendinning, M. and Muthesius, S. 1994: *Tower Block: Modern Public Housing in England, Scotland, Wales and Northern Ireland*. New Haven: Yale University Press.

Glynn, S. 1975: *Urbanisation in Australian History 1788–1900*. Sydney: Nelson.

Godschalk, D. R. (ed.) 1974: *Planning in America: Learning from Turbulence*. Washington, DC: American Institute of Planners.

Goetze, R., Goodman, R., Grenell, P., Linn, C., Peattie, L., Terner, D., and Turner, J. 1968: Architecture of Democracy. *Architectural Design*, 38, 354.

Goist, P. D. 1969: Lewis Mumford and "Anti-Urbanism." *Journal of the American Institute of Planners*, 35, 340–7.

Goist, P. D. 1974: Patrick Geddes and the City. *Journal of the American Institute of Planners*, 40, 31–7.

Goist, P. D. 1983: Seeing Things Whole: A Consideration of Lewis Mumford. In: Krueckeberg, D. A. (ed.) *The American Planner: Biographies and Recollections*, 250–75. New York and London: Methuen.

Gold, J. R. 1993: "Commoditie, Firmenes and Delight": Modernism, the MARS Group's "New Architecture" Exhibition (1938) and Imagery of the Urban Future. *Planning Perspectives*, 8, 357–76.

Gold, J. R. 1997: *The Experience of Modernism: Modern Architects and the Future City 1928–53*. London: Spon.

Gold, J. R. and Ward, S. V. (eds.) 1994: *Place Promotion: The Use of Publicity and Marketing to Sell Towns and Regions*. Chichester: John Wiley & Sons, Ltd.

Goldfield, D. R. 1979: Suburban Development in Stockholm and the United States: A Comparison of Form and Function. In: Hammarström, I. and Hall, T. (eds.) *Growth and Transformation of the Modern City: The Stockholm Conference September 1978*, 139–56. Stockholm: Swedish Council for Building Research.

Goldsmith, W. W. 1982: Enterprise Zones: If They Work We're in Trouble. *International Journal of Urban and Regional Research*, 6, 435–42.

Goldstein, S. and Sly, D. F. (eds.) 1977: *Patterns of Urbanization: Comparative Country Studies*. Dolhain (Belgium): Ordina.

Goodall, B. and Kirby, A. (eds.) 1979: *Resources and Planning*. Oxford: Pergamon.

Goodall, L. E. and Sprengel, D. P. 1975: *The American Metropolis*. Second edition. Columbus, OH: Charles E. Merrill.

Goodman, P. and Goodman, P. 1960: *Communitas: Means of Livelihood and Ways of Life*. Second edition. New York: Vintage Books.

Gopnick, A. 2007: From "Cities and Songs." In: Mennel, T., Steffens, J., and Klemek, C. (eds.)
    Block by Block: Jane Jacobs and the Future of New York. Princeton: Princeton Architectural
    Press.
Gordon, D. L. A. 1998: A City Beautiful Plan for Canada's Capital: Edward Bennett and the
    1915 Plan for Ottawa and Hull. *Planning Perspectives*, 13, 275–300.
Gordon, D. L. A. 2010: The Other Author of the 1908 Plan of Chicago: Edward H. Bennett –
    Urban Designer, Planner and Architect. *Planning Perspectives*, 25, 229–41.
Gordon, I. 2004: The Resurgent City: What, Where, How, and for When? *Planning Theory
    and Practice*, 5, 371–9.
Gordon, P., Kumar, A., and Richardson, H. W. 1989a: Congestion, Changing Metropolitan
    Structure, and City Size in the United States. *International Regional Science Review*, 12,
    45–56.
Gordon, P., Kumar, A., and Richardson, H. W. 1989b: The Spatial Mismatch Hypothesis –
    Some New Evidence. *Urban Studies*, 26, 315–26.
Gordon, P., Kumar, A., and Richardson, H. W. 1989c: The Influence of Metropolitan Spatial
    Structure on Commuting Time. *Journal of Urban Economics*, 26, 138–51.
Gordon, P. and Richardson, H. W. 1996: Employment Decentralization in US Metropolitan
    Areas: Is Los Angeles the Outlier or the Norm? *Environment and Planning A*, 28,
    1727–43.
Gordon, P., Richardson, H. W., and Jun, M. 1991: The Commuting Paradox – Evidence from
    the Top Twenty. *Journal of the American Planning Association*, 57, 416–20.
Gottdiener, M. 1977: *Planned Sprawl: Private and Public Interests in Suburbia*. Beverly Hills:
    Sage.
Gould, P. C. 1988: *Back to Nature, Back to the Land, and Socialism in Britain, 1880–1900*. New
    York: St Martin's Press.
Grabow, S. 1977: Frank Lloyd Wright and the American City: The Broadacres Debate. *Journal
    of the American Institute of Planners*, 43, 115–24.
Grabow, S. 1983: *Christopher Alexander: The Search for a New Paradigm in Architecture*.
    Stocksfield: Oriel Press.
Gradidge, R. 1981: *Edwin Lutyens: Architect Laureate*. London: Allen and Unwin.
Graham, H. D. and Gurr, T. R. (eds.) 1969: *Violence in America: Historical and Comparative
    Perspectives*. 2 vols. Washington, DC: Government Printing Office.
Graham, S. and Marvin, S. 1996: *Telecommunications and the City: Electronic Spaces, Urban
    Places*. London: Routledge.
Grant, J. and Serle, G. (eds.) 1957: *The Melbourne Scene: 1803–1956*. Melbourne: Melbourne
    University Press.
Grant, N. L. 1991: *TVA and Black Americans: Planning for the Status Quo*. Philadelphia:
    Temple University Press.
Grava, S. 1978: Locally Generated Transportation Modes of the Developing World. In: *Urban
    Transportation Economies: Proceedings of Five Workshops as Priority Alternatives,
    Economic Regulation, Labor Issues, Marketing, and Government Financing Responsibilities*.
    Final Reporting March 1978. Washington, DC: Department of Transportation, 84–95.
Gravier, J. -F. 1947: *Paris et le désert français*. Paris: Flammarion.
Greater London Council 1969: *Tomorrow's London: A Background to the Greater London
    Development Plan*. London: GLC.
Greater London Regional Planning Committee (GLRPC) 1929: *First Report*. London: Knapp,
    Drewett.

Greater London Regional Planning Committee (GLRPC) 1933: *Second Report* (includes Interim Reports). London: Knapp, Drewett.

Green, C. M. 1963: *Washington: Capital City, 1879–1950.* Princeton: Princeton University Press.

Green, C. M. 1965: *The Rise of Urban America.* New York: Harper and Row.

Green, H. A. 1979: Urban Planning in Nigeria. *Journal of Administration Overseas,* 18, 22–33.

Green, R. E. 1991: *Enterprise Zones: New Directions in Economic Development.* Newbury Park: Sage.

Greer, G. and Hansen, A. H. 1941: *Urban Redevelopment and Housing: A Program for Post-War.* (Planning Pamphlets, no. 10). Washington, DC: National Planning Association.

Greer, S. 1965: *Urban Renewal of American Cities: The Dilemma of Democratic Intervention.* Indianapolis: Bobbs-Merrill.

Gregg, D. J. 1986: The Origins and Philosophy of Parkways with Particular Reference to the Contribution of Barry Parker. *Planning History Bulletin,* 8/1, 38–50.

Gregory, J. and Gordon, D. L. A. 2012: Introduction: Gordon Stephenson, Planner and Civic Designer. *Town Planning Review,* 83, 269–78.

Grenell, P. 1972: Planning for Invisible People. In: Turner, J. F. C. and Fichter, R. (eds.) *Freedom to Build: Dweller Control of the Housing Process,* 95–121. New York: Macmillan.

Griffith, E. S. 1974: *A History of American City Government: The Conspicuous Failure, 1870–1900.* New York: Praeger.

Grigsby, W. G. 1963: *Housing Markets and Public Policy.* Philadelphia: University of Pennsylvania Press.

Grindley, W. C. 1972: Owner-Builders: Survivors with a Future. In: Turner, J. F. C. and Fichter, R. (eds.) *Freedom to Build: Dweller Control of the Housing Process,* 3–21. New York: Macmillan.

Grote, L. (ed.) 1974: *Die deutsche Stadt im 19. Jahrhundert: Stadtplanung und Baugestaltung im industriellen Zeitalter.* München: Prestel Verlag.

Gugler, J. 1980: "A Minimum of Urbanism and a Maximum of Ruralism": The Cuban Experience. *International Journal of Urban and Regional Research,* 4, 516–35.

Gugler, J. and Flanagan, W. G. 1977: On the Political Economy of Urbanization in the Third World: The Case of West Africa. *International Journal of Urban and Regional Research,* 1, 272–92.

Gugler, J. and Flanagan, W. G. 1978: *Urbanization and Social Change in West Africa.* Cambridge: Cambridge University Press.

Gupta, S. K. 1974: Chandigarh: A Study of Sociological Issues and Urban Development in India. *Architectural Design,* 44, 362–8.

Gurley, J. G. 1975: Rural Development in China 1949–72, and the Lessons to Be Learned from It. *World Development,* 3, 455–71.

Gurr, T. R. 1969: A Comparative Study of Civil Strife. In: Graham, H. D. and Gurr, T. R. (eds.) *Violence in America: Historical and Comparative Perspectives,* 443–86. 2 vols. Washington, DC: Government Printing Office.

Gutheim, F. 1977: *Worthy of the Nation: The History of Planning for the National Capital.* Washington, DC: Smithsonian Institute Press.

Gutman, H. G. 1977: *Work, Culture, and Society in Industrializing America. Essays in American Working-Class and Social History.* Oxford: Blackwell.

Guttenberg, A. Z. 1978: City Encounter and Desert Encounter: Two Sources of American Regional Planning Thought. *Journal of the American Institute of Planners,* 44, 399–411.

Gwynne, R. N. 1985: *Industrialisation and Urbanisation in Latin America*. London: Croom Helm.

Haar, C. M. 1975: *Between the Idea and the Reality: A Study in the Origin, Fate and Legacy of the Model Cities Program*. Boston: Little, Brown.

Haar, C. M. 1996: *Suburbs under Siege: Race, Space and Audacious Judges*. Princeton: Princeton University Press.

Hague, C. 1984: *The Development of Planning Thought: A Critical Perspective*. London: Hutchinson.

Hake, A. 1977: *African Metropolis: Nairobi's Self-Help City*. London: Chatto and Windus (for Sussex University Press).

Hall, J. 1992: The LDDC's Policy Aims and Methods. In: Ogden, P. (ed.) *London Docklands: The Challenge of Development*, 19–24. Cambridge: Cambridge University Press.

Hall, J. M. 1982: *The Geography of Planning Decisions*. Oxford: Oxford University Press.

Hall, J. M., Griffiths, G., Eyles, J., and Darby, M. 1976: Rebuilding the London Docklands. *The London Journal*, 2, 266–85.

Hall, P. 1968: The Urban Culture and the Suburban Culture. In: Eels, R. and Walton, C. (eds.) *Man in the City of the Future: A Symposium of Urban Philosophers*, 99–145. New York: Arkville Press.

Hall, P. 1971: Spatial Structure of Metropolitan England and Wales. In: Chisholm, M. and Manners, G., *Spatial Policy Problems of the British Economy*. Cambridge: Cambridge University Press.

Hall, P. 1973: England in 1900. In: Darby, H. C. (ed.) *A New Historical Geography of England*. Cambridge: Cambridge University Press.

Hall, P. 1977: Green Fields and Grey Areas. *Papers of the RTPI Annual Conference, Chester*. London: Royal Town Planning Institute.

Hall, P. 1978: Can Cities Survive? The Potential and Limits of Action. *The Ditchley Journal*, 5/2, 33–41.

Hall, P. 1979: The European City in the Year 2000. In: Hammarström, I. and Hall, T. (eds.) *Growth and Transformation of the Modern City: The Stockholm Conference September 1978*, 157–62. Stockholm: Swedish Council for Building Research.

Hall, P. 1980: *Great Planning Disasters*. London: Weidenfeld and Nicolson.

Hall, P. (ed.) 1981: *The Inner City in Context: The Final Report of the Social Science Research Council Inner Cities Working Party*. London: Heinemann.

Hall, P. 1982a: *Urban and Regional Planning*. Third edition. London: George Allen and Unwin.

Hall, P. 1982b: Enterprise Zones: A Justification. *International Journal of Urban and Regional Research*, 6, 416–21.

Hall, P. 1984: *The World Cities*. Third edition. London: Weidenfeld and Nicolson.

Hall, P. 1985: The People: Where Will They Go? *The Planner*, 71/4, 3–12.

Hall, P. 1994: *Abercrombie's Plan for London – 50 Years On: A Vision for the Future*. (Report of the 2nd Annual Vision for London Lecture 1994). London: Vision for London.

Hall, P. 1995: Bringing Abercrombie Back from the Shades: A Look Forward and Back. *Town Planning Review*, 66, 227–41.

Hall, P. 1998: *Cities in Civilization*. London: Weidenfeld and Nicolson.

Hall, P. 1999: Planning for the Mega-City: A New Eastern Asian Urban Form? In: Brotchie, J. F., Batty, M., Blakely, E., Hall, P., and Newton, P. (eds.) *Cities in Competition*, 3–36. Melbourne: Longman Australia.

Hall, P. 2000: Cool Brazil: A Pilgrimage to Curitiba. *Town and Country Planning*, 69, 208–9.

Hall, P. 2008: Catching Up with Our Visions. *Town and Country Planning*, 77, 444–9.

Hall, P. 2011a: In Context – Rioting: A Theory from the 1970s. *Planning*, August 26. http://ww.planningresource.co.uk/article/1086903/context---rioting-theory-1970s (accessed December 19, 2013).

Hall, P. 2011b: In Context – Riots Shine Light on Underclass. *Planning*, November 4. http://www.planningresource.co.uk/article/1102070/context---riots-shine-light-underclass (accessed December 19, 2013).

Hall, P. 2012: Can We Reverse the Long Downward Slide? *Town and Country Planning*, 81, 252–4.

Hall, P., Breheny, M., McQuaid, R., and Hart, D. A. 1987: *Western Sunrise: The Genesis and Growth of Britain's Major High Tech Corridor*. London: Allen and Unwin.

Hall, P. and Hass-Klau, C. 1985: *Can Rail Save the City? The Impacts of Rail Rapid Transit and Pedestrianisation on British and German Cities*. Aldershot: Gower.

Hall, P. and Hay, D. 1980: *Growth Centres in the European Urban System*. London: Heinemann.

Hall, P., Thomas, R., Gracey, H., and Drewett, R. 1973: *The Containment of Urban England*. 2 vols. London: George Allen and Unwin.

Hall, P. and Ward, C. 1998: *Sociable Cities: The Legacy of Ebenezer Howard*. Chichester: John Wiley & Sons, Ltd.

Hall, T. 1979: The Central Business District: Planning in Stockholm, 1928–1978. In: Hammarström, I. and Hall, T. (eds.) *Growth and Transformation of the Modern City: The Stockholm Conference September 1978*, 181–232. Stockholm: Swedish Council for Building Research.

Hall, T. 1991a: *Planning and Urban Growth in Nordic Countries*. London: Spon.

Hall, T. 1991b: Urban Planning in Sweden. In: Hall, T. (ed.) *Planning and Urban Growth in Nordic Countries*, 167–246. London: Spon.

Hall, T. 1997: *Planning Europe's Capital Cities: Aspects of Nineteenth Century Urban Development*. London: Spon.

Hall, T. and Vidén, S. 2005: The Million Homes Programme: A Review of the Great Swedish Planning Project. *Planning Perspectives*, 20, 301–28.

Halliman, D. M. and Morgan, W. T. W. 1967: The City of Nairobi. In: Morgan, W. T. W. (ed.) *Nairobi: City and Region*, 98–120. Nairobi: Oxford University Press.

Hamer, D. 2000: Learning from the Past: Historic Districts and the New Urbanism in the United States. *Planning Perspectives*, 15, 107–22.

Hamilton, F. E. I. 1976: *The Moscow City Region*. London: Oxford University Press.

Hamm, M. F. (ed.) 1976a: *The City in Russian History*. Lexington: University of Kentucky Press.

Hamm, M. F. 1976b: The Breakdown of Urban Modernization: A Prelude to the Revolutions of 1917. In: Hamm, M. F. *The City in Russian History*, 182–200. Lexington: University of Kentucky Press.

Hamm, M. F. 1977: The Modern Russian City: An Historiographical Analysis. *Journal of Urban History*, 4, 39–76.

Hammarström, I. and Hall, T. 1979: *Growth and Transformation of the Modern City: The Stockholm Conference September 1978*. Stockholm: Swedish Council for Building Research.

Hamnett, S. and Freestone, R. (eds.) 2000: *The Australian Metropolis: A Planning History*. Sydney: Allen and Unwin.

Hamzah, S. 1964: Urbanisation. In: Wang, G. (ed.) *Malaysia: A Survey*, 82–96. London: Pall Mall Press.

Handlin, O. and Burchard, J. (eds.) 1963: *The Historian and the City*. Cambridge, MA: MIT Press and Harvard University Press.

Hansen, A. H. 1927: *Business-Cycle Theory: Its Development and Present Status*. Boston: Gunn.

Hansen, A. H. 1932: *Economic Stabilization in an Unbalanced World*. New York: Harcourt Brace.

Hansen, G. 1889: *Die drei Bevölkerungsstufen: Ein Versuch, die Ursachen für das Blühen und Altern der völker Nachzuweisen*. München: J. Lindauer.

Hansen, N. M. 1981: Development from Above: The Centre-Down Development Paradigm. In: Stöhr, W. B. and Taylor, D. R. F. (eds.) *Development from Above or Below? The Dialectics of Regional Planning in Developing Countries*, 15–38. Chichester: John Wiley & Sons, Ltd.

Hardinge of Penshurst 1948: *My Indian Years 1910–1916*. London: John Murray.

Hardwick, P. A. 1977: The Transportation Systems. In: Kay, G. and Smout, M. A. H. (eds.) *Salisbury: A Geographical Survey of the Capital of Rhodesia*, 94–112. London: Hodder and Stoughton.

Hardy, C. O. and Kuczynski, R. R. 1934: *The Housing Program of the City of Vienna*. Washington, DC: The Brookings Institution.

Hardy, D. 1979: *Alternative Communities in Nineteenth Century England*. London: Longman.

Hardy, D. 1983a: *Making Sense of the London Docklands: Processes of Change*. Enfield: Middlesex Polytechnic (Geography and Planning Paper no. 9).

Hardy, D. 1983b: *Making Sense of the London Docklands: People and Places*. Enfield: Middlesex Polytechnic (Geography and Planning Paper no. 10).

Hardy, D. 1989: War, Planning and Social Change: The Example of the Garden City Campaign, 1914–1918. *Planning Perspectives*, 4, 187–206.

Hardy, D. 1991a: *From Garden Cities to New Towns: Campaigning for Town and Country Planning 1899–1946*. London: Spon.

Hardy, D. 1991b: *From New Towns to Green Politics: Campaigning for Town and Country Planning, 1946–1990*. London: Spon.

Hardy, D. 2000: Quasi Utopias: Perfect Cities in an Imperfect World. In: Freestone, R. (ed.) *Urban Planning in a Changing World: The Twentieth Century Experience*, 61–77. London: Spon.

Hardy, D. 2005: Utopian Ideas and the Planning of London. *Planning Perspectives*, 20, 35–49.

Hardy, D. and Ward, C. 1984: *Arcadia for All: The Legacy of a Makeshift Landscape*. London: Mansell.

Hargrove, E. C. and Conkin, P. K. (eds.) 1983: *TVA: Fifty years of Grass-Roots Bureaucracy*. Urbana: University of Illinois Press.

Harloe, M. 1991: Social Housing and the "Urban Question": Early Housing Reform and its Legacy. In: Smith, M. P. (ed.) *Breaking Chains: Social Movements and Collective Action*, 69–107. (*Comparative Urban and Community Research*, 3). Brunswick: Transaction.

Harris, B. 1975: A Fundamental Paradigm for Planning. *Symposium on Planning Theory, 1* (Planning Papers, 1). Philadelphia: Wharton School.

Harris, C. D. 1945: The Cities of the Soviet Union. *Geographical Review*, 35, 107–21.

Harris, C. D. 1970a: *Cities of the Soviet Union*. Chicago: Rand McNally.

Harris, C. D. 1970b: Population of Cities in the Soviet Union, 1897, 1926, 1939, 1959 and 1967 with Tables, Maps, and Gazetteer. *Soviet Geography: Review and Translation*, 11, 307–444.

Harris, R. and Hay, A. 2007: New Plans for Housing in Urban Kenya, 1939–63. *Planning Perspectives*, 22, 195–223.

Harris, W. D. 1971: *The Growth of Latin American Cities*. Athens, Ohio: Ohio University Press.

Harrison, B. 1982: The Politics and Economics of the Urban Enterprise Zone Proposal: A Critique. *International Journal of Urban and Regional Research*, 6, 422–28.

Harrison, J. B. 1980: Allahabad: A Sanitary History. In: Ballhatchet, K. and Harrison, J. *The City in South Asia: Pre-Modern and Modern*, 166–95. London: Curzon Press.

Harrison, M. 1991: Thomas Colgan Horsfall and "the Example of Germany." *Planning Perspectives*, 6, 297–314.

Harrison, P. 2002: Reconstruction and Planning in the Aftermath of the Anglo-Boer South African War: The Experience of the Colony of Natal, 1900–1910. *Planning Perspectives*, 17, 163–82.

Harrison, P. F. 1972: Planning the Metropolis – A Case Study. In: Parker, R. S. and Troy, P. N. (eds.) *The Politics of Urban Growth*, 61–99. Canberra: ANU Press.

Harrison, P. F. 1974: Planning the Metropolitan Areas. In: Burnley, I. H. (ed.) *Urbanization in Australia: The Post-War Experience*, 203–20. London: Cambridge University Press.

Hart, D. A. 1976: *Strategic Planning in London: The Rise and Fall of the Primary Road Network*. Oxford: Pergamon.

Hart, D. A. 1983: Urban Economic Development Measures in West Germany and the United States. In: Young, K. and Mason, C. (eds.) *Urban Economic Development: New Roles and Relationships*, 9–33. London: Macmillan.

Hartman, C. 1964: The Housing of Relocated Families. *Journal of the American Institute of Planners*, 30, 266–86.

Hartman, C. 1966a: The Housing of Relocated Families. In: Wilson, J. Q. (ed.) *Urban Renewal: The Record and the Controversy*, 293–335. Cambridge, MA: MIT Press.

Hartman, C. 1966b: A Comment on the HHFA Survey of Location. In: Wilson, J. Q. (ed.) *Urban Renewal: The Record and the Controversy*, 353–8. Cambridge, MA: MIT Press.

Hartman, C. 1984: *The Transformation of San Francisco*. Totowa: Rowman and Allanheld.

Hartman, C. and Kessler, R. 1978: The Illusion and Reality of Urban Renewal: San Francisco's Yerba Buena Center. In: Tabb, W. K. and Sawers, L. (eds.) *Marxism and the Metropolis: New Perspectives in Urban Political Economy*, 153–78. New York: Oxford University Press.

Hartmann, K. 1976: *Deutsche Gartenstadtbewegung: Kulturpolitik und Gesellschaftsreform*. München: Heinz Moos Verlag.

Hartog, R. 1962: *Stadterweiterungen der Zweiten Hälfte des 19. Jahrhunderts*. Darmstadt: privately published.

Harvey, D. 1973: *Social Justice and the City*. London: Edward Arnold.

Harvey, D. 1982: *The Limits to Capital*. Oxford: Blackwell.

Harvey, D. 1985a: *Consciousness and the Urban Experience: Studies in the History and Theory of Capitalist Urbanization*. Baltimore: Johns Hopkins University Press. Oxford: Blackwell.

Harvey, D. 1985b: *The Urbanization of Capital: Studies in the History and Theory of Capitalist Urbanization*. Baltimore: Johns Hopkins University Press; Oxford: Blackwell.

Harvey, D. 1989: *The Condition of Postmodernity: An Enquiry into the Origins of Cultural Change*. Oxford: Blackwell.

Hasegawa, J. 1999: Governments, Consultants and Expert Bodies in the Physical Reconstruction of the City of London in the 1940s. *Planning Perspectives*, 14, 121–44.

Hass-Klau, C. 1990: *The Pedestrian and City Traffic*. London: Belhaven.

Hausner, V. (ed.) 1987: *Critical Issues in Urban Economic Development*. 2 vols. Oxford: Oxford University Press.

Hayden, D. 1976: *Seven American Utopias: The Architecture of Communitarian Socialism, 1790–1975*. Cambridge, MA: MIT Press.

Hayden, D. 1984: *Redesigning the American Dream: The Future of Housing, Work, and Family Life*. New York: W. W. Norton.

Hayek, F. A. 1944: *The Road to Serfdom*. London: George Routledge.

Hays, F. B. 1965: *Community Leadership: The Regional Plan Association of New York*. New York: Columbia University Press.

Haywood, R. 1997: Railways, Urban Form and Town Planning in London: 1900–1997. *Planning Perspectives*, 12, 37–70.

Headey, B. 1978: *Housing Policy in the Developed Economy: The United Kingdom, Sweden and the United States*. London: Croom Helm.

Hearle, E. F. R. and Niedercorn, J. H. 1964: *The Impact of Urban Renewal on Land-Use*. Santa Monica: The RAND Corporation (Memorandum RM-4186-RC).

Heath, T. 2010: Nottingham: "A Consistent and Integrated Approach to Urban Design." In: Punter, J. (ed.) *Urban Design and the British Urban Renaissance*, 148–64. Abingdon: Routledge.

Hebbert, M. 1992: The British Garden City: Metamorphosis. In: Ward, S. V. (ed.) *The Garden City: Past, Present and Future*, 165–96. London: Spon.

Hebbert, M. 1998: *London: More by Fortune than Design*. Chichester: John Wiley & Sons, Ltd.

Hebbert, M. 2010: Manchester: Making it Happen. In: Punter, J. (ed.) *Urban Design and the British Urban Renaissance*, 51–67. Abingdon: Routledge.

Hecker, M. 1974: *Die Berliner Mietskaserne*. In: Grote, L. (ed.) *Die deutsche Stadt im 19. Jahrhundert: Stadtplanung und Baugestaltung im industriellen Zeitalter*, 273–94. München: Prestel Verlag.

Heclo, H. and Madsen, H. 1987: *Policy and Politics in Sweden: Principled Pragmatism*. Philadelphia: Temple University Press.

Hee, L. and Ooi, G. L. 2003: The Politics of Public Space Planning in Singapore. *Planning Perspectives*, 18, 79–103.

Hegemann, W. 1930: *Das steinerne Berlin: Geschichte der grossten Mietkasernenstadt der Welt*. Berlin: Gustav Kiepenheuer.

Hegemann, W. 1936: *City Planning: Housing. First Volume: Historical and Sociological*. New York: Architectural Book Publishing Co.

Heineman, H. -E. (ed.) 1975: *New Towns for Old: Housing and Services in Sweden*. Stockholm: The Swedish Institute.

Held, D. 1980: *Introduction to Critical Theory: Horkheimer to Habermas*. Berkeley: University of California Press.

Helmer, S. D. 1980: *Hitler's Berlin: Plans for Reshaping the Central City Developed by Albert Speer*. Ann Arbor: University Microfilms.

Henderson, S. R. 1994: A Setting for Mass Culture: Life and Leisure in the Nidda Valley. *Planning Perspectives*, 10, 199–222.

Henderson, S. R. 2010: Römerstadt: The Modern Garden City. *Planning Perspectives*, 25, 323–46.

Herbers, J. 1987a: Poverty of Blacks Spreads in Cities. *The New York Times*, January 26.

Herbers, J. 1987b: Governors Urge Welfare Work Plan. *The New York Times*, February 22.

Herbert-Young, N. 1998: Central Government and Statutory Planning under the Town Planning Act 1909. *Planning Perspectives*, 13, 341–55.

Herlitz, E. 1977: Fran byalag till miljörelse. *Plan*, 31, 216–22.

Heseltine, M. 1987: *Where There's a Will*. London: Hutchinson.

Heskin, A. D. 1980: Crisis and Response: An Historical Perspective on Advocacy Planning. *Journal of the American Planning Association*, 46, 50–63.

Hess, A. 1992: Styling the Strip: Car and Roadside Design in the 1950s. In: Wachs, M. and Crawford, M. (eds.) *The Car and the City: The Automobile, the Built Environment, and Daily Urban Life*, 167–79. Ann Arbor: University of Michigan Press.

Hewlett, R. G. and Anderson, O. E., Jr 1962: *The New World, 1939/1946*. (*A History of the United States Atomic Energy Commission*, vol. I). University Park: Pennsylvania State University Press.

Hightower, H. C. 1969: Planning Theory in Contemporary Professional Education. *Journal of the American Institute of Planners*, 35, 326–9.

Hill, D. R. 1993: A Case for Teleological Urban Form History and Ideas: Lewis Mumford, F. L. Wright, Jane Jacobs and Victor Gruen. *Planning Perspectives*, 8, 53–71.

Hines, T. S. 1974: *Burnham of Chicago: Architect and Planner*. New York: Oxford University Press.

Hirsch, A. R. 1983: *Making the Second Ghetto: Race and Housing in Chicago, 1940–1960*. Cambridge: Cambridge University Press.

Hirsch, F. 1977: *Social Limits to Growth*. London: Routledge and Kegan Paul.

Hirt, S. 2012: Jane Jacobs, Modernity and Knowledge. In: Hirt, S. (ed.) *The Urban Wisdom of Jane Jacobs*, 37–48. Abingdon: Routledge.

Hofmeister, B. 1975: *Bundesrepublik Deutschland und Berlin*. (*Wissenschaftliche Länderkunde*, 8). Berlin: Wissenschaftliche Buchgesellschaft.

Hogdal, L. 1981: 50-talet. *Arkitektur*, 81/5, 14.

Höjer, J., Ljungqvist, S., Poom, J., and Thörnblom, I. 1977: Vällingby, Tensta, Kista, vada? *Arkitekt*, 77/2, 16–21.

Holcomb, B. and Beauregard, R. 1981: *Revitalizing Cities*. Washington, DC: Association of American Geographers.

Holm, L. 1977: Miljö och miljoner. *Plan*, 31, 223–58.

Holm, L. 1981. Trettio ars erfarenhet – grunden för en ny planlag. *Plan*, 35, 57–60.

Holm, P. 1957: *Swedish Housing*. Stockholm: Swedish Institute.

Holm, P. 1977. Det långa perspektivet – om planeringsproblem och planeringsideolgier då och nu och sedan. *Plan*, 31, 184–93.

Holston, J. 1990: *The Modernist City: An Anthropological Critique of Brasília*. Chicago: University of Chicago Press.

Holt, R. T. and Turner, J. E. 1962: *Soviet Union: Paradox and Change*. New York: Holt, Rinehart, Winston.

Holyoak, J. 2010: Birmingham: Translating Ambition into Quality. In: Punter, J. (ed.) *Urban Design and the British Urban Renaissance*, 35–50. Abingdon: Routledge.

Home, R. 1990: Town Planning and Garden Cities in the British Colonial Empire 1910–1940. *Planning Perspectives*, 5, 23–37.

Home, R. 1996: *Town Planning and British Colonialism: The Making of British Colonial Cities*. London: Spon.

Home, R. 1997: *Of Planting and Planning: The Making of British Colonial Cities*. London: Spon.

Home, R. 2013: *Of Planting and Planning: The Making of British Colonial Cities*. Second edition. Abingdon: Routledge.

Home, R. K. 2000: From Barrack Compounds to the Single-Family House: Planning Worker Housing in Colonial Natal and Northern Rhodesia. *Planning Perspectives*, 15, 327–47.

Hood, C. 1992: Going from Home to Work: Subways, Transit Politics, and Metropolitan Spatial Expansion. In: Ward, D. and Zunz, O. (eds.) *The Landscape of Modernity: Essays on New York City, 1900–1940*, 191–212. New York: Russell Sage Foundation.

Hood, C. 1995: *722 Miles: The Building of the Subways and How They Transformed New York*. Baltimore: Johns Hopkins University Press.

Hopkins, K. 1972: Public and Private Housing in Hong Kong. In: Dwyer, D. J. (ed.) *The City as a Centre of Change in Asia*, 200–15. Hong Kong: Hong Kong University Press.

Horowitz, D. L. 1983: Racial Violence in the United States. In: Glazer, N. and Young, K. (eds.) *Ethnic Pluralism and Public Policy: Achieving Equality in the United States and Great Britain*, 187–211. London: Heinemann Education.

Horsey, M. 1988: Multi-Storey Housing in Britain: Introduction and Spread. *Planning Perspectives*, 3, 167–96.

Horsfall, T. C. 1904: *The Improvement of the Dwellings and Surroundings of the People: The Example of Germany*. Manchester: Manchester University Press.

Hoskins, G. and Tallon, A. 2004: Promoting the "Urban Idyll": Policies for City Centre Living. In: Johnstone, C. and Whitehead, M. (eds.) *New Horizons in British Urban Policy: Perspectives on New Labour's Urban Renaissance*, 25–40. Aldershot: Ashgate.

Howard, E. 1898: *To-morrow: A Peaceful Path to Real Reform*. London: Swan Sonnenschein.

Howard, E. 1902: *Garden Cities of To-morrow*. London: Swan Sonnenschein. (Repr. 1946: London: Faber and Faber.)

Howe, I. 1976: *The Immigrant Jews of New York: 1881 to the Present*. London: Routledge and Kegan Paul.

Hoyle, B. S., Pinder, D. A., and Husain, M. S. 1988: *Revitalizing the Waterfront: International Dimensions of Dockland Redevelopment*. London: Belhaven Press.

Hubbard, P. and Faire, L. 2003: Contesting the Modern City: Reconstruction and Everyday Life in Post-War Coventry. *Planning Perspectives*, 18, 377–97.

Hubbard, P. J. 1961: *Origins of the TVA: The Muscle Shoals Controversy, 1920–1932*. Nashville: Vanderbilt University Press.

Hubbard, T. K. 1923: *A Manual of Information on City Planning and Zoning: Including References on Regional, Rural, and National Planning*. Cambridge, MA: Harvard University Press.

Hubbard, T. K. and Hubbard, H. V. 1929: *Our Cities, Today and Tomorrow: A Study of Planning and Zoning Progress in the United States*. Cambridge, MA: Harvard University Press.

Hudson, R. and Williams, A. 1986: *The United Kingdom (Western Europe: Economic and Social Studies)*. London: Harper and Row.

Hughes, J. and Sadler, S. 2000: *Non-Plan: Essays on Freedom Participation and Change in Modern Architecture and Urbanism*. Oxford: Architectural Press.

Hughes, M. (ed.) 1971: *The Letters of Lewis Mumford and Frederic J. Osborn: A Transatlantic Dialogue 1938–70*. New York: Praeger.

Hughes, T. P. and Hughes, A. C. 1990: *Lewis Mumford: Public Intellectual*. New York: Oxford University Press.

Hulbert, J. 1984: Children as Parents. *New Republic*, September 10, 15–23.

Hunter, R. 1901: *Tenement Conditions in Chicago: Report by the Investigating Committee of the City Homes Association*. Chicago: City Homes Association.

Hussey, C., 1953: *The Life of Sir Edwin Lutyens*. London: Country Life.

Hutchings, A. 1990: The Colonel Light Gardens Suburb in South Australia: The Continuing Influence of the Garden City Tradition. *Planning History*, 12/1, 15–20.

Hyndman, H. M. 1884: *The Coming Revolution in England*. London: William Reeves.

Imrie, R. and Thomas, H. 1993: Urban Policy and the Urban Development Corporations. In: Imrie, R. and Thomas, H. (eds.) *British Urban Policy and the Urban Development Corporations*, 3–26. London: Paul Chapman.

Irving, R. G., 1981: *Indian Summer: Lutyens, Baker, and Imperial Delhi*. New Haven: Yale University Press.

Isard, W. 1960: *Methods of Regional Analysis: An Introduction to Regional Science*. Cambridge, MA: MIT Press.

Jackson, A. A. 1973: *Semi-Detached London: Suburban Development, Life and Transport, 1900–39*. London: George Allen and Unwin.

Jackson, F. 1985: *Sir Raymond Unwin: Architect, Planner and Visionary*. London: Zwemmer.

Jackson, J. A. (ed.) 1969: *Migration*. (Sociological Studies, 2). Cambridge: Cambridge University Press.

Jackson, K. T. 1973: The Crabgrass Frontier: 150 Years of Suburban Growth in America. In: Mohl, R. A. and Richardson, J. F. (eds.) *The Urban Experience: Themes in American History*, 196–221. Belmont, CA: Wadsworth.

Jackson, K. T. 1981: The Spatial Dimensions of Social Control: Race, Ethnicity and Government Housing Policy in the United States, 1918–1968. In: Stave, B. M. (ed.) *Modern Industrial Cities: History, Policy and Survival*, 79–128. Beverly Hills: Sage.

Jackson, K. T. 1984: The Capital of Capitalism: The New York Metropolitan Region, 1890–1940. In: Sutcliffe, A. (ed.) *Metropolis 1890–1940*, 319–54. London: Mansell.

Jackson, K. T. 1985: *Crabgrass Frontier: The Suburbanization of the United States*. New York: Oxford University Press.

Jackson, P. (ed.) 1985: *Implementing Government Policy Initiatives: The Thatcher Administration 1979–83*. London: Royal Institute of Public Administration.

Jacobs, A. B. 1976: *Making City Planning Work*. Chicago: American Society of Planning Officials.

Jacobs, A. B. 1983: 1968: Getting Going, Staffing Up, Responding to Issues. In: Krueckeberg, D. A. (ed.) *Introduction to Planning History in the United States*, 235–57. New Brunswick, NJ: Rutgers University, Center for Urban Policy Research.

Jacobs, J. 1962 (1961): *The Death and Life of Great American Cities*. London: Jonathan Cape.

Jahn, M. 1982: Suburban Development in Outer West London, 1850–1900. In: Thompson, F. M. L. (ed.) *The Rise of Suburbia*, 93–156. Leicester: Leicester University Press.

James, H. 1907: *The American Scene*. New York: Harper and Brothers.

Janowitz, M. 1969: Patterns of Collective Racial Violence. In: Graham, H. D. and Gurr, T. R. (eds.) *Violence in America: Historical and Comparative Perspectives*, 317–40. 2 vols. Washington, DC: Government Printing Office.

Jeffcoate, R. 1984: *Ethnic Minorities and Education*. London: Harper and Row.

Jencks, C. 1981: *The Language of Post-Modern Architecture*. New York: Rizzoli.

Jencks, C. 1992: *Rethinking Social Policy: Race, Poverty, and the Underclass.* Cambridge, MA: Harvard University Press.

Jencks, C. and Peterson, P. E. (eds.) 1991: *The Urban Underclass.* Washington, DC: Brookings Institution.

Jenkins, D. 1969: *Sweden: The Progress Machine.* London: Robert Hale.

Jephcott, P. 1971: *Homes in High Flats: Some of the Human Problems Involved in Multi-Story Housing.* Edinburgh: Oliver and Boyd. (University of Glasgow Social and Economic Studies, Occasional Papers no. 13).

Joad, C. E. M. 1937: The People's Claim. In: Williams-Ellis, C. (ed.) *Britain and the Beast,* 64–85. London: J. M. Dent.

Johansson, B. O. H. 1975: From Agrarian to Industrial State. In: Heineman, H. -E. (ed.) *New Towns for Old: Housing and Services in Sweden,* 22–52. Stockholm: The Swedish Institute.

Johnson, C. 1991: *The Economy under Mrs Thatcher 1979–1990.* Harmondsworth: Penguin.

Johnson, C. D. 1941: *Growing Up in the Black Belt: Negro Youth in the Rural South.* New York: Shocken Books.

Johnson, D. A. 1984: Norris, Tennessee on the Occasion of its Fiftieth Anniversary. *Planning History Bulletin,* 6/1, 32–42.

Johnson, D. A. 1988: Regional Planning for the Great American Metropolis: New York between the World Wars. In: Schaffer, D. (ed.) *Two Centuries of American Planning,* 167–96. Baltimore: Johns Hopkins University Press.

Johnson, D. A. 1996: *Planning the Great Metropolis: The 1929 Regional Plan of New York and its Environs.* London: Spon.

Johnson, D. L. 2008: Disturbing Evidence: Adelaide's Town Plan, 1835–7. *Planning Perspectives,* 23, 225–31.

Johnson, J. H. 1964: The Suburban Expansion of Housing in Greater London 1918–1939. In: Coppock, J. T. and Prince, H. (eds.) *Greater London,* 142–66. London: Faber and Faber.

Johnson, J. H. (ed.) 1974: *Suburban Growth: Geographical Processes at the Edge of the Western City.* Chichester: John Wiley & Sons, Ltd.

Johnson, P. B. 1968: *Land Fit for Heroes: The Planning of British Reconstruction, 1916–1919.* Chicago: University of Chicago Press.

Johnson, T. F., Morris, J. R., and Butts, J. T. 1973 (1962): *Renewing America's Cities.* Westport, CT: Greenwood Press.

Johnston, N. J. 1983: Harland Bartholomew: Precedent for the Profession. In: Krueckeberg, D. A. (ed.) *The American Planner: Biographies and Recollections,* 279–300. New York and London: Methuen.

Johnston, R. J. 1979: *Geography and Geographers: Anglo-American Human Geography since 1945.* London: Edward Arnold.

Johnston, R. J. 1986: The General Good of the Community. Some Perspectives on Town Planning and Residential Segregation: A Mount Laurence Case Study. *Planning Perspectives,* 1, 131–45.

Jones, B. 1982: *Sleepers, Wake! Technology and the Future of Work.* Oxford: Oxford University Press.

Jones, D. 1982: *Crime, Protest, Community and Police in Nineteenth Century Britain.* London: Routledge and Kegan Paul.

Jones, D. W., Jr 1985: *Urban Transit Policy: An Economic and Political History.* Englewood Cliffs, NY: Prentice Hall.

Jones, P. N. 1998: "… a fairer and nobler City" – Lutyens and Abercrombie's Plan for the City of Hull 1945. *Planning Perspectives*, 13, 301–16.

Judd, D. R. and Mendelson, R. E. 1973: *The Politics of Urban Planning: The East St Louis Experience*. Urbana: University of Illinois Press.

Kalia, R. 2006: Modernism, Modernization and Post-colonial India: A Reflective Essay. *Planning Perspectives*, 21, 133–56.

Kallus, R. 1997: Patrick Geddes and the Evolution of a Housing Type in Tel-Aviv. *Planning Perspectives*, 12, 281–320.

Kampffmeyer, H. 1908: Die Gartenstadtbewegung. *Jahrbücher für Nationalökonomie und Statistik*, III. Series, 36, 577–609.

Kampffmeyer, H. 1918: Die Gartenstadtbewegung. In: Fuchs, C. J. (ed.) *Die Wohnungs- und Siedlungsfrage nach dem Kriege: Ein Programm des Kleinwohnungs- und Siedlungswesens*, 331–49. Stuttgart: Wilhelm Mener-Ilschen.

Kantor, H. A. 1973a: Charles Dyer Norton and the Origins of the Regional Plan of New York. *Journal of the American Institute of Planners*, 39, 35–42.

Kantor, H. A. 1973b: The City Beautiful in New York. *New York Historical Society Quarterly*, 57, 149–71.

Kantor, H. A. 1973c: Howard W. Odum: The Implications of Folk, Planning, and Regionalism. *American Journal of Sociology*, 79, 278–95.

Kaplan, H. 1963: *Urban Renewal Politics: Slum Clearance in Newark*. New York: Columbia University Press.

Karl, B. 1963: *Executive Reorganization and Reform in the New Deal: The Genesis of Administrative Management, 1900–1939*. Cambridge, MA: Harvard University Press.

Karyd, A. and Södersten, B. 1990: The Swedish Housing Market from a Distributional Perspective: Market and Policy Interactions. In: Persson, I. (ed.) *Generating Equality in the Welfare State: The Swedish Experience*, 157–78. Oslo: Norwegian University Press.

Katz, M. (ed.) 1993: *The "Underclass" Debate: Views from History*. Princeton: Princeton University Press.

Katz, P. 1994: *The New Urbanism: Toward an Architecture of Community*. New York: McGraw-Hill.

Kay, G. 1967: *A Social Geography of Zambia: A Survey of Population Patterns in a Developing Country*. London: University of London Press.

Kay, G. 1970: *Rhodesia: A Human Geography*. London: University of London Press.

Kay, G. and Smout, M. A. H. (eds.) 1977: *Salisbury: A Geographical Survey of the Capital of Rhodesia*. London: Hodder and Stoughton.

Keeble, L. 1959: *Principles and Practice of Town and Country Planning*. London: Estates Gazette.

Kelbaugh, D. *et al.* (eds.) 1989: *The Pedestrian Pocket Book: A New Suburban Design Strategy*. New York: Princeton Architectural Press in association with the University of Washington.

Keles, R. and Payne, G. 1984: Turkey. In: Wynn, M. (ed.) *Planning and Urban Growth in Southern Europe*, 165–97. London: Mansell.

Kellner, D. 1987: Baudrillard, Semiurgy and Death. *Theory, Culture & Society*, 4, 125–46.

Kemeny, J. 1981: *The Myth of Home Ownership*. London: Routledge and Kegan Paul.

Kendall, H. 1955: *Town Planning in Uganda: A Brief Description of the Efforts Made by Government to Control Development of Urban Areas from 1915 to 1955*. London: Crown Agents for Oversea Governments and Administrations.

Kent, T. J. 1964: *The Urban General Plan*. San Francisco: Chandler.

Kent, W. 1950: *John Burns: Labour's Lost Leader*. London: Williams and Norgate.

Kenward, J. 1955: *The Suburban Child*. Cambridge: Cambridge University Press.

Kessner, T. 1977: *The Golden Door: Italian and Jewish Immigrant Mobility in New York City 1880–1915*. New York: Oxford University Press.

Keynes, J. M. 1936: *The General Theory of Employment, Interest, and Money*. London: Macmillan.

Killingworth, C. M. 1968: The Continuing Labor Market Twist. *Monthly Labor Review*, 91/9, 12–17.

Kilmartin, L. A. 1973: Urban Policy in Australia: The Case of Decentralisation. *The Australian and New Zealand Journal of Sociology*, 9/2, 36–9.

Kilmartin, L. A. and Thorns, D. C. 1978: *Cities Unlimited: The Sociology of Urban Development in Australia and New Zealand*. Sydney: George Allen and Unwin.

Kimble, G. H. T. 1951: The Inadequacy of the Regional Concept. In: Stamp, L. D. and Wooldridge, S. W. (eds.) *London Essays in Geography*. London: Longmans, Green.

King, A. 1990: *Global Cities: Post-Imperialism and the Internationalization of London*. London: Routledge.

King, A. D. 1974: The Language of Colonial Urbanization. *Sociology*, 8, 81–110.

King, A. D. 1976: *Colonial Urban Development: Culture, Social Power and Environment*. London: Routledge and Kegan Paul.

King, A. D. (ed.) 1980a: *Buildings and Society: Essays on the Social Development of the Built Environment*. London: Routledge and Kegan Paul.

King, A. D. 1980b: Exporting Planning: The Colonial and Neo-Colonial Experience. In: Cherry, G. E. (ed.) *Shaping an Urban World*, 203–26. London: Mansell.

King, A. D. 1980c: Historical Patterns of Reaction to Urbanism: The Case of Britain 1880–1939. *International Journal of Urban and Regional Research*, 4, 453–69.

King, A. D. 1984: *The Bungalow: The Production of a Global Culture*. London: Routledge and Kegan Paul.

King, A. D. 1996: Worlds in the City: Manhattan Transfer and the Ascendance of Spectacular Space. *Planning Perspectives*, 11, 97–114.

Kirby, A. 1978: *The Inner City: Causes and Effects*. Corbridge: Retailing and Planning Associates.

Kirkby, R. J. R. 1985: *Urbanisation in China: Town and Country in a Developing Economy, 1949–2000 A.D.* London: Croom Helm.

Kitchen, P. 1975: *A Most Unsettling Person: An Introduction to the Ideas and Life of Patrick Geddes*. London: Victor Gollancz.

Klapheck, R. 1930: *Siedlungswerk Krupp*. Berlin: Wasmuth.

Klein, M. and Kantor, H. A. 1976: *Prisoners of Progress: American Industrial Cities 1850–1920*. New York: Macmillan.

Kleniewski, N. 1984: From Industrial to Corporate City: The Role of Urban Renewal. In: Tabb, W. K. and Sawers, L. (eds.) *Marxism and the Metropolis: New Perspectives in Urban Political Economy*, 205–22. New York: Oxford University Press.

Knapp, J. M. 1895: *The Universities and the Social Problem*. London: Rivington Percival.

Knevitt, C. 1975: Macclesfield: The Self-Help GIA. *Architects' Journal*, 162, 995–1002.

Knevitt, C. 1977: Down your Way: Current Projects by Rod Hackney. *Architects' Journal*, 166, 630–4.

Knight, C. G. and Newman, J. L. (eds.) 1976: *Contemporary Africa: Geography and Change*. Englewood Cliffs: Prentice Hall.

Kopp, A. 1970: *Town and Revolution: Soviet Architecture and City Planning, 1917–1935*. London: Thames and Hudson.

Krause, A. S. 1886: *Starving London*. London: Remington and Co.

Krause, R. 1958: *Der Berliner City: frühere Entwicklung/gegenwärtige Situation, mögliche Perspektiven*. Berlin: Duncker and Humblot.

Kropotkin, P. 1906: *The Conquest of Bread*. New York: Vanguard Press.

Kropotkin, P. 1908: *Modern Science and Anarchism*. New York: Mother Earth.

Kropotkin, P. 1913 (1898): *Fields, Factories and Workshops: Or Industry Combined with Agriculture and Brain Work with Manual Work*. New, revised, and enlarged edition. New York: G. P. Putnam's Sons.

Kropotkin, P. 1920: *The State: Its Historic Role*. Fifth edition. London: Freedom Press.

Kropotkin, P. 1971a (1927): Anarchist Morality. In: Baldwin, R. N. (ed.) *Kropotkin's Revolutionary Pamphlets: A Collection of Writings by Peter Kropotkin*, 79–113. New York: Vanguard Press. (Repr. 1971: New York: Dover Publications.)

Kropotkin, P. 1971b (1927): Modern Science and Anarchism. In: Baldwin, R. N. (ed.) *Kropotkin's Revolutionary Pamphlets: A Collection of Writings by Peter Kropotkin*, 146–94. New York: Vanguard Press. (Repr. 1971: New York: Dover Publications.)

Kropotkin, P. 1971c (1927c): Anarchism – Encyclopaedia Britannica Article. In: Baldwin, R. N. (ed.) *Kropotkin's Revolutionary Pamphlets: A Collection of Writings by Peter Kropotkin*, 283–302. New York: Vanguard Press. (Repr. 1971: New York: Dover Publications.)

Krueckeberg, D. A. 1980: The Story of the Planner's Journal, 1915–1980. *Journal of the American Planning Association*, 46, 5–21.

Krueckeberg, D. A. (ed.) 1983a: *The American Planner: Biographies and Recollections*. New York and London: Methuen.

Krueckeberg, D. A. 1983b: From the Backyard Garden to the Whole USA: A Conversation with Charles W. Elliot, 2nd. In: Krueckeberg, D. A. (ed.) *The American Planner: Biographies and Recollections*, 350–65. New York and London: Methuen.

Krueckeberg, D. A. (ed.) 1983c: *Introduction to Planning History in the United States*. New Brunswick, NJ: Rutgers University, Center for Urban Policy Research.

Krueckeberg, D. A. 1983d: The Culture of Planning. In: Krueckeberg, D. A. (ed.) *Introduction to Planning History in the United States*, 1–12. New Brunswick, NJ: Rutgers University, Center for Urban Policy Research.

Krueckeberg, D. A. 1997: Planning History's Mistakes. *Planning Perspectives*, 12, 269–79.

Krumholz, N. 1983: A Retrospective View of Equity Planning: Cleveland, 1969–1979. In: Krueckeberg, D. A. (ed.) *Introduction to Planning History in the United States*, 280–94. New Brunswick, NJ: Rutgers University, Center for Urban Policy Research.

Kuhn, T. S. 1962: *The Structure of Scientific Revolutions*. Chicago: University of Chicago Press.

Ladd, B. 1990: *Urban Planning and Civic Order in Germany, 1860–1914*. Cambridge, MA: Harvard University Press.

Lahti, J. 2008: The Helsinki Suburbs of Tapiola and Vantaanpuisto: Post-War Planning by the Architect Aarne Ervi. *Planning Perspectives*, 23, 147–69.

Lancaster, O. 1959: *Here, of All Places: The Pocket Lamp of Architecture*. London: John Murray.

Lanchester, H. V. 1914: Calcutta Improvement Trust: Precis of Mr. E. P. Richard's Report on the City of Calcutta. *Town Planning Review*, 5, 115–30.

Lanchester, H. V. 1918: *Town Planning in Madras: A Review of the Conditions and Requirements of City Improvement and Development in the Madras Presidency*. London: Constable and Co.

Lanchester, H. V. 1925: *The Art of Town Planning*. London: Chapman and Hall.

Lane, B. M. 1968: *Architecture and Politics in Germany, 1918–1945*. Cambridge, MA: Harvard University Press.

Lang, J. 2000: Learning from Twentieth Century Urban Design Paradigms: Lessons for the Early Twenty-First Century. In: Freestone, R. (ed.) *Urban Planning in a Changing World: The Twentieth Century Experience*, 78–97. London: Spon.

Lang, M. H. 1982: *Gentrification amid Urban Decline: Strategies for America's Older Cities*. Cambridge, MA: Ballinger.

Langdon, P. 1986: *Orange Roofs, Golden Arches: The Architecture of American Chain Restaurants*. New York: Knopf.

Lange, A. 1972 (1961): *Berlin zur Zeit Bebels und Bismarcks: zwischen Reichsgründung und Jahrhundertwende*. Berlin: Das Neue Berlin.

Lappo, G. M. 1973: Trends in the Evolution of Settlement Patterns in the Moscow Region. *Soviet Geography: Review and Translation*, 14, 13–24.

Lappo, G. M., Chikishev, A., and Bekker, A. 1976: *Moscow – Capital of the Soviet Union*. Moscow: Progress Publishers.

Larkham, P. J. 2007: The Place of Urban Conservation in the UK Reconstruction Plans of 1942–1952. *Planning Perspectives*, 18, 295–324.

Larkham, P. J. and Lilley, K. D. 2012: Exhibiting the City: Planning Ideas and Public Involvement in Wartime and Early Post-War Britain. *Town Planning Review*, 83, 647–68.

Lärmer, K., 1975: *Autobahnbau in Deutschland 1933 bis 1945: zu den Hintergründen*. Berlin (East): Akademie-Verlag.

Larsen, K. 2008: Research in Progress: The Radburn Idea as an Emergent Concept: Henry Wright's Regional City. *Planning Perspectives*, 23, 381–95.

Larsson, L. O. 1978: *Die Neugestaltung der Reichshauptstadt: Albert Speers General-bebauungsplan*. Stockholm: Almqvist and Wiksell.

Larsson, Y. 1977: *Mitt Liv i Stadshuset. Andra Delen* (vol. II) *I Tjänst hos denna stolta Stad*. Uppsala: Almqvist and Wiksell.

Lash, S. 1990: *Sociology of Postmodernism*. London: Routledge.

Laska, S. B. and Spain, D. (eds.) 1980: *Back to the City: Issues in Neighborhood Revitalization*. New York: Pergamon.

Lavedan, P. 1952: *Histoire d'urbanisme. Époque contemporaine*, Paris: Henri Laurens.

Lavedan, P. 1959: *Geographie des villes*, Paris: Gaillimard.

Lavedan, P. 1960a: *Histoire de Paris*. Paris: Presses Universitaires de France.

Lavedan, P. 1960b: *Les Villes françaises*. Paris: Éditions Vincent, Fréal.

Lavedan, P. 1975: *Historie de l'urbanisme à Paris*. Paris: Hachette.

Lawless, P. 1986: *The Evolution of Spatial Policy: A Case Study of Inner-Urban Policy in the United Kingdom 1968–1981*. London: Pion.

Lawless, P. 1991: Urban Policy in the Thatcher Decade: English Inner-City Policy 1979–90. *Environment and Planning C: Government and Policy*, 9, 15–30.

Le Corbusier 1929: *The City of Tomorrow and its Planning*. London: John Rodher. Translated by Frederick Etchells from *Urbanisme*, eighth edition (Repr. 1947: London: Architectural Press.)

Le Corbusier 1937: *Quand les cathédrales étaient blanches: Voyage aux pays des timides*. Paris: Plon.

Le Corbusier 1948: *Concerning Town Planning*. London: Architectural Press. (Translated by Clive Entwistle from *Propos d'urbanisme*.)

Le Corbusier 1959: *L'Urbanisme des trois établissements humaines*. Paris: Éditions de Minuit.

Le Corbusier 1967 (1933): *The Radiant City*. London: Faber and Faber.

Le Corbusier 1998: *Essential Le Corbusier: L'Esprit Nouveau Articles*. Oxford and Boston: Architectural Press.

Le Corbusier 2007: *Toward an Architecture*. Translated by John Goodman. Los Angeles: Getty Research Institute.

Le Corbusier-Saugnier 1923: *Vers une architecture*. Paris: G. Crès.

Leavitt, H. 1970: *Superhighway–Superhoax*. Garden City, NY: Doubleday.

Lebas, E., Magri, S., and Topalov, C. 1991: Reconstruction and Popular Housing after the First World War: A Comparative Study of France, Great Britain, Italy and the United States. *Planning Perspectives*, 6, 149–67.

Ledgerwood, G. 1985: *Urban Innovation: The Transformation of London's Docklands 1968–84*. Aldershot: Gower.

Lee, C. E. 1966: *Sixty Years of the Piccadilly*. London: London Transport.

Lee, R. 1992: London Docklands: The Exceptional Place? An Economic Geography of Inter-Urban Competition. In: Ogden, P. (ed.) *London Docklands: The Challenge of Development*, 7–18. Cambridge: Cambridge University Press.

Lees, A. 1979: Critics of Urban Society in Germany, 1854–1914. *Journal of the History of Ideas*, 40, 61–83.

Lees, A. 1984: The Metropolis and the Intellectual. In: Sutcliffe, A. (ed.) *Metropolis 1890–1940*, 67–94. London: Mansell.

Lees, A. 1985: *Cities Perceived: Urban Society in European and American Thought, 1820–1940*. Manchester: Manchester University Press.

Lees, L. 2003: Visions of Urban Renaissance: The Urban Task Force Report and the Urban White Paper. In: Imrie, R. and Raco, M. (eds.) *Urban Renaissance? New Labour, Community and Urban Policy*, 61–82. Bristol: Policy Press.

Lees, R. and Mayo, M. 1984: *Community Action for Change*. London: Routledge and Kegan Paul.

Lefebvre, H. 1968: *Le Droit à la ville*. Paris: Éditions Anthropos.

Lefebvre, H. 1972: *Espace et politique: Le droit à la ville II*. Paris: Éditions Anthropos.

Lehning, A. (ed.) 1973: *Michael Bakunin: Selected Writings*. London: Jonathan Cape.

Leonard, S. G. 1999: The Regeneration of the Old Town of Edinburgh by Patrick Geddes. *Planning History*, 21, 33–47.

Lepawsky, A. 1976: The Planning Apparatus: A Vignette of the New Deal. *Journal of the American Institute of Planners*, 42, 16–32.

Lerner, D. 1967: Comparative Analysis of Processes of Modernisation. In: Miner, H. (ed.) *The City in Modern Africa*, 21–38. London: Pall Mall Press.

Letwin, S. 1992: *The Anatomy of Thatcherism*. London: Fontana.

Lewis, D. N. (ed.) 1971: *The Growth of Cities*. (Architects' Year Book, XIII.) London: Elek Books.

Lewis, J. W. (ed.) 1971: *The City in Communist China*. Stanford, CA: Stanford University Press.

Lewis, N. P. 1916: *The Planning of the Modern City: A Review of the Principles Governing City Planning*. New York: John Wiley & Sons, Inc.

Lewis, O. 1952: Urbanization without Breakdown: A Case Study. *The Scientific Monthly*, 75, 31–41.

Lewis, O. 1961: *The Children of Sanchez*. New York: Random House.

Lewis, O. 1966: The Culture of Poverty. *Scientific American*, 215/4, 19–25.

Lewis, O. 1967: *La Vida: A Puerto Rican Family in the Culture of Poverty – San Juan and New York*. London: Secker and Warburg.

Lewis, R. A. and Rowland, R. H. 1976: *Urbanization in Russia and the USSR, 1897–1970*. In: Hamm, M. F. (ed.) *The City in Russian History*, 205–21. Lexington: University of Kentucky Press.

Liebs, C. H. 1985: *Main Street to Miracle Mile: American Roadside Architecture*. Boston: Little, Brown.

Lilienthal, D. E. 1944: *TVA: Democracy on the March*. New York and London: Harper and Brothers.

Lin, T. -B., Lee, R. P. L., and Simonis, U. -E. (eds.) 1979: *Hong Kong: Economic, Social and Political Studies in Development*. Folkestone: Dawson.

Lindblom, C. E. 1959: The Science of "Muddling Through". *Public Administration Review*, 19, 79–88.

Lindström, J. 1977: Hur kunde det gåsåilla?: Dialog fackmänallmänhet viktigast. *Plan*, 31, 203–5.

Ling, A. 1943: *Planning and Building in USSR*. London: Todd.

Lipton, M. 1977: *Why Poor People Stay Poor: Urban Bias in World Development*. London: Temple Smith.

Little, K. L. 1974: *Urbanization as a Social Process: An Essay on Movement and Change in Contemporary Africa*. London: Routledge and Kegan Paul.

Lloyd, P. C. 1979: *Slums of Hope? Shanty Towns of the Third World*. Manchester: Manchester University Press.

Lloyd, P. C., Mabogunje, A. L., and Awe, B. (eds.) 1967: *The City of Ibadan*. Cambridge: University Press.

Lokjine, J. 1977: *Le Marxisme, l'état et la question urbaine*. Paris: PUF.

London County Council 1913: *Housing of the Working Classes in London: Note on the Action Taken between 1855 and 1912 for the Better Housing of the Working Classes in London, with Special Reference to the Action Taken by the London County Council between the Years 1889 and 1912*. London: Odhams.

London County Council 1928: *Housing: With Particular Reference to Post-War Housing Schemes*. London: P. S. King.

Long, N. E. 1966: Local Government and Renewal Politics. In: Wilson, J. Q. (ed.) *Urban Renewal: The Record and the Controversy*, 422–34. Cambridge, MA: MIT Press.

Longstreth, R. 1992: The Perils of a Parkless Town. In: Wachs, M. and Crawford, M. (eds.) *The Car and the City: The Automobile, the Built Environment, and Daily Urban Life*, 141–53. Ann Arbor: University of Michigan Press.

Longstreth, R. 1997: *City Center to Regional Mall: Architecture, the Automobile, and Retailing in Los Angeles, 1920–1950*. Cambridge, MA: MIT Press.

Los Angeles, County Regional Planning Commission 1943: *Freeways for the Region*. Los Angeles: The Board.

Lösch, A. 1954 (1940): *The Economics of Location*. Translated by W. H. Woglom and W. F. Stolper. New Haven: Yale University Press.

Lotchin, R. 2003: World War II and the Growth of Southern City Planning: A Gigantic Force? *Planning Perspectives*, 18, 355–76.

Lowe, J. R. 1967: *Cities in a Race with Time: Progress and Poverty in America's Renewing Cities*. New York: Random House.

Lowitt, R. 1983: The TVA, 1933–45. In: Hargrove, E. C. and Conkin, P. K. (eds.) *TVA: Fifty Years of Grass-Roots Bureaucracy*, 35–65. Urbana: University of Illinois Press.

Lowry, I. S. 1964: *A Model of Metropolis*. Santa Monica: RAND Corporation. (RM-4035-RC).

Lowry, I. S. 1965: A Short Course in Model Design. *Journal of the American Institute of Planners*, 31, 158–66.

Lubetkin, B. 1932: Recent Developments of Town Planning in USSR. *Architectural Review*, 71, 209–14.

Lubetkin, B. 1933: Town and Landscape Planning in Soviet Russia. *Journal of the Town Planning Institute*, 18, 69–75.

Lubove, R. 1960: Homes and "A Few Well Placed Fruit Trees": An Object Lesson in Federal Housing. *Social Research*, 27, 469–86.

Lubove, R. 1962a: *The Progressives and the Slums: Tenement House Reform in New York City, 1890–1917*. Pittsburgh: University of Pittsburgh Press.

Lubove, R. 1962b: New Cities for Old: The Urban Reconstruction Program of the 1930s. *The Social Studies*, 53, 203–13.

Lubove, R. 1963: *Community Planning in the 1920s: The Contribution of the Regional Planning Association of America*. Pittsburgh: Pittsburgh University Press.

Lubove, R. 1967: *The Urban Community: Housing and Planning in the Progressive Era*. Englewood Cliffs: Prentice Hall.

Lubove, R. 1969: *Twentieth-Century Pittsburgh: Government, Business, and Environmental Change*. New York: John Wiley & Sons, Inc.

Lugard, F. T. 1919: *Revision of Instructions to Political Officers on Subjects Chiefly Political and Administrative 1913–1918*. London: Waterlow & Sons.

Lundqvist, J. 1981: Tanzania: Socialist Ideology, Bureaucratic Reality, and Development from Below. In: Stöhr, W. B. and Taylor, D. R. F. (eds.) *Development from Above or Below? The Dialectics of Regional Planning in Developing Countries*, 329–49. Chichester: John Wiley & Sons, Ltd.

Lundqvist, L. 1984: Strategies for the Swedish Public Housing Sector. *Urban Law and Policy*, 6, 215–51.

Lutyens, E. 1982: *Lutyens: The Work of the English Architect Sir Edwin Lutyens (1869–1944)*. London: Arts Council of Great Britain.

Lutyens, M. 1980: *Edwin Lutyens*. London: John Murray.

Lyall, K. 1982: A Bicycle Built-for-Two: Public–Private Partnership in Baltimore. In: Fosler, R. S. and Berger, R. A. (eds.) *Public–Private Partnership in American Cities: Seven Case Studies*, 17–57. Lexington, MA: Lexington Books.

Lynch, K. 1960: *The Image of the City*. Cambridge, MA: MIT Press.

Lynd, H. M., 1945: *England in the Eighteen-Eighties: Toward a Social Basis for Freedom*. Oxford: Oxford University Press.

Lyotard, J. -F. 1984: *The Postmodern Condition: A Report on Knowledge*. Manchester: Manchester University Press.

Mabin, A. and Smit, D. 1997: Reconstructing South Africa's Cities? The Making of Urban Planning 1900–2000. *Planning Perspectives*, 12, 193–223.

Mabogunje, A. L. 1967: The Morphology of Ibadan. In: Lloyd, P. C., Mabogunje, A. L., and Awe, B. (eds.) *The City of Ibadan*, 35–56. Cambridge: University Press.

Mabogunje, A. L. 1968: *Urbanization in Nigeria*. London: University of London Press.

Mabogunje, A. L. 1980: *The Development Process: A Spatial Perspective*. London: Hutchinson University Library.

Mabogunje, A. L., Hardoy, J. E., and Misra, R. P. 1978: *Shelter Provision in Developing Countries: The Influence of Standards and Criteria.* (Scope, 11). Chichester: John Wiley & Sons, Ltd.

Macdonald, M. C. D. 1984: *America's Cities: A Report on the Myth of Urban Renaissance.* New York: Simon and Schuster.

Macfadyen, D. 1933: *Sir Ebenezer Howard and the Town Planning Movement.* Manchester: Manchester University Press.

MacFarland, J. R. 1966: The Administration of the New Deal Greenbelt Towns. *Journal of the American Institute of Planners,* 32, 217–25.

Machedon, F., Machedon, L. and Scoffham, E. 1999: Inter-war Bucharest: City in a Garden. *Planning Perspectives,* 14, 249–75.

Machler, M. 1932: Town Development in Soviet Russia. *Journal of the Town Planning Institute,* 18, 94–7.

MacKaye, B. 1925: The New Exploration. *The Survey,* 54, 153–7, 192.

MacKaye, B. 1928: *The New Exploration.* New York: Harcourt Brace.

MacKaye, B. 1930: The Townless Highway. *The New Republic,* 62, 93–5.

MacLeod, G. and Ward, K. 2002: Spaces of Utopia and Dystopia: Landscaping the Contemporary City. *Geografiska Annaler,* 84B(3–4), 153–70.

MacPherson, K. L. 1994: The Head of the Dragon: The Pudong New Area and Shanghai's Urban Development. *Planning Perspectives,* 9, 61–85.

Madanipour, A. 2010: Newcastle upon Tyne: In Search of a Post-Industrial Direction. In: Punter, J. (ed.) *Urban Design and the British Urban Renaissance,* 132–47. Abingdon: Routledge.

Madgin, R. 2010: Reconceptualising the Historic Urban Environment: Conservation and Regeneration in Castlefield, Manchester, 1960–2009. *Planning Perspectives,* 25, 29–48.

Mairet, P. 1957: *Pioneer of Sociology: The Life and Letters of Patrick Geddes.* London: Lund Humphries.

Makielski, S. J. 1966: *The Politics of Zoning: The New York Experience.* New York: Columbia University Press.

Malone, D. 1936: *Dictionary of American Biography,* vol. XX. New York: Charles Scribner's Sons.

Malpass, P. 2000: Public Utility Societies and the Housing and Town Planning Act, 1919: A Re-examination of the Introduction of State-Subsidized Housing in Britain. *Planning Perspectives,* 15, 377–92.

Malpass, P. 2003: Wartime Planning for Post-War Housing in Britain: The Whitehall Debate, 1941–5. *Planning Perspectives,* 18, 177–96.

Mandelbaum, S. J. 1980: Urban Pasts and Urban Policies. *Journal of Urban History,* 6, 453–83.

Mandelbaum, S. J. 1985: Thinking about Cities as Systems: Reflections on the History of an Idea. *Journal of Urban History,* 11, 139–50.

Mandler, P. 1999: New Towns for Old: The Fate of the Town Centre. In: Conekin, B., Mort, F., and Waters, C. (eds.) *Moments of Modernity: Reconstructing Britain 1945–1964,* 208–27. London and New York: Rivers Oram Press.

Mangin, W. (P.) (ed.) 1970a: *Peasants in Cities: Readings in the Anthropology of Urbanization.* Boston: Houghton Mifflin.

Mangin, W. (P.) 1970b: Urbanization Case History in Peru. In: Mangin, W. (P.) (ed.) *Peasants in Cities: Readings in the Anthropology of Urbanization,* 47–54. Boston: Houghton Mifflin.

Mangin, W. P. and Turner, J. C. 1969: Benavides and the Barriada Movement. In: Oliver, P. (H.) (ed.) *Shelter and Society*, 127–36. London: Barrie Rokliff: The Cresset Press.

Manieri-Elia, M. 1979: Toward an "Imperial City": Daniel H. Burnham and the City Beautiful Movement. In: Ciucci, G., Dal Co, F., Manieri-Elia, M., and Tafuri, M. *The American City: From the Civil War to the New Deal*, 1–142. Cambridge, MA: MIT Press.

Mann, E. 1968: Nairobi – From Colonial to National Capital. In: Berger, H. (ed.) *Ostafrikanische Studien: Ernst Weigt zum 60. Geburtstag*, 141–56. Nürnberg: Friedrich-Alexander-Universität, Wirtschafts- und Sozialgeographische Institut.

Mann, L. D. 1972: Social Science Advances and Planning Applications: 1900–1965. *Journal of the American Institute of Planners*, 38, 346–58.

Marchand, B. and Cavin, J. S. 2007: Anti-Urban Ideologies and Planning in France and Switzerland: Jean-François Gravier and Armin Meili. *Planning Perspectives*, 22, 29–53.

Marcuse, P. 1980: Housing Policy and City Planning: The Puzzling Split in the United States, 1893–1931. In: Cherry, G. E. (ed.) *Shaping an Urban World*, 23–58. London: Mansell.

Markelius, S. 1957: The Structure of Stockholm. In: Kidder Smith, G. E. *Sweden Builds*, 22–7. London: Architectural Press.

Markelius, S. 1962: Stockholms City. *Arkitektur*, 62, 274–87. (English summary: xxxvi–xxxvii).

Marmaras, E. and Sutcliffe, A. 1994: Planning for Post-War London: Three Independent Plans, 1942–3. *Planning Perspectives*, 9, 455–65.

Marris, P. 1961: *Family and Social Change in an African City: A Study of Rehousing in Lagos*. London: Routledge and Kegan Paul.

Marsh, J. 1982: *Back to the Land: The Pastoral Impulse in England, from 1880 to 1914*. London: Quartet.

Marshall, A. 1884: The Housing of the London Poor. I. Where to House Them. *Contemporary Review*, 45, 224–31.

Martin, R. 1982: The Formulation of a Self-Help Project in Lusaka. In: Ward, P. M. (ed.) *Self-Help Housing: A Critique*, 251–74. London: Mansell.

Martín-Ramos, Á. 2012: The Cerdà Effect on City Modernization. *Town Planning Review*, 83, 695–716.

Masser, I. 1980: An Emerging World City. *Town and Country Planning*, 49, 301–3.

Massey, D. 1982: Enterprise Zones: A Political Issue. *International Journal of Urban and Regional Research*, 6, 429–34.

Massey, D. 1984: *Spatial Divisions of Labour: Social Structures and the Geography of Production*. London: Macmillan.

Massey, D. and Meegan, R. 1982: *The Anatomy of Job Loss: The How, Why and Where of Employment Decline*. London: Methuen.

Masterman, C. F. G. 1909: *The Condition of England*. London: Methuen.

Masterman, C. F. G. *et al.* 1901: *The Heart of the Empire: Discussion on Problems of Modern City Life in England with an Essay on Imperialism*. London: T. Fisher Unwin.

Matzerath, H. 1978: Städtewachtum und Eingemeindungen im 19. Jahrhundert. In: Reulecke, J. (ed.) *Die deutsche Stadt im Industriezeitalter*, 57–89. Wuppertal: Peter Hammer.

Matzerath, H. 1984: Berlin, 1890–1940. In: Sutcliffe, A. (ed.) *Metropolis 1890–1940*, 289–318. London: Mansell.

Mawson, D. 1984: T. H. Mawson (1861–1933) – Landscape Architect and Town Planner. *Journal of the Royal Society of Arts*, 132, 184–99.

Mawson, T. H. 1927: *The Life and Work of an English Landscape Architect*. London: Richards Press.

May, E. 1961: Cities of the Future. *Survey*, 38, 179–85.

May, R. 2003: Planned City Stalinstadt: A Manifesto of the Early German Democratic Republic. *Planning Perspectives*, 18, 47–78.

Mayer, H. M. and Wade, R. C. 1969: *Chicago: Growth of a Metropolis*. Chicago: University of Chicago Press.

McCann, L. D. 1996: Planning and Building the Corporate Suburb of Mount Royal, 1910–1925. *Planning Perspectives*, 11, 259–301.

McCarthy, J. 1999: The Redevelopment of Rotterdam since 1945. *Planning Perspectives*, 14, 291–309.

McCarthy, M. P. 1970: Chicago Businessmen and the Burnham Plan. *Journal of the Illinois State Historical Society*, 63, 228–56.

McCarthy, T. A. 1978: *The Critical Theory of Jürgen Habermas*. Cambridge, MA: MIT Press.

McClendon, D. 1984: Rail Transit in North America. *Planning*, 50/6, 22–3.

McCraw, T. K. 1970: *Morgan vs. Lilienthal: The Feud within the TVA*. Chicago: Loyola University Press.

McCraw, T. K. 1971: *TVA and the Power Fight, 1933–1939*. Philadelphia: Lippincott.

McGahey, J. 1990: "Bolt-Holes for Weekenders": The Press and the Cheap Cottages Exhibition, Letchworth Garden City 1905. *Planning History*, 12/2, 17–18.

McGee, T. G. 1967: *The Southeast Asian City: A Social Geography of the Primate Cities of Southeast Asia*. London: Bell.

McGee, T. G. 1971: *The Urbanization Process in the Third World: Explorations in Search of a Theory*. London: Bell.

McGee, T. G. 1979: The Poverty Syndrome: Making Out in the Southeast Asian City. In: Bromley, R. and Gerry, C. (eds.) *Casual Work and Poverty in Third World Cities*, 45–68. Chichester: John Wiley & Sons, Ltd.

McKay, D. H. and Cox, A. W. 1979: *The Politics of Urban Change*. London: Croom Helm.

McKelvey, B. 1963: *The Urbanization of America. 1860–1915*. Brunswick: Rutgers University Press.

McKelvey, B. 1968: *The Emergence of Metropolitan America, 1915–1966*. New Brunswick: Rutgers University Press.

McKelvey, B. 1969: *The City in American History*. London: George Allen and Unwin.

McKelvey, B. 1973: *American Urbanization: A Comparative History*. Glenview, IL: Scott, Foresman.

McLeod, R. 1971: *Style and Society: Architectural Ideology in Britain, 1835–1914*. London: RIBA Publications.

McLoughlin, J. B. 1969: *Urban and Regional Planning: A Systems Approach*. London: Faber and Faber.

McMaster, D. N. 1968: The Colonial District Town in Uganda. In: Beckinsale, R. P. and Houston, J. M. (eds.) *Urbanization and its Problems: Essays in Honour of E. W. Gilbert*, 330–51. Oxford: Blackwell.

McShane, C. 1994: *Down the Asphalt Path: The Automobile and the American City*. New York: Columbia University Press.

McVicar, K. G. 1968: Pumwani – The Role of a Slum Community in Providing a Catalyst for Culture Change in East Africa. In: Berger, H. (ed.) *Ostafrikanische Studien: Ernst Weigt zum 60. Geburtstag*, 157–67. Nürnberg: Friedrich-Alexander-Universität, Wirtschafts- und Sozialgeographische Institut.

Meadows, J. 1985: The Changing Pattern of Central–Local Fiscal Relations 1979–83. In: Jackson, P. (ed.) *Implementing Government Policy Initiatives: The Thatcher Administration 1979–83*, 145–68. London: Royal Institute of Public Administration.

Mearns, A. 1883: *The Bitter Cry of Outcast London: An Inquiry into the Condition of the Abject Poor*. London: James Clarke.

Meehan, E. J. 1975: *Public Housing Policy: Convention versus Reality*. New Brunswick, NJ: Rutgers University, Center for Urban Policy Research.

Meehan, E. J. 1977: The Rise and Fall of Public Housing: Condemnation without Trial. In: Phares, D. (ed.) *A Decent Home and Environment: Housing Urban America*, 3–42. Cambridge, MA: Ballinger.

Meehan, E. J. 1979: *The Quality of Federal Policymaking: Programmed Failure in Public Housing*. Columbia: University of Missouri Press.

Mehr, H. 1972: Stockholm. In: Robson, W. A. and Regan, D. E. (eds.) *Great Cities of the World*, vol. II, 873–901. Third edition. London: George Allen and Unwin.

Meier, A. and Rudwick, E. 1969: Black Violence in the 20th Century: A Study in Rhetoric and Retaliation. In: Graham, H. D. and Gurr, T. R. (eds.) *Violence in America: Historical and Comparative Perspectives*, 307–16. 2 vols. Washington, DC: Government Printing Office.

Meiler, H. E. (ed.) 1979: *The Ideal City*. Leicester: University Press.

Meller, H. 1990: *Patrick Geddes: Social Evolutionist and City Planner*. London and New York: Routledge.

Meller, H. 1995: Philanthropy and Public Enterprise: International Exhibitions and the Modern Town Planning Movement, 1889–1913. *Planning Perspectives*, 10, 295–310.

Meller, H. 1997: *Towns, Plans and Society in Modern Britain*. Cambridge: Cambridge University Press.

Menzler, F. A. A. 1951: Lord Ashfield. *Public Administration*, 29, 99–112.

Meyerson, M. 1961: Utopian Traditions and the Planning of Cities. *Daedalus*, 90/1, 180–93.

Meyerson, M. and Banfield, E. C. 1955: *Politics, Planning and the Public Interest*. New York: Free Press.

Mill, J. S. 1909: Principles of Political Economy, with Some of Their Applications to Social Philosophy. Seventh revised edition. London: Longmans, Green and Co.

Miller, C. L. 2004: Theory Poorly Practised: The Garden Suburb in New Zealand. *Planning Perspectives*, 19, 37–55.

Miller, D. L. 1989: *Lewis Mumford: A Life*. New York: Weidenfeld and Nicolson.

Miller, M. 1983: Letchworth Garden City Eighty Years On. *Built Environment*, 9, 167–84.

Miller, M. 1989a: *Letchworth: The First Garden City*. Chichester: Phillimore.

Miller, M. 1989b: The Elusive Green Background: Raymond Unwin and the Greater London Regional Plan. *Planning Perspectives*, 4, 15–44.

Miller, M. 1992: *Raymond Unwin: Garden Cities and Town Planning*. London: Leicester University Press.

Miller, M. 2000: Transatlantic Dialogue: Raymond Unwin and the American Planning Scene. *Planning History*, 22/2, 17–28.

Miller, M. 2002: The Origins of the Garden City Residential Neighborhood. In: Parsons, K. C. and Schuyler, D. (eds.) *From Garden City to Green City: The Legacy of Ebenezer Howard*, 99–130. Baltimore and London: Johns Hopkins University Press.

Miller, M. and Gray, A. S. 1992: *Hampstead Garden Suburb*. Chichester: Phillimore.

Milner, H. 1990: *Sweden: Social Democracy in Practice*. Oxford: Oxford University Press.

Miner, H. (ed.) 1967: *The City in Modern Africa*. London: Pall Mall Press.

Minney, R. J. 1958: *Viscount Addison: Leader of the Lords*. London: Odhams Press.

Mitchell, B. R. 1975: *European Historical Statistics, 1750–1970*. London: Macmillan.

Mitchell, J. C. 1969: Structural Plurality, Urbanization and Labour Circulation in Southern Rhodesia. In: Jackson, J. A. (ed.) *Migration*, 156–80. (Sociological Studies, 2). Cambridge: Cambridge University Press.

Mitchell, N. 1972: *The Indian Hill Station: Kodaikanal*. University of Chicago, Department of Geography, Research Paper, no. 141.

Mitchell, R. B. and Rapkin, C. 1954: *Urban Traffic: A Function of Land Use*. New York: Columbia University Press.

Mitchell, W. J. 1995: *City of Bits: Space, Place, and the Infobahn*. Cambridge, MA: MIT Press.

Mitchell, W. J. 1999: *e-topia: "Urban Life, Jim – But Not as We Know It."* Cambridge, MA: MIT Press.

Mohl, R. A. and Richardson, J. F. (eds.) 1973: *The Urban Experience: Themes in American History*. Belmont, CA: Wadsworth.

Mollenkopf, J. H. 1978: The Postwar Politics of Urban Development. In: Tabb, W. K. and Sawers, L. (eds.) *Marxism and the Metropolis: New Perspectives in Urban Political Economy*, 117–52. New York: Oxford University Press.

Mollenkopf, J. H. 1983: *The Contested City*. Princeton: Princeton University Press.

Monclús, F. -J. 2003: The Barcelona Model: An Original Formula? From "Reconstruction" to Strategic Urban Projects (1979–2004). *Planning Perspectives*, 18, 399–421.

Monkkonen, E. H. 1988: *America Becomes Urban: The Development of US Cities and Towns, 1780–1980*. Berkeley: University of California Press.

Montgomery, R. 1985: Pruitt–Igoe: Policy Failure or Societal Symptom. In: Checkoway, B. and Patton, C. V. (eds.) *The Metropolitan Midwest: Policy Problems and Prospects for Change*, 229–43. Urbana: University of Illinois Press.

Moore, C. 1921: *Daniel H. Burnham: Architect, Planner of Cities*. Boston and New York: Houghton Mifflin.

Moore, C., Becker, P., and Campbell, R. 1984: *The City Observed – Los Angeles: A Guide to its Architecture and Landscapes*. New York: Vintage Books.

Morgan, A. E. 1974: *The Making of TVA*. Buffalo: Prometheus Books.

Morgan, W. T. W. (ed.) 1967: *Nairobi: City and Region*. Nairobi: Oxford University Press.

Morizet, A. 1932: *Du vieux Paris au Paris moderne: Haussmann et ses prédécesseurs*. Paris: Hachette.

Mort, F. 2004: Fantasies of Metropolitan Life: Planning London in the 1940s. *Journal of British Studies*, 43, 120–51.

Moynihan, D. P. 1965: *The Negro Family: The Case for National Action*. Washington, DC: US Department of Labor Office of Policy Planning and Research.

Moynihan, D. P. 1986: *Family and Nation: The Godkin Lectures, Harvard University*. New York: Harcourt Brace.

Muench, L. H. and C. Z. 1968: Planning and Antiplanning in Nigeria: Lagos and Ibadan. *Journal of the American Institute of Planners*, 34, 374–81.

Muller, J. 1992: From Survey to Strategy: Twentieth Century Developments in Western Planning Methods. *Planning Perspectives*, 7, 125–55.

Muller, T. 1976: *Economic Impacts of Land Development: Economic, Housing and Property Values*. Washington, DC: The Urban Institute.

Mullin, J. R. 1977a: American Perceptions of German City Planning at the Turn of the Century. *Urbanism Past and Present*, 3, 5–15.

Mullin, J. R. 1977b: City Planning in Frankfurt, Germany, 1925–1932: A Study in Practical Utopianism. *Journal of Urban History*, 4, 3–28.

Mumford, E. 1995: The "Tower in a Park" in America: Theory and Practice, 1920–1960. *Planning Perspectives*, 10, 17–41.

Mumford, L. 1923: *The Story of Utopias*. London: Harrap.

Mumford, L. 1925a: The Fourth Migration. *The Survey*, 54, 130–3.

Mumford, L. 1925b: Regions – To Live In. *The Survey*, 54, 151–2.

Mumford, L. 1930: Mass-Production and the Modern House. *Architectural Record*, 67, 13–20, 110–16.

Mumford, L. 1932: The Plan of New York. *New Republic*, 71, 121–6; 146–54.

Mumford, L. 1934: *Technics and Civilization*. New York: Harcourt Brace.

Mumford, L. 1938: *The Culture of Cities*. London: Secker and Warburg.

Mumford, L. 1944: *The Condition of Man*. London: Secker and Warburg.

Mumford, L. 1946: The Garden City Idea and Modern Planning. In: Howard, E. *Garden Cities of To-morrow*, 29–40. London: Faber and Faber.

Mumford, L. 1954: The Neighbourhood and the Neighbourhood Unit. *Town Planning Review*, 24, 256–70.

Mumford, L. 1961: *The City in History: Its Origins, its Transformations, and its Prospects*. New York: Harcourt, Brace & World.

Mumford, L. 1964: *The Highway and the City*. New York: Mentor Books.

Mumford, L. 1982: *Sketches from Life: The Autobiography of Lewis Mumford: The Early Years*. New York: Dial Press.

Murphey, R. 1977: *The Outsiders: The Western Experience in India and China*. Ann Arbor: University of Michigan Press.

Murphey, R. 1980: *The Fading of the Maoist Vision: City and Country in China's Development*. London: Methuen.

Murphey, R. 1984: City as a Mirror of Society: China, Tradition and Modernization. In: Agnew, J., Mercer, J., and Sopher, D. E. (eds.) *The City in Cultural Context*, 186–204. Boston: Allen and Unwin.

Muschamp, H. 1983: *Man about Town: Frank Lloyd Wright in New York City*. Cambridge, MA: MIT Press.

Muthesius, H. 1908–11: *Das englische Haus: Entwicklung, Bedingungen, Anlage, Aufbau, Einrichtung und Innenraum*. 3 vols. Second revised edition. Berlin: Ernst Wasmuth.

Myers, G. A. 2003: *Verandahs of Power: Colonialism and Space in Urban Africa*. Syracuse, Syracuse University Press.

Myhra, D. 1974: Rexford Guy Tugwell: Initiator of America's Greenbelt New Towns, 1935 to 1938. *Journal of the American Institute of Planners*, 40, 176–88.

Myrdal, G. 1944: *An American Dilemma: The Negro Problem and Modern Democracy*. New York: Harper and Brothers.

Nadin, V. 2007: The Emergence of the Spatial Planning Approach in England. *Planning Practice & Research*, 22, 43–62.

Nairn, I. 1955: Outrage: A Special Number of the Architectural Review. *Architectural Review*, 117, 363–454.

Nairn, I. 1965: *The American Landscape: A Critical View*. New York: Random House.

Negroponte, N. 1995: *Being Digital*. London: Hodder and Stoughton.

Nehru, J. 1936: *An Autobiography: With Musings on Recent Events in India*. London: John Lane – The Bodley Head.

Neild, S. M. 1979: Colonial Urbanism: The Development of Madras City in the Eighteenth and Nineteenth Centuries. *Modern Asian Studies*, 13, 217–46.

Nelson, J. J. 1959: The Spread of an Artificial Landscape over Southern California. *Annals of the Association of American Geographers*, 49, Supplement to no. 3, 80–99.

Nelson, W. H. 1967: *Small Wonder: The Amazing Story of the Volkswagen*. London: Hutchinson.

Nettlefold, J. S. 1914: *Practical Town Planning*. London: The St Catherine Press.

Neue Gesellschaft für Bildede Kunst 1977: *Wem gehört die Welt? Kunst und Gesellschaft in der Weimare Republik*. Berlin: Neue Gesellschaft für Bildede Kunst.

Neufang, H. 1963: Die Siedlungsverband Ruhrkohlenbezirk (1920–1963). *Die öffentliche Verwaltung*, 16, 812–19.

Neuman, M. 2011: Ildefons Cerdà and the Future of Spatial Planning: The Network Urbanism of a City Planning Pioneer. *Town Planning Review*, 82, 117–43.

Neumeyer, F. 1978: Zum Werkwohnungsbau in Deutschland um 1900. In: Siepmann, E. (ed.) *Kunst und Alltag um 1900*. Lahn/Giessen: Anabas Verlag.

Neuse, S. M. 1983: TVA at Age Fifty – Reflections and Retrospect. *Public Administration Review*, 43, 491–9.

Neutze, G. M. 1977: *Urban Development in Australia: A Descriptive Analysis*. Sydney: George Allen and Unwin.

Neville, R. J. W. 1965: The Areal Distribution of Population in Singapore. *The Journal of Tropical Geography*, 20, 16–25.

Nevins, A. 1954. *Ford: The Times, The Man, The Company*. New York: Charles Scribner's Sons.

"New Townsmen" 1918: *New Towns after the War: An Argument for Garden Cities*. London: J. M. Dent.

Newman, I. and Mayo, M. 1981: Docklands. *International Journal of Urban and Regional Research*, 5, 529–45.

Newman, O. 1972: *Defensible Space: Crime Prevention and Urban Design*. New York: Macmillan.

Newman, O. 1980: *Community of Interest*. Garden City, NY: Anchor/Doubleday.

Niethammer, L. 1981: Some Elements of the Housing Reform Debate in Nineteenth Century Europe: Or, On the Making of a New Paradigm of Social Control. In: Stave, B. M. (ed.) *Modern Industrial Cities: History, Policy and Survival*, 129–64. Beverly Hills: Sage.

Njoh, A. 2009: Urban Planning as a Tool of Power and Social Control in Colonial Africa. *Planning Perspectives*, 24, 301–17.

Nocks, B. C. 1974: Case Studies: A Decade of Planning Education at Three Schools. In: Godschalk, D. R. (ed.) *Planning in America: Learning from Turbulence*, 206–26. Washington, DC: American Institute of Planners.

Nolen, J. (ed.) 1916a: *City Planning: A Series of Papers Presenting the Essential Elements of a City Plan*. New York: D. Appleton.

Nolen, J. 1916b: The Subdivision of Land. In: Nolen, J. (ed.) *City Planning: A Series of Papers Presenting the Essential Elements of a City Plan*, 19–47. New York: D. Appleton.

Novak, F. G., Jr (ed.) 1995: *Lewis Mumford and Patrick Geddes: The Correspondence*. London: Routledge.

Oberlander, H. P. and Newburn, E. 1999: *Houser: The Life and Work of Catherine Bauer*. Vancouver: UBC Press.

O'Carroll, A. 1996: The Influence of Local Authorities on the Growth of Owner Occupation: Edinburgh and Glasgow 1914–1939. *Planning Perspectives*, 11, 55–72.

O'Connor, A. M. 1981: *Urbanization in Tropical Africa: An Annotated Bibliography*. Boston: G. K. Hall.

O'Connor, A. M. 1983: *The African City*. London: Hutchinson University Library for Africa.

O'Connor, T. H. 1993: *Building a New Boston: Politics and Urban Renewal, 1950–1970*. Boston: Northeastern University Press.

Ödmann, E. and Dahlberg, G. -B. 1970: Urbanisation in Sweden: Means and Methods for the Planning. Stockholm: Allmanna Forlaget.

Odum, H. W. 1910: *Social and Mental Traits of the Negro: Research into the Conditions of the Negro Race in Southern Towns: A Study in Race Traits, Tendencies and Prospects.* (Studies in History, Economics and Public Law, 37, no. 3.) New York: Columbia University.

Odum, H. W. 1926: *An Approach to Public Welfare and Social Work*. Chapel Hill: University of North Carolina Press.

Odum, H. W. 1936: *Southern Regions of the United States*. Chapel Hill: University of North Carolina Press.

Odum, H. W. and Jocher, K. (eds.) 1945: *In Search of the Regional Balance of America*. Chapel Hill: University of North Carolina Press.

Odum, H. W. and Johnson, G. B. 1925: *The Negro and his Songs*. Chapel Hill: University of North Carolina Press.

Odum, H. W. and Moore, H. E. 1938: *American Regionalism: A Cultural-Historical Approach to National Integration*. New York: Henry Holt and Co.

Ogden, P. (ed.) 1992a: *London Docklands: The Challenge of Development*. Cambridge: Cambridge University Press.

Ogden, P. 1992b: Introduction: Some Questions of Geography and History. In: Ogden, P. (ed.) *London Docklands: The Challenge of Development*, 1–6. Cambridge: Cambridge University Press.

Olds, K. 1995: Globalization and the Production of New Urban Spaces: Pacific Rim Megaprojects in the Late 20th Century. *Environment and Planning A*, 27, 1713–43.

Oliver, P. (H.) (ed.) 1969: *Shelter and Society*. London: Barrie Rokliff: The Cresset Press.

Oliver, P. (H.) (ed.) 1975: *Shelter in Africa*. London: Barrie and Jenkins.

Oliver, P. (H.), Davis, I., and Bentley, I. 1981: *Dunroamin: The Suburban Semi and its Enemies*. London: Barrie and Jenkins.

Orlans, H. 1952: *Stevenage: A Sociological Study of a New Town*. London: Routledge and Kegan Paul.

Orwell, G. 1939: *Coming up for Air*. London: Secker and Warburg.

Osborn, F. J. 1934: *Transport, Town Development and Territorial Planning of Industry*. London: Fabian Society.

Osborn, F. J. 1936: *London's Dilemma: The Only Way Out*. London: Garden Cities and Town Planning Association.

Osborn, F. J. 1937: A Lecture to London. *Journal of the Town Planning Institute*, 23, 45–51.

Osborn, F. J. 1938: The Planning of Greater London. *Town and Country Planning*, 6, 97–102.

Osborn, F. J. 1942: *New Towns after the War*. London: J. M. Dent.

Osborn, F. J. 1950: Sir Ebenezer Howard: The Evolution of his Ideas. *Town Planning Review*, 21, 221–35.

Osborn, F. J. 1955: How Subsidies Distort Housing Development. *Lloyds Bank Review*, N. S. 36, 25–38.

Osborn, F. J. 1970: *Genesis of Welwyn Garden City: Some Jubilee Memories*. London: Town and Country Planning Association.

Owens, S. E. 1984: Spatial Structure and Energy Demand. In: Cope, D. R., Hills, P. R., and James, P. (eds.) *Energy Policy and Land Use Planning*, 215–40. Oxford: Pergamon.

Owens, S. E. 1986: *Energy, Planning and Urban Form*. London: Pion.

Owens, S. E. 1990: Land-Use Planning for Energy Efficiency. In: Cullingworth, J. B. (ed.) *Energy, Land and Public Policy*, 53–98. Newark, DE: Transactions Publishers, Center for Energy and Urban Policy Research.

Owens, S. E. 1992a: Energy, Environmental Sustainability and Land-Use Planning. In: Breheny, M. J. (ed.), *Sustainable Development and Urban Form*. (*European Research in Regional Science*, 2). London: Pion.

Owens, S. E. 1992b: Land-Use Planning for Energy Efficiency. *Applied Energy*, 43, 81–114.

Owens, S. E. and Cope, D. 1992: *Land Use Planning Policy and Climate Change*. London: HMSO.

Pahl, R. E. (ed.) 1968: *Readings in Urban Sociology*. Oxford: Pergamon.

Paris 1978: Anonymous news contributions. *Macadam*, 4, 4–9.

Paris 1979a: Anonymous news contributions. *Architecture*, 1, 7–17.

Paris 1979b: Anonymous news contributions. *Building News*, 437, 4; 438, 1; 456, 8.

Paris 1979c: Jeu de l'Oie des Halles de Paris. *Macadam, 8/9*, 12–13.

Park, R. E. 1925a: The City: Suggestions for the Investigation of Human Behavior in the Urban Environment. In: Park, R. E., Burgess, E. W., and McKenzie, R. D. *The City*, 1–46. Chicago: University of Chicago Press.

Park, R. E. 1925b: Community Disorganization and Juvenile Delinquency. In: Park, R. E., Burgess, E. W., and McKenzie, R. D. *The City*, 99–112. Chicago: University of Chicago Press.

Park, R. E. 1928: Human Migration and the Marginal Man. *The American Journal of Sociology*, 33, 881–93.

Park, R. E., Burgess, E. W., and McKenzie, R. D. 1925: *The City*. Chicago: University of Chicago Press.

Park, R. L. 1962: The Urban Challenge to Local and State Government: West Bengal, with Special Reference to Calcutta. In: Turner, R. (ed.) *India's Urban Future*, 382–96. Berkeley: University of California Press.

Parker, B. 1932: Highways, Parkways and Freeways: with Special Reference to Wythenshawe Estate, Manchester, and to Letchworth Garden City. *Town and Country Planning*, 1, 38–43.

Parker, B. and Unwin, R. 1901: *The Art of Building a Home: A Collection of Lectures and Illustrations*. London: Longmans, Green.

Parker, R. S. and Troy, P. N. (eds.) 1972: *The Politics of Urban Growth*. Canberra: ANU Press.

Parkin, D. J. (ed.) 1975: *Town and Country in East and Central Africa*. London: Oxford University Press (for International African Institute).

Parkins, M. F. 1953: *City Planning in Soviet Russia: With an Interpretative Bibliography*. Chicago: University of Chicago Press.

Parsons, K. C. 1992a: America's Influence on Stockholm's Post World War II Suburban Expansion. *Planning History*, 14/1, 3–14.

Parsons, K. C. 1992b: British and American Community Design: Clarence Stein's Manhattan Transfer, 1924–74. *Planning Perspectives*, 7, 181–210.

Parsons, K. C. 1998: *The Writings of Clarence S. Stein: Architect of the Planned Community*. Baltimore: Johns Hopkins University Press.

Parsons, K. C. 2002: British and American Community Design: Clarence Stein's Manhattan Transfer, 1924–1974. In: Parsons, K. C. and Schuyler, D. (eds.) *From Garden City to Green City: The Legacy of Ebenezer Howard*, 131–58. Baltimore and London: Johns Hopkins University Press.

Partners for Livable Places 1982: *Towards Livable Communities: A Report on Partners for Livable Places, 1975–1982*. Washington, DC: Partners for Livable Places.

Pass, D. 1973: *Vällingby and Farsta – From Idea to Reality: The New Community Development Process in Stockholm*. Cambridge, MA: MIT Press.

Patterson, O. 1982: *Slavery and Social Death: A Comparative Study*. Cambridge, MA: Harvard University Press.

Pawlowski, C. 1967: *Tony Garnier et les débuts de l'urbanisme fonctionnel en France*. Paris: Centre de Recherche d'Urbanisme.

Payne, G. K. 1977: *Urban Housing in the Third World*. London: Leonard Hill.

Payne, G. K. 1982: Self-Help Housing: A Critique of the Gecekondus of Ankara. In: Ward, P. M. (ed.) *Self-Help Housing: A Critique*, 117–39. London: Mansell.

Payton, N. I. 1995: The Machine in the Garden City: Patrick Geddes' Plan for Tel Aviv. *Planning Perspectives*, 10, 359–81.

Pearlman, J. 2000: Joseph Hudnut and the Unlikely Beginnings of Post-modern Urbanism at the Harvard Bauhaus. *Planning Perspectives*, 15, 201–39.

Pearson, S. V. 1939: *London's Overgrowth and the Causes of Swollen Towns*. London: C. W. Daniel.

Peattie, L. 1968: Reflections on Advocacy Planning. *Journal of the American Institute of Planners*, 34, 80–8.

Peel, J. D. Y. 1980: Urbanization and Urban History in West Africa. *Journal of African History*, 21, 269–77.

Pehnt, R. (ed.) 1974: *Die Stadt in der Bundesrepublik Deutschland*. Stuttgart: Philipp Reclam.

Peil, M. 1976: African Squatter Settlements: A Comparative Study. *Urban Studies*, 13, 155–66.

Peltz-Dreckmann, U. 1978: *Nationalsozialistischer Siedlungsbau*. München: Minerva.

Pendlebury, J. 2002: Conservation and Regeneration: Complementary or Conflicting Processes? The Case of Grainger Town, Newcastle upon Tyne. *Planning Practice & Research*, 17, 145–58.

Pendlebury, J. and Strange, I. 2011: Urban Conservation and the Shaping of the English City. *Town Planning Review*, 82, 361–92.

Pepler, G. L. 1911: Greater London. In: Royal Institute of British Architects *Town Planning Conference – Transactions*, 611–20. London: RIBA.

Pepper, S. and Richmond, P. 2009: Homes Unfit for Heroes: The Slum Problem in London and Neville Chamberlain's Unhealthy Areas Committee, 1919–21. *Town Planning Review*, 80, 143–71.

Perera, N. 2004: Contesting Visions: Hybridity, Liminality and Authorship of the Chandigarh Plan. *Planning Perspectives*, 19, 175–99.

Perkins, K. L. 2007: Roosevelt and Rexford: Resettlement and its Results. *Berkeley Planning Journal*, 20, 25–42.

Perlman, J. E. 1976: *The Myth of Marginality: Urban Poverty and Politics in Rio de Janeiro.* Berkeley: University of California Press.

Perloff, H. S. 1965: New Directions in Social Planning. *Journal of the American Institute of Planners*, 31, 297–304.

Perloff, H. S. (with Klett, F.) 1974: The Evolution of Planning Education. In: Godschalk, D. R. (ed.) *Planning in America: Learning from Turbulence*, 161–80. Washington, DC: American Institute of Planners.

Perloff, H. S., Berg, T., Fountain, R., Vetter, D., and Weld, J. 1975: *Modernizing the Central City: New Towns Intown … and Beyond.* Cambridge, MA: Ballinger.

Perroux, F. 1961: *L'Économie du XXe siècle.* Paris: Presses Universitaires de France.

Perroux, F. 1965: *La Pensée économique de Joseph Schumpeter: Les Dynamiques du capitalisme.* (Travaux de Droit, d'économie, de Sociologie et de Sciences Politiques, 34.) Genève: Droz.

Perry, C. A. 1929: *The Neighborhood Unit: A Scheme of Arrangement for the Family-Life Community* (Regional Study of New York and its Environs, VII, Neighborhood and Community Planning, Monograph One, 2–140). New York: Regional Plan of New York and its Environs.

Perry, C. A. 1939: *Housing for the Machine Age.* New York: Russell Sage Foundation.

Perry, M., Kong, L. and Yeoh, B. 1997: *Singapore, A Developmental City State.* Chichester: John Wiley.

Persson, I. (ed.) 1990: *Generating Equality in the Welfare State: The Swedish Experience.* Oslo: Norwegian University Press.

Peters, J. 1982: Interstates: Nearing the End of the Road. *Planning*, 47/12, 12–15.

Petersen, W. 1977: The Ideological Origins of Britain's New Towns. In: Allen, I. L. (ed.) *New Towns and the Suburban Dream: Ideology and Utopia in Planning and Development*, 61–81. Port Washington: Kennikat.

Peterson, J. A. 1976: The City Beautiful Movement: Forgotten Origins and Lost Meanings. *Journal of Urban History*, 2, 415–34.

Petsch, J. 1976: *Baukunst und Stadtplanung im dritten Reich: Herleitung/Bestandsaufnahme/ Entwicklung/Nachfolge.* München: Carl Hanser.

Petz, U. von 1990a: Margarethenhöhe Essen: Garden City, Workers' Colony or Satellite Town? *Planning History*, 12/2, 3–9.

Petz, U. von 1990b: Urban Renewal under National Socialism: Practical Policy and Political Objectives in Hitler's Germany. *Planning Perspectives*, 5, 169–87.

Petz, U. von 1999: Robert Schmidt and the Public Park Policy in the Ruhr district, 1900–1930. *Planning Perspectives*, 14, 163–82.

Petz, U. von 2010: News from the Field: City Planning Exhibitions in Germany, 1910–2010. *Planning Perspectives*, 25, 375–82.

Pfautz, H. W. 1967: *Charles Booth on the City. Physical Patterns and Social Structure.* Chicago: University of Chicago and London Press.

Phares, D. (ed.), 1977: *A Decent Home and Environment: Housing Urban America.* Cambridge, MA: Ballinger.

Phillips, W. R. F. 1996: The "German Example" and the Professionalization of American and British City Planning at the Turn of the Century. *Planning Perspectives*, 11, 167–83.

Philpott, T. L. 1978: *The Slum and the Ghetto: Neighborhood Deterioration and Middle-Class Reform, Chicago, 1880–1930.* New York: Oxford University Press.

Pick, F. 1927: Growth and Form in Modern Cities. *Journal of the Institute of Transport*, 8, 156–74.

Pick, F. 1935: Some Reflections on the Administration of a Public Utility Undertaking. *Public Administration*, 13, 135–45.

Pick, F. 1936: The Organisation of Transport: with Special Reference to the London Passenger Transport Board. *Journal of the Royal Society of Arts*, 84, 207–19.

Pick, F. 1937: London Fifty Years Hence. *Journal of the Town Planning Institute*, 23, 61–6.

Pick, F. 1938: Evidence of London Passenger Transport Board. In: GB Royal Commission on the Geographical Distribution of the Industrial Population 1937–9: *Minutes of Evidence*, Day 12. London: HMSO.

Pick, F. 1941: *Britain Must Rebuild: A Pattern for Planning*. (The Democratic Order, no. 17.) London: Kegan Paul, Trench, Trubner.

Piven, F. F. and Cloward, R. A. 1977: *Poor People's Movements: Why They Succeed, How They Fail*. New York: Pantheon.

Piven, F. F. and Cloward, R. A. 1982: *The New Class War: Reagan's Attack on the Welfare State and its Consequences*. New York: Pantheon.

Poëte, M. 1931: *Une vie de cité: Paris de sa naissance à nos jours*. 3 vols. Paris: Auguste Picard.

Pollock, N. C. 1968: *The Development of Urbanization in Southern Africa*. In: Beckinsale, R. P. and Houston, J. M. (eds.) *Urbanization and its Problems: Essays in Honour of E. W. Gilbert*, 304–29. Oxford: Blackwell.

Pons, V. 1969: *Stanleyville: An African Urban Community under Belgian Administration*. London: Oxford University Press.

Popenoe, D. 1977: *The Suburban Environment: Sweden and the United States*. Chicago: University of Chicago Press.

Popper, F. J. 1981: *The Politics of Land-Use Reform*. Madison: University of Wisconsin Press.

Porfyriou, H. 1992: Artistic Urban Design and Cultural Myths: The Garden City Idea in Nordic Countries, 1900–1925. *Planning Perspectives*, 7, 263–302.

Portes, A. 1979: Housing Policy, Urban Poverty, and the State: The Favelas of Rio de Janeiro, 1972–1976. *Latin American Research Review*, 14/2, 3–24.

Powell, J. M. and Williams, M. 1975: *Australian Space, Australian Time: Geographical Perspectives*. Melbourne: Oxford University Press.

Power, A. and Mumford, K. 1999: *The Slow Death of Great Cities? Urban Abandonment or Urban Renaissance*. York: Joseph Rowntree Foundation.

Poxon, J. 2000: Solving the Development Plan Puzzle in Britain: Learning Lessons from History. *Planning Perspectives*, 15, 73–89.

Prescott, J. 2003: Quoted in "Prescott Demands More 'Wow' and Less 'Noddy.'" http://www.architectsjournal.co.uk/home/prescott-demands-more-wowand-less-noddy/146911.article (accessed December 19, 2013).

Prescott, N. C. 1968: The Development of Urbanization in Southern Africa. In: Beckinsale, R. P. and Houston, J. M. (eds.), 304–29.

Preston, J. and Wall, G. 2008: The Ex-ante and Ex-post Economic and Social Impacts of the Introduction of High-speed Trains in South East England. *Planning Practice & Research*, 23, 403–22.

Priemus, H. 2004: From a Layers Approach Towards a Network Approach: A Dutch Contribution to Spatial Planning Methodology. *Planning Practice & Research*, 19, 267–83.

Proudfoot, P. R. 1996: The Symbol of the Crystal in the Planning and Geometry of the Design for Canberra. *Planning Perspectives*, 11, 225–57.

Punter, J. 2010a: Reflecting on Urban Design Achievements in a Decade of Urban Renaissance. In: Punter, J. (ed.) *Urban Design and the British Urban Renaissance*, 325–52. Abingdon: Routledge.

Punter, J. (ed.) 2010b: *Urban Design and the British Urban Renaissance*. Abingdon: Routledge.

Purdom, C. B. 1917: *The Garden City after the War*. Letchworth: privately printed.

Purdom, C. B. (ed.) 1921: *Town Theory and Practice*. London: Benn.

Purdom, C. B. 1925: *The Building of Satellite Towns: A Contribution to the Study of Town Development and Regional Planning*. London: J. M. Dent.

Qian, Z. 2012: Post-reform Urban Restructuring in China: The Case of Hangzhou 1990–2010. *Town Planning Review*, 83, 431–55.

Queen, S. A. and Carpenter, D. B. 1953: *The American City*. New York: McGraw-Hill.

Rabinowitz, F. 1969: *City Politics and Planning*. New York: Atherton Press.

Radford, G. 1996: *Modern Housing for America: Policy Struggles in the New Deal Era*. Chicago: University of Chicago Press.

Rae, J. B. 1971: *The Road and the Car in American Life*. Cambridge, MA: MIT Press.

Raffe, W. G. 1936: The Reconstruction of Moscow: The Ten Year Plan. *Town and Country Planning*, 4, 53–9.

Raines, A. R. 2011: Wandel durch (Industrie-) Kultur (Change through (Industrial) Culture): Conservation and Renewal in the *Ruhrgebiet*. *Planning Perspectives*, 26, 183–207.

Rainwater, L. 1967: Fear and the House-as-Haven in the Lower Class. In: Bellush, J. and Hausknecht, M. (eds.) *Urban Renewal: People, Politics and Planning*, 437–50. Garden City, NY: Anchor.

Rainwater, L. 1970: *Behind Ghetto Walls: Black Families in a Federal Slum*. Chicago: Aldine.

Rainwater, L. and Yancey, W. L. 1967: *The Moynihan Report and the Politics of Controversy*. Cambridge, MA: MIT Press.

Rasmussen, S. E. 1937: *London: The Unique City*. London: Jonathan Cape.

Rave, R. and Knöfel, H. -J. 1968: *Bauen seit 1900 in Berlin*. Berlin: Kiepert.

Ravetz, A. 1974: From Working-Class Tenement to Modern Flat: Local Authorities and Multi-Storey Housing between the Wars. In: Sutcliffe, A. (ed.) *Multi-Storey Living: The British Working-Class Experience*, 122–50. London: Croom Helm.

Ravetz, A. 1980: *Remaking Cities: Contradictions of the Recent Urban Environment*. London: Croom Helm.

Read, B. 1993: LA Rail Network Blossoms. *International Railway Journal*, June, 43–6.

Read, J. 1978: The Garden City and the Growth of Paris. *Architectural Review*, 113, 345–52.

Reader, D. H. 1961: *The Black Man's Portion: History, Demography and Living Conditions in the Native Locations of East London, Cape Province*. Cape Town: Oxford University Press.

Reclus, E. 1878–94: *The Earth and its Inhabitants: The Universal Geography*. Edited by E. G. Ravenstein and A. H. Keane. 19 vols. London: J. S. Virtue.

Reclus, E. 1905–8: *L'homme et la terre*. 6 vols. Paris: Librairie Universelle.

Regional Plan of New York and its Environs (1927–31): *Regional Survey of New York and its Environs*, 8 vols. (in 10). I. Major Economic Factors in Metropolitan Growth and Development. IA. Chemical, Metal, Wood, Tobacco and Printing Industries. IB. Food, Clothing & Textile Industries. Wholesale Markets and Retail Shopping & Financial Districts. II. Population Land Values and Government. III. Highway Traffic. IV. Transit and Transportation. V. Public Recreation. VI. Buildings: Their Uses and the Spaces about them. VII. Neighborhoods and Community Planning. VIII. Physical Conditions and Public Services. New York: The Regional Plan.

Reich, R. B. 1991: *The Work of Nations: Preparing Ourselves for 21st-Century Capitalism*. New York: Random House.

Reid, A. 2000: *Brentham: A History of the Pioneer Garden Suburb 1901–2001*. Ealing: Brentham Heritage Society.

Reiner, T. A. 1963: *The Place of the Ideal Community in Urban Planning*. Philadelphia: University of Pennsylvania Press.

Reiss, R. L. 1918: *The Home I Want*. London: Hodder and Stoughton.

Reith, J. C. W. 1949: *Into the Wind*. London: Hodder and Stoughton.

Reps, J. W. 1965: *The Making of Urban America: A History of City Planning in the United States*. Princeton: Princeton University Press.

Reulecke, J. (ed.) 1978: *Die deutsche Stadt im Industriezeitalter*. Wuppertal: Peter Hammer.

Revell, K. D. 1992: Regulating the Landscape: Real Estate Values, City Planning, and the 1916 Zoning Ordinance. In: Ward, D. and Zunz, O. (eds.) *The Landscape of Modernity: Essays on New York City, 1900–1940*, 19–45. New York: Russell Sage Foundation.

Rex, J. 1973: *Race, Colonialism and the City*. London: Routledge and Kegan Paul.

Richards, J. M. 1946: *The Castles on the Ground*. London: Architectural Press.

Richards, J. M. 1953: The Failure of the New Towns. *Architectural Review*, 114, 29–32.

Richmond, J. E. D. 2005: *Transport of Delight: The Mythical Conception of Rail Transit in Los Angeles*. Akron: Akron University Press.

Rickaby, P. A. 1987: Six Settlement Patterns Compared. *Environment and Planning B*, 14, 193–223.

Rickaby, P. A. 1991: Energy and Urban Development in an Archetypal English Town. *Environment and Planning B*, 18, 153–76.

Rickaby, P. A., Steadman, J. B., and Barrett, M. 1992: Patterns of Land Use in English Towns: Implications for Energy Use and Carbon Monoxide Emissions. In: Breheny, M. J. (ed.) *Sustainable Development and Urban Form* (European Research in Regional Science, 2), 182–96. London: Pion.

Riesman, D. 1950: *The Lonely Crowd: A Study of the Changing American Character*. New Haven: Yale University Press.

Riis, J. A. 1890: *How the Other Half Lives: Studies among the Tenements of New York*. New York: Scribner's Sons.

Riis, J. A. 1901: *The Making of an American*. New York: Macmillan.

Riley, R. B. 1967: Urban Myths and the New Cities of the South-West. *Landscape*, 17, 21–3.

Rittel, H. W. J. and Webber, M. M. 1973: Dilemmas in a General Theory of Planning. *Policy Sciences*, 4, 155–69.

Robbins, G. W. and Tilton, L. D. (eds.) 1941: *Los Angeles: A Preface to a Master Plan*. Los Angeles: The Pacific Southwest Academy.

Roberts, S. I. 1961: Portrait of a Robber Baron, Charles T. Yerkes. *Business History Review*, 35, 344–71.

Robertson, D. S. 1998: Pulling in Opposite Directions: The Failure of Post War Planning to Regenerate Glasgow. *Planning Perspectives*, 13, 53–68.

Robertson, K. A. 1997: Downtown Retail Revitalization: A Review of American Development Strategies. *Planning Perspectives*, 12, 383–402.

Robinson, C. M. 1901: *The Improvement of Towns and Cities: Or, The Practical Basis of Civic Aesthetics*. New York: G. P. Putnam's Sons.

Robson, W. A. 1939: *The Government and Misgovernment of London*. London: George Allen and Unwin.

Robson, W. A. and Regan, D. E., 1972: *Great Cities of the World*. Third edition. 2 vols. London: George Allen and Unwin.

Rodgers, C. 1947: *American Planning: Past, Present and Future*. New York: Harper Bros.

Rodwin, L. 1965: Ciudad Guayana: A New City. *Scientific American*, 213/3, 122–32.

Rogers, R. and Power, A. 2000: *Cities for a Small Country*. London: Faber and Faber.

Romanos, A. G. 1969: Illegal Settlements in Athens. In: Oliver, P. (H.) (ed.) *Shelter and Society*, 137–55. London: Barrie Rokliff: The Cresset Press.

Rooijendijk, C. 2005: Urban Ideal Images in Post-War Rotterdam. *Planning Perspectives*, 20, 177–209.

Roos, D. and Altshuler, A. 1984: The Future of the Automobile: The Report of MIT's International Automobile Program. London: George Allen and Unwin.

Roosevelt, F. D. 1932: Growing Up by Plan. *Survey*, 67, 483–5, 506–7.

Roosevelt, F. D. 1938: *The Public Papers and Addresses of Franklin D. Roosevelt,* vol. 1, *The Genesis of the New Deal 1928–1932*. New York: Random House.

Roper, L. W. 1973: *F.L.O.: A Biography of Frederick Law Olmsted*. Baltimore and London: Johns Hopkins University Press.

Rose, M. H. 1979: *Interstate: Express Highway Politics, 1941–1956*. Lawrence: University of Kansas Press.

Rosenfeld, R. A. 1980: Who Benefits and Who Decides? The Uses of Community Development Block Grants. In: Rosenthal, D. B. (ed.) *Urban Revitalization* (*Urban Affairs Annual Reviews*, no. 18), 211–36. Beverly Hills: Sage.

Rosenthal, D. B. (ed.) 1980: *Urban Revitalization* (*Urban Affairs Annual Reviews*, no. 18). Beverly Hills: Sage.

Rosenwaike, I. 1972: *Population History of New York City*. Syracuse: Syracuse University Press.

Ross, R. and Telkamp, G. J. (eds.) 1985: *Colonial Cities: Essays on Urbanism in a Colonial Context.* (*Comparative Studies in Overseas History*, vol. 5). Dordrecht: Martinus Nijhof.

Rosser, C. 1971: Housing for the Lowest Income Groups – the Calcutta example. *Ekistics*, 31, 126–31.

Rosser, C. 1972a: Housing and Planned Urban Change: The Calcutta Experience. In: Dwyer, D. J. (ed.) *The City as a Centre of Change in Asia*, 179–90. Hong Kong: Hong Kong University Press.

Rosser, C. 1972b: *Urbanization in India*. (International Urbanization Survey. Working Papers 278.) New York: Ford Foundation.

Rossi, A. 1982: *The Architecture of the City*. Cambridge, MA: MIT Press.

Rossi, P. H. and Dentler, R. A. 1961: *The Politics of Urban Renewal: The Chicago Findings*. New York: The Free Press of Glencoe.

Roth, G. 1967: *Paying for Roads: The Economics of Traffic Congestion*. Harmondsworth: Penguin Books.

Roth, G. and Butler, E. 1982: *Private Road Ahead*. London: Adam Smith Institute.

Roth, G. and Wynne, G. G. 1982: *Free Enterprise Urban Transportation* (Learning from Abroad, 5). New Brunswick and London: Transaction Books.

Rothenberg, J. 1967: *Economic Evaluation of Urban Renewal: Conceptual Foundation of Benefit–Cost Analysis*. Washington, DC: The Brookings Institution.

Royal Institute of British Architects 1911: *Town Planning Conference – Transactions*. London: RIBA.

Rubenstein, J. M. 1978: *The French New Towns*. Baltimore: Johns Hopkins University Press.

Ruble, B. A. 1994: Failures of Centralized Metropolitanism: Inter-War Moscow and New York. *Planning Perspectives*, 9, 353–76.

Ruskin, J. 1903–12: *The Works of John Ruskin*. Edited by E. T. Cook and A. Wedderburn. 39 vols. (20. *Oxford Lectures on Art*; 34. *To the Clergy on the Lord's Prayer*.) London: George Allen.

Ruttan, V. W. 1983: The TVA and Regional Development. In: Hargrove, E. C. and Conkin, P. K. (eds.) *TVA: Fifty Years of Grass-Roots Bureaucracy*, 150–63. Urbana: University of Illinois Press.

Sable, M. H. 1971: *Latin American Urbanization: A Guide to the Literature*. Metuchen, NJ: The Scarecrow Press.

Saint, A. 1976: *Richard Norman Shaw*. New Haven: Yale University Press.

St Clair, D. J. 1981: The Motorization and Decline of Urban Public Transit, 1935–1950. *Journal of Urban History*, 41, 579–600.

Salau, A. T. 1977: A New Capital for Nigeria: Planning, Problems and Prospects. *Africa Today*, 24/4, 11–22.

Salisbury, H. E. 1958: *The Shook-Up Generation*. New York: Harper and Brothers.

Salisbury, R. 1964: Urban Politics: The New Convergence of Power. *Journal of Politics*, 26, 775–97.

Sandercock, L. 1976: *Cities for Sale: Property, Politics and Urban Planning in Australia*. London: Heinemann.

Sandercock, L. 1998a: *Towards Cosmopolis: Planning for Multicultural Cities*. Chichester: John Wiley & Sons, Ltd.

Sandercock, L. (ed.) 1998b: *Making the Invisible Visible: A Multicultural Planning History*. Berkeley and Los Angeles: University of California Press.

Sanders, H. T. 1980: Urban Renewal and the Revitalized City: A Reconsideration of Recent History. In: Rosenthal, D. B. (ed.) *Urban Revitalization* (*Urban Affairs Annual Reviews, no. 18*), 103–26. Beverly Hills: Sage.

Sarin, M. 1979: Urban Planning, Petty Trading, and Squatter Settlements in Chandigarh, India. In: Bromley, R. and Gerry, C. (eds.) *Casual Work and Poverty in Third World Cities*, 133–60. Chichester: John Wiley & Sons, Ltd.

Sarin, M. 1982: *Urban Planning in the Third World: The Chandigarh Experience*. London: Mansell.

Sassen, S. 1991: *The Global City: New York, London, Tokyo*. Princeton: Princeton University Press.

Saunier, P. -Y. 1999: Changing the City: Urban International Information and the Lyon Municipality, 1900–1940. *Planning Perspectives*, 14, 19–48.

Saushkin, Y. G. 1966: *Moscow*. Moscow: Progress Publishers.

Savitch, H. V. 1988: *Post-Industrial Cities: Politics and Planning in New York, Paris and London*. Princeton: Princeton University Press.

Sawers, L. 1978: Cities and Countryside in the Soviet Union & China. In: Tabb, W. K. and Sawers, L. (eds.) *Marxism and the Metropolis: New Perspectives in Urban Political Economy*, 338–64. New York: Oxford University Press.

Sawers, L. 1984: The Political Economy of Urban Transportation: An Interpretative Essay. In: Tabb, W. K. and Sawers, L. (eds.) *Marxism and the Metropolis: New Perspectives in Urban Political Economy*, 223–54. New York: Oxford University Press.

Scarpa, L. 1983: *Martin Wagner e Berlino: casa e città nella Repubblica di Weimar 1918–1933*. Roma: Officina Edizioni.

Schaffer, D. 1982: *Garden Cities for America: The Radburn Experience.* Philadelphia: Temple University Press.

Schaffer, D. 1984: The Tennessee Transplant. *Town and Country Planning,* 53, 316–18.

Schaffer, D. 1986: Ideal and Reality in the 1930s: The Case of the Tennessee Valley Authority. *Planning Perspectives,* 1, 27–44.

Schaffer, D. (ed.) 1988: *Two Centuries of American Planning.* Baltimore: Johns Hopkins University Press.

Schaffer, D. 1990: Benton MacKaye: The TVA Years. *Planning Perspectives,* 5, 23–37.

Schaffer, D. 1992: The American Garden City: Lost Ideals. In: Ward, S. V. (ed.) *The Garden City: Past, Present and Future,* 127–45. London: Spon.

Schiffer, J. 1984: *Anatomy of a Laissez-Faire Government: The Hong Kong Growth Model Reconsidered.* Hong Kong: University, Centre of Urban Studies and Urban Planning, Working Paper.

Schill, M. H. and Nathan, R. P. 1983: *Revitalizing America's Cities: Neighborhood Reinvestment and Displacement.* Albany: State University of New York Press.

Schlereth, T. J. 1983: Burnham's *Plan* and Moody's *Manual*: City Planning as Progressive Reform. In: Krueckeberg, D. A. (ed.), 1983a: *The American Planner: Biographies and Recollections,* 75–99. New York and London: Methuen.

Schlesinger, A. M. 1933: *The Rise of the City, 1878–1898.* (A History of American Life, vol. X). New York: Macmillan.

Schlosser, E. 2001: *Fast Food Nation: What the All-American Meal Is Doing to the World.* Harmondsworth: Allen Lane the Penguin Press.

Schmetzer, H. and Wakely, P. 1974: Chandigarh: Twenty Years Later. *Architectural Design,* 44, 350–61.

Schmitt, P. J. 1969: *Back to Nature: The Arcadian Myth in Urban America.* New York: Oxford University Press.

Schnur, R. 1970: Entwicklung der Rechtsgrundlagen und der Organisation des SVR. In: Anon. *Siedlungsverband Ruhrkohlenbezirk 1920–1970, 29. Schriftenreihe Siedlungs verband Ruhrkohlenbezirk.* Essen: SVR.

Schoener, A. (ed.) 1967: *Portal to America: The Lower East Side, 1870–1925.* New York: Holt.

Schon, D. A. 1971: *Beyond the Stable State.* New York: Random House.

Schon, D. A., Cremer, N. S., Osterman, P., and Perry, C. 1976: Planners in Transition: Report on a Survey of Alumni of MIT's Department of Urban Studies, 1970–71. *Journal of the American Institute of Planners,* 42, 193–202.

Schorske, C. E. 1963: The Idea of the City in European Thought: Voltaire to Spengler. In: Handlin, O. and Burchard, J. (eds.) *The Historian and the City,* 95–114. Cambridge, MA: MIT Press and Harvard University Press.

Schrader, B. 1999: Avoiding the Mistakes of the "Mother Country": The New Zealand Garden City Movement 1900–1926. *Planning Perspectives,* 14, 395–411.

Schubert, D. 2000: The Neighbourhood Paradigm: From Garden Cities to Gated Communities. In: Freestone, R. (ed.) *Urban Planning in a Changing World: The Twentieth Century Experience,* 118–38. London: Spon.

Schubert, D. 2004: Theodor Fritsch and the German (*volkische*) Version of the Garden City: The Garden City Invented Two Years before Ebenezer Howard. *Planning Perspectives,* 19, 3–35.

Schubert, D. and Sutcliffe, A. 1996: The "Haussmannization" of London? The Planning and Construction of Kingsway–Aldwych, 1889–1935. *Planning Perspectives,* 11, 115–44.

Schultz, S. K. 1989: *Constructing Urban Culture: American Cities and City Planning, 1800–1920*. Philadelphia: Temple University Press.

Schultz, S. K. and McShane, C. 1978: To Engineer the Metropolis: Sewers, Sanitation and City Planning in Late-Nineteenth-Century America. *Journal of American History*, 65, 389–411.

Schwartz, B. (ed.) 1976: *The Changing Face of the Suburbs*. Chicago: University of Chicago Press.

Schwartz, J. 1993: *The New York Approach: Robert Moses, Urban Liberals and Redevelopment of the Inner City*. Columbia: Ohio State University Press.

Scobie, J. R. 1974: *Buenos Aires: Plaza to Suburb, 1870–1910*. New York: Oxford University Press.

Scott, A. J. and Roweis, S. T. 1977: Urban Planning in Theory and Practice: An Appraisal. *Environment and Planning A*, 9, 1097–119.

Scott, A. J. and Storper, M. (eds.) 1986: *Production, Work, Territory: The Geographical Anatomy of Industrial Capitalism*. London: Allen and Unwin.

Scott, M. 1969: *American City Planning since 1890: A History Commemorating the Fiftieth Anniversary of the American Institute of Planners*. Berkeley: University of California Press.

Scully, V. 1969: *American Architecture and Urbanism*. New York: Praeger.

Segal, H. P. 1985: *Technological Utopianism in American Culture*. Chicago: University of Chicago Press.

Sellier, H. and Bruggeman, A. 1927: *Le problème de logement: son influence sur les conditions de l'habitation et l'aménagement des villes*. Paris and New Haven: Presses Universitaires de France and Yale University Press.

Selznick, P. 1949: *TVA and the Grass Roots: A Study in the Sociology of Formal Organization*. Berkeley: University of California Press.

Sennett, R. 1971 (1970): *The Uses of Disorder: Personal Identity and City Life*. London: Allen Lane.

Shaffer, M. 2001: Scenery as an Asset: Assessing the 1930 Los Angeles Regional Park Plan. *Planning Perspectives*, 16, 357–82.

Shaftoe, H. and Tallon, A. 2010: Bristol: Not a Design-Led Urban Renaissance. In: Punter, J. (ed.) *Urban Design and the British Urban Renaissance*, 115–31. Abingdon: Routledge.

Shannon, A. H. 1930: *The Negro in Washington: A Study in Race Amalgamation*. New York: Walter Neale.

Sharp, T. 1932: *Town and Countryside: Some Aspects of Urban and Rural Development*. London: Oxford University Press.

Sharp, T. 1936: *English Panorama*. London: Dent.

Sharp, T. 1940: *Town Planning*. Harmondsworth: Pelican Books.

Shaw, C. R. *et al.* 1929: *Delinquency Areas: A Study of the Geographic Distribution of School Truants, Juvenile Delinquents, and Adult Offenders in Chicago*. Chicago: University of Chicago Press.

Shaw, C. R. and McKay, H. D. 1942: *Juvenile Delinquency and Urban Areas: A Study of Rates of Delinquents in Relation to Differential Characteristics of Local Communities in American Cities*. Chicago: University of Chicago Press.

Shaw, D. and Sykes, O. 2005: European Spatial Development Policy and Evolving Forms of Territorial Mobilisation in the United Kingdom. *Planning Practice & Research*, 20, 183–99.

Shaw, K. and Robinson, F. 2010: UK Urban Regeneration Policies in the Early Twenty-First Century: Continuity or Change? *Town Planning Review*, 81, 123–49.

Sheail, J. 1981: *Rural Conservation in Inter-War Britain*. Oxford: Oxford University Press.

Sheail, J. 1995: John Dower, National Parks, and Town and Country Planning in Britain. *Planning Perspectives*, 10, 1–16.

Sherrard, T. D. (ed.) 1968: *Social Welfare and Social Problems*. New York: Columbia University Press.

Short, J. R., Fleming, S., and Witt, S. J. G. 1986: *Housebuilding, Planning and Community Action: The Production and Negotiation of the Built Environment*. London: Routledge and Kegan Paul.

Shostak, L. and Lock, D. 1984: The Need for New Settlements in the South East. *The Planner*, 70/11, 9–13.

Shvidovsky, O. A. (ed.) 1970: Building in the USSR, 1917–1932. *Architectural Design*, 40, 71–107.

Sidenbladh, G. 1965: Stockholm: A Planned City. *Scientific American*, 213/3, 107–18.

Sidenbladh, G. 1968: Stockholm: A Planned City. In: (*Scientific American*) *Cities: Their Origin, Growth and Human Impact*, 75–87. New York: Knopf.

Sidenbladh, G. 1969: Debatt om samhällsplanering hösten – 68. *Plan*, 23, 16–19.

Sidenbladh, G. 1977: Idedebatt och praxis i efterkrigstidens Samhällsplanering. *Plan*, 31, 196–202.

Sidenbladh, G. 1981: *Planering för Stockholm 1923–1958*. Uppsala: Almqvist and Wiksell. [Monografier Utgivna av Stockholms Kommunalförvaltning 22:V3.]

Sies, M. C. 1997: Paradise Retained: An Analysis of Persistence in Planned, Exclusive Suburbs, 1880–1980. *Planning Perspectives*, 12, 165–92.

Sigurdson, J. 1975: Rural Industrialization in China: Approaches and Results. *World Development*, 3, 527–38.

Simmance, A. J. F. 1974: Urbanization in Zambia. *Journal of Administration Overseas*, 13, 498–509.

Simmie, J. (ed.) 1994: *Planning London*. London: UCL Press.

Simon, E. D. *et al.* 1937a: *Moscow in the Making*. London: Longmans.

Simon, E. D. 1937b: Town Planning: Moscow or Manchester. *Journal of the Town Planning Institute*, 23, 381–89.

Simon, R. and Hookham, M. 1954: Moscow. In: Robson, W. A. and Regan, D. E. (eds.) *Great Cities of the World*, 383–41. Third edition. 2 vols. London: George Allen and Unwin.

Simpson, M. A. 1976: Two Traditions of American Planning: Olmsted and Burnham. *Town Planning Review*, 47, 174–9.

Simpson, M. A. 1985: *Thomas Adams and the Modern Planning Movement: Britain, Canada and the United States, 1900–1940*. London: Mansell.

Sinclair, R. 1937: *Metropolitan Man: The Future of the English*. London: George Allen and Unwin.

Sinha, P. 1978: *Calcutta in Urban History*. Calcutta: Firma K. M. Private Ltd.

Sit, V. F. S. 1978: Hong Kong's Approach to the Development of Small Manufacturing Enterprises. *U.N. Economic and Social Council, Small Industry Bulletin for Asia and the Pacific*, 15, 89–98.

Sitte, C. 1901: *Der Städte-Bau nach seinen künstlerischen Grundsätzen: ein Beitrag zur Lösung moderner Fragen der Architektur und monumentalen Plastik unter besonderer Beziehung auf Wien*. Third edition. Vienna: Graeser.

Sjöström, J. 1975: The Form and Design of Housing. In: Heineman, H. -E. (ed.) *New Towns for Old: Housing and Services in Sweden*, 104–27. Stockholm: The Swedish Institute.

Skilleter, K. J. 1993: The Role of Public Utility Societies in Early British Town Planning and Housing Reform, 1901–36. *Planning Perspectives*, 8, 125–65.

Smith, A. E. 1925: Seeing a State Whole. *The Survey*, 54, 158–60.

Smith, D. H. 1933: *The Industries of Greater London*. London: P. S. King.

Smith, G. 1928: A Town for the Motor Age. *Survey*, 59, 694–8.

Smith, M. P. (ed.) 1991: *Breaking Chains: Social Movements and Collective Action*. (*Comparative Urban and Community Research*, 3). Brunswick: Transaction.

Smith, R. 1974: Multi-Dwelling Building in Scotland, 1750–1950; A Study Based on Housing in the Clyde Valley. In: Sutcliffe, A. (ed.) *Multi-Storey Living: The British Working-Class Experience*, 207–43. London: Croom Helm.

Smout, M. A. H. 1977: The Townscape. In Kay, G. and Smout, M. A. H. (eds.) *Salisbury: A Geographical Survey of the Capital of Rhodesia*, 26–40. London: Hodder and Stoughton.

Snell, B. C. 1974: *American Ground Transportation: A Proposal for Restructuring the Automobile, Truck, Bus, and Rail Industries. (Subcommittee on Antitrust and Monopoly, Committee on the Judiciary, US Senate)*. Washington, DC: Government Printing Office.

Sociological Society, Cities Committee 1919: Towards the Third Alternative: I. The Civic School of Applied Sociology. *Sociological Review*, 11, 62–5.

Soja, E., Morales, R., and Wolff, G. 1983: Urban Restructuring: An Analysis of Social and Spatial Change in Los Angeles. *Economic Geography*, 59, 195–230.

Sommer, J. W. 1976: The Internal Structure of African Cities. In: Knight, C. G. and Newman, J. L. (eds.) *Contemporary Africa: Geography and Change*, 306–20. Englewood Cliffs: Prentice Hall.

Sonne, W. 2004: Specific Intentions – General Realities: On the Relation between Urban Forms and Political Aspirations in Berlin during the Twentieth Century. *Planning Perspectives*, 19, 283–310.

Soria y Puig, A. 1968: *Arturo Soria y la Ciudad Lineal*. Madrid: Revista de Occidente.

Southall, A. 1967: Kampala-Mengo. In: Miner, H. (ed.) *The City in Modern Africa*, 297–332. London: Pall Mall Press.

Southall, A. 1971: The Impact of Imperialism Upon Urban Development in Africa. In: Turner, V. (ed.) *Colonialism in Africa 1870–1960*, vol. 3. *Profiles of Change: African Society and Colonial Rule*, 216–55. Cambridge: Cambridge University Press.

Southall, A. W. 1966: The Growth of Urban Society. In: Diamond, S. and Burke, F. G. (eds.) *The Transformation of East Africa: Studies in Political Anthropology*, 463–92. New York: Basic Books.

Southall, A. W. 1973: *Urban Anthropology: Cross-Cultural Studies of Urbanization*. New York: Oxford University Press.

Spann, E. K. 1996: *Designing Modern America: The Regional Planning Association of America and its Members*. Columbus, OH: Ohio State University Press.

Spear, A. H. 1967: *Black Chicago: The Making of a Negro Ghetto, 1890–1920*. Chicago: University of Chicago Press.

Speer, A. 1970: *Inside the Third Reich*. London: Weidenfeld and Nicolson.

Spencer, J. E. and Thomas, W. L. 1948/9: The Hill Stations and Summer Resorts of the Orient. *Geographical Review*, 38, 637–51; 39, 671.

Spengler, J. J. 1967: Africa and the Theory of Optimum City Size. In: Miner, H. (ed.) *The City in Modern Africa*, 55–89. London: Pall Mall Press.

Spengler, O. 1934 (1918): *The Decline of the West*. London: George Allen and Unwin.

Stamp, G. 1982: New Delhi. In: Lutyens, E. *Lutyens: The Work of the English Architect Sir Edwin Lutyens (1869–1944)*, 33–43. London: Arts Council of Great Britain.

Stamp, L. D. 1962: *The Land of Britain: Its Use and Misuse*. London: Longman.

Starkie, D. 1982: *The Motorway Age: Road and Traffic Policies in Post-War Britain*. Oxford: Pergamon.

Starr, K. 1990: *Material Dreams: Southern California through the 1920s*. New York: Oxford University Press.

Starr, S. F. 1971: Writings from the 1960s on the Modern Movement in Russia. *Journal of the Society of American Architectural Historians*, 30, 170–8.

Starr, S. F. 1976: The Revival and Schism of Urban Planning in Twentieth-Century Russia. In: Hamm, M. F. (ed.) *The City in Russian History*, 222–42. Lexington: University of Kentucky Press.

Starr, S. F. 1977: L'Urbanisme utopique pendant la révolution culturelle soviétique. *Annales: Économies, Sociétés, Civilisations*, 32, 87–105.

Stave, B. M. (ed.) 1981: *Modern Industrial Cities: History, Policy, and Survival*. Beverly Hills: Sage.

Stedman Jones, G. 1971: *Outcast London: A Study in the Relationship between Classes in Victorian Society*. Oxford: Oxford University Press.

Stein, C. 1958 (1951): *Toward New Towns for America*. Liverpool: Liverpool University Press.

Stein, C. S. 1925: Dinosaur Cities. *The Survey*, 54, 134–8.

Steinberg, S. 1981: *The Ethnic Myth: Race, Ethnicity, and Class in America*. New York: Atheneum.

Stern, R. A. M. 1986: *Pride of Place: Building the American Dream*. Boston: Houghton Mifflin.

Stern, R. A. M. and Massingale, J. M. (eds.) 1981: The Anglo American Suburb. *Architectural Design*, 50/10 and 11, entire double issue.

Sternlieb, G., Hughes, J. W., and Hughes, C. O. 1982: *Demographic Trends and Economic Reality: Planning and Markets in the 80s*. New Brunswick: Center for Urban Policy Research.

Sternlieb, G. and Listokin, D. 1981: *New Tools for Economic Development: The Enterprise Zone, Development Bank, and RFC*. Piscataway, NJ: Center for Urban Policy Research, Rutgers University.

Stewart, J. Q. 1947: Empirical Mathematical Rules Concerning the Distribution and Equilibrium of Population. *Geographical Review*, 37, 461–85.

Stewart, J. Q. 1956: The Development of Social Physics. *American Journal of Physics*, 18, 239–53.

Stewart, J. Q. 1959: Physics of Population Distribution. *Journal of Regional Science*, 1, 99–123.

Stewart, J. Q. and Warntz, W. 1958: Macrogeography and Social Science. *Geographical Review*, 48, 167–84.

Stewman, S. and Tarr, J. A. 1982: Four Decades of Public–Private Partnerships in Pittsburgh. In: Fosler, R. S. and Berger, R. A. (eds.) *Public–Private Partnership in American Cities: Seven Case Studies*, 59–128. Lexington, MA: Lexington Books.

Stilgoe, J. R. 1989: *Borderland: Origins of the American Suburb, 1820–1939*. New Haven: Yale University Press.

Stockard, J. 2012: Jane Jacobs and Citizen Participation. In: Hirt, S. (ed.) *The Urban Wisdom of Jane Jacobs*, 49–62. Abingdon: Routledge.

Stockholm, Information Board 1972: *Kista, Husby, Akala: A Digest for Planners, Politicians and Critics.* Stockholm: The Board.

Stockholm, Stadsplanekontor 1952: *Generalplan för Stockholm.* Stockholm: Stockholms Stads Stadsplanekontor.

Stockholm, Stadsplanekontorets Tjänsteutlåtande 1947: *Angående Ny Stadsoplan för Nedre Norrmalm avigivet den 31 Maj 1946.* Stockholm: K. L. Beckmans Boktrycken. [Stadskollegiets Utlåtenden och Memorial, supplement no. 60].

Stoddart, D. R. 1986: *On Geography: and its History.* Oxford: Blackwell.

Stöhr, W. B. 1981: Development from Below: The Bottom-Up and Periphery-Inward Development Paradigm. In: Stöhr, W. B. and Taylor, D. R. F. (eds.) *Development from Above or Below? The Dialectics of Regional Planning in Developing Countries,* 39–72. Chichester: John Wiley & Sons, Ltd.

Stöhr, W. B. and Taylor, D. R. F. (eds.), 1981: *Development from Above or Below? The Dialectics of Regional Planning in Developing Countries.* Chichester: John Wiley & Sons, Ltd.

Stokes, C. J. 1962: A Theory of Slums. *Land Economics,* 38, 187–97.

Stone, P. A. 1959: The Economics of Housing and Urban Development. *Journal of the Royal Statistical Society A,* 122, 417–76.

Stone, P. A. 1961: The Impact of Urban Development on the Use of Land and other Resources. *Journal of the Town Planning Institute,* 47, 128–34.

Stone, P. A. 1963: *Housing, Town Development, Land and Costs.* London: Estates Gazette.

Storper, M. 2001: The Poverty of Radical Theory Today: From the False Promises of Marxism to the Mirage of the Cultural Turn. *International Journal of Urban and Regional Research,* 25, 155–79.

Strauss, A. L. 1908: *The American City: A Sourcebook of Urban Imagery.* London: Allen Lane.

Stren, R. 1972: Urban Policy in Africa: A Political Analysis. *African Studies Review,* 15, 489–516.

Strömdahl, J. 1969: Vem planerar du för samhällsplanerare? *Plan,* 23, 26–8.

Strong, A. L. 1971: *Planned Urban Environments: Sweden, Finland, Israel, the Netherlands, France.* Baltimore: Johns Hopkins University Press.

Strong, A. L. 1979: *Land Banking: European Reality, American Prospect.* Baltimore: Johns Hopkins University Press.

Sussman, C. (ed.) 1976: *Planning the Fourth Migration: The Neglected Vision of the Regional Planning Association of America.* Cambridge, MA: MIT Press.

Sussman, E. 1989: Introduction. In: Sussman, E. (ed.), *On the Passage of a Few People through a Rather Brief Moment in Time: The Situationist International 1957–1972,* 1–15. Cambridge, MA: MIT Press.

Sutcliffe, A. 1970: *The Autumn of Central Paris: The Defeat of Town Planning 1850–1970.* London: Edward Arnold.

Sutcliffe, A. (ed.) 1974a: *Multi-Storey Living: The British Working-Class Experience.* London: Croom Helm.

Sutcliffe, A. 1974b: A Century of Flats in Birmingham, 1875–1973. In: Sutcliffe, A. (ed.) *Multi-Storey Living: The British Working-Class Experience,* 181–206. London: Croom Helm.

Sutcliffe, A. 1977: A Vision of Utopia: Optimistic Foundations of Le Corbusier's Doctrine d'Urbanisme. In: Walden, R. (ed.) *The Open Hand: Essays on Le Corbusier,* 216–43. Cambridge, MA: MIT Press.

Sutcliffe, A. 1979: Environmental Control and Planning in European Capitals 1850–1914: London, Paris and Berlin. In: Hammarström, I. and Hall, T. (eds.) *Growth and*

Transformation of the Modern City: The Stockholm Conference September 1978, 71–88. Stockholm: Swedish Council for Building Research.

Sutcliffe, A. (ed.) 1984: *Metropolis 1890–1940*. London: Mansell.

Sutcliffe, A. 1990: From Town–Country to Town Planning: Changing Perspectives in the British Garden City Movement, 1899–1914. *Planning Perspectives*, 5, 271–83.

Sutcliffe, A. 1993: *Paris: An Architectural History*. New Haven: Yale University Press.

Svetlichny, B. 1960: Les villes de l'avenir. *Recherches Internationales*, 20–1, 208–29.

Swenarton, M., 1981: *Homes Fit for Heroes: The Politics and Architecture of Early State Housing in Britain*. London: Heinemann.

Swenarton, M. 1985: Sellier and Unwin. *Planning History Bulletin*, 7/2, 50–7.

Swenarton, M. 2002: Tudor Walters and Tudorbethan: Reassessing Britain's Inter-War Suburbs. *Planning Perspectives*, 17, 267–86.

Tabb, W. K. and Sawers, L. (eds.) 1978: *Marxism and the Metropolis: New Perspectives in Urban Political Economy*. New York: Oxford University Press.

Tabb, W. K. and Sawers, L. 1984: *Marxism and the Metropolis: New Perspectives in Urban Political Economy*. Second edition. New York: Oxford University Press.

Tahmankar, D. V. 1970: *Sardar Patel*. London: Allen and Unwin.

Taneja, K. L. 1971: *Morphology of Indian Cities*. Varanasi: National Geographic Society of India.

Taper, B. 1983: Charles Abrams: Lover of Cities. In: Krueckeberg, D. A. (ed.) *The American Planner: Biographies and Recollections*, 366–95. New York and London: Methuen.

Tarn, J. N. 1973: *Five Per Cent Philanthropy: An Account of Housing in Urban Areas between 1840 and 1914*. Cambridge: Cambridge University Press.

Taylor, N. 1998: *Urban Planning Theory since 1945*. London: Sage.

Taylor, N. 1999: Anglo-American Town Planning Theory since 1945: Three Significant Developments but No Paradigm Shifts. *Planning Perspectives*, 14, 327–46.

Taylor, R. R. 1974: *The World in Stone: The Role of Architecture in the National Socialist Ideology*. Berkeley: University of California Press.

Teaford, J. C. 1984: *The Unheralded Triumph: City Government in America, 1870–1900*. Baltimore: Johns Hopkins University Press.

Teitz, M. B. 1974: Toward a Responsive Planning Methodology. In: Godschalk, D. R. (ed.) *Planning in America: Learning from Turbulence*, 86–110. Washington, DC: American Institute of Planners.

Teran, F. de. 1978: *Planeamiento urbano en la España contemporánea: Historia de un proceso imposible*. Barcelona: Gustavo Gili.

Tewdwr-Jones, M. 1999: Reasserting Town Planning: Challenging the Representation and Image of the Planning Profession. In: Allmendinger, P. and Chapman, M. (eds.) *Planning Beyond 2000*, 123–49. Chichester: John Wiley & Sons, Ltd.

The Editors of *Fortune* 1958: *The Exploding Metropolis*. Garden City, NY: Doubleday Anchor.

Thernstrom, S. 1973: *The Other Bostonians: Poverty and Progress in the American Metropolis 1880–1970*. Cambridge, MA: Harvard University Press.

Thernstrom, S. and Sennett, R. (eds.) 1969: *Nineteenth-Century Cities: Essays in the New Urban History*. (Yale Studies of the City, 1.) New Haven: Yale University Press.

Thienel, I. 1973: *Städtewachstum im Industrialisierungsprozess der 19. Jahrhundert: der Berliner Beispiel*. Berlin: de Gruyter.

Thies, J. 1978: Hitler's European Building Programme. *Journal of Contemporary History*, 13, 413–31.

Thomas, D. 1970: *London's Green Belt*. London: Faber and Faber.

Thomas, M. J. 1978: City Planning in Soviet Russia (1917–1932). *Geoforum*, 9, 269–77.

Thomas, W. H. 1901: *The American Negro: What He Was, What He Is, and What He May Become*. New York: Macmillan.

Thomas, W. I. and Znaniecki, F. N. 1927 (1918): *The Polish Peasant in Europe and America*. 2 vols. New York: Knopf.

Thompson, F. M. L. (ed.) 1982: *The Rise of Suburbia*. Leicester: Leicester University Press.

Thompson, J. B. and Held, D. 1982: *Habermas: Critical Debates*. Cambridge, MA: MIT Press.

Thompson, R. 1975: City Planning in China. *World Development*, 3, 595–606.

Thompson, W. S. 1947: *Population: The Growth of Metropolitan Districts in the United States: 1900–1940*. (US Department of Commerce, Bureau of the Census.) Washington: Government Printing Office.

Thompson-Fawcett, M. 1998: Leon Krier and the Organic Revival within Urban Policy and Practice. *Planning Perspectives*, 13, 167–94.

Thomson, J. 1880: *The City of Dreadful Night, and Other Poems*. London: Reeves and Turner.

Thorne, D. C. 1972: *Suburbia*. London: Macgibbon and Kee.

Thorne, R. 1980: *Covent Garden Market: Its History and Restoration*. London: Architectural Press.

Thornley, A. 1991: *Urban Planning under Thatcherism: The Challenge of the Market*. London: Routledge.

Thornton White, L. W., Silberman, L., and Anderson, P. R. 1948: *Nairobi: Master Plan for a Colonial Capital. A Report Prepared for the Municipal Council of Nairobi*. London: HMSO.

Thrasher, F. M. 1926: The Gang as a Symptom of Community Disorganization. *Journal of Applied Sociology*, 11, 3–20.

Thünen, J. H. von. 1966 (1826): *Von Thünen's Isolated State*. Translated by C. M. Wartenberg, edited by P. Hall. Oxford: Pergamon Press.

Tilton, T. 1991: *The Political Theory of Swedish Social Democracy: Through the Welfare State to Socialism*. Oxford: Oxford University Press.

Titmuss, R. M. 1950: *Problems of Social Policy*. (History of the Second World War, United Kingdom Civil Series.) London: HMSO and Longmans, Green.

Tobe, E. 1977: Kommunal planering 1947–77. *Plan*, 31, 206–9.

Tobin, G. A. 1976: Suburbanization and the Development of Motor Transportation: Transportation Technology and the Suburbanization Process. In: Schwartz, B. (ed.) *The Changing Face of the Suburbs*, 95–111. Chicago: University of Chicago Press.

Toll, S. I. 1969: *Zoned American*. New York: Grossman.

Tomlinson, S. 1983: *Ethnic Minorities in British Schools: A Review of the Literature, 1960–82*. London: Heinemann Education.

Topalov, C. 1993: The City as *Terra Incognita*: Charles Booth's Poverty Survey and the People of London, 1886–1891. *Planning Perspectives*, 8, 395–425.

Towers, G. 1973: City Planning in China. *Journal of the Royal Town Planning Institute*, 59, 125–7.

Treves, A. 1980: The Anti-Urban Policy of Fascism and a Century of Resistance to Industrial Urbanization in Italy. *International Journal of Urban and Regional Research*, 4, 470–84.

Trip, J. J. 2008: Urban Quality in High-speed Train Station Area Redevelopment: The Cases of Amsterdam Zuidas and Rotterdam Centraal. *Planning Practice & Research*, 23, 383–401.

Tripp, H. A. 1938: *Road Traffic and its Control*. London: Edward Arnold.

Tripp, H. A. 1942: *Town Planning and Road Traffic*. London: Edward Arnold.

Tuck, M. and Southgate, P. 1981: *Ethnic Minorities, Crime and Policing: A Survey of the Experiences of West Indians and Whites* (Home Office Research Study, 70). London: HMSO.

Tugwell, R. G. and Banfield, E. C. 1950: Grass Roots Democracy – Myth or Reality? (Review of Selznick, P., 1949), *Public Administration Review*, 10, 47–55.

Tunnard, C. 1953: *The City of Man*. London: Architectural Press.

Tunnard, C. 1968: *The Modern American City*. Princeton: Van Nostrand.

Tunnard, C. and Reed, H. H. 1955: *American Skyline: The Growth and Form of our Cities and Towns*. Boston: Houghton Mifflin.

Turner, J. F. C. 1963: Village Artisan's Self-Built House. *Architectural Design*, 33, 361–2.

Turner, J. F. C. 1965: Lima's Barriadas and Corralones: Suburbs versus Slums. *Ekistics*, 19, 152–5.

Turner, J. F. C. 1967: Barriers and Channels for Housing Development in Modernising Countries. *Journal of the American Institute of Planners*, 33, 167–81.

Turner, J. F. C. 1968a: *Uncontrolled Urban Settlement: Problems and Policies*. (International Social Development Reviews, 1: Urbanization: Development Policies and Planning.) New York: United Nations.

Turner, J. F. C. 1968b. The Squatter Settlement: Architecture that Works. *Architectural Design*, 38, 355–60.

Turner, J. F. C. 1969: Uncontrolled Urban Settlement: Problems and Policies. In: Breese, G. (ed.) *The City in Newly Developing Countries: Readings on Urbanism and Urbanization*, 507–35. Englewood Cliffs: Prentice Hall.

Turner, J. F. C. 1970: Barriers and Channels for Housing Development in Modernizing Countries. In: Mangin, W. (P.) (ed.) *Peasants in Cities: Readings in the Anthropology of Urbanization*, 1–19. Boston: Houghton Mifflin.

Turner, J. F. C. 1971: Barriers and Channels for Housing Development in Modernizing Countries. In: Lewis, D. N. (ed.) *The Growth of Cities*, 70–83. (Architects' Year Book, XIII.) London: Elek Books.

Turner, J. F. C. 1972a: The Reeducation of a Professional. In: Turner, J. F. C. and Fichter, R. (eds.) *Freedom to Build: Dweller Control of the Housing Process*, 122–47. New York: Macmillan.

Turner, J. F. C. 1972b: Housing as a Verb. In: Turner, J. F. C. and Fichter, R. (eds.) *Freedom to Build: Dweller Control of the Housing Process*, 148–75. New York: Macmillan.

Turner, J. F. C. 1976: *Housing by People: Towards Autonomy in Building Environments*. London: Marion Boyars.

Turner, J. F. C. 1982: Issues in Self-Help and Self-Managed Housing. In: Ward, P. M. (ed.) *Self-Help Housing: A Critique*, 99–113. London: Mansell.

Turner, J. F. C. and Fichter, R. (eds.) 1972: *Freedom to Build: Dweller Control of the Housing Process*. New York: Macmillan.

Turner, J. F. C. and Roberts, B. 1975: The Self-Help Society. In: Wilsher, P. and Righter, R. (eds.) *The Exploding Cities*, 126–37. London: André Deutsch.

Turner, J. F. C., Turner, C., and Crooke, P. 1963: Conclusions (to special section, Dwelling Resources in South America). *Architectural Design*, 33, 389–93.

Turner, R. (ed.) 1962: *India's Urban Future*. Berkeley: University of California Press.

Turner, V. (ed.) 1971: *Colonialism in Africa 1870–1960*, vol. 3. *Profiles of Change: African Society and Colonial Rule*. Cambridge: Cambridge University Press.

Tuttle, W. M., Jr 1970: *Race Riot: Chicago in the Red Summer of 1919*. New York: Atheneum.

Tyler, W. R. 1939: The Neighbourhood Unit Principle in Town Planning. *Town Planning Review*, 18, 174–86.

Tym, R. and Partners 1984: *Monitoring Enterprise Zones: Year Three Report*. London: Roger Tym and Partners.

Tyrwhitt, J. (ed.) 1947: *Patrick Geddes in India*. London: Lund Humphries.

US Department of Housing and Urban Development 1986: *State-Designated Enterprise Zones: Ten Case Studies*. Washington: HUD.

US Housing and Home Finance Agency 1966: The Housing of Relocated Families: Summary of a Census Bureau Survey. In: Wilson, J. Q. (ed.) *Urban Renewal: The Record and the Controversy*, 336–52. Cambridge, MA: MIT Press.

US Library of Congress, Congressional Research Service 1973: *The Central City Problem and Urban Renewal Policy*. Washington, DC: Government Printing Office.

US National Advisory Committee on Civil Disorders 1968: *Report*. New York: Dutton.

US National Resources Committee 1935: *Regional Factors in National Planning and Development*. Washington, DC: US Government Printing Office.

US National Resources Planning Board 1937: *Our Cities: Their Role in the National Economy*. Washington, DC: Government Printing Office.

Uhlig, G. 1977: Stadtplanung in den Weimarer Republik: sozialistische Reformaspekte. In: Neue Gesellschaft für Bildende Kunst: *Wem gehört die Welt? Kunst und Gesellschaft in der Weimare Republik*, 50–71. Berlin: Neue Gesellschaft für Bildende Kunst.

Unikel, L. 1982: Regional Development Policies in Mexico. In: Gilbert, A. (ed.) *Urbanization in Contemporary Latin America: Critical Approaches to the Analysis of Urban Issues*, 263–78. Chichester: John Wiley & Sons, Ltd.

United Kingdom. 1991: *Hansard Parliamentary Debates*. Commons, written answers, 6th ser., vol. 190. http://www.publications.parliament.uk/pa/cm199091/cmhansrd/1991-05-08/Writtens-7.htmln (accessed March 10, 2014).

Unwin, R. 1902: *Cottage Plans and Common Sense* (Fabian Tract no. 109). London: The Fabian Society.

Unwin, R. 1912: *Nothing Gained by Overcrowding!: How the Garden City Type of Development May Benefit both Owner and Occupier*. London: P. S. King.

Unwin, R. 1920 (1909): *Town Planning in Practice: An Introduction to the Art of Designing Cities and Suburbs*. London: T. Fisher Unwin.

Unwin, R. 1921: Distribution. *Journal of the Town Planning Institute*, 7, 37–45.

Unwin, R. 1930: Regional Planning with Special Reference to the Greater London Regional Plan. *Journal of the Royal Institute of British Architects*, 37, 183–93.

Unsworth, R. and Smales, L. 2010: Leeds: Shaping Change and Guiding Success. In: Punter, J. (ed.) *Urban Design and the British Urban Renaissance*, 68–84. Abingdon: Routledge.

Urban Land Institute, Research Division 1980: *UDAG Partnerships: Nine Case Studies*. Washington, DC: Urban Land Institute.

Valladares, L. do P. 1978: Working the System: Squatter Response to the Resettlement in Rio de Janeiro. *International Journal of Urban and Regional Research*, 2, 12–25.

Van Rooijen, M. 1990: Garden City versus Green Town: The Case of Amsterdam 1910–1935. *Planning Perspectives*, 5, 285–93.

Van Velsen, J. 1975: Urban Squatters: Problem or Solution. In: Parkin, D. J. (ed.) *Town and Country in East and Central Africa*, 294–307. London: Oxford University Press (for International African Institute).

Van Zwanenberg, R. M. A. and King, A. 1975: *An Economic History of Kenya and Uganda: 1800–1970*. London: Macmillan.

Vance, J. E., Jr 1964: *Geography and Urban Evolution in the San Francisco Bay Area*. Berkeley: Institute of Governmental Studies.

Vandervelde, E. 1903: *L'exode rural et le retour aux champs*. Paris: Felix Alcan.

Veiller, L. 1900: *Tenement House Reform in New York, 1834–1900*. New York: The Tenement House Commission.

Venturi, R., Brown, D. S., and Izenour, S. 1972: *Learning from Las Vegas*. Cambridge, MA: MIT Press.

Veronesi, G. 1948: *Tony Garnier*. Milano: Il Balcone.

Vigar, G. 2001: Reappraising UK Transport Policy 1950–99: The Myth of "Mono-modality" and the Nature of "Paradigm Shifts." *Planning Perspectives*, 16, 269–91.

Ville de Suresnes 1998: *Idées de cité-jardins: L'exemplarité de Suresnes*. Suresnes: Ville de Suresnes.

Vogel, I. 1959: *Bottrop: eine Bergbaustadt in der Emscherzone des Ruhrgebietes* (Forschungen zur Deutschen Landeskunde, 114). Remagen: Bundesanstalt für Landeskunde.

Voigt, P. 1901: *Grundrente und Wohnungsfrage in Berlin und seinen Vororten*, part 1. Jena: Gustav Fischer.

Voigt, W. 1989: The Garden City as Eugenic Utopia. *Planning Perspectives*, 4, 295–312.

Wachs, M. 1984: Autos, Transit, and the Spread of Los Angeles: The 1920s. *Journal of the American Planning Association*, 5, 297–310.

Wachs, M. and Crawford, M. (eds.) 1992: *The Car and the City: The Automobile, the Built Environment, and Daily Urban Life*. Ann Arbor: University of Michigan Press.

Wade, R. C. 1968: Urbanization. In: Woodward, C. V. (ed.) *The Comparative Approach to American History*, 187–205. New York: Basic Books.

Walden, R. (ed.) 1977: *The Open Hand: Essays on Le Corbusier*. Cambridge, MA, MIT Press.

Walker, R. A. 1950: *The Planning Function in Urban Government*. (Social Science Committee, University of Chicago, Social Science Studies, 34.) Chicago: University of Chicago Press.

Wallman, S. (ed.) 1979: *Ethnicity at Work*. London: Macmillan.

Wallman, S. 1984: *Eight London Households*. London: Tavistock.

Wallman, S. *et al.* 1982: *Living in South London: Perspectives on Battersea 1971–1981*. Aldershot: Gower.

Walters, A. A. 1976: *The Outer Limits and Beyond*. (Discussion Paper no. 12). London: Foundation for Business Responsibilities.

Walters, A. A. 1979: *Costs and Scale of Bus Services*. (World Bank Staff Working Paper no. 325). Washington, DC: World Bank.

Walton, J. and Masotti, L. (eds.) 1976: *The City in Comparative Perspective*. New York: John Wiley & Sons, Inc.

Wang, G. (ed.) 1964: *Malaysia: A Survey*. London: Pall Mall Press.

Wannop, U. 1986: Regional Fulfilment: Planning into Administration in the Clyde Valley 1944–84. *Planning Perspectives*, 1, 207–29.

Ward, C. (ed.) 1973a: *Vandalism*. London: Architectural Press.

Ward, C. 1973b: *Anarchy in Action*. London: Allen and Unwin.

Ward, C. 1976: *Housing: An Anarchist Approach*. London: Freedom Press.

Ward, D. 1971: *Cities and Immigrants*. New York: Oxford University Press.

Ward, D. and Zunz, O. (eds.) 1992: *The Landscape of Modernity: Essays on New York City, 1900–1940*. New York: Russell Sage Foundation.

Ward, P. M. 1976: The Squatter Settlement as Slum or Housing Solution: The Evidence from Mexico City. *Land Economics*, 52, 330–46.

Ward, P. M. (ed.) 1982: *Self-Help Housing: A Critique*. London: Mansell.

Ward, R. 1986: London: The Emerging Docklands City. *Built Environment*, 12, 117–27.

Ward, S. V. 1990: The Garden City Tradition Re-examined. *Planning Perspectives*, 5, 257–69.

Ward, S. V. (ed.) 1992a: *The Garden City: Past, Present and Future*. London: Spon.

Ward, S. V. 1992b: The Garden City Introduced. In: Ward, S. V. (ed.) *The Garden City: Past, Present and Future*, 1–27. London: Spon.

Ward, S. V. 1994: *Planning and Urban Change*. London: Paul Chapman.

Ward, S. V. 1998: *Selling Places: The Marketing and Promotion of Towns and Cities 1850–2000*. London: Spon.

Ward, S. V. 2000a: Practice: The Tony Garnier Urban Museum, Lyon, France. *Planning History*, 22/2, 29–35.

Ward, S. V. 2000b: Re-Examining the International Diffusion of Planning. In: Freestone, R. (ed.) *Urban Planning in a Changing World: The Twentieth Century Experience*, 40–60. London: Spon.

Ward, S. V. 2002a: Ebenezer Howard: His Life and Times. In: Parsons, K. C. and Schuyler, D. (eds.) *From Garden City to Green City: The Legacy of Ebenezer Howard*, 14–37. Baltimore and London: Johns Hopkins University Press.

Ward, S. V. 2002b: The Howard Legacy. In: Parsons, K. C. and Schuyler, D. (eds.) *From Garden City to Green City: The Legacy of Ebenezer Howard*, 222–44. Baltimore and London: Johns Hopkins University Press.

Ward, S. V. 2002c: *Planning the Twentieth-Century City: The Advanced Capitalist World*, Chichester: John Wiley & Sons, Ltd.

Ward, S. V. 2005: Consortium Developments Ltd and the Failure of "New Country Towns" in Mrs Thatcher's Britain. *Planning Perspectives*, 20, 329–59.

Ward, S. V. 2007: Cross-National Learning in the Formation of British Planning Policies 1940–99: A Comparison of the Barlow, Buchanan and Rogers Reports. *Town Planning Review*, 78, 369–400.

Ward, S. V. 2010: What Did the Germans Ever Do for Us? A Century of British Learning about and Imagining Modern Town Planning. *Planning Perspectives*, 25, 117–40.

Ward, S. V. 2012a: Soviet Communism and the British Planning Movement: Rational Learning or Utopian Imagining? *Planning Perspectives*, 27, 499–524.

Ward, S. V. 2012b: Gordon Stephenson and the "Galaxy of Talent": Planning for Post-War Reconstruction in Britain 1942–1947. *Town Planning Review*, 83, 279–96.

Ward, S. V., Freestone, R., and Silver, C. 2011: The "New" Planning History: Reflections, Issues and Directions. *Town Planning Review*, 82, 231–61.

Warner, S. B., Jr 1972: *The Urban Wilderness: A History of the American City*. New York: Harper and Row.

Warren, H. and Davidge, W. R. (eds.) 1930: *Decentralisation of Population and Industry: A New Principle of Town Planning*. London: P. S. King.

Watanabe, S. -I. J. 1980: Garden City Japanese-Style: The Case of the Den-en-Toshi Company Ltd., 1918–28. In: Cherry, G. E. (ed.) *Shaping an Urban World*, 129–43. London: Mansell.

Watanabe, S. -I. J. 1992: The Japanese Garden City. In: Ward, S. V. (ed.) *The Garden City: Past, Present and Future*, 69–87. London: Spon.

Wates, N. 1982a: Community Architecture Is Here to Stay. *Architects' Journal*, 175/23, 42–4.

Wates, N. 1982b: The Liverpool Breakthrough: or Public Sector Housing Phase 2. *Architects' Journal*, 176/36, 51–8.

Weaver, C. 1981: Development Theory and the Regional Question: A Critique of Spatial Planning and its Detractors. In: Stöhr, W. B. and Taylor, D. R. F. (eds.) *Development from Above or Below? The Dialectics of Regional Planning in Developing Countries*, 73–106. Chichester: John Wiley & Sons, Ltd.

Weaver, C. 1984a: *Regional Development and the Local Community: Planning, Politics and Social Context*. Chichester: John Wiley & Sons, Ltd.

Weaver, C. 1984b: Tugwell on Morningside Heights: A Review Article. *Town Planning Review*, 55, 228–36.

Weaver, R. C. 1964: *The Urban Complex: Human Values in Urban Life*. Garden City, NY: Doubleday.

Weaver, R. C. 1966: *Dilemmas of Urban America*. Cambridge, MA: Harvard University Press.

Weaver, R. C. 1967. The Urban Complex. In: Bellush, J. and Hausknecht, M. (eds.) *Urban Renewal: People, Politics and Planning*, 90–101. Garden City, NY: Anchor.

Webb, B. 1926: *My Apprenticeship*. London: Longmans Green.

Webber, M. M. 1963: Order in Diversity: Community without Propinquity. In: Wingo, L., Jr (ed.) *Cities and Space: The Future Use of Urban Land*, 23–54. Baltimore: Johns Hopkins University Press.

Webber, M. M. (ed.) 1964a: *Explorations into Urban Structure*. Philadelphia: University of Pennsylvania Press.

Webber, M. M. 1964b: The Urban Place and the Nonplace Urban Realm. In: Webber, M. M. (ed.) *Explorations into Urban Structure*, 79–153. Philadelphia: University of Pennsylvania Press.

Webber, M. M. 1968/9: Planning in an Environment of Change. *Town Planning Review*, 39, 179–95, 277–95.

Webber, M. M. 1976: *The BART Experience – What Have We Learned?* Berkeley: University of California, Institute of Urban and Regional Development and Institute of Transportation Studies. (Monograph no. 26).

Weber, A. 1929 (1909): *Alfred Weber's Theory of the Location of Industries*. Translated by C. J. Friedrich. Chicago: University of Chicago Press.

Weber, M. 1966: *The City*. London: Collier-Macmillan.

Weimer, D. R. (ed.) 1962: *City and Country in America*. New York: Appleton-Century-Crofts.

Weis, D. 1951: *Die Grossstadt Essen: Die Siedlings-, Verkehrs- und Wirtschaftliche Entwicklung des heutigen Stadtgebietes von der Stiftsgrundung bis zur Gegenwart*. (Bonner Geographische Abhandlungen, 7). Bonn: Geographische Institut.

Weiss, M. A. 1980: The Origins and Legacy of Urban Renewal. In: Clavel, P., Forester, J., and Goldsmith, W. W. (eds.) *Urban and Regional Planning in an Age of Austerity*, 53–80. New York: Pergamon.

Weiss, M. A. 1990: Developing and Financing the "Garden Metropolis": Urban Planning and Housing Policy in Twentieth-Century America. *Planning Perspectives*, 5, 307–19.

Weiss, M. A. 1992: Density and Intervention: New York's Planning Traditions. In: Ward, D. and Zunz, O. (eds.) *The Landscape of Modernity: Essays on New York City, 1900–1940*, 46–75. New York: Russell Sage Foundation.

Welfeld, I. H., Muth, R. M., Wehner, H. G., Jr, and Weicher, J. C. 1974: *Perspectives on Housing and Urban Renewal*. (American Enterprise Institute Perspectives II.) New York: Praeger.

Wells, H. G. 1902: *Anticipations of the Reaction of Mechanical and Scientific Progress upon Human Life and Thought*. London: Chapman and Hall.

Wells, H. G. 1905: *A Modern Utopia*. London: Chapman and Hall.

Wells, H. G. 1994 (1899): *When the Sleeper Wakes*. Edited by John Lawton: London: Everyman.

Werner, F. 1976: *Stadtplanung Berlin: Theorie und Realität*. Teil 1: *1900–1960*. Berlin: Verlag Kiepert.

Western, J. 1984: Autonomous and Directed Cultural Change: South African Urbanization. In: Agnew, J., Mercer, J., and Sopher, D. E. (eds.) *The City in Cultural Context*, 205–36. Boston: Allen and Unwin.

Westman, T. 1962: Cityregleringens Fortsättning. *Arkitektur*, 62, 288–97.

Westman, T. 1967: Cityreglering – nu. *Arkitektur*, 67, 348–9.

White, L. T., III 1971: Shanghai's Polity in Cultural Revolution. In: Lewis, J. W. (ed.) *The City in Communist China*, 325–70. Stanford, CA: Stanford University Press.

White, M. G. and White, L. 1962: *The Intellectual versus the City: From Thomas Jefferson to Frank Lloyd Wright*. Cambridge, MA: Harvard University Press and MIT Press.

White, P. M. 1979: *Urban Planning in Britain and the Soviet Union: A Comparative Analysis*. (CURS Research Memorandum, 70). Birmingham: University, *Centre for Urban and Regional Studies*.

Whyte, W. H. 1956: *The Organization Man*. New York: Simon and Schuster.

Whyte, W. H. 1958: Urban Sprawl. In: Editors of *Fortune* (ed.) *The Exploding Metropolis*, 115–39. Garden City, NY: Doubleday Anchor.

Wibberley, G. P. 1959: *Agriculture and Urban Growth*. London: Michael Joseph.

Wiebenson, D. 1969: *Tony Garnier and the Cité Industrielle*. London: Studio Vista.

Wiedenhoeft, R. 1985: *Berlin's Housing Revolution*. Ann Arbor: UMI Research Press.

Wiener, N. 1948: *Cybernetics*. Cambridge, MA: MIT Press.

Wigglesworth, J. M. 1971: The Development of New Towns. In: Dwyer, D.J. (ed.) *Asian Urbanization: A Hong Kong Casebook*, 48–69. Hong Kong: Hong Kong University Press.

Wildavsky, A. 1973: If Planning Is Everything, Maybe It's Nothing. *Policy Sciences*, 4, 127–53.

Wilde, A. (ed.) 1937: Famous Women Demand Planning for Health and Beauty. *Town and Country Planning*, 5, 132–5.

Wilde, A. (ed.) 1938: Wanted – A National Plan for Town and Countryside. *Town and Country Planning*, 6, 24–30.

William-Olsson, W. 1961: *Stockholm: Structure and Development*. Stockholm: Almqvist and Wiksell.

Williams, F. B. 1916: Public Control of Private Real Estate. In: Nolen, J. (ed.) *City Planning: A Series of Papers Presenting the Essential Elements of a City Plan*, 48–87. New York: D. Appleton.

Williams, F. B. 1922: *The Law of City Planning and Zoning*. New York: Macmillan.

Williams, S. 1992: The Coming of the Groundscrapers. In: Budd, L. and Whimster, S. *Global Finance and Urban Living: A Study of Metropolitan Change*, 246–59. London: Routledge.

Williams-Ellis, C. 1928: *England and the Octopus*. London: Geoffrey Bles.

Williams-Ellis, C. 1933: What's the Use? In: Council for the Preservation of Rural England: "Penn Country" Branch: *The Penn Country of Buckinghamshire*, 103–86. London: CPRE.

Williams-Ellis, C. (ed.) 1937: *Britain and the Beast*. London: J. M. Dent.

Wilsher, P. and Righter, R. (eds.) 1975: *The Exploding Cities*. London: André Deutsch.

Wilson, J. Q. (ed.) 1966: *Urban Renewal: The Record and the Controversy*. Cambridge, MA: MIT Press.

Wilson, W. H. 1974: *Coming of Age in Urban America, 1915–1945*. New York: John Wiley & Sons, Inc.

Wilson, W. H. 1983: Moses and Skylarks. In: Krueckeberg, D. A. (ed.) *Introduction to Planning History in the United States*, 88–121. New Brunswick, NJ: Rutgers University, Center for Urban Policy Research.

Wilson, W. H. 1989: *The City Beautiful Movement*. Baltimore: Johns Hopkins University Press.

Wilson, W. J. 1978: *The Declining Significance of Race: Blacks and Changing American Institutions*. Chicago: University of Chicago Press.

Wilson, W. J. 1987: *The Truly Disadvantaged: The Inner City, the Underclass, and Public Policy*. Chicago: University of Chicago Press.

Wilson, W. J. 1996: *When Work Disappears: The World of the New Urban Poor*. New York: Knopf.

Wingo, L., Jr (ed.) 1963: *Cities and Space: The Future Use of Urban Land*. Baltimore: Johns Hopkins University Press.

Witherspoon, R. 1982: *Codevelopment: City Rebuilding by Business and Government*. Washington: Urban Land Institute.

Wohl, A. S. (ed.) 1970: *The Bitter Cry of Outcast London*. Leicester: Leicester University Press.

Wohl, A. S. (ed.) 1977: *The Eternal Slum: Housing and Social Policy in Victorian London*. London: Edward Arnold.

Wohl, A. S. 1983: *Endangered Lives: Public Health in Victorian Britain*. London: J. M. Dent.

Wohlin, H. 1969: Plandemokrati. *Plan*, 23, 20–6.

Wohlin, H. 1977: Arvet. *Plan*, 31, 261–7.

Wolfe, T. 1987: *The Bonfire of the Vanities*. New York: Farrar, Straus.

Wollen, P. 1989: Bitter Victory: The Art and Politics of the Situationist International. In: Sussman, E. (ed.), *On the Passage of a Few People through a Rather Brief Moment in Time: The Situationist International 1957–1972*, 20–61. Cambridge, MA: MIT Press.

Wolters, R. 1978: *Stadtmitte Berlin: Stadtbaulich Entwicklungsphasen von den Anfängen bis zur Gegenwart*. Tübingen: Wasmuth.

Wood, R. C. 1959: *Suburbia: Its People and their Politics*. Boston: Houghton Mifflin.

Wood, S. E. and Heller, A. E. 1962: *California Going, Going …* Sacramento: California Tomorrow.

Woodcock, G. 1962: *Anarchism: A History of Liberation Ideas and Movements*. Cleveland and New York: Meridian Books.

Woods, R. A. 1914: The Neighborhood in Social Reconstruction. *Publications of the American Sociological Society*, 8, 14–28.

Woodward, C. V. (ed.) 1968: *The Comparative Approach to American History*. New York: Basic Books.

Woolf, P. J. 1987: "Le Caprice du Prince" – The Problem of the Bastille Opera. *Planning Perspectives*, 2, 53–69.

Wright, F. L. 1916: Plan by Frank Lloyd Wright. In: Yeomans, A. (ed.) *City Residential Land Development: Studies in Planning*, 96–102. Chicago: University of Chicago Press.

Wright, F. L. 1945: *When Democracy Builds*. Chicago: University of Chicago Press.

Wright, G. 1981: *Building the Dream: A Social History of Housing in America*. Cambridge, MA: MIT Press.

Wright, H. 1925: The Road to Good Houses. *The Survey*, 54, 165–8, 189.

Wright, H. 1935: *Rehousing Urban America*. New York: Columbia University Press.

Wrigley, R. A. 1983: The Plan of Chicago. In: Krueckeberg, D. A. (ed.) *Introduction to Planning History in the United States*, 58–72. New Brunswick, NJ: Rutgers University, Center for Urban Policy Research.

Wu, C. T. and Ip, D. F. 1981: China: Rural Development – Alternating Combinations of Top-Down and Bottom-Up Strategies. In: Stöhr, W. B. and Taylor, D. R. F. (eds.) *Development from Above or Below? The Dialectics of Regional Planning in Developing Countries*, 155–82. Chichester: John Wiley & Sons, Ltd.

Wu, V. 1998: The Pudong Development Zone and China's Economic Reforms. *Planning Perspectives*, 13, 133–65.

Wu, Y. L. 1967: *The Spatial Economy of Communist China: A Study on Industrial Location and Transportation*. New York: Praeger.

Wynn, M. (ed.) 1984a: *Planning and Urban Growth in Southern Europe*. London: Mansell.

Wynn, M. 1984b: Spain. In: Wynn, M. (ed.) *Planning and Urban Growth in Southern Europe*, 111–63. London: Mansell.

Wynn, M. (ed.) 1984c: *Housing in Europe*. London: Croom Helm.

Yago, G. 1984: *The Decline of Transit: Urban Transportation in German and US Cities, 1900–1970*. Cambridge: Cambridge University Press.

Yazaki, T. 1973: The History of Urbanization in Japan. In: Southall, A. (ed.) *Urban Anthropology: Cross-Cultural Studies of Urbanization*, 139–61. New York: Oxford University Press.

Yelling, J. A. 1986: *Slums and Slum Clearance in Victorian London*. London: Allen & Unwin.

Yelling, J. A. 1989: The Origins of British Redevelopment Areas. *Planning Perspectives*, 3, 282–96.

Yelling, J. A. 1992: *Slums and Redevelopment: Policy and Practice in England, 1918–1945, with Particular Reference to London*. London: University College Press.

Yelling, J. A. 1994: Expensive Land, Subsidies and Mixed Development in London, 1943–56. *Planning Perspectives*, 9, 139–52.

Yelling, J. A. 1999a: The Development of Residential Urban Renewal Policies in England: Planning for Modernization in the 1960s. *Planning Perspectives*, 14, 1–18.

Yelling, J. A. 1999b: Residents' Reactions to Post-War Slum Clearance in England. *Planning History*, 21/3, 5–12.

Yeomans, A. B. (ed.) 1916: *City Residential Land Development: Studies in Planning*. Chicago: University of Chicago Press.

Young, K. and Mason, C. (eds.) 1983: *Urban Economic Development: New Roles and Relationships*. London: Macmillan.

Young, M. and Willmott, P. 1957: *Family and Kinship in East London*. London: Routledge and Kegan Paul.

Young, T. 1934: *Becontree and Dagenham: The Story of the Growth of a Housing Estate*. A Report Made for the Pilgrim Trust. London: Becontree Social Survey Committee.

Zimmer, B. 1966: The Small Businessman and Location. In: Wilson, J. Q. (ed.) *Urban Renewal: The Record and the Controversy*, 380–403. Cambridge, MA: MIT Press.

Zipf, G. K. 1949: *Human Behavior and the Principle of Least Effort*. Cambridge, MA: Addison-Wesley.

Zorbaugh, H. W. 1929: *The Gold Coast and the Slum: A Sociological Study of Chicago's Near North Side*. Chicago: University of Chicago Press.

Zukin, S. 1992: The City as a Landscape of Power: London and New York as Global Financial Capitals. In: Budd, L. and Whimster, S. *Global Finance and Urban Living: A Study of Metropolitan Change*, 195–223. London: Routledge.

Zwerling, S. 1974: *Mass Transit and the Politics of Technology: A Study of BART and the San Francisco Bay Area*. New York: Praeger.

Index

Note: Page numbers in *italics* refer to illustrations